Mutual Aid Groups
And The Life Cycle

To Dessie,

I enjoyed our collaboration.
Your thoughtfulness, interpersonal
sensitivity and professional competence
were very much appreciated.

Mutual Aid Groups And The Life Cycle

EDITED BY:

Alex Gitterman and
COLUMBIA UNIVERSITY

Lawrence Shulman
BOSTON UNIVERSITY

 F.E. PEACOCK PUBLISHERS, INC. ITASCA, ILLINOIS 60143

In Memory of William Schwartz

Contents

Contributing Authors

Yetta H. Appel, Professor, School of Social Work, Rutgers, The State University of New Jersey, New Brunswick, N.J.

Toby Berman-Rossi, Assistant Professor, Columbia University School of Social Work, New York, N.Y.

Judith Bloch, Director, Variety Pre-Schooler's Workshop, Syosset, N.Y.

Alex Gitterman, Professor, School of Social Work, Columbia University, New York, N.Y.

Penny Goldberg, Director, Social Work Services, Hospital for Joint Diseases—Orthopaedic Institute, New York, N.Y.

Elizabeth Graham, Director, Division of Day Care, New York City Department of Health, New York, N.Y.

Samuel Indelicato, Instructor, University of Delaware, Newark, De.

Carol Irizarry, Lecturer, School of Social Sciences, The Flinders University of South Australia, South Australia, AUSTRALIA

Margaret Jones, Counselor in Private Practice, Vancouver, British Columbia, Canada

Judith A. B. Lee, Associate Professor, School of Social Work, University of Connecticut, West Hartford, Connecticut

Derryl Lubell, Social Worker, Health Sciences Centre—Psychiatric Unit, University of British Columbia, Vancouver, British Columbia, Canada

Judith Margolis, Assistant Director, Special Projects, Variety Pre-Schooler's Workshop, Syosset, N.Y.

Alice Nadelman, Licensed Clinical Psychologist, Hackensack Medical Center, Hackensack, N.J.

Amy Nierenberg, Social Worker, Northside Center for Child Development, Inc., New York, N.Y.

Alberta L. Orr, Executive Director, East Bronx Council on Aging, Bronx, N.Y.

Dorothy Poynter-Berg, Clinical Coordinator and Private Practitioner, Community Psychiatric Institute, Maplewood, N.J.

Daniella Pozzaglia, Social Worker, New York City Board of Education, Committee on the Handicapped, Bronx, N.Y.

Diana S. Schaefer, Pediatric Social Worker, Memorial Sloan-Kettering Cancer Center, New York, N.Y.

Lawrence Shulman, Professor, School of Social Work, Boston University, Boston, Massachusetts.

Sheila Small, Social Worker, Center for Mental Health, Interfaith Medical Center, Brooklyn, N.Y.

Carol R. Swenson, Associate Professor and Chair, Clinical Practice Sequence, Simmons College School of Social Work, Boston, Massachusetts

Dale Trimble, Counselor in Private Practice, Vancouver Family Court, Assaultive Husbands' Project, Vancouver, British Columbia, Canada

Joyce M. Vastola, Social Worker, S.U.N.Y. Downstate Medical Center, Brooklyn, N.Y.

Foreword

This book is a tribute to William Schwartz—a valued friend, colleague and mentor, who died August 1, 1982. While neither of us was a student of Bill's, we were both influenced by his seminal ideas about social work practice in general and group work practice in particular. Some chapters in this book were contributed by Bill's former students and colleagues who were eager to share in the endeavor. This was an opportunity to pay tribute to his influence in the way he would have most appreciated—by demonstrating in detail what their practice looked like in the real world, with real clients facing real problems. Other chapters were written by practitioners, who while not specifically rooted in Bill's practice framework, nevertheless incorporate his concept of mutual aid in their practice.

Thus, the book represents a personal and professional statement of thanks to Bill for laying the groundwork which piqued our curiosity about method and gave direction to our ongoing inquiry into the subject of practice.

January 15, 1985   Alex Gitterman and Lawrence Shulman

Preface

Part one of this book contains a number of chapters that set out the theoretical model guiding the practice. In chapter 1, Shulman and Gitterman introduce three major sets of ideas: the life model as an approach to understanding and helping clients; a mutual aid approach to working with groups; and mediation as a functional role for the group leader. In chapter 2, Shulman elaborates on the practice theory by describing and illustrating the specific core skills used by the social worker as he or she puts the mediating function into action. The dynamics and skills involved are illustrated with detailed excerpts of practice drawn from the chapters that follow. Thus, this chapter will serve to introduce the reader to each of the mutual aid groups described in balance of the book. In chapter 3, Gitterman addresses the issues and skills involved in the critical group formation process. The steps between a worker's conceptualization of the need for a group and a successful first meeting need careful consideration if the group is to be well launched.

In part two, the focus is on the childhood stage of life. Chapter 4 by Vastola, Nierenberg, and Graham describes a group for children who have lost a parent or close relative. The authors' sensitive practice excerpts and discussion illustrate some of the unique ways in which children express their ambivalence about discussing painful feelings. The group is called by the members "The Lost and Found Group," which poignantly describes their commonality in having lost meaningful adults while finding each other. In chapter 5, Bloch and Margolis describe work with young children who have handicapped siblings. This discussion of the unique problems involved in contracting with young children helps to add to our understanding of the importance of differential approaches to practice. The central theme of feelings of shame, shared by the children, focuses our attention on an important and often overlooked population—the sibling.

Part three of the book examines mutual aid groups and the adolescent population. In chapter 6, Irrizary and Appel illustrate their work with a community-based, preadolescent group. They provide a sensitive description of the normative tasks facing this population with special attention to cultural factors. In chapter 7, Nadelman shares her work with teenage girls in a residential setting. These youngsters, who have lost contact with meaningful adults in their lives, must learn how to meet their needs for intimacy with their peers. Nadelman demonstrates how apparently tough and hardened young clients can be helped to discover their ability to help each other. When one group member, reluctant to give another advice, says: "I ain't no expert in personality," Nadelman presses her to take some responsibility for offering help and credits all of them as having something to give. The two articles offer interesting comparisons as we see the similarity of the developmental tasks with both groups of teens, as well as the differences created by the institutionalization of the second group. Finally, in chapter 8, Small examines work with a similar age group, but one in which the status of being a "learning disabled teenager" adds unique issues. Taken together, the three articles illustrate the normative tasks of growing up, which are important for all the group members, and the variations on the theme introduced by culture, institutionalization and a handicap.

Part four of the book takes us into work with adult populations. In chapter 9, Shulman examines a short-term group experience for single parents. The group life lasted one evening and the following full day, and yet the depth of the concerns discussed raises interesting issues about the impact of time on group process. Also, the discussion highlights the capacity of group members to respond to a group leader's "demand for work" much more quickly than many of us would have guessed.

In chapter 10, Indelicato and Goldberg deal with the problems of learning disability from the perspective of the parents. They illustrate sensitively how "harassed and alone" these parents often feel and the many ways in which they can help each other, not the least of which is the support of finding others "in the same boat." It is an example of a situation in which one of the best ways of helping the children is by providing support to the parents.

In chapters 11 and 12, Jones and Trimble break important ground as they illustrate process with groups concerned with family violence. Jones's group is for the nonoffending parent of sexually victimized children. The group represents a recognition that there are many victims of this crime and that nonoffending parents also need help with their guilt as well as some concrete assistance on how to provide support for their children. The title "Speaking the Unspoken" alludes to the strong taboos which make it difficult to face the issue and the importance of doing so if healing is to begin. Trimble's chapter on work with men who batter their wives or women they live with represents an important evolution in thinking about working with the offender. As Trimble points out, it is crucial for the worker to be in touch with his or her own anger if there is any hope of reaching past the deviant behavior and beginning to help the offender as a client in his own right. Groups such as this have often failed because of the inability of the group leader to understand the artificial dichotomy between support and demand. Trimble demonstrates the necessity of using authority and confronting the group members on the issue of personal responsibility, while simultaneously synthesizing the demand with caring.

In chapter 13, Lee tackles another very current and pressing social issue: the problem of homeless women with "no place to go." In an interesting mixture of direct practice skill with clients and social action activity around the problem, we see the social worker's dual function of helping group members to cope with the realities of today while simultaneously trying to organize to change those realities. Her work also nicely illustrates some of the beginning-stage problems in engaging a difficult, often hostile and mistrusting population. Similar themes are also addressed by Poynter-Berg in chapter 14, as she focuses on the task of helping institutionalized schizophrenic women get connected to both the worker and each other. When contrasted with the homeless women in chapter 13, we can see that the connection between these women and their social surroundings is only faintly visible, and then only if the worker searches for it. For the chronic schizophrenic women, on the extreme end of the breakdown continuum, patience and persistence on the worker's part are important if the connection is to be reestablished.

Chapter 15, by Lubell, deals with the impact of catastrophic illness on a client's developmental life cycle. Her clients, all of whom now have to live with a kidney failure and a future linked to a dialysis machine, must cope with the impact of this fact upon their lives. This impact varies, depending upon the stage of life and the life tasks to be confronted. For all the group members, however, the transition into the role of an individual with an illness is an experience in common. In chapter 16, Schaefer and Pozzaglia document the impact of a traumatic illness on the parent of a child with cancer. In this situation, sociocultural issues are also important, as the group consists of Hispanic parents. They must face the horrifying nightmare of a child ill with a possibly terminal illness and deal with it in a strange culture and under great economic stress. Once again, mutual aid offers one avenue of help.

In part five of the book, work with the elderly completes the journey through the life cycle. Orr, in chapter 17, describes her work with the visually impaired elderly living in the community. For these group members, the mutual aid group is an important substitute for other support systems (such as friends or relatives) which are not always available to them. In a dramatic meeting, the worker presses the group participants to deal with the death of a valued and loved group member. The internal dialogue of each member, in which part of them wants to face the hurt and part of them wants to deny it, is acted out in the group discussion as different members voice the two sides of the ambivalence. With the gentle, caring, yet firm support of the leader, the members enter the taboo area of discussion about death and face the loss of this member, their sense of loss of others close to them, and their own impending deaths. The powerful forces for support inherent in mutual aid are clearly evident in these process recordings.

In chapter 18, Berman-Rossi examines the plight of the institutionalized aged who must fight against feelings of hopelessness and despair.

In an interesting illustration of the social worker's mediating, or third-force function, Berman-Rossi demonstrates how support combined with demand can help the group experience strength in numbers as they tackle the institution's dietary practices. Berman-Rossi combines a number of complicated tasks in her illustration of her role in action. She helps mobilize the members and yet, at the same time, offers assistance and support to the institution's staff. She demonstrates the importance of keeping the common ground between staff and client in mind. The anger in the group over the institution's food preparation is closely connected to their underlying depression over the fact that they no longer can cook for themselves. As she helps the group members find the strength to tackle the institution, an effort which really symbolizes the choice of life over resignation, she also reaches for the themes which underlie the work with the organization.

In part six of the book, in chapter 19, Lee and Swenson reach back into our history for a scholarly examination of the mutual aid theory, reminding us of the roots of group work and social work practice. We think this historical view of mutual aid will have more meaning to the reader after vivid illustrations of its modern-day implementation.

Part One
Mutual Aid: An Introduction

Lawrence Shulman
Alex Gitterman

CHAPTER 1

The Life Model, Mutual Aid, and the Mediating Function

The perspective on practice presented in this book emerges from the convergence of three major sets of ideas: a life model for understanding and helping clients, a mutual aid approach to group work, and a theory of practice which views the role of the worker as mediating the individual-group engagement.

Perhaps the easiest way to introduce these sets of ideas is by illustrating them with an example from this book. In chapter 15, Lubell describes her work with a group of hospital patients with kidney disorders which may require them to be dependent upon a dialysis machine. Employing elements of the life model (as described by Germain and Gitterman) to understand these clients, each of the group members can be viewed as facing the normative life transitions for their age (for example, entering young adulthood, preparing for retirement), while simultaneously having to cope with a transition from the status of well person to one of coping with a traumatic illness.[1] The impact of this status change will be different for a person just beginning adult life as compared to one ready to retire.

In Lubell's chapter, we see these patients brought together in a mutual aid group so that the energies of the group members can be mobilized to help each other. The concept of mutual aid in groups, one of Schwartz's major contributions to the literature, shifts the source of the helping from the group leader to the members themselves.[2] For example, as members in this group discover that they are not alone in their feelings, a powerful healing force is released. With the help of the group leader, members can support each other, confront each other, and provide suggestions and ideas from their own fund of experiences, concomitantly helping themselves as they help each other.

The third set of ideas, the mediating function of the worker, which was also proposed by Schwartz, provides a role statement for the group leader.[3] While the potential for mutual aid is present in the group, members will need the help of the worker to activate its power and to overcome the many obstacles that can frustrate its effectiveness. For the worker to carry out his or her tasks in the group, a clear and precise statement of function is necessary.

Schwartz proposed a general functional statement for the social work profession as that of mediating the individual-social engagement.[4] If one views the small group as a microcosm of our larger society, then the worker's role can be described as mediating the individual-group encounter. Thus, in our group for dialysis patients, we see the worker assisting each member to reach out to the group for help while simultaneously helping the group members to respond. Even if a group member presents a pattern of denial and refuses to face the impact of the illness, the worker's mediating function may involve providing support to that member using the worker's capacity for empathy, while also confronting the member's denial and reaching for the underlying fears and apprehensions. And if the other group members appear to turn away from a member's direct and emotional appeal for help (for example, changing the subject or looking uninterested) possibly because the issue raised their own level of anxiety, the mediating function would call for the worker to confront the group members on their evasion and denial.

These three sets of ideas, the life model, mutual aid, and the mediating function, are discussed in more detail in the balance of this chapter.

THE LIFE MODEL

The Life Model is an operationalization and specification of the ecological perspective and offers a view of human beings in constant interchanges with their environment.[5] People are changed by their physical and social environments and in turn change them through processes of continuous reciprocal adaptation. In these complex interchanges, disturbances often emerge in the adaptive balance (in the "goodness-of-fit") between individual needs and capacities and environmental qualities. These disturbances challenge and disrupt customary coping mecha-

nisms and create stress.[6] The Life Model proposes a useful and viable approach to professionals for understanding and helping clients to deal with life stresses and their consequences. Clients' "troubles" are identified as arising from three interrelated problems of living: (1) life transitions, (2) environmental pressures, and (3) maladaptive interpersonal processes.

Life Transitions

There is a well-developed literature describing the process by which we all proceed through biologically induced "life cycle" changes. Though biologically induced, these processes are shaped by psychological, socioeconomic, and cultural forces. These dynamic, interacting processes have been conceptualized by Erikson as occurring in epigenetic stages of development.[7] Each stage requires changes and redefinitions in relationships with significant others, negotiations with the external environment, and struggles with one's self-definitions and self-identity. Successful mastery of the tasks in one stage sets the foundation for successful mastery of the tasks associated with the next stage. Personal, familial, and environmental resources support or frustrate an individual's ability to develop a sense of mastery and competence. Unsuccessful task resolutions create troubles and confusions which often poses problems at later stages.

During the infancy period (birth to approximately six years), according to Erikson, we learn and achieve the acquired qualities of "trust," "autonomy," and "initiative." In the first years of life, the child is totally dependent upon parental figures. For trust to be developed, they have to be trustworthy and dependable. For autonomy and initiative to be accomplished, they have to encourage and support such behaviors. Using the ideas of "cog wheeling" between generations, Erikson identifies a potential "goodness-of-fit" between, for example, child's need to be nourished and parents' own stage-specific needs for intimacy and caring.

This potential for reciprocal fulfillment of intergenerational needs is profoundly influenced by the external environment. For parents to nurture children (and meet their own needs as well), they need the support of relatives, friends, and neighbors (in other words, "social networks") as well as responsive economic, educational, and health structures. When such supports are available, the opportunities for personal growth, family integration, and social benefits are increased. When, however, a child is unable to respond to parents, or parents are unable to nourish the child, or social institutions are unable to provide required supports, they become potent sources for continuous stress and interfere with successful adaptation. And, consequently, in this and subsequent stages, the individual as well as the family and environmental systems have to deal with the psychological and behavioral residues of "distrust," "shame," and "guilt."

When a child enters school, he or she has to master two new developmentally linked relationships—teachers and peers. A child who develops comfort in and acceptance from these new relationships and masters required learning tasks and social skills, may incorporate a sense of "industriousness" into the self-concept. However, a child who is unable to trust, to separate, to initiate may become frightened and overwhelmed by the demands for new relationships with adult authorities as well as for intimacy with peers. A handicapped child (cognitive, emotional, or physical) may experience similar difficulties as might the child of a parent who "holds on" and experiences difficulties with separation. If any of these more vulnerable children also confront an unresponsive school or peer system, their self-concepts may introject feelings of self-doubt and "inferiority." For example, in a study in which children with sickle cell anemia were compared to a group of similar children on all characteristics except the sickle cell anemia, dramatic differences in self-concept, in feelings of self-worth, and in feelings of wholeness were found. These experiences may well persist and be carried for life.[8]

"Who am I?" "Who am I becoming?" are the questions adolescents ask in search of "identity." The adolescent experiences major biological changes (such as physical growth and sexual characteristics) and an emerging awareness of sexuality. These physiological and self-image changes elicit direct responses from parents, siblings, relatives, and institutional representatives. Turmoil and crises often characterize family interaction patterns as the adolescent demands greater autonomy and simultaneously struggles with dependency needs. To cope with the independence/dependence ambivalence and increased sexuality, the adolescent turns to the "teenage culture" for comfort and acceptance. In exchange for a sense of belonging, the teenager must meet peer expectations and pressures about dress, demeanor, behavior, and other matters. Since peer and family norms often conflict, the adolescent experiences heightened stress in the search for a clearer sense of self.

Most adolescents (and their families) somehow survive this painful life period and grow out of this stage and its perpetual crises with a more intact and integrating sense of individual and collective identity. Others, however, do not. Adolescents whose families are unable to tolerate testing behavior or to provide the essential structure may experience profound confusion. Adolescents who were abandoned, institutionalized, or abused by their families may develop a sense of helplessness, learning to believe that they are unworthy and incapable of influencing life events.[9] Similarly, handicapped adolescents (such as orthopedic, learning disabled) or adolescents who deviate from peer norms (such as obese, shy) may experience peer group rejection and be denied a powerful source of support. Adolescents growing up in an unjust and hostile environment may introject negative stereotypes and prejudices into their self-identities.[10] These adolescents are vulnerable to "identity confusion" and "role diffusion," which may carry over to adulthood.

To the request for criteria for the mature adult, Freud has been reported to have responded: *"Lieben und Arbeiten"* (love and work). The young adult faces these two developmental transitions: the development of an "intimate" relationship (marriage or couplehood) and the accomplishment of work (employment and career). The young adult, for example, has to form an initial dyadic relationship characterized by the task of establishing interpersonal intimacy (caring and giving to another person) without losing his/her own identity.[11] If a partner has not mastered prior developmental stages and tasks or is withdrawn or abusive or experiences such unforeseen events as unemployment or illness, disillusionment and conflict may block the establishment of interpersonal intimacy. A child born into such situations may intensify parental stress as new accommodations are necessary to care for the needs of the dependent infant. Still other life transitions such as children entering school or leaving for college, the

loss of social support associated with a geographical move, the trauma of a separation and divorce, or the struggle related to reconstituting two families may create crises and generate feelings of isolation and alienation.[12]

As children mature and leave home (psychologically and/or physically), adults have to restructure their life space and change patterns of relating to the children, spouse, and others. The parental dyad rediscovers each other and forges a new level of caring and giving. The single parent develops other intimate relationships. Work provides career and financial advancement and meets creativity and self-esteem needs. The adult becomes concerned about others and future generations. When these tasks are achieved, the adult experiences a period of "generativity," an excitement with life.[13] When, however, the adult is unable to separate from children or to forge new relationships, or work provides limited opportunities to demonstrate creativity and competence, the adult may experience a period of "stagnation," or depression with life.[14]

In later adulthood, one attempts to integrate life experiences within the reality of declining physical and mental functions. Added to these biological changes, older adults face numerous other sources of stress. They may have to relinquish the status of worker (and its associated roles) and assume the status of retirees. Older adults may lose their spouses, relatives, or close friends. At some point, they may be institutionalized. These life transitions and crises are extremely stressful and may create bitterness, despair, and even depression. Children, grandchildren, relatives, close friends, community, and organizational ties, however, can buffer these insults. And with these essential supports, older adults are better able to come to terms with the meaning of their lives and achieve a sense of emotional integrity.

Environmental Pressures

While the environment can support or interfere with life transitions, it can itself be a significant generator of stress. For lower-income people, the environment is a harsh reality. By nature of their economic position, they are often unable to command needed goods and services. Similarly environmental opportunities for jobs, promotions, housing, neighborhood, and geographic and social mobility are extremely limited. As a consequence, lower-income families are less likely to remain intact, and life expectancy is lower. For lower-income black families, the rate of physical illness is higher, life expectancy is shorter, and loss of employment greater.[15] Thus, the environment is a powerful source of trouble and distress, and often its intransigence overwhelms us. By specifying assessment and intervention methods, the Life Model attempts to broaden the profession's practice repertoire (for example, problem definition, points of entry, and so on).

The social environment is primarily comprised of *organizations* and *social networks*.[16] Health, education, and social service organizations are established with social sanctions and financial support to provide services. Once they are established, there develop external and internal structures, policies, and procedures which inevitably impede effective provision of the very services they are set up to provide. The organization proliferates, taking on a life of its own, and its maintenance assumes precedence over client needs. Latent goals and functions displace manifest goals and functions. An agency, for example, may create complex sets of intake procedures which screen out prospective clients whose problems are immediate and urgent and do not lend themselves to delays and postponements congenial to agency style.

Low-income families are unable to compete for social resources; their leverage on social organizations is relatively weak. Similarly, hospitalized or institutionalized clients may be overwhelmed by their own vulnerability and relative powerlessness. With limited power, ignorance about their rights, and little skill in negotiation, such service users often become resigned to the unresponsiveness of various organizations' services. Because of cultural expectations and perceptions, physical or emotional impairments or lack of role skills, others may be unwilling or unable to use organizational resources that are actually available and responsive.

Social networks are increasingly recognized as important elements of the social environment. People's social networks can be supportive environmental resources in that they provide a mutual aid system for the exchanges of instrumental assistance (such as money, child care, housing) and affective (emotional) supports. When a goodness-of-fit exists between an individual's concrete, social, and emotional needs and available resources, it buffers intra-psychic, interpersonal, and environmental pressures. Some networks have available resources, but the individual does not want or is not able to use them. Others, however, encourage maladaptive patterns; for example, drug-oriented networks reinforce and support deviant behavior. Some exploit and scapegoat a more vulnerable member, taking unfair advantage of vulnerability. Still other social networks are loosely knit and unavailable for support. Finally, some individuals are without any usable social networks and are extremely vulnerable to social and emotional isolation. For these individuals, the network (or lack of one) is a significant factor in adding to distress.

Maladaptive Interpersonal Processes

In dealing with life transitional and environmental issues, families and groups are powerful mediating forces. They may, however, encounter obstacles caused by their own patterns of communication and relationships. When this occurs, maladaptive family and group interpersonal patterns generate tensions in the system and attenuate the mutual aid processes. These maladaptive patterns are often expressed in withdrawal, factionalism, scapegoating, interlocking hostilities, monopolism, and ambiguous messages.

While these maladaptive patterns are dysfunctional for most members, they often serve latent functions of maintaining a family's or group's equilibrium. When a family or group is characterized by factions, the subcliques provide its members greater affirmation and security than does the larger system. Similarly, the scapegoating of a member declared deviant enables the other members to contrast themselves favorably and thereby enhance their sense of self. The status of scapegoat offers such secondary gains as attention and martyrdom.[17] After a while these relationship patterns become fixed, and potential change becomes exiguous. At the same time, however, the status quo makes all members vulnerable and thwarts the nurturing character of mutual aid.

Interpersonal obstacles are generated by various sources. Group composition is an important factor. A group of athletic preadolescents which includes a single very unathletic member has a built-in potential for a scapegoat (chapter 3 examines formation issues). Family and group structures can be another source for interpersonal difficulties.[18] Some families and groups lack boundaries. Members come and go as they please. The individual member enjoys a high degree of autonomy and privacy but sacrifices a requisite sense of group belonging and security. When the boundaries are unclear and unstable, members lack a sense of reciprocity, coordination, and integration. Family members, for example, eat meals separately, pursue individual interests, and become unavailable to and for each other. On the other hand when family and group boundaries are too rigid and enmeshed, members have limited freedom. To be sure, the individual member enjoys a strong sense of collective belonging and security, but it is costly to autonomy and privacy. The family or group demands unequivocal loyalty, as individual interests threaten the collective enterprise.

Family or group members may also become overwhelmed by environmental expectations and limitations. In a school system, for example, children may scapegoat a slow learner because the institution makes them all feel "dumb." Similarly, parents may be harsh with each other and with their children because they feel mistreated by the outside world. In response to a nonnurturing or oppressive environment, some families or groups turn inward, displace, and act out their frustrations, while others withdraw and become functionally apathetic.

Transitional stages of development also contribute to maladaptive communication patterns. Entrances, such as the birth of an infant, addition of a new group member, and exits, such as the departure of adolescents for college, or loss of a group member may create interpersonal distress and problematic responses. When a family or group is unable to move through a collective stage of development, they may turn away from or turn on each other. And the potential resources for mutual aid become dissipated.

The purpose of a group mutual aid system is to help members to help each other with their day-to-day problems in living. The next section discusses mutual aid and its processes as well as the obstacles which can block its powerful forces.

THE MUTUAL AID GROUP

The idea of a group as a system for mutual aid is rooted in a broader conception of the nature of the relationship between people and society. Schwartz, drawing upon the ideas of Dewey, Mead, Kropotkin, and others, postulated a view of reciprocity between individuals and their social surround.[19] In part six of this book, Lee and Swenson explore the historical roots of mutual aid in more detail. For our immediate purposes, the crucial idea as proposed by Schwartz is that of a "symbiotic" relationship between the individual and societal needs, "each needs the other for its own life and growth and reaches out to the other with all possible strength at a given moment."[20] Schwartz perceived the individual to have a natural impetus toward health and growth and belonging, with a similar impetus on the part of society to integrate its parts into a productive and dynamic whole.

If one then considers the small group to be a special case of this larger individual-social engagement and one carries this notion of symbiosis into the small-group encounter, then Schwartz's definition of a social work group logically follows:

The group is an enterprise in mutual aid, an alliance of individuals who need each other, in varying degrees, to work on certain common problems. The important fact is that this is a helping system in which the clients need each other as well as the worker. This need to use each other, to create not one but many helping relationships, is a vital ingredient of the group process and constitutes a common need over and above the specific tasks for which the group was formed.[21]

The Mutual Aid Process

There are a number of mutual aid processes that can be identified when one watches an effective small group in action. These have been described in some detail elsewhere and are illustrated through process recording excerpts in the chapters that follow.[22] The nine processes briefly described in this section include the following: sharing data, the dialectical process, entering taboo areas, the "all-in-the-same-boat" phenomenon, mutual support, mutual demand, individual problem solving, rehearsal, and the strength-in-numbers phenomenon.

In sharing data, group members can provide each other with ideas, facts, beliefs, and resources, which they have found helpful in coping with similar problems. For example, in a welfare mothers' group, members had suggestions for how to use the rules of the system to make maximum use of available benefits as well as what places to shop for the best buys. In a married couples group, the older couples could often share their experiences from earlier in their marriages, some of which were similar to current crises experienced by the younger couples. The knowledge that the issues were universal and the suggestions as to how to deal with them were often most helpful. While the content of the data varies according to the group type, the essential idea is that people facing similar problems can often be a resource for each other.

The dialectical process consists of one or more members advancing a thesis, other members countering with an antithesis, and the group members attempting to develop their own synthesis. This form of disputation process can be very helpful as one tries to develop insights into difficult problems. A group member can put forth a tentative idea (often only after the worker has helped the group develop a culture of trust and respect) and have other members respond as sounding boards to the views. Other members may change their mind and be open to new ideas as they listen to a view being challenged. One extremely interesting process to observe in a group is the way in which the group may encourage a debate between two members, or two subgroups, in which each side appears to take an opposing view to the other. For example, in a parents of teenagers group, one side argued impressively for the need to be "tough" and to set limits. The other argued just as passionately for the importance of providing support and of being able to communicate. The apparent dichotomy is of course a false one, with the skillful parent learning early of the need to integrate both support and limits at precisely the same time. In fact, each parent carries out the same dialogue internally, trying to find a way of resolving the split. In the group, one part of each parent's ambivalence may be assigned to an individual group member or subgroup, and the dialectical process becomes a public airing of each individual's private confusion.

Of course, the assignments are not made consciously. A premeeting was not held for the purpose of deciding which group member would articulate which view.

This group process emerges from the group's need to articulate and resolve an apparent schism, while simultaneously maintaining the split to avoid having to face it. Bion, in his pioneering work on group processes, observed the way in which immature groups often go into "flight" (changing the subject) or "fight" (strenuous debates and personal attacks) when faced with difficult or frightening issues. He described the group leader's job as pointing out the process and educating the group on its way of working to aid it in becoming a more mature group. In the model suggested here, the worker could identify the common ground, even at the point of conflict, by articulating the part of each group member which really agreed with the "other side." For example: "You're all arguing your points so strenuously; yet, I can't believe that some part of each of you isn't struggling to find a way to put together your love for your child with your sense of the importance of setting some limits and providing some structure."

A third area of mutual aid involves the help members can give each other in discussing a taboo subject. For example, while all group members in the married couples group may have some issues related to their sexual relationships, they also may see discussing this subject as taboo. An unstated norm of behavior exists in our society which forbids honest discussion of our fears and concerns in this area. We can joke about such subjects, but real talk is forbidden. Since the sense of urgency about dealing with the subject may be stronger for some couples than others, or the fear of discussion may be less powerful, one couple may take the initiative and lead the group into the formerly forbidden area. As group members listen to the discussion and they see the courageous members supported and credited (often by the leader but just as often by other members), they find their own courage to participate.

In another example of this process in action, some group members may not be in touch with their own feelings if they believe these feelings to be inappropriate (for example, a parent of a handicapped child who feels anger at the child and the burden he or she represents). As these members hear others speak the unspeakable, it may cause them to experience openly the same emotions.

The mutual experiencing of ideas and emotions leads to yet another powerful mutual aid process: the "all-in-the-same boat phenomenon." This is the healing process which occurs when one realizes that one is not alone and that others share the problem, the feeling, the doubts, and all the rest. Students learning to practice social work are greatly relieved to find that other beginning students also wonder if they are right for the field. Parents who experience "improper" thoughts and feelings judge themselves less harshly when they find they are not alone.

A fifth mutual aid process can be observed in the way in which group members provide support for each other. When a group member is in difficulty or has experienced a trauma (such as a death in the family) or is revealing painful feelings which have been long repressed, one can see direct and indirect efforts on the part of individual group members and the group as a whole to provide empathic support. Carrying a burden is often easier if others express their understanding. Having peers try to share in your painful feelings can be experienced as a form of a "gift," much more meaningful than artificial efforts to cheer you up. In a single parents group, one member began to cry with deep, heartfelt sobs as she described her tremendous sense of rejec-

tion by her ex-spouse. The leader could see the member next to the one in distress fidgeting and turning, apparently wanting to reach out. When the leader commented on this and asked if she wanted to hold the woman next to her, she replied that she did and then took her hand. This was a physical comforting which was followed by words of support by the other group members. As they were supporting this member in her feelings of rejection, they were also helping themselves with their own similar feelings. Thus, the giving of empathic support is often as helpful to the one who gives as the one who receives. In the small group, the support of peers can be even more powerful in its healing potential than the support of the worker.

While support is a crucial ingredient for mutual aid to take place, it is not enough by itself. The change process requires mutual demand as well. The artificial split between support and demand can be commonly observed in group practice. For example, Trimble (chapter 12) describes his early efforts in working with male batterers in which he felt that creating an accepting, empathic atmosphere was the key element in bringing about changes in behavior. Experience demonstrated that caring was not enough and that he had to integrate it with confrontation and demand, in which he needed to dig and push to get these men to accept responsibility for their actions and the change process. The key to the success of his work is the integration of the two essential elements in simultaneous action, rather than structuring his groups to be all confrontation and no support. It is exactly at the moment that group members are confronted that they will need all the support they can get.

It is not unusual to observe groups in which the members are more ready than the worker to confront each other. The worker may hesitate, concerned about the member's possible fragility, and then sit back in wonder as the "fragile" member responds with strength to the peer group's demands. Somehow, it is easier to accept a confrontation from one who really knows what it is like than from an "outsider," however caring and empathic. Group members who share the problem may also be more astute in picking up the defenses, the denials, the many ways in which we all "con" ourselves out of facing the truth when it is painful. They are astute observers of these methods of avoidance because they can see them in their own behaviors.

Another simple, yet powerful way in which mutual demand operates in a group, can be the expectation felt by the member that he or she take some difficult action. For example, a men's group discusses a member's difficulty communicating with his boss at work, and after support, discussion, even role-play of how he should handle the conversation on the job, the group members expect to hear what happened when they return the next week. Group members have said they would rather face the boss than have to return the following week and reveal to their peers that they "chickened out."

While group members can help each other through general discussion of common themes of concern, such as the feelings of loneliness of a single parent coupled with the fear of risking being hurt again in a new relationship, they must also offer help on a member-by-member, specific-example-by-specific-example basis. In fact, effective mutual aid groups are constantly moving back and forth between the specific case and the general issue. Individual problem solving is one of the important ways a mutual aid group works. As the group members help the

individual with a specific problem, they are actually also helping themselves with their own variations on a theme. Workers who are unclear about this specific-general interaction often make the mistake of keeping the discussion on an overly general level. They express fears of "doing casework in the group." If one is clear that a mutual aid group involves members helping each other and that there is usually a connection between the individual's specific problem and the group's general purpose, then this issue of the individual need versus the group's need is revealed as yet another artificial dichotomy.

Take the example of a parents group discussion about the difficulty in raising teenage children. One member raises it at the start of a group meeting as follows: "I have been thinking recently about how hard it is to raise teenage girls these days, what with the changes taking place in ideas about morality. It just isn't as clear as it was when I was a kid." The group leader who fears "casework in the group" might turn to the other members and ask for their comments on the issue. The resultant general discussion can become an "illusion of work," and meanwhile, the initiator of the conversation may be sitting there still churning away over the fight she had the night before with her fifteen-year-old when she didn't return home until 3:30 in the morning.

If the leader is clear about the individual problem-solving process in mutual aid groups, he or she might ask the mother if she had a specific incident in mind. As the mother describes the fight, the worker would help the mother share the incident with the other group members, invest the presentation with feelings, describe the actual conversation with the daughter, and mobilize the group members to offer feedback and advice. As they discuss this particular parent trying to cope with changing morals and parental responsibility, they will move back and forth between the specific problem and the general issues. As the group members offer help to this mother, they will be formulating new ideas for how they can handle similar issues with their children.

Discussion of the interaction with the daughter may reveal that the mother was so distraught and worried about her daughter's safety that she may have translated that concern into an outburst of anger when the daughter returned. While the anger may have been appropriate, it often covers the fear, anxiety, and caring from which it springs. If the group members and the leader help the mother see how she needs to share these feelings as well, then rehearsal, a form of role-play in the group, can help the mother find the words and feelings for a follow-up discussion with her daughter. Sometimes just practicing a difficult task, with support and advice from the group members, can give the member enough confidence to attempt it. In addition, as the member struggles through the role-play, he or she often reveals ambivalent feelings about the issue which were not present during the discussion. For example, does some part of the mother not want to have such a discussion with the daughter because she is afraid of what she might hear? It is better if the ambivalence emerges in the group, where it can be explored, rather than in the conversation at home.

Finally, there is the strength-in-numbers phenomenon. Individual members often feel powerless to deal with large institutions and agencies, helping professionals (even the group leader), and apparently overwhelming tasks. In unity, however, one often finds strength. Take for example a group of welfare mothers living in a public housing development in which the management is insensitive to their needs, exploitative (for example, levying excessive charges for repairs), and authoritarian (threatening to evict them if they "make trouble"). For such a group, the idea of confronting the management, dealing with city hall if they meet resistance, in other words, standing up for their rights, can be frightening and risky. In one such group, they faced the additional problem of fear of reprisals from youth gangs in the project if they complained about the drug use in the halls, the welfare checks stolen from their mailboxes, and their general sense of lack of security.[23] It was only through patient work by the group leader and a willingness to recognize the fears lurking beneath the surface that these group members were able to find the strength in numbers which allowed them to take a small first step.

This section has described a number of mutual aid processes that can be observed in a group. Of course, these will not necessarily happen by themselves. In fact, it is the difficulty for most groups in learning how to release these powerful forces for change and growth that creates the need for the group worker. In the next section, we describe a number of obstacles which can block the mutual aid process, followed by a section describing how a group leader can assist the group in overcoming these problems.

Obstacles to the Mutual Aid Process

While the *potential* for mutual aid is present in the group, hard work by the group leader and all of its members is required if it is to emerge. In the next chapter on group work skills and in the illustrative chapters which follow, you will see example after example of the delicate moments in which the ability of the group member to take help and the ability of the group to provide help seem to lie in balance. For example, group members will be struggling with feelings and ideas about which they may feel ashamed. "I am that handicapped child's mother! How can I feel such strong feelings of anger toward my own child?"

Strong societal taboos, which declare some areas of discussion or some feelings out of bounds (for example, sexual issues), operate to prevent us from honest discussion. These taboos will be brought from the broader society and enacted in the microcosm of the small group. As the small group gingerly approaches the taboo area, employing indirect communications such as "hints," the worker will have to call the group members' attention to the barrier and assist them in dealing with it, through a combination of support and demand. The members, for their part, will have to find the courage to enter the formerly forbidden areas, in response to the worker's gentle pushing, and begin to discover they are "all in the same boat." The feelings for which they judged themselves so harshly are normal for their situations. The subjects they felt were not for open discussion, the feelings they experienced as possibly too painful to be faced, all take on a manageable status as the healing power of mutual aid begins its work.

A group's culture (norms, taboos, rules of behavior, and so on) is just one example of the many obstacles that may frustrate the emergence of mutual aid in the group. Another common problem is the inability, in the early phases of the life of a group, for members to see the connection between their own sense of urgency and that of the other members. "What can these other people know of my problems and worries; their lives must be so different?" The connection between the agency service and the individual member's felt needs may also be unclear at the beginning. Particularly in a mandated service, where involuntary participation is common, the group member may begin with strong expressions of denial, resistance, and anger to the offer of a group service. Skill will be required on the part of the group worker to help the members overcome their initial reactions to authority and their initial inability to see their stake in the agency service or in the other group members. The contracting process, described in the next chapter, can be the start of this change. Sensitivity to these issues is demonstrated in many of the group examples in the book as workers attempt to reassure members that they still maintain control of their inner lives. Trimble, in chapter 12, illustrates this beautifully in his opening statement to a group of men forced to come to a group for men who batter their wives. After recognizing that they may have been forced to attend (for example, by a judge's order), he speaks directly to the issue of control as he states: "but no one can reach into your mind and heart and order a change. That's where you have complete control."

These obstacles as well as others can serve to frustrate the emergence of the mutual aid potential. One way to view the role of the group leader is by seeing his or her job as that of helping the group to learn how to be a better mutual aid system. For example, the group leader can model effective helping behavior in the way he or she intervenes in the group. Another way of helping would be to call the group members' attention to the obstacles blocking their path. ("Every time someone raises an issue dealing with your difficulties in the sexual area, someone else changes the subject.") The group leader would need to provide support as the group members enter the previously taboo area ("Is it too scary or painful to deal with such a sensitive subject in this group?"), while at the same time, making a demand for work by asking the group to explore and conquer the obstacle ("What is it that makes it hard to talk to each other about sex? Perhaps if we understand that, it might make it easier to risk.") As the group members discuss the obstacle, they are simultaneously overcoming its power to frustrate their efforts at mutual aid. Obstacles revealed are usually much less powerful than those that remain hidden from view and discussion.

Some obstacles, as Gitterman describes in chapter 3, may be avoided by skillful group composition and formation. All groups, however, experience some obstacles, problems, conflicts, and a process which often seems to go two steps forward, and three steps back. These are not signs of the lack of mutual aid potential in the small group; rather, they are indicators to the worker of normative group issues which need to be handled with skill and sensitivity. The effective mutual aid group is not one without problems, but rather, one in which the leader and members become more sophisticated about how to cope with the inherent problems. When they are dealt with, a number of important benefits can be observed in a mutual aid group. In the next section, we propose a statement of function which may help the group leader in his or her efforts to help the group.

THE MEDIATING FUNCTION OF THE GROUP WORKER

A worker must be clear about his or her function in the group. Function is defined here as a description of the specific role of the worker, that is, his or her part in the proceedings. All the interpersonal skill in the world will be of no use to a group worker without a clear sense of the job description. Group process can become very complex, and a worker without a clear, internalized sense of how one helps in the group will inevitably become as lost as the group members.

For example, when a group of teenage boys begins to scapegoat a smaller, weaker member, and that member exhibits a pattern of inviting the abuse, what will the worker say and do? When an individual raises a deeply felt issue and the group seems to turn away from the member, changing the subject, or downplaying the significance of the issue, how will the worker intervene? When a group splits into two opposing camps, seemingly unable to come to a decision or appearing unwilling to listen and to understand each other, how will the worker help? When a group of foster adolescents begins to discuss their use of drugs or their involvement in some illegal activity, what is the group leader's responsibility? When group members espouse positions which are the opposite to the strongly held values of the worker, should he or she challenge them? The list of questions could go on for pages. What is common to each of these examples is that they describe moments when the worker will feel on the spot and unsure how to intervene.

No matter how well armed with interpersonal skills the worker may be, the question remains, to what immediate function will he or she harness those skills? If the worker is not clear about the question of role and is suffering from a form of functional diffusion (taking on many different roles, thus diffusing the clarity of the job description), then the intervention will often flow from the worker's past experiences, current sense of panic, personal value systems, and other sources. For example, the worker might start to protect the scapegoat, or exhort the group members who have turned away from the member in pain, or preach to the adolescents about the evils of drugs. In each case, as they protect, exhort, or preach, they will cut themselves off from the group members and lose their ability to help effectively.

Fortunately, functional diffusion is not a terminal illness. It can be treated with a dose of functional clarity. Schwartz, building on the assumption of the symbiotic relationship between the individual and the group, proposed the role for the worker of mediating the individual/group engagement.[24] This worker function within the group was an extension of his statement of the general function of social work in society as implemented in the small group modality.

If we return to some of those critical moments in the life of a group which we described earlier, then we can illustrate how functional clarity, and in particular, this mediating role, might help the worker intervene effectively. In the teenage scapegoating example, instead of taking the scapegoat's side and alienating the group, the worker would realize that he or she has two "clients" at this critical moment—the individual scapegoat and the group as a whole. One of the central tasks of the mediating function, as described by Schwartz, involves the worker's effort to "search out the common ground between the individual and the group."[25] Thus, the worker needs to understand the purpose of scapegoating in the group, which is often displacing the feelings of the members on the individual who represents the worst example of their own "sins."[26] Scapegoating was part of the ancient Hebrew tradition, which is the source of the word itself. The Hebrews invested the skin (scape) of a goat with the sins of the people, and placed it upon another goat's back, driving the goat into the wilderness. Thus, for another year, the community was absolved of its sins.

With this understanding of the meaning of the scapegoating pattern in mind and with the mediating function as a guide, the worker can implement Schwartz's second set of tasks, that of challenging the obstacles which obscure the common ground between the individual and the group.[27] Rather than siding with one versus the other, the worker must emotionally be with both at the same time. As the worker points out the way in which the group members and the scapegoat have chosen to avoid their own feelings, he or she must provide support to both clients. In chapter 2, the specific skills for implementing this functional role are described and illustrated. For now, the important point is that clarity of function provides the worker with a clear direction for intervention.

In the second example provided earlier, rather than getting mad at the group for apparently rejecting the member in need, the worker mediates the engagement by helping the member articulate the pain of the issue while *simultaneously* acknowledging the group members' pain which causes them to withdraw. For example: "Are Frank's feelings hitting you all so hard that you're finding it difficult to stay with him? Do you have so much pain yourself that it's hard to find any room left in your heart for his pain?" The worker has two "clients" in the mediating framework and must help both to reach out to each other. If the worker is busy trying exhortation to shame the group, he or she cannot be tuned in to the group members' pain which is expressed indirectly through their behavior. The worker is in the ironic situation of demanding that the group members feel for the individual, while lacking empathy for them.

In the third example mentioned earlier, what will the worker do when the group polarizes around an issue with each side taking apparently opposite points of view and holding firm, not even listening to the other half of the group? If the worker's sense of function is diffused and the worker tries to play the role of expert, throwing support to the "right" side in the debate, once again a chance to help may be lost. In the mediating role, the worker would try to look deeply into the connections between the apparent dualism instead of getting lost in what may well be a phony dichotomy. The worker has a point of view about life and needs to share it in the course of the work of the group—what Schwartz described as another task—sharing data.[28] However, whatever the worker's opinions, he or she still has the general function of mediation in the group and sharing data is only one task.

An example from a parent-teen discussion group may help. At one point, the teenagers articulated their need for more freedom from their parents and less structure. They wanted some recognition of their new status. The parents countered with their need to have a say in the lives of their children. The specific examples dealt with curfew times, supervision of schoolwork, the use of alcohol and/or drugs, and sexual freedom. A worker who is unclear about his or her role might get caught up in the details of the debate. For example, siding with the parents if the teens suggested curfew times which were too late, or with the teens if the parents seemed overly protective. As the worker listened to the group, energy would be directed into making "expert" judgments on who was "right." Group members might even ask the worker to play the role of judge.

As the worker becomes caught up in these roles, he or she would fail to play the crucial role of mediating the engagement. Thus, the worker might not listen to the argument unfolding, attempting to tune in to the stake that parents have in seeing their teenage children make a responsible transition to young adulthood. The parents have an investment in their children's learning to take responsibility for themselves, which is essentially what the teens are looking for. At the same time, what is the stake the teens have in having parents who still care enough to want to provide some structure? Would they really want their parents not to care about them any longer? A simple debate on the issue of curfew may change, with the intervention of the worker, into a more basic discussion of a life transition for both the parents and the teens, one that is never easy, one that has no clear and simple answers, and one that must involve some struggle. The worker's investment must not be in a specific curfew time, but rather, in bringing these mixed feelings into the open, in identifying the transitional questions, in helping the parents and teens truly understand what the other is saying and feeling as they experience a normative crisis. With this kind of help, both parents and teens may develop the skills of dealing with the many specific structure/freedom issues they must face and master if they are to keep the family relationship sound through the transition work ahead of them. Functional clarity can help a worker implement this task.

In the final example, dealing with ideas, values, or beliefs expressed by the group members which trouble the worker, a clear sense of function is important. We suggested in the previous illustration that the worker should share his or her view of life, a process Schwartz described as "lending a vision."[29] However, the view of life which the worker *lends* (implying members are free to take it or leave it), must be relevant to the current work of the group and not immediately available to the members. This means that the worker shares from his or her fund of life experience when the group members need access to it, not when the worker decides they need to be "educated." If the worker has a "hidden agenda" which guides the worker's activity, then the members will have to start to invest their energy into guessing what the worker has up his or her sleeve. They have probably already experienced professionals who are doing things to them in indirect ways. In fact, that is usually the reason for their early wariness about the worker's motives. If one believes that the only way to help people is by doing *with* instead of doing *to* them, then the crucial questions are as follows: What are the group members working on at this moment in the group? Do I have information, beliefs, values, and so on that may be helpful to them? How can I share these in such a way that the group members treat them as just one more source of data—not the final word from the final authority?

An example might help at this point. It comes from work with middle-class, white children in a suburban community center in a neighborhood undergoing a change from an all-white to a racially mixed community. In the course of one group meeting, a disparaging comment was made about some of the new black children who had entered the local school. The worker, feeling a great sense of responsibility for "teaching" the right attitudes, intervened and chastised the group member for having expressed a racist comment. The conversation changed immediately, and the worker felt the lesson had been learned. During the week before the next meeting, the worker tuned in (developed some empathy) for what these children might be experiencing at home, in school, and in the community during a tense transition period. He began the next session by reopening the discussion, explaining that he had reacted quickly because of his own strong feelings on the matter, and wondered if this kind of discussion was taking place in their homes and at the school. If they wished, he would try to help them talk about it, if it troubled them. The result was an outpouring of feeling about what they were hearing and experiencing, the pressures they were feeling from parents (in some cases) and peer group to act in certain ways toward the new members of the community. For many of them, there was a real dilemma, as they felt torn between what they felt was right to do and what they felt they were being forced to do. Because of the worker's skillful catching of his mistake, his clarifying in his own mind what his functional role was, he was able to help the group members create a place where they could really talk about the issues.

In an adult illustration of the same issue, staff at a transition house for battered women felt so strongly about their own feminist ideology that they found it hard to accept the views expressed by women who were just starting to develop a positive sense of themselves as women and a belief in their rights. When these women expressed views such as "Sometimes I asked for the beating," "My man really loves me and can be nice to live with most of the time," and "Living with him is really better than being alone," staff members found it hard to understand a view so different from their own. Lectures and admonishments designed to change the group members' attitudes often only drove them underground. The group members learned to participate in an "illusion of work" where they said what they thought the workers wanted to hear. The tragedy was that often, at the end of their time in the shelter, the women returned to the abusing spouse.

It was not that the ideology was wrong. In fact, it is in helping clients to deepen their understanding of gender issues which affect their lives, helping them to see how role stereotypes have been oppressive to them, helping them to understand how they have internalized these stereotypes and have lost touch with their sense of their own value as individuals and as women—it is these steps and others which will help them grow, change, and develop the strength to reject a life of abuse. The problem rested with the group leaders' sense of their function in the group, which was to "preach" these ideas. With functional clarity, the leaders might express their genuine understanding of the dilemmas expressed by the group members and then help them to help each other in learning how to cope when you feel two ways at the same time. For example: "That's the struggle for you, isn't it? You know you can't live with him when he is this way. You know he can be dangerous to you and your kids. And yet, a part of you still feels you love him and need him and you're afraid to be without him. How about others in the group? Have you felt the same way as June? What can she do about this?"

Often, the group members can offer support and advice, since June's struggle may be theirs as well. The workers can and must share their ideas about how and why women find themselves in this position. However, these must be shared when appropriate to the immediate work of the group member. That is the only time they can be heard, understood, and remembered. No matter how sound or important the ideas, values, and beliefs may be,

the worker cannot substitute his or her experience for the work the group member must do.

In addition to thinking about the worker's function in relation to the group and its processes, one also has to consider the worker's function in relation to the problems being explored (the content of the discussions). The Life Model proposes a schema for understanding and helping group members to deal with life stresses and their consequences. As previously described, clients' "troubles" are identified as arising from three interrelated problems of living: (1) life transitions, (2) environmental pressures, and (3) maladaptive interpersonal processes. With life changes, the social work function is to help the group and its members to meet the particular task associated with developmental stages and the accompanying status and role demands and crisis events. Helping a group and its members move through life transitions so that their adaptive functions and problem solving skills are supported and strengthened is a valuable and important professional activity.

The social work function with environmental concerns is to help the group and its members to use available organizational and network resources and to influence these environmental forces to be responsive. Mobilizing and strengthening the goodness-of-fit between natural and formed groups and their social environments provides social work with a core mediating function. With maladaptive interpersonal group processes, the social work function is to help group members to recognize the obstacles and to learn to communicate more openly and directly and attain greater mutuality in their relationships.[30]

The Life Model offers a normative perspective on the troubles people experience. Whatever a client's diagnosis, he or she still has to manage life problems. The problems-in-living schema (life transitions, environmental pressures, and maladaptive interpersonal processes) accounts for the troubles of most clients. It enables the worker to design preventive services (see chapter 3) as well as to develop clinical strategies in an orderly and focused way. To illustrate, a worker was assigned to a group of recent widows. In the fifth session, the members were agitated and complained about their sense of loneliness and isolation. At this particular moment were the members asking for help with the life transition—that is, with exploring their grief and helping them through their mourning stages? Or were they at this particular moment asking for help with environmental isolation—that is, with getting connected to new networks to do things to combat their loneliness? Or were they at this particular moment indirectly complaining that the worker and group experience were being unhelpful and requesting attention to their interpersonal concerns—that is, in dealing with their struggles about the worker's competence or the member's ability to help? At each moment the worker has to consider whether the members are asking for help with life transitional, environmental, or interpersonal issues and to be responsive to their primary concerns. Unfortunately, too often our interventions are not based upon an examination of members' latent messages, but rather upon our own (or our agency's) preoccupations. A worker committed to "advocacy" practice might direct the group to environmental issues; the worker committed to "sensitivity work" might direct the members to interpersonal issues; and the worker committed to "psychological practice" may direct the members to life transitional issues. Group members are not responsible for confirming and conforming to our interests; our professional responsibility is to join their natural life processes, to follow their leads and to be responsive to their cues.

CONCLUSION

We have given a number of examples of how functional clarity can come to the aid of a group worker when the going gets tough. While the mediating function was suggested as a helpful one in understanding this complex task, it is certainly not the only way to describe the group worker's part in the proceedings. We are still at the beginning stage of our theorizing and research in the field, and we are far from being ready to vote on such issues. This statement of function has been shared as one that has proved helpful to the authors of this chapter as they struggle to find ways of deepening their understanding of practice. In the next chapter, the specific skills required to put this function into action in the various phases in the life of the group (preliminary, beginning, work, and transition/ending) will be described and illustrated. The ideas drawn from the Life Model view of the client and the concept of mutual aid will also be elaborated and illustrated in the group examples which follow.

NOTES

1. Carel B. Germain and Alex Gitterman. *The Life Model of Social Work Practice* (New York: Columbia University Press, 1980).

2. For his seminal work on the mutual aid model, see William Schwartz, "The Social Worker in the Group," in *New Perspectives on Services to Groups: Theory, Organization and Practice* (New York: National Association of Social Workers, 1961), pp. 7-34; and *Social Welfare Forum, 1961* (New York: Columbia University Press, 1961), pp. 146-77. See also Lawrence Shulman, *The Skills of Helping Individuals and Groups, Second Edition* (Itasca, Ill.: F. E. Peacock Publishers, Inc., 1984).

3. William Schwartz, "Social Group Work: The Interactionist Approach," in *Encyclopedia of Social Work,* Vol. 2, ed. John B. Turner (New York: National Association of Social Workers, 1977), pp. 1328-38.

4. Ibid.

5. See Carel B. Germain, "An Ecological Perspective in Casework Practice," *Social Casework* 54 (July 1973): 323-330.

6. People feel stress when they experience an imbalance between a *perceived* demand and the *perceived* capability to meet the demand through the use of available internal and external resources.

7. Erik H. Erikson, "Growth and Crises of the Healthy Personality," in Erik H. Erikson, *Identity and the Life Cycle: Psychological Issues,* Monograph 1 (New York: International Press, 1959), pp. 50-100.

8. For examples of issues related to self-worth, see S. I. Allyne et al., "Psychosocial Aspects of Sickle-Cell Disease," *Health and Social Work* 1 (November 1976): 104-119; S. Conyard, M. Krishnamurthy, and H. Dosik, "Psychosocial Aspects of Sickle-Cell Anemia in Adolescents," *Health and Social Work* 5 (February 1980): 20-26; Lepontois, Joan, "Adolescents with Sickle-Cell Anemia Deal with Life and Death," *Social Work in Health Care* 1 (Fall 1975): 71-80.

9. Carol Hooker, "Learned Helplessness," *Social Casework* 21 (May 1976): 194-98.

10. See Lean W. Chestang, "Character Development in a Hostile Environment," in *Life Span Development,* ed. Martin Bloom (New York: Macmillan Publishing Co., 1980), pp. 40-50; and William H. Grier and Price M. Cobbs, *Black Rage* (New York: Harper & Row, 1968).

11. Rhodes identified seven sequential stages of family development. See Sonya L. Rhodes, "Developmental Approach to the Life Cycle of the Family," *Social Casework* 58 (May 1977): 301-311.

12. Golan has described eleven adult life transitions. See Naomi Golan, *Passing Through Transitions* (New York: Free Press, 1981).

13. While our developmental knowledge is primarily based upon the nuclear family, we are becoming more aware of the developmental tasks confronting the single parent. We remain, however, relatively uneducated about other family forms such as the gay or homosexual couple, the reconstituted family, the extended family, and communal families. We also need to be better educated about the developmental varieties due to ethnicity, social class, and gender.

14. Levinson and Sheehy offer poignant insights into adult life issues and struggles. See Daniel J. L. Levinson, The *Seasons of a Man's Life* (New York: Alfred A. Knopf, 1978); Gail Sheehy, *Passages: Predictable Crises of Adult Life* (New York: E. P. Dutton, 1976).

15. Barbara S. Dohrenwend and Bruce P. Dohrenwend, "Class and Race as Status Related Sources of Stress," in *Social Stress,* ed. S. Levin and N. Skotch (Chicago: Aldine Publishing Co., 1976), pp. 111-142.

16. Due to space limitations, the physical environment, the built world and the natural world, will not be discussed.

17. Lawrence Shulman, "Scapegoats, Group Workers, and Pre-emptive Interventions," *Social Work* 12 (April 1967): 37-43; Ezra F. Vogel and Norman W. Bell, "The Emotionally Disturbed Child as the Family Scapegoat," in *The Family,* ed. N. Bell and E. Vogel (Glencoe, Ill.: Free Press, 1968), pp. 412-427.

18. Over time, a family or group elaborates a division of roles and tasks through which responsibilities are allocated, patterns of com-

munication through which interaction takes place, and patterns of affective ties through which relationships are established. The interrelationship of these patterns represents the concept of social structure.

19. Schwartz, "The Social Worker in the Group." See also Petr Kropotkin, *Mutual Aid: A Factor of Evolution* (New York: Alfred A. Knopf, 1925); George Herbert Mead, *Mind, Self and Society* (Chicago: University of Chicago Press, 1934).

20. Schwartz, "The Social Worker in the Group," p. 15.

21. Ibid., p. 19.

22. Shulman, *The Skills of Helping Individuals and Groups*, chapter 7.

23. Ibid., 378–85.

24. Schwartz, "The Social Worker in the Group."

25. Ibid., p. 21.

26. *The American Heritage Dictionary of the English Language* (Boston: American Heritage Publishers, and Houghton Mifflin, 1969), p. 1159.

27. Schwartz, "The Social Worker in the Group," p. 25.

28. Ibid., p. 27.

29. Ibid., p. 28.

30. Germain and Gitterman, *The Life Model,* pp. 77–296.

CHAPTER 2

Group Work Method

This chapter focuses on skill: what the group leader does when he or she tries to help group members help each other.[1] Most of the skills used by the group leader are core communications, relationship, and problem-solving skills which are important in all helping modalities (such as individual or family work). Some skills are unique to work with more than one client at a time. Since so many of the skills are generic in nature, readers who have worked with people in other modalities will soon discover that they already know more about group work than they had imagined.

In order to provide illustrations of the skills in action, process recording excerpts have been drawn from the articles found in this book. Thus, the skill will be named, described, and illustrated with examples of real workers responding to real group members on a moment-by-moment basis.

This attention to the details of method was central to Schwartz's work.[2] He stressed that the worker's knowledge and values were made known to the client through the worker's actions. He pointed to a need to describe method in a way that was specific, but not overly prescriptive, thereby developing a structure for practice which provided freedom for spontaneous and artistic responses. For example, although a number of specific empathic skills will be described in this chapter, the way in which each group leader demonstrates his or her capacity to empathize with clients might differ depending upon highly personal factors. One worker's facial expressions might convey as much meaning to the client as another's hand on a shoulder or another's tears. The injunction against an overly prescriptive approach cautioned against mechanical descriptions of process in which each client behavior called forth a specific worker response. Attention to method had to be at a level that provided answers to the worker's legitimate need to know how to practice, while still leaving room for individual artistry.

In order to simplify the complex task of describing the helping process in groups, Schwartz borrowed ideas about time and its impact on process from Taft.[3] He then built upon these to develop his four phases of work: the preliminary, beginning, work, and ending/transition phases. The preliminary phase involves the worker's activity before the first group meeting. Gitterman describes the worker's tasks in setting up a group in chapter 3.[4] The beginning phase refers to the first sessions in which important contracting work takes place. The work phase is the ongoing or middle period, and the ending/

transition phase comes into play as the group completes its work.

These phases are useful when thinking about group work, since each one contains its own interesting dynamics and calls for specific worker activity. This framework is used to organize the balance of this chapter.

In addition to being useful in understanding the life process of a group over time, the phases-of-work concept is also helpful in understanding each individual group session, which has its own preliminary, beginning, work, middle, and ending phase. Thus, the framework is used to understand the life of the group over time as well as the dynamics of each individual session.[5]

THE PRELIMINARY PHASE OF WORK

A major skill in the preliminary phase of work is the development of the worker's preparatory empathy. This technique can be used before the first meeting. Schwartz termed this process *"tuning in."*[6] It involves the worker's efforts to get in touch with potential feelings and concerns which the group members may bring to the encounter. The four major areas for tuning in include issues related to the authority of the group leader (for example, "What kind of person will this leader be?"), concerns related to the group ("Who are these other people and how will they react to me?"), concerns related to the purpose of the group (for example, the guilt often experienced by parents of handicapped children when faced with their angry feelings toward their child), and the indirect ways in which the group members may use group process to communicate (such as scapegoating).

The rationale for employing the tuning-in skills is related to the indirect nature of communications used by group members, particularly in the early sessions before a climate of trust can be developed. Group members will often only hint at their real feelings in relation to taboo subjects (such as authority, dependency, death, sexuality). By tuning in, the group leader can be more sensitive to the group members' indirect cues.

This increased sensitivity compliments a second skill, *responding directly to indirect communications* and when used together, can significantly speed up the work of the group allowing the leader and the members to deal more quickly with significant issues. The responding skill involves anticipating and putting into words the thoughts and feelings of the group members. I have referred to this skill elsewhere as "articulating the client's feelings."[7] In addition to speeding up the work of the group, the use of this skill reveals to the group members early in the life of the group the worker's capacity to be empathic, honest, and direct. Each of these qualities is important in the building of the working relationship.

For example, when a member of a group for parents of handicapped children inquires in the first session if the worker is married, a direct response might be as follows: "No, I'm not married, and I don't have children. Are you wondering if I'm going to be able to understand what it's like for you?" Such a response, if said with genuine feeling and not merely as an intellectual inquiry, will often help to open up the working relationship. The alternative response of defensively describing the worker's credentials (such as, "At my school of social work I took a course in working with developmentally handicapped children") will often serve to distance the worker and group members further.

Of course, if the worker is to respond directly and without defensiveness, he or she must have tuned in to their own normal feelings of insecurity, which may arise during the preparation for such a first meeting. Being sensitive to one's own feelings and fears lessens the likelihood of responding inappropriately; however, the group leader should anticipate that he or she will make mistakes. In fact, effective practice is described in this chapter as shortening the time between making and catching a mistake. Perfect work is a myth. Group leaders who are viewed as paragons of virtue—always tuned in and always correct in their responses—are a part of this fiction. This image tends to immobilize new leaders. A more forgiving and reasonable view would expect a new group leader to miss the first cues of concern about his or her understanding of the group members and their problems. Acknowledging a mistake can be helpful to the group work. For example, the group leader questioned about his or her marital status could begin the next session by saying: "When you asked if I had children last week, I felt on the spot and told you about my training. I thought about it during the week, and I think you may have really been wondering if I could understand what it was like for you to raise children with a handicap. If I'm going to help, I'm going to have to understand what it feels like for each of you. Can you let me know?" Not only has the group inquiry been answered, the worker has also begun to demonstrate a desire to understand.

Tuning in also includes sensitizing oneself to potential client concerns about the work of the group and anticipating some of the indirect ways in which these concerns may be communicated. For example, in married couples groups I have led, issues of a sexual nature were difficult to discuss both between the partners in the marriage and within the mutual aid groups. Tuning in to sources of stress may make it easier to pick up the call for help which is often raised through conflicts over other issues. Tuning in can help to clarify the common pattern in which sexual dysfunctioning leads to a vicious cycle of mutual blaming stemming from each partner's own feelings of inadequacy. A worker who has tuned in effectively can more easily pick up the cues, reach for the hidden agenda, and then help members deal with the difficult feelings—the ones which when revealed, often offer the possibility of reestablishing a caring and supportive relationship.

Finally, in the group situation, one needs to learn to tune in to the language of the group as a whole.[8] This is one of the skills unique to group and to family work which helps to differentiate group work practice from individual work. In addition to the individual indirect communications of group members, the group itself may communicate through its process of interaction. Often operating on an unconscious basis, the group acts as a dynamic organism where the movements of each member are affecting and being affected by the interaction. Thus, a group of teenage boys struggling with issues of male identity may scapegoat a member who embodies the ambivalence they fear in themselves as their way of "speaking" to the group leader. Preliminary-phase work, both before the first session and from week to week, can help a group leader to identify patterns of interaction and to understand the particular functions played by these individual members. Of course, experience over time helps the group leader to understand better this subtle language of the group.

THE BEGINNING PHASE OF WORK

First meetings in all helping relationships are important. If handled well, they can lay a foundation for productive work, begin the process of strengthening the working relationship between group leader and members, as well as beginning the process of helping the group members develop a productive culture for work (such as mutual trust). If handled badly, they can turn the group members away from the services. The skills involved in making a positive start can be grouped together under the rubric of *contracting*. The general goals of this contracting process include clarifying to group members the agency's purpose in offering the group (agency service) and identifying the common ground between these purposes and the group members' sense of immediate urgency (client needs). The overlapping area between services and needs, as pictured by Schwartz in Figure 2-1, provides the core of the working contract.[9]

will be understandably raised until the contracting process eases their minds. In addition, unless group members can perceive a clear and immediate stake in the work of the group, they will not invest themselves in a meaningful way. This connection is often subtle, partial, and changeable over time; however, some clear stake must exist for effective work to proceed. If group members suspect that the agency, through its agent, the group leader, has a "hidden agenda" aimed at changing them or indirectly influencing them, then their participation will be, at best an "illusion of work."

In addition to a clear idea about group purpose, group members also need some reassurance about the way in which the group leader will help. They may initially fear the power of this authority figure, a fear arising from previous experiences with symbols of authority (such as teachers, other helping professionals, and so on). By understanding that the worker's job lies in helping them to help each other,

FIGURE 2.1

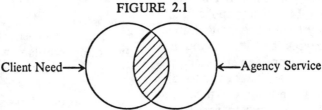

Client Need⟶   ⟵Agency Service

The contracting process also involves specifying for the group members the role that the worker will play, the mutual need members have for each other, and the mutual expectations and obligations of the group leader and the group members.

The argument is made that group members desperately need some clear structure in order to free them to work. They begin a new situation with some anxiety about what will happen to them, or perhaps be done to them, and their defenses

group members become increasingly able to make effective use of the worker's assistance.

Group members must also appreciate how the other members of the group relate to their own concerns. They often feel that they are alone with their feelings and are reassured when they discover that the group members are often experiencing similar feelings. Finally, group members need to know the rules of the game, such as what the leader and other group members will expect of them and what they can expect in return. Confidentiality is another important area to address in a first meeting.

While the contracting agenda is an imposing one, it does not have to be completed in the first session. In fact, first sessions should be seen as the beginning of this process. The leader may need a number of sessions to work it through. As the group begins to work, its purpose becomes clearer to members as specific issues are raised and discussed. As group members watch the worker in action, he or she gives meaning to the description of the group leader's role articulated in the first session. As group members listen to the concerns and feelings of others, they discover their common ground in deeply meaningful ways. Working contracts thus may evolve and change over time.

In order to accomplish the task of contracting, the following skills are needed: clarifying purpose, clarifying role, reaching for member feedback, defining mutual expectations and obligations, and encouraging intermember interaction.

The skills of clarifying purpose and role can be encompassed in the worker's efforts to make an "opening statement" to the group members, one which clearly states the worker's agenda (for offering the group) and the way in which the worker wishes to help. It is crucial in this statement to avoid the use of typical professional jargon (such as "facilitate," "enhance," and "enable") and to find ways of verbalizing purpose in words that can have direct meaning to the group members. It is often useful to prepare such a statement and to try it out with colleagues or clients in order to develop an effective opening. The statement of role should be simple and may be similar to the following: "My job will be to help you talk to and listen to

each other, to share your problems, and to help you help each other. Whenever useful, I'll throw my own ideas in along the way."

Reaching for feedback can be done through a simple exercise in which members are asked to share, *with each other*, the concerns and issues they feel should be part of the agenda. The sharing with each other, a form of "problem swapping," is also the way in which the worker begins the process of encouraging intermember communications. Group members are used to talking to the leader, the symbol of authority; therefore, they require help to see that their work is really with each other. Mutual expectations and obligations, which can be discussed at the start or the end of the first session, provide an open statement of the group's structure as it has been negotiated with the group members. Issues of confidentiality, attendance, expectations of participation of all members, and the like can be discussed at this time.

Some examples of this process, drawn from the following chapters, illustrate the skills and the variations in the contracting process introduced by setting, client population, issues of mandatory versus voluntary involvement, and so on. In the first excerpt, drawn from Indelicato and Goldberg's description of their work with parents of learning disabled children (chapter 10), purpose is carefully partialized into potential themes of concern and offered to group members as "handles" with which they begin their work. The simple question at the end demonstrates the reaching for feedback skill.

Worker: In the letter we stated that we would like to try to set up parent groups to give parents a place to talk with each other about their concerns involving their children. We've noted that parents who come to the clinic usually express some concern about their child's ability to keep up with the schoolwork, difficulty in making and keeping friends, or not getting along with brothers and sisters. Do these sound like some of the things you have experienced with your child?

In a second example, Berman-Rossi in her work with a group of institutionalized aged (chapter 18) tries to explain how she will play the mediating role between the residents and the staff:

In the midst of a heated discussion of their relationship with some nursing staff members, Mrs. Mann said she thought I should go and tell them off for them. Mrs. Rosen said she didn't agree, because if I did, the staff would never listen to me again. They would think I was on the residents' side. There was a hush, and Mrs. Mann looked at me and said, "Aren't you on our side? Don't you agree with us?" I said that I thought she was asking an important question. I said that actually, I thought I was on neither side, but rather on the side of working out the troubles between them and nursing. To do that, I had to have a special relationship with each, where each knew I was listening to them, while not siding with the other. Mrs. Mann thought and said, "That's pretty tricky." I said I agreed. I thought she had put her finger on what was the hardest part of being a social worker—listening hard to both sides in a conflict, siding with neither, while working in the middle to help with the conflict between them. Mrs. Mann winked at me, smiled and said, "But you really know we are right." We all laughed. I let the comment go as I recalled staff making a similar bid for my allegiance. We moved on to thinking through the next steps in their work with nursing staff.

In a third and final example the issue of authority and the mandatory nature of a group is dealt with directly by Trimble as part of his opening statement to a group of male batterers (chapter 12), most of whom have been forced to come to the group by a judge or through the threat of losing their marriages. While not evading his authority nor soft-pedaling the demands he will place on the men, he still demonstrates sensitivity to the underlying issue of control in their lives:

Leader: (After explaining attendance rules and expectations of participation on members, as well as the mandatory reporting role of the group leader). I'm sure it is possible to follow all these rules and not change, not open up to facing yourself or to the other men here. You can probably get through this group and not really change. That's up to you. The judge may order you to be here or your wife may be saying that she won't come back unless you get help. And as I have said, we require your anger diary and regular attendance in order for you to stay here, but no one can reach into your mind and heart and order a change. That's where you have complete control.

THE WORK PHASE

Describing the skills of the group worker using the phases of work to organize the discussion can be misleading. In many ways, these skills cross boundaries and are important in every phase of work. Even phase-related skills, such as the contracting skills, become important again at crucial points in the life of the group as contracts are renegotiated to reflect the changing nature of the group process. The use of time as a backdrop to the discussion is a somewhat artificial device; however, it can be helpful in partializing a complex process.

In the work phase, sometimes referred to as the middle or ongoing phase, the general goal of the worker is to help the group develop an effective mutual aid system. The worker recognizes that effective contracting is crucial for laying the foundations of a good working group. However, it is only the beginning. The worker's task is not completed with contracting. He or she must be an active participant in the process of helping the group members and the group as a whole overcome the barriers to effective work that are inherent in any small group system.

The idea of expecting things to go wrong in the group is a crucial one, especially for those new to group work who tend to take total responsibility for the process. If the group could work effectively on its own, the group leader would not be needed. While groups vary from those which are immature (where members are unable to see their connections, much less work on them), to those which are more mature working groups (where members can freely share more difficult and taboo feelings, to reach out and offer direct support and help), most groups need the worker's help to become more efficient mutual aid systems. When there is a problem in the group, the work seems to stop, members turn away from each other, and the group regresses, the group leader is not failing, but rather the group is giving signals to the leader that it needs intervention. Assistance is required to help the group cope with the many different ways in which the mutual aid process can and will be sidetracked during the life of the group. As group leaders increase their sense of competency, the obstacles become less threatening. The worker's energy is then free to invest in his or her tasks designed to help the group members take increasing responsibility for their work.

This chapter is too short to allow for a full discussion of the dynamics and skills of this phase of work.[10] In an oversimplified summary, however, the major goals of the leader in the work phase are to help the individual group members to reach out for help from the group as a whole, to help the group members pro-vide mutual aid to others (thus helping themselves), and to help the group as a whole pay attention to its own developmental tasks, such as developing a consensus on the directions of work and developing a climate of trust.

For the reasons cited in the discussion of the preliminary phase, group members will reach out for help with some ambivalence. They may raise their concerns and then deny they have them. They may hint at serious problems by sharing problems that are safer to discuss. They will share their anger, often directing it at group members or the leader, while trying simultaneously to hide and reveal the deep hurts which are just below the surface. Since they cannot get help unless the group understands their true feelings, a third force, the group leader, must concentrate on helping the individual reach out to the group even at those times when he or she appears to be turning away.

The group worker in the mutual aid model has a unique responsibility in that he or she always has "two clients." The first is the individual member, and the second is the group as a whole. Thus, at precisely the same time that the leader is emotionally with the individual, he or she must also be able to identify with the second client, the group.

This function is illustrated when an individual raises painful feelings which are shared by the group members. It is not uncommon for the group to seem to turn away from the member, ignore the offering, change the subject, rush in to provide premature and artificial reassurances (such as, "Don't worry, you will get over it.") or even attack the member. If the group leader identifies with the member, for example by siding with or protecting him, then the leader will miss the communications from the group members about their feelings related to the issue. In this specific example, the mediating function calls for the leader to search out the common ground between the two clients. For example, "You all seem to be angry at Frank right now for feeling helpless and hopeless, and yet isn't that what you have all felt yourselves from time to time? It must be hard for you to hear it from Frank."

In the third general area of work, the group leader needs to educate the group as a whole as to how it will operate and must help it to develop the structures it requires to work more effectively. For example, in my married couples groups, the first direct issue in the sexual area often comes at the "door knob" as members are ready to leave. This, of course, makes it hard to deal with the subject and serves to protect the member raising it. A discussion of why it is difficult to talk about sex and of why it is so often raised at the end of the session may help the group to develop a more open culture for work in this area, with more accepting norms of behavior and a greater ability to deal with taboo subjects. Members who are made aware of their tendency to raise issues at the end may become members who have the courage to raise them more directly at the start. A group that acknowledges its dependency on trust, honesty, and a willingness to risk will work on creating conditions which support and even demand such behavior on the part of members.

Important skills for group leaders as they carry out this mediating function and work on these three major tasks include the following: sessional tuning in, sessional contracting, elaborating, empathic, sharing worker's feelings, demand for work, pointing out obstacles; sharing data and sessional ending.[11] These skill groupings will be discussed and illustrated in the balance of this section.

Sessional Tuning In

Sessional tuning in is similar to the general tuning in described earlier. In this case, it is the preparatory empathy the worker endeavors to develop prior to *each* group meeting. In some cases, the events of the group session itself can be used to deepen one's feelings for the work, as illustrated in this excerpt from Berman-Rossi's work with the institutionalized aged (chapter 18).

Many years ago, at the end of my first group meeting with older people (average age eighty-four) I said to the members that I would see them next week. Mrs. Gross rose slowly, turned, looked at me and said, "God willing." She slowly continued walking. I was stunned. Could it mean that she did not know from week to week whether she would be alive? What was it like to live with the reality that life might end at any instant? I was only twenty-nine years old and had just given birth to my first daughter. I could hardly grasp the meaning of what had just occurred between us. It would be a while before I understood how this incident would affect our work together, individually and in the group.

At other times, it may be the worker's awareness of events which take place in the life of the group members between meetings which activates the tuning in process. For example, Orr, writing about her work with the elderly in a community setting (chapter 17), describes her attempts to put herself in her group members' shoes after hearing about the death of a member.

Worker: (Putting herself in her group members' place and carrying on a form of internal dialogue) It really hits hard when a member of the group dies; it hits so close to home. I could be next. So Maddie died; I'll hear about two more people soon; you know they always happen in threes. It's not just Maddie. Maddie's death reminds me of when my closest friend died, not so long ago. It makes me go back to when I lost a husband. That was so terribly difficult for me. Whenever someone else dies, I remember how long it took me to get over it. You never get over a death of someone close to you. Maddie's husband will certainly have a hard time. He was devoted to her. That's how it was with my husband. It makes you feel so empty, like the world's caving in . . . like there is no way of knowing when your time is up.

As Orr skillfully demonstrates in her description of the meeting which followed this tuning-in exercise, her preparation helped her to hear the indirect cues of many of these concerns and, in turn, made it possible for her to help her elderly members deal with them.

Sessional Contracting

It was earlier suggested that the phases of work could be used to understand each individual group session. Thus, each meeting has a beginning phase in which the central task is to identify what the individual members, or the group as a whole, will work on in that session. Because of the many indirect ways in which individuals and the group itself may raise issues, the worker must be tentative in the first part of each session, listening carefully to pick up the often difficult to perceive thread of the current theme of concern. Therefore, it is important for the worker not to latch onto a concern too quickly until he or she really knows what the group is working on. Even if the group members had all agreed on an agenda at the previous meeting, events between sessions can often change their current sense of urgency.

In the example which follows, Schaffer and Pozzaglia, describing their work with a group of Spanish-speaking parents of children with cancer (chapter 16), reach past the safe, opening conversation on housing and transportation for the deeper theme of the session—the group members' fears for their children.

Mrs. J.: Oh, you're from Chile. So where are you living now?

Mr. P.: In a hotel.

Mrs. J.: You live in a hotel and not an apartment?

Mr. P.: Yes, because all of the apartments are either very far away from the hospital or if they're close, they're too expensive. So, we are living on 32nd Street, but it is still far and taxis are expensive.

Mrs. M.: You can catch a bus right out front.

Mr. P.: No, because of Gloria's disease she could get an infection being around so many other people on the bus.

Worker: It sounds as if it could be dangerous for her to get an infection. Why is that?

Mr. P.: Gloria has extremely low blood counts since her bone marrow transplant. I worry about how unprotected she is, so I try my best to keep her away from crowds.

Mrs. M.: What does she have?

Mr. P.: Leukemia.

Mrs. J.: So does my son. (Period of silence.)

Worker: (To the group) How did it affect you when you discovered that your children had leukemia?

Mrs. J.: I was, like crazy. I couldn't believe that this could happen to my child. I kept asking, "Why, why?" This disease is terrible. I was in a state of despair.

Mr. P.: (To Mr. J.) When someone tells you something like that, it's terrible. I was sure my child was going to die, but thank God she's lived longer than the doctor originally thought; but we're still scared.

The assumption underlying sessional contracting is that the agenda for work emerges from the sense of urgency felt by the members, and that the group leader's task is not to select the agenda but rather to help the members identify the issues they need and want to work on. That does not mean that the worker never raises an issue for discussion. Some items may be raised because the agency structure requires the group to pay some attention to them (for example, a change in agency policy). In other cases, the worker may be aware of an important event in the lives of the members, and rather than waiting for the group to deal with it, the worker may tackle it directly . The following example from Poynter-Berg's work with institutionalized schizophrenic women illustrates the point as she starts a meeting by referring to the death of a patient on the ward.

I said something had happened on the unit on Friday that I felt they must have feelings about and wondered if they wanted to talk about it—that was, Mrs. James, a patient, had died on the unit on Friday (a natural death). Pause. Beverly said, "Mrs. James died?" I nodded and asked if they all knew who she was. Nods. I asked if they knew she'd died. Beverly said, "I heard about it—it's a sad thing to think about." I said it is a sad thing to think about and asked if they had any questions or thoughts about it they wanted to share with the others. Rhoda had tears coming to her eyes, and I gently pointed this out to her, asking if she was feeling sad. She said, "No." Beverly again said, "It *is* sad." I nodded. I said it's kind of a scary feeling, wondering if it will happen to someone else, and maybe to us. Marie and Beverly nodded. Arlene was extremely calm and silent today. Beverly said, "I don't feel scared—just sad." She said, "It 'minds me of my father and mother who died; my father five years ago and my mother three years ago." She held up her fingers to indicate the years. She said, "But I still have my brother, who visits on Sundays." I said that was good. Rhoda was tearing, and I asked gently if she was thinking about someone who had died. She said, "Yeah, my father died."

Elaborating Skills

The elaboration skills are those used by the worker to help the client tell his or her story. These same skills are important in individual counseling, with the difference in the group context that the member is helped to talk to the other members. Thus, as the worker helps the individual to elaborate, he or she simultaneously *encourages intermember communications.*

In order to implement these elaborating skills, the worker must first demonstrate *the skill of containment.* Simply put, the worker keeps quiet as the member speaks and contains the impulse to jump in with solutions, interpretations, a change of subjects, and so on. This skill appears to be a passive one; however, in reality, the temptation to take over the session and to "help" can be so powerful that I view containment as an active skill.

As the worker contains him or herself, *the skill of focused listening* is important. Focused listening involves listening while keeping in mind both the purpose of the group and the tuning-in exercises. All conversation, even the premeeting chatter which often precedes the official start of the meeting, can be understood as potential indirect communications to the worker and the group. Not only is conversation important, but actions (such as a nervous new member spilling a cup of coffee), nonverbal cues (depressed expressions, arms folded with face flushed—apparently signaling resistance) can be significant cues to the underlying communications. In one example, used later in this section, an empty chair in the circle signals the group members' need to talk about a member who died during the week. While focused listening is important in all counseling, once again, the group variation emerges from the "two client" idea; the worker must listen to the individual members *and* to the group as a whole.

Another skill useful in helping the client tell the story is *the skill of questioning*. The worker seeks to help the member elaborate on the question, statement, problem, conflict, or incident. For example, take the following seemingly simple question asked in an adoption group: "How do you tell your child he was adopted?" The worker who does not use containment and instead uses the question as an opening for a prepared lecture on the "right" way to handle this difficult question, may miss the real issue. Instead, by asking the member to speak some more, to explain why he or she is raising the question right now, or to explain why the question is troubling the worker may yield a number of difficult (themes of) concerns which go beyond the simple phrasing of an answer to an adopted child. Often, it is not the adoptive child's feelings about the adoption which are at issue, but rather those of the adopting parents: "Will I be able to handle the stresses of raising such a child?" "Can we love this child as one of our own?" "Will this child still love us or want to find his or her *real* parents?" In effect, the worker and the group need to know much more about the question before they can provide meaningful answers.

Often, indirect communications are most evident when the subject is taboo. In those cases, a strategy that *helps the members discuss taboo subjects* is needed. In the following example, the taboo subject is death, a particular concern to Lubell's group of patients with kidney failure (chapter 15). Many of the skills cited in this section thus far are illustrated in the process recording.

At the next group meeting, the patients included an empty chair in the circle. When the social worker commented on it, Victoria said it must be for John, who had just died. The worker said it must be hard on them when someone dies with whom they were close. Victoria acknowledged that you get to know everyone in the program very well. Others nodded. They discussed how depressed John had been. The worker asked if his death made them think more about their own situation. There was silence. Suzanne said she worried about it a lot. Others shared their fear of being alone and their preoccupation with death. Then they started to recount the details of every death that had occurred among patients in the unit. Victoria said most people who died were depressed at the time or just could not accept dialysis. The worker asked whether it made it easier for them to accept someone's death if that person were somehow different from the other patients in the dialysis unit, if they could attribute the death to something other than kidney failure. The patients agreed.

The first "offering" of the (theme of) concern was the empty chair of the dead member. The second offering emerged with the help of the worker's elaborating skills as they discussed the death directly. With further help from the worker, the third offering finally lands on the taboo theme—their own fears for their lives.

The silence in the example, right after the worker confronts the issue head on, raises another important set of elaborating skills: the *skills of exploring silences*. Silences in group meetings can be stressful for workers. They often feel something may have gone wrong and have a difficult time containing themselves. Actually, as in this preceding example, the silence meant that the worker had intervened effectively. In one of my early studies of practice skill, we analyzed 120 hours of videotaped social work practice, half with individuals (sixty sessions) and half with groups (sixty sessions).[12] Employing a categorized observation system developed in the project, we were able to identify and code interactions at three-second intervals and then analyze these numeric patterns by computer. Most often, when faced with three seconds or more of silence, the worker changed the subject. Silences were clearly uncomfortable for the workers. Helpful skills in exploring silences include *remaining silent in the face of silence* and *reaching inside the silence.*

Remaining silent in the face of silence simply means respecting the quiet in the group. If emotions are being felt, the worker allows the members time to feel them while trying to connect to his or her own feelings. If it's a thoughtful silence, time to think can help. It is important that the silence not go on too long, since it could easily turn into a battle of wills as worker and group members wait for the other to speak. At those moments, exploring the silence might be attempted by saying: "You're quiet now. What are you thinking?" or "Are your feelings hitting you hard right now?" or "You are all so quiet right now. What's going on?" If the worker can sense the feeling under the silence, it can be helpful simply to articulate it.

The final elaborating skill, a crucial one in all counseling situations, involves *reaching from the general to the specific.* Group members often raise specific concerns through overly general questions or comments. For example, "Men are harder to deal with these days" may really be "My husband and I had a terrible fight last night, and I think he is ready to walk out." The skilled worker will encourage the group member to be specific in response to general comments, to the point of asking for the specific conversation of the fight: "What did he say to you?" "What did you say back?" "How did you feel

when he said that?" It is only in the particulars of the situation that the group members can be helpful to the individual raising the example and at the same time be helpful to themselves.

Empathic Skills

The empathic skills are those through which the worker communicates to the group members his or her capacity to experience their feelings. These include *reaching for feelings, acknowledging feelings, and articulating feelings.* In reaching for a group member's (or the group's) feelings, the worker is asking for the affect associated with the information. For example, "How did it make you feel when your son said that to you?" Acknowledging feelings requires the worker to communicate his or her understanding of feelings already expressed by the members. The skill of articulating feelings involves expressing the *unstated* affect about one half a step ahead of the client. For example:

Group Member: I was furious at my daughter when she responded that way to me.
Worker: You must have felt really hurt and unappreciated.

Before illustrating these skills, it is important to deal with a number of issues associated with the use of the empathic skills. First, it is crucial that the expression by the group leader be genuine. That is, the leader must really be feeling something when he or she expresses empathy. The emergence of prescriptive training programs which appear to encourage artificial responses to clients without the worker genuinely experiencing the affect is a serious problem for the profession. Clients see workers who mechanically echo them as artificial. (for example: *Cli-*

ent: "I am really angry at that kid."
Worker: "You are really angry at that
kid.") Commonly used expressions, such
as "I hear you saying . . .," when used by
the worker ritualistically without affect,
will also come across to group members
as phony. The major problem with these
more mechanical approaches is not the
words themselves. I have heard very skillful workers use the phrase "I hear you
saying . . . ," and because they are really
feeling the emotions, they came through
to the group members as genuinely caring. The problem is evident when the
words or expressions become a substitute for the much more difficult task of
really feeling with our clients.

For beginning workers who are leading
their first groups, it is very understandable that the only thing they may feel in
their first meetings is their knees knocking. That is why it is so important to
incorporate into the idea of skillful work
catching one's mistakes as soon as possible. As workers become more comfortable with affect, both their own and those
of their group members, each group meeting will teach the worker more about the
group members' lives. The workers' capacity for genuine empathy will grow, not
only in the professional context, but in
their personal lives as well.

The second major issue relates to the
reasons for dealing with affect. Why inquire about feelings in the first place? It
is not uncommon for workers who involve themselves in the feelings of the
group and who empathize with their clients to be stuck for words when I ask
them why they are interested. One responded: "Because I'm a social worker."
That answer is not good enough.

There are three major reasons why affect
is important in our work. First, the
worker's capacity to empathize with the
group members contributes to the devel-

opment of a positive working relationship. Group members who perceive that
a worker is trying to be with them in
feeling will have a greater degree of trust
in the worker and will be more ready to
risk difficult feelings. They will not experience the worker as judging them harshly.
Nonjudgmental acceptance by the worker
creates the conditions which help group
members to lower their defenses. By articulating even the most taboo feelings,
the worker sets the stage so that group
members know that *when they are ready*
to deal with these feelings, the worker
will also be ready. This fund of positive
feeling between the group members and
the worker then allows the worker to make
a demand for work on the group, a form
of confrontation in which the worker insists that the group invest their work with
meaning and not tolerate the illusion of
work. These concepts, the illusion of work
and the demand for work, are discussed
in the next section. For now, the important point is that a worker must express
caring through empathy before he or she
can confront and demand.

The second major reason that affect is
important has to do with the way in which
the group leader models his or her beliefs
about how one relates to other people.
Schwartz described this as part of the task
of "lending a vision."[13] When group
members observe the worker as a caring,
supportive, and yet at times demanding
person, they are free to experiment and
adopt some of these qualities in their relationship to each other and to others
who are important in their lives. This
"vision" is shared by example, not subtly
or directly imposed upon the members
by the worker. They are free to use the
worker as a model if they wish.

Finally, feelings must be dealt with in
pursuit of purpose. There is a connection
between how we feel and how we act,

what I call the "feeling—doing" connection. Group leaders are always looking for the often subtle connections between the clients' emotions and their actions in order to help the clients understand and deal with the feelings. For example, a foster adolescent who has been rejected by his own parents and has been through a number of group homes and foster parents could well begin to feel he has no value as a person. This lack of self-esteem easily translates into activities which confirm the judgment (such as drug use, criminal activities, prostitution). The deepening sense of depression and low self-judgment can lead to self-destructive behavior. Understanding this vicious cycle can be the start of breaking it, and as the group member begins to cope more effectively with his feelings and takes some small steps to change his life, the positive responses to these steps strengthen the self-esteem, allowing further positive action. The foster adolescent's feelings of low self-esteem are dealt with in pursuit of the purpose of the group—to help foster adolescents cope with their problems of living.

In another less dramatic but very common example, we have the foster child who has been rejected often. He or she begins each new alternative care placement assuming the rejection is coming. The inevitable acting out fulfills the prophecy. As one teenager put it, speaking of his relationship with a child care counselor he really liked, "I didn't build it [the relationship] too high because I knew it wasn't a forever place."

In the following example of the empathic skills, Indelicato and Goldberg describe a dramatic moment in their group for parents of learning disabled children (chapter 10). In this excerpt, the worker reaches for the anger experienced by many parents in this situation, feelings which they believe they are not supposed to have. Just hearing these feelings expressed by others is a healing process as group members discover they are "all in the same boat" and that their "evil" feelings are quite understandable.

Mrs F. described how on Monday, her son would not get out of bed to go to school. She said: "I kept reminding him to get up, since I know he is very particular about his hair and he needs extra time to get ready. I knew he was pretending to be asleep so I smacked him in the face. He went into a rage, started kicking the covers and screaming. I ran out of the room crying. I sometimes want to hurt him. . . ."

I told Mrs. F. that I noticed when we talked earlier about the situation with her son, her hands were clenched, and her face was intense. I encouraged her to bring us on board about what she was experiencing. She responded: "Yes, I get very angry, so angry I want to hit him." I asked what do you get angry about the most? She replied: "Wasting time! He has to go to school, has to learn, to get a job, raise a family. He can't stay dependent on me!"

Mrs. M. spoke about her own fear of loss of control: "I don't hit my children because I'm afraid I'll hurt them. It's just the frustration, the hurt, the anger, mostly the hurt. I look at my child, thinking, I have done everything I know, given you my time and look what you're doing. You're totally disrupting my life. Everything else is OK, but sometimes I get caught up in the feelings of how much he disrupts my schedule."

As members listen to others describe strong feelings, they may be put in touch with similar feelings within themselves which they have long denied. We can often easily see in other people those things which we have the most difficulty seeing and facing in ourselves. In the following example from my single parents group (chapter 9), one member described her frustration at trying to get her ex-spouse to be "more of a Dad" for their five-year-old boy. He appeared to reject this boy, while at the same time showing his love for the youngest child. I put her feelings into words by articulating how hard it must be on her when the child questions the father's rejection. I also connect feelings to purpose when I inquire as to how she deals with it.

I told Ginette I thought this must have put her in an awful bind with the child, when for example, he asked her, "When is Daddy going to visit me?" I wondered how she dealt with it. Ginette described her conversation, which indicated she tried to cover up the problem, told "white lies," and did what she could to avoid dealing with the child's feelings. I acknowledged to her, and the group, that I could appreciate the bind she felt.

June, a new member who had been listening quietly all morning, began to speak. She spoke with a low, soft voice, and began to cry before she could complete her comments: "I have been sitting here listening to Ginette thinking that what she is describing is my problem exactly. And now, I think I realize that I'm going to have to face my own rejection by my husband, who walked out on me, before the healing can start . . . and I can help my kids face their rejection."

With deep emotions triggered by Ginette's comment, June moved the whole group into the underlying theme of rejection, beautifully stating the connection between their own need to resolve their feelings and their ability to help their children do the same. As is often the case, group members are moved and concerned by such a strong display of emotion. In the mediating role, I tried to help the group members release that part of them which wants to reach out to June, but might be embarrassed to do so. Note also, how much help is available from members in the group. This is a relief for

the worker, who does not have to provide all of the help but can concentrate instead on releasing the group's inherent potential for mutual aid.

We all felt very moved by June's words. I could see the group members were upset. Marie was sitting next to June, and I could tell she was very agitated—looking around the room, looking at June, and literally moving in her seat. I said: "I think June's feelings have hit all of us very hard. I have a feeling you would like to reach out to June, wouldn't you, Marie?" Marie said she really would. When I asked her: "Why don't you?", she said: "Well, I'm afraid to." After a slight pause, she reached over and took June's hand, holding it tightly. June responded warmly to the gesture. I reassured Marie that it was OK to share her feelings with us and that her tears were an important part of how she felt. I told her that I felt she spoke for all of the group members, and they quickly assured her that I was correct.

We then returned to Ginette and her difficulty in being honest with her children and allowing them to express their feelings. She said, "I want my son to share his feelings within certain guidelines." I responded, "You mean, you want him to share the feelings that are not too tough for you." The group members, including Ginette, laughed in recognition of the point. Ginette admitted she realized she had to be honest with him. The group members, at my suggestion, agreed to help her role-play the conversation so she could find a supportive way of being honest.

It is important to note how the group, in response to the leader's demand, did not get lost in the feelings of rejection, and instead, began specific work on how to deal with their children effectively. This is what is meant by the expression used earlier, dealing with feelings in pursuit of purpose. As these parents help their children with their sense of rejection, they will be helping themselves cope with identical feelings. This is another example of the feeling-doing connection.

Sharing Worker's Feeling Skills

Many models of professional practice have suggested the importance of separating the personal self from the professional self. The skillful worker is described as one who is in control at all times. There is an element of truth to this construct. As workers develop, they learn the importance of not judging people against their own personal standards, of not stereotyping people, of not acting out and expressing inappropriate feelings, of not turning the group meeting into a discussion of their own personal problems. However, this is not the same as a process in which workers monitor their feelings and never openly express them. A group leader's spontaneous reactions, including the moments when he or she is angry with group members, can be important contributions to the development of group process.

For the new worker, this appears to pose a paradox which might be expressed as follows: "First he [Shulman] tells me to be honest and spontaneous, and then he tells me not to do all of the things I probably will do if I follow his advice." The apparent paradox can be resolved by recalling the advice about allowing oneself to make mistakes, to learn from them, and then to make more sophisticated mistakes. I would argue that honesty and spontaneity are central elements to professional practice. The real paradox arises when we tell our group members that they should be open, honest, nondefensive, and ready to risk their most deeply held feelings while at the same time modeling a role as group leader in which we do just the opposite. As helping professionals, we need to learn to trust our feelings and to

use them in implementing our helping function.

If workers wait until they are certain that they are going to say exactly the right thing, they will never say anything at the right time. Thus, they have to be willing to risk making mistakes and be prepared to apologize to their clients if they are wrong. The image workers will then project is not one of the all-knowing group leaders, who have all of life's problems worked out, who are always in control, and never make mistakes but rather that of real human beings who more closely resemble their clients. It is a great relief to group members to see that the worker is *not* a paragon of virtue. Also, workers can model for clients the very skills they are helping them to develop in their interpersonal relationships (the "lending a vision" task).

If group leaders sit on their feelings and churn away inside while pretending to be calm, the energy they need to invest in the lives of the group members, to feel their feelings, will simply not be available. Thus, the task workers need to work on all during their work lives is how to synthesize personal and professional selves, not how to split them into two artificially separate entities.

For example, I often have participants in workshops describe a problem with a group or group members, which is a common middle or work phase issue. The group has begun well, developed a clear working contract, but now seems to be doing a "dance," an illusion of work. The group leader has been supportive for weeks, has genuinely expressed empathy for the group members' dilemmas; however, he or she gets a very strong feeling that the group is resisting taking the next step, perhaps not taking responsibility for their own part in their problems. When I ask what the worker is feeling, it is often frustration and anger at the group members, feelings generated because the worker really does care for these clients. When I ask if he or she has let the group know these feelings, the worker often looks shocked and says: "But that wouldn't be professional."

I would argue that it would be very professional indeed, and as will be discussed in the next section, that this kind of confrontation (a form of demand for work) may be just what the group members need at the moment. Close analysis of the worker's feelings often reveals that the worker is simply afraid to take the risk. When group leaders say, "But is the group ready for that?" they often really mean, "Am I ready for that?"

In a study of social work practice skill, I found that the capacity to share thoughts and feelings honestly was one of the highest correlating skills with developing a good working relationship and with helping effectively (as judged by clients).[14] These findings were replicated in my studies of supervision and medical practice.[15]

It is not only the angry feelings which need to be shared openly. Often, group leaders can be as moved as the members by the work of the group. In my own groups, I have found myself in tears in response to strong emotions expressed by group members. Group members did not see this as weakness. They interpreted my strong emotions as a gift to them of my willingness to experience their feelings. Other group leaders communicate this gift differently, through respectful silence, an arm on the shoulder, facial expressions, or whatever. There is much room for individual difference and style. The important point is that the group leader's feelings are shared when appropriate to the work of the group, to implement the leader's professional function.

Workers often fear they may be immobilized by their feelings. For example, they fear they will feel as hopeless as a client about a problem and therefore not be able to help. In one example, a group member described the experience of learning that her young husband had a terminal illness. As she spoke, she cried, and the worker as well as the group members cried with her. There would be time later for the "demand for work" which would help this woman face the many issues she needed to deal with (such as telling the children, supporting her husband, obtaining support for herself). At the moment, however, the gift of sharing in the feelings was what was needed and what was helpful.

In the example which follows, Orr helps a group of blind senior citizens face the death of one of their group members (chapter 17). At one point, they talk about all of the losses they have experienced, and one of the members suggests that they stand for a moment of silence.

(Silence)

Worker: (speaking of the dead member) I guess what's always most difficult for me is when I feel there was no closure, that I didn't have a chance to say goodbye, and a feeling that I've been deprived of having that person with me longer.

Tessie: That's what hurts so much about Maddie, that I tried and tried to call and couldn't get through. They didn't know I was calling. That's what I feel deprived of, making sure that she knew I cared.

Allen: But you've called so many times while she was sick. She knew you cared.

The Demand for Work

Reviewing the helping skills discussed thus far, we see a premium placed upon preparation (tuning in), on clarifying a working contract to provide a structure for work, on skillful sessional contracting and elaboration skills designed to help the clients tell their story, and on the empathic skills and sharing one's own feelings designed to invest the work with affective substance and to strengthen the worker-member and member-member relationships. While all of these skills and processes are necessary in setting the stage for work, another essential dynamic must be introduced, the dynamic embodied in what Schwartz termed the *demand for work*.

This process becomes clearer if one considers ambivalence to be central to all human change processes. A part of us wishes to move ahead, to grow, challenge life, confront difficult tasks, be responsible, and so on. Another part of each of us fears such changes, does not want to take risks, is hesitant to experience painful emotions, feels deeply responsible for our own problems and thus sets up elaborate defenses to deny responsibility and blame others. For some, depending upon many personal, historical, and socioeconomic factors, the forces for change may be stronger or the forces of resistance may dominate. As helping professionals, our work involves engaging these forces in our clients. We must understand and have compassion for the forces which block change, synthesizing this support with a continuous expression of our belief in the client's strength for change, however faint it may be. The many skills contained in making a *demand for work* are found in the way in which the group leader puts this basic assumption of client strength into action.

For example, consider an employment group leader working with middle-aged women whose children have grown up. The women have expressed a desire to find a job and to become independent of welfare. The group focuses on job-

finding skills (resume writing, interview skills, and so on), and a number of possible positions are identified. Suddenly, the worker perceives resistance to the idea of applying for a new job. Upset that the group members are not taking up the opportunity with gusto, and in fact seem to be finding superficial reasons to avoid it, the worker pressures them and then is disappointed when they miss or "blow" the arranged interviews. After all, jobs are difficult to find in this economy, and the worker is rated on how many of these women she can place.

In her eagerness to accomplish her *task*, the worker loses sight of the *process*. She is so anxious to *do* something for the women that when she perceives the resistance, she is upset by it and tries to override it using exhortation as a major tool. If instead of being upset by the resistance, she could have been guided by the understanding that *resistance is part of the work*, she could have tuned in to the part of the group members' natural fears and concern which led to the ambivalence and then offered them support. The resistance was a signal to the worker not that the group was going badly but that the group was going well.

She was at a crucial point in her work, when these women had to face what could be termed the *second decision* about changing their life status from homemaker to employed person. The first decision, that of coming to the group, was the easier one to make. Now that the real crisis was imminent, the group members would need all the help they could get from the worker and each other.

The skill of *exploring the resistance* would be one way in which the worker could make a demand for work. The general and superficial discussion about going to an interview and getting a job was an example of the illusion of work in which the real fears and anxieties are left for the bus ride home. Such questions as: "Am I still competent after so many years at home?" "Can I compete with younger women who have all these new skills I know nothing about?" "Are my kids really old enough for me to work? Ever since I started this program Jane is regressing—having trouble at school—is it too soon for her?" "Everyone else in the group seems so confident, so competent. The worker keeps telling us we can do it, but in my heart, I'm scared stiff." "Before we split up, my husband told me for years that all I was good for was housework and raising kids. Maybe he was right?"

Workers often sense the "lurking negatives" and ambivalences under the surface in their groups. However, they fear their power and try to override them. The thought is "If I can just push them through, they will be all right." Actually, it is the negatives remaining below the surface which have all the power. When brought to light in a mutual aid group, they often lose their ability to block growth and change. The "all-in-the-same-boat" phenomenon helps people put their feelings into a better perspective. In addition, hearing how others have overcome a similar problem, having group members challenge others' own low estimation (for example, "It's funny to hear you say you were afraid you couldn't make it in the work world. I've been sitting here for weeks thinking of how strong you seem.") These and other supportive forces can be brought into play if the group leader understands and works with resistance rather than avoiding it. In fact, if the resistance is not evident (for example, if everyone agrees it will be a piece of cake to go to the interviews), the smart leader would be wise to look *for trouble when everything is going his or her way.* In this example, it might sound like this:

Worker: You know it's great to hear your enthusiasm about the job interviews. However, you have been out of the work field for a long time. I wonder if in addition to your enthusiasm, there aren't also some doubts and concerns. You know, for example, "Do I still have it to compete out there after fifteen years of diapers and carpools?"

Ambivalence and resistance are very much a part of the life of the group as well as its individual members. Thus, the illusion of work in a group may be a signal of the collective hesitation about entering a difficult or taboo subject area. Once again, the skillful leader must provide a subtle blend of support and demand as he or she helps this second client, the group, to identify the obstacles blocking effective work and to deal with them. In many ways a group can be seen as more or less sophisticated in its ability to work effectively. Part of the group leader's responsibility is to help the group's individual members and the group as a whole to mature. In a poignant example from Vastola, Nierenburg and Graham's work with children who have had close relatives die (chapter 4), we see one child, Mark, play the role of "deviant member" as he acts out the way in which all of the children have learned to cope with the pain of the deaths of close relatives, through denial and acting-out behavior. As the group leaders help Mark to face the feelings, they are also helping their other client, the group, learn to tolerate and to talk about painful experiences. By examining Mark's behavior closely, one can see a classic example of a client calling for attention and help, while seemingly denying it is needed. The worker's understanding of ambivalence led to the intervention which reaches for the call for help.

Eleven-year-old Mark was repeatedly writing Bob (his grandfather's name) on a sheet of paper in front of him.

Carl: Mark, your grandfather died?

Mark: I don't want any damn body talking about my grandfather or I'll kick their butt.

Leader: You sound pretty angry.

Mark: I'm not angry. I just don't want anybody talking about my grandfather.

Leader: I guess it must be very difficult.

Mark: It's not difficult; I just don't want anybody saying anything about him. (His anger was escalating and others in the group expressed similar feelings. "Nobody wants to talk about nobody dying.")

Dick: Yes, we don't want to talk about that.

Leader: (Exploring the resistance) Why?

Gloria: (Insightfully noted) That's why he is running around. You can't force him if he doesn't want to.

Leader: Are you saying that perhaps that's why you're running around, so you won't have to talk about something so upsetting?

Mark: Nope.

Leader: You may feel it's too hard to talk about.

Mark: No, it's not hard for me to talk about anything ... but that reminds you and you could be dreaming.

Carl: Yup, you dream for about a week when you talk about your mother, then it takes about five days to try to get over it, but it comes back again and it stops and it comes back again ... nightmares ... I hate—I hate talking about my mother.

Once again, the synthesis of *content* (the substance of the work) and *process* (the way of working) is clear. As the worker explores the resistance expressed through Mark's acting-out behavior, a deeper level of feeling is revealed which is important for all of the group members. Thus, the other artificial dichotomy, that between the individual and the group, also dissolves as we search out the connection between the one (Mark) and the many (the group). The worker does not have to chose between dealing with Mark's behavior *or* working with the group. Mark's behavior speaks for the group; that is his role.

In another illustration of the importance of the demand for work, the dynamic of the illusion of work, and the way in which individual members play a role in the group, Lubell describes a moment in her group for patients on kidney dialysis machines (chapter 15) when *facilitative confrontation* is required. In this case, Charlie plays the role of group clown, serving as an informal "gatekeeper" and preventing the group from having to face difficult realities. The group encourages Charlie, since in some ways he represents that part of all of the group members which would rather evade the difficulty of the work. As the leader confronts Charlie and the group, she is helpful to both clients. As the group members begin to confront Charlie, they are really dealing with the part of themselves that they see in Charlie.

During a discussion of how hard it was to stick to the diet, Charlie, a professional entertainer, offered to sing a song. The others laughed and encouraged him. The social worker acknowledged how much easier it was to sing and joke than to deal with the sometimes overwhelming problems they were all facing. When Charlie continued to clown, the worker pointed out that although he was usually the one to district the group, he also had the most difficulty in following the diet. The others agreed, but Charlie began to give excuses. Brad told him he'd have to change some of his habits and added that he himself no longer went to the pub where he was tempted to drink but arranged to see his friends at other times instead. Suzanne added that Charlie did not take the diet seriously enough and that he was the only one to abuse it flagrantly every week. Charlie again claimed that he had to accept drinks from patrons between shows and rejected Maureen's suggestions about how he might explain the situation. When asked how she handled similar situations, Maureen gave an example of how she had responded to dinner invitations, adding that if she acted matter of factly, people accepted it easily. The social worker pointed out that it is hard to deal with other people's reactions unless you are feeling comfortable with the situation and have accepted it yourself. There were general nods.

Charlie continued to deny. In this example, however, the ball was now in his court. With help from the worker, the group confronted Charlie. The outcome of this confrontation now depends upon what Charlie himself will do with it, which is not the responsibility of the group leader or the members.

In some situations, the worker must deal with the group members' apathy about influencing their systems (even the agency employing the worker). For example, in chapter 18, Berman-Rossi tries to help a ward group of senior citizens take responsibility for influencing the dietary department of their long-term care facility. She can make this demand for work, in part, because she has not given up *her* belief in their ability to influence the system. It is often difficult for workers to continue to press this demand because of their own ambivalent feelings about the systems they work in. It is important for the worker to keep alive a belief in the ability of systems to change, through negotiation, mediation, advocacy with social pressure, or whatever means can be helpful.[16]

Pointing out Obstacles

This skill is a collection of activities in which the worker brings the members' attention to the various obstacles blocking the group's ability to work effectively. Many of the earlier examples illustrated these skills in action. Two themes emerge here which require special attention—the "authority" and the "intimacy" themes in group dynamics. These ideas are drawn from the group dynamics literature, particularly the work of Bennis and Sheppard.[17] Their theories were based on the interactions they observed in T-Groups (training groups). While some of their views are probably unique to that type of group, the two central constructs have meaning for all groups. The first is that the group members have to deal, early in the life of the group, with their relationship to the leader—the authority theme. Many of the central issues have to do with dependency; that is, how dependent will the group members be on the leader. In the model presented here, the mutual aid group is seen as having to take responsibility for its own processes, with the help of a leader. Since most people bring to the group an image of all-powerful leader, one who takes responsibility for the work of the group, the leader must teach the group members a new way of thinking about the division of labor between leader and members.

For example, in one of my married couples groups, during a middle-phase session, one couple had a long conversation on an issue without getting to the point. I noticed the group looking bored, and I asked what was going on.

Fran responded by saying it was getting boring and she was waiting for me to do something. Since this was well into the middle phase, I found myself angry that everyone was waiting for me and I said, "How come you are all waiting for me to do something? This is your group, you know, and I think you can take some responsibility."

The resulting discussion indicated that they felt it was risky to say things like that to each other, so they left it to me.

I asked them to talk about what made it risky for them. They discussed their reluctance to embarrass people, their reticence about being critical, their fear of angry reactions, and other similar feelings. We continued to discuss how we could set ground rules about honesty in the group in which they also would take responsibility for helping the group work effectively.

This discussion dealt simultaneously with both the authority theme and the second major driving theme in a group, that of intimacy. The intimacy theme has to do with the way in which the group members will deal with each other. Since all group members bring into the group some clearly established norms of "polite" behavior, many of which lead to the obstacles which result in the illusion of work, the leader must help the group members examine these assumptions and develop new ways of working which are more honest. Bennis and Sheppard describe the struggle in terms of how "personal" members wish to be with each other.[18] One example would be deciding whether to risk intimate personal details with people who are still strangers. Members learning to trust each other is as important as, and often more difficult, than their learning to trust the worker.

Another way of conceptualizing these ideas is that at any one time the group may be working on their *contract* (issues of content which bring them together) or on their *way of working* (the process or interaction). The way of working will break down into two major subthemes: the group member-leader relationship (authority) and the member-member relationship (intimacy). As illustrated earlier, even this division between *content* and *process* is artificial, since examination of process issues (for example, the resistance of the young boy Mark and the other group members to talking about death) often leads us more deeply into the content (in this case, the difficulty of coping with the pain of the loss of a loved one).

It is not possible in this section to discuss adequately the major issues of authority and dependency in group process. However, one issue requires some discussion. As the group works, strong feelings toward the group leader, both positive and negative, will be generated. This process is sometimes referred to in individual counseling as "transference."[19] These feelings may be an important source of energy which can help to power the activity of the group. This affect must be discussed at appropriate times. For example, when the group leader makes his or her demands for work, some anger will be generated. This anger is healthy and is a normal part of the process. It can be brought out in the open, discussed, understood, and accepted. In fact, if a group is *never* angry at the leader, there is a good chance that the leader has not pressed hard enough.

Alternatively, there will be times when the group members may feel positive affection for the leader whom they perceive as a caring and nurturing person. In my married couples group, members raise this aspect of the authority theme. One of the members had come into the group alone, sat next to me, and shared a frightening problem she was facing. She cried during the presentation. The other group members and I tried to comfort her.

Fran said, "I knew this was Jan's night to get help the minute she walked in the door." When I inquired as to how she knew, she said, "Because she sat in the crying chair." She went on to point out that all of the people who had cried in sessions, four of the ten group members, had sat in that chair at the beginning of the session. Other members nodded in recognition. I inquired if they had any thought about why that was so. Rose said, "Because that's the chair next to you, and we sit there to get some support when the going gets rough." I encouraged them to elaborate on what they felt they got from me, since that was also what they probably wanted from each other.

Louise said, "It's because we can feel free to say anything to you, and you won't judge us. We can tell you our feelings." Rose continued, "And we know you really feel our hurt, it's not phony—you really care." Lou said, "It's safe next to you. We can share our innermost feelings and know that you won't let us get hurt." As I listened to the members, I felt myself deeply moved by the affect in their voices, and I shared that with them. "You know, it means a great deal to me to have you feel that way—that you can sense my feelings for you. I have grown to care about you quite a bit. It's surprising to me, sometimes, just how hard things in this group hit me—just how important you have really become."

It is important to recognize that the group members will also generate feelings in the worker. These feelings must also be understood and accepted.

Sharing Data

Sharing data involves the worker communicating to the group members his or her ideas, facts, beliefs, view of life, biases, and so on. There is much misunderstanding about the use of this skill in group work. At the one extreme there are those who argue that the worker should be neutral, never sharing an opinion which might influence the group members. Self-determination is raised as the sacred value. At the other extreme, it is argued that the group leader should clearly establish him or herself as the "expert," so that the group members are more likely to accept the "right" views. Group leaders who try to be impartial often fall victim to the pressure to influence their clients indirectly. That is, they ask questions which are de-

signed to lead their group members to the "right" ideas, or they encourage members to provide their ideas, and then quickly question the offered viewpoint when it does not conform to the accepted doctrine. Group members quickly suspect that this impartial worker really does have a hidden agenda and redirect their energy to determining what the worker wants them to think or to do.

At the other extreme, the worker who tries to use "expert power" to convince group members of the right view makes the mistake of confusing his or her view of life with reality. In the last analysis, the worker, no matter how "correct" his or her ideas may be, is only one resource among many. The group members must work to develop their *own* view of the real world. Assuming the task of making judgments for the group members is futile and, in fact, dangerous, since it is the group members who must live with the results. In fact, as a group leader, I would begin to worry when group members appeared to be too dependent upon me for their answers.

The argument made at this point might be that we are always attempting to influence people; that is what effective practice is all about. However, it must be done openly and honestly. The group members should be encouraged to weigh the worker's contributions as they weigh those made by other group members and by other significant people in their lives. The worker's ideas must be open to challenge and accepted only if they have merit, not because the worker is the expert on life.

The other requirement when a worker shares data is that the information be relevant to the work of the group members. Information which *we* think is important for them but is not related to their current sense of urgency will be experienced as a hidden agenda. I remember my student days as a group leader in a community center working with middle-class, white adolescents in a neighborhood undergoing racial tensions between whites and blacks. I would not miss an opportunity to slip in comments encouraging positive racial attitudes, even when such ideas were irrelevant to the group's immediate work. My hidden agenda soon became obvious to the group, and they avoided such comments in my presence. In retrospect, I realize that if I had not been so busy trying to preach to the youngsters, I would have been able to hear the real struggles they were experiencing in relation to this conflict. Coping with parents, a peer group, and others in relation to the race issue was at times of deep concern to them. They needed to discuss these concerns with an adult who could listen and understand their struggles, who would not immediately judge them and lecture them. In my eagerness to teach them my values, I lost many opportunities to help them with the complex process of developing values of their own.

Finally, not only does a group leader allow the members to have access to his or her views of the world, but the mediating function also calls for the worker to help members tap each other's fund of experience. Each group member is an expert in their own areas of concern. A fundamental form of mutual aid involves freeing the group members to give and take help in this way. In the illustration which follows, drawn from my single parents group (chapter 9), we see members providing specific ideas to a woman who has just discovered that she lost her positive credit rating of twenty-five years when her husband left her.

Carrie told her [Rose] she had given up too soon. She said that Rose was going to have to assert herself if she wanted to obtain her rights. I asked Carrie how she thought Rose could do this, and she suggested the following plan. She advised Rose to visit the credit bureau and discuss her desire to establish a credit rating. She pointed out that Rose was making monthly payments on a number of bills, for example, rent, telephone, and utilities, and that she could use this to impress the credit bureau with her credit worthiness. She should also speak to the bank manager directly and point out that she had been part of the family that had given his bank all of her business up to that point, and that she would like his cooperation in developing a plan to establish a credit rating on her own.

The group members agreed this might be a first step. They also felt that if she ran into difficulty with this approach, she consider bringing this to the attention of the bank's head office, by writing to the president. Another member suggested that she contact the Provincial Human Rights Commission, since this actually constituted a form of discrimination. It was obvious that everyone was angry at her situation. Rose agreed she could do more than she had thus far. She said, "I guess I began to believe that they were right about me not having earned a credit rating. It never occurred to me to refuse to accept the decision." Carrie said, "The hard part is understanding that you're going to have to fight for your own rights, because nobody else is going to do it for you."

Sessional Endings and Transitions

The skills required in this subphase are those which help to bring a session to a close and to make the transition to future events. The future events may be activities of the group member which flow either from the session, such as a member trying to open up communications with a boss or a family member after having discussed the problem at the group meeting, or from an activity of the group such as moving into a new area of discussion, continuing a theme, or inviting a speaker.

Summarizing the discussion is one of these skills. This may or may not involve a formal, point by point review of the issues, observations, or decisions. In a community action group, such as a tenants association, a formal review may be appropriate. In my married couples group, a few words at the end to help to articulate the major themes or observations may serve the same purpose (for example, "It seems that all of the couples here have put their finger on how hard it is to talk to each other about sexual matters without becoming defensive").

Another skill that is often useful in the ending subphase of a group meeting is moving from the specific to the general. This is the reverse of the skill discussed earlier—that of moving from the general to the specific. The worker in this instance points out the connections between the particular work of the session and the concerns, issues, or observations which emerged in earlier sessions. For example, continuing with the practice excerpt after I summarized the problem of communicating about sexual issues, I said, "You know, this sounds very similar to the issues we have been discussing thus far. Every time you describe how you deal with a sensitive issue such as sexual functioning, sharing responsibilities in the home, or conflicts with the kids, it seems you have all admitted feeling defensive and guilty, and the conversation with your spouse breaks down into mutual blaming. It seems to be a common pattern." Thus, looking back over the sessions allows the group members to gain insight and perspective into their patterns of behavior or responses in particular situations.

Another connected skill would be that of *identifying next steps*. It is important to articulate what next steps are needed for the individual member or the group.

It is not unusual for this apparently simple step to be overlooked. Most readers have probably experienced sitting through a committee or staff meeting during which decisions were made and later discovering that nothing happened because no one was identified to take responsibility for implementing the action. Actually, avoiding being specific about the next step can be a subtle form of resistance. It is one thing to decide to confront a difficult problem, perhaps even role playing how to handle it, and then quite another actually to do it. When specific next steps are identified, an additional demand is placed on the members to implement them. In the example of the married couples group, after generalizing about the communication problem, I said, "Since this issue seems important to all of you, do you want to begin with it next week? If so, maybe we could look at some of the things you have discovered thus far about dealing with touchy areas and then examine how they would apply in this particularly difficult one."

Another useful skill in ending group sessions is one I call the *skill of rehearsal.* This involves using the group for a form of role-play in which the member tries out what he or she will say in an actual conversation outside of the group (such as handling an employment interview). Role-play is a useful group learning device; however, it is often used in such a formal way that it increases the pressure on the members. Even the use of the words "role-play" can set up a mind set which increases tension. Setting up special chairs in the middle of the group places the group members too much "on stage." Compare these formal approaches with the following excerpt from an employment counseling group for ex-convicts.

Worker: It sounds like the job interview has you really worried. No wonder it's scary. It's been a while since you've had to face this. You're probably also wondering how you're going to explain the three-year gap in your work record.

Lou: That's it exactly! What do I say when he asks me where I've been?

Worker: Why don't we try it out in advance right here? I'll be the interviewer, and I'll ask you questions, and the rest of the group can give you some ideas about how you handle the answers. How about it? Is that OK with you, Lou, and with the rest of you?

Lou: Well . . . I'll give it a try. (Group members nod).

Worker: Welcome, Mr. Franklin. Why don't you have a seat here and we can talk about the job. . . .

THE ENDING AND TRANSITION PHASE

The fourth and final phase in the life of the group involves endings and transitions. The endings and transitions of the previous section were sessional in that they applied to each group meeting. In this section, I refer to the phase of work in which the worker and the group members bring to a close their experience together. This phase has its own unique dynamics and skills.[20]

First, one often observes a form of denial as a first stage in the process. Members seem to forget the impending ending of the group. To make sure the process begins early enough to have time to discuss the ending and to ensure that the ending is not experienced as abrupt or as a form of rejection, the worker should use the strategy of *pointing out the endings early*. For example, simply commenting on the number of weeks remaining may set the process in motion. The timing of this strategy depends on how long the group has been meeting. In a short-

term, three-session group, the worker might comment on the last session at the end of the second meeting. In my married couples group, which lasted nineteen weeks, I reminded the group of the ending the third meeting from the last. Sometimes, a signal from the group may trigger the worker's beginning discussion. For example, a comment after a break in the flow of meetings or a session canceled by the worker because of illness may mark the first signs of concern.

A second stage in the ending process often involves the emergence of anger toward the group leader, sometimes expressed indirectly in the form of missed sessions or acting-out behavior in a children's group. The reader may have already noted the parallel between these stages of endings and those described by Kübler-Ross in her work on death and dying.[21] This anger is followed by a period of mourning. This sadness may be expressed through apathy and listlessness at group meetings or through other verbal and nonverbal means. For example, in my married couples group, I entered the meeting room at the start of the third from the last session to find the lights still off and the normal premeeting conversation missing. I commented that the room reminded me of a wake and one of the member responded: "Yes, and it's for this group." As the group moves through the ending phases, the worker can help the members to take control of the process, rather than just letting it happen to them, by using the strategy of *identifying the stages*.

This approach seeks to avoid the possibility that the group will be so overwhelmed by the ending that it will end prematurely by withdrawing from meaningful work. Since the ending phase has the possibility of being the most significant time in the work of the group due to the increased urgency brought on by the lack of time, the worker wants to ensure that the ending process does not become an obstacle to what could be the most powerful period of work. For example, in the group of older foster teens who were preparing to leave the care of the child welfare agency, a discussion of the ending process in the group can be directly related to the many endings they have faced both from their families and from foster homes, and of how these experiences make it difficult for them to risk themselves in new relationships.

The next noticeable stage is the one in which the group appears to be trying the ending on for size. In the situation where the group worker is leaving, there may be discussion about the new worker. The worker may notice members trying to cope with problems and demonstrate their abilities to handle things on their own. During the ending of my groups, I found the group members almost ignoring me, eager to work on their own without my intervention and help. The final stage in the process has been described by Schwartz as the "farewell party syndrome."[22] This is the tendency for the group members to avoid the painful feelings of endings by planning a party for the last session, or by padding the experience by remembering only the positive aspects of the group, not the problems. Worker's skills that I have already identified are important in this phase and include the following: sharing his or her own feelings about the endings (for example, "I wanted you all to know that I'm going to miss you and think about you a great deal"), reaching for the ending feelings of the group members ("You all seem down this week. Are you starting to think about missing the group?"), and reaching for the negative feelings as well as the positive ("It can't always have been the best group you have

ever been in. Let's also talk about the meetings that weren't so great").

Just as structure is important in the beginning, it can also be helpful in the ending phase. I usually ask members to prepare for the last session by identifying ideas in the group that have been important to them, areas that they still feel they need to work on, the strengths of the group and my leadership, as well as the problems with both. Even if the group has gone badly and both the members and the worker are glad to see it end, an honest evaluation may be helpful to both in any future efforts to lead or participate in a mutual aid group.

The last session can be used to summarize the work as the members share their understandings and feelings with each other, completing a process which began in the first session when they shared their concerns in the problem swapping. The sense I hope to convey is not that they have solved all their problems, but rather, that they have learned something about how to deal with them and how to get help along the way. Transition issues can include the question of where they can get help in the future and how they can use their learning in the group to cope more effectively with the issues that first brought them together. Although the last session may have a more formal ending structure, this process should be viewed as taking place over time.

In the following illustration, from Poynter-Berg's work (chapter 12) with institutionalized women, we observe the worker initiating the process six months after the group's beginning and seven weeks before the termination date.

I said I had something important I wanted to talk with them about. They all looked up from working on the clay. I asked if they remembered when we started working together, a long time ago, that I said I'd be here until June. Silence. I said that June will be here in a few weeks—six weeks after today, when I will be leaving the hospital. Beverly said, "Why do ya have ta leave?" I explained about school and that it ends in June. Beverly said, "When will ya be back after that?" I explained that my leaving in six weeks wouldn't be like the vacations I've had, when I was gone for a while and came back; that I would be leaving for good in June, not coming back. Beverly said, "Ya mean ya won't come back—ever?" I nodded. Silence. I said they were very quiet and wondered if they were thinking about what I'd said. Nods. I said I'd wanted to tell them now, since we'd been working together a long time and it's taken them a long time to be able to talk about some very hard things—but they could talk about them now—and it will take time for us to think about and talk about my leaving. Beverly said, "Six more weeks? That's good." She then said, "What will happen to the group?" I said the group could still meet together with another worker and asked if they wanted to talk about that now. Silence. I said it's a hard thing to talk about. Beverly said, "Ya, talk later." When it was time to clean up, they sat longer than usual. I said I felt what we'd talked about today—my leaving soon—made it harder to leave today. Nods.

CONCLUSION

This chapter has been used to set out a framework for viewing group work practice through the Preliminary, Beginning, Work, and Ending and Transition Phases, and to identify some of the core dynamics as well as core worker skills useful in leading groups. It is an effort to describe a methodology for putting the ideas of chapter 1, such as the mediating function, into action. In the chapters that follow, which are organized according to the stages of the life cycle, these skills will be evident as workers try to help their clients make use of the powerful healing force of mutual aid.

Before we proceed to examples of these skills in action, the crucial issue of group formation needs to be addressed. In the next chapter, Gitterman examines some of the pitfalls and strategies central to the process of forming a group.

NOTES

1. This chapter is an expanded version of a paper presented at the Jane Addams School of Social Work, Chicago, Illinois, at a 1983 school memorial service for William Schwartz, a former faculty member.

2. For examples of the work of William Schwartz, see "Social Group Work: The Interactionist Approach," in the *Encyclopedia of Social Work*, vol. 2, ed. John B. Turner (New York: National Association of Social Workers, 1977); "Between Client and System: The Mediating Function," in *Theories of Social Work With Groups*, ed. Robert W. Roberts and Helen Northern (New York: Columbia University Press, 1976).

3. Jessie Taft, "Time as the Medium of the Helping Process," *Jewish Social Service Quar-*

terly 26 (December 1949):230–243. See also William Schwartz, "Social Group Work: The Interactionist Approach."

4. See also: Carel B. Germain and Alex Gitterman, *The Life Model of Social Work Practice* (New York: Columbia University Press, 1980).

5. For a complete description, see Lawrence Shulman, *The Skills of Helping Individuals and Groups, Second Edition* (Itasca, Ill.: F. E. Peacock Publishers, Inc., 1984). See also *The Skills of Helping* (a series of three video tape programs). (Montreal, Quebec: The Instructional Communications Centre, McGill University, 1978).

6. Schwartz, "Between Client and System: The Mediating Function," pp. 186-88.

7. Shulman, *The Skills of Helping Individuals and Groups, Second Edition,* pp. 65-71.

8. Ibid., pp. 293–322.

9. William Schwartz, "Social Group Work: The Interactionist Approach," p. 456.

10. See Shulman, *The Skills of Helping Individuals and Groups, Second Edition,* pp. 51–97. See also Germain and Gitterman, *The Life Model of Social Work Practice,* pp. 77–202.

11. Shulman, *The Skills of Helping Individuals and Groups, Second Edition,* pp. 51–97.

12. Lawrence Shulman, *Identifying, Measuring and Teaching the Helping Skills* (New York: Council on Social Work Education and the Canadian Association of Schools of Social Work, 1979), chapter 3.

13. William Schwartz, "The Social Worker in the Group," in *New Perspectives on Services to Groups: Theory, Organization and Practice* (New York: National Association of Social Workers, 1961), pp. 7-34; and *The Social Welfare Forum, 1961* (New York: Columbia University Press, 1961), pp. 146-177.

14. Shulman, *The Skills of Helping Individuals and Groups,* 2d ed.

15. Ibid.

16. Shulman, *The Skills of Helping Individuals and Groups, Second Edition,* chapters 16 and 17. See also George Brager and Stephen Holloway, *Changing Human Service Organizations: Politics and Practice* (New York: Free Press, 1978).

17. Warren G. Bennis and Herbert A. Sheppard, "A Theory of Group Development," *Human Relations* 9 (1948):415–437.

18. Ibid.

19. For a discussion of the transference phenomenon in social work practice, see Herbert S. Strean, *Clinical Social Work Theory and Practice* (New York: Free Press, 1978).

20. Shulman, *The Skills of Helping Individuals and Groups, Second Edition,* chapter 15.

21. Elizabeth Kübler-Ross, *On Death and Dying* (New York: Macmillan, 1969).

22. Schwartz, "The Social Worker in the Group."

CHAPTER 3

Developing a New Group Service: Strategies and Skills

Why develop group services? Why bring people together in a group? Mutual aid, the subject of this book, is a primary rationale for the development of group services. By its very nature, the group mutual aid system has the potential to universalize individual problems, reduce isolation, and mitigate stigma. This potential evolves from powerful, yet quite subtle, interpersonal processes.

As members develop a sense of purpose and commonality, they begin to share common experiences and concerns. Initially, safer and less threatening issues are presented to test the worker's and each other's genuineness and competence. The worker's authority—function and boundaries—receives primary attention.[1] And through a testing process, group members begin to develop and reinforce mutual bonds and alliances as they figure out where the worker belongs in the interpersonal system. A few years ago the author worked with a group of high school girls. They were uncomfortable with a male adult stranger (as was the writer with a group of adolescent girls). At our third meeting, a member with the support of others confronted the discomfort by asking the worker to share a happy and a painful life experience. At that moment,

the group coalesced to test the worker's willingness to "belong" to the group. Upon sharing a happy experience as well as a painful loss, members responded by sharing their own experiences, and the work began, focused and intense. A social work student, for another example, was assigned to a group of recently released mental patients who had been meeting for a year:

After a short pause, I stated that I understood that this patient group has been meeting for about a year. Ms. B interrupted by saying, "I don't like being called a patient." I asked her why, and Ms. B suggested in effect that "patient" connoted sickness. I asked the group how they felt about it. Ms. C agreed that she did not like to be classified as a patient either. Mr. A asked her what she wanted to be called. Ms. C paused thoughtfully for a moment and said she would like to be called a "client." I asked the rest of the group how they felt about that. Ms. B said that was all right, and she would just like to be called a "member." The group responded positively to this, nodding, with a few members saying that they like that better. I said that since I was new to the group and they had been *members* for some time, could they bring me up to date on how the group began, what they talked about, dealt with, and so on.

The group members challenge the worker. Her openness encourages the elaboration of mutual support. In contrast, if she had turned their concerns into manifestations of psychological problems or had treated the content with lack of seriousness and respect, members might have become withdrawn or engaged in exploitative behavior such as scapegoating the dissonant participants.

From this type of experience and collective support, group members develop increased comfort and a willingness to risk personal and sometimes taboo concerns. This process alone helps members to experience their difficulties and problems as being less unique and deviant. And as members share and reach out to each other, they experience a "multiplicity of helping relationships" with all members invested and participating in the helping process rather than only the worker assuming that function and role.[2] Members may receive support for their perceptions and behaviors or they may be challenged to examine them further. Since their experiences have been similar (in other words, they are "in the same boat"), they are often receptive to each other's views and suggestions. Moreover, the group experience itself is a microcosm of members' interpersonal self-presentation and therefore serves as a rich arena for members to examine their respective adaptive as well as maladaptive perceptions and behaviors. From these exchanges, members are helped to develop and practice new interpersonal and environmental strategies and to receive feedback on such efforts.

Finally, the mutual aid group also has the potential to be a force for people to act and to gain greater control and mastery over their environments. Collective action has greater visibility and is more likely to gain organizational or community attention, mitigating individual isolation and reprisals, diminishing potential risks, and increasing chances for success. To be passive, to retreat from one's environment, inevitably leads to a sense of incompetence and impotence. In contrast, to be active in a group, to influence one's environment, provides opportunities to experience a sense of competence and efficacy.

These powerful mutual aid processes and potentials are marvelously illustrated in the practice chapters that follow. However, despite growing interest and efforts in the field to develop group services, the actual outcomes are quite uneven and sometimes discouraging.[3] After much effort, some groups never begin, others begin and then disintegrate, and still others seem to reinforce deviant and maladaptive behaviors.

Practitioners often attribute these problems to the clients' lack of motivation and resistance. Administrators may question the motivation and competence of the staff. Though these factors may contribute to the problem, they do not explain the persistent false starts, the attendance problems, the scapegoating, the factionalism and other internal group difficulties. Other organizational and structural factors may be more relevant and salient.

ORGANIZATIONAL FACTORS

Too often, the group service is an anomaly added to workers' existing caseloads. Or it may be an idiosyncratic expression of a particular worker's interests, an exception to the primary service, inadequately conceptualized and supported by agency structures and procedures. Too often, an idea for a group is developed, but somehow it never gets off the drawing board or becomes unsatisfactorily implemented, and therefore never institutionalized. Too often agencies, workers, and clients experience these failures and become reluctant to be involved with a group again. Inattention to formal and informal organizational structures and processes accounts for many of these difficulties.

Organizational sanctions are essential to the development and institutionalization of group services. Without vertical, administrative approval, the worker "walks on egg shells." In response to any perceived problem, such as "uncooperative patients" in a hospital or "noisy children" in a school or social agency, the medical or psychiatric chief, the school principal, or the agency director may precipitously terminate the group. Similarly, without horizontal, interdisciplinary, and peer staff involvement, the service is easily undermined or sabotaged. It may be time for the group to begin, yet co-workers have not referred appropriate clients, or nurses suddenly have to take the patients' temperatures, or teachers decide to punish children for class behavior by disallowing group participation.

Along with organizational sanctions, structural supports are also essential to the development and institutionalization of group services. Without them, group services are doomed to fail. If children are to participate freely, a worker's office or an auditorium may inhibit activity or encourage destructive behavior, and therefore, more suitable space is required. If working parents are to be engaged, the agency has to be open in the evening or on weekends. If young single mothers are to participate, child care assistance is essential. If the agency is located in a large catchment area or if special populations are to be recruited, transportation may be necessary. If group members are to be welcomed, petty cash for refreshments

may be helpful. If workers do not have confidence and skill in providing group services, supervision, consultation, or in-service training will be needed. If workers are to maintain investment, time for preparation and follow-up, statistical credit for the service must be allowed. When these supports are not negotiated beforehand, the result is administrative, worker, and client frustration.

To acquire institutional sanctions and supports, the worker begins by analyzing which environmental, organizational, and interpersonal forces are apt to support or to restrain the development of group services.[4] An organizational analysis is made to determine whether and what types of group services are feasible.[5] Since environmental forces affect all organizational processes, the worker must evaluate features in the environment that may affect the desired outcome. With the current demands for accountability, federal, state, and local reimbursement mechanisms increasingly circumscribe time and services. Thus, for example, in developing outpatient hospital group services for Medicaid patients, a worker had to become an "expert" in reimbursement policies and procedures. This expertise can make a group service feasible. Similarly, many agencies have increased their reliance upon computer technology. Unfortunately, this technology is often used against clients to determine ineligibility, to decrease entitlements, and to violate confidentiality. Computers, however, may also be used on behalf of clients' interests and needs. In a child welfare agency with a large catchment area, computers were used by the author to locate clusters of children and adolescents in diverse geographic areas and to provide outreach group services. Because of insurmountable transportation barriers, all prior efforts to offer group services at the agency had failed.

Internal organizational structures also affect the feasibility for group services. In agencies characterized by a high degree of formal structure, a proposed new service that challenges established routine will likely confront resistance. Thus, for a group service to be accepted in a hospital or school setting, it had to be responsive to the nurses' and teachers' daily schedules. The service has to be adapted to existing structures rather than disruptive of them.

Complex agencies, characterized by a large number of professional disciplines, have been found to be more responsive to programmatic innovation.[6] The diversity and advanced training create a greater openness to new ideas, methods, and technologies and therefore offer the worker a certain degree of organizational maneuverability. At the same time, the actual program implementation requires complex coordination with numerous turf-conscious disciplines, because a division of labor is required to allocate and specify work roles and tasks. And the differential role assignments are conducive to the development of a preoccupation with one's own role and function. One's own turf takes on increasing personal importance, and protecting that turf becomes the driving concern. A latent consequence of a "protectionism" culture is that client needs may be held "hostage" to turf interests. Consequently, the worker should anticipate that departments and staff may resist sharing and referring their clients to a newly formed group service (behaving as if the clients "belonged" to them). Based upon an assessment of this organizational characteristic, the worker develops a strategy to involve the staff and to address their self-interests. The group has to be "owned" by the setting and its staff. To achieve this institutional ownership, the author, for example, has encouraged hospital social workers to collaborate with nurses and doctors in developing and co-leading groups. This arrangement is more productive than staff and departments competing for clients. In one setting, the author observed the same patients simultaneously invited to four newly formed groups conducted respectively by an occupational therapist, a nurse, a rehabilitation counselor, and a social worker!

Since the work group develops a system with its own culture of values, norms, and expectations as well as its own system for distributing rewards and punishments, informal organizational structures need to be assured. Just as the formal structures socialize each organizational participant to the agency culture, the informal system socializes the participants to its own culture. And since the informal system significantly influences participants' perceptions and behaviors, it affects the development of group services. A new worker, for example, attempted without success to develop a group in a mental health clinic. She confronted a long-standing psychoanalytic orientation which channeled all clients into long-term individual psychotherapy. In requesting referrals for "her" group, none were received, and subsequent requests were similarly ignored. Moreover, the worker experienced interpersonal ostracism as she violated, without realizing it, a powerful peer norm.

In addition to analyzing the potential effect of environmental forces and organizational characteristics, the worker identifies the key participants who will affect and be affected by the proposed group service and attempts to estimate their likely response. To gauge their potential reactions, the worker evaluates the impact of the group service on the participants' job performance and satisfaction.

If the group service increases the participants' self-esteem, visibility, praise, or influence, then their support can be anticipated. Conversely, if the group service threatens the participants' self-interests, then resistance can be anticipated.

The worker also has to assess where he/she is located in the organization's formal and informal structures. The worker's structural location may or may not provide opportunities to interact with and therefore influence key participants. Some workers isolate themselves in their organizations, as though they were engaged in private practice. They do their work and leave. Their conception of professional function is limited to client contact; consequently, their potential to develop group services is limited. If the worker has limited access to influential organizational participants, his/her position has to be improved before sanctions and supports can be acquired.

The worker, moreover, also has to take stock and assess how he/she is viewed by significant others in the organization. In developing this specialized self-awareness, the worker must differentiate between how he/she would like to be perceived and how he/she is actually perceived. The worker might consider such questions as: Am I considered competent? Am I viewed as a valuable colleague? Am I thought of as being fair? Am I someone colleagues seek out for advice, for informal socializing, or for favors? A newly employed social worker illustrates this process:

After six months, my position in the agency (child welfare) is somewhat mixed. I am fairly sure I am perceived as smart, competent, and enthusiastic about the work at the agency. I have a solid, constructive relationship with my supervisor. With the most senior worker, I have the beginning of a personal friendship.

With another prestigious worker I collaborated extensively on a family case and thus also have a strong working relationship.

I have recently become aware of a problem in my agency participation. I tend to be somewhat oppositional and critical of agency procedures. While I do see many problems with the extremely loose way in which agency operations have evolved, I have been insensitive to the fact that both my supervisor and senior worker have been with the agency since its inception. Despite their general respect for me and my ideas, I have become aware that at times I offend them with an adversarial and caustic stance in some of my comments. I realize to change the written policies and loose decision making, I will have to alter my stance.

Self-awareness in an organizational context provides guidelines for professionally effective behaviors.

Through the analysis of environmental, structural, and interpersonal forces, the worker evaluates feasibility—that is the potential to develop a group service. Where forces strongly promote the valued outcome, a group service has an excellent potential for success. Where forces strongly restrain a group service, service objectives and means for implementation have to be reevaluated and, most likely, changed. Where forces neither promote nor restrain a group service, the supports have to be courted and mobilized before the service can be implemented. And, finally, where forces strongly promote as well as strongly oppose a group service, the resulting unpredictability and potential conflict requires a low-key approach to test the waters before selecting appropriate strategies.

After assessing feasibility, the worker attempts to develop a receptive organizational climate.[7] Since practitioners usually have limited formally ascribed authority, they have to achieve organizational influence. Visible professional competence is a major pathway to being influential. A social work student describes her efforts to make her competence more visible in a hospital in order to gain staff confidence and receptiveness for developing a group service on a neurology ward:

I have made a conscientious effort to show my competence to staff in ways that would encourage their support for the group. For example, during discharge planning meetings, I have contributed knowledge about community resources as well as helped nurses deal with certain difficult patients. Four of the patients who were management problems became more cooperative with nursing staff in caring for their own needs, and going for tests because of my helping efforts. My own enthusiasm and willingness to take on "difficult" placement cases and work with their families allowed staff to view another area of my competence as I discussed my work with them. I conscientiously adhere to the hospital's value system, i.e., planning for discharge and getting the job done, and gained respect for adhering to the dominant value system.

Recognized knowledge and expertise gains prestige, respect and, in effect, informal influence.

Another pathway is involvement in the agency's interpersonal network. The worker who is an "insider," attentive to colleagues' interests and concerns, acquires support systems and allies. Since an organization's informal system represents the "grease" that makes the machinery run, an effective presence in the informal system is essential to the development of group services.

I gave myself a pep talk and decided to change my quiet, shy image. In the lunch room, I began to talk to my new colleagues so that they would get to know me and vice-versa. I began to relax a little—rather than avoid coffee machines, elevator, main office—I began to be more sociable. At Christmas time, I joined the party planning committee. This enabled me to get to know other staff members on a more personal level. They began to invite me into their offices for coffee breaks. Recently, at a staff meeting, the senior case supervisor was overly critical of my handling of a case assignment. To my surprise, several colleagues supported me and enabled me to assert my position.

Involvement in the informal system provides the worker with potential support and alliances in the sanction-building process.

Similarly, in the formal system, active and skillful involvement in committees, teams, consultations, conferences, and staff meetings provides still another significant arena for appropriately positioning oneself. And, finally, clients themselves represent a critical resource. Their informal opinions and feedback or more formal needs assessment provide essential data.

Before the worker presents the idea for a group service to the appropriate formal organizational structure and representatives, he/she decides upon an overall strategy from among demonstration, collaboration, and persuasion.[8] When there is some recognition of the need for group services and the worker's competence has been recognized, demonstration is a particularly effective strategy. By skillfully showing the value of group services, the worker may solidify organizational support before restraining forces have had the opportunity to mobilize resistance. In appropriate situations, action speaks louder than words.

In relatively open and fluid organizations where goal consensus and close interpersonal ties exist, collaboration is an effective strategy. The problems associated with the lack of group services are openly discussed with key participants invited to explore and develop programmatic ideas. In this process, the worker has to be careful about "overselling," rather than inviting genuine feedback. The problems are illustrated when a worker, relatively new to the hospital, approaches an established head nurse and attempts to "sell" a group.⁹

I said to Miss Ford that I had been doing some thinking which I would like to share with her. I told her that I had been on the ward quite a bit and felt quite at home on it. I said to her that I, as everyone else on the ward, am here to try to service the patients to the best of my ability. I then asked her what she thought of a group having any value on the ward. She said that it has been suggested before, so that it was nothing new. She said that the room full of ladies could do with something of that sort but that that's the only ladies' room there is. I asked if she thought that only ladies could benefit from a group experience and she said "no," but that she was thinking in terms of room number 1403. She asked what the group would be about and for. I said that I'm open to suggestions but that perhaps the basic purpose could be for the patients to discuss their hospitalization, frustrations, etc. It would be open to all patients.

The nurse quickly sensed the worker's agenda when she left unexplored the suggestions about the patients in room 1403. In being preoccupied with selling, the worker could not listen and be open to a collaborative exploration. In response, the nurse became agitated.

Miss Ford asked how the patients would know or how I would tell them. I told her that in order to make it a voluntary thing, perhaps written invitations to each patient would be a good idea. She asked when and where it would be held. I told her that I hoped she could help make the decision, especially the

time, because I realize they are busy. As far as the room goes, perhaps an empty bedroom or the sunroom. She said that by October 16th all rooms should be filled up. I suggested we could decide on that at a later date. I asked if she could, however, talk to the doctors and staff about this, get some ideas, and we could discuss it again next week at rounds. She said that would be fine.

Miss Ford did not seem too enthusiastic and was quite resistant (mentioning no rooms, how would patients know, etc.). However, I feel she can see some value in a ward group. Next week I plan to give her some examples of why I can see a need for the group.

In collaboration, premature agreement and superficial closure often become unraveled at a later date. Unexpressed negatives fester and often lead potential allies to sabotage the group service. The nurse changed her attitude when her concerns were addressed:

I told Miss Ford that I felt I may have been too pushy about the ward group. I said that I had asked for her participation and interest, yet I hadn't given her a chance to express herself, and I wasn't really listening to her. I then apologized and suggested that we might go back to the beginning. I said I was interested in knowing her true feelings regarding the group. She said she thought the group would be very good for most patients, but she was worried about the manpower of nurses. She said it was difficult enough to get all the nurses to attend her ward conference without having them attend a patients' group. I asked if she was thinking in terms of all the nurses going to the group at once. She said she didn't know and wondered what I thought. I said that the decision of nurses was up to her. I suggested that it might be just as effective to have one nurse drop in on the group or have the nurses rotate. . . .

I suggested that one important gap existed between patients and doctors or patients and nurses. I explained further that I believed that if a patient could release some of his anxieties or fears about his medical problems or share his hostilities in the group, he might be an easier patient to cope with. Rather than expressing his feelings in an undesirable way, he might be happier on the ward and easier to deal with. Miss Ford agreed with this and then asked about the resident on the ward. How could we keep him involved? We discussed this for a while.

As the discussion continues, the nurse becomes more involved, active, and collaborative.

Miss Ford asked how the patients would know about the group, who would go, etc. I suggested that the nurses see all the patients, and they could tell who could benefit from a group experience, who was ready to go. She asked how patients would find out about the group. I suggested we stick notices to their bedside tables. She said it would not be a good idea because the tables must be washed. She suggested we put them in the bathrooms where the beauty salon advertises. I said it was a good idea, and we went to the bathroom to select the best spot. I then brought up the subject of confidentiality. I asked how Miss Ford felt it should be handled. For example, if one patient or more complained about a certain nurse or herself, would she like to know or not? Rather than directly answering, she told me about a patient on the ward who would complain of different shifts of staff and play one against the other. I asked her if the gist of her story was that it was better to know the complaints so that they can be investigated and dealt with. She said "yes." I told her I felt the same way and that I would like to know when patients made complaints about me.

We then talked about where the group could be held. I again suggested the sunporch. This time, Miss Ford said that it would be all right because patients used it anyway. We then discussed further clearances in the hospital and set up a meeting with the nursing staff to clarify the group purpose and to select members.

Through the collaborative process, a critical organizational participant develops a stake in the group service. A worker has to engage colleagues in collaborative problem solving through a shared search for data, resources, and exploration of potential problems.

In situations characterized by goal dissent and disparity in power, persuasion (a process of argumentation and bargaining) may be the appropriate strategy. Because the status quo represents the established way of thinking and practicing, efforts to persuade others to change requires careful preparation. How one defines the need for a group service determines to a large extent the parameters of continued discussion and potential resistance. Thus, the worker has to make an effective case for an unmet need using relevant data to support this definition. Case excerpts or anecdotal experiences make the need more clearly understandable and more readily recognizable. After the unmet need is established, those opposed may turn their attention to dismissing or negating the proposed solution—a group service. Opponents usually attack a proposed solution in two areas: its feasibility, and its desirability. The worker prepares to deal with these oppositional arguments, building a case for feasibility and desirability. If significant resistance is anticipated, persuasion research suggests the two-sided argument (statement of one's own commitment to group services and the potential oppositional counterargument) is more effective in disarming resistance and influencing more neutral participants.[10] Throughout the process, the give and take, the worker's posture needs to reflect respect for others' opinions and a pressing of one's own position out of professional concern and organizational identity and loyalty.

After sanction for a group service has been obtained, a program still has to be put into action. For the practitioner much work and frustration may still lie ahead. Organizational machinery may move too slowly to sustain key participants' interest. Some organizational structures may be incompatible with group services. Staff assigned to lead groups may lack the knowledge and skill or may be overwhelmed by the additional demands and suffer from competing pressures. Thus, even after the idea for group service has been adopted, the worker must pay continued attention to acquiring and maintaining structural and interpersonal supports. Therefore, before a group service is implemented, the worker attempts to make needed modifications in existing structures (such as agency hours, intake procedures) to increase the chances for success. Before the group service is implemented, the worker concerns him/herself with the organizational participants who will be assigned responsibility for the group service, providing a clear conception about group purpose and role requirements.[11]

FORMULATION OF GROUP PURPOSE

Lack of clarity about group purpose is a common problem.[12] A group has to evolve from a common need/concern/interest around which prospective members can be brought together.[13] The commonality provides the foundation for and is essential to the development of a mutual aid system. In contrast, if members' needs are too divergent, or an agency's agenda is discrepant with group interest, or a worker's conception of group purpose is ambiguous, then members may withdraw, test incessantly, or act out. Mu-

tual aid is more likely to evolve in a group where members need each other to deal with common needs/concerns/interests. Thus, it is essential for the worker to develop a clear conception about potential group purpose, translating commonality into specific operational tasks. Groups can be formed around natural life stresses or problems in living that people experience.[14]

Life Transitional Stressors

Life transitions are often stressful. Group services can be designed to help people with developmental changes over the life cycle, such as adolescents dealing with issues of sexuality and ethnic identity, and problems of independence/dependence.[15] Developmental stress may be exacerbated by physiological, cognitive, and emotional impairment. A group experience for young adult diabetics or learning disabled adolescents can be effective in helping members to deal with their common and distinctive struggles for competence, mastery, and a sense of identity.[16]

Similarly, groups can be helpful for people with difficult life statuses, such as siblings of retarded youngsters, adolescents in residential treatment, homeless adults, adults on renal dialysis, single parents, abused children and adults, and so on.[17] These stressful life events carry heavy adaptive burdens and complex interpersonal and environmental demands.

Life changes are equally stressful.[18] Natural school transitions require children and parents to deal with the status changes associated with beginning elementary, junior high and high schools, and college. Also, marriage and parenthood are both exciting and complex life transitions. Recent retirees or parents confronting the "empty nest" phenomenon encounter acute status loss and may experience depression. Organizational transitions such as agency admission require coping with the new status of patient, client, or resident; agency discharge requires coping with new demands and expectations. Some status changes may come too early in life such as adolescent pregnancy. Others may come too late in life such as elderly people carrying primary responsibility for child rearing. Since most status changes can be stressful, they represent viable points of entry for group services.

Crisis events also represent a difficult life transition. People may confront various crises: pre- or post-surgery (cardiac, mastectomy); chronic or acute illness (sickle cell anemia); physical trauma and assault (amputation, rape); loss of a loved one (child, spouse, parent). When a sudden, unexpected, overwhelming loss occurs (or is about to occur), the client and relatives need emotional support from significant others. Group services can provide those "significant others" to help cope with the overwhelming stress.

Environmental Stressors

Environments are a major source of stress. A group formed to help with life transitional issues may also need to deal with external organizational concerns. Parents of mentally retarded children, for example, can be helpful to each other in dealing with child-rearing concerns. But they may also need to work on the lack of community resources and deal with the unresponsiveness of organizational representatives. Similarly, a group formed for life transitional issues may also need to deal with intra-organizational obstacles including the agency's structure (for example, lack of evening hours) or the quality of services (such as institutional food).

Group services may be also formed to address internal and/or external organizational issues explicitly. Thus, groups may be formed to involve consumers more fully within the agency's planning and decision-making structures. A planning committee, an advisory group, or a leadership council fulfill important functions for both members and agencies. Groups may also be organized with a social action focus to help consumers negotiate organizational structures and services (such as welfare rights, tenants' associations). These services enable people to act to gain greater control and mastery over their environments.[19]

In contemporary environments, many people are vulnerable to social and emotional isolation. Social network and self-help groups provide social and emotional linkages and establish "life lines," such as groups for new tenants in public housing, new immigrants, elderly residents of a building or neighborhood, recently released mental patients, patients with a chronic physical condition, groups for widows and widowers. Social network and self-help groups provide concrete day-to-day assistance in which interpersonal belonging and caring replace day-to-day despair, and hope replaces isolation and alienation. Unfortunately, some agencies and practitioners seem unsure about the therapeutic value of attention to environmental concerns and do not offer such services. However, for people to act upon their environment and develop social and emotional connections is, in fact, most therapeutic. These processes engage cognition and perception, improve emotional and physical well-being, and provide social identity and a sense of belonging, competence, and human relatedness.[20]

Interpersonal Stressors

Natural units such as families, patients on wards, students in classrooms, roommates in hospitals or dormitories may experience relational and communication problems. These units may develop maladaptive patterns that promote scapegoating or that reinforce mutual withdrawal. In a residential cottage, for example, child care staff and children may experience difficulties in living, working, and communicating together.[21] Or in a classroom teacher and children may find themselves at cross purposes. A social worker can intervene within the natural unit (the cottage, the classroom, the hospital ward) and identify and challenge the maladaptive patterns and facilitate communication.[22] Beyond intervening in natural units, groups can be formed with an explicit interpersonal focus. Couples and multifamily groups, for example, provide a natural modality to examine and work on relational and communication patterns.

Life transitional, environmental, and interpersonal problems in living offer a conceptualization for the provision of a variety of group services. Some groups may be formed with an *educational* focus through which participants acquire relevant knowledge and information, for example, in sex education, parent education, preparation for parenthood, pre-/post-surgery, and health education groups.[23] Other groups may be formed with a *problem-solving* focus through which members help each other to examine personal behavior in its situational context and develop new perceptions and skills, such as newly married couples, retirement, and post-cardiac groups.[24] Other groups may be formed with a *behavioral-change* focus through which the group serves as a context for individual treatment and change, such as smoking-cessation, phobia, and eating-disorder groups.[25] Still other groups may be formed with a *social* focus through which members learn skills, make friends, and build emotional and social connections, such as a regressed schizophrenics coffee club, widow/widowers group, men's cardiac club, Parents Without Partners, and senile elderly music reminiscence group.[26] And, finally, still other groups may be formed with a *task* focus through which participants use their talents to complete prescribed objectives, such as planning committees, advisory and social action groups, ad hoc task forces, and the like. The problems-in-living conceptualization emphasizes life stressors and natural life processes around which people at risk or in need or with common interests may be clustered. And clarity of commonality increases the likelihood of eliciting organizational sanctions and supports, as well as for engaging members' motivation and strengths in the mutual-aid and problem-solving processes.

GROUP COMPOSITION FACTORS

The composition of the group affects its development and direction and dictates whether the group will move toward mutual aid, disintegration, or parasitism. Group purpose provides the context for its composition. Within this context, groups composed of members with common backgrounds (age, sex, ethnic and social class), and common personality capacities and behaviors (ego functioning, role skills, authority/intimacy orientations) tend to be stable and supportive, more quickly developing a group identity and esprit de corps. Similar life experiences, concerns, interests, and adaptive styles provide members with a sense of *commonality* and a collective *stability.* While these commonalities create a sense of immediate closeness and support, they also reflect a lack of *diversity* and *vitality.* Members may be too alike, and their "likeness" may reinforce maladaptive patterns. This is sometimes seen in a gang that supports antisocial and delinquent behavior, or in a depressed patients' group that exacerbates hopelessness and despair. Overly homogeneous groups limit the diversity essential to challenge the status quo, to create the necessary tension for change, and to provide models for alternative attitudes and behaviors.

Groups composed of members with diverse backgrounds (age, sex, ethnic, social class) and diverse personality capacities and behaviors (that is, in ego functioning, role skills, authority/intimacy orientation) tend to be less stable and less predictable. They may experience difficulty in developing a sense of group identity and cohesion. Differing life experiences, concerns, interests, or adaptive styles create internal obstacles to achieving a common agenda and open communication. Members are too different, and their differences become the central issue rather than the group purpose and tasks. The author, for example, formed a racially balanced group of youngsters with school difficulties. The racial heterogeneity, however, led to factionalism and scapegoating. These internal barriers inhibited the group from working on its purpose. On the other hand, if such a group can overcome its internal problems, however, it has the potential for dramatic impact. The inner diversity provides vital and rich resources for members to draw upon.[27]

Ideally, groups require both stability (homogeneity) and diversity (heterogeneity).[28] At the very least, prospective members need to have common concerns and interests—a commonality of purpose. Once these have been identified, then key background and personality factors may be specified. For each such factor, the desired range of commonness or difference must be determined. In developing a group service for pregnant adolescents, for example, the following factors should be taken into account: their common concerns about delivery; available services and resources; relationships with parents, boyfriends, school representatives; future plans for their babies. These will bind members together and provide collective stability. The worker then needs to think through the relative advantages of commonality or difference for such other factors as age, first pregnancy, religion, ethnicity, parental and boyfriend relationships, health, stage of pregnancy, geographic location, and others.

As a rule of thumb members usually tolerate and use greater diversity when common interests and concerns are experienced intensively. Thus, for example, when the author helped to organize a group of women with cancer and a limited life expectancy, their profound commonality made differences in age, class, and ethnicity seem inconsequential. In contrast, youngsters in the racially balanced school group were identified by school personnel as problem students, while they experienced the need for the group service less intensely. Thus, the less members perceive common concerns and interests, the more homogeneous the group composition must be.

In composing a group, a worker must be particularly careful not to isolate and potentially scapegoat a member because he/she is different and alone on important background or personality factors as a "butterfly chaser" would be in a group of athletic youngsters. A client poignantly describes the experience and consequence of being different:

My previous social worker referred me to a group at a mental health clinic. She told me it would give me something to do and people other than my children to talk to. Then I found out it was a group for recently released hospital patients, many of whom were still psychotic. They talked to themselves and sometimes lost sight of reality for moments. I was frightened by them, and also upset that I was placed in a group with them. Look, I know I'm nuts, but I'm not that nuts. Maybe someday I will be, but let me get there in my own time. When I have a nervous breakdown, I want it to be my very own and not taught to me by members of my therapy group.[29]

To avoid potential isolation and alienation, each member should have at least one other member on factors assessed to be important.[30] Beyond these compositional guidelines, more elaborate and precisely designed scales are available and particularly useful for residential settings.[31]

TIME, SIZE, AND SPACE FACTORS

Many groups are long term and open ended with departing members replaced by new members. These groups have two chronic problems: (1) the ongoing, long-term nature may lead worker and members to lose their original sense of purpose and vitality, and (2) the shifts in membership may require ongoing contracting and recontracting and result in the group's inability to move beyond an early stage of group development. In contrast, planned short-term and time-limited services are associated with more positive outcomes.[32] The *time boundary* helps members focus quickly and maintain purpose, direction, and a sense of urgency. Thus, a one-session orientation

group, a two-session post-surgical group, a four-session adoptive parents group, an eight-session couples group, or a twelve-session group of foster care adolescents may be more productive than an ongoing, long-term service. For certain populations, a time limit is imperative. The group of cancer patients previously mentioned with a limited life expectancy would have been devastated by a gradual loss of membership, even if new members had been substituted. As the group nears completion of its tasks, however, members and worker may decide on the basis of evaluation to recontract another cycle or a specific number of additional sessions. Similarly, the group and worker may decide on additional sessions after a certain time set aside for experimentation and integration has passed.

Other time considerations are the *frequency* and *duration* of sessions. Many agencies offer group services on the traditional weekly hour, rather than structuring and arranging time in ways that are responsive to the special needs of the population being served. In providing group services for young children having difficulty with school, for example, the author discovered that weekly sessions for an hour were insufficient. During the interval between sessions, the youngsters confronted various school crises, and the group was unavailable for assistance. Consequently, meetings were restructured for greater frequency (twice or three times weekly) and for shorter duration (thirty or forty minutes). This time change made dramatic impact upon both the substance and intensity of our work. Generally, children and mentally impaired adults are responsive to more frequent and shorter sessions, while well-functioning adolescents and adults are responsive to weekly and longer sessions (one and a half to two hours). More frequent sessions, however, are required for adolescents and adults in states of crisis, such as pre-surgery groups or discharge groups, especially those facing difficult consequences. In medical settings, physical discomfort and pain necessitate sessions of shorter duration. Essentially, developmental stages or special population attributes and their effect on attention span and capacity for session-to-session carryover, need to be taken into account in the creative structuring of time.

Group *size* needs to be related to group objectives, primary interventive methods, and client needs. The larger the group, the more formalized it becomes through establishing rules, procedures, and possibly electing officers. Communication tends to be channeled through the formal or indigenous leader with limited opportunity for individual attention, accessibility to the worker, and intimate, spontaneous participation. For some mental patients or the frail elderly, the size of community meetings may be overstimulating and confusing, leading to inappropriate behavior or withdrawal. To shy, anxious, or less adequate members, however, the large group may provide a sense of identification and belonging without a loss of autonomy and the desired degree of interpersonal anonymity. A large group also obtains community and organizational visibility and can be an effective means for self-help and influence. Thus purposes and objectives influence the selection of appropriate group size.

Group purposes and objectives also affect the selection of appropriate interventive methods. A primarily didactic method may be used in a one-session orientation group to introduce new members to an agency's or community's available resources and requisites. In this instance, a large group (fifteen or more members) can be effective in achieving the purpose and objectives. A one-session pre-surgery preparation group may use didactic methods to present factual data, while also reaching for underlying concerns and inviting ventilation of feelings. In this instance, purpose and objectives can best be achieved in a small group (approximately three to five members).

Appropriate group size is also related to members' needs and communication styles. Small groups offer greater opportunity for individualization, providing each member with sufficient time and accessibility to peers and the worker. Members in crises, for example, often need the attention afforded by small groups. Similarly, emotionally deprived children need the continued and special attention more likely in a small group.

Small groups, however, do make greater demands for participation, involvement, and intimacy. For shy, anxious, or less adequate members, the pressures may be too great. The level of demand may exceed their level of tolerance. A moderate size group (approximately seven to nine) can provide regressed schizophrenics, for example, the necessary interpersonal space that may be unavailable in a smaller group. Moreover, a small group may have insufficient resources for diversity and vitality, or for linking up with a "buddy." Finally, absences leave a small group extremely vulnerable to disintegration.[33]

The *physical setting* also has a significant impact on a group's activities and interactions. Light, ventilation, room size, and furniture arrangement facilitate or inhibit the development of a mutual aid system. Within the limits imposed by space and design, the worker must consider the usefulness of structuring space, and defining expectations and boundaries. Children meeting in a large room need spatial boundaries to structure their activities and interactions. Prearranged tables and chairs symbolize spatial limits. As members (and the worker) develop comfort and security, available space can be used more flexibly.

In arranging space, the worker assesses members' comfort and interactional style. When the author met with the group of adolescent girls, he discovered they were initially uncomfortable with chairs arranged in a small, intimate circle. They were self-conscious about what to do with their hands, feet, and so on. The small circle also can be threatening to members who do not seek or are not ready for the degree of physical and emotional intimacy such a structure demands. In these situations, tables provide the necessary spatial boundary and distance members require. If, however, members need physical movement, the tables are restrictive. Predicting members' spatial needs may be difficult; members have to be involved in assessing and planning for their own spatial needs, including changes during a session and overtime.[34]

GROUP RECRUITMENT FACTORS

Referral is a frequent method of recruitment. To obtain referrals, the worker has to have an organizational presence. By cultivating interpersonal relationships and by demonstrating day-to-day professional competence, the worker establishes a reservoir of goodwill. To receive appropriate referrals of potential group candidates, group purpose and membership criteria have to be clearly identified and communicated. As they are received, the worker examines available data and may conduct individual or even small group intake sessions to interpret service, assess need and interest, answer questions and determine appropriateness.

Workers also develop groups from their own assigned services and caseloads. In hospitals, for example, natural group clusters exist in particular medical services or wards. In these situations, as well as in developing a group from a worker's caseload, the worker and client know each other; their relationship may lead to a quick service involvement, and often propels the group past the typical "feeling out" and testing phase characteristic of group beginnings. At the same time, members have greater difficulty in refusing the service and certainly in sharing the worker with others. In fact, sharing the same worker in itself does not necessarily provide commonality and a shared purpose.

Still another method of recruiting members for the group is random invitation: using a central card file with common criteria in mind, and sending invitations. Putting up signs, inserting notices in a union newsletter, and community publicity are other random recruitment methods. In all these, wording must be clear and should capture the attention and interest of the reader. Random open invitations invite voluntary participation, place least pressure for involvement, and may even recruit new "customers" for the agency. At the same time, the worker has only limited control over composition. This "pot luck" quality will characterize groups recruited by random methods. These methods also tend to be quite impersonal and rarely reach nonjoiners and nonreaders. Follow-up telephone calls, home visits, and group intakes can personalize the offer of service to some degree and simultaneously clear up misconceptions and screen out inappropriate candidates.

Whichever recruitment method is used, the worker must maintain professional responsibility for group composition. This is a specialized area of our professional expertise. To relinquish this responsibility invites a teacher to compose a group with only acting-out children or a nurse to compose a diabetic group with severely mixed symptomatology (such as early and amputative stages). Such groups end in despair, decreasing the probability that worker and client will invest themselves in a future group.

STAFFING THE GROUP

Staffing the group is still another important factor in the development of group services. The usual and most effective model for the staffing of groups is one worker who possesses substantive knowledge and practice skills. Modifications may sometimes be considered.

When roles are clearly delineated as in some interdisciplinary settings, coleadership may be an effective arrangement. A nurse or doctor for medical expertise and a social worker for interpersonal and environmental expertise can jointly provide a more integrated service that is responsive to patients' total needs than either one can do alone. For the arrangement to be effective, it is critical to reach explicit agreement on the respective roles and the tasks, particularly in beginning, ending, and focusing sessions. It is also helpful to contract respective coleadership roles with group members. As previously mentioned, coleadership may be used also to gain sanctions for group services by providing two disciplines, mutual accountability and by acquiring interdisciplinary involvement and support. Finally, it can be used to institutionalize group services. In developing group ser-

vices at an adoption agency, for example, the author developed a structure in which a primary and secondary leader offered a particular group service. Having gained experience and a sense of competence, the secondary leader assumed primary responsibility for the next group, breaking in a new secondary leader. Through this staffing structure, numerous staff developed on-the-job training and comfort in working with the group modality.

Coleadership, however, should only be used purposively and discriminately. While numerous rationales are offered, coleadership too often reflects workers' discomfort and anxiety about working with groups; "There are so many of them and only one of me." Besides being an uneconomical arrangement, it adds a complex dynamic to group process, namely, the workers' struggles to synchronize their interventions and to cope with role ambiguities, competitiveness, and discrepant interventions.[35] Unwittingly, this arrangement, therefore, may inhibit the group's mutual aid processes by encouraging withdrawal, testing, or identification with one worker at the expense of the others.

At the turn of the century, our profession's pioneers grappled with enormous problems associated with industrialization and urbanization. A few leaders believed a special institution was needed to help people cope and survive mass dislocation and poverty. The settlement house was born to stand against the forces of isolation, alienation, and anonymity. And within the settlements, the group modality served as the primary mechanism to focus on people's fundamental needs to belong and to express themselves socially and intellectually. In contemporary society, pervasive social and emotional isolation continues to call forth the extraordinary potentials inherent in the offering of group services. And so we discover the same themes exist today as in the past, altered only by the growth and changes in

our society. Groups have and can continue to serve as a powerful healing force for people who share common needs and aspirations.

NOTES

1. See James Garland, Hubert Jones, and Ralph Kolodny, "A Model of Stages of Development in Social Work Groups," in *Explorations in Group Work,* ed. Saul Bernstein (Boston: Boston University School of Social Work, 1968), pp. 12–53.

2. William Schwartz, "The Social Worker in the Group," in *New Perspectives on Services to Groups: Theory, Organization, Practice* (New York: National Association of Social Workers, 1961), p. 18.

3. Alex Gitterman, "Survey of Group Services in Maternal and Child Health," in *Social Work with Groups in Maternal and Child Health* (New York: Columbia University School of Social Work, Conference Proceedings, June 1979), pp. 8–14.

4. Lewin's "force-field analysis" helps the worker visualize the salient forces promoting and resisting change. Kurt Lewin, "Group Decisions and Social Change," in *Readings in Social Psychology,* ed. Eleanor E. Maccoby, Theodore R. Newcomb, and Eugene L. Hartley (New York: Holt, Rinehart & Winston, 1952), pp. 207–211.

5. Brager and Holloway, and Germain and Gitterman apply "force-field analysis" to organizational innovation and change. George Brager and Stephen Holloway, *Changing Human Service Organizations: Politics and Practice* (New York: Free Press, 1978), pp. 107–108; and Carel B. Germain and Alex Gitterman, *The Life Model of Social Work Practice* (New York: Columbia University Press, 1980), pp. 307–319.

6. Haige and Aikens review the relationship between organizational properties and innovation. Jerald Haige and Michael Aikens, *Social Change in Complex Organizations* (New York: Random House, 1970).

7. For elaboration, see Brager and Hollo-

way, *Changing Human Service Organizations,* pp. 157–176; Gene Dalton, "Influence and Organizational Change," in *Organizational Change and Development,* ed. G. Dalton, P. Lawrence, and L. Greiner (Homewood, Ill.: Irwin and Dorsey Press, 1970), pp. 234–237; Germain and Gitterman, *Life Model of Social Work Practice,* pp. 311–319; David Mechanic, "Sources of Power of Lower Participants in Complex Organizations," in *New Perspectives in Organizational Research,* ed. W. Cooper, H. Leavitt, and M. Shelly, II (New York: John Wiley, 1964), pp. 136–149.

8. Brager and Holloway specify three broad "tactics": collaboration, campaign, and contest. Brager and Holloway, *Changing Human Service Organizations,* pp. 129–153. Germain and Gitterman identify four "engagement phase strategies: demonstration, collaboration, persuasion and conflict." Germain & Gitterman, *Life Model of Social Work Practice,* pp. 319–326. Morris and Binstock describe six "pathways to influence": obligation, friendship, rational persuasion, selling, coercion, and inducement. Robert Morris and Robert Binstock, *Feasible Planning for Social Change* (New York: Columbia University Press, 1966), pp. 116–127.

9. This practice illustration is reprinted with the author's permission from Lawrence Shulman, *The Skills of Helping Individuals and Groups* (Itasca, Ill.: F. E. Peacock Publishers, 1984), pp. 178–183.

10. Marvin Karlins and Herbert I. Abelson, *Persuasion: How Opinions and Attitudes Are Changed* (New York: Springer, 1970), pp. 24–26.

11. See Jeffrey Pressman and Aaron Wildavsky, *Implementation* (Berkeley, Calif.: University of California Press, 1973), pp. 87–124.

12. Discussions about formulation of group

purpose; group composition factors; time, size, and space factors; and group recruitment factors are elaborated from the author's prior publications. See Alex Gitterman, "The Use of Groups in Health Setting," in *Social Work with Groups in Health Settings,* ed. Abraham Lurie, Gary Rosenberg, and Sidney Pinsky (New York: Prodist, 1982), pp. 6–21; and idem., "Development of Group Services," in *Social Work with Groups in Maternal and Child Health* (New York: Columbia University School of Social Work, Conference Proceedings, June 1978), pp. 15–22.

13. Schwartz defines a group as "a collection of people who need each other in order to work on certain common tasks in an agency that is hospitable to those tasks." William Schwartz, "On the Uses of Groups in Social Work Practice," in *The Practice of Group Work,* ed. William Schwartz and Serapio Zelba (New York: Columbia University Press, 1971), p. 7.

14. Germain and Gitterman conceptualize stress as emerging from three interrelated areas of living: life transitions, environmental pressures, and interpersonal processes. Germain and Gitterman, *Life Model of Social Work Practice,* pp. 77–254.

15. See Emanuel Tropp, "Social Work: The Developmental Approach," *Encyclopedia of Social Work,* 16th ed. (New York: National Association of Social Workers, 1971), pp. 1246–1252.

16. See Jean Fraher and Marvin McNally, "Group Work with Physically Disabled Adolescents," *Social Work with Groups* 2 (Winter 1979): 321–330; Naomi Pines Gitterman, "Group Services for Learning Disabled Children and their Parents," *Social Casework,* 60 (April 1979): 217–226; Judy Lee, "Group Work with Mentally Retarded Foster Adolescents," *Social Casework* 58 (March 1977): 164–173.

17. See Jean B. Peterson and Calvin H. Sturgies, "Group Work with Adolescents in a Public Foster Care Agency," *The Practice of Group Work,* pp. 122–143.

18. See James A. Cardarella, "A Group for Children with Deceased Parents," *Social Work* 20 (July 1975): 328–329); Michael Roskin,

"Life Change and Social Group Work Intervention," *Social Work with Groups* 2 (Summer 1979): 117–128.

19. See Hal Lipton, "The Social Worker as Mediator on a Hospital Ward," In *The Practice of Group Work,* pp. 97–121; Hyman J. Weiner, "Social Change and Group Work," *Social Work* 9 (1964): 106–120.

20. See George Getzel, "Group Work with Kin and Friends Caring for the Elderly," *Social Work with Groups* 5 (Summer 1982): 91–102; Carol Swenson, "Social Networks, Mutual Aid, and the Life Model of Practice," in *Social Work Practice: People and Environments,* ed. Carel B. Germain (New York: Columbia University Press, 1979), pp. 215–238.

21. See David Birnbach, "The Skills of Child Care," in *The Practice of Group Work,* pp. 176–198.

22. See Hyman J. Weiner, "The Hospital, the Ward, and the Patients as Clients: Use of the Group Method," *Social Work* 4 (October 1959): 57–64.

23. See Judith Lee, "The Foster Parents Workshop: A Social Work Approach to Learning for New Foster Parents," *Social Work with Groups* 2 (Summer 1979): 129–144.

24. See Alex Gitterman, "Social Work in the Public Schools," *Social Casework* 58 (February 1977): 111–118; Stephen J. Stephenson and Michael F. Boler, "Group Treatment for Divorcing Parents," *Social Work with Groups* 4 (Fall and Winter 1981): 67–78.

25. See Sheldon Rose, *Group Therapy: A Behavioral Approach* (Englewood Cliffs, N.J.: Prentice-Hall, 1977); Irving Yalom, *The Theory and Practice of Group Psychotherapy* (New York: Basic Books, 1970).

26. See George Getzel, "Poetry Writing Groups and the Elderly," *Social Work with Groups,* 6 (Spring 1983): 65–76.

27. For discussion about the impact of age, sex, ethnicity, socioeconomic status and personality factors on group composition, see Margaret E. Hartford, *Groups in Social Work* (New York: Columbia University Press, 1972), pp. 98–120. Helen Northern, *Social Work with Groups,* New York: Columbia University Press, 1969, pp. 86–143. Schutz developed an instrument, Fundamental Interpersonal Re-

lations Orientation, to measure interpersonal compatibility. William C. Schutz, *F.I.P.O.: A Three Dimensional Theory of Interpersonal Orientation* (New York: Holt, Rinehart & Winston, Inc., 1958), and idem., "On Group Composition," *Journal of Abnormal Social Psychology* 62 (1961): 275–281. See also William Shalinsky, "Group Composition as an Element of Social Group Work Practice," *Social Service Review* 43 (March 1964): 42–49; S. R. Slavson, "Criteria for Selection and Rejection of Patients for Various Kinds of Group Therapy," *International Journal of Psychotherapy* 5 (1955): 3–30, and idem., *A Textbook in Analytic Group Psychotherapy* (New York: International Universities Press, 1964), pp. 178–232; John Wax, "Criteria for Grouping Hospitalized Mental Patients," *Uses of Groups in Psychiatric Settings* (New York: National Association of Social Workers, 1960), pp. 91–100.

28. Redl defines this balance as the "law of optimum distance." Fritz Redl, "Art of Group Composition," in *Creative Group Living in Children's Institutions*, ed. Suzanne Schulz (New York: Association Press, 1951), pp. 76–96.

29. Edited excerpt from Alex Gitterman and Alice Schaeffer, "The White Professional and the Black Client," *Social Casework* 53 (May 1972): 280–291.

30. Yalom refers to this compositional principle as the "Noah's Ark Principle." Irving Yalom, *The Theory and Practice of Group Psychotherapy* (New York: Basic Books, 1970), pp. 192–207.

31. See Harvey J. Bertcher and Frank Maple, "Elements and Issues in Group Composition," in *Individual Change Through Small Groups*, ed. Paul Glasser, Rosemary Sarri, and Robert Vinter (New York: Free Press, 1974), pp. 186–208.

32. See Norman Epstein, "Brief Group Therapy in Child Guidance Clinic," *Social Work* 15 (July 1970): 33–38; Martin Strickler and Jean Allgeyer, "The Crisis Group: A New Application of Crisis Theory," *Social Work* 12 (July 1967): 28–32.

33. For a review of research related to the impact of group size, see, Robert F. Bales and Edgar F. Borgatta, "Size of Group as a Factor in the Interaction Profile," in *Small Groups*, ed. Edgar F. Borgatta and Robert F. Bales (New York: Alfred A. Knopf, 1965), pp. 495–512; Margaret E. Hartford, *Groups in Social Work* (New York: Columbia University Press, 1972), pp. 160–169.

34. For an informative discussion about the impact of space on perception, cognition, and behavior, see Carel B. Germain, "Space: An Ecological Variable in Social Work Practice," *Social Casework* 59 (November 1978): 515–522; Carel B. Germain, "Using Social and Physical Environments," in *Handbook of Clinical Social Work*, ed. Aaron Rosenblatt and Diana Waldfogel (San Francisco: Jossey-Bass, 1983), pp. 110–133.

35. Middleman raises serious questions about the usefulness of coleadership in student training. Ruth R. Middleman, "Returning Group Process to Group Work," *Social Work with Groups* 1 (Spring 1978): 15–26.

Part Two
Mutual Aid and Children

Joyce Vastola
Amy Nierenberg
Elizabeth H. Graham

CHAPTER 4

The Lost and Found Group: Group Work with Bereaved Children*

For children, the death of a loved one is earth-shattering because the world, as they know it, will never be the same. There are few experiences in life capable of generating more pain than the death of someone the child depends on for love and daily care. Even for those children who have caretakers readily available this tragedy can be unbearable.

The loss of a loved one is very difficult for children and adults alike. Adults, however, are able to receive support and love from their spouses, children, and dear friends. Children, by contrast, invest almost all of their energies and love in the parent. The parent is the source of sustenance and their very existence.

Cheryl was nine when her mother was killed. She had been living with her mom, three younger sisters, two cousins, and her maternal grandmother. Following her mother's death, the maternal grandmother, Mrs. W., became the sole guardian for all six children.

Overwhelmed with her massive responsibilities, Mrs. W. spent little time with Cheryl. The two avoided talking about the death, each living alone with the pain.

Cheryl began having trouble sleeping, fearing that the man who killed her mother would come back to kill her, too. She lost her appetite and suddenly became a picky eater. She taunted one of her cousins (living with the family), whose father had died earlier, repeating in sing-song fashion, "Your daddy's dead." Cheryl's teachers reported distinct behavioral changes following her mother's death; she became upset easily; she provoked peers; she stopped handing in schoolwork, and within six months her grades dropped dramatically. She busied herself daydreaming the school hours away, plotting how and when to find and kill her mother's murderer.

Cheryl's sleeping, eating, behavior, and academic problems are common among bereaved children and adolescents. Few experiences have a longer impact than the death of a primary caretaker when one is yet too young to become self-sufficient and capable of satisfying one's own basic needs. The death of a parent not only interrupts a child's accustomed daily routine, but also has the potential for interfering with the future course of development. Psychiatric illnesses and

*We would like to acknowledge gratefully Dr. C. V. Koh, who developed and directed this project: without her support and guidance our work would not have been possible. The work of Gail Barresi, Barbara Lino, and Richard Mayer is also acknowledged as making an important contribution to this project.

various pathological disturbances can result.[1]

Recently, attention has been focused on the need to help these high-risk children and their families. Immediate intervention to bereaved families as a preventive measure has been stressed. A paramount goal for the worker and the child's family is to help him confront and accept the death, so that he may eventually be able to form new attachments. The child and family may require assistance in understanding the impact of the loss. The worker also needs to draw attention to the similarities and differences in the mourning processes of adults and children. For instance, when Mrs. W. was helped to see that Cheryl's school and sleep problems and her increasingly provocative nature were part and parcel of the child's mourning reaction, Mrs. W.'s understanding and tolerance of these behaviors increased. In the process, Mrs. W. confronted her own unresolved feelings about her daughter's death, which in turn brought Cheryl and Mrs. W. closer together.

Understandably, children need time and much support to cope with the tragic death of a parent. Designing a plan to aid both children and their reconstituted families to understand the universality of death, to legitimize their feelings and reactions, and finally to help them identify how their lives can proceed in spite of their losses, is indeed a formidable task, but nonetheless a task that is well worth undertaking. It is toward this aim that we have focused our work with bereaved children.

DEVELOPMENTAL TASKS OF CHILDHOOD

The developmental tasks of childhood are the most enormous of life's challenges. The child moves from a helpless state of total dependence on the parent to become an independent, distinct human being—one with unique thoughts, beliefs, feelings, and a sense of self.

In working with children, it is crucial to consider their age and stage of development. We found Erikson's framework—The Stages of Man—[2] to be a useful model for conceptualizing their changing needs and struggles.

1. Trust versus Mistrust—In this first stage of life, children develop basic trust in the world. This comes about as the infant has his basic physiological needs met by a caretaker who provides a consistent experience and a loving environment for the baby. The infant's first social achievement is seen in his ability to let his mother out of his sight without experiencing undue fear and anger. He is able to do this because the mother has become an inner certainty as well as an outer predictability.

When a parental death occurs during this stage, the child's capacity for the development of this basic trust may be compromised.

Carlos was almost eighteen months old when his mother died, an innocent victim caught in the firing line of a drug shootout. Later, as Carlos walked through the streets with his aunt, he would point to young women walking by and cry out: "Mommy, Mommy." At home he would cling to his aunt and follow her from room to room. Understandably, he was afraid to let her out of his sight.

2. Autonomy versus Shame and Doubt—During this period, the child matures biologically and experiences support and structure from his environment. She develops a sense of self-control and a clearer notion of himself. She learns how to balance love and hate, cooperation and willfulness, and self-expression and suppression.

Joan was two and a half when her mother died. At the age of eleven she still exhibited some of the difficulties associated with a loss sustained at the untimely age of two. Joan, now eleven and being raised by her grandmother, glanced fearfully at her grandmother each time a question was asked of the young girl. It seemed she felt she needed permission from this parental figure before speaking.

3. Initiative versus Guilt—During this third stage, children begin to explore the world with vitality and vigor. The child sets out to achieve small goals with a sense of initiative. He begins to identify with those around him; a conscience starts to take form. A parental loss during this stage—particularly a same-sex parent—can result in tremendous guilt feelings. These feelings can interfere with his pursuit of goals and tasks of development.

James's father died of cancer when James was three years old. At age nine, when he entered our group, he came across as a shy, sad boy in need of a great deal of encouragement to speak up and say what was on his mind. After many weeks of quiet participation, he disclosed to the others his strong belief that he was responsible for his father's death. When asked why he thought so, he replied that he had demanded too much attention and was hard to care for. In school, teachers reported that he often sat in the back of the classroom, walled off from the others. James seemed frightened to approach his teacher as well as his peers.

4. Industry versus Inferiority—This stage signifies the beginning of the latency period and entrance into school life. Children must now learn to harness their energy and conform to the structure and rules of school. During these years, youngsters develop a sense of industry, of being part of a productive system. Socially, it is one of the most important stages, for it demands the skill of working with others. A loss here can engender feelings of inferiority, inadequacy, and inhibitions in learning. This child may show reluctance to venture out into the world and meet the challenges of life.

John's mother died when he was seven. Later that year his teacher noticed a sudden decline in his schoolwork to a level markedly below his potential. He seemed uninterested throughout the remainder of the school year, lacking the pride he had formerly taken in his work. Despite Herculean efforts and tremendous sensitivity on the part of his teacher, John was unable to regain the motivation necessary to succeed in school.

A picture emerges of the types of developmental tasks that pose obstacles to bereaved children.[3] Over all, the nature of the obstacle corresponds to the child's age and developmental stage at the time of the mother's or father's death. Guilt, fear, and doubt, among other emotions, can penetrate the child's inner world and color his performance of tasks and his relationships with others, including the relationship between himself and his new caretaker.

AGENCY CONTEXT AND THE GROUP MODALITY

A group work program for bereaved latency-aged children was developed at a child guidance center in an inner-city area. The center provides a comprehensive range of services to children and their families including individual, group, and family counseling, remedial education, medical examinations, a children's library, therapeutic day school, and an outreach program. In a retrospective review of clinical charts it was noted that 10 to 12 percent of children referred to the clinic for help had experienced the death of a parental figure, or even multiple losses, within two years prior to referral to the center. This finding was not surprising, since according to the 1970 census profile of the catchment area, the death rate due to chronic illness or violence is about 70 percent higher than it is in the rest of the city.[4] In addition, the rate of single-parent families in the area is over 60 percent. Thus, it would follow that the children of this catchment area are at a significantly greater risk of losing a primary caretaker and usually at a younger age than the general population.

What was surprising was the lack of attention paid to this problem by both our agency, the referral agencies, and remaining caretakers. The review of intake data indicated that there was not necessarily an increase in referrals of bereaved children. The problem had existed all along; however, its impact on child and family functioning was not fully appreciated by the referral source, the family, or the mental health community. Prior to the initiation of this specialized service, the fact of a parental death was rarely mentioned in referral data, nor was the question asked. Rather, a set of behavioral symptoms was identified as the target problem. More often than not the current caretaker was unaware of the child's conflicts and assumed that the child "got over it" because he no longer talked about the parent's death.

Johnny, age eight, was referred to the therapeutic day school, diagnosed learning disabled. The child and family history from the referring school mentioned only Johnny's current family constellation and made no reference to his mother's untimely death two years earlier. It was only at intake, when Johnny's grandmother was asked about the boy's mother and father, that the social worker learned that his mother had died and that his father had abandoned the family years earlier.

Johnny's grandmother, loving and caring, reported that he rarely, if ever, mentioned his mother. They assumed he had "gotten over it."

It became increasingly clear that his loss was unresolved and his grief was manifested in academic and behavioral difficulties. His way of coping with the trauma was either ignored or misunderstood by those around him. On an individual, family, and institutional level, the denial of this terrible event became clear in Johnny's case and in many others.[5]

Once aware of the children's need for help, we thought about forming groups. Both workers in the clinic's Loss and Bereavement Program and non–Loss and Bereavement workers had questions about the modality. "Would these groups be too painful for children to sit through? Would children be willing and/or able to disclose their personal stories? Would nine-year-old bereaved children be supportive, hurtful, or oblivious to others when they disclosed their hurt?"

Despite the fact that we had no known precedent in the literature, we decided that groups had potential to help these children, so we formed groups for them. We felt that the use of a group modality would provide an atmosphere in which children who had lost a parent could come together with other children who had similar experiences and understand what life had been like for them.

This setting allows for experiences and feelings to be universalized and accepted by others. This is crucial in working with bereaved children, for a major task is to help normalize the child's feelings and fantasies concerning the death. Most children will fantasize about rejoining the dead parent, either through thoughts of suicide or some supernatural event that will bring the parent back. The child needs to recognize that this is a common part of the bereavement process and that it does not signify that he is crazy. This realization can emerge quite naturally in a group setting.

Parental death creates fear and anxiety in other children, so the child who loses a parent often is stigmatized and faces a secondary separation from friends.[6] The group can serve as a corrective experience for these children.

Groups seem particularly indicated for children whose families have difficulty mourning. In this setting, children are given permission to mourn with appropriate adult models and children of similar circumstances.

It is clear that just as children have curiosity about where people come from, they also want to know where people go.[7] Thus, the group serves an educative function. It provides a much-needed opportunity for children to pursue their curiosity about death, however morbid, without rebuff or ridicule.

The group experience can also address many of the other developmental needs and tasks of bereaved children.

Our group program was a new one and was partially funded by outside sources. Friction developed at once between the bereavement clinicians and clinicians outside the program. Our selection process was the main focus of the conflict. When we began to implement our program, we did not have enough new referrals to form a group, so we singled out those bereaved children who were already being seen individually by clinicians. We were quite surprised by the rather strong resistance we met from those clinicians. They questioned the appropriateness of the group modality for some of their individual child clients. A second and less often expressed issue had to do with these workers' feelings about "sharing" these cases with a group worker—especially a worker in-

volved with a new program that was receiving a considerable amount of attention.

Even clinicians who were seeing new clients for intakes were reluctant to refer bereaved children to us. This conflict created much tension and many obstacles in the implementation of our program.

We quickly realized that we had not sufficiently involved other clinicians in the project in a collaborative way. More time and effort should have been expended initially educating them about our program and reaching for their ideas and feedback. These oversights proved critical to the evolution of the program. The tensions between the clinicians did not abate for several months, at which time clinic staff began to recognize the positive impact of the groups upon their clients.

THEMES OF WORK

The following material was culled from work with a group of children who had lost a parent, caretaker, or a close relative through death. (This was one of several groups formed for such children at our clinic.) Group membership was open; children entered it as they were referred to the clinic. On average, five children, black and Hispanic, ranging from age nine to thirteen, met for twelve weekly sessions with the group leader. (Over the course of the twelve weeks, nine different children participated.) Additionally, some members received individual and/or family counseling.

We would like to highlight the following phases of work and the issues that were salient during each phase. They are:

1. *Beginnings*—Getting the helping process started: facing fear and denial.
2. *Work Phase*—Helping children with

the work of bereavement, especially with the longing for the lost parent and moving from the general to the specific.

3. *Endings*—Dealing with the clients' pain and the worker's mix of uneasy feelings.

Getting Started

Schwartz has noted that group beginnings are inherently difficult and call out deep feelings in both members and workers.[8] Thus, it was not surprising to find self-protectiveness quite high during the initial group sessions. When the children were brought together, each had a different set of expectations and fears of the unknown. These unknown fears were compounded by a very real fear of the group's purpose: coping with the death of a parent and acknowledging the painful loss. These were difficult tasks but of critical importance if the group process was to be effective.

In our pregroup individual meetings with the children they all expressed a strong desire to join the group. They came readily at the appointed time, sat down quietly and cooperatively, and seemed invested in being "good" group members. The following process illustrates our first session and our contract with the group. The children move quickly to open up and share their experiences.

After everyone went around the room introducing themselves, I asked who knew why we were meeting like this as a group.

Carl: "I know—this is for children whose parents have died."

Gloria: (Adding quickly) "Well *my* parents didn't die—my grandfather died."

Carl: "Well, parents and grandparents."

Leader: "Yes—that's true—but why would we meet?"

Gloria: "To talk and maybe to play."

Leader: "Well yes, mainly to talk. What kinds of things would we talk about?"

Matt: "School?"

Leader: "Well, sometimes it might be important to talk about school—but mainly this group is for kids all of whom have had something very sad happen to them—someone very close to them has died. (Most of the children were looking down at the floor.) And other people don't always understand what that's like. This group will give you the chance to meet with other kids who know what this has been like for you and to help each other through this hard time. What do you think?"

(The children nodded in agreement.)

Leader: "It might be hard at first to talk, because some of you don't know one another and me. What do you think about being here?"

Dick: "It's good."

Gloria: "Yeh, my mother's friend's son, he should be here too—his father died."

Leader: "What about you?"

Gloria: "Well, my grandmother died."

Leader: "How did she die?"

Gloria: "She had a stroke."

Dick: (Chiming in) "My mother *and* my father died, and then my aunt who was taking care of me, she died too."

Carl: "That's terrible—who is taking care of you now?"

Dick: "My other aunt."

Leader: "So Dick, you've had a lot of people close to you die."

Dick: "Yeh . . . my mother and father—they died when I was a baby. I didn't know them so well. My aunt died last year from a heart attack."

The worker must be cautious and not assume that this initial sharing reflects a group intimacy and readiness to work. In the next session the children's ambivalence is readily apparent. From the open sharing of the previous week, the children clam up and actively avoid the work of the group.

Eleven-year-old Mark was repeatedly writing "Bob" (his grandfather's name) on a sheet of paper in front of him.

Carl: "Mark, your grandfather died?"

Mark: "I don't want any damn body talking about my grandfather or I'll kick their butt."

Leader: "You sound pretty angry."

Mark: "I'm not angry. I just don't want anybody talking about my grandfather."

Leader: "It's very difficult."

Mark: "It's not difficult. I just don't want anybody saying that he died." (His anger is escalating.)

Gloria: (Picking up on Mark's anger, expressed similar feelings.) "Nobody wants to talk about nobody dying."

Dick: "Yes, we don't want to talk about that."

Leader: "How come?"

Gloria: "That's why he is running around. You can't force him if he doesn't want to."

Leader: "Are you saying that perhaps that's what makes you run around—so you won't have to talk about something upsetting?"

Mark: "Nope."

Leader: "You may feel it's too hard to talk about."

Mark: "No, it's not hard for me to talk about anything . . . but that reminds you, and you could be dreaming."

Carl: "Yup, you dream for about a week when you talk about your mother, then it takes about five days to try to get over it, but it comes back again and it stops and it comes back again . . . Nightmares I hate. I hate talking about my mother."

In this excerpt, the worker moves to sanction members' feelings. Specifically, she reaches for the sadness and anger brewing inside Mark and gives him permission to feel these emotions. Later, she identifies the obstacles that the children erect in their efforts to avoid experiencing the pain and anger. She relies on labeling and interpreting their nonverbal behavior as her primary interventions in the process.

Avoiding the Hurt

The children often valiantly defended against the expression of their pain and anger. The difficult task of the group leader was to convey to the children that the experience of this pain would not be destructive or totally overwhelming to them. In the fourth session the children were trying to protect themselves from the pain stirred up by a new member whose loss was very recent.

This was the first meeting for Tim, whose grandfather died earlier in the week. The leaders introduced Tim by asking the group what they remembered the purpose of the group to be.

Chuck: "For death, this is the death group."

Leader: "What do you mean?"

Chuck: "You know, when somebody dies in your family."

All the children went around the room describing who had died in their families. The leader stated the purpose of this group was to have a time where children who have lost someone important to them could help each other . . . that sometimes it seemed other people did not understand how sad, hurt, and mixed up they felt. (Tim was gently nodding.) The leader noted it would probably take some time before Tim could feel comfortable in the group, but Tim was asked to try to share with the group what had happened to him. He stated softly, "My grandfather died." Tim went on to describe how his mother received a phone call in the middle of the night and was informed that his grandfather had died. As he told the story, his voice started to quiver. The other children were listening intently and the room was very still. Tim stopped and said he felt he couldn't go on. He was holding back tears. Gloria quickly added, "That's right, we don't want a Niagara Falls in here." I asked what she meant. "You know, sad stuff and that." Chuck said, "That's right, we don't want none of that in here." Dick nodded affirmatively. There was a solemn attentive tone in the room.

The leader noted that everyone seemed to be feeling sad but at the same time needed to avoid their feelings.

Gloria: (continuing) "Yeh, I don't want any of that here . . . we don't want any crying."

Dick: "That's right."

Leader: "What would happen if people cried?"

Gloria: "I told you. It would be like Niagara Falls."

Leader: "Are you saying that you still have a lot of sad feelings?"

Gloria: "Yes."

Dick: "That's right. No crying in here."

Leader: "But sometimes you feel better after you cry. Do you ever feel that way?"

Gloria: "Yes, but I don't like to cry."

Dick: "Me neither."

Leader: "I know it feels painful to cry, and no one here is going to force you to cry, but this is a place where you can express those feelings. It's OK to cry in here. A lot of sad, hurtful things have happened to all of you." (The group then picked up where it had left off . . . discussing Tim's grandfather's death.)

The introduction of a new member into an ongoing group is a difficult process, one that requires considerable skills. Initial interventions were aimed at explaining the group's purpose to the new member and at helping to bring Tim on board. The worker reaches out and encourages him to tell his story to the group.

When Tim and the other members began to run from Tim's powerful message, the worker intervenes. Her message is that, though it's painful to experience and express feelings about death, this is a safe place to share these same feelings.

She first "steps up the weak signals" the group is giving out by saying they all seem to be feeling sad.[9] She makes the problem—sadness—the group's problem.[10] She goes on to offer them an alternative way of dealing with the sadness: instead of bottling it up, why not let it out.

The group leader had to encourage this sharing supportively in several successive sessions, as the children's reluctance to verbalize their feelings surfaced at the start of these sessions. Members often resorted to behavioral expressions of their wish to avoid such a hurt. Just like adults, these children tried to ward off discomforting feelings as they crept into consciousness.

Dick: "This group is boring."

Leader: "What do you find boring about the group?"

Dick: "To talk about death all the time." (The other members nodded.)

Leader: "Well, maybe you can help me to understand something. What would be the best way to help a child who had a death in his family?"

Tim: (Looking up) "Put him in a group, of course."

Leader: "How could being in a group be helpful to the child?"

Tim: "Well, they could talk about how they were feeling and ask questions about what happened to others and talk about what happened to them."

Dealing with the Pain

This discussion served as a catalyst and reflected the group's burgeoning development of mutual trust. The leader poses a problem, and "[developing] . . . a group" is one member's solution. The bereavement work had begun. It was difficult initially for the children to confront their own feelings about their losses. Speaking about losses indirectly, by offering advice of how one might help a child who had lost a parent, enabled them to speak about their own fears, worries and fantasies.

Leader: "What are some of the things children worry about when there's a death in the family?"

Matt: "Well, sometimes kids worry about if they are going to die or who's going to take care of them."

Gloria: "I know Sam—the son of my mother's friend who died—worried about who was going to take care of him."

Leader: "It seems like that's a big concern for children who have a death in the family ... who's going to take care of them ... what's going to happen to them?" (Tim nodded vigorously.)

Dick: "I don't have to worry about who's going to take care of me because my father and mother died, and if my aunt dies, my other aunt will take care of me, and if she dies, I can get taken care of by my grandmother."

Leader: "You really have thought out the matter and you've been concerned about it." (Leader, addressing the entire group, commented that it seems to be a big worry for children and asked if that could be one of the reasons it is so difficult to talk about. Everyone in the group nodded.)

Tim: (turning to Dick) "You had both your mother and father die. Who took care of you?"

Dick: "Well, after that my aunt took care of me, and then she died."

Tim: "God, that's terrible."

The group went on to support Dick in an empathic way but also touched upon their concern that they could be faced with multiple losses as well.

In this excerpt, the worker moves the group fully into the bereavement work. She elicits and labels their feelings and their fears. She fosters an atmosphere in which the children can feel free to voice their concerns and mutually support one another.

As the group progressed, the children were able to speak at length about their various experiences. They were encouraged to draw pictures of the lost parents, the cemetery, and the funeral parlor. In so doing, they displayed intense feelings of longing for the deceased parent.

Dick: "What is the name of this group anyway? Does this group have a name?"

Leader: "No. We don't have a name. Do you think we should?" (All the children nodded.)

Tim: "It's the death group."

Matt: "No, the dying group."

Gloria: "No, it's the loss group."

Dick: (Mentioned above, who lost two parents and a caretaker) "Let's call this 'The Lost and Found Group.' "

Leader: "Why do you think that's a good name?"

Matt: "Well, I lost my mother, and now I'm trying to find her."

The group's struggle in trying to find a name for itself reflects its wish to move toward an intimacy and a clearer identity. The worker helps them in their struggle with this task and helps them identify their common purposes.

Members were encouraged to bring in pictures and personal mementos and to share these in group. These mementos, as well as remembrances from church services and funeral parlors, served as catalysts for group discussion.

Mark: "I have some stuff that I brought in—the stuff you wanted to see."

Matt: "Well, what is it?"

Tim: "Well, this is the paper that they passed out from the church. It has my grandfather's picture on the cover ... and inside it says he was in the army ... and he had three children and twelve grandchildren ... and over here it tells you to pray for him. And this is a scrapbook from where he worked as a security guard, and his picture here in the security uniform."

Gloria: "He was a handsome man."

Tim: (Rather wistfully) "He was."

Leader: "It sounds like he did many things in his life—being in the army, and a security guard ... [having] three children and twelve grandchildren."

Tim: "He did."

Carl: "Was he nice?"

Tim: "Yup. I used to go see him sometimes. And he had a dog. His dog died before he did."

Leader: "Sounds like you miss him."
Tim: (Fighting back tears.) "I do. Now I can't go see him anymore."
Gloria: "Dag."
Leader: "What do you mean by that?"
Gloria: "That's a shame."
Leader: "What?"
Gloria: "That his grandfather died, and he can't see him anymore."
Leader: "It sounds like a sad thing."
Gloria: "It is." (Tim nods.)

In this excerpt, the worker tries to help Tim express his feelings of longing for his grandfather. She pushes him to put these powerful feelings into words.

The children's longing for the lost parent was also evident in the many dreams and fantasies they shared. In one session, Art spoke about hearing rustling and doors opening and closing at night. He was convinced that his dead mother was calling to him and returning home. Carl (after silently debating whether or not the group would consider him crazy), divulged that he had many sleepless nights during which he clutched a baseball bat in order to defend himself against reappearing images of his father.

It is crucial for children to work through this period of longing (as fully as possible) in order to progress and complete the task of mourning. During this period, the worker's role is to be sensitive to the child's feelings and to communicate an understanding of these feelings. Additionally, it is incumbent upon the worker to help put the children's feelings into words and to help them confront the myriad feelings.

The group format proved an appropriate modality for universalizing some of the common fears and fantasies children have secondary to the death of a significant family member. The children in our group(s) were relieved to find that others share similar imageries and concerns.

Many indicated they were afraid that they, and they alone, had these thoughts. They were certain that this indicated they were "going crazy." We found in our groups that members were greatly relieved to find others with the same imageries and concerns.

Along with emotional support, children need concrete, factual information about illness and death. They asked many questions about death and about the preservation of life.

Right before the end of one meeting Tim looked up and said: "Can I ask you a question?"
Leader: "Sure."
Tim: "Why do people die?"
Leader: "That's a very hard thing to understand sometimes. Does anyone know why do people die?"
Chuck: "They die of natural causes."
Leader: "What does 'natural causes' mean?"
Chuck: (Uncertain, squirms in his seat.)
Leader: "Sometimes people are like cars—when they get older, their body starts to wear out, like a car. It's kind of like your body wearing out when it's old."
Chuck: "Is cancer natural causes?" (Chuck's mother had died of cancer.)
The group then had a discussion about the meaning of cancer. They tried to sort out why some people die of disease and others of "natural causes."

Here the worker supports the children as they delve into taboo areas. She shares information at a level that the children are capable of understanding.

The group also served as a vehicle for clarifying other issues that aroused feelings of vulnerability. Questions about abortion and adoption surfaced in another session.

Tim: "What is the difference between adoption and abortion?"

Leader: "Does anyone in the group know?" (No response.) Leader explains the difference.

Tim: "You know, people should think about having children before they go and have them and don't want them. That's a terrible thing to do."

Leader: "You're right. People should think carefully about having children. Sometimes they have problems though and aren't able to think about them."

Tim: (Angrily) "I can't believe people would do that to a child and not want a child." (The others nodded.)

Leader: "It looks like everyone has strong feelings about that."

Gloria: "That's right."

Leader: "Tim, you seem particularly upset about that."

Tim: (Silent, nods.)

Leader: "I wonder if something has happened to make you feel so upset."

Gloria: "It's his birthday next week."

Leader: (Looks toward him for validation.)

Tim: "That's right, and my sister, she left the house . . . you know, because she's gonna have a baby."

Chuck: "Are you gonna celebrate?" (Tim shrugs.)

Gloria: "Are you gonna get presents?" (Tim shrugs.) "Well, I would make sure to tell them what I want."

Leader: "It sounds like everything is up in the air."

Tim: "It is."

Chuck: "They'll have a party for you. Don't worry."

Leader: "Tim, it sounds like you're not sure."

Tim: "I'm not because everyone is talking about my sister this, and my sister that."

Here the worker moves in to give the group factual information and clarify questions about having babies. She looks beyond their global concerns as she zeros in on Tim's quiet suffering. Members are able to fill in missing information, that Tim's birthday is next week. As the excerpt unravels, it becomes clear that Tim is upset about his birthday going unno-

ticed by his family. He feels left out and uncared for and probably displaced by his sister. The children attempt to reassure Tim, but do so prematurely. The worker checks this with Tim. In so doing, she keeps the focus on the pain. Members are forced to face the subtle resistance they erected in their efforts to avoid feeling Tim's discomfort.

In another session, the children struggled with issues regarding their own vulnerabilities, and they requested information about their parents' illnesses.

The children began by discussing their anger toward physicians.

Tim: "Don't talk that way about doctors. They need doctors to find medicine for new diseases like herpes and AIDS for babies, because babies come out with these diseases." (Gloria and Chuck giggled.) "That's not funny."

Leader: "Sometimes people laugh when they're nervous."

The children proceeded to talk about a number of children in school and asked many questions about their problems. The children giggled anxiously.

Leader: "I hear you talking about kids you know who have problems, but perhaps some of you have concerns about being sick, and whether or not kids can get sick from their parents."

Dick: "They can."

Tim: "How do you think that baby in that hospital got AIDS, that's dying? People don't want it no more."

Leader: "What do you think about that?"

Tim: "People don't want to catch that disease."

The children then continued to debate why parents don't want to keep their children. They brought up the example of a retarded child.

Leader: "What does retarded mean?"

Gloria: "Mentally ill."

Matt: "Kleptomaniac."

Tim: "No, it doesn't mean that—it means that they aren't able to do some things—but some retarded people are able to live in their own homes."

We went on to clarify what retarded means and what other diseases they brought up entailed.

The children were hungry for information. They wanted to know all about various aspects of the funeral process. One week, the children were encouraged to draw pictures of the funeral parlor. This discussion followed:

Gloria: "What do they do when they take the body to the funeral parlor?"

Leader: "Who can answer that question?"

Dick: "They take all the stuff out and put on makeup and everything."

Gloria: "Yuck . . . What stuff?"

Dick: "You know, the blood and guts and everything."

Matt: (to leader) "Really?"

Leader: "Well, it depends. Most times they remove the blood and replace it with a chemical to help preserve the body. Do you know what preserve means?"

Gloria: "To keep it fresh—so it doesn't stink." (The group giggled.)

Leader: "Yet, sometimes when there is an autopsy they remove some of the parts of the body inside."

Doug: "What is an autopsy?"

Leader: "Who knows?"

Tim: "It's like after you're dead—they operate on you to see why you died."

Leader: "That's right."

Tim: "They look at your liver, and your heart and stuff and see what went wrong."

Gloria: "So what happens when they bury the bodies?"

Dick: "Do worms eat you up?"

Gloria: "They do?"

Leader: "Well, because of all the chemicals they use to preserve you, the body lasts a long time. Eventually, though, the body does waste away."

Here the worker tries to help the group answer one another's questions. She shares with them facts that may further the children's cognitive understanding of death and the events surrounding it.

The children also asked many questions about the specific illnesses that befell their parents, such as cancer, hypertension, and heart disease. Childhood diseases, such as measles, chicken pox, and earlier problems, including jaundice and forceps deliveries, were also areas of concern for them. They even wanted information about the Heimlich maneuver. In addition, they used the group to work through previous separations and to anticipate other changes in their lives. Recognizing that the group was formed to help children cope with the death of a parent, it was important to acknowledge their fears, answer their questions, and clarify their misconceptions in order to help them mourn.

It is important to note that while the children struggled with their fears and concerns, the worker was by no means immune. In fact, parallel processes of self-protectiveness on the part of the leader and the members became evident. One of the last and greatest taboos of the Western world is our fear of dying.[11]

It is no wonder that during the initial stages of the group—with fears, inhibitions, and acting out rampant—that the worker as well as the members frequently questioned the appropriateness of the group modality.

It becomes critical for the worker to deal with personal feelings about death and dying in order to help overcome these obstacles and to help the group with bereavement. She must reexamine her own losses in life, with an eye on the scars these left and on patterns she may have adopted to shield these scars.

The worker also struggles with a whole

host of other disquieting feelings. She experiences guilt in the realization that the child's pain is deep. And, along with this is the shattering of her own grandiosity as she helplessly realizes that nothing can be done to bring back a lost loved one for the child. The following excerpt illustrates the worker's attempts to close off feelings of pain.

Gloria: "I have a lot of nice things that my grandmother left me."

Leader: "What are they?"

Gloria: "Well ... nice jewelry, with little diamonds in it, and her hats from church, which I like to put on, and my mother has her diamond ring ... and my mother said ... one day, when I'm older ... I can have it for myself."

Tim: "Wow. She left you a diamond ring?"

Gloria: "That's right, and that's worth a lot of money."

Matt: "So. My mother has a diamond ring!"

Dick: "Well, I have something from my mother."

Leader: "What is it?"

Dick: "This." (He whips out a very old picture of his mother as a teenager. It is worn and frayed at the edges.)

Leader: "Who is this?"

Dick: "My mother, when she was a teenager."

Leader: "She was a pretty woman. You know you can get this picture laminated in a five and ten so it won't wear out like that." (Leader and Dick then continued with a discussion about laminating the picture.)

Here the worker prematurely closes off a painful area for Dick by making suggestions which will keep the picture "alive." In so doing, she avoids getting into what the picture means to Dick. The worker cannot face this discussion and the powerful feelings it promises to evoke.

Endings

A series of twelve sessions was contracted for at the start of the group. Clearly, the work of mourning cannot be completed within this rigid time constraint. Instead our goals were to promote a mutually supportive forum within which feelings and concerns would be addressed.

For any group, termination is a difficult process. It evokes memories of previous endings and separations for member and worker alike. For these children, who earlier faced tragic losses, termination was a highly stressful transition.

The following process illustrates the children's anger and other reactions to the upcoming abandonment. Dick, ostensibly fantasizing about what will happen to the group leader, discloses instead what actually happened to him, the loss of three caretakers.

At the beginning of the session, the group discussion wandered without focus. The children seemed to be avoiding the work at hand.

Leader: "I noticed that no one has mentioned that next week is our last meeting."

Dick: "It is?" (He looked stunned, as if he were hearing this for the first time.)

Gloria: (Angrily) "Shoot!"

Leader: "That's right. Next week is our last meeting."

Dick: "So. What are you gonna do after next week?"

Leader: "What do you think I might be doing?"

Dick: "Have another group."

Leader: "Maybe you feel you are going to be replaced?"

Tim: "Well, maybe."

Dick: "With other people ... let them get a chance ... then after their weeks are up ... then they're gonna be replaced ... then after that, it goes on and on and on till everybody is dead."

Leader: "It sounds like that is what life has been like for you—many people replacing each other." (Dick nodded.) "I am wondering if the others are feeling that they can be replaced." (Tim started to name other children he felt should be in the group.) "I see your concern for the other children, but I'm wondering what the end of the group means for you."

Tim: "It means I won't be coming up here every week. That's what it means."

Leader: "How do you feel about that?"

Tim: "I don't really care."

Gloria: "That's right. Why should he care?"

Leader: "It sounds to me like you're both angry." (No response.) "And I'm wondering if this ending of the group and thoughts of people replacing one another reminds you of other people who have been replaced in your life?" (Silence.)

Tim: (After a few minutes) "Why should we tell you anything—if you really cared about it, you wouldn't end the group."

Dick: "That's right! It's not fair."

Leader: "It seems many things have happened in your life that aren't fair."

Gloria: "That's right."

Leader: "Like people who you have loved, dying."

Matt: "That's not fair! Other kids have their parents."

Leader: "And what is that like for you?"

Matt: "It makes me mad."

Here, the worker understands, reaches for, and sanctions the children's anger and sadness. These were veiled in their fantasies of replacement. The worker identifies, in part, the feelings related to endings.

We felt that in the termination stage especially it was important to review with the youngsters what they had gained in group and how they can use this knowledge in the future. This helps prepare them for the future, for the hurt, pain, anger, and problems connected to the tragic loss are far from resolved. In the same vein, it's essential to help the children internalize a way to recognize and express their feelings to significant others in their lives. These others, in turn, can help them cope

not only with this initial death but with future losses and separation in their lives as well.

Leader: "What I'd like to know is, supposing what you feel in your dreams, the things that you said you used to feel about the person who died—supposing they come back again. What would you do?"

Dick: "Be sad again."

Leader: "What would you do with your sadness?"

Dick: "Just think about it until it goes away."

Leader: "What came up in the group about that?"

Gloria: "To talk about those things."

Leader: "So, what are things that kids can do when they feel very sad?"

Tim: "Cry."

Leader: "It seems like you're feeling sad right now?"

Dick: "Yeh, and you can tell your mother and father, or your grandmother." (He named a number of people.)

Leader: "But sometimes it's hard for kids to tell adults how they are feeling—like it is for you now."

Dick: "Well . . . tell one of their friends or their teacher." (He proceeded to name a bunch of people.)

Leader: "Well, what could you tell a grown up?"

Tim: "That somebody in the family died?" (Silence.)

Here the worker helps the members to review how they might use the skills learned in group. Meanwhile, she continues to reach for feelings about ending. Issues associated with earlier stages in the group process did reemerge. The self-protectiveness seen in the beginning phase reemerged. So did the work phase's characteristic longing for the deceased parent, and the pleas during this phase for support and cognitive understanding. The fears and feelings about loss and displacement associated with termination were also, naturally, witnessed during the ending phase. Add to these the worker's struggles throughout, and a picture of the complex factors involved in group work with bereaved children emerges. We have highlighted these as they represented the most striking and fascinating issues we have seen thus far in our work.

CONCLUSION

A loss in childhood which is un-

mourned remains active in the personality, influencing all aspects of dealing with feelings and the making of lasting relationships. We hope we have successfully communicated the need for increased attention to this tragedy in childhood, as well as the effectiveness of group work in helping bereaved children.

NOTES

1. Psychoanalytic research indicates that persons who suffered parental loss via death in childhood are more prone to psychiatric illness than those who did not suffer such a loss. M. Wolfenstein, "How Is Mourning Possible?" in *Psychoanalytic Study of the Child*, ed. R. Eisler, A. Freud, H. Hartmann, and M. Kris, 39 vols. (New York: International Universities Press, 1966), vol. 25, pp. 93–123. See also Erna Furman, *A Child's Parent Dies* (New Haven, Conn.: Yale University Press, 1974). For information on correlation between constricted cognitive development and early parental loss, see M. Lifshitz, D. Berman, A. Galili, and D. Galad, "The Effect of Mother's Perception and Social System Organization on Their Short Range Adjustment," *Journal of the American Academy of Child Psychiatry* 16 (1977): 272–284. For information on early parental loss as an etiological factor in schizophrenia, see N. F. Watt and A. Nicholi, "Early Death of a Parent as an Etiological Factor in Schizophrenia," *American Journal of Orthopsychiatry* 49 (1979): 465–473. For information on association between early loss of a parent and later development of adult depressive disorders, see B. Pfohl, D. Stangl, and M. Tsuang, "The Association Between Early Parental Loss and Diagnosis in the Iowa 500," *Archives of General Psychiatry* 40 (1983): 965–967. See also F. Brown, "Depression and Childhood Bereavement," *Journal of Mental Science* 107 (1961): 754–777. For studies on

correlation between early parental death and children's emotional, intellectual, and learning problems, see W. R. Keller, "Children's Reaction to the Death of a Parent," in: *Depression*, ed. Paul H. Hach and Joseph Zubin (New York: Grune and Stratton, 1954), pp. 109–120.

2. H. E. Erikson, *Childhood and Society* (New York: W. W. Norton, 1963), pp. 247–274.

3. The developmental needs and tasks of bereaved children have been identified by Erna Furman and are as follows. Children need to know that someone will be available to care for them; they need to accept the reality of the death; they need the opportunity to express their longing for the deceased; they need to be able to identify with the lost parent; they need permission to express their anger and sadness and to recognize that many of their dreams and fantasies are likely to be a part of this process; they need consistent routines and a stable environment; they need clear, age-appropriate conceptions of death and its finality; they need active sanctioning and permission to experience this myriad of feelings from a caring, empathic adult; and finally, they eventually need to accept new adults into their lives whom they can trust and love. Furman, *A Child's Parent Dies*.

4. United States Census, 1980 (United States Census Bureau, Washington, D.C., 1980).

5. This denial and resistance to discussing death may be related to universal fears of death

which make it especially difficult to observe objectively in children those aspects which cause anxiety in adults. Harrison, Davenport, and McDermott have described how, on a children's psychiatric ward, the staff's upset over President Kennedy's death interfered with their ability to observe the children's reactions and to handle them appropriately. S. I. Harrison, C. W. Davenport, and J. F. McDermott, "Children's Reactions to Bereavement," *Archives of General Psychiatry* 17 (1967): 593–597.

6. In studies of nursery school children, McDonald noted that children had difficulty expressing their empathy to children whose parents died until they were reassured about their own concerns. M. McDonald, "A Study of the Reactions of Nursery School Children to the Death of a Child's Mother," in *Psycho-analytic Study of the Child,* ed. R. Eisler, A. Freud, H. Hartmann, and M. Kris, 39 vols. (New York: International Universities Press, 1964), pp. 321–337 and pp. 358–376.

7. G. Kliman, "Mourning and Bereavement Process in Children" (New York Hospital, Westchester Division, Grand Round Presentation, October 25, 1983).

8. W. Schwartz and S. R. Zalba, *The Practice of Group Work* (New York: Columbia University Press, 1971), pp. 3–24.

9. Lawrence Shulman, *A Casebook of Social Work with Groups: The Mediating Model* (New York: Council on Social Work Education, 1968), pp. 77–92.

10. Ibid.

11. E. Kübler-Ross, *On Death and Dying* (New York: Macmillan, 1969).

Judith Bloch
Judith Margolis

CHAPTER 5

Feelings of Shame: Siblings of Handicapped Children*

In the last decade work with handicapped children has progressed, becoming broader and deeper. It now includes early intervention, mandated schooling, and expanded parent education. Although autobiographical material, anecdotal records, research results, and common sense indicate the possibility of increased vulnerability and risk for other family members, little interest has been seen among parents or professionals in understanding or addressing the impact the presence of a handicapped child has on the development of siblings.

We know from our work with parents of such children that stress is often pervasive in these households. Marital problems, divorce, alcohol abuse, and single-parent households are not uncommon.[1] Child abuse is documented in the literature. These factors, as well as the handicapped child's need for extraordinary care, can produce a state of chronic tension and joylessness that has a negative impact on each family member.

Children in our special education classes are classified according to New York State Education Department guidelines; included are children with attention deficit disorders, conduct/behavior disorders, autism, mental retardation, pervasive developmental disorders, and speech impairments between the ages of fifteen months and seven years. They all have problems with learning, language, and behavior, which typically were not evident at birth. Most begin their preschool special education at three years of age. The school's social work department provides counseling and support services to their families.

The first stress point in most of these families is the initial phase of identification of their child's handicapping condition.[2] There are many uncertainties that attend the diagnosis of these preschoolers. The "hidden" nature of the child's disability, its delayed emergence, the differences among professionals regarding diagnosis, etiology, and remediation exacerbate the parental state of confusion and distress.

Characteristically, this stage of first identification produces a resounding parental silence which keeps the extended family and siblings in ignorance. Most

*We thank Martin Seitz, M.S.W., associate professor, Adelphi University School of Social Work, for his contribution to the development of this approach, his participation in the Sibling Program, and his supervision of the sibling group leaders.

parents are likely to struggle privately and even secretly with this newly perceived possibility that their child may have a handicap. Even as parents arrange for their child's evaluation, there is hope mixed with resistance to the possibility of a confirmation of handicap.

THE FAMILY ADAPTS TO THE DISABLED CHILD

Families rarely move with tranquility from one with well children to one which includes a developmentally disabled child. Planning for parenthood and anticipating the birth of a child are major developmental milestones in family life. The wish to become a parent is prompted by a variety of needs and expectations, among which is the desire to expand one's circle of loved ones—to love and be loved. People choose parenthood for many different reasons, but the hope is always that this will be a time of emotional enhancement.

With conception and parenthood come aspirations for the family; dreams of love, security, and achievement. The plan is for a healthy, happy child. The expectation is that the child will be an asset, although the specific form of this fulfillment depends on individual parental needs and fantasies. For many this is a critical way to meet their need for purpose and responsibility. Some see parenthood as another opportunity to satisfy their own unfulfilled childhood needs or adult ambitions. Still others may hope that parenthood will be a means of providing protection and care for themselves in their old age. Most expect that their children will do at least as well as they did in life, or better. Because of these fundamental and deep-seated yearnings, families do not move with ease from one with well children to one which includes a de-

velopmentally disabled child. A thwarted dream is not easily abandoned.

The first crisis, "identification and evaluation," creates a family maelstrom. Primary parental hopes are threatened by a suggestion of impairment. Many families seem shattered, not strengthened, by this adversity. Parental behavior at this point is often characterized by anxiety, uncertainty, anger. The intensity of these reactions sometimes provides "justification" to clinicians evaluating the child regarding the nurturing capabilities of their parents.

We have found it is normal for parents to react in this "abnormal" fashion to this life crisis. It is understandable that parents who are threatened with the loss of their parental dream may at first deny the presence of the problem or tend to minimize the magnitude of the disaster. We need to remember that these reactions are not unusual. It takes times to deal with grief and to come to terms with changed life circumstances. Parental "denial" serves that important purpose.

This first trauma alters the normative family states and their attending parenting tasks. Instead of celebrating their toddler's milestones, parents are compelled to make crucial judgments about evaluation and the need for preschool special education. Yet with rare exceptions these children are born into families who have neither the knowledge, the skills, nor the support systems to deal with these matters. But their situation requires immediate decision making. At this stage the parents' first adaptive task is to meet the needs of their young disabled child. This alone can be overwhelming. In addition, this period of family life is often complicated by other factors. Often there is more than one child under five years of age in one family, or there is a need for extraordinary child care because the disabled child presents serious behavior problems or is not yet achieving self-help milestones. These situations further contribute to the chaos in the household. The couple's capacity to assume their parenting responsibilities, negotiate their differences in this area, support each other, and adequately nurture all their children are critical.[3]

This predictable phase-specific issue can become a crisis when parents react in a nonfunctional manner. If they are overwhelmed with grief, fear, and shame, or their stress exacerbates old marital problems or creates new ones, maladaptive patterns may begin to take place. If they continue to deny the significance of the disabled child's pathology and refuse a preschool special education placement, or if at the other extreme, the needs of the disabled child continue to remain paramount and override all other family considerations, additional problems will emerge. The overburdening of one parent or a sibling and the disengagement of a father carry a potential for harm. At this time most families must reorganize internally and make shifts in responsibilities.

After the first crisis of identification, there are other issues which will emerge as the developmentally disabled child matures. Some of these are addressed in this chapter. They may serve to prepare social workers for the possible consequences of the handicap on the family system.

Placement in a preschool special education program produces another predictable stress phase in the lives of these families. This placement decision creates a need for an internal affective change and adjustment to a new status as "identified parents" of a disabled child. This phase is often characterized by a preoccupation with outcome. Parents seek professional reassurances that their disabled child will improve rapidly. They hope their child will be eligible for "regular" public school at age five. And if this does not happen when the child is of kindergarten age, there is a repeated violation of family expectation. Another stress phase emerges.

When parents from our school with recently admitted children press for a forecast of their disabled child's future, we are optimistic about the possibility of change. At this time we focus on the family as well as the child. We highlight the need to promote family strength and minimize risk factors. We underscore the interactive component of the disability. We acknowledge its impact on all family members and emphasize the need for all members to adjust to their changed status and relationships. We share our experience which indicates that the disabled child's progress is mostly related to the child's intrinsic potential life's circumstances (illness, wealth), the quality of our special education program, and the quality of their family life. We present the school programs that support family life and offer to help parents make appropriate choices.

We also focus on immediate concerns. When the children begin school, we know that their parents are worried about a successful separation from home. Many of the children have never had a babysitter or been away from their parents or on a bus. Our social workers make themselves valuable with information that gives assurances that the children are adjusting to school and are in competent, caring hands in a safe place. The parents can then begin to appreciate the school placements' potential for remediation and their respite from the total burden of child care.

Understandable parental preoccupation with long-term outcome at this time is best postponed. The professional who confronts parents with a grim prognosis, who chooses to focus on the child's later serious and irreversible limitations, is premature. This approach destroys necessary parental hope and energy needed for remediation. It compels parents to face and work through and complete a normative parenting task which under the best of circumstances can take two decades. Coming to terms with a child's capabilities and integrating those realities with parental wishes and dreams is a long-term issue. All parents struggle to adapt their "outcome" expectations. In the normal family these revisions are gradual. While it is true that good parenting decisions are based on a realistic perception of a child's capability, this initial phase of identification is not the time for professionals to expect parents with a young disabled child to confront and accomplish this task.

It is important to remember that disabled children are part of a family system. Its plight will affect the outcome for the handicapped child. Time alone does not necessarily ease the pain and disappointment an entire family experiences when they live with a disabled child. Worry and the extraordinary burdens of child care often erode family strength.

We have seen families in which the marital dyad becomes weak and joyless. Anxious, responsible mothers have submerged themselves in child-rearing problems and been undermined by their inability to change their child's functioning or behavior. We have heard mothers struggling with their natural feelings of irritation and disappointment, berating themselves when they could not reconcile those feelings with their own expectations that they should always and only love their child. Sometimes fathers become totally consumed with their financial responsibility for providing. They become disengaged from parenting and resentful of their wife's preoccupation with their disabled child.

Boundaries that permit necessary subsystems to work are not maintained well. Since at first the needs of the disabled child are so pressing, the pain of the parents, siblings, and grandparents is often overlooked or inadvertently ignored. But all family members must learn to cope with their changed family status.

We know too well that sometimes the family system does not function in a way that meets the needs of all its members. We have seen families become isolated and life's pleasures muted. There remained little time or energy for social activities. Family life became problematic and unsatisfying. Chronic stress and anxiety combined to create patterns which contribute to pathological or marginal functioning, and in many cases families were destroyed.

Parents in these households often convey overtly as well as covertly expectations that persuade their well children to put aside their own "childish" needs and mature before their time. There are indeed many problems to address which may require considerable sacrifice or self-denial.

There are extra household chores and child care, as well as additional emotional burdens. These well children often become a part of the care-giver system. They struggle to deal with and deny their tumultuous feelings of rage and shame. They hide or deny their angry feelings and may even attempt to "be good" at all times. These conflicts can overburden the children. They can become depleted and resentful. We often saw a premature definition of role that prevented these children from exploring and experimenting with options.

Thorough and recent reviews of the literature by Lobato,[4] Seligman,[5] Trevino,[6] and Schell[7] revealed many limitations in the research, but there were still significant indications that siblings in these families have a potentially more problematic and complicated emotional life than is generally assumed. This sibling experience also produces sequelae which seem to have a pervasive and persistent influence in adult functioning and later intimate relationships. As reported by Seligman, different authors and clinicians view the potential for psychological harm somewhat differently. The most pessimistic conclusions about the effects of a handicapped brother or sister on normal sibling adjustment are reported by Poznanski and Trevino. Poznanski reports that psychiatrists treat more siblings of handicapped children than handicapped children themselves.[8] Trevino focused on the relationship between sibling status and adult personality. While there is appreciation for the fact that these sibling bonds and attachments shape character, there is no conclusive consensus about the form this takes. Significant factors include family size, ordinal position, and the sex of the well sibling. Trevino concludes that prospects for the normal siblings appear to be the worst for families in the following four instances: "(1) there are only 2 siblings, a normal and a handicapped child; (2) the normal sibling is close in age or younger than the handicapped sibling, or is the oldest female child; (3) the normal and handicapped child are the same sex; (4) the parents are unable to accept the handicap."[9] Grossman states that siblings seemed "more tolerant, more compassionate, more aware of prejudice and its consequences; sometimes more focused, both occupationally and personally, than comparable young adults without such experiences."[10] Nevertheless, real concerns remain that early unresolved or adaptive reaction adjustments can become serious psychological problems and impair one's later ability to maintain intimacy, invest deeply in family life, and parent. While Farber's study has been challenged, it is still worth noting because of his conclusion that normal siblings, both boys and girls, were similarly and significantly influenced in one view: their value of family life. Both showed less interest in focusing their adult life around marriage and family. Surprisingly, girls too have given a lower rank to this later life goal than they did to that of becoming a "highly respected community leader."[11] Did family life become so onerous and joyless, so burdened with extraordinary responsibilities that career goals both reflect and deflect this experience?

Major developmental markers for siblings create new crises. At age five, these well children separate from home and adjust to their own school. They are often expected to explain their sibling's handicap to their classmates but have little preparation or information to deal with this task. Their own unarticulated fears and uncertainties only further complicate this social issue for them. They are usually without resources to cope with their first introduction to peer attitudes of ignorance or prejudice.

Just as parents searched frantically for reasons, causes, and cures for their family catastrophe, we anticipated that their well children would have similar preoccupations. In the same way that parents might mourn the loss of a perfect child, we also noticed that these siblings felt cheated and sometimes embarrassed by their handicapped sibling. In addition, they suffered from the seemingly "unfair" distribution of parental time and energy. Some were flooded with resentment and anger. But their simultaneous awareness (if not understanding) of their handicapped sibling's needs and their parents' pain prevented them from owning or justifying these feelings. Instead they struggled privately and often silently with their intense feelings of shame and anxiety.

Clearly, these children also need attention. They must learn to cope with unexpected demands and disappointments. We knew, too, that their social competence was related to their identity development and that this in turn was influenced by their reactions to this significant family change and to their sibling bonds. They had to learn to deal with their personal dilemmas; to better understand these issues and their relationships to their disabled sibling and family.

It is easy to understand that, at first, the needs of the well sibling may be overlooked by parents who may believe they have adequately masked their own fears. They may accept the misleading but appealing notion that their silence continues to protect their well children. While this initial attitude can be appreciated, we must wonder why it continues. Clearly there had to be other factors operating that contribute to this avoidance pattern, because we know from our experience that their parents care or that their concerns surfaced and became worrisome at regular intervals. Why then do parents choose to believe that this sibling will somehow heroically cope with and overcome major obstacles quietly, independently, and without personal penalty?

AGENCY CONTEXT AND THE GROUP MODALITY

What about the professional silence? Why is there such general reluctance and discomfort when it comes time to identify the needs of the well sibling? Perhaps it is related paradoxically to two core and basic professional skills: empathy and perception. Professionals understand the persistent, natural wish of parents for a healthy child. It is so powerful that it makes intolerable any suggestion of a problem related to their well sibling. Professionals know too that parents want to believe (even more than ever after one disappointment) that all other siblings are perfect. Indeed the desire for the well sibling to perform and achieve is so intense and pressing that it may account for the numerous parental anecdotes that illustrate the ways their well child has benefited and even grown from this experience, almost a "trial by fire," but all for the good. Given these factors, which include parental fears that professional offerings that suggest client status for still another child, are unacceptable and may even carry a potential for harm, what could be done? How could our agency and its professional staff provide services to meet this family need? Was there a way to sensitize parents to the value of early identification and intervention for this child without frightening or alienating them?

Our agency developed a model to address this problem. Since direct suggestions for individual counseling or family therapy were often disregarded or responded to with distress or anger, another approach had to be found. Parents responded to the agency's recommendation for a group for their well siblings with a mixture of hope and fear. On the one hand it met their own need for help in answering their child's painful questions. It recognized their understanding of their child's need to know. On the other hand they were afraid that the child might be exposed to unacceptable behavior and ideas in the group. They thought they might reveal family secrets. Maybe the worker's suggestions would be incompatible with their family values. Parents knew they wanted their siblings to grow with love and loyalty for one another. Perhaps this group experience would make things worse. Despite these spoken and unspoken concerns, parents took the risk and registered and prepared their children for the group.

Two sibling groups were put in place as part of a newly funded Wednesday afternoon after-school program for families with children in special education classes with social, recreational, and therapeutic modules. Child care for the handicapped siblings was provided as well as parent education meetings for mothers. As a result membership in the sibling groups was "captive" and somewhat assured, although there was extensive outreach to expand this group. The two groups were divided by age: one from age five and a half to seven, consisting of ten children, and the other from seven to nine with nine children. Two children from the same family were not put in the same group, and consideration was not given to the diagnosis or age of the handicapped sibling. Each group ran for eight consecutive weeks—one series in the fall and one in the spring. There was a two-month midyear hiatus with one leader/child/parent contact to ensure participation in the spring series and to deal with individual parent/child issues that had emerged in the fall.

Standard social work supervision procedures were maintained. Process recordings were required, as well as weekly reviews with the group-work supervisor. As the groups completed their first eight-week segment, 90 percent working membership had been maintained. A commitment to resume again in two months for the next eight-week series was made by the children and their parents. Although different practice issues had emerged in

each group requiring separate resolutions, both became functioning and cohesive units and their members saw their group as safe and valuable.

The agency saw the group as an appropriate and helpful place for the children to identify their concerns, which often paralleled those of the parents. Working with siblings in groups appeared to be a logical way to provide the youngsters with an experience where they could begin to deal with issues that were of importance to them. A group experience would provide the children with an opportunity to discover that their situation and fears were shared by others; they were not alone or unique. They would meet others with similar life circumstances which would diminish their sense of isolation and loneliness. The group would provide emotional supports, and relief and comfort in the sharing of feelings of anger, resentment, fear, and shame that typically plague so many of these youngsters. Since all the children had a similar life crisis, the group created an arena in which the children not only shared their feelings, but also acquired essential information as well as attitudes they needed to cope with their common life circumstance.

The short-term format described was developed and adopted for a number of reasons—some practical and fiscal, and others clinical and philosophical. The structure was a product of our understanding of the developmental capacities and needs of this age child as well as the agency's capabilities and approach to families.

The agency's experience with groups demonstrated that the children could develop a mutual aid system.[12] They could verbalize, empathize, explore, and share their mutual concerns and fears as long as there were appropriate and timely play activities. Permission had to be given and plans made to help the children discharge intolerable tensions. The groups helped the children to understand that they were not the only ones with this problem and their "bad" thoughts and feelings were commonplace. They shared worrisome ideas and attitudes. This diminished their anxiety. They also helped each other, first and most simply, by their presence and participation in play activities which reduced their sense of isolation. The structure provided and enhanced essential social and recreational experiences.

THEMES OF WORK

A few themes have been selected to illustrate salient issues in work with children. Confidentiality and establishing group purpose are particularly important issues.

Confidentiality

The establishment of trust between the social worker and the children was a basic and primary prerequisite. It had to be developed in order to allow the group members to begin to work together. The children needed to know that their ideas and feelings would not be used against them. In these groups this issue was complicated because guarantees about confidentiality as they ordinarily operate had to be modified. The children's ages and the nature of the work were the main reasons that the traditional social work assurances regarding confidentiality could not be made easily and firmly. To give children ages five to eight too much independent control and power in view of their dependent position in their families is unrealistic, and in the long run will prove to be unproductive. Instead, trust had to be achieved through skillful work

with the group and clearly expressed attitudes on the part of the social worker. The group experience had to produce continuing evidence that the social worker was attuned to family relationships and interactions, and caring and protective of the well child's perspective. The children had to understand that sharing information with their parents would not hurt them but could be helpful.

We chose to maintain a family and intergenerational perspective because we knew that sibling dynamics were fundamentally related to the larger family context. We could not exclude their parents. But the children in the group needed to know that they would be involved in any decisions to share information, and this would be done only to help them communicate more openly with their parents when appropriate, that is, to share their reactions to stressful family incidents or to sensitize their parents to their problems and pain.

Clearly, all relationship issues could not be addressed in this brief group format. As a result we found our family approach had two advantages: it was more likely to enable the social worker to engage parents as allies and was also designed to use the group better to gain entree to the family system if further work became necessary.

This excerpt is from the third group meeting. The social worker already knows from Lisa that there are problems at home regarding her handicapped brother. In the first two weeks of the group, Lisa has expressed her disappointment with her parents and criticized the way her mother manages her brother. Lisa has reached out for support from the social worker and has used the group to share her wish that life could be different for her at home. The social worker is not surprised when Lisa's mother makes contact at this early stage of the group sequence. She knows she must not alienate the mother and must ease her anxiety, or she may not permit Lisa to continue to participate. Yet she must not prematurely share the child's disclosures regarding family life. She can use this opportunity to restate the group's purpose. If she is successful, this will give Lisa's mother a better idea of the value of the group without violating the child's trust. The social worker validates the need for Lisa to share her feelings with the group and obtains the mother's permission for this to continue with an expectation that this will ultimately lead to more appropriate communication at home.

Lisa comes early to the meeting with her mother. She asks if the other children are there, and I say no, that they may be in the gym. She goes there. As soon as she leaves, her mother asks me what is going on in the group. The mother implies Lisa is a problem at home, is very angry at her brother but holds this inside until she can't contain it anymore. She then loses control and screams, cries, and beats up her sibling. The mother is concerned that Lisa does not get enough attention at home. Both she and her husband work and don't have enough time even to see the kids. When she heard about the sibling group, she was so happy because it seemed perfect. Lisa is very excited about the group, looks forward to it, and talks about the fun she has and the other children in the group. When Lisa's mother asks her whether she talked about her brother, Lisa clams up. Mother says this is a pattern for Lisa and asks whether this is a fun or a talk group.

Mother is asking me what's going on, looking for some kind of help in dealing with her children. Meanwhile, Lisa is peeking out from the door of the gym, watching. I told the mother that we do talking around activities, so there is ample opportunity to express feelings about family life including siblings. I said to the mother, "Perhaps at some future time, you, Lisa and I can discuss some of the things

that take place in the group. That might be a way for you to understand better what the group is all about, and I think Lisa might find it helpful and comforting." She seemed only partially reassured and appreciative of the information about the group but acknowledged my suggestion. Later I took Lisa aside to acknowledge my conversation with her mother. I said I wanted to let her know that I told her mother about our activities and the talking we do to express feelings and share ideas about having a sibling in a family who needs extra attention. Perhaps at some time in the future the three of us can talk together. She said "okay" and stayed close to me.

In this exchange the worker is "in the middle." She must protect her relationship with Lisa and at the same time initiate a working relationship with her mother if she hopes to effect any change in this family system. The social worker clarifies the group purpose for Lisa and for her mother and supports the idea that the expression of feelings in the group will lead to a better later dialogue at home. The social worker is able to assure Lisa that her mother understands the need for the group and has indeed given her permission to express and expose her thoughts and feelings. This is not a betrayal of her own family. Both Lisa and her mother received reassurances from the social worker about the value of expressing feelings and the group as a safe place to do this. There is a gentle suggestion to both that appropriate sharing of information with each other may help ease family tensions and relationships, and this three-way dialogue is a possibility and goal for the future.

Establishing Group Purpose

Since the children were young and the group experience had been proposed by the agency and selected by the parents, we knew that the children would need to be told again about the purpose of the group and how it could be helpful to them. Although the children had been prepared for the group by their parents, it was still important for the leader to help the children understand that this was a place to get help with any real or perceived difficulties arising out of the presence of a disabled sibling in their family. This needed to be clarified or the children might remain puzzled about the nature of this group and could mistakenly assume it was simply another social or recreational activity. By establishing a special time, place, and leader, the agency provided sanction and structure for the group's activities and purpose.

We found that introduction of group purpose with children of this age was a complicated and sensitive task. All leaders began by telling the group that they knew that living with their sibling could create special problems. They were here to talk about that. But this traditional direct, initial statement of purpose and its usual attending discussion seemed to frighten some, to heighten their anxiety, and to result in "flight" or in acting-out behavior. Yet we knew it was important for the children to understand the reason they were in this particular kind of group, their responsibility as participants, and the role of the social worker.

Finding a balance between "directness" and "indirectness" seemed the most effective way to deal with the establishment of group purpose. Different leaders approached this task differently. One worker, having been initially trained as a special education teacher, felt more comfortable in dividing the meeting time into defined segments. She called it "talk time" with the expectation that the children would address the purpose of the group and use the remainder of the group for play and activities. In her first meeting she focused on establishing this agenda with the children, and at the second meeting the worker implements her plan. Her directness seems to create difficulties.

In the following excerpt, the worker reminds the children of the schedule. While she notes their resistance, she persists in an effort to fulfill her agenda and attempts to deal with their discomfort with humor and fun.

I reminded the children of last week when we discussed the format of the sibling group. I recalled for them that we had planned to set aside "Talk Time" as the place during the meeting when we could share feelings about having a handicapped brother or sister. The children did not respond; they seemed resistant. There was a knock on the door and Andrew, a new child, entered. I suggested everyone introduce himself to Andrew. When Chris's turn came, he said, "I'm going to do something funny." I joined the group with some more antics regarding attendance, hoping this humor would deal with their resistance and they would begin to talk and share problems.

It appears that during this second meeting that the worker's wish that the children address the purpose of the group leads to a premature telling of family secrets that result in a group disrupture. The children respond to the warmth of the leader and attempt to give the worker what she is asking for even though they are not prepared to deal with the material. The worker takes note that the children are too uncomfortable. She tries to put them at ease and changes the nature of the group discussion.

Anna is sitting quietly next to me and whispers something about her little brother. She says that her brother says "F" words. I asked her what happens when he says "F" words.

She says he gets hit or the chair. I ask her how she feels when this happens, and she says a little sad. I say that I think the other children would be interested in what she said and would she like to tell the group? She says "no" and seems to withdraw. I ask her if I can bring it up with the group. She says "yes." I relay the story to the children, and they respond by telling similar stories about their families. Andrew says, "I hate my brother." I'm not sure if he said "hate" or "hit" and I ask him. Other children begin talking, interrupting and walking around the room. Elizabeth say she has an idea for next week, "We can all pull down our pants." I say,"I don't think that's such a great idea for our group." Finally, I get the hint. I say, "It sounds like many children don't want 'Talk Time' today." They enthusiastically agree. "I guess some things in the group will be the way I want them. Today we will do things the way you want. Let's stop talking and start our pictures."

The worker knew she was in trouble with the children when the material began to overstimulate some of the members. While many of the things that the children were talking about were important issues, it was too early in the life of the group to share, much less tolerate. It is important for the group members to experience very slowly what it means to hear one talk and listen to one another. They must learn to use the leader as a model to see how they should receive such "family secrets." Since the worker was a sensitive, caring, and responsive person, she was able to realize this and gain enough credibility with the members to help them through this second meeting and ultimately decide to continue and return.

The following excerpts are from the group worker who chose an indirect approach, used natural opportunities throughout the meeting to discuss painful material. Throughout the first meeting, the group worker's informal, episodic,

and seemingly casual interventions were focused on establishing a "talk contract" with the children. But she creates a balance between directives and indirectives. She found as many natural situations as she could to introduce and explain the group's purpose. While the approach in some of the excerpts to follow may seem fragmented, it was a deliberate one. The group worker had to monitor carefully and evaluate the children's capacity for this kind of discussion. The effectiveness of this approach is documented by the appropriate quality of the children's participation and the later success of the group.

The group worker's first interventions are designed to establish the purpose of the group. She begins by welcoming the children, helping lingering parents to depart, and starting the group on time. The place of meeting, a special education classroom, added further clarity to the group's purpose. The group worker introduced the first session with information that each member had a handicapped sibling in a special school. The worker reviews for the children how the group came to be and why the agency chose to offer a group for siblings of handicapped children. She told them that the agency had meetings with parents and learned that the children had some of the same worries and concerns they expressed. This reporting of events tended to universalize the problem. The children were given to understand that their fears and hopes were similar to those of other children and families. It indicated that their parents supported the idea that it was okay to talk about them.

During the first meeting, the group worker had to be sensitive to the children's anxiety reactions. This group is probably the first one in which they have publicly acknowledged their relationship to a handicapped brother or sister. In the following excerpt the worker responded to a child's intense expression of anxiety in order to help her remain part of the group.

After the children settled in and introduced themselves, they began spontaneously to offer stories about their handicapped brothers and sisters. Joan, a five-and-a-half-year-old girl, appears tense and uncomfortable. She persists in telling her story in an extremely agitated manner. Joan didn't pay much attention or seem to hear the other children trying to tell stories about their siblings. I reached out to Joan and sat next to her. My physical proximity seemed to reduce her anxiety enough so that she could listen to the other children and then wait for her turn to tell her story.

All the children were encouraged to speak, and this was made as easy as possible. Initially interruptions were tolerated, but the group worker took responsibility for telling the children that each person must have a turn. She tried to discourage any one child from monopolizing the conversation, from disclosing too much information, or from interrupting others. She used pictures and materials in the classroom to initiate and support observations about handicapped children. She used both play and discussion opportunities to facilitate member interaction, to help the children listen to each other, and to establish ground rules for behavior. The next excerpt further clarifies group purpose. It deals with a child's confusion about appropriate behavior in each setting.

Mary states that she hates school. She has a teacher who is very strict and she always feels she has to be very good. You cannot scream or hit in her classroom. If you do, the teacher sends you out of the room. I said it sounded to me that Mary was frightened and unsure

about the rules here. What was it going to be like for her in this group? What would I accept? Was it all right to speak about feelings that others found unacceptable, or could she share very angry feelings? I said that it was too bad that her teacher was so strict and that perhaps we could talk about that a little bit later. I said that it must be difficult to feel that you always have to be very good. I said that here, in this group, we could talk about things that she may not talk about in school.

Some of the most pressing issues for siblings of handicapped children, concerns that evoke a great deal of feeling, are centered on privacy, protection of property, time with parents, and responsibility for the handicapped sibling. These same themes consistently emerge in parent discussion groups. In the following excerpt we see the children acknowledge these problems. Discussion of these subjects during the first meeting helped to establish and underscore the children's common needs, circumstance, experience, and problems and to clarify the group purpose further. The group worker helps the children become part of a working group by identifying the problems they share. She helps them explore these sensitive but necessary areas, always remaining aware of their tolerance to participate in the discussion.

Some of the children only listened. I asked the group what they do when they have problems with their siblings. John, Mary, and Susan said that they tell the sibling to stop, that they try to move away from the sibling, that they try to keep their things away from their sibling, and some of them said that they tell their parents right away. I asked them what they felt helped the most. Mary said that she very rarely has time when her sister is not bothering her. John said that his brother wanted to be around him all the time and he resented this. The children said they wanted time with their parents alone, and they didn't want to have their things touched by their siblings. They didn't want to help their sibling all the time. Laura said she was an interpreter for her parents because they could not always understand her brother. Sara said she always had to take care of her siblings and didn't like it. Maria spoke of how angry her father gets at her sibling, but it is the only way he can get her brother to do what he is supposed to do.

In the following excerpt the group worker does not terminate the discussion between Wanda and Steven or redirect with play activity. Instead she remains focused on Steven's painful disclosures. She appropriately assumes some of the other children have similar conflicts and she tries to help the other children understand Steven's distress. She hopes that such a discussion will lead the group members to think about different options of oehavior when they also must deal with similar situations at home.

Wanda said that she doesn't understand Steven. "Why does he want to change his name?" I said we should see if we can find out. There must be an important reason. Steven told the group that his friend has a family that he thinks is fun. They have a nice home. He showed us a picture of a family and a house he had drawn. It was a family that he wanted to live with, that he liked. The worker said that she guessed he felt those families didn't have problems and worries. Maybe it was easier in those families.

The group worker's continuing focus on establishing the common bond is again seen in the following excerpt:

Wanda discussed her feelings about all her responsibilities at home—not in relation to her brother, but for herself. She told the group that her mother worked as a nurse on the late shift from 11:00 to 5:00 or 6:00 A.M. and she missed her a lot. When her mother was home, she was tired, and so Wanda made her own

breakfast, and sometimes she also had to make her own dinner, too. She was often lonely and wanted her mother to be there with her and do those things for her.

The group worker had to help the children see that the group provided an opportunity to speak freely. This was a place to be heard without being criticized. The group worker listened to Wanda and linked her wish that her family circumstances could be different to Steven's wish to be in a different family. Both children were expressing feelings of being overburdened. The social worker understood that in their families these appropriate childish needs could not always be met.

The social worker had to remember to help each child deal with the pain that this exposure and disclosure of strong feelings produced. The social worker had to gauge the children's tolerance for discussion and help them understand that dealing with these relationship issues and their feelings was the work of this group. She remained sensitive to their distress and acknowledged the pain their feelings produced. She put their struggle into words for them. In the following excerpt the leader identifies the children's common themes and fears and helps them to perceive the similarities in their experiences.

I said that sometimes when things are hard for us, we wish we could be somewhere else; that happens to everyone. It can be difficult to talk about things that really bother us. Take Steven, it is easier for him to yell out or run around than it is for him to tell us what worries him. At the same time Steven couldn't tell us why he wanted to be called Christopher, and so he yelled, but it would be better to talk and not yell because that makes people feel bad. Wanda said she'll call him Christopher.

The social worker has promoted discussion but prevented premature or excessive personal exposure. The children seem to understand that the group is "theirs." They must also believe their secrets are safe. We knew that ultimately the leader's earlier nonjudgmental acceptance of angry outbursts would lead to more open sharing of deeper and sometimes more painful feelings.

As the leader begins to close the first meeting, some of the children begin to demonstrate their identity as group members, and their beginning sense of belonging (to this group) is seen in the following excerpt.

I said to the children, in this group you will learn from each other and have fun with each other. You will see that many of you have had similar experiences with your brothers and sisters. Sometimes they need more attention than you do, and sometimes your parents give it to them. While this short discussion was going on, one of the siblings came bursting into the room—a parent had opened the door. Sara got up and pushed the sibling out of the room, saying very clearly, "This is my room and you can't come in." I then asked the parent to close the door because we were not finished with our group meeting.

The children's open expression of feelings and stories about their handicapped siblings reflects their growing understanding of the group's purpose. At the conclusion of this first meeting, the children seemed to understand that this group had a specific task. They did not behave as if the group was imposed upon them by their parents and the agency but rather that it was something they found important and helpful. The social worker's informal and episodic interventions had established a clearly defined contract.

Learning About Handicaps

The group became a place where questions could be asked. The children wanted and needed reliable and current information about their siblings' handicap. They wanted to know more about their handicapped siblings. The children began to reveal their siblings' handicaps and the problems they had discussing these matters at home. The children were preoccupied with thoughts about their sibling that revolved around the following:

- What did they have?
- How did they get it?
- Why did it happen?
- Could it be fixed?
- Could the well sibling get it too?

As a rule, parental reactions to their disabled child and the problems they generated provided a critical diversion. Their well children often incorporated and reflected their parents' fears and concerns. The worker had to listen carefully in order to understand the way the children said their parents dealt with the disability. Was there open communication in the household? Did parents readily acknowledge and discuss their own feelings? What did they tell their friends and relatives?

The group's expression of confusion and anxiety in the face of a handicapped child's need for surgery and a prosthesis seemed to be heightened by their ignorance. In the following excerpt the worker moves from the specific disability to the general theme that includes all the members of the group. She points out their common fears related to handicaps.

Barbara presented a problem that her brother was having with his foot. She explained how her parents were going to care for him. He was recuperating from his operation, and uncomfortable and in pain. Barbara's brother's foot became a very important theme for the group. Barbara said her brother was going to the hospital. She said her mommy was going with him to have his leg fixed. He has a "prosthesis." I asked if anyone knew what that was. Some said yes, but most said no. Barbara would not explain it. I said I thought it was hard to talk about what is different about our brothers and sisters. Perhaps this made Barbara sad or frightened. She nodded. Lisa said she knew what it was, but she then said she didn't. Barbara then explained it. Another child mentioned that his sibling also has a short foot. He couldn't walk right. He had an operation. I asked if they knew what happens in an operation. The two said they try to fix the foot so they could walk and stand.

Barbara then told everyone about her brother's operation. He had to have his "foot cut off." She was obviously confused about this and why it happened. She told us about a cut she once had on her foot which she seemed to think was comparable to her brother's disability. We discussed the way her cut was very different from her brother's. I explained what happened to her brother during the operation. In order for the prosthesis to fit on his leg, the leg had to be shaped for it and a part of his foot removed. We talked about the fact that many of the members seemed worried. Maybe they thought that what happened to their brothers and sisters could also happen to them.

In this excerpt the children were curious. They wanted to know more about a particular handicap. They seemed to have very little understanding or information about this physical disability. Open communication and a dialogue in which questions were permitted and encouraged was of demonstrable value in reducing the children's confusion and fears.

Having Fun

The group experience showed the children that satisfying recreational and social activities could take place even though all the members were part of a family with a particular problem. Many of the mothers had spoken of the way their concerns and obligations interfered with relaxed, spontaneous, joyful family activities. Yet, they did not want their children to be deprived of these experiences, although they found they had too little energy, time, money, or opportunity to provide them. They sometimes discouraged playfulness inadvertently. Childish, spontaneous activities were not always welcomed or accepted. This kind of behavior was perceived of as self-indulgent or inappropriate in a household overburdened with reponsibilities. Well siblings sometimes took on this serious view of life. They deprived themselves of essential social contacts and recreational experiences important in personality development in so many critical ways, and invaluable in discharging tension and facilitating coping skills.

The following excerpts show that some of the children were not comfortable with age-appropriate activities. Spontaneity and pleasure with art materials, even when messy, are activities most children enjoy, but not in this instance. Childish impulses to experiment, get dirty, and participate in a disorganized fashion were neither natural nor even comfortable options.

The group's next activity was mixing some paint in different colors and putting it on, sharing colors, and also looking at themselves in the mirror that I had set up in the room. This activity lent itself to a lot of interesting interaction. Barbara would not participate. She said that it was too babyish. It she were five she might but she was too old at age seven. Sara had trouble with the activity because she said she was worried about what her mother would say. The worker explained that the paint washed off and perhaps she could try a little so she too could have fun with the group. Sara said that in her house her mother always liked everything to be very organized. She said that this was the way her mother said it had to be, that we must do things in certain ways. The worker said that at home they did have to cooperate with their parents, and sometimes carry extra responsibilities. But in this group we didn't have to do everything in one particular way. They all had a chance to decide how things should be done and what games should be played. They knew that these activities and this group were for them and that they could do things the way they liked.

A number of children had already acquired adaptive responses to highly organized households which had established rigid routines in order to meet their responsibilities of caring for a handicapped youngster. The group provided a brief, different, and important experience for these children which allowed for group and individual play, choice, and spontaneity.

Beginning Mutual Aid

The group experience showed that even children as young as five and a half could form a viable group, reactive to each other, and helpful to one another in their struggle to cope with a common life situation. The leader's interventions continually clarified the purpose of the group, encouraged member interaction, and put the children's feelings into words for them. With this help the children in the groups slowly moved from the place of only talking at each other to listening and responding (sometimes empathically) and exchanging ideas with each other.

As the meetings continued and the chil-

dren began to react to one another, the worker facilitated their exchanges and communications. She told the children that in this group they would be learning new things about their brothers and sisters. In the following excerpt she begins to establish the theme of mutual need by helping the children understand that they must listen to one another and respond to the person who is talking. She also helps Steven feel more comfortable with this new group of strangers.

I started to talk to the group about Joan's feelings toward her sibling and that Joan seemed to want some responses from the group. Steven was the next child to want to share. He seemed to want to talk to his peers about his relationship at home. He shared quite quickly his relationship with his close friend at home and talked about their aggressive play. Steven seemed to miss his friend a great deal. We talked a bit about how he might make new friends in this group and that these children might have something in common with him. Perhaps they would become his friends also. He seemed to feel very comfortable with this.

In the section to come, the worker focused on a common problem: the children's shared resentment and disappointment when their property was not protected. They discussed their options in responding and adapting. Group or individual projects which culminated in a creation, such as a painting, had to be planned carefully. Some children anticipated parental expectations that they produce and bring home a similar object for their sibling. Others planned for the likelihood that work once brought home would be damaged by their sibling.

The worker went on to the next activity which was making hats from construction paper. Florence explained how to do this. Betty proceeded to make two hats, and I had wondered why she had two hats. She told me one hat was for her sibling to ruin. The worker repeated this to the group and wondered if anyone else felt like this. As we talked, she noticed that other children had done the same thing. Larry made a couple of hats. One he kept flying in the air like an airplane. She said he must feel something about this too because he was running around so much. Lisa said it made her mad, not angry, when her things were ruined.

The following excerpt illustrates the children's beginning attempts at mutual problem solving and the worker's interventions in facilitating the exchange:

The worker asked: "Do your parents help take care of your things when you're unhappy?" Lisa said no, at her home it was not taken care of because her brother messes everything up. Barbara said her mother tries. Billy shook his head no. The worker said it sounded like they were saying that their parents weren't really able to help take care of these problems so they were unhappy about it and disappointed. The worker asked, "What did they do?" Larry again stated, he beats his sister up. The worker asked the group if they thought this would work it out. Sara said, you could tell your mother. The worker asked if she meant she could tell her mother how she felt about it. She said yes. Lisa agreed. The worker asked if this was a way they could work it out. Could they tell their parents how they felt? Some said they could, others could not. The worker said she guessed that it might be hard for some of them really to talk about how they feel about these things. Sometimes we all have trouble talking about what really worries us and bothers us, to adults and to each other. Maybe we could find some ways to make that easier.

CONCLUSION

Personal reactions generated by this sibling experience are variable. But we do know that brothers and sisters have lifetime bonds and serve important functions for each other. Their early interactions provide significant experiences in attachment and identification, as well as rivalry, aggression, loyalty, and responsibility. Whether the well youngster matures without serious damage or scars or acquires compensatory skills and strength is complex. In all likelihood development is related to individual temperament and intrapsychic organization, as well as the nature of the handicapped sibling's disability and the quality of family life.

This well-sibling group met an important family objective. It responded to the adult's need for relief from some of their parenting stress while addressing the well child's need for support and information. Many of the same elements thought to be useful only to older children participating in groups were found to be of value to this age child as well. For the professional this model created an entry into the family system. It opened a dialogue among family members and between parent and worker. It established an early intervention and prevention practice for families with handicapped children.

Community-based programs should respond to this recently identified family and sibling need, which has become more pressing and visible with the advent of P.L. 94–142 and the change in public policy to educate and maintain handicapped children at home. Families will benefit from local support systems which also include groups for the well sibling, which provide for education, support, and problem solving.

NOTES

1. Gregory C. Schell, "The Young Handicapped Child: A Family Perspective," *Topics in Early Childhood Special Education* I (October 1981): 24.

2. Judith Bloch, "Impaired Children: Helping Families Through the Critical Period of First Identification," *Children Today* 7 (November-December 1978): 4.

3. Sonya L. Rhodes, "A Developmental Approach to the Life Cycle of the Family," *Social Casework* 58 (May 1977): 308.

4. Debra Lobato, "Siblings of Handicapped Children: A Review," *Journal of Autism and Developmental Disorders* 13 (December 1983): 347.

5. Milton Seligman, "Siblings of Handicapped Persons," in *The Family With a Handicapped Child, Understanding and Treatment,* ed. M. Seligman (New York: Grune and Strattor, 1983), p. 153.

6. Fern Trevino, "Siblings of Handicapped Children: Identifying Those at Risk," *Developmental Disabilities No Longer a Private Tragedy,* 6 (October 1979): 488.

7. Schell, "The Young Handicapped Child," p. 22.

8. E. Poznanski, "Psychiatric Difficulties in Siblings of Handicapped Children," *Pediatrics* 8 (April 1969): 232–234.

9. Trevino, "Siblings of Handicapped Children," p. 490.

10. Francis Kaplan Grossman, *Brothers and Sisters of Retarded Children: An Exploratory Study* (Syracuse: Syracuse University Press, 1972), p. 176.

11. Bernard Farber, "Effect of a Severely Retarded Child on Family Integration," *Monographs of the Society for Research in Child Development* 24 (1959), p. 78.

12. William Schwartz, "On the Use of Groups in Social Work Practice," in *The Practice of Group Work,* ed. W. Schwartz and S. Zalba (New York: Columbia University Press, 1971), p. 7.

Part Three
Mutual Aid and Adolescents

Carol Irizarry
Yetta H. Appel

CHAPTER 6

Growing Up: Work with Preteens in the Neighborhood

Social work intervention with children has always had to pay attention to developmental issues. The child's stage of development, cognitively and psychosocially, presents both opportunities and constraints for the social worker, and more often than not the "problems" to be worked on have developmental components. Thus, a life-span perspective which focuses on the bio-psychosocial transitions that need to be negotiated through the life cycle is an indispensable framework within which social workers are able to engage clients, particularly children, on the presenting problems or issues.

This chapter presents a social group worker's intervention with a naturally formed group of female preadolescents who were attempting to cope with the typical developmental tasks and stresses of this transitional stage, in the context of their being members of ethnic minority groups (black and Puerto Rican) as well as being subject to the socioeconomic deprivations associated with low-income status in American society. These youngsters can be viewed as experiencing a "double marginality."

By virtue of being preadolescent, they were at the cognitive stage where they could begin to grasp, very likely for the first time, their marginal position; what it feels like to be passing from childhood, with some sense of loss at being compelled to give up this stage, into the unknown stage that was looming, that of early adolescence, and to feel oneself as not belonging fully to either. But as ethnic minority preadolescents, this psychosocial stage presents a "double crisis" in Miranda's terms. He notes that a developmental perspective sensitizes the professional to the increased vulnerability to both psychological and physical disorders that stage transitions can initiate. However, Miranda suggests that ethnic minority individuals have to cope with

> the added stress created by society's reaction to their ascribed status [which] seriously increases the potential for breakdown. The developmental process thus becomes part of a double crisis at each stage of unfolding.[1]

These youngsters not only had to cope with developmental issues common to all preadolescents in our society, but also had at their disposal a somewhat different array of strengths and weaknesses when compared with their white, middle-class counterparts.

DEVELOPMENTAL TASKS OF PREADOLESCENCE

Erikson's epigentic formulation of the psychosocial stages of development has been widely incorporated within social work's knowledge base, but there has been a discernible tendency to emphasize the crucial nature of the early stages of childhood, such as establishing basic trust versus mistrust, achieving autonomy versus shame/doubt, initiative versus guilt, and then usually focusing on the identity crisis of adolescence.[2] Relatively little attention tends to be given to the "in-between" stage of industry versus inferiority, although some highly significant psychosocial development takes place. This is the stage, for example, where peers become as meaningful to the growing child as one's family, and sometimes more so. Sullivan and Piaget, more than Erikson, have perceived this stage as needing to provide the child with critical social experiences with age mates which, if absent, can have a detrimental impact on later social functioning.[3] Because of the work of Sullivan and Piaget, and the symbolic interactionist school which traces its beginnings to George Herbert Mead, social experiences with peers both in groups and in paired relationships have begun to be accorded almost as much importance as the family with regard to the achievement of mature social functioning.[4]

When one views adult social functioning in American society from a life-span perspective, the psychosocial importance of this preadolescent stage becomes clearer. Much adult behavior depends greatly on peer associations, peer interaction, and developing interpersonal competence with peers. This interpersonal competence requires learning to be comfortable with equals, a redefinition of one's relationship to authority, and eventually becoming able to use authority and becoming able to establish close working relationships, including intimate relationships, with strangers. It is the contention of Sullivan and Piaget that this development begins in the preadolescent period, between the ages of nine and twelve, and is further elaborated and consolidated in the stage of adolescence.

The preadolescent period needs to be recognized as a "bridging" stage in which the child is dealing with the transition from childhood, of relinquishing, with resistance, some of the earlier, still-gratifying dependency, and beginning hesitantly to anticipate becoming a teenager in our society and more autonomous. For this one needs peer experiences. In *Human Social Development*, Blitsten argues that the family is a necessary but insufficient socializing institution if one is to become socially mature.[5] Families in almost all societies are organized around clear divisions of labor and authority. In families, children experience a unilateral direction of authority, from adults toward themselves.

The predominant interactional pattern is one of dominance-submission, as the family, according to Blitsten, is essentially not a democratic institution. Significant inequalities exist between members. But in the preadolescent stage, the child begins to emerge from the enveloping social boundary provided by the family, and with the help of peers begins to address the psychosocial tasks of this developmental period between childhood and adolescence.

The developmental tasks that have been identified for this psychosocial stage tend to be largely instrumental in nature. It is the stage in which the growing child learns how to use one's body more skillfully as the child's gross and fine motor coordination continually progress. These years have been viewed as relatively stable and quiescent, as generally "untroubled," since there are no major biophysical changes occurring (as will all too soon become evident with puberty), and a modicum of self-regulation with regard to instinctual demands has been achieved by the child.

However, there is a significant gender difference. For girls aged ten to twelve the biological changes of puberty are imminent and will be experienced by the end of this stage, whereas for boys this stage is prolonged and the experience of puberty will occur later chronologically. For both boys and girls, the pubertal changes become the means by which peers recognize one's developmental maturity, and those who are "early maturers" begin to differentiate themselves from those who are still untouched by this biological watershed. As puberty looms, both sexes tend to experience greater anxiety and to search for information in order to understand the bodily changes which are making their physical selves—so taken for granted—unpredictable.

Because the organism is more quiescent biologically, the preadolescent can concentrate on developing technical and social skills, in particular how to "connect" with age mates, and to be able to function in a nonfamily environment. In Erikson's view, the child is exploring "how things work," and "how to make things." This stage is one in which the developing juvenile needs to experience a growing sense of mastery. Thus school becomes a major, if not dominating, institution in the juvenile's expanding social environment, for it is the arena wherein one's level of mastery tends to be continually tested.

In the process of relating to strange children and strange adults, which attendance at school essentially initiates and which becomes extended through formal and informal group associations, the child begins to develop a repertoire of social skills and to gain "social" knowledge which becomes the basis for later extensive social development in adolescence and young adulthood.

If one is to be able to make friends, one has to develop skill in expressing oneself verbally, in communicating one's needs especially to strangers, and in establishing and maintaining relationships with others in a nonfamily environment. This becomes the child's "work" in the preadolescent stage, and it is enormously facilitating for children's social development to be able to begin to do this initially with peers. One can probably date the beginning of interpersonal sensitivity to this stage. True relationships which acknowledge the intrinsic value of another, and in which one is gratified by the experience of providing satisfactions to another, "the satisfaction in giving satisfaction" as Sullivan has stated it, emerges at the end of this stage.[6]

Piaget's work has demonstrated also that the cognitive resources available to the preadolescent enable the child to move into more socially demanding situations.[7] The young juvenile, cognitively, is in Piaget's stage of concrete operations, which is characterized by a decreasing subjectivity, by the ability to decenter, that is, to begin to be able to view things from another's perspective. The child at this stage can begin to think about things and demonstrates conservation in the physical sphere, that is, that the essential nature of an object does not change even if its appearance can be variously manipulated. Greater precision in the use of language becomes evident, and memory becomes a repository of experience which tends to be more orderly and subject to relevant recall. An example of this is one of the girls remarking to the worker that when they had earlier refused to let her discuss "periods and babies," it was "because we were younger then."

Just as nurturing adults need to be available as the child takes its first faltering steps in learning to walk, parental and adult support need to be available to the preadolescent. This support involves modeling interaction with strangers, encouraging the youngster to explore the physical and social environment, providing a range of experience and activities in which the child will be able to develop appropriate social skills and technical mastery, but also providing a "home base" where failures will be understood and accepted. To acquire a feeling of mastery, of "industry" in Erikson's terms, requires that the juvenile experience some degree of success which, in turn, helps the child to cope with the inevitable failures. If the youngster has little or no experience of success, does not progressively feel able to accomplish things, perceives oneself to be socially inept, impaired self-esteem and a pervasive sense of inferiority can become entrenched.

For minority preadolescents, subject to the "double crisis" identified by Miranda, negotiation of these developmental tasks tends to present additional stresses. Understanding in what ways this transitional stage was similar and different for them was critical for the worker in intervening with this group of female preadolescents.

In our society as presently structured, children growing up in low-income families in general, but especially ethnic minority children, may have little opportunity to experience success and mastery, to feel valued. Sullivan was one of the first neo-Freudians to recognize that a child's emotional health in the juvenile and preadolescent stages can become impaired if the "school, neighborhood, and other social environments are blighted by poverty, economic injustice, intellectual stagnation, widespread vice, and ethnic prejudices."[8] This view of Sullivan's has received empirical support in the work of Jerome Kagan.

Kagan suggests that it is primarily through initiation into the school environment that a child comes to understand the attributes that our society values and devalues. He has found that American children come to view material wealth and possessions, various cognitive skills, and certain occupations as of higher value. Unskilled labor by parents, limited literacy, excessive drinking on the part of parents, homes shabbily furnished or in disrepair can become sources of shame and embarrassment. He contends that for the child,

> the family's social class position and the specific psychological characteristics of parents and siblings influence the degree to which the child's conception of himself is positive or negative.[9]

Middle-class children, both within the dominant white majority and ethnic minorities, have more opportunities to experience some measure of success as they become involved with the wider social environment. They *expect* to be able to achieve, according to Kagan, which becomes in part a self-fulfilling prophecy.[10] Their families expect this as well because they can provide more material resources, and they do not feel as alienated from the majority culture to which they proceed to introduce their children. In contrast, socioeconomically deprived and socially oppressed parents cannot readily do this, and may well reinforce a sense of isolation and alienation in their children by keeping them "ghetto-bound."

This was evident in this group of

preadolescents, who demonstrated considerable fearfulness toward venturing "off their block" into surrounding areas, which could have provided access to desired recreational activities. These possibilities were literally at their doorstep. Psychologically, however, they could not leave their "block," and were never "off their block," even when they began to experience some of these activities through group trips organized by the worker. Their sense of exclusion, of not fully belonging, of being different and possibly performing inadequately seemed to induce anxiety and extreme self-consciousness, which affected their behavior on trips out of the neighborhood. As one of the girls indicated following their eviction from a subway train due to noisy and generally disruptive behavior, "I feel funny on the subway, people stare."

This youngster was revealing, in part, the lack of opportunity to develop expected social behaviors and to acquire the social knowledge that helps middle-class preadolescents appear more socially competent in the wider social environment. Moreover, parents continually facing material privation and living with their children in impoverished circumstances tend to communicate their own sense of helplessness and powerlessness. Defeatist feelings with regard to being able to succeed in the larger society may thus be subtly reinforced in their children.

Nowhere was this more evident than in these preadolescents' feelings about, and actual performance in, the neighborhood schools they attended. School was almost always an anxiety-provoking experience and perceived as an alien place. The girls viewed the schools as primarily rule-enforcing institutions. But the "rules" bore little relationship to the social context in which these preadolescents found themselves, a context which included their being poor and from diverse subcultural backgrounds, specifically, black and Puerto Rican. For a good many, Spanish was the native language as well. The schools they attended all but ignored these contextual factors.

Thus school was not a place where they could expect to achieve even small successes. Instead of beginning to acquire the technical skills which engender a sense of instrumental mastery, of "how things work," their school experiences tended to instill feelings of failure, ineptness, and lowered self-esteem. Nor did they have access to alternative forms of expressive and/or recreational activities (given their impoverished circumstances) through which they might be helped to develop some sense of accomplishment, and a more positive self-image.

Living in poverty or occupying what has been labeled as lower-class status also exposes children to a quite different experience of authority relations. As has been noted, all families tend to be undemocratic. However, there is accumulating evidence that families continually confronting material privation and the associated interpersonal stresses stimulated by such privation are not as able as more affluent families to be "looser" and to encourage "participatory" processes in the rearing of their children.[11] All but one of the girls lived in mother-only families, and there was pervasive material deprivation.

Most of these mothers wanted their daughters to "do better," not to follow their own life patterns. Yet the stress levels in these families and the mothers' own handicapping socialization experiences seemed to prevent them from involving their children in any kind of decision making or working out compromises by trying to view things from their daughter's perspective. Also, there was little support for the verbal expression of feelings and concerns, which tended to reinforce acting-out behavior.

For example, these preadolescent girls increasingly and quite appropriately raised questions about sexual functioning as a consequence of the onset of puberty. In response, the mothers were highly prescriptive emphasizing what the girls "shouldn't do," but were unable to discuss with their daughters the pubertal changes and their implications. (The worker had to be very cognizant of this maternal prescriptiveness when she attempted to respond to the developmentally appropriate needs of these preteens for accurate sexual information.)

Punishment was routinely experienced by these youngsters in order to secure their compliance, but it could be arbitrary and unpredictable. In response to the authoritarian behavior of their parents, the girls were outwardly submissive and obedient. At the same time, they were deeply dependent on their mothers for nurturance and protection which engendered conflicting, ambivalent feelings they found difficult to recognize and express. These preteens were still in need of adult caring and support related to their stage of development, but were receiving such support inconsistently, if at all. Thus, there tended to be veneration and hostility/defiance at one and the same time toward adult authority figures perceived to be in nurturant roles. Unpredictable and arbitrary behavior can make it appear that both good and bad things happen to one without rhyme or reason.

In the school system, their experience of authority was similar although for different reasons. Coercive approaches tended to prevail; compliance was demanded and was secured through bribes and/or punishment. The girls portrayed their teachers as arbitrary and insensitive when comparing them to the worker, who did not "fit" their conception of an adult authority figure. In time, they verbalized to her that they only outwardly complied with the teachers' demands, but really didn't "respect" them. For at this point in their development, they were distrustful, as they put it, of all "grown-up people."

AGENCY CONTEXT AND THE GROUP MODALITY

A settlement house in New York City was the locus for this social work service. Traditionally, settlement houses have attempted to provide supplementary educational, recreational, and social services to the neighborhood's residents. These residents frequently have been disadvantaged populations, including many waves of immigrants. As is well known, the settlement has served in the past as a vehicle for immigrant groups in particular to achieve some upward mobility.

As with all innovative approaches, institutionalization overtook the settlement house movement. A discernible tendency to become more restrictive regarding membership and to set standards for behavior on their premises and the use of their facilities took hold. Increasingly, they appeared to gear their programs to the upper strata of the lower-income population, to working and lower middle-class groups. They also tended to ignore the newer waves of immigrants, primarily Spanish-speaking, who were arriving in large numbers in New York City in the 1950s.

A number of the settlements began to recognize the distancing that had occurred, and attempts to remedy this took the form of outreach programs of various kinds. A particular target group were young adolescents, usually very streetwise, who could not tolerate the degree of structure and some of the restrictiveness inherent in traditional settlement house programs.

The social work intervention to be described below was part of a settlement's outreach program in a densely populated area of New York City. The settlement contracted for the use of a neighborhood housing project's basement which served as the physical base for this program. Contact was made with groups of preadolescents in the neighborhood who were known to be engaged in antisocial activities of various kinds. Master's level social workers made these contacts and offered service to start a clublike group on a frequent and ongoing basis for some of the natural friendship "cliques" of preadolescents ranging in age from nine to thirteen years. Typically, the groups formed averaged about ten preadolescents.

The only other condition was that the worker would be available to family members of the club group. A daily log was kept by the worker for as long as she was involved with the group.

The population designated for outreach in this delinquency prevention project were ten to thirteen-year-old preadolescent girls in a natural friendship group who lived in a poverty area of New York City. They had been identified by the school system as "trouble makers" and were often asked to leave the regular settlement house programs due to antisocial behavior. The challenge of the project was to offer the social work service to this hard-to-reach, socially isolated population in a way that fit with the needs and interests of girls at this particular stage of development, while clearly and honestly representing the professional role of the worker and her commitment to an agency base.

The designated girls were initially visited in their homes by the worker and the project supervisor, an agency staff member who was well known and accepted in the community. The offer was made to form "a club" for the girls which would meet three times a week for the summer using a nearby housing project basement as headquarters. The statement was made to the girls and their parents that the worker, Carol, would be responsible for the club but that as part of her job she would also be available to help other family members if requested.

THEMES OF WORK

The group included three cultural strands: white, black, and Hispanic-Puerto Rican. The youngsters were quite aware of their cultural differences and the social discrimination experienced by minorities of color. Those preadolescents in the group who were black and Puerto Rican appeared more aware of their marginality, of their being pulled between two cultures. As a result, they seemed to be confronting emerging identity issues earlier. One of the black members of the group, very aware of society's prejudices toward her race, revealed her struggle with achieving some self-acceptance as a black human being when she shared with the worker her poignant observation that "black don't look good on nobody."

Because they had to live in and negotiate a culturally diverse, complex environment, they tended to be rather wary and to have learned quite early and accurately how to "read" people and their intentions, particularly with adults. They used nonverbal cues, paid close attention to body language, and appeared to have a heightened interpersonal sensitivity that belied their years.

The individual members of this natural friendship group manifested a number of personal strengths that had not been initially anticipated. In addition to the accuracy of their perceptions of others' attitudes and intentions (their "reading" of people), they had a basic reality orientation, an ability to look at life realistically. Learning to survive in a frequently violent, unpredictable, depriving environment, which they certainly were doing, required de-illusionment, the giving up of childish naiveté and illusions. Because so much less was hidden from them in the homes in which they were growing up, they were not as confused about their feelings. They expressed directly their anger and frustration, their being "mad." They could express just as directly what and whom they liked. And they could abandon themselves to the existential moment, at the moment they were enjoying themselves, from which they derived sustenance.

Also, one needs to recognize that they demonstrated some mastery, but not as conventionally defined. Given their social context, the only available outlet for them was to be "good at being bad," which they demonstrated on many an occasion. This sense of "negative" mastery created a strong bond among the members of the group.

With this strong group subculture, they developed a considerable ability to handle various crises by themselves, using the inherent impetus within the group toward mutual aid.

The girls immediately responded with enthusiasm to the idea of any club which would enable them to take trips and hid any reservation they might have felt. The evolvement of a contract between the girls and the worker took many weeks and presented numerous struggles. Negotiation with this new adult in their lives became

the first overt theme of work, a theme which reflected their ambivalences around striving for independence while experiencing the necessity for compromise and cooperation.

Getting Started

The contract presented the vehicle around which the theme surfaced. The group presented the medium through which it could be expressed. The mutual aid process gave rise to the impetus for a successful resolution.

At the first formal meeting, the girls identified their interest in having a club to "go places and have fun." They indicated that this was only possible with the assistance of the adult worker, conveying the attitude that due to this practical necessity, she would be tolerated. The girls were slightly aloof in affect, listened but did not respond to her comments, excluded her from any intimate exchanges, and particularly avoided any suggestions regarding the worker's availability for family members.

The worker's task was to respond to their concrete presentation of need, to help them to "have fun," while continuously finding ways to present her broader role and function and seek out their feedback. Simultaneously, she needed to be attuned to developmental issues and needs, that is, to help with growth and change. Almost immediately (the second meeting) such an issue surfaced, that of having a party but "with boys," which became the means for further specification of the worker's role.

The second meeting was a trip to the local swimming pool (help with concrete need). As the girls were walking home, plans were discussed for next week and became the first interaction around the contract. Carmen asked if they would have a party, and Nilda added "with the boys?" Margarita said that they could tell their mothers it was just a party—then later sneak the boys in. I asked what the reaction would be if I brought up the idea of inviting boys at the first parents' meeting to be held the following week. The girls all responded that the mothers would never allow it. Nilda became quite angry and said she didn't know why the mothers had to know everything. I said that I could see they were upset about my wanting to talk to their parents about it. Nilda asked why the mothers had to meet at all anyway. I said that this was part of my job—to work with families as well as with them. Margarita exclaimed, "Well, if that's what she's supposed to do, Nilda, then that's what she's supposed to do." Nilda replied maybe, but she didn't think any parents would come to the meeting anyway.

The group saved face by Nilda's comment that no one would come to the meeting, but an important step had been made in their recognition of the "job" classification of the worker's activities and the parameters this presented. Subsequent discussions with the girls led to agreement that the topic of boys could be introduced at the parents' meeting. When it was agreed that the party would be allowed, with the supervision of settlement house staff, the girls were ecstatic, and their attitude toward the worker shifted to one of sudden curiosity. She was temporarily seen as a miracle worker, one who really possessed the key to new and possibly forbidden "adult" experiences.

Trusting and Testing a Stranger

The first theme of adult negotiation continued, but the second theme of work also emerged this early: trusting and testing a stranger. This powerful theme took many forms and dominated all aspects of interaction between the worker and the girls. It appeared in its infancy linked to sort-

ing out her role and function as the worker continuously tried to clarify the unique aspect of her involvement with the group.

During the first few weeks on a picnic to Central Park, the girls kept referring to me as a teacher. When I inquired into this, I was told it was because I looked like a teacher and because teachers also took them places. I said that this was probably why they did call me a teacher, but then maybe they would feel toward me what they felt toward teachers. Nilda replied, "Oh, no, we like you." Then followed a series of complaints about teachers who shout a lot, punish unfairly, and never listen.

The primary nonfamilial authority figure with whom the girls had constant interaction was, of course, a teacher, and the comparison was obvious. It was many months before the differences in roles were experienced and accepted as easily as the similarities. The worker did impose limits, but they were directly related to their personal safety or possible destruction of property. She did not censor verbal expressions or physical behavior that fell outside of these parameters.

The worker used the term social worker frequently and informally in referring to herself and her purpose in spending time with the group. Since the actuality and visibility of an agency was minimal and the external manifestations of the professional stance were significantly limited while sitting on the steps of a tenement building, the importance of verbal repetition of purpose and function was great. Over the summer months with the worker's help the girls began to experience a sense that this new adult in their lives was different from others they had known in the family or school and that her responses were unique.

The testing of the few worker-imposed limits did happen, but it was almost always obvious to the girls and verbalized by the club president, Nilda, that they would not be allowed to continue going on trips if there were injuries. The club existed from the girls' point of view so that they could "go places and do things," a feat not easily accomplished by preadolescent girls living in a restricted, impoverished urban environment. The group members immediately identified with their stake in working together to enable the club to continue functioning, and as a consequence of their being a strong, natural friendship group they had their own well-oiled system of internal control. The worker on many occasions, such as in the following example, had only to use and strengthen this system by pointing it in the direction of self-interest.

Mrs. Vilar spoke to the worker one day about Carmen (her daughter) being afraid of Tata beating her up in the club. For this reason she didn't like Carmen coming. I spoke with the president, Nilda, who at the time was the only one with influence over Tata. I explained that I felt responsible to their mothers if someone was hurt, although I knew Carmen also teased Tata a lot. Nilda, Tata, and I had a meeting, and Nilda told Tata to stop beating up Carmen because her mother was mad about it. Tata refused to discuss the matter at all with the worker, but responded to Nilda and stopped.

This type of intervention was frequent and smooth, easily recognized and accepted by the girls for what it was—a way to help them stay together as a group. This part of the social worker's role still closely resembled other authority figures in their lives—especially the teacher. The specific characteristics of the social worker's responses lay in the exploration of the girls' behavior rather than the censorship of it. This they had not experi-enced before, and it confused them. The testing in this area came first in the form of imitation and ridicule of the worker's gestures, manner of speech, and personal idiosyncracies, in particular from Tata, the group member who often acted out the most extreme feelings in the group. The worker did not respond to this behavior.

Swearing, or "cursing" as the girls called such language, was a normal part of conversation when adults were not present, as was public unsocial behavior, such as rude gestures or insults, to pedestrians or subway riders. Very quickly the testing for worker reaction moved into the arena of expressing some type of antisocial behavior.

All such behavior was embarrassing and unpleasant, but it was also obvious that stringent demands from various authority agents in society, familial and nonfamilial, had not been successful in inhibiting its expression. A new process was begun with the presence of a nonjudgmental adult. The group members were left to feel and react to the impact of their behavior themselves. The worker was not passively accepting of all and any behavior. She watched for and used opportunities to help the girls examine together what they wanted for themselves.

Becoming Autonomous

The girls hovered on the threshold of the first step toward autonomy, that is, of making decisions about themselves and their behavior that were not simply reactions to external demands to avoid punishment. This third theme of work was a painful struggle of hestitatingly testing new responses and retreating to safer, previously familiar patterns. Only by recognizing the impetus toward self-motivated decisions could the worker use intervention that mirrored their behavior back to the group for scrutiny and exploration.

In midsummer an extensive trip was planned to Coney Island, a distance of one and a half hours by subway. As usual on the subway, the restraint of space and apparent scrutiny by passengers led to noisy behavior by the girls. During the trip the antisocial quality and subsequent interaction with passengers increased. The worker was glanced at frequently but not spoken to directly and sat without comment in her seat. Eventually, the authorities evicted the girls from the train and the worker accompanied them. The event was treated as a great joke even though the trip itself was aborted and the group returned home due to lack of funds. I was excluded from discussion about the event as the bravado attitude prevailed.

The next day while we were eating cookies at the center, the whole episode was spontaneously reviewed. Judy remarked, quite somberly, that she imagined passengers thought they were girls on a trip from a "loony house." Nilda added, without laughter, "We all looked crazy—no wonder people stared." Comments ensued about various crazy people from the neighborhood and how they acted. The worker asked if they wanted people to think that about them. Carmen instantly replied no but that it was the worker's fault because she hadn't screamed at them and made them stop.

I said I hadn't thought I was a policeman to go around watching how they behave, and that they were always telling me how much they didn't like their teachers bossing them around so much. Nilda said I could be in some ways like a teacher. Judy agreed—to tell them to sit down. I said that I was willing to remind them to sit down if they wanted me to, but also asked them if they thought it would really stop them. Tata led the general response that no one could stop them when they got going "like that." I said that I thought one of the hardest things for anyone to learn in life was to act the way they really wanted. There was silence. Nilda said, "I feel funny on the subway, people stare!"

The group members immediately ended the discussion and rushed into other activities. But as the mirror was held up, it had been looked into, and things would never be as simple again. The worker had introduced the idea of how hard it is to obtain desired personal outcome—the message was also a challenge to work rather than simply establishing blame.

Exploration of behavior with preadolescent girls living in stressful socioeconomic conditions often accompanying racial or cultural minority status could feel like a double exposure. Not only were they feeling the self-consciousness that accompanies the change from childhood to early adolescence, but they had to deal with the very powerful impact of being identified by society as "different." Interpreting and reacting to this difference seemed always a part of their attempts to define themselves and their relationship to this outsider, the worker, whom they saw as belonging to the mainstream of society.

The impetus of the girls toward growth and change was strong and strengthened by the bond of the group. What was fascinating was the way in which the themes of work merged together. The negotiating with the adult authority continued, but took on new dimensions as trust deepened. Self-exploration surfaced around not only increasingly threatening areas but around subjects which were seldom talked about with this population.

One of the first things that came up was a discussion of cursing, raised at a Christmas party. Judy said she wondered what their mothers thought of the worker when she let them curse in front of her. Everyone seemed in agreement that I should be "teaching" them good things and that teachers at school would never let them curse. I responded by saying that if everyone else, like teachers and so on, was teaching them all these things, they did not need me to do it. There was some engagement around what cursing meant to them, how "everyone always said that anyway" when they were angry. (The "everyone" referred to people on the block and in the area.) This particular meeting was ended by Margarita concluding that the worker really didn't want them to curse, and they should do it no more around the center.

The worker consistently continued clarifying her role and purpose. She gave legitimacy to subjects relating to discussion of behavior and feelings toward societal authority figures. She understood and accepted the girls' ambivalent feelings.

By the end of the summer the girls were meeting twice a week in the center after school.

On day Tata and Kathy seemed upset because they did not have a certain kind of ball. They ran around awhile, then lay down on the table laughing and chanting, "We hate (substitute name)." Everyone's name in the center was mentioned except the worker's. She sat saying nothing, and gradually the "I hate" started to include gestures toward her. After fifteen minutes Tata looked at her and said, "Well?" The worker knew what Tata meant—What was she going to do? I told her that I really didn't know what to say to them, since they seemed to be angry and mad, and that I wasn't sure if they wanted me to say anything about it. Kathy said they were mad, and Tata agreed. I said I could see this and asked them if they knew what it was they were so mad at. Kathy said yes, but that they weren't going to tell her. She went on, "Why should we always tell you everything, you never tell us your personal life." The worker responded "No, I don't, and I guess that makes you feel bad." Kathy asserted that it did and then asked why the worker wanted to know anyway. I said that the reason I wanted to know was because their being so mad today seemed to have stopped them from doing anything. Tata said that they didn't want to play anyway, and I remarked that this was unusual, since they usually liked to play.

I said that they really didn't have to find a thing to say that they were mad at—maybe it made them mad to feel both hate and liking for someone. This was too much and again they began laughing and chanting that she knew who it was they really hated, and that it was her. Margarita stayed in the club room and showed her disapproval of Tata and Kathy by saying, "You should respect Carol" (the worker) and by suggesting to Carol that she should make them respect her. The worker replied that she really was more interested in what they were feeling, even if those feelings were hard to talk about. Kathy shouted, "And don't think we respect our teachers just because we're polite to them, 'cause we don't. We don't like any grown-up people."

The worker sought out the underlying ambivalence usually felt toward authority figures at this stage of development but which was intensified with a population who felt excluded from society in so many ways. The response from the girls in the group was an expression of this ambivalence. The worker's intervention was one of the strongest statements she would ever make to facilitate work on developmental issues—she was more interested in what they were feeling than in making them respect her. No matter how threatening or difficult it was to talk about something, she would try to help.

Verbally Exploring Taboo Concerns

This intervention lent the group a specific tool for addressing their issues of concern: experience and support in talking about subjects which were usually not addressed verbally. This tool was particularly significant, since the girls' environment presented a dearth of socially acceptable opportunities to explore feelings and attitudes verbally. In the group context they felt less self-conscious about experimenting with verbal (group) discussions and in helping each other to articulate confusing and threatening feelings. Drawing on the support of the worker and each other, more taboo subjects started to be approached.

As the girls were returning from swimming, Carmen remarked that she was so tired she felt "old enough to be a mother." When I inquired how old she thought this was, Carmen replied that she didn't know, but that it had to be older than they were. Judy laughed, saying that wasn't true because since she had "started" a few months ago, she had stopped "fooling around with boys." I said that any time after a girl started her period, she was able to have a baby. Several girls exclaimed uncomfortably at this, and Tata told her that she shouldn't "say it." When I asked them if it was my talking about a girl's period that upset them, Tata started jumping around exclaiming, "What you said, what you said!" The others imitated her, and the conversation ended for that time.

When they were back in the center, I asked them why they had been so upset before on the street. The president, addressing the worker in great seriousness, said that she had almost called a policeman. To the inquiry of why, she replied that people weren't allowed to talk about things like that, and he would have stopped it. Another girl added that they were too young to know about babies and that the worker shouldn't be "giving them advice on them." As if to make the final point, Tata added that if her mother knew they talked about things like that in the club, she would take her out of it immediately. The others seemed to agree with this immediately, and when I asked if they ever had seen any movies on menstruation at school or talked about it in health class, I received the same negative answer, and again the comment from someone that her mother would take her out of school if such a thing happened.

As a natural consequence of self-exploration, the girls had plunged headlong into a taboo area—sex. The fact that sex-

ual identity and a need for information was of central developmental concern did not alter the fact that family and cultural restraints on the expression of sexual interest were firm. The worker could only allow the girls to set the pace for further discussion and give them sanction and support for entering taboo areas.

References to sex took the form of third-person jokes, fantasies, or spontaneous remarks for several months. The worker was asked nothing directly and not included in the interaction. She remarked occasionally that there seemed to be interest in the subject of sex. This was always denied.

One afternoon the girls rushed into the center saying how upset they had been at school that day. Tata began shouting that they had been talking about "periods and that stuff" at school and added that they had called it "hygiene, or something." (This was said in a disgusting tone as if to indicate "hygiene" was a coverup.) I replied that I had noticed that they got upset when they talked about periods or sex.

Tata explained the health class further, saying the teacher had asked fresh things like who had their period. She had said the eggs turned to blood and came out of them, but not to look for them because they were too small to see. I said that I didn't think the egg exactly turned to blood, but that it came out of you and after that the blood came. Judy said that's what the teacher had said, and the worker suggested that it must be hard to understand just what the nurse was saying, especially if they felt upset about her even talking about it.

Kathy asked if it were true that we had eggs inside of us. I replied that they were inside of every girl, and that when she got her period, this meant the egg came out of you, once a month, since it wasn't going to grow into a baby. Kathy said she (the teacher) has said it was where a baby came from, and I agreed with this, saying it was terribly small like a little seed, but that the baby started from that.

Tata said she had never known this, and Judy said that was why you had to stop fooling around with boys when you got your period. The worker didn't reply. Lydia declared emphatically that she knew the boys were listening at the door when the teacher asked those fresh questions. Margarita said that in her school they had the same kind of meeting with the girls, and the nurse had said not to be embarrassed about it, but that if they got their period, they should come and ask for "a-a-a-I think she said a sanitary napkin or something." (Seemed to be a lack of understanding of what this was.) Tata replied that their nurse had said not to be shy either, and I asked if this stopped anyone from being shy. Everyone laughed, saying they weren't going to talk about "those things." I asked if there had been a question time when they could ask questions about sex. Judy replied, "Hell, yes, but who's going to open their big mouth?" Again laughter. I said that it must be very hard for them, since probably, like most girls, they had questions they wanted to ask but they couldn't do it there.

Tata said, "Why can't you answer our questions?" Cautioned by their previous reactions, the worker replied that she remembered having brought up a discussion before with them in the summer about periods and babies, and they were so upset that they wanted to call a cop. This produced some smiles of recollection. Tata explained the situation by saying, "Well, it's because we were younger then." I replied, "Oh," and said that I felt that they should know about it, if they wanted to, and that was her feeling. Margarita said she thought girls should know, too, especially after they had their periods.

Working Through Sexual Issues

The worker, at last, could be very active as the girls tackled the subject. She gave information, clarified misconceptions, helped find comfortable words to use, acknowledged the anxiety around the subject, supported the girls around the risk of talking about a taboo subject, and always accepted the level and speed at which the work could progress.

Timing was crucial. Any response to the question, "Why can't you answer our questions?" which shifted control from the girls' pace to the worker's preconceived idea of how the discussion should proceed might have stopped the action. The correct timing involved remembering and using everything she had experienced and learned about this group and how the mutual aid process operated with this population. The girls worked together to solve a problem around gaining sex-related information and expressing feelings related to the subject. The worker intervened in supplementary ways, with her responses attuned to their natural helping efforts which were reflected in such responses as the rationale which made it permissible now to discuss sex: "We were younger then." This rationale possessed a wisdom far beyond the girls' years, and yet was uniquely within their framework and culture. The work continued moving further into the even more threatening topics of babies and rape.

Tata asked again if Carol was sure you couldn't have a baby before you had your period, and I replied yes, I was sure. Tata said that when she was a little girl, she had gone into the hall to get something and that some strange man had talked to her nicely, then he "took" her right there, and she didn't even know what it was all about. I said she must have been very scared, and she replied that she cried and cried, and her mother tried to arrest him, but he had run away. Margarita said that at least she couldn't have a baby, and Tata said, no, that she didn't have her period. In fact, she didn't know why she didn't even have it yet. Lydia shouted hadn't she even heard what the nurse had said—it comes anywhere between ten and sixteen or seventeen. There was some discussion of who started when, and so on. Judy said the worker must remember when she started, in the summer, as she came to the center that day, and I said that I did remember. Judy added that if she "fooled around" after that time, she would be able to have a baby. Judy said she still wanted to know how babies came, and before I could respond, everyone started screaming at her. Tata said she didn't know why Judy was always talking about those things—babies and periods. Everyone chimed in on this. Lydia didn't know why she had brought it up in the first place, and Kathy ridiculed her for thinking kissing made babies.

The worker had a feeling that this was the moment and raising her voice in a louder scream than all of theirs, she shouted, "Maybe it's that everyone has this question and only Judy is brave enough to say it." Her words created immediate silence, everyone looking at each other. Kathy responded quietly, "Well, I brought it up anyway; I asked if we really had eggs." Margarita added, "There is no reason why girls shouldn't know." (She had said this before). I said, "No, there isn't any reason why you shouldn't know, although I do remember your saying your mothers would take you out of the center if they knew you talked about it." Margarita smiled, "And who tells their mother everything?" Everyone laughed.

The worker reframed Judy's continued pressing for information about sex as bravery and acknowledged the appropriateness of their curiosity on the subject. The girls were deep into the discussion, but checking that the pace was not moving faster than they could handle, the worker reminded the group of the parental censorship on the subject of sex. Margarita's response of, "Who tells mother everything?" was perfect, as once again the preadolescents chose their own age-appropriate explanations to help them keep working. The laughter broke the ice; it also told the worker she was a part of their more private and intimate thinking and that the discussion could continue.

Kathy, Lydia, and Margarita left the room (for a drink of water?) leaving Noemi, Tata, and Judy. Judy turned to the worker and said, "Well, Carol, I still want to know—if a guy starts messing around with me and does me wrong, I'll get a baby, won't I?" I said that it depended on what she meant by messing around, and Judy said it was F (pronouncing the letter). I said that people used F to mean different things and that maybe I should just tell her what happened between two people to make a baby. She said yes.

I said that they knew a man had a thing on his body, and asked Judy what word she used for it. She said a "dick," and I said that in books it was usually called a penis, but that I wanted to talk so they would understand me. Judy said she hadn't heard the other word—they called it dick, and they began laughing. The worker asked Tata if they were laughing because it was strange to hear about, and she said no—that some men were named Dick and that when they heard the name, they thought of the other thing. I said oh and continued. I said that when a man put his dick inside of a woman, he became very excited and that some white stuff comes out. When the white stuff meets the egg that they had been talking about before, it made the egg start to be a life and that from that moment it began growing into a baby.

Judy said, "That's all?" and I replied that this was the main thing that happened. Tata asked if anything else could make you pregnant, and I replied no, not kissing, hugging, grinding, or a boy touching or putting his fingers into you. Tata shouted, "What did you say? Fingers could do it?" Judy explained, "No, nothing but the dick, right, Carol?" I replied "Right." Tata asked if the boy was going to the bathroom, and I replied that was why I said it was kind of white stuff because it wasn't like going to the bathroom, that this was special stuff which was the only thing that could join with an egg to make a baby.

Kathy, Lydia, and Margarita returned —there hadn't been laughing until they arrived; then Tata and Judy started, "Oh, guess what Carol is telling us, she is telling us about babies," in a chanting fashion. Margarita closed the door, and I said that I had been telling them what happens to make a baby, and Judy said, "Fingers can't do it, either." Kathy said she wanted to know, and Judy said "Tell it again, Carol, like you did."

I repeated the explanation as before—everyone was more relaxed and listened intently. Kathy asked why each contact didn't result in a baby, and Judy asked the purpose of the monthly bleeding. The questions were answered, and they continued.

Lydia asked if the white stuff was "scum," and I said it was called that sometimes too. Kathy asked why a guy's "dick" had a rubber thing on it sometimes. I replied that guys put them on sometimes in order to have less chance to have a baby, because then when the white stuff came out, it stayed inside of the rubber thing and didn't meet with the egg inside of the woman. Judy added that only when they met did a baby start, and I said yes. Tata asked why the rubber thing didn't work all the time, and I said that sometimes it broke and then the stuff came out. Lydia asked how she knew all about it. Judy replied that Carol had a fiancé, and Tata said, "You haven't slept with him, or have you, Carol?" The worker replied. "I remember from last week that you felt mad when you couldn't know more about my personal life, but I don't think it really matters here whether I sleep with him or not. There are lots of ways to find things out about sex—the hard thing is to talk about it. As a matter of fact, you are always asking me what I have to learn to be a social worker, and one of the things they try to teach us is how to help people talk about things, like sex, that are usually hard to talk about!"

The discussion had taken close to two hours and broke up with a game requiring physical activity and contact.

The worker had helped the girls to feel secure enough in a taboo area to gain information which was vital to their stage of development. Within the supportive context of the group an important educational function had been performed by the worker. The restraint of the taboo was broken through by legitimizing the desire for information and for labeling it as normal. This was only possible when trust had been established between the girls and the worker (a "stranger" representing broader societal sanctions). Timing, as always, was pivotal, because only at this point could the worker's support be accepted and the real questions arising out of the girls' curiosity be asked. It is only when real questions surface that they can be answered. The answer can only be heard when fear doesn't deafen the response.

The girls had always shared intimately with each other, fiercely reacting and responding to pent-up emotions and feelings. With the entrance of a nonjudgmental worker into their inner world they gained access to additional help besides each other in dealing with their feelings.

Confronting Racial Differences

Sexual interest was indeed a strong taboo, but it paled in light of the emerging recognition and fight against the implications of racial minority status. Developmentally the girls needed to experience success and accomplishments. Coinciding with this need was the increasing impact of racial and cultural stereotyping on their lives. The worker had no greater area of strain than was experienced in helping elicit real emotions and feelings around racial concerns, largely because it was inevitable that such tensions be expressed to her personally.

The pattern was similar to other emotionally stressful areas; tentative and superficial exploration of the subject expressed indirectly in front of the worker but not involving her. Worker response at this stage was important—it was a time for observation, restraint, and identification of patterns, as shown in the following three excerpts.

On a summer trip to the swimming pool we were changing from our bathing suits into clothes when Noemi (a Puerto Rican group member) came running into the dressing room screaming and crying. She reported that she had been out in the hall looking for the front door when "a black man" had started following her and, frightened that he was going to grab her, she had come racing back to the rest of us. She ignored any questions I asked about the episode and in a few minutes was fooling around with the other girls as if nothing had happened.

For a brief period in the fall, the girls joined a "Y" out of their neighborhood, in a predominantly white area. There was frequent conversation among themselves about the other girls in attendance there. Margarita had mentioned how boring our club was compared to the "Y." There was general agreement on this, and Noemi started describing how many pretty girls she had seen, how many blondes with "eyes like in the books." Tata said she thought she was pretty "smart" to be going there, and again several voices indicated agreement. Judy, one of the black girls in the group, proudly described the ballet class, adding casually that she was the only "colored" girl there. Then glancing nervously at me, she left for a drink of water.

I was walking unnoticed behind Kathy, the darkest girl in the club and Lydia, a light-skinned blonde girl, as they left the pool. Lydia asked Kathy if she could borrow her hair brush, and Kathy handed it to her. Lydia started combing her hair, then stopped to pull out the little pieces of black hair which were stuck in the brush. Kathy watched silently while Lydia struggled in vain to fix the brush to her liking, and then handed it back saying, "Thanks anyway." Kathy looked at this brush and asked, "Was it dirty?" Lydia nodded yes and then ran to join the other girls, shouting at Kathy to "come on." Kathy continued walking alone, hitting her leg with her brush as she walked.

The most common form of interaction around ethnicity or race was in the form of insults hurled at each other, and any girl in anger would scream "dirty nigger," "spic," or "black bastard" to any other girl in the club. One afternoon when Tata was particularly vexed with the worker, she thrust her arm in the worker's face and pointing to her own skin she shouted, "I'm glad you're whiter than I am."

The worker had originally been an authority to be negotiated, a stranger representing adulthood and wider society. As the group members gained strength from successfully negotiating one small part of this outside world and in making sense out of some of their behavior and feelings, a deeper level of their original lack of trust emerged. The worker represented the white, middle-class world, the world of teachers, policemen, nurses, dentists, and "directors" of society. The girls clearly felt not only themselves but their families were excluded from an effective and active role in the community. The avenue of resentment was directed toward each other and eventually included the worker.

The intervention was a difficult one— it was not to respond to the girls' derogatory remarks or insults about race and not to interfere in their conversations with each other on the subject. Gradually, they began to be less self-conscious and to stop glancing up nervously whenever a derogatory remark was made about "guineas," "paddies," or "niggers." A deliberate choice was made not to use these opportunities to teach a preferred approach to racial differences, but to wait until an opening presented itself where the energy of group members was directed toward working on the issue.

One afternoon Judy and Tata came first to the center and into the club room where I was sitting. They were laughing and after a few minutes of fooling around Tata started telling me about a lady who had "called down" Judy. She stopped and asked Judy if it was all right to tell me. Judy nodded consent. Tata continued about a "guinea" lady on the street who had passed them and called Judy something. They couldn't remember the name but it was "something blackie." Judy said she didn't even know what name it was but that she had told her teacher, and he had tried to look serious but then laughed when he turned away. They were laughing loudly this whole time, and I remarked on their laughter, saying it sounded to me as if what the lady had said would make Judy feel bad—not like laughing. Judy responded that she didn't laugh at that old guinea, that she had called her down right back. She included some of the insults. I told Judy that I thought she probably felt mad and hurt by this lady. Judy replied that she had been told she had knots in her hair, and added that she didn't want straight old hair anyway. I said that I didn't think anyone liked being called names and I was sorry she had been hurt. Judy looked surprised and asked me if I thought her hair, which was always very neat, looked nice. I replied yes but that I doubted if that would help her feel better about the insults she had received.

The other girls had started to arrive and had been listening carefully. Tata rushed in at this point again laughing and making jokes and the subject was changed. But the ice had been broken, more raw feelings had been presented directly to the worker, allowing for her recognition of their impact and her sharing in their pain. It became more acceptable to say angry things about white people in general, but it was Kathy, a black girl, who was very popular in the group, who first related this general anger specifically to the worker.

One day Kathy was continually hitting a little six-year-old girl, who was waiting in the center, on the head. I insisted that she stop, and she started calling me "white trouble," saying she wouldn't stop. Several of the others gasped at this and tried to hush Kathy. I replied that I was sure I did seem like "white trouble" to her right now but that I wanted her to stop hitting the little girl.

On another occasion several of the girls were talking about which pool they liked best, and Noemi asked me my preference. I gave my opinion, and Kathy jumped on the answer saying of course I liked that one since "all the guineas went there." Again the others looked worried about her remark, and Noemi tried to reassure me that she liked that pool also. I replied that I didn't blame Kathy for saying what she had, since white people often did not like to swim with black people and likely they weren't sure about my reasons.

One afternoon six months after the club had started the girls became very upset when they could only find a golf ball to take to the park. When I did not agree to give them the money for a new ball, Kathy and Tata started shouting that I was "cheap," gradually changing this to "cheap white." When I asked if they thought I didn't like them when I didn't give them something, they both replied that I "couldn't" like them. Both Tata and Kathy went through a whole hour of "hating" me, following the above episode, but even in the anger of that moment they couldn't seem to relate their hatred directly to my color or their own but instead alluded to it through subtle remarks and insults.

As the intensity of feelings around the subject increased, the worker focused on the feelings behind the accusations rather than responding to or defending herself from attacks.

This approach was carried out when the attacks were toward her or other group members. She was aware of the fact that all group members were deeply identified with the content of interactions on this subject, as evidenced by their intense concentration.

I'm not sure exactly how it started, but Kathy asked me for something I couldn't give her (potato chips, I believe) and then shouted I was "no good." Tata said the whole club was no good and that they were never given anything around here. I told Kathy that I was sorry because I knew she always got upset when I couldn't give her something she wanted. She responded, "Shut up!" Judy remarked that you couldn't do anything with white people anyway, and Kathy agreed, saying none of them were any good, they were cheap and never gave you anything. I opened my mouth, and Kathy shouted, "Shut up, you white cracker." She looked surprised herself at the remark, and I mentioned this to her. Kathy just called me a "white cracker" and repeated this over and over.

During my talk with Kathy, Tata had begun laughing and continued doing so, pointing to Lydia. She motioned to Kathy who apparently caught on immediately and joined her in the laughter. Lydia looked embarrassed and told them to stop. Tata continued laughing, Noemi and Rosa imitated her. Their laughter intensified as she told the story of "a girl" at school who had arrived in the morning with a dirty line around her neck. The point was that she had apparently washed only her face and not her neck. It was not mentioned who this girl was although there was increased laughter and pointing at Lydia. Finally Lydia jumped up and shouted, "It wasn't me, you know." Immediately Tata and Kathy began shouting that it was her and that she knew it was and that she was "dirty" and didn't wash, etc. Lydia was becoming increasingly upset and exasperated, and in desperation turned to me on the verge of tears insisting, "It wasn't me, Carol, it was another girl. I never did such a thing." I said it didn't seem like such a big deal anyway whether someone forgot to wash their neck. Tata screamed, "Well, it left a line around her neck, that's why."

I sensed there was something much deeper behind this and looking at Tata replied, "Maybe what you're really saying is that because Lydia is a lighter color, the line showed more." Tata just stared, Kathy jumped up shouting, "White bastard, that's a white bastard for you. Shut up, you white cracker box."

I replied to Kathy that she should know by now that I was not very good at shutting up.

Yvette, one of the quieter group members, said she thought the others were mean to Lydia "for no reason." Tata became quite serious and explained she did have a reason, since Lydia had previously insulted her. Noemi, Judy, and Rosa said they hadn't meant to hurt Lydia. The girls started to talk pulling their chairs spontaneously together in a circle. The discussion centered on asking each other about being black or Puerto Rican, which names were most insulting, and how much color differences were noticed and used against them. The conversation was serious, the girls deeply involved in it, and the circle drew closer and closer. The session ended with the conversation again reverting to the worker when Yvette reminded everyone how they had asked the Bingo man at Coney Island to announce that I was a "cheap white." After general laughter Noemi quickly added, "But we were only kidding," to which they all strongly gave accord. Tata summed up the afternoon by emphatically proclaiming to the girls, "Well, Carol always said we could get mad at her!" Then shifting her glance nervously added, "Right, Carol?"

The subject of racial tensions and confusions began to move into the domain of things that could be talked about with the worker. The group's taboo against it turned to a group norm in support of sharing feelings. More dramatically than with other subject areas, the worker faced the dilemma of being perceived as too lenient in her responses for not establishing and enforcing codes of behavior and language which were more socially acceptable. Certainly the girls expected this role and continually tried to provoke a more familiar response.

The worker's decision to not respond to the girls' interactions, negative or positive, in relation to racial attitudes was based on an awareness that at this stage of development they were ready to examine attitudes which had been handed to them by various influences and were in the process of being accepted as their own. Younger children are more directly influenced by role modeling and respond to the security of tighter boundaries. Adolescents have moved even further from direct adult influence, and carry out their struggle for autonomy in relation to the thoughts, ideas, and codes of their peers. The preadolescent stands in between, a child still wanting and reaching for adult involvement while at the same time experiencing a strong pull to break away from earlier adult controls. Most typically, the adult feels and responds to the first part of this duality expressed by the preadolescent and treats them in a way that would be successful with a younger child. The effect is often the opposite of what is intended when in response the preadolescent gains impetus for turning away from adults and leans more exclusively on peers for help with the task of sorting through and selecting attitudes, values, and self-concepts.

The worker observed from the beginning that the girls were very verbal with each other. Her focus was to become a part of the conversations where threatening topics were discussed. In terms of racial and ethnic issues there was no way to smooth the hurt. There was no way to avoid their real confusion—a rejection of and identification with the same attitudes. This was not necessarily a permanent state, for many future influences and experiences would undoubtedly shape and contribute to new identifications. But for the moment, it was painful and confusing, and as with anyone who deeply feels a hurt that cannot be removed, the worker's most important job was to stand close and help the client know that she had been understood.

At Coney Island Judy and I were standing alone while the others were on a ride. Judy asked if we were going to the beach, and I said I thought so if they all wanted to go. Judy said she couldn't understand why some people wanted to get tans. She looked up at me pointing to her skin, "You know, most colored people would like to take their color away," and she laughed as if it were the funniest joke. I didn't laugh or say anthing, and she added, "It really isn't so pretty." I replied, "On you it looks good, Judy." "No," she answered, "black don't look good on nobody." She didn't move away as I had expected but just stood beside me, now with a perfectly serious face. She seemed to have expressed so directly and with such feeling the essence of this whole issue and struggle. I felt very moved by her words and said, "I guess it is easy for me to say that just standing here looking at you. But the hard part is to know what you are really feeling like inside your skin." We were interrupted by everyone rushing back, screaming from the ride and with them I began gathering up things to move to another place. As we started walking along, Judy slipped her arm through mine.

Understanding and reflecting that understanding in a way that can be accepted by a preadolescent requires a constant interpretation of what is happening and what feelings are being expressed. In terms of racial attitudes, ambivalence can often cause great unrest and anxiety.

One afternoon, Tata, Noemi, and Elisa sat down to do homework, but Kathy started knocking things off the table. When I asked if she had something she wanted me to help her with, she shouted that she was leaving now. I said I thought she had seemed pretty restless all afternoon, and she replied that she was sick of this center. The other three were working at a table and ignoring her. Kathy put on her coat and started for the door, then returned and knocked over chairs by the door.

When she didn't stop in a few minutes, I went over and asked her to stop, since kids from our club and the other clubs were doing homework. She shouted, "Shut up, white cracker," and I suggested that since she didn't feel like going, that she at least come and sit down. She sat down at the table saying something about white people and how they were no good and always making trouble, and without stopping she just continued along in that vein. I said that I had a pretty good idea about some of the things she felt about white people but that I didn't really think she felt just this way about me. She shouted that she did, started for the door, knocked over a few chairs, and returned continuing along the same lines.

Noemi told her to shut up, and Kathy lowered her voice. She said she knows what happened to me, anyway, that when I was being baptized, they had dipped me into white paint by mistake, thinking it was water. We both started laughing at this, and Kathy added, "You're really black, just black, painted white." She seemed to be afraid to stop talking and continued without ceasing about how this "accident" had happened to me, and how it was going to wash off in the rain or she was going to wash it off. I tried to answer her and said, "Maybe, Kathy, you would really like to think that I was black because you like me."

She stopped laughing and replied, "But my people don't like your people!" There was a silence, then returning to her former tone, she started again about white bastards and how they couldn't be trusted, etc.

I said that I thought she had a problem. She asked, "What problem do I have?" I said that I thought she liked me but was afraid, in case she wasn't supposed to or because she'd always thought white people were the same. She immediately shouted they were "all the same, all those crackers were bastards," then she stopped and looked at me. I said I still thought she was at least thinking it all over and that it was going to be pretty hard for her to figure it out.

She left for a drink of water and returned, asking quietly if she could have her two cookies, since she'd missed them before. I got her the cookies and said I'd see her Thursday. She calmly and casually replied, "Yeah, see you Thursday. Bye." As if nothing had happened, she went out the door.

Only after clear bonds of affection had developed, could the worker risk this level of interpretation and confrontation. It had taken eight to ten months of contact in various degrees of intimacy to feel secure in a judgment of the girls' feelings. But the bond had been formed, the affection was strong, and the group had experienced using a worker, in addition to each other, to find their way through the maze of preadolescent emotions pertaining to racial attitudes.

Saying Goodbye—Termination

No emotion catches one as unaware as the feelings associated with loss. The worker's resignation to marry and move away introduced all the realities of grief to this group of girls. It is evidence of their stage of development that they experienced the loss acutely—they had loved another outside of themselves and realized the implications in that person's leaving. It is evidence of the strength of the mutual aid process, as fostered by the worker, that the group moved through the termination process with awareness and self-disclosure, eventually making the connection to a new worker.

Five months before her departure the worker introduced the fact that she would be leaving at the end of summer. The reaction was anger and disengagement, a message that the information had been heard but could not yet be accepted.

Judy asked if I was going away when I was married. I replied yes, that I would be living in Puerto Rico. Tata insisted that she didn't see why I had to leave; after all, Shirley, the center's secretary, was married . . . lived in New York. Rosa said it was because Shirley's husband was here. Noemi asked why mine couldn't stay here, too. I answered that he was in school, and there were questions about why he couldn't change and move here.

Finally Noemi said brightly that she might go to Puerto Rico for a visit, and Tata shouted, "I don't ever want to go to Puerto Rico just to see you!"

I said that I couldn't blame her or any of them for being mad when I had helped them make a club, had taken them places, and had lots of fun with them. Maybe they were even getting to like me, and now I was getting married and moving away. I added I thought anyone would hurt at this.

There was surprise and no one spoke for a few minutes.

Then Carmen asked if I would be here for the summer, and I answered that I would be for most of it and it was still a long time away. This seemed to bring general relief and agreement, and the conversation ended with Noemi demanding they all be invited to the wedding.

The worker acknowledged the hurt that was embodied in Tata's anger, recognizing the loss which the girls instantly felt in relation to the "fun" they had shared together, and with her. But she did not push them to talk about how they were feeling. The impact of the shock associated with the news meant that the girls needed time to retreat, to speak with each other, and to put space between the news and themselves. The worker knew that the news was heard and that the subject would be raised again.

A few weeks later I was walking the girls home when Noemi and Tata started to complain that I "never" came to their houses any more. I remarked that they had been saying this a lot lately and asked if they were worried about something. Tata asked why the club couldn't meet on Saturdays and Sundays. I answered that maybe even if we met every day, it wouldn't seem enough and that maybe they were really worried about my leaving in the summer. There was no response.

The worker expected that feelings about her leaving might be raised indirectly, and she related one concern of the girls to the possible deeper issue of termination. The fact that they didn't overtly agree with her is not as important as the message she had given them that she realized they must feel bad about the event and that she cared. For leaving is associated with not caring, and whether or not they were loved permeated the girls' concern over the next few months.

The girls continued insisting that I loved my fiancé more than them. I said I wonder if what they were really asking was if I could love him *and* love them. Tata replied, "Don't tell me you do!" I said, "Yes, Tata, I do," and she responded "Huh." Noemi questioned how I could know such a thing, indicating that I couldn't. I told her that I thought people got a feeling when they started to feel love for someone else and this feeling could tell them when they liked someone or someone liked them.

Kathy commented on that time when they had said how much they "hated" me in the other room. I replied "Oh, well, I don't mean that when you love a person, it doesn't mean you can't feel mad at them or hate them too."

The discussion diverted at this point to talking about the paradox of loving and hating, particularly mothers. The worker ended by pointing out how hard it is many times, to know what you really feel.

The intervention here was to lay the groundwork for the gradual unraveling of the complexities of saying good-bye. The worker did state that she loved them for the first time using the word directly but also acknowledged the anger of "hate" that someone can feel for the same person who is loved. The agony in termination is exactly that issue, the experiencing of affection and anger for someone at the same time. The girls are once again not asked what they are feeling, but rather given the message that it is hard to sort out feelings of such intensity.

For several months the subject of "the leaving" was not mentioned, but as summer drew nearer, it again surfaced in the form of behavior indicative of the beginning stage of the group's development.

Walking back from the bus, I noticed again what had frequently been happening lately: the girls were very "busy" talking to themselves and teasing each other, and although it looked as if we were together, I was quite obviously apart. At one point, they actually walked in front of me, laughing over some joke, while I walked behind alone.

This had essentially not happened for a year, and I felt much as I had then—isolated from them. It made me very sad, a feeling that must have reflected in my face, for suddenly Judy "noticed" I was walking alone and came and took my arm condescendingly. Tata's response was, "Shit on her," at which she, Judy, Carmen, and Kathy laughed hysterically.

When we were eating in the center, I said that I thought they had seemed kind of unhappy with me lately and asked if they wanted to talk about it. Kathy said they weren't unhappy about *anything*. I asked, "Even about my leaving in the summer?" Tata jumped up and shouted, "Nobody gives a shit about your leaving. Go ahead and leave now if you want to!" There were tears in her eyes as she spoke.

I replied I really didn't think she meant that. Kathy interrupted, jumping up, raising her hand and shouting with authority, "We are not talking about this anymore!"

This time the worker was trying to reach for more direct involvement to interpret the actions via the feelings they represent. The girls were not ready, and when Kathy insisted that they were not talking about "this" anymore, the worker conformed to their wishes. Shortly after that afternoon, the anger surfaced again.

We were playing tag until I ran into a table and hurt my leg. Tata immediately began remarking how stupid I was and how my "husband" would be so mad he wouldn't let me come to the center again. I said I thought I'd live without too much trouble, but she continued along this line. I replied that I thought maybe *she* was the one who was mad at *him*. She answered that she couldn't care less about him, that he could marry me tomorrow and take me away, for all she cared. I answered that I thought it was very hard to have someone leave when you didn't want her to, and that I could really understand if she felt mad. She responded, "Huh" and walked away mumbling, "I don't know why you always talk that way!"

The worker again indicated that anger was an understandable response to her leaving. She accepted the verbal and nonverbal expressions of anger as appropriate to the occasion. The girls had developed a joke about her over the year, telling her that she didn't "talk" like other people. They would, at times, imitate her with each other. They recognized her response as distinctively hers and as connected to her being a social worker. Tata's reference to not knowing why she talks "that way" was deeply affectionate.

The group members continued indirect references to the worker's leaving and appeared uninterested in the new worker, Joanne.

Nilda asked me again why we were having club only three days a week. I replied that I knew it was hard for them, but that I had many things to finish before I left and needed two days a week to do them. As soon as I mentioned leaving, Nilda turned away and started looking at pictures on the bulletin board. She asked if it would be the same all fall, and I said she'd have to check again with Joanne when she came. She asked, "Who's Joanne?" and I answered that she was the social worker who was taking my place. Nilda turned from the board, insisting emphatically, "Carol, we don't talk about *her*!" I replied that I had noticed this and guessed that it must be pretty hard for them to talk about her. Nilda hurried from the room saying it was her turn to give out the cookies.

Again, the worker identified how difficult these feelings were to discuss. She opened opportunities and waited for a response. A group discussion was too anxiety-provoking, but individual group members cautiously approached the subject while others listened.

As Lydia and I were walking slightly apart from the others, she asked when the club would end. I said I didn't think it was ending as far as I knew and inquired if she was thinking about my leaving. She said she was wondering what would happen when I left. I told her another social worker was coming to take my place and that they could still have the club. Lydia responded, "But I may not like her." I nodded in agreement, and she went on to say that if she didn't like her, she wasn't coming to the club. I said I thought most of the girls felt this way and they would have time to see what they thought of her. She felt this was a good thing, since she didn't know how it would be. I added that they weren't too sure of me in the beginning and asked if she remembered how they didn't like to talk to me much when I first came but mostly whispered together. Lydia roared with laughter.

By this time the others had joined us, and the laughter increased. Spontaneously the girls began telling stories about the early club days— how "weird" I had seemed. One after another led off with another "Do you remember?" They described in minute detail a trip, a conversation, a party, a fight, or an episode. Even at this stage, after so much time together the girls surprised me with the total recall of so much of the worker's words, actions, and expression. Never lacking a sense of drama, they acted out with great flare different gestures and comments I had made months before. I ended the sessions with the comment, "A lot sure happened, and it's fun to remember." The smiles of satisfaction showed agreement.

The worker had initiated a looking back at past feelings and experience. She had linked Lydia's fear over a new "stranger" to the earlier fear of the worker. The tone of Lydia's comment was reflective and thus led naturally to remembering. This was an important influence in choosing an intervention aimed at reviewing the past, for both reflective moods and laughter are more conducive to reminiscing than emotions such as anger.

Having once gained the experience and pleasure of reviewing the past, the girls openly and frequently referred to events from the previous year. It was obvious that the girls did not want the club to end, that the impetus for planning for the future after the worker left was strong. Finally, only a few weeks before the new worker's arrival for introductions, the girls engaged in the first direct conversation with the worker around her leaving.

We were eating on the Coney Island Beach when suddenly Tata blurted out, "When is that other girl coming anyway?" I answered that it would be in the middle of August, in about a month. She shouted, "We are going to kick her ass!" I said that didn't surprise me. She added, "Well, you better tell her about us!"

Nilda asked me if I had seen her and talked to her. I replied that I'd seen her a few times. Tata asked if I'd told her about them. Kathy answered immediately, "Of course! What do you think they'd talk about?" I agreed with Kathy, saying Joanne had asked me about them and I'd said they might feel like kicking her ass at first but this didn't mean they wouldn't get to like her. Everyone laughed, and I said I was serious, that this was just what I'd told her. Judy asked me how tall she was, and I answered that she was a little taller than I am. Nilda exclaimed, "My God, another tall one," and asked if she was older than I. I replied, no, younger. Tata said she'd be too young to take care of them, and Judy asked how old she was. I said she was the same age as I was when we had started the club. She said, "Oh, that's all right."

Laura, who hadn't spoken until that point, said she didn't see why they had to have another girl. Everyone was quiet, and by this time the air was pretty heavy with gloom. I said that I kept wanting to say something to them about leaving, but nothing I could find to say seemed to make any of us feel any better. Judy was the only one who spoke, "Well, you can write to us." I said of course I would.

The worker had helped the girls to partialize their loss into pieces of emotion which could be faced in the singular. They had experienced and expressed the avoidance, denial, projection, and anger involved in grief and had these feelings accepted by the worker without judgment. Inevitably, the more poignant feelings of sadness began to emerge, and left on their own, they were clearly an essential aspect of saying good-bye.

Thus followed the saddest and yet closest of moments. The intensity of feelings increased as the time shortened, and gingerly the worker began to share some of her own emotion. This was done with caution because the girls were overwhelmed enough by their own concerns. What helped them was seeing their sadness mirrored in the person who had witnessed so much of their inner world.

The weekend before a scheduled meeting with the new worker, Joanne, the girls went on an overnight camping trip. A wonderful, carefree time was experienced until, exhausted, everyone piled on the bus. Only then did the mood change.

The girls relayed to Bill, the bus driver, everything that had happened with special emphasis on the terror experienced when a raccoon had frightened them at night. Then they sat down sleepily. I was sitting with Judy and overheard Noemi telling the others how I had held her when she was crying in her sleep. Kathy said that I had done this with everyone when they cried, and Tata said she had only been able to go back to sleep because I held her.

I told them I wanted them to feel good. Nilda asked, "Will you miss us a lot?" I answered, yes, that I would miss them and think of them a lot too.

Kathy said, "We're going to miss you so much." Judy put her head in my lap and cried.

I asked Kathy if she would write to me, and she shrugged. Noemi said she would. I told her I was sure Joanne would help her mail the letter. Norma asked, "Who's Joanne?" Laura answered slowly, "The new girl."

There was quiet.

Tata said, "She's coming Monday, right?" I nodded and everyone insisted it couldn't be so soon. Nilda asked me if I was sure. I said I was and that I had wanted to be with them to help them meet her and look her over because I knew it would be hard at first.

Noemi asked if she would really help them mail a letter to me. I answered that I was sure she would.

Monday, the long-anticipated day, finally arrived.

Joanne arrived at the center before the girls, and we had a few moments of apprehension and waiting. Tata came in, her first question being if "she had come." I replied yes and introduced them. Tata smiled (very politely) and stood close to me, holding my arm while looking Joanne over carefully. Joanne and I continued talking to give her a few minutes to do so quietly. She then interrupted us, asking if we were going to stand around talking all day or go over to pick up the other girls.

Walking over to their street, Tata walked between Joanne and me, talking mostly to Joanne. She began asking about her name, how to spell it, and say it, and where she had picked up such a funny one. From this she continued asking questions and talking easily and warmly to Joanne. I never remembered seeing her as open or moving out so quickly to a stranger; her approach to volunteer teachers had always been a period of initial insulting and ignoring. None of this occurred that first day with Joanne. From the beginning Tata seemed to feel comfortable with her.

Tata's reaction and response to Joanne was unprecedented, as her initial relationship with the worker had been honed through hostility, aggression, and mistrust. The worker had allowed expression of these feelings and encouraged talking about them individually and among group members. She had not tried to change feelings but acknowledged them as appropriate within the context of the life stage and environmental experience of the girls. Tata had accepted the emotional support of an outsider to both her family and peer system. She feared this "new stranger" less and, along with the other girls, she possessed negotiation skills, built on her relationship to the current worker as a beginning point for interacting with a new worker.

Noemi, Nilda, and Judy were waiting on the street. They were a little shyer with Joanne than Tata had been and tended to avoid conversation, but I think Tata's attitude had an effect on all of them. She continued acting as if having Joanne there was the most natural thing in the world. We walked to the pool, picking Kathy up on the way. There were some whispered comments and giggling behind our backs, but during most of the walk the girls were really just looking Joanne up and down; a few remarked on her height. Joanne didn't say much but responded to their questions and occasionally asked a few about the neighborhood or the pool. By and large, she was very quiet, just giving them the time to study her.

In the pool a series of comparisons started, when Noemi tried getting Joanne into the pool and Joanne hesitated because it was too cold. Tata shouted, "Just like Carol, doesn't like cold water," and they splashed her and coaxed her in which set everyone into fits of laughter. Judy wanted to know if Joanne had long hair,

too, and proceeded to take down Joanne's hair and examine it. It wasn't as long as mine, but it was fairly long, and Judy said that it would soon be "really long."

But the real excitement came when in a series of pointed and direct questions Tata asked Joanne if she could come on the rides with them at Coney Island. Joanne responded that she'd love to go with them to Coney Island, but not on the rides because they made her dizzy. "Just like Carol, just like Carol!" Tata started shouting in a mocking yet delighted tone. It was agreed by the rest that this was the ultimate and most striking coincidence, and Tata added, "But I suppose you won't mind the merry-go-round." Joanne agreed this would be just her speed. I was sure by this time that each of them was thoroughly convinced that at least women social workers didn't have the guts for real thrills at Coney Island. The similarities were so striking that by this time both Joanne and I found ourselves laughing as much as the girls. The example of the merry-go-round (the only ride I had ever gone on with them) was preserved as the classical one, and in the next week or so I would hear Tata and the others telling it to impress people with the like qualities of Joanne and me.

I told all the girls as we were standing in front of Noemi's house that I was glad today had gone pretty well because I knew they had been worried about it for a long time. Nilda said, "She's nice," with a big smile at Joanne. The others sort of smiled. Tata said she didn't know why all their social workers had to be tall.

The girls were looking for ways in which the workers were alike and had exaggerated external manifestations of similarities. The two workers also held similar beliefs about what they were there to help with and had spent considerable time planning for the transition. With myself, the term social worker had been a word with little concrete meaning. In meeting Joanne, the girls now had expectations related to professional function. They expected her to listen to them, to talk "that way" about behavior and emotions, and to be more related to what they were feeling than what they were doing. It was, of course, necessary to test out some of their assumptions, and the worker helped through this transitional phase.

Behavior in public had been fairly calm for most of the school year, but it was inevitable that the classic subway scene would be repeated for Joanne's benefit. I had a totally different response in this situation than previously, based on my relationship over time with the girls and my interpretation of the meaning of the behavior. On a trip to the beach, the girls were noisy and provocative as they walked to the subway.

Everyone got on the subway and the whole thing started again. This time with cursing at a man in another train who answered them back in the same tones. The train moved away and the running up and down continued much to the other passengers' annoyance. This didn't stop the girls who kept looking at Joanne and me, mostly Joanne, to see our reactions. We both didn't react too much, although it was obvious I wasn't pleased. Joanne's face was a little more noncommittal. I kept waiting for the girls to sit down, but they didn't, although I noticed they kept looking more and more frequently in my direction. After ten or fifteen minutes I got up and very authoritatively told everyone to sit down, which they did with little resistance. I said that they probably wanted to see what Joanne was going to do, and that she wasn't going to do anything, and that I didn't feel like having them make so much noise so they should sit still or we'd go back. They looked relieved and no one protested. Judy asked Joanne if she liked girls that acted like that, and Joanne replied she didn't dislike them because of the running around, etc. Nilda asked if she was mad. Joanne replied no, but that she could see how they might be worried about what she was thinking.

That was just about the end of the noisy behavior—it broke out now and then but in a very mild form.

The worker interpreted the girls' furtive glances as a request for an excuse to stop the behavior without losing face. She had learned (from them) how they felt about themselves in such situations, and once they had seen Joanne's reaction, they felt they would want to end the demonstration. Timing and interpretation are again crucial to the intervention. The behavior was not felt to have been primarily generated by anxiety, and, in addition, explorations of various behaviors by the girls among themselves and with the worker had given the worker tools for intervention that were not available earlier in the group's existence.

The worker's role continued right into the good-bye party, helping the girls to adjust to Joanne and fit her into their world.

Nilda came into the office while the others were getting the food ready, asking me to come and get some. When I got up she asked exactly when I was leaving. I explained the days to her. She said she hadn't realized it was so close. I said it did seem pretty close now, and I asked her how she liked Joanne. She repeated what she'd said Monday, "She's nice," but I noticed she was hesitating and asked, "What else?" She answered, "Well, you know what my mother and father say?" I replied that I didn't, and she explained that although they liked Joanne, they didn't think she was "one of us, like you are." I asked her if she thought it was because I spoke Spanish to her parents, and she said yes, and because I understood how they felt. She added that her mother felt good about this and let Nilda come with me. I told Nilda that I was glad her mother and father felt that way, because I did try to understand how they were feeling, but I asked her if she remembered the last summer when I started with the club. She said yes, why? and

I answered that I didn't think her parents felt right from the beginning that I was one of them and understood them. She started to protest, and then smiled as she started to remember her parents' negative attitudes to the club.

I said that it was too bad Joanne didn't know much Spanish yet, that I thought she did want to understand, and that maybe together they would find a way. Nilda said, "Maybe." I said I would never forget how much she (Nilda) had helped me in the beginning. Nilda grinned at this and remarked that I had needed a *lot* of help! Noemi and Judy came in to see what we were doing, and Nilda said we should go to eat.

The worker had tried to make the transition as easy as possible, and it had gone well. The girls were launched into a new helping relationship. The other part of leaving—the inevitable sense of loss—could not be removed. The sadness was open and real. "Termination" is the professional designation for the ending of the work between a group and a social worker. But who can completely define or understand what passes between human beings who, under the most difficult of situations, break through barriers of fear, prejudice, and years of mistrust, to reach some degree of communication and love? Truly, this is an intimate part of any explanation of the helping process.

The worker's final log entry, difficult as it was to experience and write, captures the remarkable capacity of the preadolescent for emotional growth and expression.

After a few minutes of playing with the others, Noemi came out of the pool and sat alone beside me "to get some sun." She was strangely quiet and avoided any conversation or questions I asked. I knew she was sad, and I was feeling the same way myself, but there didn't seem any way to put it into words. I was avoiding looking at her because of my feelings but suddenly I felt my hand getting wet. Noemi was playing with my fingers and crying. She tended to cry a lot, with big loud sobs that attracted attention and response. Just the way she was crying, without moving and without a word or sound was heartbreaking.

I said, "You are very sad, aren't you, Noemi?" She nodded her head and mumbled that she didn't see why I had to go. I replied, "You know I feel very, very sad, too. It's really hard to say good-bye."

She looked up, "It is?" I added, "But I want you to remember that I love you very much and that I won't ever forget you."

She started to cry and put her head in my arms and said quietly, "Promise you won't ever forget me."

I answered that I wouldn't forget her, that I was sure I would think of her many, many times.

The others were busy playing in the water and Noemi stayed that way for a long time. It was one of the saddest moments I ever remember, and I'm sure both of us shared in the same despair.

CONCLUSION

The social work intervention with this group of preteens illustrates the interweaving of developmental issues with the themes of work which emerged as a result of the initiation of a social work process. That there was growth and change is evident in the way the girls moved into the relationship with the new worker in the process of dealing with impending separation and loss.

They had changed enough to trust a stranger and to develop close affectional bonds with a nonfamilial figure—a giant step in their psychosocial development. In retrospect, it can be said that considerable developmental strides were made in being able to establish an intimate relationship with a stranger. With this to build on, it might be possible for them to face the psychosocial crisis of establishing intimacy with another, the central concern of late adolescence and young adulthood, which was looming ahead, with less in the way of developmental deficits.

Throughout, the worker and these preteens struggled together to deal with developmental issues these youngsters identified because of the transitional stage they were confronting. Yet, it must be emphasized that the developmental gains that were apparently achieved occurred because of the worker's focus on the social work process, that is, the pace of the work, attention to timing, to the strengthening of the mutual aid process within the group, and to the choice of themes of work that reflected the particular problems in social functioning presented by this natural friendship group.

In intervention with children and adolescents, social workers can be "seduced" to focus primarily on developmental needs. Thus developmental concerns may become the focal issue instead of the facilitation of the mutual aid process in the group which needs to become the vehicle for addressing these developmental concerns.

In this group, the work on becoming more autonomous, in responding differentially to authority figures, in developing greater environmental mastery, in confronting taboo issues depended greatly on these preteens being engaged with a nonjudgmental, nurturant professional who enabled them to develop significant social skills, especially how to present themselves and to articulate their needs. Because of this, a significant measure of social competence was added to the strengths they had brought initially to this social work encounter.

NOTES

1. Manuel R. Miranda, "The Life Cycle: An Ethnic Minority Perspective," in *The Social Welfare Forum, 1979* (New York: Columbia University Press, 1979), p. 111.

2. Erik H. Erikson, *Childhood and Society* (New York: W. W. Norton, 1950).

3. See Harry S. Sullivan, *Conceptions of Modern Psychiatry* (New York: W. W. Norton, 1940); Jean Piaget, *The Moral Judgment of the Child* (New York: Free Press, 1965).

4. George H. Mead, *Mind, Self, and Society* (Chicago: University of Chicago Press, 1946); see also James Youniss, *Parents and Peers in Social Development* (Chicago: University of Chicago Press, 1980).

5. Dorothy R. Blitsten, *Human Social Development* (New Haven, Conn.: College and University Press, 1971), pp. 69–73.

6. Sullivan, *Conceptions of Modern Psychiatry,* p. 42.

7. Jean Piaget, "Piaget's Theory," in *Carmichael's Manual of Child Psychology,* ed. Paul Mussen (New York: John Wiley, 1970), pp. 703–732.

8. A. H. Chapman, *Harry Stack Sullivan: His Life and His Work* (New York: G. P. Putnam's Sons, 1976), p. 179.

9. Jerome Kagan, "The Child in the Family," *Daedalus* 106, no. 2 (Spring 1977): 35.

10. Ibid.

11. See Harry Eckstein, "Civic Inclusion and Its Discontents," *Daedalus* 113, no. 4 (Fall 1984): 126–131.

BIBLIOGRAPHY

Blitsten, Dorothy R. *Human Social Development.* New Haven, Conn.: College and University Press, 1971.

Chapman, A. H. *Harry Stack Sullivan: His Life and His Work.* New York: G. P. Putnam's Sons, 1976.

Damon, W. *The Social World of the Child.* San Francisco: Jossey-Bass, 1977.

Eckstein, Harry. "Civic Inclusion and Its Discontents." *Daedalus* 113:4 (1984): 107–145.

Erikson, Erik H. *Childhood and Society.* New York: W. W. Norton, 1950.

Kagan, Jerome. "The Child in the Family." *Daedalus* 106:2 (1977): 33–56.

Lewis, M., and L. A. Rosenblum, eds. *Friendship and Peer Relations.* New York: John Wiley, 1975.

Mead, G. H. *Mind, Self, and Society.* Chicago: University of Chicago Press, 1946.

Miranda, M. R. "The Life Cycle: An Ethnic Minority Perspective," In *The Social Welfare Forum, 1979.* New York: Columbia University Press, 1979.

Piaget, Jean. *The Origins of Intelligence in Children.* New York: W. W. Norton, 1963.

———. *The Moral Judgment of the Child.* New York: Free Press, 1965.

———. "Piaget's Theory." In *Carmichael's Manual of Child Psychology.* Ed. Paul Mussen, pp. 703–32. New York: John Wiley, 1970.

Sullivan, Harry Stack. *Conceptions of Modern Psychiatry.* New York: W. W. Norton, 1940.

———. *The Interpersonal Theory of Psychiatry.* New York: W. W. Norton, 1953.

Youniss, James. *Parents and Peers in Social Development.* Chicago: University of Chicago Press, 1980.

Alice Nadelman

CHAPTER 7

Sharing the Hurt: Adolescents in a Residential Setting

But you're not all alone, you have us. We'll help you, and sometimes you'll help us.

With these simple words, a fourteen-year-old girl living away from home in a residential treatment institution crystallized the meaning of her experience in a mutual aid group. Such groups may be better suited to adolescence than to any other age. One of the essential characteristics of adolescence involves turning away from primary family ties and turning toward peers for norms, values, and support.[1] Simply stated, adolescents look to each other, where they used to look to their parents or to other adult authorities. They evaluate their own behavior against group norms; they judge themselves according to the standards of their peers. They may not always help each other, but they most certainly influence each other in profound ways.

This phenomenon is nowhere clearer than for institutionalized adolescents who have been placed in constant and intimate interaction with their peers because of their ejection/rejection from parental homes. Regardless of the individual reasons for their removal from family, or their individual needs and personality traits, or even the characteristics of each

specific institution, the powerful impact of peer culture in institutions has been documented clearly. Polsky has stated succinctly, "institutionalized adolescents are probably socialized more by their peers than any other young people in American society."[2]

A crucial question for those responsible for the socialization of institutionalized adolescents, and perhaps for all of society, is whether adolescent mutual aid will be essentially constructive or destructive. The small-group experience, with a trained social worker as group leader, can provide an opportunity to harness some of the tremendous power of adolescent peer influence for positive, growth-promoting outcomes.

ADOLESCENTS IN INSTITUTIONS

Adolescence has been defined as a period of tremendous and rapid physiological, sexual, intellectual, emotional, and social changes.[3] Anna Freud has called adolescence a "developmental disturbance" because of the severity and extent of the upheaval of this period.[4]

141

The essential developmental tasks of adolescence may be conceptualized as follows:[5]

1. To establish a stable identity.
2. To accept one's sexuality and assume a mature sexual role.
3. To establish independence from family.
4. To make educational/vocational/career choices.

During this seven-to-ten-year period, the young person must move from being a dependent child to being an independent adult. The resolution of the developmental tasks of adolescence determines the resources with which the young adult will face the world. Havighurst has defined developmental task as "a task which arises at or about a certain period in the life of the individual, successful achievement of which leads to his happiness and to success with later tasks, while failure leads to unhappiness in the individual, disapproval by the society, and difficulty with later tasks."[6]

The already complex demands of adolescence are further complicated for those youngsters living in institutions, in which the environment itself is not always supportive of the struggles of adolescence. Maier has defined three inherent features of institutional living as anonymity, standardization, and authoritarianism.[7] These features present obstacles to institutionalized adolescents trying to negotiate their daily world. It is doubly hard to answer the question, "Who am I?" in an anonymous, standardized, and authoritarian environment.

In addition, institutionalized adolescents must come to terms with the meaning of their ejection from their families. Regardless of the objective assignment of "blame" for their removal from their families, institutionalized adolescents generally feel a profound sense of rejection, failure, and isolation. They also have fewer supports and resources than adolescents living successfully with their own families.

The concerns of adolescents in an institution become superimposed on the general tasks of adolescence. The overriding concern is day-to-day coping —how to negotiate the institutional system with its myriad and sometimes contradictory subsystems. There are at least two, and generally more, cultures within an institution—that of the staff (or subgroups within the staff) and that of the residents. Polsky has documented this in his research. "The belief that ... [RTC] is a unified therapeutic milieu is a cultural fiction and contributes to the disparity between the cottage peer group and staff values. The staff and cottage subcultures are, in fact, quite insulated from each other."[8]

Adolescents must make their way among the discrepant cultures in the institution, trying to minimize the frustrations and maximize the satisfactions. The general tasks of adolescence may be translated into more specific tasks of institutionalized adolescents in the following manner.

1. Identity

Feeling alone in an impersonal environment; cared for by strangers; ashamed of having been "put away" by family; doubting one's own abilities and value; thrust into constant togetherness with mates not of one's own choosing; continually exposed to standards and pressures of "the group"; how do I begin to answer the questions: Who am I? What do I want? What do I believe?

2. Sexuality

Living in a structured and controlled environment, under close scrutiny of authority and peers, where freedom and privacy are at a premium, how do I begin to discover myself sexually? What must I do, or say I did, to become popular? to become respected? Do I follow the rules—follow the crowd—follow my own desires?

3. Independence from family

Having already been separated physically from my family, with or without my consent, how do I begin to separate emotionally? How far can I go without losing my family ties completely? Do I really want to keep them? Did I ever really have them? Will I define myself by becoming everything my family is not—or everything they don't want me to become? Can I still be part of my family?

What about my new institutional family—in many ways more controlling, less flexible, and less caring than my own family—how can I become independent in a place where dependence and conformity are rewarded and independence is frequently viewed as defiance?

4. Educational/Vocational

Living in a place of limited options and opportunities because of the label "disturbed" and likely with significant intellectual, academic, and social limitations, what choices are really available to me? How can I make something of myself? What do I want to do with my life?

These concerns and tasks must be tackled within the institutional setting. Birnbach has defined the Residential Treatment Center as "a total institution in which all aspects of the child's life take place in the limited arena of the institution's own grounds. Its function is to offer the individual child a number of related experiences that are designed to help him regain some control over his life and the circumstances surrounding it. The unique feature of residential treatment is the group living situation, in which the child spends the greatest part of his time in the institution."[9]

THE AGENCY CONTEXT AND THE GROUP MODALITY

Residential treatment, being a group living situation, consists of a network of groups. Whether by choice or by assignment, adolescents in residential treatment find themselves in many groups. Schwartz's definition of a group as "an enterprise in mutual aid, an alliance of individuals who need each other, in varying degrees, to work on common problems" is particularly relevant.[10] Since adolescents need and value peer experiences, and since they need each other to accomplish many of their life tasks successfully within the institution, the basic energy for work and growth is provided.

Into this arena steps the social worker, hoping to help harness that energy toward constructive ends. Birnbach describes the professional task as being "to find the viable and operational connections between the institution's need for 'a tight ship' and the client's need to develop autonomy and to negotiate within and among the various systems with which he must come to terms."[11] The worker's task further involves helping the members of each group communicate with and use each other in solving problems of daily living and in working on common tasks.

The particular Residential Treatment Center (RTC) being discussed was co-ed, housed two hundred youngsters from six to eighteen years of age, and was located in a major metropolitan suburb. The children lived in cottages of fourteen to sixteen youngsters, supervised by three live-in cottage parents. The children attended a specialized, on-grounds school which was geared to their academic and social needs. The RTC was designed for two essential purposes:

1. To provide an alternate living and educational setting for youngsters who could not function successfully at home, at school, and in their communities.
2. To provide necessary therapeutic and remedial services to the youngsters and their families, so they could resolve their problems and return home or return to the community.

The specific functions of the RTC included:

1. To provide food, shelter, and clothing for the children.
2. To provide schooling for the children and to include remedial services for learning disabilities.
3. To provide a complete recreational program.
4. To provide individual psychotherapy for the children.
5. To provide family therapy, whenever appropriate, to resolve family problems.

The RTC needed to maintain itself as an orderly and viable institution which could offer an array of services to its residents and their families. These services were designed to facilitate the children's cooperation with, and adjustment to, the routines of the institution and to develop coping skills which would facilitate their return to families and the community.

AN ADOLESCENT GIRLS GROUP—PRENTIA THEMES

The decision to offer problem-solving groups came from the conviction that the youngsters would benefit from an opportunity to share and work on common concerns with their peers. The purpose of this particular adolescent girls group was to give five girls, who lived together in a cottage, a chance to talk about and try to help each other deal better with common problems. These included general concerns of adolescent girls as well as specific concerns related to living away from home in a RTC. Among these concerns were:

1. Getting along in the cottage and larger institution; living within the rules while gaining personal satisfaction; getting along with adult authorities and feeling listened to and cared about; getting along with cottage mates and classmates; making and keeping friends.
2. Dealing with family problems which had necessitated placement.
3. Dealing with emerging sexual feelings, physical and sexual development, and relationships with boys.
4. Dealing with school, learning, achievement, aspirations, feelings of competence or incompetence.

All the girls in the group were white and were between thirteen and fifteen years of age. Each girl had at least one living parent who had been unable to provide an adequate home. Each girl had had some problems at home with which her parents were unable to cope. These included difficulty in getting along with family members; poor peer relationships; unsatisfactory academic and social functioning in school; minor delinquency such as lying, truanting, and running away.

Beth, age thirteen, came to the RTC because of her explosive temper at home and school and a hostile, often violent relationship with her mother.

Donna, age fourteen and a half, had been ping-ponged between her divorced parents since she was two and had been abused and rejected by both stepparents. When she came to the RTC, she was quite depressed and withdrawn, feeling that no one wanted her.

Gladys, age thirteen and a half, had been in various foster homes since birth because her unmarried mother could not take care of her but refused to surrender her for adoption. She had been in one foster home for several years but was sent to the RTC because of worsening problems of defiance, tantrums, and lying.

Jill, age fourteen, had been placed in foster care by her father when her mother deserted the family. She was sent to the RTC because of repeated runaways from her foster home.

Margie, age thirteen, had become increasingly depressed and uncommunicative. Her mother had died three years earlier, and her father was unable to provide a stable home. She was not responding to psychotherapy while living at home.

The worker, here called Miss D., was a twenty-five-year-old white woman who had worked at the RTC for two years prior to the formation of this group. She was the individual caseworker for each girl in the group as well as for all their cottage mates. She knew the girls and their families quite well and was also very familiar with cottage life.

The worker had the following assumptions prior to beginning the group:

These girls live together in a cottage, away from home and family. They know each other well, share daily experiences, and affect each other's lives. They confront similar, as well as different, tasks and problems. Each girl, in her own way, is trying to grow up, get more satisfaction from her life, and make some kind of "peace" with other people—family, friends, outside authorities.

Within this framework, how can they be helped to help each other to recognize and tackle some of the problems they face individually and as a group? How can they use each other to learn more about themselves, to begin to meet more of their needs, to find new ways of dealing with difficult situations? How can they develop enough trust in each other so they can share honestly some of the pain and problems they experience? How can they develop an investment in helping each other and themselves?

Before addressing herself directly to these considerations by discussing ideas for groups with the girls, the worker tried to "tune in" to some of the girls' feelings about groups, to put herself in their shoes, so that she could be more sensitive to their reactions and work *with* them rather than *on* them in establishing meaningful groups: "I'd like to be in a group with *some* kids, the ones I like and get along with, they understand me, they want to help me. I can trust them with my real feelings and problems." "I'm not going to tell my personal secrets to *them,* it's none of their business, what'll they think of me, they'll use it against me." "I'm not crazy like the rest of them, I don't need them to help me—I just mind my own business until I get out of here." "How can we help each other when we can't help ourselves? We'll mess up and ruin things, we're just hopeless." "What's it all about? What do you really want from me?" "How do I play the game?" "Can I really expose myself in front of others? How will I stack up to them? What will they think of me?"

The worker also tried to tune in to possible feelings about herself—"What will you do with the information you find out about us—whom will you tell? Will you use it to hurt us? Will you play favorites in the group? Will you like the others more than me? What will you think of me? Will you continue to like me if I don't perform as you want? What if I say too much? What if I embarrass myself? Will you protect me, help me, condemn me? Will I be good enough? Will I satisfy you, the others, myself?"

Following this period of "tuning in," the worker approached each girl individually to discuss possible groups, offering her own ideas and reaching for feedback. In general, the responses of the girls, with the exception of one, were hesitantly positive: "Let's give it a try. We got something out of it last year, you've never double-crossed us before, maybe it'll work for us." The worker selected the members for each group and set up the first meetings.

THEMES OF WORK

The main task of the beginning of the group was to answer the questions, "Why are we here and what are we going to do together?" Schwartz has defined this "contracting" phase as the time during which the worker helps the group members "to understand the connection between their needs, as they feel them, and the agency's reasons for offering help and hospitality."[12]

Getting Started

For these adolescent girls, the contracting phase was particularly significant because it touched on their need to run their own show. They began to tackle the question "Is this *our* group? Do we really have a say in what we're doing together and how we'll do it?" This is an important issue for all adolescents, but even more so in an institution, where so many opportunities for autonomy and control have been limited.

It was essential that the worker make a clear statement about group purpose and then reach for genuine feedback.

I began the meeting by saying that I'd like to try to tell them my ideas about a group like this, and how it could work and then get their reactions. I said that they were all living away from home and in the same cottage at the center. They were all girls, all around the same age. Although they were each different, unique I'd say (there were giggles), they did have many things in common. Jill piped up, "Yeah, like getting out of here!" The girls cheered! Gladys added, "And keeping the cottage parents off our back!" There were more cheers. I said, "That's it exactly. You're dealing with many of the same concerns and problems, and maybe you can help each other figure out how to handle them." Beth said, "I'd like to handle a few of the boys around here." There were giggles. I said, "We can talk about boys, too, and anything else that's important to you— like things going on at the center, or with friends, or at home, or with your families." Jill said, "I get it—we talk about whatever we want to, whatever is on our minds, and we help each other?" Gladys said, "Yeah, that's right, but we only want kids in the group who are friends." And they all began saying, "Yeah, we don't want Harriet. We don't want Harriet."

Gladys said, "And I don't want Beth either." Jill picked up and said, "Yeah, we want to have a good group—no creeps." Beth hung her head. Margie said, "Hey, Beth is O.K. I want her—just not Harriet!" Gladys said she wasn't sure.

The girls spent the major part of the first meeting discussing who should be in their group, what they would expect of each other, and how they would work together. Despite their differences and brief temper flareups, they did a good job of beginning to settle these issues. The worker credited their work as an actual demonstration of how their group could function. She then helped them reach out to each other to resolve the remaining obstacles in beginning.

After a while I said, "It looks to me like you kids really can begin to work with each other, even though you have a lot of differences, and you really are doing quite well." Margie smiled and said, "I knew that we could do it." Jill said, "Yeah, I think it's worth a try with this group." Once again Gladys tightened up and said, "No, I absolutely refuse. I won't have *her* in this group." I turned to the others and said to them, "How do you react?" They tried to persuade Gladys and reason with her, but she absolutely wasn't having any of this. I turned to her and said, "I have to intervene here and repeat that I can't leave it up to you whether or not Beth is in the group. It looks like the others feel that it is worth a try, and to me that means Beth is in the group, and I hope that you will be in it also, but you don't have the right to kick her out." Gladys then turned and said, "Well, then I won't come." I turned to the others and said, "Is that what you want? Can you tell Gladys how you feel?" Once again the kids tried to reason with her and explain, but Gladys just sat there with her hands crossing, "No, no, no." At one point I interrupted and I turned to her and said, "Look, Gladys, can I ask you one thing? Are you in one of those moods when you're just being obstinate and unreachable, or is it still worthwhile to reason with you?" Gladys seemed to be taken by surprise and said to me, "What do you mean?" I said, "You know. We've talked about this before. There are times that you become impossible to reach and it really doesn't matter what kinds of arguments —you've made up your mind and you won't hear them, and the wisest thing to do is to come back and talk to you at another time. And, if you're in that kind of a mood now, why don't you tell us because then there's no point in going on with this." Gladys kind of thought about it for a minute, and then she said, "No, I'm still reachable. You can reason with me." Once again, and this time I was in it also, everyone was really trying to persuade Gladys at least to give it a try. Finally, Gladys turned to us and said, "O.K., I'm not happy

about it, but I'll be willing to give it a try." Everybody heaved a sigh of relief.

The worker was able to reach for input from all the girls in the group, encouraging them to express their ideas, needs, and feelings, even when these were painful. While she encouraged them to work out their own disagreements, she made clear the limits of their control and those areas of her own and agency responsibility. Although these limits were tested and negotiated repeatedly over time, the beginning contracting set the stage for future work together. The girls seemed satisfied with their degree of freedom and control, while appearing relieved that the worker's authority could be a protection for them. This conflict between the need to feel in control and the need to feel protected is common to adolescents, and was an important area of ongoing work. The girls needed to know that they would not have the "freedom" to mistreat each other and would, therefore, be protected from mistreatment. While there were times of painful confrontation, they were in the interest of the work of the group— problem solving, facing or clarifying an issue, giving up a self-defeating behavior—and not just for the sake of confrontation. The worker's limits actually gave the girls greater freedom, because it enabled them to risk becoming vulnerable to each other.

During the twenty-five sessions of this group, the girls dealt with all five major concerns of adolescents living in residential treatment centers:

1. Coping with daily living in the RTC— living with rules, getting along with staff and peers.
2. Dealing with their emerging sexuality.
3. Confronting family relationships and problems.

4. Developing a positive sense of unique identity.
5. Making use of educational, recreational, and vocational opportunities at the RTC.

However, they did not deal with these concerns equally, in terms of time, energy, or intensity of emotional involvement. The most important issues to these five girls were clearly the first three. Although the identity question or "Who am I?" did seem to underlie many of the other issues, it was usually not dealt with explicitly.

The process of developing and using their mutual aid system was similar, regardless of the issue the girls were tackling. They first needed to learn how to talk to each other in a real way, about real concerns, and with real feeling—revealing pain, doubt, fears, weaknesses, thereby leaving themselves vulnerable. The girls needed to learn to listen to each other, to try to put themselves into each others' places, accepting each other for what they were. They had to learn how to give real feedback—not intellectual platitudes, sentimental reassurance, or diffusely angry attacks. They needed to ground their questions in real curiosity and caring, and learn to express their own suggestions, opinions, support, and criticism. They needed to learn to identify commonalities as well as differences—in background, needs, styles, and goals. Ultimately, each girl needed to learn to take what she could from the group and use it in her own unique way. All of this involved taking risks with the group—with each other and with the worker—and putting their fragile self-esteem on the line.

The worker functioned alongside the girls, using her skills to help them with their work of developing a mutual aid network in the group and using it to deal with their concerns. She tried to be careful not to intrude into the girls' work but to focus on her own job of helping the girls to do their work.

This is illustrated in the excerpt below, in which the girls tried to include a silent group member. The worker was careful not to join the chorus demanding that the girl talk, but maintained a mediating position between the isolated member and the rest of the group. Worker skills included encouraging intermember interaction and clarifying mutual obligations and expectations.

The girls were talking excitedly about drinking, when someone noticed that Gladys wasn't talking but was making strange clucking noises. Jill yelled, "Hey, what's wrong with you, are you an animal?" Gladys didn't answer. Beth and Jill began yelling at her to talk. Gladys just hung her head. I said that Gladys seemed upset about something, and the others seemed angry about her silence. Margie said gently, "Can you tell us?" Gladys shook her head. The others again began yelling at Gladys, demanding that she talk to them. I said they seemed so angry, as if they felt insulted by her silence. Was it possible to be too upset to talk, even with people you trusted? I looked toward Gladys, who remained silent. Margie began to say something, then stopped. I encouraged her, asking if she could reach out to Gladys without attacking her. Margie said, "Would you like us to leave you alone until you're ready or should we keep trying?" I touched Gladys's arm and said, "Can you respond?" Gladys nodded and whispered, "Give me a few minutes, then I'll talk more."

The themes that occupied the major part of the girls' time and energy in the group involved coping with daily demands of the RTC, dealing with their emerging sexuality, and dealing with their families.

Coping with Residential Living

The ongoing concern about dealing with the many daily demands in the RTC consumed the greatest amount of group time, although not necessarily with the greatest intensity. The girls did their share of griping, blaming others, and denying their own roles in whatever happened to them. However, there was a part of each girl that really wanted to make things work at the RTC, and the worker (and later the girls themselves) relentlessly reached for that part, to supply the energy to keep working.

The most frequent topic related to institutional life was making and keeping friends. This touched on the girls' need for acceptance, affection, and genuine closeness, as well as their fear of rejection and their defensive provocations. The worker tried to bring these complex factors to their attention, so that they could confront them together.

Then somebody picked up on the point that Beth had made about Donna not having any real friends. Gladys said, "Yeah, Donna, you let everybody use you and take advantage of you, and that's not real friends." Beth said, "Gladys, didn't you ever think that maybe Donna can't face the truth that she has no friends? And, at least it's better to have make-believe friends than nobody at all, so she just tries not to think about it." Gladys said, "Well, she can't live like that. She's here to be helped, and part of her help means she has to face the truth." Beth said to her, "But can't you understand how hard that is?" I said, "It sounds like you're talking from experience, like you really know how it feels." Beth said that she did, that many times she'd do anything to have a friend, and even though she knew that these kids weren't being true to her, that she couldn't stand the thought of it so she just tried to fool herself, and she thought that that's what Donna was doing, too. Donna hung her head. Gladys said, "But, don't you see that in

order to change, you have to face it? You can't deny the truth—that's just running away." I said to all of them, "Maybe you can help Donna face it a little bit rather than only screaming at her." Beth smiled and said, "Well, I'm no adviser on personality." I said, "Sure you are. Go ahead. You all are." Beth talked to Donna about trying to figure out if even one kid liked her just for being her, and she could get close to her. Then, if you had one friend, it wasn't as hard to admit that maybe the others weren't as real friends. Gladys said, "I'd rather be all alone and the most unpopular kid in the world than have a false friend." The other kids just kind of looked at Gladys. I said, "I think they're realizing how terribly that would hurt—to have no one." Gladys said, "Well, I had to take it. I had to learn how that would feel, and I had to learn a lot more of really hurting things, and there's still more that I have to learn, but that's the only way I'm going to get well."

Just as all the girls became "advisers on personality," they became advisers, challengers, and comforters on everything else. The worker encouraged them to risk themselves as they tried to tackle problems together. Continually making a "demand for work" while being sensitive to the difficulties of such risk taking, the worker used skills of holding to focus, reaching for feelings, and pointing out their responsibility to each other.

In the following excerpt, from the fourteenth meeting, the girls confronted their responsibility to each other at those times when they lost control.

While they were discussing how to have friends, Beth kept running back and forth, looking out of the window, and was very wild. The kids were kind of laughing and encouraging her, and she just got wilder and more disruptive. At one point, I kind of blew up at them and I said that here, on the one hand, we were trying to talk about Beth's difficulty in getting along with Gladys, and they were pretending to be helping her try to work it out, when right at the moment Beth was acting wild and out of control and they weren't reacting at all; if anything, they were encouraging her. They weren't even acting like they cared, they were just allowing her to get wilder and wilder, and if they really meant it when they said that they cared about her and they wanted to help her, this was the opportunity to do it.

They all seemed kind of stunned for a moment, including Beth. Margie said, "You mean you expect us to try to stop Beth when she acts crazy?" I said, "What do you expect from each other? Beth, what do you expect from them?" Beth said, "Well, I do expect them to help me if they're my friends." Jill said, "Well, we do try to help you." Margie said, "We try to keep you out of trouble." Gladys said, "When we try to stop you from acting crazy, sometimes you get mad at us and you turn on us."

Beth said something like, "Yeah, I can't take it very much, but don't give up."

As they began to experience their real ability to help each other, the girls experienced satisfaction, pride and greater closeness with each other.

I said to the girls, "You notice how different Gladys is now than from what she was at the beginning of the meeting—how much calmer, how much more at peace." All the kids said "Yeah," that it was amazing—she was like a different person. Gladys said, "And I feel very different—I feel like I just got a million pounds off my back." I asked how did the others feel. Beth said that she felt good, too—that helping people make her feel good. I said to them, "You really did help Gladys." Beth said "Gladys helped herself—she helped herself with our help." And Margie said, "Gladys helped herself by telling us, by opening up to us and by trusting us." Donna said, "It would have hurt her to keep quiet—to hold things in. It was the best thing for her to get it out of her system." Gladys shook her head, and once again she began to cry. She said that that was

true. Again there was a moment of quiet in the room. I said, "This is exactly it—how you're helping each other right now." Beth said to Gladys, "People may say that they hate you, and even we say that once in a while—but no one likes you more than the people up here at the school, and no one likes you more than the people in this room, and the more you let us get to know you, and the more we understand you, the more that we feel close to you and then we want to help you and we want to like you." Gladys said to her, "Thanks. That means a lot to me." I said, "This closeness to each other, this helping each other—what does that feel like?" Gladys said, "It makes me feel great." Beth said it made her feel good, too. Margie said that in a way it was half and half—she felt good that they had helped Gladys, and yet she felt depressed because Gladys had had such a hard life and because there was so much pain.

Their growing conviction that they could help each other despite each girl's "hard life" gave them the strength to tackle many problems. The worker credited their accomplishments, pointing out when they really reached or came through for each other. The girls learned that pain could lead to growth and closeness, that even while Gladys cried, she was feeling something positive, of which they were all a part. Margie's apt description of "feeling half and half" was a beginning identification of the ambivalence which characterized their feelings about so many things in their lives.

Another major concern of the girls was their relationship with authority figures at the RTC, particularly cottage parents. The girls grappled with such issues as whether the staff really cared about them or just tolerated them in order to be paid; whether they could really trust the cottage parents; whether they would be hurt if they became too attached to or dependent on staff members.

This was sometimes a difficult process, because the girls needed to get along with the cottage parents and feared that any negative comments would be reported back to them. They were sometimes unsure whether they could trust each other, or the worker, to keep their confidences.

The worker identified obstacles to their working effectively, even when she herself was one of the obstacles. She persisted in reaching for real feelings about herself and other staff members. She recognized and respected their feelings of powerlessness in the face of adult authority, but shared her belief that their opinions and desires did matter, and that they could have an impact on the authority figures in their lives.

I said, "You're saying that the cottage parents are doing things you don't like." Beth said, "Aw, there isn't anything we can do about it anyway." I said, "Is that how the rest of you feel?" And there was no answer. Then I said, "What's happening here? Are you all afraid to speak?" Margie said, "The cottage parents know that we talk about them with you, and they really hate it. They don't want us to do it." I said, "Is that what you're afraid of—that if you talk about them now, that I'll go back and tell them?" Margie said, "Well, we're supposed to be able to talk about them with you." I said, "Yeah, that's right. So what's getting in the way?" Again there was no response. I said, "Look, I feel as if I'm not helping you with this, and I want to. Can you tell me—is there something that I'm doing that's cutting you off?" There was no response to that, and then they began talking about other things, something that had happened in school. They would talk, and then they would stop talking.

I asked once again, "Are you telling me that you want me to tell you that whatever you raise in here now about the cottage parents, I won't tell them?" The kids said, "Yeah, we don't want you to tell them." I said, "But you don't really believe me? You think that I will go back and tell them?" Donna said, "Yeah,

you have in the past." But nobody picked up on that, and there was a tone of hopelessness. I said, "Wow, you seem to feel so helpless, like there's nothing you can do, like it doesn't even do any good to talk about it, like there is nothing I can do to help you. Is that how you're feeling?" There was no response to that.

Then they talked about E., the cottage parent, who is supposed to come back from her vacation this week, and they said they were happy she was coming back because she cared about them. Gladys said no, that E. does not, E. only works for the money. Then they said that G. only works for the money and that G. had told them that she was only here to get the experience until she could move on to something else. Then they said at least L. cared about them and really wanted to work with them. They felt like B. was going to leave the school and go work someplace else and they were on the verge of losing her. I said, "Wow, it sounds like you're feeling that the cottage parents really don't care about you that much, that they're only here to tell you what to do and boss you around, but somehow they really don't care." A couple of them said, "Well, they don't." I said, "Well, where does that leave you? How does that make you feel?" There were silent shrugs and then someone changed the subject.

In dealing with their feelings about authority figures in their lives, the girls were encouraged to talk directly to the worker about their feelings toward her. This, too, was sometimes difficult and painful, especially when ambivalent feelings were involved. The worker tried to reach for honest feedback from the girls, even when it was critical or negative, to demonstrate that a relationship could continue, and even grow, despite negative feelings.

We were discussing the coming staff meeting about Beth. She said she was afraid that no one would stick up for her. Jill said, "Yeah, who sticks up for us at these meetings?" I said, "I would hope that everybody at that meeting will have as their purpose to stick up for you, but I know that when I have a meeting on you, I like to think that I'm sticking up for you, and I guess what you're telling me is that you don't really believe that, that you don't really trust me to act in your interest." I said, "Maybe I've hit on an important thing and also a hard thing to talk about, my doing things that you kids don't always like, and maybe you really don't trust me not to hurt you."

Nobody responded to that, and they continued to talk about how they can't trust the cottage parents, and the cottage parents don't tell them things, and they want to be at the meetings, and they have a right to be at the meeting. I tried to pull them back and I said, "Come on, give it a try, talk to me directly about my role in these things in your lives, and what power I have over you, what I'm going to do for you. I know it's hard, but I think that that's what you're thinking about." Donna said, "Well, I don't feel like anybody sticks up for me when you have meetings. Everybody is trying to do what they want to, and nobody sticks up for me." Margie said, "Miss D. is the one who's going to stick up for you. That's what she's telling us." I said, "But you don't believe that for one minute. You think that's a lot of shit." Jill smiled and said, "That's true. I don't believe it. I don't think you stick up for us." I said, "I'm glad you could tell me that." Donna said, "Well, I don't think you stick up for me, either, because when I wanted to go home, you were making plans for me to go to another institution." They began remembering times when I had not "stuck up" for them and became quite critical of things I had done in the past. Suddenly, they became silent, as if they had gone too far in their criticism. I said, "Hey, it's O.K.; it's O.K. for you to tell me these things. I know I don't always do what you think I should. I'm glad you can tell me about it."

The above two excerpts reflect the worker's persistence in pursuing and validating the girls' right to have negative feelings about authority figures. She did not take herself or the girls off the hook easily by accepting evasion or glib superficialities. Rather, she hung in there, exposing herself to criticism, as she modeled the risk-taking behaviors she asked of the girls. She was sensitive to the girls' fears of retaliation and loss of love and approval if they criticized those in charge of them. She encouraged them and credited their efforts. The worker had to stay close to the girls' feelings, matching their intense mood and affect with her own. Her use of profanity and slang reflected her attempts to stay on the same wave length, to use "real talk," which she demanded of them.

As always, the worker needed the sensitivity to know when to back off, to stop pushing, to credit the work, and assuage some of their fears.

Dealing with Emerging Sexuality

The theme which generated the greatest excitement, not surprisingly, was sex. Like many mid-adolescents, the girls had difficulty in discussing sexual matters in any depth or detail. The seriousness of their interest and concern was somewhat masked by the silliness and wildness that accompanied their discussions about sex. However, they did make a beginning at putting their concerns openly on the table, to be shared with each other and their worker, rather than just whispered and giggled about in secret. The worker encouraged this sharing of common concern and common embarrassment, reaching inside awkward silences, moving from general to specific issues, as she supported the exploration of this, as well as other, "taboo" material.

As the girls came into the room, it was apparent that they were talking about their boyfriends, whom they liked and were making out with. They were enthusiastic about it, and they continued talking about it even while in the room, and I said to them, "It sounds to me like you want to talk about boys," and they all said, "Yeah." Beth said, "Boys, boys, boys—that's what we live for," and all the girls began to laugh. They were talking about Beth's hickey, and they told Beth to come up and let me look at it. She did, and I looked at it, and Jill said she had one also. I said to Beth, "Wow, you wear that like a badge of honor—what does it mean?" Then the kids began telling me that when a boy gives you a hickey, it means that he really likes you and that you like him and it is an honor to have it. They talked about making out. Their conversation was sprinkled with slang and profanity. Also, they talked about marriage, and they talked about loving these boys forever. At one point, I picked that up and said that it was like they really, really like a boy and wanted him to really, really like them. They wanted to feel like it would last forever. They began telling me about their individual boyfriends, whom they really did like and felt they'd marry them, like it was true love and it was the real thing. The conversation was coming fast and furious—it was loud and it was very enthusiastic. There was a lot of talking all at once and interrupting of each other. Then Beth began talking about how her boyfriend had tried to go too far last night and put his hand on her ass and she didn't like that. I asked if this had happened to a lot of them, with boys trying to go too far, and they said, "Yeah, the boys always try, but it was up to the girl to stop them and the girl had to keep control, because the boy always tried to get as much as he could." They said it was hard to say no, because the boys kept pushing them.

Relationships with Families

The girls' most compelling concern, and the one to which they returned repeatedly, involved their relationships with their families. Initially, the girls seemed to feel isolated from each other, each alone in her pain of family rejection, feeling that she was the only one who had "nobody

who cares." While the concerns about coping with the daily hassles of the RTC were clearly shared by all, and the excitement and embarrassment about sex seemed to be universal, the pain of being rejected by one's own family seemed to be a private matter. As the girls began to share family experiences and feelings, they not only recognized the commonality of their "private" pain, but were able to help each other deal with it.

This process of using the peer group to deal with family problems is a basic part of adolescence. Polsky has stated, "The translation of personal insecurities into public issues, resolving them constructively in the group, and yet retaining individual responsibility, is a dilemma ... that faces all adolescents."[13]

Initially the worker was quite active in pointing out commonalities and helping the girls tell each other about difficult family experiences. But as the girls became absorbed in each other's stories, they were able to provide their own energy and momentum.

The girls were talking about their wish for a volunteer Big Sister. Jill and Donna said they really wanted and needed one. Donna said, "I really have no one—nobody in my family really cares for me." Gladys responded by saying, "Well, who do you think I have? I have nobody either." Donna said, "At least you have a mother." Gladys said, "To hell with her. Having somebody like her is like having no one." Donna said, "Well, my mother is in Chicago. She doesn't even want to be near me." Jill said, "My mother is in Puerto Rico, and I'll probably never see her again." Donna said, "My stepmother treats me lousy, and it just makes it worse."

The girls continued exchanging notes on how terrible it was not to have a mother who cared about you. I said, "What I hear coming from all of you is how rotten it feels to have been gypped, not having a mother who would care for you." Donna said, "You know how it makes me feel? It makes me feel so bad that I can't even cry. I just get numb, and I can't even feel the sadness anymore." Gladys said, "Shit. My life's been like that since the day I was born." Jill said, "Eight years of my life have been ruined because I haven't had a family." Then she turned to Donna and said, "At least when you go home, you have stepbrothers and stepsisters. I have nobody. I used to have a stepbrother, but he died." As Jill said this, she began to cry a little bit. I said in a soft voice, "That's really rough for you." Donna said to Jill, "Gee, I didn't even know that your stepbrother died. I'm really sorry." Gladys said, "Yeah, I can imagine how bad it must make you feel. I wish there was something that I could say to make you feel better." Jill said it was really terrible to lose somebody who you loved. There was a moment of real closeness and a real trying to reach out to each other in their grief, and it was kind of quiet in the room.

As they continued to share with each other, they reached more deeply into themselves. Donna turned to the group and said, "I want to tell you all a thing that I've never told anybody before. But, I think I can trust everyone here. When I was living in Texas with my real mother, she kicked me out of the house two times and told me she didn't want me any more, and I felt so bad that I wanted to die." Jill said, "Oh my God, that's terrible. You must have felt so bad. There were times I felt real bad in the foster home too—like I wanted to get out because they really didn't care for me." Gladys said, "Me too—same here." Donna said, "A lot of times I feel like I want to kill her because she treated me so bad, because she walked out on me." Jill said, "How about me? My mother walked out on six kids. She just walked out on us like she didn't even care for us." Then Jill switched and began knocking her foster mother and talking about times she didn't feel like the foster mother cared for her either.

Then there was a quiet and a tension in the room, almost like the kids had become frightened of what they were talking about. I said, "Is it scaring you a little talking like we are about your real mothers and the terrible hurts

you've had?" Gladys said, "It's O.K. I want to talk about it even though it hurts. I remember getting all my hopes up about my real mother and hoping and working on it so that things could be ironed out between us, but after a while I realized that it was impossible and I just gave up. Then that happened in the foster home too, and I had to give up." Jill said, "Yeah, that happened to me, too. I couldn't keep knocking my brains out. I knew it wouldn't work in the foster home, and I just gave up and stopped trying." Donna said that lots of time she had given up everywhere and didn't know where she would go from here.

Again there was quiet in the room. And I said, "This is very hard, and it's also very sad." The kids nodded and just kind of hung their heads. Then Gladys said, "But you don't really give up. You keep on looking for people to be close to." I nodded to her and said, "Like when you reach out for a Big Sister?" She said, "Yeah, and I know because I love D. There are people in the world who can love me."

The girls' remarkable ability to share painful memories and revelations with each other primarily seemed to be due to their trust that such material would be received with respect and empathy. Their discovery that they were all "in the same boat" reduced their shame and guilt about family problems. As they became able to give support and help as well as to receive it, they began to feel less helpless. Their experience of themselves as capable help givers increased their feelings of competence and self-worth. This, in turn, made it easier for them to risk revealing further problems and weaknesses.

The worker's earliest interventions mainly involved reaching for and displaying understanding of the girl's feelings, as well as sharing her own. She encouraged them really to listen to each other and to respond to the feelings behind the words. Gradually, she began to help them to partialize and specify their needs and concerns. This enabled them to break down the overwhelming problem of family disruption into more manageable ones, such as looking for people who would care about them. Always, the worker tried to convey her own caring for the girls, her belief that they were capable of giving and receiving love, and were deserving of that love.

The girls returned to the theme of family relationships at several subsequent meetings, deepening their probing, revealing more of their pain. As they faced their essential aloneness and need to make it without adequate family support, they experienced the gamut of painful emotions, from rage to bitterness, to fear to despair. But they did not sink into their own despair. Out of their pain, and the sharing of that pain, and their growing sense that others really understood and cared, emerged those parts of themselves which were hopeful and alive. They began to discuss what they could do to make things better for themselves. They began to look toward other sources of "family" within the RTC, within their cottage, and especially with each other.

The worker helped the girls to listen and respond to each other, sticking with the pain, not rushing to "fast and easy" solutions. She helped them to partialize, to generalize, and to use each other for real problem solving. Whenever faint glimmerings of hope and energy emerged, she nurtured them, without rushing them. She tried to help the girls to reach for growth out of their pain, to see themselves as being able to gain something positive from even the most difficult experiences.

Beth asked Gladys about her real father. Gladys hung her head and said she never knew him. Beth said, "Gee, that's sad—maybe he ran away from your mom because he couldn't stand her either—just like you don't want to have anything to do with her." Gladys nodded her head and was on the verge of tears. Beth said, "It must really hurt you very much." Gladys nodded her head, and everybody was quiet. Beth said to Gladys, "I wonder if you ever think that if he had really cared about you, he wouldn't have left, even if he couldn't get along with your mom." Gladys said that she tried not to think about it—that it hurt so much that she never really had a father, that she really didn't know if she had a father. Margie said to her, "Well, everybody has to have a father." Gladys said, "No, no, that's not what I mean." I said to her, "Can you tell us what you mean?" Gladys nodded, and with tears now streaming out of her eyes she said, "I mean, I don't know if my parents were ever married. I don't know if I ever really had a family. Maybe my mom had me just for kicks, like she went out and got pregnant and that was that." Then Gladys put her head down on the table and began to cry.

Everybody got very quiet. Beth said, "I didn't mean to hurt you. I'm sorry." I said to her, "No, that's O.K. I think Gladys wants to talk about it, even though it hurts very much. And, I think she needs to get it out of her system and be able to talk about it. It's O.K. to cry and to feel hurt." I turned to her. Gladys lifted up her head and nodded, and she said to them, "I have to talk about it." I turned to them and said, "And you're helping her to do that, even though it hurts very much." Beth said, "I don't like to see anybody this unhappy. It makes me very sad." I nodded and everybody else nodded. Margie said, "It makes me feel very bad for Gladys." Gladys said to her, "I don't want you to feel bad for me." Margie said, "No, no, I don't mean I feel pity. I mean I know a little what it feels like and what you're going through," and Margie began talking about when her mom had passed away and what it felt like to lose her mom, and that she had cried all the time for almost a year, and the terrible, terrible pain that had been in it for her. She said that now she could talk about it and it didn't bother her anymore. I said, "And, I think part of the reason that you are stronger about it now is because you were able to cry, and you were able to feel all that hurt and all that pain and get it out of you. And that's why Gladys has to cry."

Margie said, "Yeah, in a way that's true. Because I remember how bad I felt, and how lonely I felt. But then gradually I got over it." Then they all began talking about sad things that had happened to them and that the best way to handle it was to let yourself feel really bad, and to cry, and to get it out of your system. Margie said, "But maybe in a way it's easier for us to talk, because even though we've all had hurts, none of us has been hurt as much as Gladys has, not even to know her father." Beth said, "Yeah, that that was true"—that even though she had had a hard time at home with her parents, at least she had parents and that Gladys didn't even have that. Gladys said that that was true and it made her very lonely and frightened. Beth then said to Gladys, "Maybe your father was a good guy. I bet that he did care about you, but he couldn't cope with your mom." Gladys said that maybe that was true—that she just didn't know, that she often wondered about it. I asked if this was on her mind a lot. She nodded. Then Margie asked if Gladys had ever talked about this with her mom. Gladys shook her head no and said, "Are you kidding? I can't talk with her about anything."

Once again Gladys began to cry and put her head down on the table. Beth said to Gladys, "Come on, Gladys, get it out of your system, it'll help you." Donna reached over and patted her and gave her a tissue. Gladys wiped her eyes and lifted up her head. She then began to tell them of the incident where she was living in the foster home and her mom had come to visit her and had stolen some money, and her humiliation when the foster parents told her about it, and how angry she felt, and how she wanted to kill her mom and swore she never wanted to see her again.

All the girls were listening very intently. I turned to them and I said, "Can you imagine what that must have felt like for Gladys?" They all nodded and moved physically closer to her. Gladys continued talking as she was crying. They began asking her more of the details about it. And Gladys continued to tell

them, and she talked about all these years of harboring this hatred toward her mom and feeling that all her mom could ever do was ruin things for her and that she had ruined her life from the moment she was born. Margie asked if she could talk about any of this with her mom. Gladys again shook her head and said her mother would either lie about things or blow up at her and have a fit. One of the other kids asked if Gladys had been able to talk about it with anybody. Gladys shook her head no. I said, "So, there you were, all alone, holding it in, having all this anger, having all those fears of not being able to talk about it, not being able to have anybody to help you with it." Gladys nodded. Margie said, "Now I understand you more than I ever did!" The other girls said they understood more about Gladys, too, and it helped them to see her in a new way. Gladys said she was glad she finally let it out with them—she knew she could trust them.

Ending

The ending of this group was very difficult for these often-abandoned and rejected girls. It not only meant the loss of their valuable group, but it revived memories of past losses. In addition, the planned ending of the group, at the close of the school year, coincided with the worker's leaving the RTC. So, the good-byes were more final, with no possibility of "see you in September." The issue of separation and moving away from dependent ties, which is a crucial part of adolescent development, was especially poignant for these girls. For them, separation had often meant desertion, leaving them with fewer resources to cope with life tasks. They had rarely been prepared for endings, frequently not even having a chance to say good-bye.

This group ending gave the girls an opportunity to come to terms with some of their feelings about endings and separation. They were able to take the time to experience the process fully, to examine their range of feelings and reactions. They were able to experience and help each other with the issues and feelings common to endings—anger at being left and having something taken away, sadness about loss, fear of not being able to make it alone. But as the girls and their worker dealt with these painful feelings, and confronted, as well as comforted, each other, the strength and richness of what they had done together began to emerge. Even as they were saying good-bye, and even through their rage and fear and tears, they were able to experience the power of their mutual aid and mutual caring. They were able to remember the moving moments they had shared, the problems they had struggled to solve, and the closeness they had experienced. This is what they were able to take with them—hopefully as part of themselves, to be used at other times and other places—the sense of having worked together to help each other and to help themselves.

The skills of the worker during the ending phase of the group included many that she had used throughout the life of the group, but particularly emphasized the following: reaching for and sticking with the pain of saying good-bye, reaching behind the joviality and "farewell party" chatter to the real feelings about separation and loss, identifying and crediting the work each girl had done, and summing up the work of the group as a whole.

It was essential that the worker share her own feelings honestly, not to detract from or change the girls' own reactions, but to contribute fully to the richness of what they had all shared. Only in this way could the group's ending affirm the value of the life of the group itself.

In the next to last session of the group, Beth suddenly began to cry. "You can't leave. We need you. Don't leave." I said, "You mean you're afraid you won't be able to make it without me?" Margie said, "You're the best social worker I ever had. I won't be able to talk to anybody else." I said, "We have been real close, me and every one of you, and I guess the thought of starting with somebody else is scary." . . .

There was a lot more talk that they didn't want anybody new. And I said, "You're angry at me. You have a right to be, and even though your anger hurts me and a big piece of me wants to say 'Don't be angry at me,' I can understand that you are and I know the kind of pain that must be underneath, and I feel some of that pain also. It's hard as hell for me to leave you." Beth said, "If it was hard for you to leave us, then you wouldn't leave us." Margie said, "No, Beth, that's just not the truth. It was hard for me to leave home." . . .

Beth got up and walked over to Gladys and put her arms around her and said to her, "You're scared because everybody's leaving, right?" Gladys nodded her head and said, "Everybody leaves me. I have no one." One of the other kids at the table said, "We're all in that situation, too. Miss D.'s leaving us, too. Not only you." Beth said, "But maybe it is different for Gladys." Gladys said, "You have a mother and a father. Every one of you has at least a mother or a father. Who did I have?" Beth said, "You have foster parents." Gladys said, "Big deal. They don't want me." There was a hush in the room at the pain of those words, and I said, "Wow, you really know how that feels." Beth said, "I think I know how it feels. I think I know how bad it feels. And if you want to cry that's O.K., but you gotta *live*. You got to pick yourself up. You gotta face it." Gladys shook her head. "No," she said, "I can't." I said, "It seems like she's feeling so miserable and so knocked down that she feels that she can't pick herself up." Donna said, "Even when you're alone, you have to trust yourself." Margie said, "That's pretty hard to do." Beth said, "But you're not *all* alone, Gladys. You have us. We'll help you, and sometimes you'll help us." Margie said, "You gotta have confidence in your-self." I said, "How do you do that, Margie? Can you tell her?" Margie said, "You gotta think of the things that you do *right*, not only the bad things. Even when people leave you, you gotta think of what you did have with them, and all that was good. And then you gotta believe that you're going to have some-body else, too." Beth said, "You gotta learn to stand on your own feet. you gotta learn how to make friends." Jill said, "You gotta take responsibility for what you do, even when it's hard." I said, "It sounds like you feel that Gladys can do these things, even though now she doesn't think she can." Beth said, "That's right. I even mean it coming from me. Lots of times I hate her, but other times I really like her, and I remember when she was nice to me, and when she helped me, and I do believe in her, and I believe she can pick her-self up." Beth took Gladys's hand and brought her back to the table. Then Gladys said, "I feel real, real bad; Miss D.'s leaving hurts me more than anybody can know, but you've helped me and I want to thank you," and there were tears in everybody's eyes. I said, "This is what it's about. This beautiful thing that you can do in helping each other, and you've got that now. You own that. And no matter who leaves, no matter how much it hurts, you can't lose that." Beth said, "I hate you for leaving, but I know what you mean. I know you're right!"

CONCLUSION

As these compelling selections demon-strate, the small group experience, guided by a trained leader, can provide an inval-uable opportunity for mutual aid, mutu-al problem solving, and positive growth for adolescents. Since an essential char-acteristic of adolescence involves look-ing to peers for norms, values, and supports, such groups are particularly well suited to this age. This is especially true in residential treatment centers, where adolescents are in constant intimate in-teraction with each other. The already complex demands of adolescence are fur-ther complicated for institutionalized youngsters because they generally have limited psychological resources due to past deprivations, have fewer family supports, and live in an institutional en-vironment which frequently is not sup-portive of their needs. The mutual aid group provides a chance for institution-alized adolescents to "put their heads to-gether," and by pooling their resources, to deal better with their common con-cerns.

The five major concerns of institution-alized adolescents have been identified as:

1. Negotiating the day-to-day demands of the institution.
2. Developing a sense of personal identi-ty.
3. Dealing with emerging sexuality.
4. Coming to terms with family prob-lems and rejections.
5. Making constructive educational/vocational choices.

The mutual aid group can be an im-portant vehicle for dealing with these con-cerns, as well as for helping the adoles-cent develop a sense of competence, achievement, and satisfaction. The five girls in this group came away from their group experience with the beginning of those positive feelings. When their social worker summed up her own feelings at the end of the group by saying, "Wow, you kids are fantastic!" they simply re-plied, "Sure, maybe we'll become social workers too!!!"

NOTES

1. Muzafer Sherif and C. W. Sherif, eds., *Problems of Youth* (Chicago: Aldine Publishing Co., 1965), p. 286.

2. Howard Polsky, *Cottage Six* (New York: John Wiley & Sons, 1962), p. 181.

3. William Schonfeld, "The Body and Body-Image in Adolescents," in *Adolescence: Psychosocial Perspectives,* ed. Gerald Caplan and Serge Lebovici (New York: Basic Books, 1962), p. 27.

4. Anna Freud, "Adolescence as a Developmental Disturbance," in *Adolescence: Psychosocial Perspectives,* ed. Gerald Caplan and Serge Lebovici (New York: Basic Books, 1962). p. 7.

5. Guy Manaster, *Adolescent Development and the Life Tasks* (Boston: Allyn and Bacon, 1977), pp. 14–17.

6. R. J. Havighurst, *Developmental Tasks and Education* (New York: McKay, 1972), p. 2.

7. Henry Maier, "The Social Group Work Method and Residential Treatment," in *Group Work as Part of Residential Treatment,* ed. Henry Maier (New York: National Association of Social Workers, 1965), p. 33.

8. Polsky, *Cottage Six,* p. 136.

9. David Birnbach, "Residential Treatment: The Skills of Child Care," in *The Practice of Group Work,* ed. W. Schwartz and Serapio Zalba (New York: Columbia University Press, 1971), p. 177.

10. William Schwartz, "The Social Worker in the Group," in *New Perspectives on Services to Groups* (New York: National Association of Social Workers, 1961), p. 18.

11. Birnbach, "Residential Treatment," p. 181.

12. William Schwartz, "On the Use of Groups in Social Work Practice," in *The Practice of Group Work,* ed. W. Schwartz and Serapio Zalba (New York: Columbia University Press, 1971), p. 15.

13. Polsky, *Cottage Six,* p. 177.

Sheila Small

CHAPTER 8

Learning to Get Along: Learning Disabled Adolescents

Learning disabled adolescents present an interesting and exciting professional challenge. Their developmental tasks reflect those of all adolescents; however, their learning disability may make it difficult for them to achieve mastery in many areas.

Until very recently, learning disabilities received limited professional or public awareness. As a result, children with these special problems were misdiagnosed, misunderstood, and mistreated. Stymied by the academic performance and social behavior of these children, families and other social institutions often made inferences about the sources (ranging from laziness to emotional disturbances). Social services and educational policies, structures, and approaches to help these children and their families were similarly often misguided and dysfunctional.

Reflecting the excitement and limitations of a new discovery, "learning disabilities" has today become a broad concept, a catchall for diverse related problems encountered by children. There is much that is unknown about learning disabilities: their nature, source, ramifications, and effective social and professional responses. Attitudes and responses to

the learning disabled child continue to be issues for concern.

Social workers who help children and their families need to be attuned to the phenomenon of learning disabilities and to the special needs and problems of the learning disabled. They also need to be open to new knowledge as it unfolds. They need to be creative and flexible as they deliver services to these children, their families, and multiple systems involved in their lives. One approach with considerable potential is the development of groups for learning disabled children and adolescents, including the incorporation of program activities.

In developing a program for this population, one must understand the characteristics of the learning disabilities syndrome, adolescence, group work, and the nature and use of various activities.

ADOLESCENCE AND THE LIFE CYCLE

Frequently the learning disabled adolescent has failed to achieve the objectives of the latency stage. Because the child has not experienced pleasure in learning and perceives himself to be an academic failure, his motivation to achieve lessens, leading to ever-increasing gaps between his capacity and his performance.

According to Erikson, at the close of the latency period, the child has learned how to win recognition through the "pleasure of work completion by steady attention and persevering diligence."[1] The function of school was to have provided the child with the skills for a career. He further states that "the child's danger, at this stage, lies in a sense of inadequacy and inferiority."[2]

The major task of the adolescent is to achieve a sense of his own identity and role in life. He must begin to separate himself from his parents and make important decisions about his future. Physical changes he experiences as he matures bring with them new impulses and concerns about emerging sexuality. "The increasing requirements for independent judgement, abstract thinking, and interpersonal communication during adolescence sorely tax his capacities."[3]

Because adolescence also brings with it enhanced awareness of limitations relative to one's peers and heightened sensitivity to being "different," the learning disabled boy or girl is highly susceptible to psychological stress after puberty. Most common stress symptoms take the form of antisocial or withdrawn behavior, both of which can readily obscure a previously undetected neurological deficit.[4] The friendless, isolated adolescent should also be a danger sign when working with this age group. According to Meeks, "the turn towards peers is an almost universal adaptive technique for the adolescent."[5] This is based on his need for narcissistic support, the absence of a sense of individual identity, the natural grouping provided by schools and society, and the need to separate from his parents.

The learning disabilities syndrome is one of many terms used to describe a common behavioral syndrome of childhood. Other terms include Minimal Brain Dysfunction (MBD), the Hyperkinetic Syndrome, and Attention Deficit Disorder (ADD). These syndromes are reported to be subtle yet often multiple functional disturbances of the central nervous system which affect the child's ability to learn and have the potential to contribute to the development of a wide range of behavioral disturbances. Despite average or above average intelligence, most of these children have specific deficits in the learning performance.

Gitterman poignantly describes behavioral manifestations and characteristics:

> These deficits take many forms: reading problems and language or auditory difficulties; integration, memory, and perception disorders; and awkwardness in small or gross motor coordination. These disabilities, viewed in the context of life tasks, would mean, for example, that a child might have trouble not only in handwriting but in buttoning clothes; not only in reading or auditory comprehension, but in following sequential directions from parents; not only in organizing a book report, but in maintaining order in a bedroom or a desk.
>
> The learning disabled child portrait often includes evidence of behavioral dysfunction or maturational lag. A commonly identified population are those who are hyperactive, distractible, or have selective attention spans. Other children, however, may manifest their physiological problems in such areas as delayed social maturity or judgment, perseveration, weak impulse control or low frustration levels resulting in antisocial behavior, or increased emotional vulnerability. Areas of social dysfunction that are physiologically based might also include alterations in interpersonal relationships, extroversion, resistance to social demands, or slower adaptive mechanisms. The clinical picture is broad but not homogeneous. Each child's

functioning reflects a different combination of some of these learning and attendant behavioral characteristics, thus fitting into the broad unitary syndrome.

It is not uncommon for children with learning disabilities to develop secondary social and emotional problems. Family attitudes and expectations toward the disabled child and the implications of these deficits may exacerbate or modify the child's ability to cope and his self-perception. Similarly, the pressures or supports of school, including academic requirements and remediation, teachers' styles, and peer responses have a direct and sometimes cumulative effect on a learning disabled child's perception and behavior. Those who experience frequent frustrations and failures may develop a range of reactions to deal with the stress, such as fear or withdrawal reactions, somatic complaints, excessive anxiety, depression, aggressive tendencies, or pseudomaturity.[6]

All too often, the child's unmet narcissistic needs, in conjunction with negative reactions from parents and other significant figures, result in the incorporation of this dislike by the child, creating a negative self-image or internalization of the bad object. Maturation and acquired means of compensating for some deficits may have reduced some of the physical symptoms, such as hyperactivity, by the time the child reaches adolescence; however, often the social, behavioral, and intrapsychic difficulties persist.

AGENCY CONTEXT AND THE GROUP MODALITY

The agency is an outpatient psychiatric clinic of a teaching hospital located in a disadvantaged area in New York. The clinic serves primarily minority families who are low income or public assistance recipients. The clinic offers a comprehensive diagnostic, treatment, and referral service to emotionally handicapped, retarded, and learning disabled children, adults, and their families.

The staff consists of psychiatrists, pediatricians, a pediatric neurologist, social workers, psychologists, educational and learning disabilities specialists, speech therapists, and an audiologist. These professionals provide medical, therapeutic, and educational interventions.

Referrals are made primarily from schools as well as from community agencies, private physicians, and hospitals. There is also a well-organized and active outreach program in which staff members provide diagnostic services to the children in early elementary grades of local schools in order to identify problem areas. When indicated, the child and his family are then further evaluated at the clinic, as in other referrals.

The evaluation consists of a developmental history, physical and neurological examination, social assessment, psychological and educational evaluations, and (if indicated) psychiatric, speech, and hearing evaluations. This process is followed by a case conference during which an assessment is made and recommendations are formulated. The content of this conference is shared with patient and/or family members, giving them an opportunity to raise questions and concerns, and an agreed upon plan is worked out. The worker assigned to the case is then responsible for the management of the case, coordination of services, and contact with appropriate agencies involved, such as schools. With supervisory agreement, the worker may decide to use whichever modality or combination of modalities seems to meet the needs of the client best. The diverse and comprehensive services offered by this clinic are ideally suited to meet the multiple needs of learning disabled adolescents and their families.

There is considerable potential for helping learning disabled adolescents through the group modality. Groups offer an opportunity for individuals with similar problems, experiences, or concerns to identify, share, and work on them with support of other members and the leader. This experience can reduce their feeling of isolation and uniqueness as it promotes mutual aid. The opportunity for peer support is critical for all adolescents, including the learning disabled. It may need to be structured for youngsters who have suffered and incorporated the stigma associated with their limitations.

A group experience also serves to stimulate and encourage the growth of skills in interaction and communication, thereby increasing the individual member's level of social functioning. As group members provide feedback about how they perceive others and hear how they are perceived, they can become aware of their interaction firsthand; this provides an opportunity for growth and change. Learning disabled adolescents are sometimes all too aware of negative responses by others, but may not understand what they are doing to perpetuate or can do to change the nature of their interactions. Furthermore, feedback experiences need to be structured according to their cognitive level of mastery and sometimes to particular modes of communication. Formed groups can provide an arena for this structure.

This group emerged from the commitment of one worker and the problems of one learning disabled adolescent in her caseload. Recognizing the client's need for a group experience that did not currently exist in the agency, the social worker began to recruit from other clinic staff, by using the informal system. Potential group members were taken from the worker's own caseload or referred by coworkers who understood the value of a group experience, were ready to help their clients separate from them, and willing to "share" their clients. All of the girls were seen individually to determine their capacity to tolerate and participate in a group. This process resulted in the identification of six girls who could benefit from or wanted a group experience.

The group was formed for high school–age adolescent girls currently being served by this clinic, who were having difficulties with interpersonal relationships and had poor socialization skills. Some had been in individual counseling prior to the group. All were being seen individually by specialists in reading and math. All of the girls had been referred by schools for long-standing academic difficulties and were reading four to six years below grade level; most had a history of poor attendance, cutting and/or truancy. At the same time, all were evaluated to have intellectual potential.

The group was geared to youngsters with primary learning disabilities and secondary emotional problems. These emotional difficulties were exacerbated by the fact that the girls came from poor families with multiple problems and from environments with limited resources.

The group purpose was defined as helping the girls improve their social skills. These included cooperation and sharing time, attention, and materials with members and worker; and learning and development of new skills and interests. From the beginning, the contract of the group and the individuals was articulated by the members as "a place where we can learn how to make and relate to friends better."

The following material briefly describes each of the group members.

Alma, age eighteen, is an attractive,

slender Puerto Rican girl who provided the impetus for the group. At the time of referral to the clinic, she was an anxious, immature, inhibited adolescent. Alma is the fourth of five girls raised in an intact family dominated by the father's alcoholism and physical abusiveness toward his wife. Alma demonstrated restrictive, phobic-like behavior (such as refusal to be alone and fears of traveling by herself even to the store or to school). In part, this appeared to be learned behavior, through identification with her mother who is phobic; feelings of extreme self-consciousness also contributed. Alma had a history of school adjustment problems that began in elementary school, including truancy. At the time of referral, she read at the fourth grade level and was poorly motivated for achievement. After a year of individual and family therapy, she began describing situations in school which made her uncomfortable and perpetuated her truancy. She felt self-conscious about entering the classroom. She did not know how to initiate a conversation with anyone and felt uncomfortable sitting by herself when everyone else seemed to have a friend. She was thus beginning to recognize her lack of socialization skills and was looking for help in this area. At this point I recommended a group for her as I continued to see her individually.

Terry, age sixteen, is an obese black adolescent, who at the time of referral was depressed and severely withdrawn. Her physical movements were extremely slow and she had a poor attention span. When required to relate verbally, she tended to withdraw. For example, she would avert her body, avoid eye contact, turn into her coat to hide, not answer, or turn her back. Terry is the third of seven children raised by her mother. Although family members reside in the same household, they are emotionally isolated from each other, as there is only minimal interaction or communication between them. When the group began, Terry attended high school regularly and was reading on a sixth grade level. Her anxiety about the group was apparent, but after adequate preparation, she was included in the group and seen individually on an as-needed basis.

Lydia, age sixteen, is a small, immature-looking Puerto Rican girl who appears to be about thirteen years old. At time of referral, she was depressed, lacked family and peer communication skills and tended to isolate herself. Lydia is the youngest of four children raised by an overly protective and restrictive mother. She felt infantilized by her family and had no awareness of the role that her own immature responses contributed to her family's perception of her as immature and inadequate. She replicated this pattern with peers who rejected her. After six months of individual work with another therapist, Lydia began to communicate more effectively with her mother, who was helped to recognize Lydia's need for more independent functioning. She then identified her need for peer relationships as her primary concern. She continued to be seen individually by her worker and by the group leader for group-related problems.

Ernestine, fifteen and a half, is a large-boned, obese black adolescent. At the time of referral, she was an immature, depressed, anxious girl with a tendency toward withdrawal. She had poor socialization skills, which resulted in feelings of inadequacy and rejection by peers. Ernestine is the only child of a depressed, dependent, and inadequate mother, who strongly identifies with her daughter. As Ernestine withdrew from her peers, she became overly dependent upon her mother, who supported this behavior. She had a history of chronic absenteeism and was experiencing academic delays. Pressure from the school regarding her attendance and a referral for special class placement were perceived as a threat by this parent and contributed to her recognition that a problem existed. At first Ernestine used somatization as a means of canceling appointments and avoiding socialization tasks. Collateral contact with the mother was required to enable her to set limits for Ernestine and convey the expectation that she attend the group.

Sandy, age fifteen, is an immature black adolescent of average height and weight. She has poor social judgment and relates in a manner that alienates her from others (such as teasing and denigrating the efforts of others). Her overwhelming anxiety and fear of failure make it very difficult for her to risk exposing herself in interpersonal relationships. Although her performance was uneven, Sandy had grown in her capacity to interact in a one-to-one relationship and was now in need of an opportunity to develop peer relationships. Severe anxiety and paranoid concerns prevented her from using the group experience. She was terminated for therapeutic reasons.

Angela, age fifteen, is an attractive black adolescent who relates in a hostile, aggressive, and often provocative and denigrating manner. This alienates peers, causing her to feel rejected and isolated. Angela has no awareness of the effect she has on others and feels victimized. She expresses the need for friends despite her bravado which often causes her to deny this, and is seeking a supportive relationship with adults. Angela is the oldest of four children raised in a single-parent family. Her relationship with her mother, which had been conflict ridden in the past, deteriorated further when she became an adolescent. Angela perceives her mother as a punitive, rejecting, and overly controlling parent. Sibling rivalry, which is intense, is due in part to the mother's obvious preference for the younger children.

The social worker is a married, white, Jewish woman with three adolescent daughters.

The group was limited to six members to avoid arousing excessive and overwhelming anxiety. A larger number would have reduced the worker's ability to give individual attention to these very needy youngsters. In addition, the girls selected for the group were not able to interact with each other initially, thus requiring the worker to be more active in fostering group participation. A larger number would also have increased the general activity level of the group and the scope of interaction, which was thought to be more than the girls could tolerate in the beginning stages of the group. Fewer than six members would have created difficulties if members were absent and would not have provided adequate stimulation and opportunity for interaction.

The group met during the early evening hours to enable everyone to travel independently and in relative safety. The meetings were planned for one hour, as this would allow sufficient time to use activities without creating more stress than the members could tolerate.

It was also decided that the group would be ongoing and open-ended. The worker felt this would permit the group to continue despite the transitory nature of the population, the pattern of members' withdrawal from threatening experiences, and the probability of varying rates of progress and therefore possibly different time for termination as individual goals were reached.

The Use of Program

Program is a tool that can be used in groups to facilitate interaction between the members, provide opportunities for gratification through mastery, and thereby increase self-esteem, foster sublimation of aggression, and provide opportunities for mutual aid. Program, or the use of activities, can be effective in the reduction of anxiety, particularly with nonverbal group members, and enables the members to share a common experience. This reduces the feelings of isolation. Shulman states, "In the complex processes of human interaction people express feelings, ideas, support, interest and concern —an entire range of human reactions through a variety of mediums."[7] Thus, for the nonverbal adolescent, the use of activities as a medium provides the opportunity for interaction with their peers.

The selection of activities to be used by the group must be based upon the worker's assessment of the needs of the group members.

> Problems arise in selecting specific activities to achieve particular treatment objectives. The specific criteria employed in making a particular choice for a given group must be consistent, of course, with objectives for that group and its individual members.[8]

From the start, the use of program was a means through which the members could begin to experience competence, relate to each other and the group purpose, and work toward individual and group goals. Although the idea of activities was introduced in the beginning phase of individual preparation ("making and doing things together"), this was deliberately left vague, as each girl's level of functioning was not clear. As data about these girls was learned and as the girls were helped to formulate individual goals, the worker began to select and recommend program accordingly.

While most of the girls could relate verbally in a one-to-one situation with supportive adults, their ability to do so with peers and in a group situation was severely limited. These girls demonstrated a high degree of physical and social awkwardness, self-consciousness, and inhibition. While they would need to learn to verbalize in order to socialize on an age-appropriate level, this would require incremental growth. The social worker decided that rather than create another frustrating collective experience for these girls, she would begin by meeting them at their current level of interest, functioning, and communication. Therefore she decided to introduce a task-oriented program. Each activity selected would provide its own structure in a simple progression of steps that the girls could follow without becoming overwhelmed by the need to make decisions or to engage in power struggles for control. Due to the members' initial inability to participate in a group decision-making process or to assume responsibility for the group's activities, this role was assumed primarily by the worker. Over time the girls developed increasing capacity to involve themselves at this level of functioning. This was a slow process. By the end of the second year the girls had moved from nonverbal activity to verbal communication, and from use of program to focus on concerns expressed as, "After we say hello, we don't know what to say."

Before the group actually met, the girls needed to be prepared for this experience. Many of these adolescents were frightened by the prospect of new, potentially threatening situations. The following material illustrates how one prospective member was prepared for the group and for the use of activities/program as a tool.

I had introduced the possibility of participating in a group to Terry and her mother during the intake study when the issue of her isolation and poor peer relationships had emerged. When this was agreed upon as a plan, I made an appointment with Terry to prepare her for inclusion in the group.

Terry arrived on time, recalled having met me previously, and accompanied me to my office. She remained standing until shown where to sit; then sat with her body turned partially away from me. She did not remove her heavy winter pea coat, and at times seemed to disappear, sinking down and hiding in its large, upturned collar when under stress. Because of her acute discomfort and inability to respond verbally, I spoke at length about what it would be like when the group met. I generalized about how people sometimes feel in a new situation, and tried to determine what her past experiences in groups had been like. I verbalized how uncomfortable new situations are for many people and how sometimes even old situations (such as school) can be uncomfortable. She responded, "I don't talk in school," and again withdrew into her coat. I speculated how nice it would be to have a friend in class, elaborating on how hard it might be to know how to start talking to someone or what to say when someone spoke to her. Although still buried in her coat, it was clear that she was listening attentively, which encouraged me to continue in a similar vein. I then told her that other girls in the clinic had the same kind of concerns, and that the purpose of the group was to help them learn how to talk to each other and how to make friends. She emerged from her coat, although her body remained averted. I suggested that although it might be hard at first, it would become easier over time. I then explained that to help them get to know each other and feel comfortable, we would be doing things together, like arts and crafts. For the first time, Terry looked directly at me showing her interest, and when asked, responded, "I like to sew." She smiled when I said I would

remember that, and if the other girls also wanted to sew, we would. I then asked Terry if she would like to give the group a try. She asked when it would be and indicated the time was convenient for her. I reminded her of the time and date, saying I would see her then. She smiled, said good-bye, and left. She returned a few minutes later to check which day the group was to meet.

Here the worker recognized and accepted Terry's awkwardness, discomfort, and need to withdraw in what she perceived to be a new and threatening social situation. The worker's acceptance and verbalization of the feelings, using Terry's nonverbal communications as a guide, helped Terry relax sufficiently to begin to respond more appropriately. She was given information about the group and what the members would be doing together to relieve her anxiety, prepare her for the group, and enable her to make a decision about joining it. By identifying Terry's problems and relating them to the clearly and simply defined purpose of the group, "to help them learn how to talk to each other and make friends," Terry was able to hope that the group could help her.

THEMES OF WORK

Although the group was formulated with the idea of using program, the actual choice of activities was based on the individual and group contracts of learning socialization skills. While cooking and eating together could have been used to provide a fundamental learning experience, the agency's lack of a kitchen and cooking facilities eliminated this possibility. Thus the worker had to select program within organizational realities, while responding to the level of functioning of the girls.

Getting Started

In the early sessions there was a need for the members to agree together about the purpose of their group. This would provide the necessary framework both for the formulation of goals and for an understanding of why specific activities were being selected to help them achieve these goals. The purpose had been stated during the individual sessions; however, it needed to be restated and owned as a group purpose. They were able to agree that it was hard to make friends and they wanted to learn how to do it better.

The use of the program had also been introduced to the members during the individual sessions as a way to have fun while learning how to talk to each other and do things together. Their discomfort and lack of experience in communicating and interacting with others had been recognized, and although it had been accepted (it's all right to sit and sew without talking to each other *at first*), they had stated and accepted the expectation that doing things together would make it easier for them to get to know each other and be able to talk to each other. Thus, the use of program (doing things together) was to be the means of helping them achieve their goal (learning how to talk to each other and be friends).

Feedback about their preferences had been elicited (as with Terry's interest in sewing), and in the first session these were shared with the group. They were helped to agree upon their first project (sewing).

Following the agreement of the first two sessions, the choice of the first group project was to make stuffed animals as presents to give to the younger children in the clinic. This project involved cutting out prestamped (ten-inch-by-ten-inch) animal patterns, stitching them together, and stuffing them. Considerations involved in this choice were (1) the age, sex, interests, and level of functioning of the girls, (2) the simplicity of the project, which required minimal skills, (3) the expectation that the girls would work individually within a group setting, as they were not yet able to interact or work cooperatively, and (4) the encouragement of age-appropriate behavior. Although the project used elementary skills and might have seemed "babyish," the girls could actually assume adult roles by making toys to give to babies.

The girls initially worked on the project at the level of "parallel play" with no peer interaction. Interactions were primarily directed toward the leader, as individuals sought assistance and support of their efforts. Total concentration was required at first, as the girls were intent upon getting the leader's attention, establishing themselves, and completing their work. Considerable anxiety was exhibited. The girls feared a repetition of the critical denigrating responses which past experiences had taught them to expect whenever their work and inadequacies were exposed to others. This is illustrated by the third session.

After greeting everyone, I reviewed the agreement from last week to make stuffed animals and showed the girls the patterns I had brought. I asked them to select the one they wanted to work on. At first they were reluctant to make a choice and sat back looking at me. After commenting on how often they were asked to make choices during the day, Angela reached over to take one. Alma, Lydia, and Sandy followed. However, Terry had to be presented with a choice of the two remaining before she could select one. The first step was to cut out the pattern. Alma and Lydia proceeded to work independently with only minimal requests for assistance or for assurance that they were doing it correctly. Terry worked steadily without seeking attention and passively sat doing nothing whenever she needed help. I learned to recognize this nonverbal communication and responded by verbalizing her need for help and waiting for her nod of agreement before proceeding to help her. Sandy and Angela were unable to proceed without my continuous help and verbal encouragement. At times Sandy's anxiety became overwhelming, and she regressed into very demanding and provocative behavior. By the end of the session, only Alma and Lydia had completed cutting their patterns.

In this session worker introduced the materials to be used and began introducing the decision-making process by encouraging the girls to select their own designs. Nonverbal communications, which were recognized and accepted by the worker, helped the members feel they were being understood. The members were not pressured to communicate verbally; however, verbal communication was modeled by the worker in accordance with the member's contract of "learning how to talk to each other."

I often had to use restraint to accept the pace of the group members. They did everything, even walking, in a hesitant and slow-motion manner. Flexibility was required to meet the needs of each individual at her own level. For example, Angela was so immobilized by anxiety in the group that she was permitted to work at home at first. This was done with the understanding that she would bring her work to each session. Another member, Sandy, required step-by-step assistance to the extent that pieces of batting had to be handed to her to be put into the sewn animal. Their anxiety lessened as the girls began to respond to the supportive and protective atmosphere of the meetings, as well as to their visible mastery of the different stages of the project. This enabled them to begin to relate more to what was going on with the others. Although Terry no longer hid inside her coat, she was not yet able to remove it.

Making Connections

During each of the sessions, I kept up a monologue (commenting on what was happening, asking questions about school, or explaining what I was doing). At times, individual members responded and began to learn how to "chat," or they listened as they experienced being in a "social" group. As the girls gradually learned to share experiences, they also began to reveal the lack of verbal communication within their families. In commenting on aspects of group behavior, I worked at first with the nonverbal cues whenever the girls could handle my feedback. Often there was no verbal response; however, it was obvious that the girls were listening, absorbing what was said, and responding to the demonstration that they were being understood and accepted. This acceptance was exemplified by the contractual statement, "When you're ready to talk, then you will." This gave permission not to speak and the acceptance of nonverbal behavior, as well as the expectation of a goal to be reached.

Working together on this initial project, and the pride of accomplishment they felt upon its completion, was helping them feel comfortable within the group. They were starting to trust the nonthreatening atmosphere they were in, and were starting to talk to each other as they worked. Roles in the group were being established and a feeling of being connected to each other was growing. Thus, at the end of eight weeks, they were ready to make connections with the external world as represented by the greater entity of the clinic. They responded positively to my suggestion that they give the gifts to the children themselves.

They met the children and afterwards became involved in hosting a party where they would be presenting the gifts. Motivation and enthusiasm were high. They took responsibility for arranging the decorations (streamers and balloons), serving the refreshments, and helping the children. Again, the physical movements were slow, requiring two hours to hang ten balloons and a few streamers. Planning this party represented their first efforts to interact verbally and work purposefully with each other as a group. They made suggestions, negotiated differences, arrived at decisions, and shared some of their concerns about how to conduct themselves at the party. As a result of their success and the recognition of their efforts by staff and the children's parents, they felt more self-confident and began to share life concerns from school and family.

After the party experience (we had been meeting for almost five months) the girls needed to give to themselves and elected to make stuffed animals for their own use. I continued to use program as a tool, suggesting this time an activity that could be used to help them move from parallel play to involvement with another group member and would be age-appropriate as an adolescent's "thing," namely an octopus yarn doll. Strands of yarn had to be measured and cut. One girl would hold the body while the other divided the sections for braiding. Girls with reading skills were encouraged to read the instructions aloud, while the rest interpreted and followed them. The task promoted interaction among members by enabling them to assist each other; physical movement around the room further reduced their constriction. A model for learning and working together was thereby created and encouraged. During this period, Terry removed her coat.

Socializing with Boys

The group had now been together for a year. They were functioning as a cohesive unit, capable of supporting each other and working together to resolve problems. In order to increase their awareness of the progress they had made, I asked them first to reflect upon their experiences of the past year, then to identify continuing areas of concern and to formulate goals for this year. The girls recognized and were helped to verbalize ways in which they were now able to try new experiences and could talk to each other more comfortably. They agreed that their primary concern now was "how to get along with and talk to boys." After exploring the resources of the clinic with them, we were able to arrange to work with an adolescent boys' group in the clinic to plan and host the disco party the clinic was having for its teenagers. These boys shared the same anxieties and trepidations about socialization as the girls did. Being able to work together as a committee made the prospect of participating in the party seem less formidable to both groups. For the girls, it drew upon their past success and provided an opportunity for a positive, age-appropriate experience with boys, involving the learning, use, and practice of socialization skills. The girls were encouraged and helped to verbalize their anxiety and to use peer support to enable them to cope with the anxiety. This very meaningful, shared experience increased the ability of the members to present and work through their problems verbally.

Again, program was used to focus interaction in a nonthreatening context. Through discussion of how to help their guests feel comfortable, the group members were helped to relate to their own discomfort in a social setting. They began to recognize that while others coped differently, their fears were shared.

Before working together, each group met first with its own leader to anticipate and work through fears. The combined group meeting was held in "neutral territory." Before the joint meeting, the girls expressed the following:

Lydia: I don't want to go in there. What will I say?

Alma: Me neither. I don't talk to boys.

Worker: What do you think the boys are saying now?

Lydia: They're probably having a good time. They're not shy like us. (Alma and Angela agree.)

Worker: How about it, Terry? (This was addressed to Terry as the authority, as she has four brothers.)

Terry: They're shy too. Samuel never knows what to say. He doesn't talk much either.

Here the worker picked up on their anxiety and focused on helping the girls perceive the boys more realistically, so that they could establish areas of commonality and dispel the myth that boys are not afraid. Recognition of Terry as the authority increased her status in the group. The girls were able to meet with the boys' group and learned that they all shared the same anxieties about hosting the disco. The mutually planned party was a success and provided the girls with yet another positive experience, contributing to their growing self-esteem and social confidence.

Problem Solving

From these types of experiences, the members indicated their readiness for problem solving on a more verbal level. Their ability to explore incidents which had been occurring at home and at school increased. They were now beginning to focus more on dealing with internal group issues.

Lydia: (defensively began explaining her absences) I guess I must have missed the last two sessions.

Alma: More than that. (She looked to me for support of her challenge. I nodded in agreement.)

Lydia: (She began by confusedly explaining about having a kidney infection.) I had to go to the doctor. I could go Wednesday or Saturday. I didn't want to go on Saturday. My mother kept saying, "Call her up." I know I should have, but I didn't. (She addressed me) I can bring proof.

Worker: I think the girls have been wondering what happened to you. Are you all right? How come you haven't been coming or calling? They seem to have some feelings about your not being here.

Alma: I wasn't really mad. It's just that . . . we're a group—we're in it—we should all come—or call. I wasn't angry. I was wondering how big the group really is.

Worker: So the fact that Lydia didn't come affected you.

Alma: Yeah. I would like all of us to be together.

Worker: How about you, Terry?

Terry: I don't care.

Worker: You don't care? You must have some feeling about whether or not Lydia comes.

Terry: I want her to come.

Worker: Lydia, how do you feel about what the girls are saying?

Lydia: It makes me feel nice. It makes me feel like I'm wanted. . . . (hesitates)

Worker: And missed?

Lydia: And missed. Like they care. I feel good. It's like a family.

Here the worker chose not to address the anger that was being expressed, but focused instead on eliciting the positive feelings that the girls had developed about each other and about the group. Their perception was that this is a place where they can "be together like a family."

In the months that followed, the girls gradually began to reveal their deeper concerns about shyness or doubts about being crazy.

Alma: Lydia said family problems and being shy, right? I want to talk more about the shy part . . . because in some ways I'm still a little shy.

Terry and Ernestine both agreed that shyness was a problem for them also.

Lydia: I lost some of my shyness. It's not like before.

Alma: I'm not as shy as I was before—but sometimes if someone talks to me, I answer, but then I get shy again.

Worker: Like after you answer, what do you say next?

The girls agreed and after some discussion, continued.

Lydia: I'm not going to talk to strangers.

Worker: I wonder how everyone can become less like strangers to each other.

Alma: By talking to each other and doing things together.

Worker: You mean like at the party where you all helped each other?

Lydia: That was nice because everyone hung out together.

Ernestine: No one was alone.

Alma: We were all shy and we all stayed together.

Lydia: Sometimes we just keep talking about the same things.

Alma: I don't mind talking about the same things because it's my problem, and sometimes if it's not a problem I can help the others.

Worker: Sometimes it feels good to be able to help someone else. (All except Terry responded spontaneously to this.) How do you feel when some people are more willing to share their problems than others?

Ernestine: I'm not sure how I feel.

Lydia: Some people like to keep their problems to themselves while others like to let everyone know about them.

Ernestine: (Mumbled something . . . was asked to repeat it.) Sometimes it's hard to talk. I'll try.

Alma: Some people don't like to tell their problems. They like to keep them inside. But sometimes keeping it inside . . . it hurts you.

Worker: It sounds like you're all saying that you know it helps to talk about things that are bothering you but find it hard to do so. How can we help each other with this?

Alma: I would try to get someone in the group that I know more than the others. I would like to try to explain to them the problem . . . that I feel like this but I don't want to tell them, because—you know—to tell the group . . . or maybe, they would help me—you know—to tell the group.

Worker: So what you are saying is that you would like to tell the whole group, but you need some help to do it.

Lydia: Yeah, like to start it off. (All nod.)

Worker: I wonder how much of that is related to the problem of shyness.

Lydia: (Stated positively) It's shyness. (Alma and Ernestine agree.) I feel that if something bothers them in their mind—that some people have their own fantasy—they wish they were this, they wish they were that.

Ernestine: It's your imagination.

Alma: Some people might think that . . . they might not believe what you're saying. They might think . . . you are crazy or something.

Lydia: They might think you're out of your mind.

Worker: You wonder sometimes if what you're thinking is what everyone else thinks?

Lydia: Yeah. And nobody believes nobody. You gotta go through a lot. Sometimes not everyone is nice. (All agreed.)

Alma: It's a story you make up about yourself. Like sometimes when you're mad. . . . Like sometimes I wish I had another kind of parent. (Lydia and Ernestine laughed uncomfortably but with recognition. Terry had turned and had her back to us.)

Worker: It looks like you're not the only one who had that wish.

Ernestine: Sometimes I think how it would be if my family was different. (Lydia and Ernestine acknowledged similar thoughts. When asked, Terry said she never thought that way.)

Worker: It seems like most of you have had similar thoughts at times and are relieved to find that they aren't much different from anyone else's thoughts.

In this problem-solving phase of the group, the themes of the interdependence and cohesiveness of the group are addressed. Internal issues such as attendance and scapegoating were raised, and the members were able to recognize and state that belonging to the group was important to them. They have learned to trust each other and feel accepted and understood within the group. They feel comfortable discussing issues of concern and draw upon common and shared experiences as a frame of reference. Although they continue to turn to the leader for help in putting their feelings into words and in maintaining the forms, they have developed the capacity to communicate with each other in a meaningful manner.

The group, at this point, seems to accept Terry's role as a silent participant; however, there is potential for scapegoating as the members increase their feelings of intimacy created by the sharing of thoughts, feelings, and fears. The worker's purpose for raising this issue was to explore the group's feelings about their more silent members. This resulted in Ernestine contracting to try to participate more, as well as tacit permission for Terry to retain her role at this time. It was noted that they continued to include her in nonverbal activities.

Alma, Lydia, and to a more limited extent Ernestine have progressed to a level of functioning in which they no longer require an activity to sustain their ability to interact with each other. They are able at this time to identify and share problem areas using the group for feedback and support in working them through. Although Terry has not reached this level,

it is possible to evaluate the meaning that inclusion in the group has had for her. This is shown by her excellent attendance, her ability after a year to remove her coat during sessions, her increased self-confidence and progress in remediation sessions, and her ability to interact more appropriately with peers. It is notable, however, that although Terry continues to need broadening experiences, Terry has felt threatened by the need to interact verbally and has begun to show signs of withdrawal, such as not participating and turning her back to group during discussions.

Ending the Group

After two years, the group members had begun to show signs that they had achieved many of their goals and were ready to end the group. Attendance had become erratic, and the girls were indicating in their reports of their activities during the week that they were establishing new relationships in the community and were involved in age-appropriate goals and activities such as academic work and employment. The group was no longer their sole means of socialization, nor were the relationships in the group as meaningful as they had been in the past.

Alma: What are we going to be doing?
Worker: You sound angry. Are you?
Alma: Nobody ever comes anymore.
Lydia: I was busy last week. I had to go shopping with my friend, and I didn't get home until it was too late.
Ernestine: I had too much homework. Besides, I worked late.
Terry: I came.
Alma: Well, it's not the same when people don't come. I'm busy, but I came.
Worker: It sounds like some of you are saying that you are too busy now with friends, school and jobs to come to the group, while some would like to continue.

Lydia: Yeah—that's it. You said it. I don't have time anymore.

Worker: Who remembers why we started to meet together?

Alma: 'Cause we wanted to make friends.

Lydia: And to help us because we were shy. I'm not shy anymore—well sometimes—but not like before.

Worker: How about the rest of you?

All agreed that they could talk to others now, had at least one friend, and were generally feeling more socially competent. When I summed up their progress and suggested that some of them no longer had need of the group, Lydia and Ernestine were relieved, although Alma continued to press for the group to continue.

The degree of ambivalence about termination varied among the members, as participation in the group had been a gratifying experience that they were reluctant to end.

Some, such as Alma and Terry, continued to seek the support of the worker despite the progress they had made and the strong probability that they would be able to maintain these gains. For example, Alma (the "original" member) had achieved a grade level of 8+ in both reading and math, had passed her competency exams, and was eligible for a high school diploma. For them, the flexibility of the agency structure assured them that they would continue to receive the support they were seeking on an individual basis to prepare them for more independent functioning.

Others were able to assess their own role in the progress they had made realistically and felt more confident about their ability to maintain and increase these gains. Additionally, they had established new support systems in the community. They, as well as the two who would continue to be seen individually, were helped

to express their feelings about termination, reflected upon how different they felt about ending this group compared to other experiences they had, and were able to involve themselves in defining issues they wanted to resolve in the final four sessions of the group that they felt necessary to prepare them for termination.

CONCLUSION

What has been seen is one way in which program can be used as a tool, using the group modality, to provide socially immature and isolated learning disabled adolescents the opportunity for growth and change.

These youngsters felt awkward and self-conscious in social situations. They tended either to withdraw or to act inappropriately. The negative responses they received further increased their depression and sense of inadequacy. Academic functioning was severely impaired, partly as a result of their learning disability and partly because of their depression and extreme inhibition in school.

Inclusion in a group provided a way of bringing these adolescents together in a supportive, nonthreatening environment. Helping them to identify their common feeling of isolation reduced their sense of uniqueness and provided a focus for the group.

By planning activities that demanded a steadily increasing degree of interaction between its members, these adolescents developed greater social maturity as they were helped to advance from isolation to parallel play to cooperative play. As a group they learned to support each other as they moved into age-appropriate activities, such as the disco party. No longer feeling isolated and inadequate, the girls further developed the ability to communicate more appropriately with peers and began to involve themselves in school, peer, and community activities. They formed friendships and began dating. Their academic functioning improved, promoting more optimistic feelings about their futures.

The girls had achieved their goal of learning how to talk to peers and were able to form friendships. They no longer needed the support of the group in these areas and were ready to terminate. Several continued to use other services offered by the clinic, such as individual therapy, to resolve other issues.

Thus, the use of a carefully planned program was effectively used to provide the opportunity for interaction and gratification through the planning, sharing, and mastery of common experiences.[9]

NOTES

1. Erik H. Erikson, *Childhood and Society* (New York: W. W. Norton, 1963), p. 259.
2. Ibid., p. 260.
3. Irving B. Weiner, *Psychological Disturbances in Adolescence* (New York: Wiley-Interscience, 1970), p. 249.
4. Ibid., p. 250.
5. John E. Meeks, *The Fragile Alliance* (New York: Robert E. Krieger Publishing Company, 1975), pp. 22–23.
6. Naomi Pines Gitterman, "Group Services for Learning Disabled Children and their Parents." *Social Casework* 60, no. 4 (April 1979): 218.
7. Lawrence Shulman, " 'Program' in Group Work: Another Look," in *The Practice of Group Work,* ed. W. Schwartz and S. Zalba (New York: Columbia University Press, 1971), p. 221.
8. Robert Vintner, "Program Activities: An Analysis of Their Effects on Participant Behavior," *Readings in Group Work Practice,* ed. R. Vintner (Ann Arbor, Mich.: Campus Publishers, 1967), p. 96.
9. An earlier draft of this paper "A Group of Learning Disabled Adolescents," may be found in *Social Work in Maternal and Child Health: A Casebook.* New York: Columbia University School of Social Work, Monograph, 1982, pp. 37–76.

BIBLIOGRAPHY

Erikson, Erik H. *Childhood and Society.* New York: W. W. Norton & Company, Inc., 1963.

Gitterman, Naomi Pines. "Group Services for Learning Disabled Children and Their Parents." *Social Casework* 60, no. 4 (1979): 217–226.

Meeks, John E. *The Fragile Alliance.* New York: Robert E. Krieger Publishing Company, 1975.

Shulman, Lawrence. " 'Program' in Group Work: Another Look." In *The Practice of Group Work,* New York and London: Columbia University Press, 1971.

Vintner, Robert. "Program Activities: An Analysis of Their Effects on Participant Behavior." In *Readings in Group Work Practice.* Edited by R. Vintner. Ann Arbor, Mich.: Campus Publishers, 1967.

Weiner, Irving B. *Psychological Disturbance in Adolescence.* New York: Wiley-Interscience, 1970.

Part Four
Mutual Aid and Adults

Lawrence Shulman

CHAPTER 9

Healing the Hurts: Single Parents

This paper focuses on the practice issues involved in working with single parents in groups. Our understanding of the average family as a working father, a mother at home, and two to three children has become a myth. In Canada, where the group described in this chapter took place, there were over 300,000 one-parent families as of 1976.[1] That was 10 percent of all Canadian families. Of this group, women headed 85 percent of the families and men 15 percent. There were 631,000 children in these families, which means over 1 million Canadians, adults and children, were members of single-family units. These single-parent families were the result of divorce, widowhood, separation, and unmarried parenthood. With the number of single-parent families growing at a rate almost triple that of two-parent families, even these already high figures are out of date today.

DEVELOPMENTAL ISSUES

The parents and children in a single-parent family must face all the normative developmental tasks for their age and stage of life; however, in addition, they must also face the stresses generated by significant transitions in status.[2] For example, one member of the group who is discussed later in this chapter was in his late twenties and had just become a parent. His ability to cope with the transition to the parent role was severely affected by his wife's decision to leave him and the new baby. Thus, he had to deal with the change in status from nonparent to parent, a difficult enough transition, while simultaneously coping with the change in status from married partner to single parent.

The teenage children of another group participant were facing the normative transitional stresses associated with adolescence but now found themselves also having to cope with the inevitable stresses associated with the disruption of their family and the departure of their father. The impact of the change in status from child in a "normal" family to child in a "broken" family exacerbated the already difficult transitional issues associated with adolescence. Other associated status changes included a sharply decreased family income after the split. Thus, both the parent and the children were faced with changes in their economic status from "well-off" and secure, to indigent and insecure. As will be illustrated later, in the

179

discussion of the difficulties single women encounter when they try to establish their own credit, the prejudicial responses of the community may mean resources needed to cope with this change (such as credit) are unavailable.

Compounding all of these issues faced by single-parent families is the reality that the single parent often has to handle these problems alone. For this reason a mutual aid group, in which parents can share with others who are "in the same boat," can provide an important alternative source of support.

One area of unique concern for the single parent centers on the world of work. In Canada, 45 percent of single mothers work while 41 percent of them depend on welfare.[3] Many women who try to work face serious discrimination in their efforts to obtain jobs. There is the myth that they are "unreliable," that is, they have too many distractions. They often run into inflexible employers. When they do get jobs, they are often poorly paid, dead-end jobs. Between low-paying jobs and welfare, two thirds of single mothers try to live on income below the accepted poverty line, a factor which significantly adds to the stress of trying to raise a family alone.

Second, closely related problems relate to finances and housing. Many options are not available to single parents with the result that they often must pay more of their income to obtain any housing at all. If a female single parent wishes to obtain a loan for buying a house, she may be refused because of her status. This financial discrimination cuts across all forms of credit with many female single parents facing a "Catch-22" situation.

Third is the problem of dealing with friends. Many single parents report changes in attitudes toward them after separation or divorce as former close friends seem to take sides in the marital split. Another problem is sometimes referred to as the "Noah's Ark Syndrome," in which friends seem to operate under the general belief that people come "two by two." Old friends seem to slip away and new friends seem to be hard to find.

Fourth is the difficulty of trying to balance personal needs against all of the responsibilities of raising a family. At the time when the single parent is most vulnerable and most needy, he or she must also deal with school meetings, dental appointments, homework, and all the rest. Finding time for oneself can be extremely difficult.

Fifth is the ongoing relationship with the ex-spouse, whether or not he or she is still actively in the picture. A major problem becomes how to work out a new relationship which can overcome the bitterness and hard feelings associated with the split, so that the children don't feel torn between parents. Often, the ongoing legacy of anger from the marriage and from the way in which the split was handled by overzealous lawyers can remain to haunt all members of the family even when the ex-spouse is no longer around.

Finally, dealing with the children can take its toll. For example, finding child care assistance, either during the evening for a night out or during the day to facilitate working, can be extremely difficult. The makeshift arrangements which are often necessary in such situations can lead to heightened anxiety for the parent and an increased sense of guilt.

In addition to the concrete issues related to children, there are the problems of dealing with their emotional needs. These can cause even more difficulty for the single parent whose own emotions are still raw. Although reactions differ according to age and according to the specific situation, it is not uncommon for children to react to the split in the family by going through the phases of grieving similar to those associated with death and dying.[4]

First, there is the shock, followed by depression and denial. Then comes anger and a lowered sense of self-esteem. Often, there is also a feeling of being responsible for the split in the marriage. These feelings are expressed in different ways, ranging from regression for toddlers to problems in school and with peer group for young teens. The children's anger at the parent thought to be at fault, their struggle with the loyalty problem when parents force them to take sides, their feelings of sadness, depression, anger, and guilt can cut them off from friends and other close people, just at the time they need them the most. Often, one of the hardest times for the single parent is trying to help the child deal with these strains at precisely the same time they are feeling most vulnerable themselves.

I have reviewed some of the major issues facing single parents and their children. I would now like to examine the practice implications for dealing with these concerns using examples as they emerged in a mutual aid group I led for single parents. The practice skills employed to help these parents will also be identified and illustrated.

THE SINGLE PARENTS GROUP: AGENCY CONTEXT

I was the group leader for a single parents group held in a small, northern town in British Columbia, Canada. The service was offered as part of a university community psychiatry outreach program. The mission of this program included bringing psychiatric services to rural areas of the province which were lacking in resources. While individual services to single parents existed in this small community, local professionals felt that group work could also be helpful in unique ways. Since the local staff felt they lacked the skills required to initiate and conduct such a program, I was employed on a contract basis to lead the first group of this kind and to use the occasion to demonstrate the use of the group process and group leadership skills for attending professionals. Thus, the group had both service and training purposes. The presence of other professionals was also a condition of my leading the group, since I felt it was important to have back-up resources available to group members after I left town. Thus, the group members would have made direct contacts with sources of support to deal with issues which might emerge in the discussion. As will be seen in the excerpts from the first meeting, this was an important safeguard, since one member did raise the issue of suicide. One of the local professionals was able to initiate a follow-up contact, at my suggestion, following the group session.

Thus, in addition to demonstrating the processes in a single parent group, this chapter also illustrates how a social work professional, who is not employed full time by an agency, can be used to initiate outreach and developmental services in areas which are poor in resources.

The group was advertised as a mutual aid discussion group for single parents, focusing on their unique concerns and what they might be able to do about those concerns. The group met for one evening (three hours) and the following day for seven hours.[5] Participants included eight single mothers, three single fathers, and three community professionals who worked with single parents. The order in which I will discuss the issues generally follows the order in which they emerged in the group; however, I have grouped some of the excerpts together for ease of explication.

GROUP THEMES

Getting Started

The session began with our contracting work. I hoped to set the stage by using the skills of clarifying purpose and clarifying my role.[6] To help them understand the purpose, I had tuned in to possible themes of concern and included in my opening statement some handles for work by partializing the overall purpose into potential issues for discussion. This was followed by my reaching for feedback from the group members.

I explained the purpose of the group as an opportunity for single parents to discuss with each other some of the special problems they faced because they were alone. I said that my role was not as an expert with answers for them, but rather as someone who would try to help them to talk to and listen to each other and to provide help to each other from their own experiences. In addition, I would throw in any ideas I had which might be helpful. I then offered a few examples of possible concerns (these were similar to those described earlier in this paper). There was much head nodding in agreement as I spoke. I completed my opening by describing some of the phases which both parents and children go through after a separation. I invited the participants to share some of their own experiences, their concerns and problems, and suggested that we could use their issues as an agenda for our two days of discussion. There was a brief silence and then Irene asked how long it took to go through the phases. I asked her why she was asking, and she said it was three years since her separation, and she didn't think she had passed through all of them yet. The group members laughed, acknowledging their understanding of the comment. I said I thought there must have been a great deal of pain and

sadness both at the time of the split and since then to cause it still to hurt after three years. I asked Irene if she could speak some more about this.

Although Irene responded in a light-hearted manner, my tuning in prior to the group had prepared me to put into words what I felt would be the hurt they were experiencing. I wanted to be sure to communicate to the members that if they were prepared to discuss even these painful areas, I was ready as well. I felt it was crucial to do this early with a short-term group. After this particular group experience, I realized the importance of being direct this early in all of my groups regardless of the number of sessions.

Irene continued in a more serious tone by describing her ongoing depression. She described days in which she felt she was finally getting over things and picking herself up, followed by days when she felt right back to square one. Others in the group agreed and shared their own experiences when I encouraged them to respond to Irene's comments. I told them it might help just to know that they were "in the same boat" with their feelings.

I then asked if the group members could be more specific about what made the breakup difficult. A number of areas were raised by members which I kept track of in my written notes. They included dealing with money and finances, problems with the ex-spouse, problems with the kids, and the strain in their relationships with friends and family. There was a great deal of emotion expressed about discussion of this last area with anger directed toward others who "didn't understand" and related to them in ways which hurt more than they helped.

Dick, a young man in his mid-twenties, spoke with great agitation about his wife who had left him with their six-month-old baby only six weeks before. The group seemed to focus on Dick who expressed a particularly strong sense of urgency and was clearly still in a state of shock and crisis. Dick had arrived early and had carried on a long and animated discussion with another member in the premeeting "chatter," listing all of the crises he had to get through in order to get to the session that evening. I pointed out to the group that it seemed like Dick was feeling this concern about friends and relatives rather strongly and, in fact, had had a great deal of difficulty even getting here tonight. I asked if they would like to focus on friends and relatives first, perhaps using Dick's example to get us started. All agreed that would be helpful.

The similarity in the way this group began, when compared to married couples groups I have led, can be seen in the way the group members began. In both types of groups they started by externalizing the problems.[7] That is, the first offerings dealt with others who didn't understand. With the married couples group, it was the spouses or all of the psychiatrists and helping people who had not been helpful. With these single parents it was friends and family who created the problems. In both examples it was important to begin with the clients' sense of urgency and to respect their need for defenses. Since there were only an evening and a day for work with this group, I had to move rather quickly to confront the participants with the need to look at their part in the proceedings; however, it was also important that I take some time to acknowledge how it felt to them.

I would now like to examine briefly five of the major themes which emerged in the course of the discussion, illustrating each with excerpts from my recordings of the group sessions.

Relationship with Friends and Family

During the course of the following discussion I was struck by how the crisis for the single parent was simultaneously a crisis for friends and relatives. It appeared that the single parent was sending mixed messages to "significant others." On the one hand I heard, "I'm hurt, lost, overwhelmed. Help me." The contrary message was, "Don't get too close. I'm afraid of losing my independence."

After Dick described the details of his separation and his current living situation with his six-month-old child, he went on to describe the problems. He emphasized the difficulty of living in a small town and, in his particular case, being in a personal service occupation which put him in daily contact with many town residents. He said, "Sure I feel lousy, depressed, and alone. But some days I feel I'm getting over things a bit, feeling a little bit up, and everywhere I go people constantly stop me to tell me how terrible things are. If I didn't feel lousy before I went out, I sure do by the time I get home."

Dick added a further complication in that the baby had a serious case of colic and was crying all the time. He told the group that everyone was always criticizing how he handled the baby and even his mother was telling him he wasn't competent and should move back home with her. He continued by saying he was so depressed by this that he had taken to not talking to anyone anymore, avoiding his friends, staying home alone at night, and he was going out of his mind. Others in the group shared similar versions of this experience. I said to Dick, "And that's the dilemma, isn't it? Just at the time you really need help the most, you feel you have to cut yourself off from it to maintain your sense of personal integrity and sanity. You would like some help because the going is rough, but you are not sure you want to have to depend on all of these people, and you are not sure you like the costs involved." Dick nodded and the other group members agreed.

It became clear to the group members and me that Dick was actively sending two apparently conflicting messages, and not being really clear about either. It appeared that his ambivalence about the central issue of independence and dependence was the major dynamic in relating to friends and family. The crisis appeared to evoke unresolved conflicts. Dick was feeling that he wanted to give up and let someone else handle things for him. This frightened him and made it difficult for him to take any help at all. All of the group members expressed one variation or another on this same theme.

After providing recognition and support for these feelings, I tried to move the group members into an examination of what they could do about the feelings in terms of how they handled their conversations with friends and relatives. I encountered a good deal of resistance to this idea, with Dick balking each time I tried to get him to look at how he might have handled a conversation differently. He evaded this by jumping quickly to other comments or examples or by saying, "If you only knew my mother/friends, you would realize it is hopeless." When Rose, a member of the group in her early fifties with children close to Dick's age, confronted him from the perspective of his mother, he rejected her comments. I interpreted this as the point at which Dick, and all of the group members, needed to make a second decision. Coming to the group was the first decision to face their problems. Starting to take some personal responsibility for them was the second and more difficult decision. I wanted to integrate, at this moment, empathic support for their struggle with a clear demand for work.

I pointed out what was happening. I said, "It seems to me that when I or a group member suggest that you (Dick) look at your part in the proceedings, you won't take in what we are saying. I only have a day and a half with this group, so I really can't pussy foot around with you." I wondered if it was tough for Dick,

and all of them, to take responsibility for their part in their problems. Dick smiled and admitted that it was hard. He already felt lousy enough. Others joined in on how easy it was to blame everyone else and how hard it was to accept any blame themselves. I agreed that it was tough, but I didn't think I would be of any help to them if I just sat here for a day and a half agreeing about how tough things were for them. The group members laughed, and a number said they didn't want that.

At this point, Doris, one of the three workers participating in the group, surprised us all by saying that she had intended to listen and not talk during the session but that listening to Dick's problem made her want to share hers. She said she had come to the group as an observer; however, she was pregnant, unmarried and, therefore, was about to become a single parent. She thought she was having the same problem in communicating with her mother as Dick was having with his. It was a classic example of a conflict between a mother who is hurt and embarrassed and a daughter who feels rejected at a critical moment in her life. At my suggestion, Rose offered to role-play the mother as Doris tried to find a new way to talk to her mother. The group was supportive but at the same time, following my example, they confronted each other during the discussion in a healthy way.

Dick listened and participated in the work on Doris's problem, and as is often the case, was able to learn something about his own situation as he watched someone else struggling with the same concerns. When I asked him later if he had taken something from it, he said it had helped him a lot to see how he was holding back his real feelings from friends and his own mother. I pointed out to all of the group members what a shock their situation was to their friends and close relatives and how at first contact they could not respond in a way which met their needs. I said, "This does not mean they don't love you. It just means that they have feelings and aren't always able to express them. Your mixed messages also make it difficult."

Cerrise, another worker/observer in the group, joined the discussion at this point and described how she had felt when close friends had separated. She realized now that it had taken her a couple of months to get over being so angry at them for ending their marriage because she loved them both. She hadn't been able to reach out to support them. They, however, had not given up on her, and she had been able to work it out. Dick said that hearing that helped a lot. That was what was probably going on with some of his friends.

Carrie, who was both an unmarried parent and a worker in the community, described her own experiences with her mother when she split up. She shared how she had involved her mother in the process, had let her know her feelings, and that she wanted her mother's love and support but felt she had to handle the problems herself. Dick listened closely and said that this was probably what he had not been able to do. We did some role play on how Dick could handle the conversation with his mother—how he could articulate his real feelings. The group was supportive.

When I asked the group how they felt about this discussion thus far, Doris said it was helpful because I kept stressing the positive aspect, the reaching out and caring between people. Most of them had been so upset they could only see the negatives.

The discussion turned to the question of how much they needed others to talk to about what they were going through. Near the end of the session, in typical "door knob" fashion, Dick revealed that a close male friend of his, in a similar situation with a young child, had told him he was considering committing suicide. He went on to tell us, with tears in his eyes, that the friend had carried through with the threat and had just killed himself. I said, "It must have hit you very hard when that happened, and you must have wondered if you could have done something more to help." Dick agreed that was so and the group members offered him support. After some time I asked Dick if he was worried about his own situation, since he had many of the same feelings as his friend. He said he was worried, but that he thought he would be strong enough to keep going with the goal in his life to make it for his child. I told him he had shown a lot of

strength just coming to the group and working so hard on his problem. Carrie said that he was not alone and that he could call her if he needed someone to talk to as a friend, or as a worker. Rose pointed out that there was a single parent social group at the church, and Dick said he had not realized that. Others in the group also offered support. I asked Dick how he felt now and he said, "I feel a lot better. I realize now that I'm not so alone." Irene, who had opened the discussion by saying she had not yet gone through all the phases, summarized the evening's work when she said, "I guess we are all struggling to find ways of saying to friends and close relatives, please love me now. I need you." The discussion ended, and we agreed to pick up again in the morning.

Relationship to the Children

A central theme which emerged when the group members discussed their problems with their children had to do with their guilt over their feelings of failure as parents. They expressed feelings of responsibility for the marital split and therefore also felt responsible for their children's reactions. Thus, when indirect cues of the children's negative reactions emerged, they had difficulty in dealing with them. Also, the guilt made it hard for them to make appropriate demands upon their children. For example, in the first part of the discussion which follows, one mother has difficulty in asking for an older child's help in babysitting a younger child. When the mother raises the general question, I rely on the crucial skill of moving from the general to the specific, in order to obtain details for our discussion. If I had not asked for the specific incident, our discussion would have remained general and would not be helpful to the member who raised the problem or to the other members who try to help her. As in all mutual aid groups, as they help this mother, they are also helping themselves.

There were some new members in the morning, so I took some time to review the contract. The discussion picked up again with Irene raising the problem of dealing with the children. She described how tough it was on her when she asked her eleven-year-old boy to babysit his five-year-old brother. I asked if she could describe a specific incident, and she told us about one that had occurred the previous day. Her older son was about to go out to play when she asked him to cover for her, since she needed to take care of some business. His face dropped but he did not say anything. I asked her if she could tell us how she felt when she saw his face drop. She said, "Miserable!" I asked her what she said to him and she replied, "Nothing!"

I pointed out how Irene had not leveled with her son and how she had avoided a frank discussion about her expectations on him and his feelings about having to carry some of the load. I asked if she had any ideas why it was so tough on her. She said he had not been getting along with his friends for a while after the split, and in fact, was moping around alone. Now that she saw him out and around, she hated to do anything which interfered. John, a new member, revealed that he had been a son in a single-parent family and that he felt the same way her son felt. He resented having to be responsible at such a young age. He said he would have very much appreciated it if his mom had talked directly to him about it and had allowed him to get some of his feelings off his chest. I said, "I wonder if you parents really want to hear how your kids are feeling? I wonder if your kids' feelings are too close to your own."

Gary said there was a lot of guilt in these situations. You feel responsible for your kid's problems because you've split up. He went on to say, "I'm also a little bit like a third-year medical student. Every time I see any sign of trouble with my kid, I'm sure it's going to be something really terrible."

As Irene was describing her problem, I kept reaching for her feelings associated with their conversation. Clients often describe an incident without explaining their associated affect. In a sense, I was asking Irene to go back to the moment and try to remember and then share with us how it felt to her. By pointing out the gap between how she felt and what she said, I was trying to help all of the group members to see how hard it is to be honest in expression of our feelings. We often expect the other person to "divine" our feelings, without accepting the responsibility of letting them know what those feelings are. In the group situation, I wanted to move further than just understanding, since I wanted to help the group members develop the skills needed to relate differently to those people who were important in their lives. I suggested a quick role-play, consciously trying not to make it a major production (for example, Let's put two chairs in the middle of the circle ...). Role play in the group is difficult enough without the complications associated with formal structure. Irene resisted the suggestion. This resistance was important and was in many ways part of the work. Just as Rick's defensiveness in the opening session was a signal of underlying feelings, Irene's hesitation was also sending a signal. I tried to be empathic by exploring the reason for her hesitation, while simultaneously making a demand for work.

I asked if a little role-play might help here, and since John was a child in a family like this, maybe he could help by playing Irene's son. There was some hesitation by Irene who said that was hard to do. When I asked about the hesitation, she said she was afraid she would make mistakes. Carrie pointed out they would be the same mistakes they all make, so she shouldn't worry about it. Irene responded by saying it was hard to role-play. I agreed and then told her that I never said this work would be easy. She agreed to give it a try. The role-play revealed how hard it was for them to reach for the underlying feelings that they sensed were expressed indirectly by their children.

I introduced the skill of looking for trouble when everything is going your way as an active way of reaching for underlying feelings. I illustrated how they could ask the child for negative feelings even when the child seemed to say everything was fine.

There was a general recognition of how immobilized they often felt by their guilt. Irene tried again and this time was direct in opening up the question of mutual responsibility and her son's feelings. John told her that as her son he would be relieved to have it out in the open and would feel good that she respected him and needed him in this way. He still would not like to stay home and babysit but it would sure make it easier. Irene said, "I guess if I get this off my chest, it will be a lot easier for me as well."

As is often the case, when the group members saw how a first offering of a feeling-laden theme is handled, they felt safer about moving into a deeper, more painful area. The difficulties arising from their guilt and their reluctance to make demands on their children were real problems, but still, only "near problems." That is, each issue exposed just the surface of a much more difficult area of feeling. Maureen raised the issue directly in a way which touched each of the other members. Their first reaction was to avoid the feelings which were just under the surface of her question. Interesting enough, this process in the group replicates the way in which they avoid the feelings under their children's questions. Once again, the group leader's task is to confront the members, but to do it gently and in recognition of the understandable reasons for the denial.

Maureen jumped in and asked how you handle it when your kid says, "Why can't we be a normal family?" This hit the group like a bomb, and they all jumped in with their versions of how they would answer the child's question. Most of the responses were variations of defensive explanations, long analogies or examples, and so on, all designed to provide the "good parent's answer." I intervened and said, "You know, you have jumped in to answer Maureen's child's question, but I wonder if we really know what the question is?" I explain that it often takes some time for others really to tell us what they are feeling and that a quick response may not be getting at the real feelings, particularly when a question hits us in our gut and touches our feelings. I asked, "What would happen if you asked your child what he or she meant by the question?" There was a thoughtful silence in the room, and then Rose said, "Then we might really find out, and I'm not sure I want to hear."

I asked if we could get back to Maureen's example, and Maureen said, "Could we go on to someone else's example? I've been in the spotlight too long and people are probably bored with my problem." I asked the group members if this was true. They vigorously shook their heads, indicating they were very interested. I said to Maureen, "Look, they are interested. Why is it you want to get off the spot? Is it very tough to be on the spot?" Maureen replied, "It's hitting too close to home." The group members laughed in acknowledgment. I credited her for being honest and asked what she meant by "hitting close to home." She said, "I want to feel like I'm a good mother." There was silence in the room, and Lenore finally said, "I know what you mean. I feel I failed in my marriage and now I'm desperate about not wanting to feel I have failed as a mother."

This was followed by a discussion of their sense of guilt, of how harsh they were on themselves, and how their feelings of failure in their marriages and their fears of failure as parents often translated into overconcern and overprotection in relation to their children with a resulting fear of revealing the underlying, painful feelings. We returned to Maureen's example. She role-played a number of ways she might reach for her daughter's real feelings and the meaning of the question, "Why can't we be like a normal family?"

Group workers often believe they face a dilemma in having to deal either with their groups' process or its content. The dilemma is experienced only because the worker believes in the existence of what is really a false dichotomy. In this group, the process by which the members attempted to avoid the pain underlying questions raised by other group members was simply an illustration of the same problem they had with their children's question. Thus, the process and the content are synthesized, not dichotomized, and as the group worker deals with process, he or she is simultaneously dealing with content. I try to use this dynamic by asking the members to reflect briefly on the morning's discussion. The briefness is designed to ensure that the group does not lose its purpose and become lost in a discussion of its process.

Before we broke for lunch, I asked the group members to reflect on what had just happened in our group. I thought in some ways our group was an illustration of some of the problems they faced. I pointed out how Maureen had said she wanted to be off the spot because others were bored. Instead of just accepting that, I reached for other feelings which might be behind her discomfort. It turned out that she was feeling many things and her concerns were very much the concerns of the whole group. I wondered what they thought about my observation. Irene said that she could see what I meant. They had feelings they needed to talk about and they would only get to them if I helped them. The same was probably true for their kids. I said, "Lecture's over, how about lunch?"

Relationship to the Ex-Spouse

The work on the difficulty of being direct with one's child led to the subject of the relationship to the ex-spouse. The central theme for this group was related to their deep feelings of rejection. Even when they had initiated the break, it had been in response to their own feelings of rejection by the other partner. It soon became clear that their difficulty in helping the children deal with feelings of rejection related directly to their difficulty in dealing with their own similar feelings.

Ginette initiated this discussion by asking, "Is it always good to be honest?" When I asked why she raised that question, she described a situation in which her husband was rejecting their five-year-old boy while at the same time caring for their youngest child. He had refused to visit or call this son while promising to do so each time she raised it with him. When I asked her to describe her telephone conversations with the ex-spouse, it quickly became clear that she was pushing him and he was denying that any problem existed. When I asked her how all of this had made her feel, she replied, "I'm really tired of trying to get Dad to be Dad."

I told Ginette I thought this must have put her in an awful bind with the child when, for example, he asked her, "When is Daddy going to visit me?" I wondered how she dealt with it. Ginette described her conversation with her son which indicated she attempts to cover up the problem with "white lies" and to do whatever she could to avoid dealing with the child's feelings. I pointed this out to the group acknowledging that I could appreciate the bind she felt.

June, a new member who had been listening quietly all morning, began to speak. She spoke with a low, soft voice and began to cry before she could complete her comments: "I have been sitting here listening to Ginette thinking that she is describing my problem exactly. And now, I think I realize . . . (crying softly) that I'm going to have to face my own rejection by my husband who walked out on me ... before the healing can start ... and before I can help my kids face their rejection."

When a member expresses strong feelings in a group, it can be uncomfortable both for the individual and the other group members. Our societal taboos make it difficult for us to offer and accept such emotions; however, they are genuine emotions and need to be dealt with in some way. In this instance the group members seemed to turn away from June; however, it was not because they did not care. Actually, it was because they cared too much. These were their own emotions they needed to face, and June was simply expressing them. As group leader, I tried to help the members reach out to June, to overcome the norms they brought with them to the group which called for them to pretend they did not notice her pain. As they helped her with her feelings, they also helped themselves with their own.

We all felt very moved by June's words. I could see the group members were upset. Marie was sitting next to June and I could tell she was very agitated—looking around the room, looking at June, and literally moving in her seat. I said, "I think June's feelings have hit all of us very hard. I have a feeling you would like to reach out to June, wouldn't you, Marie?" Marie said she really would. When I asked her why she didn't do it, she said, "Well, I'm afraid to." After a slight pause, she reached over and took June's hand, holding it tightly. June responded warmly to the gesture. I reassured her that it was O.K. to share her feelings with us and that her tears were an important part of how she felt. I told her that I felt she spoke for all the group members and they quickly assured her that I was correct.

We returned to Ginette at this point and the issues of being honest with her children and allowing them to express their feelings. She said, "I want my son to share his feelings

within certain guidelines." I responded, "You mean, you want him to share the feelings that are not too tough for you." The group members, including Ginette, laughed in recognition. Ginette said, "I realize I have to be straight with him. When I lied and tried to make it sound that his father loved him, it didn't make any sense, just like it wouldn't make any sense to make it sound like he didn't care at all." The group members agreed to role-play the conversation, so that Ginette could find a helpful way to be honest and to recognize her child's feelings of rejection.

After a few difficult starts she finally decided on the following way of handling his questions: "Your Daddy does care about you but right now he is having a hard time and feeling very upset and bad himself. That is why he hasn't visited you or invited you to stay with him. I know it must be very hard for you to understand why he doesn't spend more time with you if he really cares. It must make you feel very bad as well." As Ginette spoke these words, she was close to tears herself. I suggested that she might share with her child how hard this was for her. Then she and her son could cry together. Ginette said the discussion had helped, and she realized there was no easy way to handle this.

Throughout this conversation and others, I was struck by the pattern in which the group members tried to deal with their own hurt through the medium of the children. Their feelings of rejection were strong; however, their sense of vulnerability made it difficult for them to admit their own feelings to the ex-spouse, the children, and even to themselves.

Relating to the World of Finances

Rose, a woman in her early fifties, raised the many financial questions she had to face when her husband had left her. Her problems related to suddenly having to take responsibility for many of the questions that her husband had always handled. One particularly frustrating example was her problem obtaining credit. When she applied for a bank credit card, she was told she would need to establish a positive credit record. She was surprised that the credit record developed over twenty years of marriage was considered to be her husband's and she was judged not to have a credit rating at all. When she enquired how she was to establish a good credit rating, she was told she needed to obtain credit and to handle it well. At this point, feeling trapped, she had just given up.

When I asked Rose how she felt about the whole experience, she replied, "Damned angry!" Carrie told her she had given up too soon. She said that Rose was going to have to assert herself if she wanted to obtain her rights. I asked Carrie how she thought Rose could do this, and she suggested the following plan. She advised Rose to visit the credit bureau and discuss her desire to establish a credit rating. She pointed out that Rose was making monthly payments on a number of bills, for example, rent, telephone, utilities, and that she could use this to impress the credit bureau with her credit worthiness. She should also speak to the bank manager directly and point out that she had been part of the family that had given his bank the family business up to that point and that she would like his cooperation in developing a plan to establish a credit rating on her own.

The group members agreed that this might be her first step. They also felt that if she ran into difficulty with this approach, she should consider bringing this to the attention of the bank's head office by writing the president. She could also consider contacting the Human Rights Commission, since this actually constituted a form of discrimination. It was obvious that everyone was angry at her situation. Rose agreed she could do more on this than she had thus far. She said, "I guess I began to believe that they were right about me not having earned a credit rating. It never occurred to me to refuse to accept the decision." Carrie

said, "The hard part is understanding that you're going to have to fight for your own rights because nobody else is going to do it for you."

Loneliness and the Fear of Risking

As is often the case, the group members seemed to leave the theme which was most difficult to deal with until near the end of the session. For most of the parents in this group the change to single-parent status, for whatever the reason, had resulted in a state of loneliness. After having experienced years of being integrated, for better or worse, as part of a couple, they were suddenly facing the problem of being differentiated and alone. While many single parents enter into new relationships, the members of this group had not. Perhaps that is why they attended the group. What became even more striking, as the following discussion reveals in a most dramatic fashion, is that the hurt they experienced in their separations has created a fear of risking in new relationships. They wanted closeness but were afraid to be vulnerable again to the pain of another separation. The crucial aspect to this work involved the group members' understanding the connections between the way they felt and the way they acted. Also, they needed to see that changing their state of loneliness might be up to them.

The conversation about finances, which was discussed in the preceding section, had actually emerged in the midst of another discussion. I would like to go back to the beginning of that segment when Rose told us she was afraid of being alone when her last child, now fifteen, grew up and moved out. All of her other children had left the home. Even though Rose wanted to deal with this question of loneliness, a part of her wanted to avoid it. It is interesting to note that the group members *and* the group leader backed off and in a silent conspiracy, allowed the subject to change to the issue of finances. What follows is the start of that discussion.

Maureen said to Rose, "Maybe the problem is you've never been Rose. You've always been somebody's mother or somebody's wife." Louise said that it was almost another form of rejection, being alone. She continued, "My kids aren't moving out, but I find myself feeling the same way just putting them on the school bus in the mornings."

I asked Rose if she could be specific about the loneliness, when did she feel it and what was it like? She said the worst time was the emptiness in the house in the evenings. After a few more comments by other group members, I noted that the discussion had shifted to the question of credit.

It was at this point that the work in the previous section took place. I intervened at the end of the credit discussion and said, "You know, it seems you have all decided to drop the issue Rose raised at the beginning, that is, how to handle the terrible loneliness of the empty house." They all laughed, recognizing they had silently agreed to drop the hot potato. Brett spoke for the first time and said that when we figured out that answer, to let her know, since she had the same problem. I commented that probably they all did and that was why it was hard to help Rose.

Carrie wanted to know what Rose did about finding friends. I said I thought that was a good start in helping Rose. Rose described how she had been invited to a dance by a group of her friends, all couples, and then spent the whole night sitting there while no one asked her to dance. I said I could imagine how uncomfortable they might all have felt. Lenore said that when she goes to a dance and no one asks her, she asks them. Connie wondered if she couldn't find a female friend to go to dances with. A pattern started to emerge with Rose saying, "Yes, but ... " to each suggestion. When I asked her if she had spoken to her friends about her discomfort directly,

so they could better appreciate her feelings, it was obvious that she had not. Instead, she had been hurt and angry and had cut herself further off from her closest friends.

As her resistance stiffened, I finally confronted her and said it appeared as though she was not willing to work at maintaining her close relationships. She seemed to be saying that she wanted friends once again to "divine" her feelings, but she was not willing to take the risk and let them know what they were. At the same time she was complaining about being alone. There was a long silence, and then with great feeling she said, "I don't want anyone to ever get close to me again." The group was somewhat stunned at the force of her feelings, since she had been speaking quietly and in control for most of the session. I asked her why she felt this so strongly. Rose went on to tell us that her husband had left her for her best friend. I said, "So you really had two losses. You must have felt very betrayed and very bitter." She replied that she still felt that way, hurt and bitter. This initiated a powerful discussion by all group members of their feelings about intimacy. Their losses made them wonder if they should ever let themselves get close to anyone again. Irene said, "I think that's what I meant last night when I asked when you get over the last phase. I realize I have been depressed because I'm holding back. I'm not risking getting hurt again." The conversation dealt with their feelings about risking with friends of the same sex as well as with members of the opposite sex. Many of them described men who had attempted to date them whom they had liked but whom they had been afraid to get to know.

I tried to take us back to Rose by asking what she thought about this conversation. She shrugged her shoulders and said, "Well, maybe in a couple of years it will get better." I said, "And maybe in a couple of years, it will get a lot worse." I pointed out how all of them had been concerned that the kids come out of the situation whole, and yet their message to their kids appeared to be that when one gets hurt, it's better not to try again. Rose pointed out how much she has done about her life, even learning to drive a car so she could be a bit more independent. I agreed that she had shown a great deal of strength in tackling the strains of being alone and that was why I felt she had the strength to even tackle this one—perhaps the hardest one for all of them. Irene said, "You're right, you know. We complain about being alone, but we are afraid to let ourselves be vulnerable again, afraid to get hurt." I said, "And that's the real dilemma, isn't it? It hurt so much to lose what you've had, you're afraid to risk. And then you find it also hurts to be alone. The important point, right now, is that you are aware of the question of loneliness and what to do about it is really in your hands."

CONCLUSION

I have tried to share some of my observations about working with single-parent families, illustrating them with excerpts from my own group work practice. I have focused on identifying the specific themes of concern and the associated feelings which are somewhat unique to this group of clients, including their ambivalence about independence and dependence in relation to their family and friends, their feelings of guilt in relation to their children, the feeling of rejection which dominated the relationship to the ex-spouse, their anger at the world of finance and business which often does not recognize them as separate individuals, and finally, the one which emerged powerfully as a "door knob" theme, their fear of risking intimacy and their desperate need for it.

When we evaluated the group in the ending phase, the participants felt it was helpful to see other people with the same problems. They also appreciated my pushing them to be specific about their problems, even to the point of asking them to recount their actual conversations. They liked getting new ideas about what to say and do and didn't feel quite so helpless about some of their concerns. They also felt it was important that I didn't let them off the hook. Finally, they felt I was really listening to them and that I could understand what they were struggling with. I pointed out that these were probably some of the same qualities their children wanted from them.

I thanked them for their honesty and for teaching me a great deal more about the problems of being a single parent. There were exchanges of positive feeling at the end and some discussion about how they might continue to stay in touch. They also discussed other sources of support in the community. The workers, who had been invited to attend the group in part to be available to the members for follow-up counseling, offered their telephone numbers and invited group members to contact them if they wanted to talk.

NOTES

1. *Canada's Families* (Ottawa: Statistics Canada, Demography Division, 1979).

2. For discussions of some of the issues facing single-parent families, see Benjamin Schlesinger, ed., *One In Ten: The Single Parent Family in Canada* (Toronto: Guidance Centre, Faculty of Education, University of Toronto, 1979); Beverly C. Barnes, *The Single Parent Experience* (Boston: Resource Communications in cooperation with The Family Service Association of America, 1980); Kristine M. Rosenthal and Harry F. Keshet, *Fathers Without Partners: A Study of Fathers and the Family After Marital Separation* (Totowa, N.J.: Roman and Littlefield, 1981).

3. Statistics Canada, 1979.

4. Elisabeth Kübler-Ross, *On Death and Dying* (New York: Macmillan, 1969).

5. For a discussion of short term groups, see chapter 14, Lawrence Shulman, *The Skills of Helping Individuals and Groups, Second Edition* (Itasca, Ill.: F. E. Peacock Publishers, Inc., 1984).

6. For a more complete discussion of the skills cited in this chapter, see chapter 2 of this book and Shulman, *The Skills of Helping Individuals and Groups, Second Edition.*

7. For a full transcript of the first session of this married couples group, see Lawrence Shulman, *The Skills of Helping Individuals and Groups,Second Edition,* pp. 197-214.

Sam Indelicato
Penny Goldberg

CHAPTER 10

Harassed and Alone: Parents of Learning Disabled Children

More than 7.5 million children under the age of eighteen in this country, suffer from a little-understood group of related physiological problems called "learning disability."[1] Ten years ago one was hard pressed to find a professional or a developmental center that recognized this imprecise and puzzling disorder. Countless numbers of the children have been mislabeled and misdiagnosed, since the symptoms of learning disabled children are frequently mistaken for those of emotional disorder or mental retardation. Though research and a knowledge base in the field are still in infancy, significant information is already known and can be applied to diagnose and treat this disorder properly. We know that learning disability is a cluster or constellation of symptoms and that they may take many forms.[2] No one neurological impairment is exactly like another. Each child's functioning depends upon the mix of a variety of possible symptoms, which exist in an almost infinite number of permutations, degrees, and proportions. The manifestations take many forms, including reading or language difficulties, gross or fine motor deficits, behavioral or maturational problems, such as poor impulse control, or perceptual problems. Therefore, it is reasonable to recognize that a hyperactive, antisocial child and a withdrawn, poorly coordinated, dyslexic child may both be considered learning disabled, though significantly different in how they present themselves.

In spite of these different combinations, two major concerns expressed by parents or educators when the child begins school are behavior difficulties and poor school performance. Some children can't match shapes, don't stay in their seats, have temper tantrums or crying spells, can't catch a ball or swing a bat, or experience difficulty grasping concepts. In our highly complex society significant pressures to perform are applied in school, even in preschool. Often the learning disabled child sees his failures, feels the rejection of peers, and begins to develop secondary emotional problems as he faces challenges beyond his capabilities. The process of growing up becomes laden with obstacles and trauma. At home his inability to follow instructions or his destructive, hyperactive behavior is often met with scolding or admonition from parents who don't understand what is wrong.

The interpretation of the child's puzzling behavior is still inadequately recognized by responsible professionals as typically masked symptoms of a learning disability. Parents are told by educators that their child is "lazy," "does not like school," "is a slow learner," is a "trouble maker," is "undisciplined," and "emotionally disturbed." Unfortunately, not enough pediatricians take a comprehensive approach to the evaluation of the symptoms. Some falsely reassure parents that their child is "just immature" and others too quickly label, "I think your child is retarded." Others say "you worry too much."

DEVELOPMENTAL CYCLE

Normal parenting is beset by strains, struggles, joys, and fears. There is, for example, anticipation of the birth of a normal baby and expectations for developmental tasks commensurate with the general course of human life, such as the stereotypic phases of growth (like terrible twos, adolescent rebellion). Parents generally expect to face these life-cycle issues and ordinarily are able to make the appropriate adaptations required by them. Germain and Gitterman point out that when there is an upset in the adaptive balance, the result is stress.[3] According to their Life Model approach, stress is viewed as a "psychosocial condition generated by discrepancies between needs and capacities, on the one hand, and environmental qualities on the other. It arises in three interrelated areas of living: life transition, environmental pressures and interpersonal processes."

In applying the Life Model concept of adaptation to the situation of parents facing the reality that there is something wrong with their child, we understand this as a critical life transition (the loss of a normal child) requiring new demands and new responses. Parents faced with inappropriate and unhelpful feedback from physicians, friends, and relatives, coupled with their own observation of their child's bewildering behavior, often live in a state of constant frustration, tension, and anxiety. Some are thrown into a state of chaos. Feelings of helplessness and failure emerge. Understandably most parents have a difficult time acknowledging that a problem exists. For those who do recognize a need to have their child evaluated and who receive a confirming diagnosis of learning disability, there are a variety of responses. They include guilt—"What did I do to cause this"; disbelief—"It can't possibly be true"; anger—"What do you know anyway, you are probably a quack doctor!"; blame—"What kind of father are you, it's your fault, if you'd have been home more, this wouldn't have happened." Parents may feel unprepared for information or may "shop" for doctors, seeking another more acceptable opinion. These reactions are normal and are expected, in view of the fact that parents are being told that their child is impaired. They feel hurt and disappointed, grieved, and upset. It may lead to overreaction, withdrawal and depression, marital, emotional, or financial strain, separation, and even divorce.

How any one parent or family meets the demands of this life stress is very much dependent upon the presence or absence of environmental support, such as schools, hospitals, and the quality of interpersonal relationships. The environment and primary relationships can either provide support or can be another source of stress. This chapter will illustrate sources of stress to parents of learning disabled children and will describe the development of a mutual aid group to meet the needs of this vulnerable population.

AGENCY CONTEXT AND THE GROUP MODALITY

The setting, a multidisciplinary, medically based center for children with developmental disabilities, combines the skills and knowledge of several professional groups: Neurology, psychiatry, social work, psychology, physical and occupational therapies, speech pathology, nursing, education, and the support of a large case management staff.

Over 1,000 children per year are served with a wide variety of developmental disabilities, such as cerebral palsy, mental retardation, seizure disorders, learning problems, and emotional difficulties. About 50 percent of the clients are learning disabled. Each child routinely receives an evaluation by the pediatric neurologist, social worker, and psychologist. Other examinations are recommended as needed. The findings and recommendations are shared at a multidisciplinary conference, with the parent(s) and child participating. In analyzing the service delivery to this population, parents of learning disabled children were virtually left to fend for themselves following the informational session describing and diagnosing their child's problem. The major service plan focused on special school placement and very little on helping the parent cope and deal with all the other ramifications of their child's situation. As a result, and unwittingly, parents of learning disabled children were being negatively affected by the individually geared diagnostic and treatment emphasis at the clinic.

In this atmosphere parents felt isolated and at times intimidated by the professional "experts" treating their child. Some were reluctant to challenge the word of the physician, with whom they imbued magical powers. Other parents became confused or frustrated by the flood of information or instructions given them to carry out in the home. Many learning disabled children manifested accompanying behavioral difficulties which often erupted in school and caused the parents to be called in to respond to "charges." Thus most parents felt anxious and defenseless against the educational system with which they often had to deal.

The mutual aid group seemed "tailor-made" to meet some of the parents' needs. Casework experiences revealed that some parents had incorporated a "bad parent" image, couching deep-seated feelings of inadequacy and guilt. Other parents seemed generally anxious and unfocused.

Schwartz has written about the mutual aid features of the group experiences.[4] The most important of these as he sees it are the ways that people support and learn from each other during this helping process. The support and incentive for members to reach for difficult themes and explore taboo areas is generated by the group interaction. Through group process the tasks of elaboration and division of problems takes place. Members from their own vantage points can swap examples, contribute to each other's ideas, and explore various facets of their problem area.

In a group we felt parents could share their experiences, feelings, and concerns, and help each other. We hoped, for example, that parents' concerns about the use of labels (as applied to their children and to themselves) such as "overprotective," "permissive," "inadequate," "crazy," or "brain damaged," would be discussed. Their common experiences provided a natural basis for the development of mutual aid, comfort, and support, a place where they could recognize that they were not alone in experiencing these painful feelings and self-doubts. The experience of isolation in our clinic was not unique, it was duplicated in other institutions (such as schools) and social networks (like neighbors), reinforcing a sense of futility and hopelessness. We hoped that through the group they would experience others "in the same boat" and develop the strength and skills to deal with unresponsive organizational and social network representatives. Professional social work intervention was vitally needed to meet the needs of this population. We therefore proposed to the administration the development of parent groups.

The group was to be of a short-term, "closed-ended," task-centered nature. This meant a contract of six sessions to be held weekly. We felt clients would be more willing to engage in a short-term commitment because many were involved heavily in other service systems with great stress on their time. According to Gitterman, "open-ended" membership seems to result in groups becoming stuck at a particular stage of development, and ongoing, long-term groups may lead to a loss of vitality and purpose.[5] The time boundary and limit of planned, short-term groups seem to help members to focus quickly and maintain purpose, direction, and a sense of urgency.

To set up groups in the agency, we had to engage the support of the entire staff in this venture. We involved staff at all levels in the group formation process; clinic administrators, social workers, doctors, case managers, and the rest. Generally staff showed enthusiasm about our proposal, indicating that the individual intervention of the clinic with clients successfully met most of their daily reality needs, but that there was a great gap in meeting the counseling needs of the clients. Much of the work involved educating the staff about group work process.

The most common question that staff

had was about the mutual aid concept of group. We explained this by citing our experience at the clinic. All of the clients seemed to share a tremendous sense of isolation about their child's disorder. By forming groups, parents would be able to hear from other parents experiencing the same situation. We wanted to create an atmosphere where parents could express and help each other with some very painful material. From this sharing experience we hoped that people could help mobilize each other to deal more effectively within a given situation.

Some workers were concerned about the intrusion upon their territorial boundaries. Since much of the workers' time at the clinic was taken up with the daily reality needs of the clients, it left little time to do any comprehensive counseling. We began to sense that workers were afraid that they would lose the few "counseling cases" they had. This issue was raised covertly by one of the workers.

Ms. Jones: I understand clearly how a group might be effective for this population, but I know dealing with these people on a day-to-day basis, that many of them won't be interested, especially the ones that are seeing a worker on a one-to-one basis. Who are you going to recruit for your group?

Worker: We're glad that you raised this issue of recruiting. The groups will be open to any parent who has a child with a learning disability, particularly when there is a significant behavior problem. We will be depending on the worker's assessment of the appropriateness of clients for the groups as well as recruiting from the older files. It would be helpful if workers could speak personally to clients who they thought might benefit from such a group.

In retrospect we had failed to open up for discussion several key concerns that the clinic workers probably had about the groups, one being the interplay of group and individual work and the other issue of confidentiality and communication between individual and group workers.

Shulman relates to the first point when he writes that clients may use both individual and group help for different issues as they see fit.[6] He sees group discussion enhancing rather than impeding individual sessions because members are given the opportunity to understand how others are experiencing problems and also see that others have fears related to their own taboo areas. These factors may put members in touch with feelings not previously evident and may help members introduce material in their individual work.

Likewise, Shulman suggests that work in individual sessions can aid a client to raise an issue in group. Some material is too personal to begin talking about in a group context. As this material is introduced in individual work and not harshly judged, the client is then encouraged to share these concerns in the group.

Schwartz deals with the second issue of confidentiality and communication between individual and group workers when he writes that the client is less concerned about intra-agency confidentiality than he is about the quality of the service he gets.[7] This would imply more communication rather than less. The sharing of such information can pose problems at the beginning. But these seem to be more easily resolved when workers learn that they can involve others in the client's work without weakening their own relationship with the client.

The lack of discussion of these two issues assured a continued cautiousness on the part of clinic workers in terms of what demands would be placed on them with the initiation of these groups and how this would affect their "counseling cases." The failure on our part to reach for these concerns is probably a major reason why we received only one referral from the staff.

The actual formation of the first group came almost entirely from reviewing files of clients who had finished the evaluation process up to a year ago.

We sent out letters to about twenty parents whose children had been evaluated for learning disability within the last year. In defining our service, we were careful not to use labels in talking about their children. From our experience in individual interviews we had found that the labels of "learning disabled, minimal brain damage, hyperactive," and the like were greatly overused by schools, peers, and extended families.

We defined our service in terms of the behavior of the child, and the consequences of that behavior. An example of this from our letter was:

We are aware that parents experience common concerns about their children which are related to behavior at school or at home. This might take the form of not getting along with brothers and sisters, an inability to keep up with schoolwork, or difficulty in making and keeping friends.

From experience at the clinic we learned that these were the three most important areas for parents. We noted that one of the aims of the group would be to learn new ways to deal with their child's behavior, a task we found where parents could be very helpful to one another. We included a reply slip with each letter to obtain feedback from them and indicated that a worker would soon call to speak further with them. Since many of the parents had been referred to our clinic from the school system, we tried to convey an empathic tone to the offer of our service by verbalizing some of the embarrassment and confusion they might have felt in receiving a call from a school official recommending that their child be evaluated. We rehearsed the phone calls by using role-plays. We found this to be valuable experience for the actual calls. Most of the parents greeted the idea with great enthusiasm and said they would definitely attend. But this did not translate into large numbers of groups. In making follow-up phone calls, and in subsequent recruiting of members, we found that a quick yes was usually a form of responding to organizational representation. We learned to explore further their conception of a group.

Another factor that was important in the formation of this first group was the size of the client "pool" we were drawing from. Because we were working almost exclusively from older files, we found that we had to enlarge our "pool" dramatically. We initially had started our mailing with twenty parents and found that we had to enlarge it to over eighty in order to secure the first group.

GROUP THEMES

We began by referring to the letter and stated that we would like to identify and discuss some of the concerns they shared about their children.

Worker: In the letter we stated that we would like to try to set up parent groups to give parents a place to talk with each other about their concerns involving their children. We've noted that parents who come to the clinic usually express some concern about their child's inability to keep up with schoolwork, difficulty in making and keeping friends, or not getting along with brothers and sisters. Do these sound like some of the things you have experienced with your child?

The importance of making a clear, uncomplicated statement of why the group is meeting is contained within Schwartz's definition of contract.[8] The contract should reflect the stake of the group members in coming together and should also reflect the agency's stake in serving them. The contract should not only reflect both stakes, but also provide a frame of reference for the work that follows. Contract work is not limited to just the beginning of groups but is seen by Schwartz as constantly being renegotiated as the concrete implications of the two stakes become clearer in the events of group life.

Many parents responded with comments and stories about the educational system. Since many of the referrals to the clinic were from the school system concerning disruptive behavior or inability to keep up with schoolwork, initial angry feelings were expressed by group members toward what they felt were the failings of the school system to educate their child. This sometimes took the form of debating the pros and cons of a special class for their children:

Mrs. Charles was discussing concern about her daughter being a slow learner, and disgust with the school system. Another member, Mrs. Frank, asked if she had tried to intervene with the school system. Mrs. Charles responded by indicating a preference for her child to attend a special class. Mrs. Frank angrily shot back that she was fighting to get her son out of a special class, as he had not progressed at all in two years.

The clinic itself also came under fire in the initial discussions. Parents complained that the evaluation process (a lengthy one requiring many appointments to complete) eliminated a few medical reasons for the cause of their child's trouble, but failed to leave them with any specific practical steps to eradicate their problem. Beginning with their frustration and anger toward the schools or clinic seemed to be the easiest way for most parents to talk about their situation.

After a period of ventilation and sharing concerns we focused the work by identifying several major areas of stress the parents wanted help with during the course of this group program. Three major themes that emerged were the relationship to the child, the status of parent of a disabled child, and familial pressures. The demands placed upon these parents to meet the special needs of their children, from an often unsupportive environment as previously described with a sense of personal loss of self combined with difficulties in their familial relationships, converged and proved overwhelming. Germain and Gitterman's Life Model supports the notion that these three major issues identified by the parents as most stressful benefit best from professional social work intervention when problem definition is located in the interface between person and environment, with intervention formulated in terms of "reciprocal adaptive processes."[9] Thus it became the task of the group leaders to help the group members strengthen adaptive capacities as well as recognize the need for increased environmental responsiveness. Although three important areas of stress were raised, the short-term nature of the group allowed only enough time for sufficient exploration of the first two themes: relationship to the child, and status of the parent. The third area, familial pressures, received only cursory group attention.

To provide group members with a sense of the group process, each member was asked to choose a situation in relation to the major themes previously mentioned that they wanted to improve upon within the six-week period. We hoped the identification of specific tasks would establish a climate within which parents would examine their situations and experiment with new coping behaviors.[10] We wanted to give the members a demonstration by focusing on one parent's concern and using it as an illustration of how we would all work together to help each other. What we found was that for parents it was usually easier to identify target problems than to identify tasks that they could begin to work on. In identifying target problems they were usually able to focus on one generalized problem or behavior. This was usually supported by feedback from other parents who had similar problems. Concerning task identification, parents sometimes responded with a sense of surprise and reluctance in that they were being asked to focus on a task that they could work on. Some of the reluctance and surprise seemed to stem from the fact that they felt "singled out" from the rest of the members in formulating the task, and although they received positive suggestions and encouragement, it seemed to heighten their sense of the uniqueness of their situations.

After talking about this with the group members, Mrs. Frank was able to risk herself by agreeing to talk about her difficulties with her son.

Worker: Mrs. Frank, what's the most difficult situation that you experience with your son?

Mrs. Frank: He never listens to me, he does everything when he's good and ready.

Worker: Is he like that throughout the entire day?

Mrs. Frank: No, it's more so in the morning. He has to catch a bus to school and I always feel pressured that he is going to miss it. He's so slow in the morning. I think he does it for spite sometimes.

Worker: What are the things that he has to do to get ready in the morning?

Mrs. Frank: After he gets out of bed, he has to wash, brush his teeth, and comb his hair. He always takes so long to comb his hair. Then he has to get dressed, which sometimes I have to help him with, and finally eat breakfast and run out for the bus.

Worker: Does anyone have any suggestions of what Mrs. Frank might try to help her situation?

Mrs. Santi: Maybe you can help him with some of the tasks and see which ones give him the most trouble.

Mrs. Frank: You mean do them for him?

Mrs. Santi: No, not do them for him but help him with them.

Worker: I think what Mrs. Santi is saying is maybe you can "walk through" the tasks with him to see where he might get stuck and maybe then see how you can help him. Is that what you were suggesting, Mrs. Santi?

Mrs. Santi: Yes, something like that.

Worker: What do you think about that idea, Mrs. Frank?

Mrs. Frank: I guess it's worth giving it a try.

Worker: Maybe you can tell us how you made out at our next session.

Mrs. Frank: O.K.

The above passage illustrates the identification of one major theme (parent's relationship to child) and the attempt to formulate a task within that area. What helped Mrs. Frank was the beginning realization that learning disabled children sometimes have trouble in following through with multiple tasks. This seemed to ease her tension and allow her to try out new ways of handling the situation.

After we defined the service, identified core themes and engaged members in task selection, we began to focus on specific situations and pieces of behavior which created stress for the parents. Through the group process members began to examine maladaptive situations and to try out specific suggestions. As they altered their dysfunctional behavior, they began to develop more confidence in their parental abilities. Of all the early group themes that emerged (relationship to child, status of parent, and familial pressures) the parents felt the most stressful problem area was their relationship to their child. This was understandable, since each parent spent the major, if not total part of the day with the child and assumed primary caretaking responsibilities. We therefore focused our initial work on this theme.

Relationship to Their Children

Members talked about their inability to understand the behavior of their children and initially tried to elicit an explanation from the leaders, the "experts" as they chose to refer to us. They sought answers to questions about their children which they felt the medical profession failed to do. As we explored this further, it became clear that the parents were hoping that the group leaders would be able to identify those aspects of their child's behavior they feared. To this end we partialized and recreated specific situations and behaviors.

Mrs. Santi spoke in broken but adequate English and explained that her son did not act right. She described him as moody and his behavior unpredictable. She feared that he might be crazy and might make her crazy. She felt confused and tired being with him.

We attempted to elicit input from the other group members so as to provide Mrs. Santi with empathic support and to develop a common ground for further work.

Mrs. Lopez responded by stating that she understood how Mrs. Santi must feel. She is frightened by what her six-year-old son has already done. She described in compulsive detail how her son pulled a knife on her. She did not know what to expect from him at any one time. She thought this might be due to his seizures or the medication he was taking. Mrs. Lopez talked of her son as a "monster."

Our efforts continued to focus on helping parents talk among themselves about their fears, perceptions, and specific behavior of the children. What emerged was almost a universal feeling among group members, the fear of no longer being able to maintain self-control, losing to their more "powerful" and demanding children. They felt they were being drained of their strength, engaging with their children in various "battle of wills." As they described their experiences, we identified their sense of loss of control and helplessness. This was highlighted by Mrs. Frank who described her frustration with her son, Alex, and her feeling that he must be retarded in some way because he does not respond to any discipline that she has tried. This made her resort often to cruel and extreme behavior. In the third meeting she explained:

On Monday Alex would not get out of bed to go to school. I kept reminding him to get up since I know he is very particular about his hair and he needs extra time to get ready. I knew he was pretending to be asleep so I smacked him in the face. He went into a rage, started kicking the covers and screaming. I ran out of the room crying. I sometimes want to hurt him.

We carefully examined the situations in which they felt loss of control and helplessness and attempted to help them gain mastery over them. We did this by asking each person, as they talked, to describe in increasing detail what they were trying to convey, so that the group could respond appropriately. The leader tried to facilitate this by saying, "try to recreate the experience, make believe you are there now and describe it just as it happened." At times members would lose focus, become tangential and involve others in broad, unspecific areas of concern. In response, we encouraged them to stay with their specific situations, maintain a clear focus.

I told Mrs. Frank that I noticed when she talked earlier about the situation with her son, her hands were clenched, her face was intense and encouraged her to bring us on board about what she was experiencing. Mrs. Frank responded, "Yes, I get very angry, so angry I want to hit him." I asked, "What do you get angry about most?" Mrs. Frank said, "Wasting time! He has to go to school, to learn, to get a job, raise a family. He can't stay dependent on me!"

For Mrs. Frank the fear of prolonged dependency of her son was a major issue and triggered her to engage in a power struggle with him. Mrs. Morse elucidated about her own fear of loss of control. She stated:

I don't hit my children because I'm afraid I'll hurt them. It's just the frustration, the hurt, the anger, mostly the hurt. I look at my child, thinking, I have done everything I know, given you my time and look what you're doing . . . you're totally disrupting my life. Everything else is O.K. but sometimes I get caught up in the feelings of how much he disrupts my schedule.

Mrs. Santi described her experience with her child, connecting it to a fear of being totally overpowered by him and her fear for the future.

Mrs. Ropar shared how she had put her son in cold water because he was so hyperactive and she knew it would stop him from running and screaming. She felt she would physically hurt him if he wasn't made to stop and articulated her fear of being or becoming an abusive parent. She went on to say that her son is three-and-a-half years old, and if she couldn't control him now, what would happen when he was older and bigger?

They shared their frustration and fear for the future, using poignant language to capture their despair. Defining observable behavior in specific terms facilitated the members' and our understanding, and facilitated attempts to change maladaptive behavior or to identify ways to avoid conflictive situations. We invited members to examine different responses. Mrs. Morse, for example, suggested that she try to avoid getting into physical battles with her son by finding some alternate response to his resistance, such as "ignore him, walk away, or try calm verbal expression." Once parents were helped to describe in detail their participation in a given situation, they were better able to assess more accurately what part they played in exacerbating the situation. From their discussions specific tasks emerged and included increasing study time, eliminating temper tantrums, increasing tolerance for delayed gratification, or reducing sibling fights. Often, evaluation of the situation implied that the parents themselves had to change. This included establishing consistent rules and limits, responding positively to a child's good behavior, or encouraging independent functioning. Although the group leaders initially helped them determine the goals, the group members became increasingly more responsible for this by the third or fourth sessions. In this way they increased their own problem-solving capacities.

We asked Mrs. Andres what bothered her the most about her son Tom. She described her overinvolvement with Tom's homework. After futher exploration with the group, Mrs. Andres finally admitted that she sat with Tom throughout the entire time he was doing his homework. This led to bitter fights and much frustration on both their parts. Mrs. Andres established for herself the goal of decreasing her involvement with her son's homework.

She planned to sit with him to help him begin his assignment, then be available to answer questions as he requested.

Sorting out problems verbally was a helpful experience, often providing insight and new skills to the members. In order to increase client participation we developed "mini contracts" as work to be done by the group members at home.

After describing her many difficulties with her son Alex, Mrs. Frank felt overwhelmed and found it difficult to focus on a specific task for home. The leader noted, "Perhaps you are expecting to handle too much from yourself. It's a lot of pressure if you try too much at once." Mrs. Morse then added, "Maybe you can focus on the morning, continue to work on that, try to control your anger by walking out of the room. Don't hit him."

Mrs. Frank resisted these and other suggestions. The leader tried to encourage her to keep trying. "Last week Mrs. Charles suggested sending him to school without his hair brushed. You weren't sure you could do it, but you did without feeling bad." Others joined in with support. Mrs. Frank finally agreed to continue her effort started last week.

Sometimes parents did not know how to implement suggestions made. In order to provide them with a repertoire of words, phrases, and feelings, we encouraged roleplaying as a means of preparing parents.

We had been talking about praising children for their good deeds. Mrs. Lopez realized that she does not frequently praise her daughter, even when it is deserved, because of built-up resentment of bad things done more frequently. After considerable discussion, Mrs. Lopez expressed, "I think I'll die when she gets off the bus today, I won't know what I could say to praise her." The worker suggested, "Why don't we make believe that it's happening now—I'll play your daughter."

Mrs. Lopez hesitantly participated and talked haltingly, became anxious and stressed.

After some struggling we suggested that it might be better if someone played Mrs. Lopez and she (Mrs. Lopez) played her daughter. Mrs. Charles volunteered and suggested that Mrs. Lopez could say something like, "That was really nice of you to make your bed before going to school today, it made my day easier, thank you." After having played both roles, and having heard another mother say things differently, Mrs. Lopez felt ready to try to respond more positively to her daughter. To help prepare her, I suggested that she practice what she would say when she got home. After several trials, Mrs. Lopez seemed to feel comfortable with her repertoire of words and facial expressions and agreed to try it at home. She reported that until she actually tried the role-playing, she didn't realize how difficult it was to praise her child.

Reflecting on Mrs. Frank's resistance and Mrs. Lopez's hesitancy and anxiety-laden behavior, we see how they felt put on the spot and how we added to their stress. We were asking them to reveal what they experienced as inadequacies in their parenting, to face their fear of criticism and being seen as a bad parent. In critiquing our interventions, we recognize that we moved too fast from the affective content, which should have been used as a barometer of what members were experiencing in the group, to problem resolution. Had we more fully explored these areas, we may have been more helpful to them by recognizing those feelings and providing a supportive environment in which they could express what they were experiencing.

In spite of this, group members were able to choose tasks and work at home on maladaptive situations. Just as the children required praise, so too the parents needed positive feedback and support from the group members upon successful completion of genuine attempts to complete a task. Mrs. Lopez, for example, in later sessions, reported back to the group that she had improved her ability to praise her daughter, and felt supported by the praise she received by other group members. Although vast changes did not always occur within our six-week sessions, parents did feel better equipped with alternatives to handle problematic situations with the children and did participate in a problem-solving approach. They seemed ready to explore further other areas of stress, namely the issue of status in relation to their child.

Status of Parent of the Disabled Child

As was stated earlier, expectant parents wish for a normal child and prepare themselves for parenting along normative developmental lines. When the child is viewed as abnormal, regardless of the age of the child, there is often a period of grief and mourning for the fantasized child, the expression of which allows parents to reach for new ways to respond and adapt to new demands. Most of these parents had not given themselves permission, nor had others, to take the time to face these highly charged feelings which then led to some maladaptive responses. At some point in these parents' lives all of them experienced feeling ashamed by their children, whether due to bizarre or hyperkinetic behavior, lack of intelligible speech, or general immaturity (inability to get along with peers). Many had been called in to school to respond to "charges." They felt attacked and exposed. Others had come under scrutiny by their own extended family members or neighbors. Others reported being embarrassed in public situations, like shopping, where their children did not act normally. These situations triggered their feelings of shame and then guilt for that feeling. They described being conflicted about how to react, often responding unnecessarily harshly with their children. Guilt over their harshness or their shame provided the backdrop for their trying to make it up to their children. That often leaned in the direction of overcompensation, indulging, and being overly permissive.

Mrs. Gardner talked about people looking at her when she brought her daughter shopping. Lisa was four years old, with little intelligible speech and often whining, irritable behavior. Mrs. Gardner stated that she was reluctant to respond by setting limits or spanking and tried instead to ignore the situation so people wouldn't stare.

Mrs. Frank remembered buying her twelve-year-old son a toy gun (a toy she stated she personally disliked) because a family member had made her feel guilty for leaving him alone when he was sick. She eventually ended up breaking the gun and feeling bad about it.

Mrs. Charles talked about being upset by her daughter being "targeted" by other children. She realized that she had tried to protect her daughter by providing a "restrictive environment." She stated, "She is very immature, can't keep friends, they move beyond her. She likes to play by herself with dolls and does the same things over and over. She says dumb things, she can't communicate and it hurts me, I feel ashamed because her infantile behavior turns me off to her, so I let her do things I wouldn't let my other kids do. They resent it, and I know I shouldn't do that. I have to be disciplined, too."

Sessions such as these provided the group members with an accepting and safe atmosphere in which to share their innermost feelings. Additionally, the leaders encouraged the members to grieve and mourn their wish for a normal child by sharing their fantasies of the kind of child they had hoped for and expected. Some members cried, others talked as if in a stream of consciousness. But each encouraged the other to find hidden and untapped strength. The group's compassionate support drew them closer together. This was eloquently illustrated in their attempt to help Mrs. Charles describe her fantasies and to find better coping mechanisms in dealing with her feelings of shame. With encouragement and through tears welling in her eyes Mrs. Charles spoke:

I was so happy to have a girl after so many boys, but right from the beginning I knew something was wrong. She just didn't act right. I had so many things planned for us to do together as she grew, but she has such a hard time learning. People, my family too, ask me "What's wrong with her?" It's as if they blame me. I want to walk away from it all, but instead I learned to withdraw from her. I know it's wrong. I feel ashamed and guilty.

The group members provided Mrs. Charles with support and acceptance but encouraged her as well to look at her own participation in the situation. By doing this, Mrs. Charles recognized that she needed to precipitate some changes in her relationship with her daughter. The group members asked Mrs. Charles to define further her wishes for experiences she had hoped for with her child. From this they established short-term goals, got Mrs. Charles to try to work on them at home, goals that seemed basically achievable. As an example:

Mrs. Charles mentioned that she always wanted her daughter to learn how to play the piano. The group encouraged Mrs. Charles to teach her just a few notes, and to play with her around those notes. They role-played the scenario and prepared Mrs. Charles for reduced, but more realistic, expectations from her daughter. Mrs. Charles agreed to try this at home and report back to the group the next week. The atmosphere was electric as Mrs. Charles described success with this. They cried together and found renewed hope from each other.

As the members felt the sense of commonality by identifying and sharing their painful experiences, they began to reflect upon "Who am I? What is there for me beyond being a full-time mother?" These were important in the third major theme that was raised, that of familial pressures.

Familial Pressures

As previously mentioned, this theme was the least developed due to the time constraints imposed by a time-limited group process. But two important issues raised and which are worth mentioning were (1) relationship to spouse, and (2) sense of self. All of the members were women who had been or who were living with the father of their child. Quite naturally, in the course of our discussions, the issue of familial support, particularly spouse involvement, was raised and examined. Group members felt the men in their lives were not emotionally available to them, or involved sufficiently in their child's daily life. The women felt abandoned and angry.

Mrs. Frank felt that her husband undermined her disciplining of Alex. Mr. Frank usually accused her of being too hard on Alex, stating this in front of the boy.

Mrs. Morse noted that her husband has always participated in caring for their nine children. She works nights; he works days. But she did not feel that he understood the special needs of her two learning disabled children and left the "burden" of care to her. She wasn't sure he understood her needs or recognized the fact that she might have needs of her own.

Mrs. Ropar stated that her son was worse at home when her husband was there. She felt this was due to the fact that she and her husband disagreed about disciplining, and about child rearing in general. They argued openly

and their son tried to play them off against each other. Mrs. Ropar felt she might be better off without her husband, that he was as much as an infant as her hyperactive three-and-a-half year-old.

The general feeling of anger with their spouses had a spillover effect in relation to how they treated their children. Germain and Gitterman refer to this process in their description of the family as a system of interacting parts where pressures and adaptive demands exceed adaptive limits.[11] One of the group members felt a need to explore this area further and began family counseling.

Some members began to reflect upon their own identities, questioning their personal goals and future. They became more assertive about their own needs and recognized that they had to find a balance between their own needs and those of their families. It seemed that for some parents the group forum presented sufficient impetus in and of itself to implement some ideas they already had.

Mrs. Gardner had expressed more strongly than any other member the desire to return to work but felt guilty at the thought of this prospect. With the group's help Mrs. Gardner was able to identify the stresses in her family situation. She thoroughly explored the pros and cons of the effect of her going to work on these stresses and decided that it might actually help the situation. More importantly, she was able to overcome her guilt at leaving her daughter and realized that she had an unfulfilled desire to pursue a career outside her home. After several weeks of employment, she reported to the group that things were well at home and that she felt better about herself since she had started working. For Mrs. Gardner, the group experience provided a cathartic atmosphere, freeing her to mobilize some of her energies in a more constructive manner.

CONCLUSION

In introducing groups into this system, as mentioned before, a significant amount of education about group process had to take place with the entire agency's staff. The purpose of training was an attempt to add a new service component to the workings of the agency. The addition of any new concept to an existing system requires that system to adapt, eliminate, or enlarge parts of its operation. In trying to establish groups for the learning disabled population we hoped to enlarge the agency's scope so that it could provide more comprehensive services within the agency itself for its clients after the evaluations were completed.

The formation and functioning of the first group helped in establishing credibility for the group work program because it no longer was a theoretical consideration but was now a concrete service that clients had used. Formation of subsequent groups of this kind went much more smoothly because workers were more confident to make referrals. This confidence seemed to come from feedback they had received from group members that the group process was helping them manage their relationship with their children more effectively but at the same time was not damaging the one-to-one relationship they had established with their institute social worker. They felt good about having other parents to turn to with the same situation but, at the same time,

were still interested in continuing individual work.

Another contributing factor in the smoother formation of the subsequent groups was that other disciplines had seen how a parents group could effectively help the institute's treatment program serve its clients more comprehensively. Doctors reported to us that they could now offer additional help (in the form of a group) to the parents at the evaluatory conference and that their recommendations would be followed up within the institute's own setting. Part of the frustration for both the doctors and social workers had been the loss of client contact after the evaluation.

The increased confidence of workers to refer members to subsequent groups helped enormously in the recruiting of parents and also seemed to improve attendance of the members at those groups. One reason for this was that the social workers helped motivate and prepare parents they referred for this group experience. The support of their individual workers seemed to have a positive effect on helping the parents overcome their reluctance to talk about their situations with others, besides their workers and families. The decrease in member anxiety in the first session of the subsequent groups (as compared to the first) seemed to support the notion that preparation for groups through individual worker's contact was very helpful in engaging members in the group process.

NOTES

1. Herbert Yahraes, "Learning Disabilities: Problems and Progress." *Public Affairs Bulletin* no. 578, Columbia Bureau of Governmental Research and Services, University of South Carolina, 1979.

2. S. Sapir and A. Nitzburg, eds., *Children with Learning Problems* (New York, Brunner/Mazel, 1973), p. 289.

3. Carol Germain and Alex Gitterman, *The Life Model of Social Work Practice* (New York; Columbia University Press, 1980), pp. 3-10.

4. William Schwartz, "Discussion" (Of three papers on the use of the group in providing child welfare services), *Child Welfare* 45 (December 1966): 572.

5. Alex Gitterman, "Development of Group Services," *Social Work With Groups in Maternal and Child Health* (New York: Columbia University School of Social Work, 1979).

6. Lawrence Shulman, *The Skills of Helping Individuals and Groups, Second Edition* (Itasca, Ill.: F. E. Peacock Publishers, Inc., 1979), p. 127.

7. Schwartz, "Discussion," p. 573.

8. William Schwartz, "On the Use of Groups in Social Work Practice," in *The Practice of Group Work,* ed. William Schwartz and Serapio Zalba (New York: Columbia University Press, 1971), p. 15.

9. Germain and Gitterman, *The Life Model of Social Work Practice,* pp. 13-14.

10. William Reid and Laura Epstein, *Task-Centered Casework* (New York: Columbia University Press, 1972).

In task identification, problems perceived by the client are elicited, explored, and clarified by the worker. The problem which the client is most anxious to resolve is normally seen as the primary target of intervention.

Once agreement on the problem has been reached, tasks are formulated and selected in collaboration with the client. A task defines what the client is to do to alleviate his problem. The task represents both an immediate goal the client is to pursue and the means of achieving the larger goal of problem alleviation. In its initial formulation, a task provides a general statement of the action the client is to undertake rather than a detailed blueprint.

In general, the client's task is based on the course of action he thinks would be most effective in alleviating his problem. Client actions provide the central means of problem-change. Hence it becomes essential to define with the client what course of action might be most effective in resolving his problem.

The task is so structured that chances of its being accomplished, in whole or in part, are high. Consequently the worker is able to convey realistic positive expectations that the client will be successful in carrying out the task.

Task provides a theoretical link between the client's problem and the worker's intervention. By definition a target problem is one that the client can act on directly on his own or indirectly through the worker.

11. Germain and Gitterman, *The Life Model of Social Work Practice,* pp. 204-208.

Margaret J. Jones

CHAPTER 11

Speaking the Unspoken: Parents of Sexually Victimized Children

Sexual assault of children has become a major focus in social work, law, and mental health practice. Incidence statistics suggest that child sexual assault has consistently increased since the mid-1970s. In British Columbia, Canada, the reported cases of child abuse increased 60 percent between 1980 and 1983.[1] The women's movement has drawn professional and public attention to the needs of children who have been sexually traumatized and to the needs of adult women who were sexually victimized as children. Reporting rates have soared in response to media attention and public education programs, creating a crisis in treatment resources for victims, offenders, and the families of each.

Correspondingly, the literature on sexual assault has shifted as more researchers report their clinical findings. Prior to 1975 a clear distinction was made between endogamous (inside the family) and exogamous (outside the family) offenders. Exogamous offenders, also called paedophiles, have a sexual deviancy based on a personality disorder, and are very difficult to treat.[2] Incest is regarded as a different clinical phenomenon, based on situational dynamics, and is perceived to be more amenable to treatment. A paedo-

phile is a fixated offender, and an incest offender is most often a regressed sexual offender.[3] These assumptions are currently being challenged by practitioners working in newly developed resources for offenders and by the women's movement.

In this essay, sexual assault is regarded as a criminal offense, and treatment decisions reflect that point of view. Sexual offenders are assumed to have some form of sexual deviancy as well as a power disorder necessitating extensive individual assessment to determine treatment planning and prognosis. Their crime is regarded as the misuse of their power through sexual activity with children. It is assumed that offending parents and nonoffending parents have quite different issues and that their treatment needs are different. Consequently offenders are excluded from the parent support group. It should also be noted that the agency is child focused. The program does not have a mandate to treat adult women suffering from sexual trauma or to treat alleged or convicted sexual offenders.

The parents group described here was part of a larger treatment program. The program has a feminist view of sexual abuse. The abuse is regarded as a criminal offense, and staff are supportive of the family (both victims and offenders) in pursuing the court process. The legal process is regarded as part of the therapy and is dealt with therapeutically in the groups. All clients have been through an investigation and validation process with a social service agency and the police. Unvalidated referrals are not accepted. They are referred for further investigation or alternate treatment. Treatment staff avoid custody suits as much as possible.

Treatment protocols offer the following guidelines to the staff:

1. Family members are interviewed individually at first contact. Therapist actively engages the family denial system through these interviews.
2. Disclosure precipitates losses which are initially met by denial. The natural grieving process takes nine months to two years if not interrupted. The loss effects changes in the family identity and in each member. Grieving is encouraged and supported therapeutically. Sgroi suggests that the mother's response and ability to adjust to the new reality is the key to how well the family handles the crisis and to the kinds of resolutions achieved.[4]
3. The offender is asked to have no contact with the family for eight weeks or longer and is asked to agree to an individual assessment done by an independent psychologist.
4. The no-contact period is used to support nonoffending parents in their decision-making process and to begin to undo the accommodation process of the child victim.[5]
5. Support is best provided through the use of peer groups and volunteers at the time of crisis.
6. Parents are encouraged to attend an educational support group to acquire information about sexual abuse and to learn from each other's experiences. They are also expected to learn about supporting the child in therapy.
7. Family work is approached through individual and subsystem interviews for the first stage of therapy.
8. Therapists avoid testifying in custody suits, if possible, since it is very difficult to continue therapeutically afterwards.
9. The therapist accompanies clients who are testifying in court. It is important for young clients testifying in criminal court proceedings to be supported by the adults in their life.
10. Therapists are aware of protection issues as they work, and they actively intervene when needed.
11. The offender, who is in individual treatment elsewhere, is incorporated into the program using joint family therapy with the offender's therapist and the child's therapist working together.

DEVELOPMENTAL CYCLE

Developmentally, the group spans several of Erikson's psychosocial stages.[6] Their ages range from seventeen to fifty, and they bring to the group all the psychosocial tasks associated with those stages.

Some members were engaged in the *adolescent task* of exploring and defining an identity within which they felt comfortable and through which they could express the major aspects of self. Typically adolescents move from one "identity" to another until they work out one that feels right. Failure to do so results in role confusion, that is, a lack of fit between self-image and needs for self-expression.

The *task of youth* is to develop a capacity for intimacy and to form intimate relationships. This stage is the time of trial relationships, first marriages, and articulation of sexual needs. Parents raise issues regarding the quality of intimacy in their marriage and in the family. Failure to develop a capacity for intimacy leads to isolation. This may be reflected in a history of serial relationships, a lack of friendship networks, a lack of community relationships, or an active attempt by the offender to separate the family from social relationships. Intimacy problems are very often enmeshed with sexual issues. In this form, they tend to be reported more openly in couples' sessions than in the parents group. Often intimacy problems coincide with the introduction of the first child into the family system and the assignment of parental role expectations.

Parents dealing with *middle-age issues* express their concerns about generativity through self-evaluative statements that indicate looking back, taking stock, or assessing the level of success they have achieved to date in their lives. The need for personal perspective combines with a sense of social concern about the welfare of the coming generations. Parental statements about the values of the younger generation, their own role as educators, the quality of life, or their responsibility in social planning and change may all reflect a need to maintain their own generativity and avoid stagnation. Hence the adage "children keep one young." The crisis of disclosure of sexual abuse has been used therapeutically to move parents away from stagnation and into new areas of personal growth.

Other family developmental tasks may be expressed in conjunction with any of these stages. These are: adjusting to and respecting the child's sexual development; adjusting parental expectations and controls to the individual child's needs, that is, supporting the individuation of each family member; and relating to community resources such as schools and social service agencies.

The normal developmental concerns of these parents center around the child's growth and progress and generally reflect desires to be a good parent or a successful parent or to have a good relationship with their child. Their responsibilities include protection from abuse, nurturing, and values education. These get expressed in child care issues, money, discipline, decision making, sex-role conditioning, and education.

Several levels of developmental disruption are possible for parents of sexually victimized children. The sexual trauma interrupts the child's growth, thereby raising parental anxiety about the child's future development. Simultaneously, the parent moves from having a relatively "O.K." child to having a child with a problem. This loss may trigger unfinished previous grief. At the same time, the sexual nature of the trauma raises sexual conflicts. The legal implications raise moral and spiritual questions and may evoke the parent's prejudice regarding the justice system.

The nonoffending parent whose spouse is the offender finds himself or herself in a crisis involving family loyalties, moral obligations, economic support, and multiple losses (such as loss of partner, loss of "O.K." child, and loss of family/friends).

AGENCY CONTEXT AND THE GROUP MODALITY

The agency is part of a larger network of resources and services available to a client within the region. The program staff work closely with social service agencies, the legal system, and other community members, participating in a monthly case review meeting.

Parent meetings are two hours long and timed to allow parents to meet family obligations. Close to the starting date, parents receive a written notice and verbal confirmation of time and place. The group is held in a large office-meeting room. Coffee is supplied. The group was developed to meet the two primary needs of education and support.

Some educational needs are general to all parents referred to the program. This information includes all aspects of sexual abuse: victim profiles; offender profiles; behaviors resulting from abuse; needs of an abused child; parenting issues with sexually abused children; causes of offending; usual parent responses to sexual abuse; normal sexual development and sexual expression; and the stages of grief.

The group is an efficient and effective learning situation. These topics could be covered in eight weeks. However, such a tightly structured approach greatly limits the leaders' flexibility in responding to group issues and themes. It also limits the supportive function of the group.

The workers chose to combine structured presentations with open-ended discussions. For example, a lecture on normal sexual development one week might be followed by a more open-ended or general discussion of sex education in the family the next week. In turn that topic usually brought forward issues related to the parents' sexual education, marital relationships, and personal sexuality. A structured presentation on sexual expression might follow that discussion. It might cover perversions, sexual forms, developmental issues, homophobia, communication with partners, and themes specific to that group.

It was important to maintain sufficient structure to keep the group anxiety level down and to help the group maintain a constructive learning atmosphere. Although parents frequently discussed personal issues and their feelings, doing so was not a requirement for attendance.

When issues requiring more individual work were raised, they were followed up in individual or family sessions. The supportive aspect of the group was more important to some parents than to others. For that reason parents enter and leave the group voluntarily, and at different times. The length of attendance varied from three months to two years. Parents requiring education would attend shorter periods of time than those wanting ongoing support. The average period of attendance was four to ten months.

This mix in the group appears to benefit all. Senior members use their new knowledge in educating new members, and they act as role models of hope and possibility. They have usually lost the public embarrassment and denial that accompany disclosure and do not regard the trauma as a shameful secret or a family skeleton. They help new members accept their own situation less judgmentally by greeting them with acceptance and understanding. Since the program is situated in a rural community, the group is a "public" community forum. Members may meet each other in Safeway or the bank. The support offered confidentially in the group transfers to the wider community— sometimes openly, sometimes more quietly.

The differences in individual and family developmental issues have also been extremely useful. Older parents have been able to offer sympathy and guidance to younger ones. Parents of young children have seen how early childhood issues affect later development. Parents of older children have relived and reworked some of their unfinished issues from earlier family stages. All parents have benefited from examining how their current parenting conflicts relate to their families or origin and their parents' parenting styles and situations.

The educational format of the group enhances mutual learning and decreases defensiveness. The lack of focus on teaching "how" to parent was experienced as freeing by members. They did not feel their families were being judged. The group was seen as safe, and the workers were regarded as supportive but confrontative on issues of protection.

GROUP THEMES

In the beginning stage the work process focuses on engagement and inclusion. Resistance to attendance is high if the parents are socially isolated, not comfortable in groups, or still caught in the secrecy and the sense of public shame that accompanies talking about sexual abuse for the first time. Engagement is achieved in several ways. The social worker may talk to the parents, giving detailed information about the group. Treatment staff may make telephone contact or have individual interviews with parents. Most parents feel comfortable once they know who the group leaders are and have a sense of what commitment they are making. Occasionally new parents will be given a phone number of a group member or rides will be arranged for new members with old members.

Inclusion is achieved through education and through using group members as educators. Some of the themes of parental concern in the initial stage are emotional confusion, concern for the child victim, denial, secrecy, and parenting skills.

Emotional Confusion and Concern for the Child Victim

Often the mother-daughter bond has been severely damaged during incest, and the mother requires help in repairing that bond, supporting her child emotionally, and processing her own reactions. This extends also to foster homes where a disclosure of sexual abuse by a natural or previous father recreates the same situation for foster mother as for mother. We also find that adopting mothers feel the mother-daughter bond is stressed and stretched thin and that is difficult to maintain a proactive stance with a child. The similarities of feelings seem to erase many of the distinctions between the parenting roles: natural, foster, and adoptive. It is extremely reassuring to natural parents to discover that foster parents have similar feelings toward the children, and similar conflicts about how to parent them.

For example, one adoptive mother felt she was neurotically compensating for her daughter's adoption. She knew she felt differently about her natural child and her adopted one. She assumed the latter's behavior problems were related to that difference. In the parent group she began to examine her guilt feelings and realized that through two unsuccessful marriages she had been accumulating guilt for not being able to protect her adopted child from physical abuse by her first husband and emotional abuse by the second. She had always known the girl was being abused but had felt powerless to stop it.

Deborah: I guess all my guilt isn't just because she's adopted. I did what I could. Now I wonder if all those problems weren't because he was sexually abusing her all that time. I felt like I've missed so much with her . . . and it could have been so different. I'm sorry I missed out on the good times.

Other parent: Don't keep dwelling on that. You'll just keep blaming yourself. You can start again from now. . . . My daughter and I are trying to do that, too.

Deborah: No. Our relationship is so bad. All we do is fight. I'm not sure I want her back home just yet, even though I can see how our problems got started, and here, I've been thinking all along I didn't love her enough.

Worker: So your guilty feelings come from several sources?

Deborah: Yes . . . some are for her adoption, but some are for her being hurt.

Denial

In the beginning stage of the group, the parents' issues and the victim's issues are enmeshed. The parents' initial response is denial. Their denial may be a grief reaction, or it may be based in anxiety related to their own issues. Because the sexual trauma interrupts the child's development, it activates parental fears about the child's future development. A desire to normalize the events or to simply forget the abuse may be expressed at this time. Delson and Clark found that parents expressed the fear that therapy would undermine the child's improvement and that a therapy group would be a negative experience for the child.[7] In the group the leaders use the experience of other parents to elicit unexpressed feelings from new parents. They also begin separating the child's issues from the family's issues.

New parent: Isn't it better to forget it than to remember all that stuff? Won't it just make her more depressed?

Worker: What do others think about that?

Sharon: No. It's not better. (very emphatically) You need to talk about it. I just pushed it away and it came out anyway. I was abused, too, you know, and later it came out at my kids.

New parent: How?

Sharon: I was standing at the kitchen sink peeling potatoes and something snapped inside, and I just threw a peeler. Fortunately, I turned myself towards the wall and I missed my kid. I could have killed him. It stuck in the wall.

Worker: Would you mind telling us how you dealt with that rage?

Sharon: (laughs, breaking the tension in the room) I divorced him! No, I did do that, but first I went to my family doctor and told him I needed help. He thought I needed a complete rest, and the only way to get it was to go to the hospital. My husband wasn't supportive. So my doctor helped me check myself into a psychiatric ward for a month. I talked about it there, and then afterwards when I came home, I had weekly sessions for quite a while.

Worker: (refocusing the group) So you were helped by your therapy?

Sharon: (talking to new parent) My situation may have been worse than your daughter's is, but I still think it helps. I know it's helping my own daughter.

Ida: But therapy won't just be roses. They do get upset by it, and they do things.

Worker: (reaching for the negative feelings) How has therapy affected your daughter?

Ida: It taught her how to analyze me! (Laughs.) No, really, now she tells me what she thinks about me and my behavior. And that's not all bad . . . but she's done things like lock herself in her room, or pick fights with her brother all the time. Has tantrums . . . little things like that.

Worker: So she's been hard for you to live with while she's been in therapy?

Ida: Yes. Now I see it's temporary . . . the feelings come up and out kinda, . . . they affect everyone, not just me. Then she moves on to the next thing. Some times you replay the same stuff over again a few times.

Worker: Is it hard to stay supportive when that is happening?

Ida: Who supports me? (to new parent) I'm a single mother. All the demands come on me. But overall it's helping her to go to her psychiatrist every week.

Worker: Is there anything we can do right now for you?

Ida: Sounding off, I guess. Just listening to me.

Worker: (to new parent) Every family is different. Do you have any sense of how your daughter's depression is affecting your family?

Secrecy

The secrecy theme may be raised in the parent's group or in family session. It usually requires some work outside the group. The child may complain that family members are talking to outsiders without her permission. The parent may complain about the lack of privacy resulting from an investigation or about the public exposure in court. Any of these may be used by the worker to clarify secrecy issues in the family.

Confidentiality is closely related to secrecy, and often the two issues are enmeshed. One family had to deal with the offender's (the father) name being printed in the local paper. The daughter's name was omitted, but her peers began guessing at school as to what happened. She became isolated. Often the offender is still trying to maintain the secret for his purposes and puts other strains on the family.

One mother and daughter expressed it this way:

Mother: I need to talk about it. And I should be able to tell my friends. I know she doesn't want everyone to know, but Sarah is my friend.

Worker: Can you understand how your daughter might feel angry or betrayed?

Daughter: (with strong anger) Well, you haven't told on Dad. No one in his family knows what he did . . . that's not fair. He gets to keep the secret 'cause it suits him. He doesn't lose his family. . . . But I lose my friends and have all yours staring at me like I'm some kind of nut case.

Mother: You don't lose your friends.

Daughter: I will if Sarah blabs to her daughter, and she's just a big gossip . . . she will. I don't want you talking about me to her.

Worker: Seems like you're mad about several things. (Worker separates and specifies the issues, also prioritizing them, so that they can begin to resolve them.) One is you're feeling you might be punished and not your father. Another is that your mother didn't ask you before talking about you. Also, it feels like she doesn't respect your "no." (turning to the mother) And it seems like your husband is getting more support from you than your daughter feels she is getting.

Mother: I'm scared to tell his family. . . . They might not believe me, and he might do something.

Worker: What do you mean?

Mother: We've been really close to his family, and it's hard to say that . . . to destroy the good feelings. I'm scared he'll hit me if I do.

Worker: You feel caught in the middle.

Mother: Yes, I do.

Worker: Let's deal with you and your daughter right now, and I'll talk to you more about the violence before we finish. (She takes the mother out of her double bind in a supportive manner.)

In this situation the worker goes on to reach for the mother's positive feelings toward the daughter and to begin rebuilding the mother-daughter trust. Later the daughter decides to tell the father's family herself, using her anger constructively to assert her own needs in the larger family system. The mother found an acceptable forum for discussing the abuse, and the daughter could give up lying about the family problems and received support. The father, who is in therapy, is both angry and relieved.

Breaking the secret open releases each family member in a different manner. The daughter develops assertiveness; the mother develops the emotional support system she needs; and the father is forced into the self-confrontation essential for his behavior to change.

Parenting Skills

Parents question their own parenting skills at this time. The questions raised most frequently are concerned with protection, ability to control acting-out behavior, ability to support the child through therapy (as expressed by Ida above), and teaching appropriate sexual values. Fears of social judgments about their parenting are expressed with fears of child protection agencies intervening in their families. The court process raises anxieties about being legally "judged" as good or bad parents. Nonoffending parents may feel that their whole private world has become public. Although they are supportive of the criminal proceedings, it is important that workers acknowledge the effects of the court process on them.

Following the introduction of two new families to the group, the worker presented a brief overview of how the children might behave, drawing on victim profiles. She related these behaviors to the effects they might have in a family, giving examples of family issues that had been discussed in the group before.

Mr. and Mrs. A. had referred their adopted daughter to the program ... Mrs. A., or Marilyn, picked up on the issues of power and authority. She was asked how do you control an acting-out young teen and be a good mother?

Marilyn: Ronnie is really hard to control. She throws fits almost if I try to discipline her in any way. She goes nuts. But my husband can sometimes manage her. Is that what you mean by it being a power issue?

Worker: Exactly. The child will work through feelings in therapy. Some of the feelings that come up are about being helpless, being physically controlled by someone else,

being threatened or frightened, being wrong or being bad ... and then they act those feelings out at home with you. So your daughter may insist on doing things her way—or insist she's right ... or refuse to follow any rules, even minor ones. ... It's an attempt to gain control of themselves.

Carol: It's like that in our house, too. We have a sixteen-year-old. She's ape with me. ... Her stepfather has a better chance with her.

Marilyn: Why you and me? Why not the men? It was men who abused them, wasn't it? I feel awful when she just walks away from me like that ... and just says no! ... or calls me a bitch ... really it's awful.

Worker: What do you mean by awful?

Marilyn: ... Frustrated ... a failure. ... I'm supposed to control her. I lose all the time. (makes a face)

Worker: How do you feel, Carol, when that happens?

Carol: All of those ... frustrated, no good, not doing my job, ... maybe ... like I'm the helpless one. I don't have any control over her. In a way she's doing to me what he did to her ... making me powerless.

Worker: What happens when you feel that way?

Carol: Lots of things! Sometimes I blow. Sometimes I ask Pete for help. Sometimes I can handle it. But always I hate being the bitch. It's really hard to make the kid do something, ... when I know it's going to cost me a week of silence ... or somehow I'm going to end up feeling like the bad one.

Worker: Marilyn, do you understand what Carol means when she says her daughter is doing what was done to her?

Marilyn: I can sort of see it. But why to the mother and not the father?

Worker: That's another issue. Does anybody want to answer that?

Using the other parent's experience at this point gives that parent a chance to say what she has learned about herself and to integrate her new ideas into her own perspective on the sexual abuse. The exchange can really be a mutual learning experience for both parents.

Sharon: (continuing from above discussion) I'll try. I live alone with my kids. My "ex" abused my daughter. She's fifteen now, and we're really going through it. She used to be good, nice, responsible ... you know, a mother's dream. Now she's a terror. I don't know what's going to happen next. She ran away last week, but it seems quiet right now. But Cindy gets mad at me a lot ... she couldn't say anything to her Dad ... couldn't talk back ... she's too scared. And he never admitted anything, so she would never get an apology. And she's mad ... I could have killed the guy myself! She's putting some of that on me. I'm safe. I'm not going to hit her or hurt her ... she knows that ... I yell at her ... I tell her I'm hurt, sometimes ... my worker says I'm "it." I agree. ... But she's really mad at him and his family. They sided with him, and they won't hardly talk to us anymore. ... So she's lost her aunts and her grandparents, too ... and he never phones ... Christmases or birthdays ... nothing ... no money for them ... nothing.

Marilyn: So you don't have a husband to help you?

Sharon: No. I don't. When it comes to dealing with Cindy, I wish I did ... but for myself ... I don't really care. I had left him before the abuse happened. This came later. So I don't miss him ... or having a husband.

Worker: But you do miss having some support and backup at home?

Sharon: Yeah, I do. That's why the group is helpful. I can let it out here. I always get ideas or just support.

Worker: Can Cindy get angry at anyone else besides you?

Sharon: Her brother. She gives him a hard time.

Worker: How about your relationship to John's family? What was your relationship with them like?

After processing some of Sharon's grief about the loss of her husband's family,

the workers refocused the group on the issues of power and discipline by asking Marilyn for a specific example that the group could discuss.

The sexually abusive act is an abuse of power. The offender has power over the child through trust, the authority of being a parent or an adult, fear, bribes, threats, violence, size, age, or cultural expectations. Often this is combined with manipulation of the child's emotional needs. After disclosure, the child has an ongoing emotional need to regain a sense of control both physically and emotionally. As discussed above, this manifests in therapy and in the home as power issues. As the child tries to establish autonomy, it is usual for the parents to experience uncomfortable feelings. Helplessness, rage, impotence, failure, guilt, and rejection are common themes.

The guilt and rejection are usually related to protection issues. Even competent, nurturing, protective parents ask themselves if they could have done something else. They feel responsible even when they know they did the right things. It seems the doubts go with the territory. Some parents have no indicators of the sexual abuse before the disclosure; some parents have indicators which they attribute to another cause; some parents realize retrospectively that the child attempted to disclose. Often a mother will look back and begin putting isolated clues together, such as times the child asked to go out, wanted to stay home, or made statements like:

"I don't like the way Daddy plays with me."

"Daddy was in my room."

"Mr. Smith reads me stories."

"I don't want to go to Gramma's with you and Dad. Can I stay home?"

Parents who have not been neglectful can be helped to deal with their doubts and guilt through learning about offender psychology. Knowing that the abusive acts often took place in planned, prearranged situations alleviates some self-doubts for the nonoffending parent.

Parents who have been neglectful need information and support in learning new parenting skills. Their guilt is much harder to loosen. This is compounded when the mother in question has been abused sexually. These mothers will see their own feelings of inadequacy as the source of the problem. It is essential to separate emotional, social, and legal issues. The parent can deal only with her own emotional issues. The worker and the legal system need to deal with the social and legal issues.

In group, time can be spent discussing the difference between emotional blaming, social expectations and consequences, and legal accountability. We talk about blaming as a relationship dynamic. We also have explored guilt as a moral response. Social expectations and consequences are related in group to sex-role conditioning and to roles in the family. Legal accountability is discussed as a societal issue. Every attempt is made to see the offender as legally responsible. This helps with the guilt described above. However, it is balanced with consideration of the particular family's situation. The legal system handles the prosecution, and that is kept as separate process.

Parents of young children may feel that their child is blaming them even when the situation has been discussed and there appears to be no cause for blame. This may be due to the child's point of view and not be related to any particular incident. For example, one child expressed the idea in therapy that parents are supposed to know everything. He felt his father always had an answer and could solve puzzles and fix things. He didn't understand why Daddy hadn't stopped the baby sitter. The father was able to relax some when he realized the source of the boy's feelings. He could forgive himself a little more and could talk to his son about adults not always knowing the answers. He used this to reinforce messages about children being able to say no to adults when the adult is doing something wrong or doing something to them that they don't like.

In the group, one mother went from discussing her self-blame to raising questions about her family.

Pat: This has happened in my family before. My father abused me. I should have been able to see it in my own family. . . . It seems almost genetic . . . except it's not, right? . . . but it's like it's in my blood.

Worker: You feel it might be related to your family?

Pat: Yes. I know that doesn't make sense.

Worker: Does anyone else have those feelings?

Ida: It is a family thing. My father abused me. My husband abused my daughter. So it's not genetic but maybe you learn it in your family.

Worker: What would you say your daughter learned in your family?

Ida: To be like me.

Worker: Can you say how she's like you?

Ida: Maybe not enough confidence? Maybe I never showed her to stand up for herself. She's scared people won't like her. Like me. She takes care of people all the time. She's always taking care of her friends.

Worker: Is that like you, too?

Ida: I always want to be the good Joe. I want everyone to like me. When she was little I was on drugs . . . I've changed a lot but maybe that's what I taught her.

Pat: Well, isn't that what's expected of you? Like Mary said the other week . . . that's what women are taught . . . but then I guess we have all learned it to different degrees.

Worker: So when you two consider what you've each said, what do you feel?

Ida: Not guilty! (laughs). Some of me is responsible for what I taught my daughter. Some of me was just doing what I was taught.

Pat: I think it would have happened anyway . . . but that my daughter needs to learn new attitudes . . . like how to say no . . . how to stand up, be more assertive.

In the middle phase, the group process work will focus on issues of control. Parents may transfer some of their old issues about control onto the worker at this time. It is helpful to identify the process that is happening without engaging in the struggle. It is also important to some parents to receive feedback from the worker at this time. Often they may be thinking the worker carries specific judgments about them and they do not know how to check them out. Feedback should be given honestly and nonjudgmentally.

The themes of parental concern focus around family-of-origin issues, power struggles, grief, and sexual attitudes. In the middle stage of the group these issues are repeated. Any of these emotional themes can be charged for a parent. Different parents have trouble with different aspects of the abuse. Almost all have some family-of-origin issues that are activated by the disclosure. The worker continually has to make choices between working with present material or family-of-origin material. Dealing with the latter gives another dimension to the learning process. However, the workers did not feel it was possible to deal with all members on that level due to time, space, emotional readiness, and the nature of the conflict.

Family of Origin and Power Struggles

Power struggles with children may evoke family-of-origin issues. For example, one mother was almost totally unable to set limits or use appropriate consequences with her oldest daughter. As in many single-parent families, her daughter had stepped into the father's role and was attempting to parent her younger sisters. The daughter had locked herself in the bathroom to avoid being abused by the boy friend when her mother was away. She knew he was abusing the younger children while she was safe. She felt guilty and impotent as a parent figure and helpless and enraged as a victim. Her feelings mirrored her mother's feelings. She began fighting with her mother and physically abusing her younger sisters. In group, mother talked of her responses.

Angela: She's a little tyrant. She just goes after them. I tell her not to hit, but she doesn't listen to me. She does it when I'm out. They sometimes tell me.

Worker: How do you respond?

Angela: I used to hit them when I was first alone. I don't do that now. Then he moved in and it was better.

Worker: He disciplined them?

Angela: Yes. She hated it. She used to tell me, "Mom, we don't need his rules." Now I know why. He was abusing her then.

Worker: How do you feel about her now?

Angela: She's still a tyrant. She has a filthy mouth. She doesn't listen to me, and I can't spend time with the other kids without her getting angry. (obviously hurt and angry, very childlike)

Worker: Does she remind you of anyone?

Angela: No. I was never like that. She's way too bossy for her age.

Sharon: Maybe she learned from your first husband . . . I mean your husband.

Angela: She started it after we left. She hasn't seen him for a long time. Could she have?

Worker: It's possible, especially if she's trying to be the daddy. What goes through your mind when you're mad at her? What words?

Angela: You can't tell me what to do! You can't talk to me like that!

Worker: Have you ever wanted to say that to anyone else?

Angela: Her! . . . and my father. I would have said that to him if I could. He did some really mean things. Cruel. She's cruel, too, like him. (looks sad, defeated)

Worker: Do you have the same feelings for each of them?

Angela: I think so . . . Mad . . . and hopeless. She makes me feel that way again.

Worker: So when you try to be a parent and tell her what to do, you feel all your old kid feelings?

Angela: Yes. When it's a fight, I feel hopeless with her.

The worker makes arrangements to explore the feelings and issues further in another session. The group focuses on what they've learned to do differently from their parents, with some discussion of old feelings that motivated them to make changes.

Grief

Parents go through a grief reaction upon learning that their child has been abused. In the group, Kübler-Ross's stages of grief can be used as a way of conceptualizing the process.[8] She recognizes, without judgment, denial, anger, and bargaining as appropriate, "normal" stages of the grief process. The theory predicts depression, acceptance, and resolution as the final stages. The idea of participating in a natural response to loss and unexpected change provides a positive basis for shared support and identification with other members. It helps establish emotional change and growth as a group norm.

Unresolved grief is a common theme in the middle stage of the group. The abuse itself may be sufficient to elicit old feelings. Often there are present losses associated with the molestation. As in Sharon's family, the family may choose sides, offender versus victim, and then stop communicating with each other. The child may be removed from the family for protection reasons. The family may become isolated in the community as a result of gossip or from fears of social judgment. The offender may go to jail. The family may move to avoid any or all of these. It is rare for there to be no losses associated with the abuse. Any of these losses may bring forward old issues. It is important to work with old grief. Opening the process up and helping the group members to move on in their grieving process frees them to move through the present issues in their life.

One family avoided therapy and social agencies until the child's behavior demanded that they get help. It soon became evident that the mother was locked in an ongoing custody battle with her first husband. She was afraid that because her child was sexually abused while in her care, the courts would return custody to her husband. As she tried to resolve some of her feelings about the divorce, her childhood responses to her parent's divorce became a focus. Shortly afterwards, she recalled her own sexual abuse as a child. Until then, she had successfully repressed the memories and had no awareness she had been abused. Working with the grief was extremely painful for her but healing in the long run. It is not possible to do this level of work in the context of a parents' group. It requires the intensity and space that are possible in individual sessions, combined with an adult women's group.

Peggy: I've listened to other women here talk about their own abuse and admired them for being able to be so open about themselves and at the same time keep on dealing with the job as a parent. As a result, I've remembered my own abuse from my childhood. I'm glad I'm in a place to talk openly and know that I'll be understood.

Carol: I still don't really remember it. I know I was though.

Ida: The first part is the worst. When the actual memories come back to you . . . and all the feelings . . . once you've remembered . . . it seems you can't put it away again . . . at least not until you've looked at it . . . cried. . . .

The group is quiet with her.

Sexual Attitudes

As a parent supports a child through dealing with a sexual trauma, his or her own feelings and attitudes about sex become a focus. Sex education is introduced in the middle phase of the group to provide a safe structure for discussions of sexuality. It is essential that this be done in a manner that maximizes the parents' comfort and trust. Besides creating a focus that gives permission for sharing personal responses, the sex education provides the skills the parents need for talking to their children.

The leaders present the materials that they would use with children and demonstrate their methods of using them. Parents can request special topics at any time. Those topics usually covered include: normal psychosexual development, age-appropriate sexual expression, teaching sexual values, sexual communication, touching, sexual effects of sexual abuse. Other topics that parents might appreciate are homophobia, homosexuality, basic anatomy, venereal disease, contraception, and adolescent sexuality. Their most frequent questions concerned when to teach what, what materials to use, teaching values, and adolescent sexuality. Pornography, prostitution, and sex-role conditioning are often discussed as a result of the focus on sexuality. While it is important to respond to the concerns and needs of your particular group, it is essential to balance this with structure and predictability. It reduces the anxiety and gives members the privacy that is sometimes needed to integrate new sexual information and knowledge. Generally, parents will lack up-to-date information about sexuality and will have some discomfort in discussing it.

If there is a good male-female mix in the group, it can be useful and fun to share their own sex education experiences. It is a positive way to lead into a discussion of male-female sex roles and social conditioning. It is important to draw out the sexist attitudes which can interfere with the protection of children, the development of intimacy, and healthy sexual development.

In one parents group, the fathers (who are nonoffenders) discovered that none of them had ever discussed their sex education with another man before. It was a shared value that "men should know about sex" and as one father put it, a man "should never be innocent."

Frank: I could never ask. My wife brought home books. I learned from that. My father died when I was quite young, so there was no one to ask.

Mark: Yeah. That's like us. We were taught you just do it. You don't talk about it.

Worker: Were you comfortable talking about the books?

Frank: Not at first. I could hardly read them! I did when my wife wasn't around. Slowly I started talking. I saw she didn't know a lot either . . . that's why she got the books. So, I didn't feel too bad. I didn't tell my friends though. In my culture [Eastern European] women aren't supposed to know anything. Married women could, but they didn't talk to the men about it.

In a later session values about touching were shared.

Worker: Men in America have been taught not to touch in nurturing and affectionate ways. What values do you want your children to learn about being boys?

Peggy: My stepson never disclosed being sexually abused because he felt he should keep it to himself, handle it alone. He's still that way. He was mad at his stepsister for disclosing for him. He thought she was weak and it was his business what happened to him. He wasn't going to go on about it like her. It really bothered him when she would openly talk about herself.

Worker: You seem to be still concerned and upset.

Peggy: I am. What if he doesn't change? His therapy isn't going well ... he doesn't want to talk ... and every one around him agrees with him ... like at school and on TV.

Ida: Does he cry?

Peggy: Only when he's mad.

Worker: Can he be affectionate, tender?

Peggy: From a distance, hugs are few. Smiles, jokes, looks ...

Worker: (Reaching for others' views and issues) Does anyone have any ideas about how he might open up his other feelings?

Pete: Talking with other boys his age.

Dave: What about his dad?

Peggy: He's just like him!

Worker: What do you mean? How does his dad open up?

Peggy: It's very hard still. He won't come to group ... (laughs) He just asks me questions when I get home. He doesn't seem mad anymore. More like he wants to know what we're doing here.

Pete: Will he talk to you?

Peggy: Yes. When he gets to a certain point he does ... but not every day ... he has to work up to it.

Worker: That sounds very difficult.

Peggy: It is. Chris and he are miles apart.

Worker: With you in the middle trying to get them to talk?

Peggy: I've given up on that. It didn't work. But still, I'm worried about Chris.

Worker: Do you have any nonverbal ways of talking? With your husband?

Peggy: Snuggles. We snuggle a lot. That's how I know how he's feeling.

Worker: But you don't with Chris?

Peggy: I've held back a lot. ... He was so upset at being touched at all. I never felt free with him.

Carol: Could you maybe tuck him into bed at night? I know I do that with the girls and they like it. I tell them I'd like a hug good night and that they can say no if they don't want a hug. I won't be offended. Or just talk with him? He sounds like a real baby.

This mixture of developmental needs and social conditioning presents many problems to parents. Finding ways to respond to the four-year-old within a fourteen-year-old can require ingenuity. Parents find each other's experience invaluable in this. Problem-solving discussions give a chance to explore new values and to change old ones. Parents also use them to give each other feedback.

Toward the end of the group issues around sexual abuse prevention, justice, the court system, saying good-bye, and helping others are explored.

Court Process

Most parents have some feelings of wanting revenge. These feelings tend to be ameliorated if the criminal court process is pursued to its fullest possibility. When the criminal aspect is downplayed or ignored, revenge feelings are fed. As more families pursue the court process, we are seeing positive outcomes for the victims and some nonoffending parents. They feel heard. They have had a chance to tell their side of the story. They have been taken seriously and considered. Some young girls feel they have faced their fear and are freer for it. Mothers feel they have contributed to protecting others. If they win, they may feel vindicated.

Courts may exacerbate family problems when the mother wants to be supportive to both the child and the alleged offender. She has to choose then between her obligations as a parent and as a wife. Family members and associated professionals may all take sides, adding to her conflict.

Saying Goodbye

Initially the workers did not clearly define the end of the group for the parents. It was left open-ended. This created difficulty for both clients and staff. A group member who had separation issues found it difficult to initiate the separation process. She simply acted it out as she did in other relationships—she picked a fight and left. Other parents have done the same thing, that is, they have said good-bye using the same style they used in previous situations by distancing, expressing feelings, being bad to get removed, or going without saying anything. Structured breaks in the group allow parents to plan their exits and to process the feelings associated with leaving. If a parent has done grief work during the group, this could be a chance to practice new responses.

Workers talk about endings and styles of separation about three sessions before an expected break. They also share with parents their own criteria for when a parent might feel ready to leave the group. The primary criteria are: ability to generate support for self either in the extended family or the community, integration of the information that was needed, ability to protect the child from further abuse, ability to recognize the children's needs and to be supportive of their therapy, and desire to move on in one's life.

This is one of the positive endings from the group:

Susan: My concerns seem so minor compared to yours. My Tanya doesn't do any of that acting-out stuff.

Sharon: My daughter didn't at first. Hers seems to be connected to being a teenager. She used to be a good kid.

Peggy: Yes. I'm scared of what will happen when Serena becomes a teenager. She's so provocative already.

Susan: Tanya used to be that way . . . when we first got her. She wanted to touch penises. She would sit on Dave's lap and touch him. But that was all she knew, poor thing. She doesn't do that anymore. She seems to ask for affection nicely, now.

Sharon: She's had help, right? She's seen someone and she's been in a group here.

Susan: Do you think that means it won't come back when she's a teenager? I won't have to go through what you're going through? I worry about her still.

Sharon: Well, hopefully.

Peggy: Therapy hasn't changed that part of Serena. She's still doing it, and she can really turn it on.

Worker: Can you see any differences between the two girls? (attempt to get the parents to separate the different issues)

Peggy: Heavens yes. Serena still has contact with the offender indirectly and Tanya doesn't. . . . She still sees her natural father, and Tanya has no contact with either parent anymore. . . . Also Serena's father is not very supportive, and he and I have an ongoing discomfort. . . . Her stepfather isn't very demonstrative with her, and she's lost contact with her grandparents! I'd say she has a lot going on in her life still! But your family sounds different, Susan . . . more settled . . . less upset.

Susan: Yes. Tanya has settled in well. She doesn't see her natural parents at all. But she still flips right out if I take her near that house. I took her in there once . . . it was empty . . . they were gone . . . just to prove to her that they weren't there anymore . . . just to confront it. Since then we've avoided it. I don't want her to ever see her mom. But when she's older and grown up, she might want to. I wouldn't let her now. If she asks me, I'll deal with it then. She doesn't seem to want to.

Worker: What about her father?

Susan: We have never had anything about him from her. Just what she's said in therapy and about the abuse. It's like he didn't exist for her.

Worker: So, listening to Peggy and Sharon, what do you think of Tanya's progress?

Susan: That she's done well. She's changed, settled into our family, seems to be thriving on the attention and care, and just wants to be normal. She doesn't want to come to therapy anymore. She used to.

Worker: How about you and Dave? Are you wanting to finish as well?

Susan: Well ... yes and no. For me and Tanya, yes. If I can just call you when I have questions about her behavior. But the court thing isn't over for custody. I want to keep coming until we have final custody. I don't want to be on my own if that goes wrong.

Worker: And if Tanya needs something later on, how will that be for you?

Susan: I know where to look for help. I'll just call you guys!

Sexual abuse prevention often is raised as an issue when the parents have resolved some of their own issues and met their own needs. There appears to be a real willingness to contribute something to the community and a desire to change the existing conditions that allow and sometimes openly support sexual abuse of children. Parents may become community volunteers. Some have contributed time to prevention programs in the schools and to educating parents in general. Some volunteer their support to a parent still in the crisis of disclosure. One has designed a coloring book on touching. Another has tried to start an advice column for parents in the local newspaper. Others have been interviewed on radio and TV and shared their poetry and art with professionals. This movement away from self and out into the community is a healthy attempt to give the abusive experience a positive meaning. It is a demonstration of compassion for others and a renewed faith in community involvement. For these parents the group has been more than a success. It has gone beyond the initial goals.

CONCLUSION

In summary, the parents help each other in several ways. The mutual sharing of details of the abuse ameliorates feelings of secrecy, shame, and guilt. Isolation is broken and social confidence is enhanced. Parents use their own experience in mutual problem solving and sometimes are able to generalize that experience into the community at large. The old group members are excellent role-model teachers for the incoming group members. They model social-emotional skills and contribute to the information-sharing process. They also bring new materials into the group.

The educational-support focus facilitates the mutual aid aspect of the group, encouraging the parents to develop new skills. Working with the strengths of group members provides a climate of safety and health that allows members to take risks and supports personal and social change. While their healthy social action does not lessen the tragedy of the sexual abuse, it does show a level of compassion and strength that is truly inspiring.

NOTES

1. *The Courier* (Vancouver, B.C.), April 1984.

2. Roland Summitt, *Beyond Belief: Sexual Abuse of Children* (Vancouver, B.C.: Justice Institute and Ministry of Human Resources, 1980), pp. 111-1 to 111-71.

3. A. N. Groth, "The Incest Offender." in *Handbook of Clinical Intervention in Child Sexual Abuse,* ed. F. Sgroi (Lexington, Mass.: Lexington Books and D. C. Heath and Co., 1982), pp. 215-17.

4. Ibid.

5. Roland Summitt, *Beyond Belief: Sexual Abuse of Children.*

6. Erik Erikson, *Childhood and Society,* 2nd ed. (New York: W. W. Norton and Co., 1963), pp. 247-274.

7. N. Delson, and M. Clark, "Group Therapy With Sexually Abused Children," *Child Welfare* 60, no. 3 (March 1981): 180.

8. Elisabeth Kübler-Ross, *On Death and Dying* (New York: Macmillan Publishing Co., 1969).

Dale Trimble

CHAPTER 12

Confronting Responsibility:
Men Who Batter Their Wives

Counseling for men who assault their wives is a relatively new phenomenon. Ten years ago what reference there was to the issue of wife assault was oriented primarily toward the masochism of the wife. Through an emphasis on the power imbalance between men and women the feminist movement has been instrumental in changing this orientation.[1] This article will focus on a group for men who have assaulted their wives. Assault is a crime for which the offender should be held responsible. At the same time, many violent men can be helped to change their behavior.

Before pursuing the specifics of our service, I would like to put it in the context of the problem of violence against women. The frequency and severity of wife assault has received increasing attention in the last few years. A U.S. study surveyed 2,143 couples and found that 16 percent had experienced one violent incident in the past year (ranging from throwing something or slapping to using a gun).[2] In 28 percent of the couples there had been at least one violent incident at some time during their marriage.[3] A study conducted in our area indicated that in a population of .5 million at least 4,000 to 5,000 women are victims of assault by their husbands every year.[4] Given the reluctance of victims to report violence, many researchers believe that figures like these could be at least double.[5]

This article will not explore theory to any great extent but will concentrate on treatment. There are many excellent surveys available now which look at the range of theoretical explanations for wife assault.[6] In "An Ecologically Nested Theory of Male Violence Toward Intimates," Dutton describes a "conceptual model of male violence towards intimates that (a) views such violence as multiply determined by forces in the individual, the family, the community, the culture and the species; and (b) views these factors as being nested within one another (i.e., that one factor operates only within limits set by another factor)."[7] I think an interactive model such as this is most useful in understanding the causes of wife assault.

Seven years ago five male workers gathered to develop the first group for violent men in our community. Due to the lack of literature to guide us, we were left to our own devices to formulate an approach. As we began the process of tuning in to the concerns of men who might attend our group, some of the themes which we identified were: the men being concerned about judgment from the group leaders, fear of intimacy and a tremendous need for intimacy, loneliness due to the loss of their wives and children, and low self-image especially as it related to "being a man."[8] Our assumption regarding fear of intimacy and male self-image was confirmed one evening by a group member.

Joe: I remember my girlfriend and I would get into these horrible arguments and I'd reach a point where I couldn't take it anymore and I'd go into the bathroom and cry. Then I'd come out and hit her. . . . I guess I was afraid to let her see me cry. I haven't cried in front of anyone since I was a kid and my dog died.

Leader: What was it about her seeing you cry that concerned you?

Joe: I didn't want to look weak in front of her, to feel like I wasn't a man.

Leader: Was that what happened when your dog died and you cried; you didn't feel like a man?

Joe: Yeah. My dad really put me down for it.

Leader: Has your wife ever put you down for crying?

Joe: No, actually she says she would feel closer to me.

Leader: So when you feel like crying, you believe that anyone around will put you down even though they aren't. It's kind of like your dad is still in the room for you.

Joe: Yeah.

DEVELOPMENTAL CYCLE

What are the life-cycle issues which are especially pertinent to a group of men who have assaulted their wives? In *The Seasons of a Man's Life* Levinson described a view of normal male adult development.[9] He divides what he calls the "male life cycle" into "eras." The majority of the assaulters in our service fit into the "Early Adulthood Era" which begins at seventeen or eighteen years of age and

ends at about forty-five. Major components with which a man must struggle, although different in each phase, are "occupation" and "marriage and family." A man experiences a "developmental crisis" in Levinson's terms when he has great difficulty with the developmental tasks of the period he is in. "In a severe crisis he experiences a threat to life itself, the danger of chaos and dissolution, the loss of hope for the future."

These words certainly reflect the feelings of many of the assaulters who have lost contact with their wife and children as a result of their violence. When we first see them, many of the men are separated from their families and do not know whether or not it will be permanent. Some of the men have no way of contacting their spouse and family because their wives will not reveal where they are for fear of threats, harassment, or further violent attacks, or they are prevented from entering the family home by a court order. Others are in the group as a term of probation under their conviction for assaulting their wives.

Several of the men coming to our service have never been in trouble with the law before, and they are trying to deal with having a criminal record. In addition, others are struggling with a withdrawal from alcohol and/or drug abuse and the habit patterns and social circle which surrounds alcoholism. Central to all of these crises is a loss of control. The man's loss of control over his anger and aggression at a crisis point of intense feeling has placed him in a situation in which control of his wife, family, and possibly place of residence have been removed from him by his partner and/or the court. In many, but certainly not all cases, this loss of control is the reverse of what the man maintained in the family through his violence, threats of violence, or verbal abuse. It's not unusual for a man to feel desperate and even suicidal and say "There's no reason to go on." Other men cope with the crisis of loss of control of their wife in the same angry and aggressive way that caused the crisis.

The "Novice Phase" covers the years of seventeen to thirty-three in Levinson's system. Most of our group fall in the twenty-eight to thirty-three-year age range. In the tasks of this period we find those with which assaulters have the most difficulty. Levinson describes the "primary, overriding task of the novice phase is to make a place for oneself in the adult world and to create a life structure that will be viable in the world and suitable for the self."[10] The ability of "having adult peer relationships with women which involve affection, friendship, collaboration and respect and emotional intimacy" is very difficult for men who are, as Ganley says, "very dependent upon those they abuse."[11]

The characteristics of assaulters are very diverse; nonetheless, a common dynamic keeps appearing. These men have a great investment in the "macho ideal" (power, money, and winning the attractive wife) and great fear and doubt about their ability to measure up. Given that part of being a "real man" is not talking about feelings of insecurity, a real pressure-cooker situation arises: expectations produce insecurities and part of the expectation is not to have and especially not to show insecurities. One of the tasks of "Early Adulthood" described by Levinson is to live out both masculine and feminine aspects of the self. To be insecure in a "macho" definition is to be feminine. In a small unpublished study I conducted in 1982 I found that violent men were more homophobic (afraid of homosexuality in themselves and others) than nonviolent men. It seems that one of the

most frightening aspects of homosexuality for men is that it is too much like being a woman; in other words, fear of the feminine in self.

This description of violent men is not meant to be either predictive or proscriptive. Not all macho men are physically abusive with their wives, although I would say that being macho is generally psychologically abusive of women. In addition, just helping a man to experience and express his feminine side will not stop his violence.

Another theorist of adult development is Erik Erikson. Within his system of the "Eight Ages of Man" the stage of "Intimacy versus Isolation" covers the twenty- to forty-year-old time of life. Erikson sees a man's task during this period as "the capacity to commit himself to concrete affiliations and partnerships and to develop the ethical strength to abide by such commitments, even though they may call for significant sacrifices and compromises. Body and ego must now be masters ... in order to face the fear of ego loss in situations which call for self-abandon."[12] Many of the assaulters I have worked with experience compromise in a marriage as emasculation: "I'm not letting a woman run my life." Any giving up of what they want is experienced as a loss of self or identity. Outbursts of domination, violence, and abuse at home may be a way for the passive man to redress a power imbalance which he experiences most of the time. More chronically domineering and aggressive men may feel that even in agreeing to go to their second choice of a movie or restaurant, their sense of self has been threatened.

Erikson describes the opposite of intimacy as "distantiation," or "the readiness to isolate and, if necessary, destroy those forces and people whose essence seems dangerous to one's own.... The danger of this stage is that intimate, competitive, and combative relations are experienced with and against the self-same people."[13] Certainly all men struggle with the tasks which Erikson and Levinson describe. With violent men the attitude and history with which they approach their tasks keeps them from struggling with the essential issues and therefore keeps them stuck. When violent men get control of their violence, they are able to return to normal developmental tasks with a sense of hope. These issues will be dealt with in some depth in the group work section of this essay.

AGENCY CONTEXT AND THE GROUP MODALITY

In the early days of the development of the project, the criminal justice system was experiencing frustration in dealing with men convicted of assaulting their wives. Some of the judges were interested in the development of a service for violent men which they might use as a sentencing option in dealing with men whom they had found guilty of assault. With support from probation officers as well we were able to arrange funding for a pilot project, jointly funded by the federal and provincial governments. Our service continues now on provincial funding alone and is currently entering its third year of operation.

The funding provides for an ongoing group containing a maximum of ten men at any one time. Each man is required to complete sixteen weekly sessions. Men who have been convicted of assaulting their wives and are required to attend the group as a term of their probation are given first priority. Referrals are also accepted from other social agencies, health practitioners, and from men themselves who have heard about our service.

The criteria for admittance to our group include: (1) an ability to converse, read, and write in English, (2) absence of mental illness, (3) participation in an alcohol or drug treatment program concurrent with the violent men's service if those substance abuse problems are present, and (4) adequate restrictions in place to protect the wife if they are of imminent necessity (such as providing space for her in a shelter or preventing him from contacting her through a restraining order).

It is important that alcohol or drug treatment begin before working on changing the man's violent behavior. Our service is based upon the assumption that men learn to be violent and they can learn other behavior to replace the violence. Learning is not possible in an intoxicated state or in an individual who is still running away from self through alcohol or drugs. Our approach demands that the man face and tolerate some pain, the pain of facing that he has hurt the person he loves, the pain and fear of being alone, and the pain and often self-disgust at having driven away his wife and children often through repeated cruelty.

During the first few years of this service most of the leadership was provided on a voluntary basis or by agencies who granted a worker a few hours a week out of his regular responsibilities to lead a group. My philosophy in working with assaulters at that time was an outgrowth of my training to lead personal growth groups. I assumed that if I showed empathy, worked at developing rapport, and tried to show the men that I judged their violent behavior and not them as people, then they would stay in counseling, learn how to experience and understand their feelings, and therefore be able to control their violence. I was disillusioned when many men would come to a few group sessions and then stop attending. When

I called them to enquire about why they had stopped, the answers given included (the implicit message is after each statement): "We've separated for good so I don't need it anymore" (The violence was provoked by her; I'm not a violent person), "We had a really good talk after the last group session. We really communicated. I know it won't happen again" (Communication problems cause violence, good communication prevents violence), "I've stopped drinking. I only hit her when I was drunk so I won't be violent again" (Booze caused my violence, not me), or "The group sessions that I attended really helped. I can control myself now" (Because I feel better, I won't be violent again). As workers we doubted that any of these men had made sufficient progress toward controlling violence in a few sessions. But the issues mentioned are common themes and defenses for violent men and sometimes for their wives and professionals who have dealt with them. These beliefs and others like them form the foundation for alibis which prevent men from taking responsibility for their own behavior.

Two factors influenced my change of focus with violent men. One was the high rate of attrition. The other was contact with workers from women's shelters in our community. They regularly saw the wives who often had severe injuries and were often in the hospital. They were effective in sensitizing me to the consequences of the men's behavior. The task for me as a worker and a primary goal for working with these men is to be able to separate feeling from action, to understand their relationship, and never to make one paramount at the expense of the other.

I was idealistic when I started this work. I wanted men to come to the service because they realized they had a problem which had hurt another person physically and psychologically and had hurt themselves. I hoped they would come to realize that they needed to change themselves even if their wives would never return. In reality few of us face our problems unless we have to. It has been my experience that most violent men who come to our group and stay long enough to make a change are there because they have to be. That "have to" is either a court order or their wives saying they won't return unless the men get some help. This does not mean that most men want to be violent but rather that most of them cannot tolerate for very long the pain and fear I mentioned earlier. Their inability to tolerate pain, fear, and loneliness forms a part of the foundation for both their violence and for the impulsivity which carries them out of the group. Because of this impulsivity an outside pressure is needed to keep them in the group past their usual tolerance level for self-confrontation.

Because of these dynamics our service uses authority more than most. For court-mandated clients, we serve partly as an arm of the law. We report nonattendance to their probation officer, who may return them to the judge for consequences. After the first session all men are required to complete an "anger diary" and hand it in as their ticket of admission to the group.[14] A man who attends without his anger diary is generally not granted admission, and that session counts as one missed group. If men are absent more than twice during their term, they may be asked to leave the group, make up the sessions, or start over.

Especially at the beginning we had real concerns about whether mandatory services would work. All my training as a helping professional led me to doubt it. I felt that trust and freewill were intrinsic to growth and change. Nonetheless, we have consistently increased the use of structure, rules, and consequences. In most instances this has brought positive results in terms of attendance and commitment to the group. The best approach for dealing with this has been an honest one in which we make the rules explicit through a written participation agreement and present them again at the beginning of the group. At this time we review the reasons for the rules, which actually is a way of teaching about the dynamics of violence as well.

One of the ways I have developed for dealing with the issue of loss of control, whether it's through a court order or through the pressure of a wife to "get help or I won't come back," is to point out to the men how much control they really still have.

Leader: I'm sure it is possible to follow all these rules and not change, not open up to facing yourself or to the other men here. You can probably get through this group and really not change. That's up to you. The judge may order you to be here or your wife may be saying that she won't come back unless you get help. And as I have just said, we require your anger diary and regular attendance in order for you to stay here, but no one can reach into your mind and heart and order a change. That's where you have complete control.

There are several reasons why we provide this service in a group format rather than individually or through family or couples sessions initially. Most men feel embarrassed about what they have done to the extent that they hide it from themselves. Some men have said that they feel "like a freak." Many men who present a cocky or belligerent attitude about their violence may feel bad underneath that exterior By showing men that there are others like them, most of them feel a relief and begin to talk about self in ways they never had. Groups can also set up a new peer group and with it a new peer pressure. In the case of being male the group can support values like not blaming other people for your violence, sharing your feelings and problems, admitting hurt does not make less of a man, and violence is a tendency I'll always have to control in myself. When a group of peers can hold values like this, it has much more impact than if one therapist tells a client in one way or another that these values are "good" for him. This is not to say that I think that a group of violent men can get together on their own and provide effective support and confrontation. A leader with authority needs to be present to push the men through their denial and to demand accountability. Self-help groups may just help the men perpetuate their denial.

I strongly agree with Ganley in her belief that family or couples sessions are very inappropriate and potentially dangerous when any threat of violence remains or when the woman does not want to reconcile.[15] As she says, work with the family unit is predicated upon an assumption that communication is possible. This is simply not true if the woman is so threatened by the man that if she mentions the violence, then "she'd better watch out." Too many therapists have inadvertently endangered women by working without an awareness of or in disagreement with this dynamic.

GROUP THEMES

Getting Started

Although this essay concentrates on the group aspect of the counseling program, service really begins with the very first contact that the man has with us. Usually this is the intake interview. In order for a man to be accepted into our group, he must meet several criteria. The primary questions we are trying to answer at that time are: Is this person in fact violent and to what extent? Does he see it as a problem? Does he want help? The manner in which these questions are asked during the interview can have a profound effect upon whether rapport is established between the man and the worker, how much of the truth is revealed in the interview, and whether the man will eventually attend and complete the group. Looking from the other side the questions that the men bring into the interview include: "Will you repeat what I say to my wife?" (confidentiality), "I know I hit her but she's part of the problem, too" (fairness), and "Do these groups work?" (Can you help me?).

The manner in which these and other questions are dealt with in the first interview and throughout is based upon a philosophy of helping which views assault as a crime for which the individual is responsible. In the areas of physical and psychological abuse and violence, experience has taught us to distrust these men. Most of them have said at least once to their wives that, "I'm never gonna hit you again. I'm sorry." (Most of them really mean it, too.) However, distrust can be separated from dislike. Empathy is no less important a quality in our groups than it is with other mutual aid groups. But assault is a *behavior,* not a *feeling.* Acquiring the skill of being able to make this distinction, especially in the midst of a crisis, is one of the primary goals of work with violent men.

One of the most difficult but important aspects of the beginning phase is getting the men to tell their stories. Most of the men with whom I have worked feel bad about their violence even if the face they present is one of justifying their actions, blaming their partner, or even defending their right to do as they please in their own homes. Many workers (and more importantly, the wives and the men themselves) mistake guilt and remorse for an ability to control behavior at a time of stress. Strong feelings of guilt are not tolerated by anyone for very long. Eventually a blurring of what happened and a clouding of responsibility set in as a defense against guilt. The problem is that, as Ganley says, "No one can change a behavior for which they don't acknowledge responsibility."[16] That is why with many men (not all) it is important at the early stage to decrease guilt to some extent through inclusion in the group and increase acknowledgment through each man's description of what he did. It is very important that this be done without editing or blaming the victim or other factors such as alcohol. Little progress can be made toward the control of aggression until this is done. When a new group of men starts the program, the first task after explaining the rules is for each new person to tell the rest of the group why he is there. What we are reaching for with each man at that stage is for him to be able to describe in clear behavior terms how he assaulted his wife.

Leader: I'd like each man who has joined the group tonight to tell the rest of the group what brought him here.

Phil: Well, my wife and I have been having marriage problems for awhile. Two weeks ago I got upset 'cause she came home really late. We started yelling at each other and I pushed her around. ... I've done it before. I came home from work the next day to find that she had left with the kids. I'm here 'cause she said she wouldn't come back until I got some help.

Leader: So you're primarily here because you want your family back?

Phil: I don't feel *good* about what I did, but I can't sleep at all since they left.

Leader: It's tough on you being alone, really lonely. It must be hard to work without sleep.

Phil: Yeah.

Leader: What do you mean, "pushed her around"? What exactly did you do?

Phil: (Goes into a story about her going out with her girlfriends more and more often ending with) Then I slapped her.

Leader: Where did you hit her?

Phil: On her face and back.

Leader: How often?

Phil: Three or four times, I guess.

Leader: You guess. So it might have been five or six times or more.

Phil: It could have been. I was really hot. I don't remember too well.

Leader: Did you hit her with your fist or with an open hand?

Phil: My fist.

Leader: I know it's hard to face it, to realize you hurt someone you love. Many men feel guilty and don't want to talk. But you can't change a problem that you try and forget. The basic goal here is to help you stop being violent. To do that we start by asking you to tell exactly what you did when you were violent with your wife.

Sam: (looking at Phil) I was in your position when I walked in here two months ago. I felt like a creep . . . thought everyone would look down on me. But it really helps to get it off your chest. We're all in the same boat here. That's really helped me. Knowing we're all here 'cause we hit our wives.

Phil: (who had been looking down looks at Sam and seems to soften) Thanks.

As I reflect on this process recording, I see some anger expressed by myself in the statement, "you guess." It's not easy to strike a balance between confrontation and support in this work. It can be especially difficult for a worker not to respond in a mimicking or angry way when faced with denial and resistance, which usually surround violence. I tried to catch myself by coming back with a response which reaches for the man's feelings: "it's hard to face" and "many men feel guilty." The feelings are not pursued in depth at this point. However, it is important to help the man be able to both acknowledge his own behavior and experience his feelings in relation to that behavior.

Every group begins with a focus upon behavior. One of the leaders writes the following words on the board: Physical, Sexual, Psychological, and Destruction of Property or Pets.[17] These words refer to the four kinds of abuse and violence which we explore in the course of the group program. At the start of the groups we go around the circle and ask each man to report to the group which of these four kinds of violence he has used in the past week. As a leader I began to find this a bit difficult, awkward, or at times boring to do. Groups which focus on process and feeling are more interesting to a worker like myself who was trained to look for and work in these areas. I dealt with this concern in the group in the following manner.

Leader: I always feel a bit awkward and artificial going around and asking each of you to report on the four kinds of violence even though I think it is really important to remember that that is why we are here. What is it like for you?

Sam: (speaking to Hank) When you were talking earlier about your wife, I really knew what you meant. I felt that my wife had done similar things to yours. (The conversation went on between Sam and Hank in an animated manner, each of them shared similar experiences. I asked my question again.)

Bill: (speaking to the leader) I think you got your answer. It's really helped. I learn a lot listening to other guys and how they handle anger. It's not easy but I know it's what I need to do. (Many of the other group members voice agreement.)

I have adapted a model presented by Dr. Irwin Drieblatt.[18] He used it to explain the development, reinforcement, and repetition of sexual abuse by paedophiliacs. The nine steps of this model are outlined in Figure 12-1. Step 1, Childhood and Life Experiences, refers to the history of violence in the man's family of origin (such as being beaten or seeing his dad beat his mother). Life experiences refers to the man's previous adult experiences when he has been violent and learned that it was effective (what I mean by "effective" will be explained in Step 7). Together these contribute to Step 2, the man's Self-Image and Expectations of the world. Some workers might call these "tapes" or "scripts." They can be recognized and even spoken out loud by the man or unconscious attitudes. Examples are: "Nobody hurts me without paying for it!" "People are just out to screw you over." "I'm not loved or lovable." "She hates me." The first two steps I have described are the "baggage" a man brings to a situation or event. Step 3, Event, may refer to something someone (in this case his wife) says to him. She might say, "Have you paid the mortgage this month?" It may also be something she does or doesn't do, like leaving dishes in the sink after a meal. An event in this context can also be a memory or thought. For example, he might recall an incident which he was angry about several years ago. It's important to emphasize in this step that the event in terms of what she did may be inconsequential, or she may have done nothing different or out of the ordinary. Many battered wives report that their abuse occurred for no identifiable reason and happened no matter how much they tried to be a "good wife." This is why I have included thought as a category under Event. In other words the man can produce a fight in his own mind for which he then blames his wife.

At Step 4, Assumption, I am referring to what he says to himself about the event, how he interprets it. So he may say, in response to the question about the mortgage, "You think I'm lazy. You never trust me." Or if he sees dishes in the sink, he might think, "I have to do everything around here. Nobody cares about how hard I work." It is interesting how the assumption step mirrors statements in the self-image step. Notice also that these are all blaming statements which produce Anger, Step 5. Anger is accompanied by physical sensations which vary from individual to individual. Men in our group have used statements like "feeling my heart pounding," "adrenalin rushing

FIGURE 12.1
Nine Steps in the Cycle of Violence

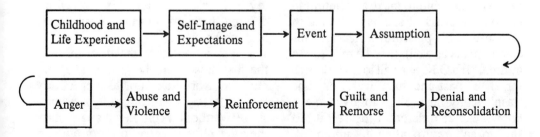

through me," "tight jaw," "clenched fists," "tight stomach," and the like to describe their experience of anger. Following his anger the man may be verbally and physically abusive. He may call her a bitch, lazy, or stupid, and may push and slap or hurl things at her up to and including using a weapon. Step 7, Reinforcement, is the key to understanding the repetitive and learned nature of violence against women by their husbands. We know from a social learning conceptualization of violence that the events that immediately follow a behavior will serve to reinforce or extinguish the behavior.[19] Violence is reinforced in many ways. First the discharge of tension accumulated in anger is a relief. We feel more relaxed if we let out a yell or hit a pillow when we've been holding our temper. Other reinforcers include the fact that the woman may often go along with the man's demands or try to remove the source of his irritation.

Most, though not all, men will experience guilt and express remorse for their behavior, Step 8. This may occur nearly immediately after hitting her or several days later. The important point from this model is that guilt and remorse do not follow the abuse; *reinforcement* does. The guilt may take the form of apologies, "I'll never do it again," or flowers and chocolates which are sent to her. But no one likes to feel guilty for long, and we probably all have defenses against it. At Step 9, Denial and Reconsolidation occur to deal with guilt and to make an attempt to resolve the crisis. If she has returned in response to his pressure (which may include threats as well), then he may say to himself, "It's O.K. She still loves me. Let's forget the past and start over." or "She wasn't really hurt. She's forgiven me. I know I can be different. I just *feel* it." If she doesn't return after his apologies, promises, or threats, then he may decide

that she is being "mean and just trying to punish me." Thus he has reconsolidated his perspective. He has nothing to change in himself and it's "her fault" for the breakup of the marriage.

This model is useful in several ways. It guards against being fooled into trusting good intentions and remorse as indicative of an ability to be nonviolent. Men may really feel guilty, or they may have learned that expressing guilt and need ("I can't live without you") will get their wife to come back. Also, although working with the men around their childhood experiences and self-image may be useful, it does not work with the dynamics of what occurs in the moment. A worker can do contactful and important work with a man around his childhood, and both the man and worker may feel that important change has taken place. If some of the work does not include training the man to know his triggers and how to control his anger, then he may not be prepared to stop his behavior next time he is under stress. As a result of this analysis the primary goals in working with violent men are (in the order of priority): (1) acknowledging the violence, (2) learning control, (3) exploring needs and feelings, and (4) experiencing and examining family background as it contributes to self-image.

The technique which we use to work on the first two goals is the anger diary. This approach to anger management was refined by Sonkin and Durphy and Ganley.[20] Our anger diary is somewhat different from any of those. An example is given below.

The men are taught the anger diary in the first session of the group. They are required to bring a completed anger diary to each group as their ticket of admission.[21] Without a completed anger diary they are refused entry to the group for that session. Through the anger diary key themes are identified which are then worked on within the group. However, the primary goal of this is always anger identification and control. Revenge, crying, manhood, and self-respect are significant issues in every group series. Curiously enough, these seemingly disparate issues are often woven together. It's not unusual for a man's diary to mention an incident when he was driving a car. Usually he would identify the trigger as being cut off by another driver.

sued after the men have gained significant control. Note how the diary parallels the central part of the nine-step process leading to violence described above. The "event" becomes the "trigger."

After six to eight weeks many of the men have made some progress in controlling their anger and aggression. At that time we move into other issues which make up the middle phase of the group. This does not mean that the diary or vio-

Trigger	How I Knew I was Angry	Rating (1-10)	Anger-Talk-up	Anger-Talk-down
Guy cuts me off while I'm driving	started yelling tense neck	8	Stupid jerk! Who do you think you are? I'll show him!	I'm angry at him. If I speed up I could cause an accident.

This kind of anger diary would generally only come from a man who has been in the group for several weeks. The talk-down shows the man taking responsibility for his anger and thinking about consequences. Earlier submissions would likely have shown the man denying his anger or not being able to conceive of a talk-down that was not really a further talk-up. For example, the man may have said, "Relax. I just won't let it bother me." Sonkin and Durphy refer to this as "stuffing it," which only leads to a growing resentment. Later in the group the men are encouraged to identify other feelings which occur before or during their anger. In this case the man may have felt frightened by a dangerous situation on the highway or he may have felt put down because another man "showed him up." These relate to issues of manhood. Masculinity myths such as "Real men aren't afraid and are always first" can be effective areas of work in our groups. However, these self-image themes are only pur-

lence control is left behind. All groups still begin with a focus on violence and abuse.

Working on the Problem

Many of the men start to say, "I've been working on my problems. When is she going to get some help?" or "When is she going to trust me or forgive me?" Often their partner has left and not indicated when or if she will come back (often she may have decided to leave and be afraid of telling him because in the past he has threatened her when she mentioned separation). If the couple is together again, she may still be very cautious and afraid of him even though she can see changes in his behavior. It's not unlikely that he may have "changed" before for brief periods of time and then gradually returned to an abusive and violent response to her. During this time the men often become impatient with their wives' "lack of goodwill." The key task is to help the men deal with their impatience, helplessness, and fear rather than expecting their wives to take it away. Successful completion of this task places the man at a new stage of maturity. He no longer requires his wife's constant approval and reassurance to feel O.K. as a person. The following process recording shows two men struggling with this same issue in different ways.

Leader: Allen said something valuable earlier. He knew it didn't take the pain away. He said, "No matter what happens with my wife (whether or not she returns), I'm going to learn something from this experience. I am going to change *me.*"

Allen: One part of me tells me to go find another girlfriend, but if I'm real honest with myself, I'd only be doing that to manipulate another person . . . to try and cover my own hurts. It wouldn't work for me anyway 'cause I wouldn't be looking at the problem. The problem (in me) never really went away.

(a few minutes later in the group)

Leader: Now your wife is saying no (to getting back together) to what you want. When you were living together and she said no, what did you do?

Mitch: I'd panic. I got mad, angry, totally outraged. Sometimes to the point where I'd actually strike her. . . . I'd panic 'cause I'm so afraid of losing . . . her.

Leader: For a lot of men it's difficult to have a woman say no to them. No to being loved when you want it, no to being taken care of when you feel you need it, or no to having sex.

Mitch: Yes, I guess it is.

Leader: About the only way a woman can say no in a relationship sometimes is to not be *in the relationship.*

Mitch: I see your point. I imagine my wife feeling that.

Leader: I imagine your wife didn't feel she had a "no." If she said no, she'd have to pay sooner or later.

Mitch: I wish she could believe she could say no to me now and don't hold it all in. Talk about it.

Coleader: Could she?

Mitch: Huh?

Coleader: Could she?

Mitch: Absolutely.

Coleader: Could she say no to you now without your going into a tailspin, panic, freaking out, getting angry?

Ralf: You're in a tailspin now.

Mitch: You know this has cost me a lot already. I don't want it to cost me my wife.

Leader: What would be necessary for you to regard your separation as positive regardless of whether your wife returns, the way Allen was talking earlier this evening? That regardless, "I've got something I can change in me," is it possible to be in his shoes, to have that attitude?

Mitch: I don't know how.

Coleader: You are doing it. You just don't want it to hurt so much. It's going to hurt. For you to be with your wife, you need to control your anger but also your panic. Though it hurts like hell. If you got back with her now, you'd hit her again.

Mitch: It started when I went to school. Guys put me down and I'd panic and then I'd talk-up. I didn't realize I've been doing that for years until I came here. That's a big plus.

Leader: The worst thing that could happen to you now would be if your wife called and said, "Let's get back together."

Mitch: You feel that would be the worst thing that would happen?

Leader: You wouldn't have the opportunity really to work with your own panic and trust yourself that you could get through it and handle it for you. Right now you're looking for Anne to bail you out. If she comes and says, "We'll get back together in six months," she's given you a safety net. You haven't had to deal with it (the panic) yourself.

Mitch: What *do* I do to deal with it?

Ralf: Just live day by day.

Leader: Just saying to yourself, "I'm not a bad person because I'm afraid, because I'm needy, because I'm hurt." I get the sense that you give yourself that message; that you are a bad person because of all of that.

Mitch: Yes, I really do (spoken with some relief).

Leader: Dealing with the panic doesn't mean turning it off. It means feeling it and not adding to it that you're a bad person.

Bill: After you have been alone, on your own, for awhile, you start to feel, well, you felt down and low and useless and nobody wants me for so long and afterwards you start to build confidence in yourself and it starts to grow and it's really a good feeling. At least that's what I experienced.

The coleader mentioned in this process recording is a woman. We have found a male-female therapy team to be very advantageous. The leaders are able to model a different kind of male-female relationship than most of the men have ever seen or thought possible. They can see a man being intellectually and emotionally equal in relation to a woman and not lose any "masculinity" in the process. In fact, they can observe how much both sexes can gain, without loss to the other, in an equal relationship. The men expressed misgivings and awkwardness when we told them that a woman coleader would be joining the group. Many felt that they would be inhibited and not be able to express themselves as easily as they did with all men. I think what sometimes passes as open communication in all-male groups still boils down to image management. No matter how hard the male leaders work at catching this, I believe that our sexual conditioning keeps all of us a little bit blind. The men also expressed appreciation that a woman would be present. Many of them looked forward to a real chance to hear from a woman about male-female relationships. One evening a man in our group said to Sue, the coleader, "Every time I hear your voice, I feel angry. It's not you personally. I realize now that I always feel that way when I hear a woman's voice." I think that as these men acknowledge, with safety, "unacceptable" feelings like these, they can increase their ability to control their behavior.

CONCLUSION

This essay will not provide space enough to explore all the themes which can be worked within the course of a group. Other useful topics to work with have included: (1) self-respect, how have they lost it and how have they gained it, (2) consequences of violence, what has verbal and physical violence done for them and what has it cost them and those close to them, (3) personal "buttons," what are the things that another person might say or do that will easily enrage them and what does that relate to in their past, and (4) practicing time-outs, getting the men to rehearse leaving a situation in which they feel their anger increasing dangerously.

I look for specific things in the behavior and feelings shown by a man for me to feel reasonably safe about him leaving the group. If a man feels that he has "fixed" his problem, that violence is behind him, then I become worried. One group member expressed it in a realistic way. He said, "It's like being an alcoholic. I have to realize that I'm always in danger of being violent again. I always have to watch myself."

Due to funding constrictions our group is shorter in length than we would like. As a partial remedy we have started a followup group which meets once a month. This acts as a support group and is run more by the men with one of the leaders present as a coordinator. We prevent men from attending the followup group who have not been in our regular group service, as we are concerned about men using it to convince their wives to return but never attending long enough for real change.

We continue to change and adjust our approach as we learn more about what is most effective in helping men to be nonviolent. The combination of confrontation of the man's violence and support for the positive changes he can make in himself remains consistent. This work is sometimes very demanding, and the burden of constant vigilance for signs of aggression or denial can be very exhausting. Many women are seriously injured and sometimes killed at the hands of their husbands. Workers need to be aware of that danger as always being present without ending up feeling helpless or enraged and burning themselves out. Certainly teamwork and networking are extremely important in this field. Effective networks in the field of wife assault are modeled after some of those which have been developed for dealing with child abuse. It is important to include members from a local women's shelter and from the different components of the criminal justice system. Maybe most important is to listen ourselves to the kind of message we keep giving to the men in our group. That is, "We can make a difference. We can change."[22]

NOTES

1. Del Martin, *Battered Wives* (San Francisco: Glide Publications, 1976).

2. M. Straus, R. Gelles, and S. Steinmetz, *Behind Closed Doors: Violence in the American Family* (Garden City, N.Y.: Anchor Books, 1980).

3. Ibid.

4. J. Downey and J. Howell, *Wife Battering: A Review and Preliminary Enquiry into Local Incidence, Needs and Resources* (Vancouver, B.C.: United Way of Greater Vancouver, September 1976).

5. James Joseph Browning, Violence Against Intimates: Toward a Profile of the Wife Assaulter (Doctoral thesis, University of British Columbia, 1983).

6. Mary Hanemann Lystad, "Violence at Home: A Review of the Literature," *American Journal of Orthopsychiatry* 45, no. 3 (April 1975): 328-35; Wini Breines and Linda Gordon, "The New Scholarship on Family Violence," *Signs: Journal of Women in Culture and Society* 8, no. 3 (1983). See also Browning, "Violence Against Intimates."

7. Donald G. Dutton, "An Ecologically Nested Theory of Role Violence Toward Intimates," paper presented at Canadian Psychological Association Annual Meeting, Toronto,
June 1981.

8. Lawrence Shulman donated his time as a consultant to aid in the formation stages of the group.

9. Daniel J. Levinson, *The Seasons of a Man's Life* (New York: Ballantine Books, 1978), p. 58.

10. Ibid., p. 72.

11. Anne L. Ganley, *Participant's Manual for Workshop to Train Mental Health Professionals to Counsel Court Mandated Batterers* (Washington, D.C.: Center for Women Policy Studies, 1981), p. 31.

12. Erik H. Erikson, *Childhood and Society* (New York: W. W. Norton & Co., 1950), p. 255.

13. Ibid., p. 255.

14. Ganley, *Participant Manual.* Presented to me in a workshop by Dr. Anne Ganley, 1982, and based on anger management work by Raymond Navaco, *Anger Control* (Lexington, Mass.: Lexington Books, 1975).

15. Ganley, Workshop.

16. Ibid.

17. Ibid.

18. From a workshop, "Treatment for Child-Sex-Offenders," given by Dr. Irwin Drieblatt, Vancouver, B.C., 1983.

19. Albert Bandura, *Aggression: A Social Learning Analysis* (Englewood Cliffs, N.J.: Prentice-Hall, 1973).

20. Daniel Jay Sonkin and Michael Durphy, *Learning to Live Without Violence: A Handbook for Men* (San Francisco: Volcano Press, 1983); and Ganley, *Participant Manual.*

21. Sonkin and Durphy, *Learning to Live.*

22. The author would like to acknowledge the following agencies and individuals for their contributions:

Funding for this service is provided by the Province of British Columbia, Ministry of the Attorney General, Corrections Branch. This service was founded by myself and Dr. Don Dutton of the Psychology Department, University of British Columbia.

The coleader mentioned in the process recordings is Dr. Sue Johnson, who is now at the University of Ottawa. Dr. Jim Browning has contributed to the development and leadership of this service.

Judith A. B. Lee

CHAPTER 13

No Place to Go: Homeless Women

Disaffiliation, transience, alienation, dispossession, and loneliness are words for our times. They are also words used to characterize the nation's homeless population.[1] While widespread unemployment, the lack of low-cost housing, and the de-institutionalization of mental patients have caused a dramatic increase in the scope of this problem, it is more than any other phenomenon a sign of our times. People who personify the meaning of these words represent the fruits of a super-industrial and space age where technology is valued and people struggle to keep up as best they can.[2] A return to Social Darwinist thinking which characterizes the conservative forces dominating the current political scene lets us know that if there are those who fall by the wayside, it is their own fault.[3] Hence social programs are aimed at giving the least service and avoiding thereby the pitfalls of dependence on government and "encouraging self-sufficiency." These are times in which the poor clearly get poorer, and those who find it difficult to manage alone are further stigmatized for needing help. These are times in which social work must reaffirm its very reason for being.

This is particularly true regarding the ever-escalating needs of homeless people. In many areas tent cities reminiscent of the "Hoovervilles" of the 1930s are springing up.[4] New York City can boast over 36,000 homeless living and dying on the city streets, many passing through the city shelters where ideally help should be given.[5] This is a "public issue" relating to the wider issues of social structure and the times in which we live, but for the sufferers it is also an intensely "private trouble." Schwartz makes an extremely powerful statement when he argues for a unified conception of social work function which does not separate private troubles from such public issues. He says that such polarization, in which we have the planners and changers on one hand and the direct practitioners, or doers, on the other "cuts off each from the other and from the reinforcing power of the other. . . . There can be no 'choice'— or even a division of labor—between serving individual needs and dealing with social problems, if we understand that a private trouble is simply a specific example of a public issue, and that a public issue is made up of many private troubles."[6] This chapter addresses my work at both levels, social work practice with homeless women particularly in small groups, and mediation on the larger or more "public" level.

The following is an example of the private trouble/public issue which speaks to the oneness of the tasks at hand. I did not know the woman I am about to describe, but I must say with regret that I know many like her whose private troubles are remarkably similar and tragic. She is not unusual in the homeless population. A curious phenomenon of our times is that the media permits us to participate passively and vicariously in the suffering of others. Usually we are far enough away to be free of direct responsibility. But sometimes it is within reach. The January 27 6 o'clock news blared out that Rebecca Smith died on the street and showed her curled up in her cardboard box "home," her feet bare and calloused in the bitter cold. She was a sixty-one-year old black woman who once had a family, was the valedictorian of her college class, and had a history of psychiatric hospitalization many years ago. She lost her public assistance in May due to "a failure to appear for recertification." Ten days before her death (she lived in her box for *eight months)* several agencies tried to convince her to enter the shelter, but she refused and died of hypothermia hours before an order to take her forcibly was obtained from the Supreme Court.[7] The number of systems failures that this tragedy represents are countless. The role of racism, classism, sexism, and ageism is also clear. The horror of it is striking as is the horror in the life of each homeless person in need of shelter and social work help.

The reality of Schwartz's formulation of social work function once again rings true: "The general assignment for the social work profession is to mediate the process through which the individual and his society reach out for each other ... (this) emerges from the fact that, in a complex and often disordered society, the individual—social symbiosis grows diffuse and obscure in varying degrees, ranging ... to where the symbiotic attachment

appears to be all but severed."[8] Rebecca Smith and all the "Ms. and Mr. Smiths" provide a prime example of this nearly severed attachment.

Schwartz believed that society was made up of "complex ambivalent systems that are hard to negotiate by all but the most skillful and best organized." He asked "How can such systems be kept functional?" He suggested, "What they need, and what each tried feebly to provide in some form or other is a force within the system itself that will act as a hedge against the system's own complexity. Its charge is to see that people do not get lost."[9] He argues, "It is this 'mediating' or 'third force' function for which social work was invented and that historically it is the function in which it has done its best work."[10] This concept of social work function motivated me to enter a municipal shelter for homeless women in one of our large cities on a voluntary basis as a direct practitioner who would also have a role in "reporting back" to the city administrators on my observations. While this mediating role was not formalized by hiring, it was a legitimate role which I negotiated openly with the administrators and the clients. In addition, using the mutual aid group would be extremely important in empowering and in building and rebuilding primary ties and human connection for this disaffiliated group of women.

THE DEVELOPMENTAL NEEDS OF HOMELESS YOUNG ADULTS AND ADULT WOMEN

While the majority of homeless people are men, the number of women who are homeless is growing at an alarming rate. Homelessness is an often life-threatening and degrading experience. While it is too early for comparative studies of how the experience affects men and women differently according to its relationship to sex-role expectations, it is clear that the feelings of loss, abandonment, and failure add to the already painful state of affairs. While some early studies and folklore and literature romanticize the plight of the male hobo,[11] there is little that can mask the devastating effects of this condition nowadays. While for the most, falling upon such hard times is far from a chosen status, there is, for some, an element of choosing this condition as one symbolic to them of freedom. But it is less the freedom of the "open road" than the freedom not to be institutionalized in mental hospitals or to be dependent on public assistance that motivates this marginal existence. It is also the choosing of one stigmatized status ("homelessness") above another ("welfare case," "mental case," "patient," "family scapegoat-outcast," and so on). When we reflect on the personal meanings of "home" for each of us, the feeling of being without in this area take on new meaning.

The dictionary defines home as "the place of one's dwelling or nurturing, with the conditions, circumstances, and feelings which naturally and properly attach to it, and are associated with it."[12] Dwelling and nurturing are indeed basic human needs; to be deprived of either takes its toll on humanity and mental health.[13] While indeed approximately 40 to 70 percent of the homeless have some history of mental hospitalization (also meaning 60 to 30 percent have no such history), the adverse effects of homelessness on anyone is drastic enough to cause serious mental disturbance.[14] We cannot dismiss this population as "mentally ill" and preferring, or able, to have no ties, for we are faced squarely with the chicken-egg nature of the dilemma. Further, we are faced with society's responsibility to its members who, for whatever reasons, are least able to negotiate its complexities and inequities. Indeed, homelessness can also be seen as a way of coping without dependence on formal institutions ranging from family to the government who have made little provision for those who are different and don't "fit in," or "toe the mark."[15] Dignity and self-worth purchased at this expense come quite high, if physical and mental health and the value of life itself are to be counted as part of the cost.

Yet, more than a place of dwelling or even nurturing, the dictionary illuminates that home is "not merely 'place' but also the 'state,' and is thus construed like youth, wedlock, health and other norms of state."[16] As to be without health is a serious blow to one's state of being in the world, so it is to be without a home. Even when housing is available, the impact of having been without a home is profound. Add to that the experience of hunger, of ill health, of fear, of living in doorways and keeping warm on steam pipes, of constantly riding the trains, or endless walking with nowhere to go, or of finally finding shelter in a place that gives three square meals and a bed but is often as frightening and unsafe as the streets and more humiliating to the spirit. It is a tribute to say that anyone survives the state of homelessness. Yet people more than survive, they help each other and even grow under these circumstances.[17] Promoting this sort of mutual aid and helping people to find new primary group ties is critical to ameliorating the effects of homelessness, for home is not restored merely with place but when a state of belonging somewhere and to someone where some level of nurturing is available. While our priorities for literally saving life must be on providing temporary and permanent shelter as a basic right of people, we must not forget that there is a next step in restoring human connection and relatedness that is crucial to restoring homes for people.[18] In this sense, having a home is a basic developmental need of all stages of adulthood.

Homeless women range in ages from eighteen to ninety. Developmentally they range from youth experiencing severe adolescent struggles for identity and individuation-separation from families, to young adults struggling with issues of intimacy versus isolation, adults striving for a measure of generativity and productivity, and older adults whose tasks of life review to attain integrity are now weighted heavily in the area of despair.[19] In another sense, looking at ego development, these are people who range from well intact and wellfunctioning people who met with calamity and crisis such as a sudden loss of income, eviction, or a combination of external events which were objectively and subjectively unmanageable, to the de-institutionalized decompensated chronic schizophrenic person, and all the shades of functioning between the two extremes. For many the level of human (object) relatedness is impaired, and the ties to significant others are weak or nonexistent, making living in the streets or seeking public shelter the only viable alternative. Many were the "different" members in families, and as family structures weakened, became outcasts or dropouts from family life. Still others lost families due to illness and death or migration and, well able to establish close ties, still find themselves alone and without primary group ties to count on. This is a highly heterogeneous population.

AGENCY CONTEXT AND THE GROUP MODALITY

A critical problem of the shelter system is that it seeks to meet differential needs in one catchall way, through offering a bed and meals and the most minimal social service help to this complex group of people, thus becoming simply a revolving door for many clients.

One can identify different groups in need of services designed to fit their special needs. First, there is a large group of young adults who have been disenfranchised from the American dream. Having extreme difficulty in finding work (the unemployment rate for black youth is staggering) and an affordable place to live, and often serious difficulty in living alone when ejected from families or couples relationships, they have established a new kind of counterculture. While some of these young people have come from middle-class and intact families, many are from poverty-level families. Many have been in foster care and other forms of group care. Some have children in foster care. Many have experienced institutionalization for juvenile or other crime, drug addiction, or mental illness. They are the children we have failed with, grown just above the age where society must plan for them. Most are hardened and streetwise. If they entered the shelters without a drug or alcohol problem or propensity for violent behavior, they are soon influenced to become part of the counterculture which boasts these attributes. They are also introduced, often with some coercion, to a rather tough lesbian/alcoholic subculture within the group. And they are faced with an army of men, including pimps and drug dealers and men from the men's shelters, who wait outside for them each day. It is a very difficult place for a young adult to find herself. As one young adult shared in a group meeting: "My bed has been next to murderers on one side and prostitutes on the other. I've seen crazy people scream at themselves and women take knives to each other. I've also met some good people, but I'm scared to death here. I can only look within myself and remember who I am." While some of these young adults "hit bottom" and find strength to move on quickly, many others make shelter life a way of survival, moving from one shelter to another. This group needs attention for many reasons. They are young and often open to help, they have and will have children to learn to mother, and, sadly, some also prey upon other shelter residents even as they are preyed upon themselves.

Another large group of people who use the shelters are those I see as "the vulnerable group." For reasons of brevity, I categorize here those who are mentally ill of all ages, the elderly, the mentally retarded, and the physically handicapped or medically ill. Shelters have made no provision of meeting any of the special needs of these people. In one of the smaller public shelters there are four medical beds, a nurse, and a part-time psychiatrist available, but in the others there is no medical staff. Neither prescribed drugs or psychotropic drugs can be administered. The "recreation room" may look more like a locked ward in a state mental hospital without the help of medication. Women hallucinate, disrobe, rage, and withdraw. While there is now some day programming in two of the shelters, this was so in only one until recently. Most remarkably there is no trained staff except part-time "medical social workers." Clients with a history of mental hospitalization who enter the shelter in a fairly compensated state decompensate quickly under these conditions. Others who may be retarded or elderly with or without organic damage also face the prospect of long empty days filled only with fear and need. Those clients who have none of these problems but have entered the shelter in an eco-

nomic or family crisis are shocked by the atmosphere and lack of service. The feel trapped and betrayed by this system.

Finally, there are within the population substance abusers of all ages. Chronic alcoholics, counterculture young adults experimenting with drugs, and hard core drug abusers are in need of a type of help, including detoxification, unavailable in such a catchall shelter service. In trying to "provide beds for all" with no attempt to group clients in order to serve them best, shelters help few clients. A shelter stay could range in time anywhere from one day to more than a year, with some coming and going in a revolving cycle.

Differential services are needed to meet these differential needs. While intensive individual work is important for many, the need for connection and human relatedness can best be served by providing a variety of group services. The overall strategy was to help restore the capacity for relatedness and to develop actual primary group ties for the group members. The common ground of the need for shelter and the need to belong somewhere made mutual aid groups, both formal and informal, an effective way to help. Three types of mutual aid groups were used: the small, homogeneous discussion/counseling group of both a planned (formal) and a spontaneous (informal) nature; the larger, heterogeneous discussion group; and activities groups where both doing and talking were vehicles of helping. This chapter will illustrate work with a smaller discussion group of young adults and with a large activities group. The homogeneous small discussion group was intended for those able to verbalize coherently, form ties more easily, and benefit from mutual sharing, support, and problem solving. The larger talking group called "The Rap Group" was somewhat different.[20] This was an open-ended meeting on a weekly basis with the intent of helping the women verbalize their concerns, exchange feeling and experiences, make suggestions on improving the shelter service, and begin to work on their concerns. The group was large, often having thirty or more people. There may be a nucleus of ongoing members or many new members each time. Since whoever wanted to could come, each meeting was unique, some dominated by the participation of the more decompensated mentally ill and some by the more intact. The large size and open-ended nature of their group had both positive and negative effects on its purpose. Women who were afraid of greater intimacy did find a place for themselves at a safe distance in the large group, and it also enabled "case finding" and outreach. But people who wanted and needed closer ties, who were frightened of large groups, or who had trouble talking at all needed the service of small groups and groups where something besides talking was the primary vehicle of service. In one shelter, a "Plant Group" served this latter function. In addition to involving people who were not able to work well by talking, it symbolically met a need for growing something and caring for it, a strong need for women deprived of such opportunities.[21]

This need to be competent in doing and producing, as well as having a nondemanding and safe place to meet other clients with similar interests and struggles, was also met by an Activity/Talking group. The activities were initially suggested by the worker(s) and then determined by the women's interests. More than one activity might take place at a time, leaving room for choice.

Activities ranged from knitting and crocheting (a favorite) to painting and drawing, making posters or collages, working in clay, printing T shirts, and so on. I initially began this group with a recent M.S.W. graduate who had skills in group work and art.[22] The response was strong, and the group was often large (fifteen to thirty-five) and heterogeneous so coworkers and sometimes other helpers were needed.[23] I worked on forming small subgroups within the larger group and on helping people to connect with each other and talk as they worked. We all worked on helping each one with successful skill mastery, never pressuring to "do it right," which is assaultive to the weakened ego, but in helping each one get "good results" as they themselves defined good results.

The informal groups, those groups naturally formed by friendship or commonality or even proximity in one of the large dormitory rooms, were also powerful helping networks the worker could help promote and strengthen. This chapter will also show the use of the group in the informal system and the development of one particular primary group.

GROUP THEMES

The first group to be discussed is a young adult mutual aid group formed by using a population approach. This approach to formation is used in a setting where clients are already present. It may be employed on a hospital ward, in a residential or neighborhood center, or in a playground, dormitory, or waiting-room setup. The common ground of being on the service may be enough to form a group. Commonality can also be increased by looking for other homogeneous factors within the population. In this case I used both age and natural friendship ties to strengthen the common ground.

My first steps were to determine the needs of the overall population with the director. We discussed possible natural clusters of clients such as the angry young people, alcoholics, and old people. From observing, I also saw the barely compensated mentally ill and pregnant women as two other distinct groups. I took a tour of the shelter with a staff member. Together we stopped and engaged people on each floor. The mood was one of depression and withdrawal as well as a high level of tension and rage about to explode. We engaged a group of loud young people. There were two leaders, Jean and Iris, and three group members. Iris raged about a woman across the room who hit her with a chair. Jean asked us to listen to several complaints: the TV was busted, the staff was rude, the toilets were stopped up, and so on. The others watched our reactions. Both of us were empathic, and I then introduced myself as a social worker and offered to meet with them later in the day to work on these grievances and to talk about getting themselves together to get out of the shelter. They enthusiastically accepted my invitation.

Getting Started

Present for the meeting were: Jean, age thirty-one; Carla, age twenty-five; Ana, age twenty-four; Iris, age twenty-four; Sheryl, age thirty-two; and Dora, age thirty-five. All are black except Ana, who is Hispanic. Jean and Sheryl were waiting for me in the appointed place. Jean called out the window and the others arrived. We put chairs in a circle and began.

I asked their names and ages and told them I was a social worker who was working here voluntarily on a part-time basis because I wanted to help. There were so many people here and not enough help to go around. "You can say that again" and "There's *no* help" were the replies. I told them the rest of the

time I was a teacher at a school of social work, but I felt concerned that women were in such trouble and living under these conditions, maybe I could help them to help each other. This group, if they wanted to become one, would be a place to talk about making this place better and about getting out and back on your feet again. I didn't need to ask what they thought because they were telling me as I spoke by saying, "yeah" and "right on." Now Iris angrily and very loudly said she didn't want to meet with me as a go-between; I should send them the director or the big boss above all the shelters. I said I couldn't do that today and I couldn't promise any fast results, but I would act as mediator or go-between until I could arrange that if they wanted to do it later. Iris reluctantly agreed. They all expressed fear that there would be reprisals for coming to this meeting. Staff would "get them" for it. I said I didn't know if that were so or not, but they should tell me if anything should happen. I asked for their concerns and they began. In a steady stream, Iris, Jean, and Carla shared what the problems were. Ana and Dora agreed with all that was said by nodding. Sheryl seemed uncomfortable with the tone and barrage. At various points, I turned to her to get her in. A few times she clarified where the others were not aware that the service they wanted did exist in some form. They went on with a list of fifteen grievances. All of this was said with much feeling of anger, depression, and desperation, and I related to these feelings with empathy as the process unfolded, naming the feelings when they were particularly strong.

In this beginning excerpt I introduced myself and my role and offered the group service. I began to negotiate the contract on the group's purpose, mutual aid and mediation. I got their feedback and asked for their specific concerns in order to begin the work. When I noted Sheryl's indirect cue that she was uncomfortable with the process, I included her. I also conveyed empathy and put the feelings into words as they strongly emerged, saying for example, "I can understand why this makes you so angry." I accepted questioning of my authority and clarified my role. I allied with their sense of injustice at this early stage of the work. My own tuning in and observations of the shelter enabled me to do this.

The Lack of Dignity and Respect, Rage and Hopelessness

Later in the meeting,

Carla said there is frequent cursing at clients and hitting of residents has also been observed. "We're all treated like we're crazy or in prison. It's hard enough to be down and out, but to be treated like dirt gets us desperate." Then Jean said, "This place is so tense, it's going to explode." Everyone agreed. Iris said she felt really close to hurting someone and going to jail. I said I understood how angry they were. I asked if Iris really wanted to go to jail; she said no. I asked the group what she could do then. Jean suggested, "Just what we're doing, talk about it here. I'm so glad you came. I don't explode, but I am so depressed." I said I heard her pain and asked how the others felt. Everyone agreed to being very depressed. Carla said you need hope, you need to know your options, how you can get out of here or you don't know what you'd do in time. Sheryl said people who felt they were so angry they would hurt someone should get some help. Many would not hurt anyone and didn't want to be hurt. I said that I heard her and understood, she didn't feel that way, and it was scary when others did. But everyone here is hurting in her own way. This brought forth more outpouring. . . .
    . . . Jean said she'll sum it up for us: "There is a lack of compassion here. Everything is hard and tough and soon you become hard and tough. You get treated like dirt, so you feel like dirt. To be treated like a criminal is the worst part of the pain. You already hate yourself for messing up and landing here. Where is the compassion?" It was a moving moment. I said I agreed and everyone nod-

ded, solemnly. I said I saw today that they cared about each other and that's why I brought them together as a group. Jean said, "God bless you for coming here. This is the first time I talked my heart out and felt caring from anyone since I got here." Everyone agreed. I thanked them for giving me a chance to hear them and work with them and share their pain and frustration. I suggested they could become a group here with me and we could worry about taking care of each other. I honestly didn't know how much I could do about the shelter system. I would be pleased to try. But I did know they could care for each other and I could help with that. Jean said, "It's happening right here, right here, right now, I'm so glad I spoke up this morning." Iris started joking and singing about everyone needing a little love.

In this excerpt my interventions were aimed at helping the group members to tell the story of life there and to reach for and show understanding of the pain they were feeling. In particular, I tried to welcome the expression of anger, not only because this brought relief but because I wanted to model an authority who did not punish them for their anger and who could "take it." While their anger was not easy to take, I also let them know what would be hard for me (the demand to change the system overnight) and that I would try. I tried to show myself as a human being who had feelings about them and their plight. I continued to include the member who felt different, recognizing her feelings. The sharing of feelings on both sides brought us to a next, more intimate phase in the meeting. As we shared a close feeling, I also broadened the contract.

Getting Back on Your Feet

I took this moment of a little warmth and tension relief to share a bag of candy. This brought further relaxing. I then said I'd like to have the group be about getting back on your feet and out of here, not just changing it here. What did they think about that? There was 100 percent agreement.

They said they want to "get back out there" and "make it in the world." I asked if each one could tell a little about why she was here and what it would take to get back on her feet. Ana suggested we go around the circle. Carla was first. Iris kept cutting in. The group put excellent pressure on her to "let Carla finish" and to quit "acting the fool." Carla said she's not from New York, and she's been here two weeks. She's had no one to tell her where to get welfare or what the housing options were or where to go for job training. I said I would make sure she got hooked up to a caseworker today. She went on that she is scared of the psychiatric cases and wonders why they are here? They need some help. Again, I agreed that she was right and recognized they could be scary. She said she worked as a social work aide at home, and she knows you have to treat psychiatric problems gently. She gave an awful example of someone hallucinating on her knees and an aide telling her "to get up off the damn floor, bitch." Now, if she knew the lady was frightened and needed a gentle talk, why didn't the aide know? Iris cut in. The group told her to let Carla continue. Carla went on to share that she had a daughter who lives with relatives and this breaks her heart. The group members empathized. Jean shared she had a daughter too and it *was* hard; she needs public assistance and a place to live. I said separation from loved ones is very hard. Everyone agreed. I asked if any one knew how to get public assistance? Sheryl knew and filled the others in. . . . They then asked about housing options; did I know anything? I told them about two possibilities they had not been told about. . . .

After Iris told a little about herself, Ana said she has her public assistance and food stamps but not enough for an apartment, since she lost her allotment for rent money when her friend "threw her out." She had nowhere to go, so here she is. Her eyes filled up. She said, "I'm only twenty-four years old. I've been here two other times when I got thrown

out. I need to learn how to make it on my own. I don't belong here." Jean put her arm around her and said, "You feel like crying, huh?" Ana wiped her tears. I looked around, everyone was feeling with them. I said, I feel like crying too, it hurts me that you're here. I felt like it when I left this morning. This is a painful place to be. Jean choked up as she said, "It's my first time, I'm never coming back here, if I can get out." Iris said, gently this time, "Never say never, here I am and here's Ana." I said it's very painful to try and not make it and come back. But I agreed with Ana, we need to help you learn how to make it on your own. Maybe we can work on that. Everyone agreed except Iris who began to complain about the staff again. Jean said, "Look, staff is shit, but we got to get out of here. I want to be in this group." Jean said she'd kill herself before coming back here. Iris said she'd kill someone else. I said they felt very depressed and angry. Let's see if we can help with this group. Jean eagerly went on with her story.

In this very moving excerpt we see a sharing of real pain on a personal level. I continued to reach for, name, and show understanding of their feelings. I established common ground between members to deepen the empathy they had for each other. I gave information and helped them to do the same. I shared my own feelings about their struggles and lent some vision of hope. This latter skill is a very important one in working with any of the shelter populations.

I credited all of the sharing and helping each other they did today. I promised to look into their grievances and do what I could. I offered to meet with them again, and for as long as a few of them remained together here. Iris said, to my surprise, if we meet next week, I have something to wait for, something is happening. It will help me hold myself together. I said I'd be back next week, and we worked out a time. Then spontaneously they began to recite the words of a song by Grandmaster

Flash.[24] I recognized it and finished it with them. They were surprised and delighted that I knew it. We repeated, "Don't push me 'cause I'm close to the edge" a few more times. I said the song told it like it was. Carla said, "It's the fruits of oppression." I said it was, and I heard they were feeling on the edge but to try to hang in there until we could get it together as a group and see if it helped. We ended on that note. They sang as we went down the stairs.

In ending the meeting, I credited their work, giving them hope of accomplishing the task and also recognizing their strengths. This also reinforced the contract and lent further vision to this enterprise in mutual aid. When we sang together, it was again a moment of sharing difficult feelings. Because the young women were in such a state of crisis, the feeling level of this meeting was deeper than many first meetings could be. It was also important for me to work on the very real grievances and in concrete ways show the meaning of mediation.

My work with this group lasted only a few sessions because half of the group was transferred to another shelter. I did begin the next meeting with followup on several specific grievances. The group did provide a vehicle for social action and contributed to empowering this relatively powerless population.[25] Jean and Carla remained in the group, but Iris became too drunk to participate. The mood was depressed although new people joined the group. After a few meetings Jean got into a fight with a security guard who cut her with a bottle. The guard was suspended, but I was able to get Jean and Carla transferred to another shelter where the atmosphere was less chaotic and tense. In the new place I continued to work with them as a dyad and individually. They became my connection to the young adult population. I was able to enter the informal network with them and also to have some

formal group meetings. I learned to treat each meeting as a "happening," a unique time together that may only come once or continue next week.

The transience of the population is a factor to reckon with. But I still found the group approach helpful on this spontaneous basis. I learned to live flexibly, turning any conversation with two or three into a possible group meeting. Over time I did have a nucleus to work with in this approach. A popular theme of the mutual aid was vocational and educational opportunities. They were good at finding and sharing resources in this area. Housing resources were highly limited but shared when found. The important developmental work of "making it on your own," separation-individuation, intimacy and identity issues were always pursued. I also attempted family mediation for Carla and Jean but found family doors shut painfully tight.

The tendency for young adults to be pulled into a substance-abusing and violent subculture was strong and was always a factor in the work. The longer the stay, the stronger the pull in this direction. Jean left after two months but not before she began drinking intermittently. It's not clear whether her leaving was growth or regression. Carla, on the other hand, stuck it out several months until we could help her get adequate housing. She became part of another group that I worked closely with ("the primary group" to be discussed below). She left with a new capacity for independent living and for greater self-esteem and improved human relatedness.

Talking and Doing

The following process excerpt shows this group at work. It is the fifth meeting of the group. There is a nucleus of six to nine that have attended all meetings; about twenty-two attended this meeting.

The room was set up with two tables and several chairs in two or three semicircles. In preparation for the coming holidays the primary activities were making cards or tree ornaments. There were also several who preferred to knit or crochet. My coworker began the meeting by welcoming everyone and demonstrating the new skill for today, decorating styrofoam balls. She also invited group members to talk about being here for the holidays or whatever else they wanted to talk about as we worked. They waited eagerly to begin, so we organized the new activity with the card making at the large table. Others preferred to paint and cast plaster ornaments at the smaller table. Those who worked with wool sat in the semicircles with a staff member helping. We moved about mingling in each grouping.

At the smaller table, Anna and Clara sat on one side. Anna is a middle-aged white Catholic woman with a history of mental hospitalization, nicely dressed, soft-spoken, and appropriate in behavior. Clara, her friend, is an older Jewish woman, more lined and hardened, also with a history of hospitalization. On the other three sides there are young adults, all are black except one: Kiki, a creative pretty and verbal twenty-year-old; Donna, a thin, quiet, intent, cautious thirty-year-old who reaches out nonverbally; and Nina, twenty-eight, obviously slow, with a deformed hand. Also in the group were Cheri, twenty-seven, recently released from a state hospital (she smells of urine and unwashed clothing and is somewhat dazed, sometimes laughing to herself); Tami is a rather agitated pregnant nineteen-year-old; and Kara, a heavy, white, twenty-five-year-old drug user. The group is remarkably tolerant of Cheri except for Tami who holds her nose and attempts to get the others to laugh but receives no response as the others are absorbed in their work.

I am working with Cheri and Nina on holding the brush and choosing colors. Anna is helping Clara. Kiki makes a point of painting all of her figures black. She comments that Christmas is for black people, too, and she is tired of white Santas. Anna said she thought it was for everyone and Santa could be any color. Kara said her baby's father is black, if she is pregnant . . . they need a black and white Santa. I agreed, and asked if she was worried about being pregnant? She poured out her fears. Tami, with concern, told her where to get a checkup and prenatal care. Tami then got up and got some paper and began to draw. Kiki encouraged Kara to get help for her drug problem and told her own story of getting off angel dust. Kara was interested in Kiki's program.

Noting the card Clara was making now, I said that there are a few people here who celebrate Chanukah rather than Christmas, introducing Clara to Lorna, an internal group leader who is a forty-five-year-old woman of observant Jewish background. Lorna came over and said she felt left out when we spoke only of Christmas. Clara agreed. Donna said it's "holidays," that's what we should call it. All agreed.

In addition to the sessional contracting skills done verbally, we see that setting up and demonstrating the activity is also necessary. Helping each member to choose and start an activity is important as is beginning to establish some level of member-to-member interaction. In a heterogeneous group such as this finding common ground is helpful (like ethnicity or a common problem like pregnancy), but the activity itself also provides a meeting place for differences. Additionally I reached for feelings in a taboo area (race and religion) as a way of helping the group to talk about real issues and to accept differences. This was also a way of giving them access to a different kind of authority, one who encourages the discussion of taboos and of feelings. We also see the beginnings of mutual aid on the nonverbal and verbal levels. Later in the meeting:

Kiki finished five objects and began to mix another batch for the group. Everyone praised her well-completed work. She said she was keeping them all. Anna said we could put hers on the tree; she couldn't keep them. I asked why not and asked her to show them to the others. They praised her work. She said she doesn't feel like Christmas inside. Cheri looked up and nodded that she agreed. I sensed the sadness all around and said it's very hard to spend your holidays here, isn't it? Tami finished her drawing and held it up. It was a great cartoon of the "Grinch Who Stole Christmas." I got the attention of the whole group and asked Tami to show it. Those who knew what it was laughed heartily. I asked her to tell the rest what it meant. She said it means some of us feel we can't really be happy enough to celebrate Christmas here. Christmas is stolen from us. "Or the holidays," Lorna said. My coworker said that was a very sad feeling. "P.J.," an articulate thirty-five-year-old black woman who did beautiful craft work, said, "But I don't feel so bad today. This is fun, and some of us are beginning to have hope, and none of us are on the street." Several others agreed. I said, "So for some of you it feels O.K. to be here now, and you can feel hopeful and some holiday happiness, and others are very sad." Tami said, "That's a sorry-looking tree. The least we could do is decorate it." Nina and others got up to put their ornaments on the tree. The others continued working and talking to each.

The themes of competence, self-esteem, and also deep sadness run through this excerpt. The activity enabled Tami to express her feelings without words, and we used it to help her and the others put words on those feelings of loss. Yet it was done with respect for the fragile defenses of several and with the balance of some laughter and some good feelings. The workers reached for and understood both the sadness and the healing power of at least being here together enjoying something. The group affords the feeling of camaraderie and competence and in that way adds balance to the understandable level of despair.

Another strategy we employed was to help group members reach out to other shelter residents who did not attend the group.

Lorna then asked me if she could bring some of the craft material down to the old people who couldn't get up to the group. I asked what the others thought of that and if anyone wanted to go with Lorna. All said it was a good idea. I said I thought it was, too. Donna and Nina said they would go, too, and I worked with them on how to show the crafts to the older people. I later went to see how they were doing and was moved to walk into another group meeting. They were duplicating what they experienced to the delight of several of the older women.

This multiplying of the mutual aid effect was also seen within the group. For example, Rina and Sally were two middle-aged black women who had exquisite knitting skills. As group members admired their work, we asked if they could become the knitting teachers. They self-consciously assumed the role but soon were sought after and spent much time during and after the groups teaching their skills. This was amazing to Sally, who had been hospitalized for depression and felt she had nothing to offer. Rina, who recently came from the West Indies, felt like "a stranger" here. This helped her find her way in and to make some new friends. We introduced people of similar backgrounds to each other. Rina was then particularly helpful to a frightened young girl from her own country. Rina and Sally became friends, and we were able to find rooms in the same newly renovated building for them. When they left, other women had learned enough to assume their teaching/helping role.

Developing a Feeling of "We"

Rina and Sally formed a small primary group quite spontaneously. Others needed help and encouragement to be able to do this. A common problem for most of the women in the shelter was the striking absence of dependable primary group ties. Some had "worn out their welcome" with families and friends for reasons ranging from severe mental illness to substance abuse to family problems and scapegoating. Others never had such ties to wear out, as they were raised in institutions or had been considered odd and outcast for most of their lives. They now found themselves in a setting with a wide range of women who were in the same boat. In addition to finding resources for housing and making the shelters more livable and service-oriented, a primary goal was to help restore the capacity for human relatedness and to help clients form some level of friendship, to re-form and restore primary group ties. For those who are alone, alienated, and isolated, "we" is a wonderful word and a statement on the road to coming back to fuller humanity.[26] Our strategy then was to observe and encourage friendship groups and to encourage greater interaction and sharing to promote closer quasi-family-like behavior.

As we look back through this essay with these lenses, we can view the work with Jean and Carla, Rina and Sally, and with Lorna, Donna, and Nina's subgroup in this light. These latter three became the nucleus of a group of four that I worked with to form deeper primary group ties. Carla was added later on. I worked with them within the larger activities group, individually, in the triad, and finally in the group of four.

Lorna and Donna were also living in the same dormitory-style room. Lorna continued to take on various leadership roles although she actually looked up to Donna for being "very smart." As Donna received, she slowly began to be able to give back a little. Donna, who had had two psychiatric hospitalizations after being severely beaten by a boyfriend, needed help in learning how to give and take in a relationship and in beginning to see how others responded to her aloof, childlike but sometimes angry quality. This was similar for Nina who completed the triad. Nina, mildly retarded and with mild physical deformity, constantly sought out Lorna, who enjoyed caring for her. But it was hard for Nina to allow Lorna space to breathe. Nina also was able to express in time that she wanted to be seen as an adult who could be capable in her own right and who in turn could help others. It was hard for the others to allow her to help them. Nina also had to learn what was appropriate to ask of others and what she could indeed do for herself. Donna, on the other hand, had to learn that it was all right to ask something of a friend as well as how to return a favor.

The basic "rules" of relating were unknown, since they had not really had friends in reciprocal relationships before. As Lorna put it, "Before, I was only a burden on others. Now I see I have something to give, too." The giving for both Lorna and Donna was easier than the taking. Lorna's family had given up on her as "worthless" when, after the death of her mother and sister ten years ago, she was bereaved and unable to function. They "placed" her with an old woman, and she did not leave the house for ten years until the woman was placed in a nursing home and she was again alone. She was directed to the shelter, where ironically she began to discover that she was capable and worthy of receiving from others. Other clients were also affected by this primary group. Networks revolved around both Lorna and Carla. Through working with them, I could influence a ripple effect of caring and helping. One of the problems Carla faced, however, was that she was easily pulled into a drinking and fighting subculture in order to show further her leadership and to get what felt like caring to her. At twenty-five, she deeply missed her mother, who had cast her out as "the black sheep of the family" after she had been raped. As Carla and I worked on this one-to-one, we both thought it might help her to be part of a different subgroup where drinking and violence were not expected. At first Lorna, Donna, and Nina expressed a fear of Carla because of who her friends were. So I encouraged her to attend the activities group and get to know them. She did this, and I began to work with the four together. Their common ground was strengthened because they were all interested in going to the same halfway house. Carla's strengths added to this group because she could deal in the outside world more effectively and teach the others.

Another area of common ground was that each woman felt bereft of family ties and was a family outcast. This held them together as a new primary group. I met with them formally or over dinner or on trips, for it was critical that they get back into the world again. The primary themes were how families have let them down and how they had to "pick themselves up" and "get back on their feet" without families, but with the help of each other. We also worked on how to be friends and how to negotiate the complex systems "on the outside." After nine months in the shelter (a statement on how scarce resources are) they are all out now. And, though not all together now (two are), they do keep in touch by letter, phone, and visits, and they do actively help each other. They were able to form some pri-

mary ties they can still count on. Each one has said, "I know I'm not alone anymore." If only for a few people, that was the goal achieved through the process of working with groups and individually in the women's shelter.

Engaging the System

Mediation between the women and the systems they needed took place on many levels. The group of young adults was a vehicle for making the shelter more responsive. Some of the specific things attained by groups were setting up a suggestion box to which the director was responsive, placing a pay telephone inside the building so clients did not have to go outside especially at night, decorating several rooms, obtaining arts and crafts materials, establishing an informational bulletin board, forming linkages with a job preparation program, and other helpful changes. Within the groups themselves mediation took place between members having difficulty with each other and in the dormitories and the informal network. Attempts were also made to mediate between clients and their families where any possibility of engaging the families existed. Mediating with welfare, housing, adult homes, foster homes, halfway houses, employment, jobs and job training, and a host of other agencies were at the very heart of the professional job in this setting.

In the areas of larger program and policy change the needs and service gaps are glaring and the bureaucratic response correspondingly slower to achieve. My primary effort in this area was to propose a design for functionally specific shelters characterized by more homogeneous groupings. For example, using age as a general dividing line, a shelter was set up to serve young adults; using a history of mental illness or current bizarre behavior as a criteria, one for the more vulnerable, including the elderly, was established, as well as one geared to the needs of substance abusers, and so on. Since there are several city shelters, there could also be one or two general shelters as currently exist for clients who can't tolerate a more specialized approach. Within the general shelters existing space could be arranged to create homogeneous groupings. This is less desirable but still better than no effort at meeting differential needs as currently exists. In the one shelter the director did set aside a floor for the elderly. This was a good start, but the next steps of differentially assigning and training staff to meet the special needs would have to be taken. The proposal took into account needs for supervision and training of staff. It also highlighted several policies that needed to be enforced such as seeing clients within twenty-four hours of arrival. It involved no new expenditure of money. This remains, however, as far as I know, the extent to which the homogeneous groupings or the specialized function idea has actually been implemented.

The pre-initiation and initiation stages of the proposal were handled from two directions.[27] I actually worked out the ideas in consultation with the administrative staff and medical social worker in one shelter to sound out reality. We also began to try out some of the notions there. My availability and direct practice "on the front lines" in this shelter was not only helpful to clients, but lent credibility to my thinking. I knew the job of caseworker because I did it. I knew how hard it was, and yet coming from outside, I could also envision how it could be different and what changes were needed to develop services. The proposal was written after several months of direct practice.

I also met with the top city administrators in charge of shelter programs on three occasions: first on entering the system, on defining my interests and mediating role; second, on discussing my proposal; and third, on how to implement the proposal in at least one shelter. My interest and ideas were welcomed. It was acknowledged that in the midst of this "housing emergency" social work service had taken bottom priority to providing beds and bathrooms in the new shelters. Everyone was warm, bright, and respectful. However, I soon got the point that nothing would move quickly, if at all, for several complex reasons. These ranged from a climate of feeling overwhelmed and reacting to instead of taking charge of the crisis; a message clearly stated that "if we give them services, they'll stay instead of leave"; the effort it would take to train staff and transfer trained workers, and a million small reasons as to "why it won't work." Basically my feeling was that I had no real leverage as an outsider to continue mediating from within. I might now be more helpful from outside, since external pressure was clearly more effective. While I do continue to make myself available to city administrators and shelter directors, supervisors, and staff, my efforts at mediation now involve seeking private funding to establish student units in the shelters, sharing my observations with the media, allying with other established groups, and advocating from outside the structure.[28] One cannot take on a bureaucratic structure single-handedly without a sanctioned role in the agency structure. But it was, nonetheless, a fruitful effort at direct service which led to helpful notions of program and policy design rooted in the reality of that practice.

CONCLUSION

It can be said, ironically, that the shelter system itself is often a cause of homelessness. Clients avoid living in such frightening and chaotic places until they are forced to do so by starvation and bitter cold winters. Moreover, the concept of "temporary shelter" is clearly nonexistent. Shelters are either long-term or revolving-door permanent, for when such meager help is given to turn lives around or to create and obtain adequate housing and other placement resources, clients remain lodged in the system.

When efforts are made to use the strengths of clients individually and in various kinds of groups, clients are able to move on and even grow from the shelter stay. Clients are able to reach out to help each other in many ways. Helping strategies which employ promoting competence and mastery, mutual aid, human relatedness, empowerment, and systems negotiation skills were particularly effective. The creation and support of primary group ties requires much effort but seems to have lasting effects in increased relatedness, competence, and actual support networks over time. While this was a relatively small-scale effort, the practice principles applied seem effective. It would be wonderful to test them empirically by a duplication of the effort. The concept is that services to this population which promote increased relatedness and build actual support networks can be effective in helping the homeless establish a home in society, with all that can mean.

Simultaneously the homeless need to be empowered by social work intervention to have an impact on shelter systems and on the broader program and policy issues that contribute to this state. They also need advocates and mediators to create the resources needed to house and support them in independent and semi-independent (for those who need this) living situations. They need social workers who see their jobs as being "the third force" who make sure that the tie is not severed and people do not get lost or cut off from their life support systems. What is needed are social workers who can make the bridges needed from private troubles to public issues, and who can understand and practice from Schwartz's interactionist approach.

NOTES

1. Ellen Baxter and Kim Hopper, "The New Mendicancy: Homeless in New York City," *The American Journal of Orthopsychiatry* 52, no. 3 (1982): 393-408; idem, *Private Lives/Public Spaces* (New York: Community Service Society, 1981); Robert E. Jones, "Street People and Psychiatry: An Introduction," *The Journal of Hospital and Community Psychiatry* 34, no. 9 (September 1983): 807-811; Frank R. Lipton et al., "Down and Out in the City: The Homeless Mentally Ill," *The Journal of Hospital and Community Psychiatry* 34, no. 9 (September 1983): 817-821.

2. *Shopping Bag Ladies: Homeless Women 1979* (New York: Manhattan Bowery Corporation, 1979); Alvin Toffler, *Future Shock* (New York: Random House, 1970).

3. Ronald Reagan, State of the Union Address, January 26, 1983.

4. George Getschow, "The Dispossessed: Homeless Northerners Unable To Find Work Crowd Sun Belt Cities," *The Wall Street Journal,* November 12, 1982.

5. Baxter and Hopper, *Private Lives/Public Spaces; The New York Times,* March 11, 1981.

6. William Schwartz, "Private Troubles and Public Issues: One Social Work Job or Two? in *The Practice of Social Work*, 2d ed., ed. Robert Klenk and Robert Ryan (Belmont, Calif.: Wadsworth Publishing Co., 1974), p. 95.

7. *New York Times,* January 27, 1982.

8. William Schwartz, "The Social Worker in the Group," in *The Practice of Social Work*, 2d ed. (Belmont, Calif.: The Wadsworth Press, 1974), p. 215.

9. Schwartz, "Private Troubles and Public Issues," p. 97.

10. Ibid.

11. N. Anderson, *The Hobo: The Sociology of the Homeless Man* (Chicago: University of Chicago Press, 1923); Walt Whitman, "The Poem of the Roads," in *The Leaves of Grass* (New York: Cornell University Press, 1961), pp. 315-328.

12. *The Oxford English Dictionary* (New York: Oxford University Press, 1971), p. 1322.

13. Charlotte Towle, *Common Human Needs*, rev. ed. (New York: NASW Press, 1957).

14. Kim Hopper, Ellen Baxter, et al. *One Year Later: The Homeless Poor in New York City* (New York: Community Service Society, 1982).

15. Baxter and Hopper, "The New Mendicancy," p. 405.

16. *The Oxford English Dictionary,* p. 1322.

17. Baxter and Hopper, *Private Lives/Public Spaces;* and Joan Shapiro, "Group Work with Urban Reject in a Slum Hotel," in *The Practice of Group Work*, ed. William Schwartz and Serapio R. Zalba (New York: Columbia University Press, 1971), pp. 25-44.

18. Carel B. Germain and Alex Gitterman, *The Life Model of Social Work Practice* (New York: Columbia University Press, 1980), p. 80.

19. Ibid., pp. 77-105; Erik H. Erikson, "Growth and Crises of the Healthy Personality," in Erik H. Erikson, *Identity and the Life Cycle: Psychological Issues, Monograph 1* (New York: International Universities Press, 1959), 1(1):50-100.

20. I credit my colleague, Jean Anmuth, with the design and implementation of this group which is now used in several shelters. I also

gratefully acknowledge her inspiration and help in all of my shelter work.

21. I credit Frank Colemen and Jose Barbosa with this group, also used in different shelters.

22. Frederica Sloan skillfully helped me to implement this group.

23. Staff member Roberta Martin and shelter administrators Karen Petterson and Dorothy Swift were also invaluable in helping this group to work so well. I also thank other facilitating actors to the whole project: Johanna Rayman, Jo Vander Kloot, Carol Maslow, Dina Rosenfeld, Lucreha J. Phillips, Carol Sturtz, and Tina Korman.

24. Grandmaster Flash and the Furious Five, "The Message" (New York: Sugarhill Records Ltd., 1982).

25. Barbara Solomon, *Black Empowerment: Social Work in Oppressed Communities* (New York: Columbia University Press, 1976).

26. Charles H. Cooley's classic definition of the primary group pertains: "By primary groups I mean those characterized by intimate face-to-face association and cooperation. They are primary in several senses, but chiefly that they are fundamental in forming the social nature and ideals of the individual. ... Perhaps the simplest way of describing this wholeness is by saying it is a 'we,' it involves a sort of sympathy and mutual identification for which 'we' is the natural expression." Charles H. Cooley, *Social Organization* (New York: Charles Scribner's Sons, 1963), p. 23. Also see Michael S. Olmsted, *The Small Group* (New York: Random House, 1959), pp. 46-81.

27. For a full description of the stages of a change process see George Brager and Stephen Holloway, *Changing Human Service Organizations: Politics and Practice* (New York: The Free Press, 1978), pp. 154-235.

28. Ibid. See also Germain and Gitterman *The Life Model*, Chapter 7; Lawrence Shulman, *The Skills of Helping Individuals and Groups, Second Edition*, (Itasca, Ill.: F. E. Peacock Publishers, 1984), chapter 16; Judith A. B. Lee, "Who's Looking Out for the Homeless?" *NASW News* 28, no. 8 (September 1983): 4-5.

BIBLIOGRAPHY

Anderson, N. *The Hobo: The Sociology of the Homeless Man.* Chicago: University of Chicago Press, 1923.

Baxter, Ellen and Kim Hopper. "The New Mendicancy: Homeless in New York City," *The American Journal of Orthopsychiatry* 52, no. 3 (1982): 393-408.

———. *Private Lives/Public Spaces.* New York: Community Service Society, 1981.

Brager, George, and Stephen Holloway. *Changing Human Service Organizations.* New York: The Free Press, 1978.

Cooley, Charles H. *Social Organization.* New York: Charles Scribner's Sons, 1963.

Erikson, Erik H. *Identity and the Life Cycle: Psychological Issues, Monograph I.* New York: International Universities Press, 1959, 1(1):50-100.

Germain, Carel B., and Alex Gitterman. *The Life Model of Social Work Practice.* New York: Columbia University Press, 1980.

Getschow, George. "The Dispossessed: Homeless Northerners Unable to Find Work Crowd Sun Belt Cities," *The Wall Street Journal,* November 12, 1982.

Hopper, Kim, and Ellen Baxter et al. *One Year Later: The Homeless Poor in New York City.* New York: Community Service Society, 1982.

Jones, Robert E. "Street People and Psychiatry: An Introduction," *The Journal of Hospital and Community Psychiatry* 34, no. 9 (September 1983): 807-811.

Lee, Judith A. B. "Who's Looking Out for the Homeless?" *NASW News* 28, no. 8 (September 1983): 4-5.

Lipton, Frank R., et al. "Down and Out in the City: The Homeless Mentally Ill," *The Journal of Hospital and Community Psychiatry* 34, no. 9 (September 1983): 817-821.

Manhattan Bowery Corporation. *Shopping Bag Ladies: Homeless Women,* 1979.

"A Journey into the Cities' Netherworld," *New York Times,* March 11, 1981, B 3:3:1.

"Woman Refuses Aid, Dies in Carton on Street," *New York Times,* January 27, 1982, A:1:1.

Oxford English Dictionary. Oxford: Oxford University Press, 1971.

Reagan, Ronald. State of the Union Address, January 26, 1983.

Shapiro, Joan. "Group Work with Urban Rejects in a Slum Hotel." In *The Practice of Group Work.* Edited by William Schwartz and Serapio Zalba. New York: Columbia University Press, 1971.

Schwartz, William. "Private Troubles and Public Issues: One Social Work Job or Two?" 2d ed. In *The Practice of Social Work.* Edited by Robert Klenk and Robert Ryan. Belmont, Calif.: Wadsworth Publishing Co., 1974.

———."The Social Worker in the Group." In *The Practice of Social Work.* 2d ed. Edited by Robert Klenk and Robert Ryan. Belmont, Calif.: Wadsworth Publishing Co., 1974.

Shulman, Lawrence. *The Skills of Helping Individuals and Groups, Second Edition,* Itasca, Ill.: F. E. Peacock Publishers, Inc., 1984.

Solomon, Barbara. *Black Empowerment: Social Work in Oppressed Communities.* New York: Columbia University Press, 1976.

Toffler, Alvin. *Future Shock.* New York: Random House, 1970.

Towle, Charlotte. *Common Human Needs.* Rev. ed. New York: NASW Press, 1957.

Whitman, Walt. "The Poem of the Road," *The Leaves of Grass.* New York: Cornell University Press, 1961.

Dorothy Poynter-Berg

CHAPTER 14

Getting Connected: Institutionalized Schizophrenic Women

Many chronically mentally ill individuals have benefited from the de-institutionalization efforts which began in the United States in the 1950s.[1] For some it has represented a chance to make it on the outside. Many others, however, considered "poor risks" for discharge,[2] are unlikely to be released, at least under the current system of service delivery.[3] Of the approximately 2 million chronically mentally ill individuals in the United States today[4] about 7 percent (138,000) reside in mental hospitals.[5] The "poor risks" for discharge include those individuals who remain severely regressed and floridly psychotic despite regular use of psychotropic medications and years of therapeutic efforts. They frequently present a mixed diagnostic picture, including a major psychiatric disorder and a combination of mental retardation, serious physical problems, and organic brain disease.[6] They require twenty-four-hour supervision and regular medical monitoring. Their families, where they even exist, are unable to care for them adequately.[7] These individuals constitute the "backwards" population who, upon closer look, are people struggling with life issues within institutions that have become their homes, even their world. The

worker's task with these individuals requires a special blend of patience, understanding, caring, and consistent optimism in order to help them move from an existence of fearful isolation and rejection to being part of a safe, supportive network of human relationships. Because of the largely nonverbal nature of this population and their chronic difficulties in interacting with their environment, groups fostering mutual aid are the method of choice.[8]

MIDDLE AGE DEVELOPMENTAL NEEDS AND TASKS

The normative aspects of middle-aged women as discussed by Theodore Lidz mark the passage into "a time of fulfillment, when years of effort reach fruition."[9] Revisions in the role of motherhood occur, as children grow up and away—into adolescence, leaving for college or independent living, and producing the "empty nest" syndrome. It is the time for experiencing grandparenthood. Some women respond to this by developing or furthering careers or becoming more involved in activities outside the home. Others experience this period with depression, feeling their primary purpose in life, that of active motherhood, is over. Physiological changes mark this period also—changing from a youthful to a "mature" body image, with subsequent influence on emotional-sexual relationships. Menopause occurs during the middle years and can result in a wide range of responses.[10] Physical health-related concerns assume greater significance in general. Siblings, parents, spouses, and peers are often lost through death during this time, contributing significantly to the developmental issues of intimacy and loss.

The potential for major life stresses during these years of transition constitutes normative crises for most people. If one's life prior to middle age has been satisfying and rewarding, the middle years can be a time of making the most out of life that has been led.[11] For those individuals who have been deprived, for a variety of reasons, of life's rewards and freedoms, the middle years can be a sad reminder of a devastated past and an expectation of a bleak future.

The normative aspects of the middle years, even when fraught with moderate amounts of stress and despair, do not compare with the extensive deprivation and shattered self-images experienced by the institutionalized person, poignantly illustrated by the following interaction.

Arlene was sitting outside my door when Doris left. I asked if she'd like to join me now to talk about the group. She nodded, quickly got up, and followed me into the room. She looked in the ashtrays, took out a "salvageable" cigarette butt, and put it in her pocket. She sat rigidly in a chair across from me, arms folded tightly across her chest. Her bright red lipstick was smeared, giving her mouth a distorted appearance. Her fingernails were long and dirty with chipped red polish unevenly applied. She talked and laughed quietly to herself, with an occasional glance in my direction. I reintroduced myself, explaining that I was a social work student and would be meeting with them in group, like Ms. K. did last year. She looked out the window and murmured something I couldn't understand. I asked her to repeat what she'd said, as I hadn't heard her. She stood up abruptly and opened the door, talking constantly and incoherently. She suddenly turned to face me, with direct eye contact, asking clearly and seriously, "Do you have an application to become a person?" She then turned and exited abruptly, talking and laughing softly to herself as she walked quickly down the corridor, seemingly unaware of the presence of others around her.

Arlene's question had an emotionally penetrating effect. It was difficult to conceive of the range of lifetime experiences which would contribute to the formulation of such a question. And yet, the question carried with it a possible indication of the nature of the work which would lie ahead for us in the group.

Arlene presents a fairly typical example of persons found in long-term institutions for the mentally ill. Their lives are an accumulation of extensive impairments encompassing all the phases of normative psychosocial development. If one considers the "building block" effect of ego development, that is, the successful resolution of each developmental phase preparing the individual to enter the next phase, one can envision the tenuous, vulnerable construction completed by middle age when begun with a shaky foundation from the earliest weeks and months of life.

Pao stresses that:

schizophrenic patients are burdened by the same kind of conflicts as any other human being. Schizophrenic patients are capable, like any other human being, of keeping their conflicts in a dormant state by means of defense mechanisms which are, however, commonly more primitive in nature (denial, introjection, projection, fusion, etc.). But, whenever the conflicts are reactivated, the schizophrenic patients do not experience anxiety as is familiar to average human beings; they experience organismic panic.[12]

Pao borrows the term "organismic panic" from Mahler's term "organismic distress," which describes the state of high physiological tension experienced by an infant in the earliest phase of life. Organismic panic, according to Pao, has its origin in the experience of chronic, overwhelming, unrelieved organismic distress during the earliest stage of the life cycle of the schizophrenic.[13]

Whether one adheres to the "nature" or "nurture" theory of the origins of schizophrenia, most literature points to a combination of biological and environmental factors which may be crystallized into potential schizophrenic symptomatology even prior to the symbiotic phase of development.[14] These symptoms may include proneness to using maintenance mechanisms. Mahler describes maintenance mechanisms (de-animation, de-differentiation, deneutralization) as preceding the development of primitive defense mechanisms of denial, projection, introjection, and fusion in the case of psychotic or potentially psychotic individuals.[15] The patient may also exhibit impaired capacity for neutralization of instincts, inadequate ability to internalize the maternal object's capacity for mastering anxiety, inability to maintain a stable sense of object and reality constancy, and an inability to integrate and blend primitive and mature cognitive and affective functioning. This complex core disturbance severely interferes with the schizophrenic individual's relations with others. Dissatisfaction with object relationships heightens aggressive urges, which the individual experiences as unable to control. Thus, close relations with others are experienced as a threat, with potential for dreaded feelings of panic, which are perceived by the individual as a life-and-death struggle. This results in an unconscious state of being "on guard," manifested by moving simultaneously toward and away from significant objects, promoting a state of constant insecurity and unsafety.[16]

Considering these theoretical explanations, one can better understand that the developmental needs of the institutionalized chronic schizophrenic individual encompass human needs associated with the entire spectrum of developmental tasks. These individuals have passed through infancy, childhood, adolescence, and early adulthood with experiences which remain largely unknown to us, struggled with a variety of difficult life issues, became part of an era of institutionalism, and find themselves in middle age with no real hope of reuniting with their families or attaining a "normal" life. They remain impoverished, isolated, and fearful—perhaps in some way protected from the reality of their life circumstances by psychosis. They require supportive persons in their environment to relieve tensions and restore homeostasis through empathic understanding and ministration.

AGENCY CONTEXT AND THE GROUP MODALITY

The hospital is state-supported, located in a predominantly black community of New York, and has been in existence there since 1906. The hospital provides services to thousands of patients, some on open (voluntary, unlocked) units, some on locked units. A full complement of skilled multidisciplinary staff is employed. The general stated purpose of the hospital is to work therapeutically with the patients and their families, whenever possible, discharging patients as soon as they manifest readiness to resume productive functioning in the community. Discharge may involve a return to family, adult foster placement, proprietary homes, day treatment programs, job training, or employment. Those patients who do not have families or supportive persons on whom they can depend are more likely to remain in the hospital for longer periods of time, due in part to the shortage of appropriate placement facilities.[17]

The hospital is a highly bureaucratized institution, illustrating the need for rigid adherence to schedules and rules. This applies to times for waking up, getting clothing (provided by the hospital), bathing, eating, recreation, resting, visiting hours, going to bed for the night, and other activities. For some this rigidity provides needed structure and limit setting. For long-term, chronic patients it provides consistency and tradition; for them, relaxing the structure or changing routines brings about anxiety and confusion, manifested by a variety of behaviors.

The hospital is mandated to provide services to all patients within its catchment area. At times it nearly bursts at the seams. Although certain units are labeled "chronic," nearly all by necessity have a heterogeneous population of acute, intermediate, and long-term or chronic patients. Due to constant policy pressures to discharge new admissions as soon as possible (for many, as soon as they are not actively suicidal or homicidal) the acutely ill patients receive the most attention. The goal is to prevent further chronicity when possible. Due largely to chronicity, lack of family involvement, and a general feeling that these are "hopeless" cases, the chronic patients generally receive minimal though quality custodial

care. They tend to sit in the same place or wander the same path all day, every day, having adjusted themselves to the basic requirements of institutional life. The unit houses approximately forty patients at any given time. There is one large room for sleeping, with forty single beds. At times, an agitated patient disrupts the sleeping of all the others. Many patients keep small personal items under their beds, always fearful that they will be stolen. All patients are awakened at the same time and, once dressed, cannot return to their beds until the appropriate time.

The hospital's organizational impact offers both support and limitations to groups within its structure: support in that groups are accepted and encouraged as part of the system's program of service delivery. It imposes limitations on the basis that groups carry a "voluntary but mandatory" expectation, so patients are "strongly encouraged" (for example, escorted to and from groups by unit attendants if necessary) because it is a hospital program norm. Resistance to this expectation is played out in a variety of overt and subtle ways, by both staff and patients. Another limitation imposed by the hospital is its expectation that groups will not be "dysfunctional to the organization."[18] For example, a group of staff and patients organized in an attempt to acquire salt and pepper shakers for the patient dining room, a seemingly simple task. This action was sanctioned by the unit's administration and was in response to complaints that the food was preseasoned and often not to the liking of individual tastes. The committee existed for two years, but no shakers were forthcoming. Thus some groups, while encouraging members to express concerns and feelings and make efforts to gain more control over their lives, can result in developing or perpetuating a sense of apathy and powerlessness. Operating within a system which itself is resistant to change even on such a minimal basis can lead to passive acceptance of the inflexible structure and a decreased effort to change one's self. It is crucial that workers maintain an objective yet hopeful outlook regarding the limitations imposed by the system and realistic potential for patient and system growth and change.

Obtaining space to meet proved to be a major focus for gaining sanction on the unit. Space was limited and carried a high priority status. Staff often shared office space, and there were no designated "group rooms" on the unit. Until the group achieved some status on the unit as viable and important, it was subject to several room changes, at times at the last minute, which resulted in the members becoming confused and frightened. One member was consistently incontinent whenever the group was held off the unit. This issue was specifically addressed to the entire unit staff, who came to understand better the problem and to accept the determination of the group's leader that the group must have one consistent, "safe" meeting space. This was arranged five weeks after the group began. It is interesting to note here that it was around the sixth week of meeting that the group began to "gel" into a working, cohesive unit.

Through experimenting with various spatial situations, it was concluded that the group members were most comfortable in a small (ten-foot-by-twelve-foot) space, which provided important spatial boundaries, an unlocked door from which they could exit when internal stresses mounted, and a table to sit around, which provided some safety through distance from physical and emotional intimacy. Gaining space appropriate to the emotional needs of the members that also carried status and organizational sanction contributed to the ultimate successful development of the group.

Group work with hospitalized patients is not new. Hospital units provide a natural milieu with potential for developing group services in a variety of settings with a wide range of patient needs.[19]

The chronically mentally ill can pose difficulties for effective intervention on an individual basis.[20] These individuals have remained isolated in spite of living in a group environment for years. Attempts to engage them in individual therapy resulted in little, if any, change. Their participation in large unit meetings was marked by behaviors such as sleeping in their chairs, hiding in the bathroom, actively responding to visual and auditory hallucinations, and pacing around the parameters of the group. They are perhaps, it would appear, unresponsive to any form of therapeutic intervention or social contact.

Considering these realities, one may then ask, "why attempt another group experience for these individuals?" According to Gitterman,

> By its very nature the group mutual aid system universalizes people's problems, reducing isolation and stigma. The group also has the potential to be a force in helping people to act and gain greater control and mastery over their environments. . . . greater visibility is more likely to gain organizational/community attention and concern, militating against individual isolation . . . and increasing chances for success.[21]

In addition to these theoretical points, the members of the group have commonalities which designate them as a homogeneous group within the larger group system. These common factors include the following: All are middle-aged, chronic, regressed schizophrenic women who have lived together in the same hospital unit for many years; all manifest withdrawn, isolated behavior; all are largely nonverbal; all have limited formal education; all have had some past work experience; all have remained single and childless; and all have previously experienced groups with student social workers.

Theoretically, with careful planning and implementation, continued group experiences could benefit these women, providing a qualitative change in their ability to interface with their immediate environment. Individuals such as these also present a unique challenge to the development of professional group work skills.

Brief case sketches will serve to illustrate the circumstances surrounding the five group members. Chronicity is illustrated in case records by a commonly found diagnosis of "dementia praecox."

Rhoda is a fifty-three-year-old, single, obese, severely diabetic Italian woman, blind in one eye, and appearing older than her stated age by at least ten years. With a single admission, she has remained hospitalized for twenty-three consecutive years.

Rhoda is very compliant and can be found at any time of the day sitting on "her" chair at "her" table on the unit, eyes closed or staring, but not sleeping. Rhoda leaves the hospital two days per year, on Easter Sunday and Christmas Day, to visit her two elderly sisters. Her mother died four years ago, but Rhoda denied that reality and continues to express wishes to return home someday to be with her mother.

Beverly is a fifty-six-year-old, single, obese Jewish woman, missing many upper teeth and appearing younger than her stated age by about fifteen years. She is borderline retarded. She has been hospi-

talized continuously in the same institution for thirty-five years.

She is no longer considered violent, although she occasionally hits other patients when they walk on floors she has just mopped. She is frequently verbally abusive to patients and staff. When she is frightened or angry, she reverts to speaking Yiddish, usually in the form of obscenities. Her response for a period of time to being reminded of weekly group sessions was shrieking, "I'm not goin' to group with a crazy fuckin' mishugana Chinaman bitch!" (referring to worker). Beverly is a heavy smoker and has found her "place" on the unit mopping the bathroom floors, rewarded by cigarettes from staff.

Golda is a sixty-two-year-old single woman. She was born in Poland and is of Jewish descent. She was hospitalized at age twenty-five and has remained for thirty-seven years. She was "catatonic, agitated type" upon admission. Two years after admission, due to "consistent resistance and unchanged and uncooperative behavior" she underwent a frontal lobotomy.

Golda has not left her "space" on the unit, according to hospital attendants, for at least fifteen years—as long as they can remember. She rarely speaks, and when she does, it is in a high squeaky pitch, often unintelligible. She is missing many upper teeth and appears self-conscious about this. She is able to manage basic personal needs and is generally compliant. In new situations she tends to avoid and withdraw. She has had no visitors or mail for many years, the hospital being her only source of interpersonal contact and support.

Arlene is a forty-year-old, single, Jewish woman, appearing younger than her stated age by about twenty years. She has been hospitalized, on second admission, for twenty-two years.

She is the most visibly actively psychotic member of the group. She talks to herself constantly in the third person, for example, "Arlene is a nice girl." She has been incontinent for many years. She is unable to verbalize her needs adequately and presents with nonverbal, autistic-like behavior. For example, she beats her head with her fists when she wants something (cigarettes), and when given some, promptly gives most of them away and soon repeats the cycle. She is often found openly masturbating on the unit. She is unable to bathe or dress herself without assistance or supervision.

Marie is a fifty-one-year-old, single, slim woman who stated she was born in Poland. She has been hospitalized for twelve years, although there is mention of previous hospitalizations dating back over three decades.

Marie's aunt and uncle are old and feel they cannot care for Marie any longer. Marie blames her aunt for not wanting her back and claims the aunt is "faking illness" to avoid this. The aunt and uncle are seventy-seven and seventy-nine years old respectively. Marie is the most talkative member of the group and seems the least socially regressed. Her physical appearance, however, is generally disheveled and dirty, and she seldom combs her hair, possible manifestations of her feelings of dejection and pessimism. She "sleeps" in a chair most of the day with her hand cupped over her mouth.

GROUP THEMES

Considering the normative developmental tasks of the group members, their current levels of functioning and environmental factors, the next step involves conceptualizing the potential for helping activities. Central themes of the work will focus on providing a safe, consistent at-mosphere in which the group members can express themselves and experience mutual understanding and empathy, particularly around the life-cycle issues of intimacy and loss. Throughout the following sections, phases of group development, group themes and practice interventions will be illustrated and discussed.

Getting Started

Prior to actually convening the group members for the first meeting, it was important to consider several factors in order to anticipate reactions to the group and to start the group on a positive note. It was important to gain an appreciation of how the women might view group participation and how the group might initially affect them. Olmsted reminds us, "For a disturbed and insecure individual, to be stripped of his protective roles and definition-of-the-situation, [the small group] can be a fairly traumatic event."[22] Leaving their isolated positions on the unit and joining a small selected group of other patients in a confined space with a "stranger" could be confusing, exposing, and frightening. In addition, since there are several ongoing discharge and predischarge groups on the unit, the women entering the group may either experience hope that they, too, will eventually be able to leave the hospital or, more likely, fear that they were selected to participate in the group as preparation for leaving the place where they have lived for most of their adult lives.

These five women had also been together in similar groups over two consecutive prior years. They experienced two leaders (student social workers) leaving. This could inhibit willingness to get involved again. Rhoda, for example, reportedly became quite attached to last year's group leader and stated she "didn't want to join another group" after Ms. K. left. Marie, with whom Ms. K. had begun predischarge planning, was angry when this could not be completed before Ms. K. left. Marie's anger and impatience around this has, a year later, become even stronger, along with her feelings of pessimism that anything will "be done" for her in the group. Beverly insists she "hates groups" and was regularly escorted to them by mental health attendants over the past two years.

As part of the preparation for entering the group, each member was interviewed individually. Mixed reactions were received. Marie said she'd like to meet to talk about leaving the hospital; Rhoda nodded her head when I asked if she would like to join the group, but did not look at me during the entire interview. Arlene, after a rapid search through the ashtrays, sat rigidly in the chair, looking past me and mumbling incoherently. She did say, "Yeah—sure" when I directly asked if she'd like to join the group. Golda did not speak at all in our initial contact and glanced at me once very briefly. She responded with silence when I asked if she'd like to meet with the group. When I approached Beverly, she had her head down on a table, resting on her arms; she glanced out briefly then returned to her original position. When I had introduced myself and stated why I was there, she looked at me and shouted, "No!" and picked up her chair and turned it so her back was facing me.

The varied initial responses to the worker's approach left the worker feeling apprehensive about the viability of forming a group with these women, wondering whether anything could be accomplished with this combination of nonverbal, unpredictable, and hostile behaviors.

Responding directly to indirect cues during the preliminary phase is essential. Institutionalized adults manifest a good deal of nonverbal and indirect expression which, if left untapped, can perpetuate a sense of not being understood.

Worker: Good morning, Marie. I'm looking forward to our first group meeting this afternoon. How about you?

Marie: (Shrugged her shoulders, head down.)

Worker: What does that mean, shrugging your shoulders?

Marie: Nothing. Nothing gets done.

Worker: Like nothing got done about your going home last year?

Marie: Yeah. Nothing gets done.

Worker: Are you wondering what's going to get done with me too?

Marie: (Looking up) Yeah—what's gonna get done?

Worker: I really can't say yet, Marie. We need to get to know each other better; then we can talk about what can get done. Are you willing to give it a try?

Marie: (With a weak smile) Guess so. Is group in back room?

Worker: Yes. I'll see you there at one o'clock.

Marie: O.K. See you there.

Marie's negative expectations of the group and the worker needed to be addressed directly. It would not have been helpful for the worker to respond with empty reassurances that things would "get done" this year. The purpose of the intervention was to convey a sense that the worker wished to understand Marie's feelings and to share an expectation that this would be part of the work in the group.

Members entered the group with different experiences and expectations. The worker, therefore, had to clarify the group's purpose and her role during the first meeting.

In spite of having met with all the group members individually and reminding them of the group time earlier in the day, none of them showed up at the appointed time. I found Rhoda and Marie in "their" chairs, and Arlene was pacing "her" path. When reminded, they came willingly. Golda sat in her chair, not responding to my invitation to join us. Beverly scurried into the bathroom shouting. "I'm not goin' to group with a fuckin' mishugana Chinaman bitch!" A unit attendant escorted Golda to the group room and another told Beverly to "get to group" and followed behind her to the room. The attendant said to me, winking and rolling her eyes, "have fun." I again told them my name and said I would be working with them in the group now and would be with them until next June, since I am a student social worker at the hospital. Beverly turned her back to the group and began to curse softly. Golda and Rhoda kept their heads lowered, avoiding eye contact. Arlene was actively talking to her reflection in the coffee pot. I said, since they had all met together in group before, they might already know why they were meeting, but I thought it would be important to go over it again. I asked if they could tell me why they had been meeting as a group. No answers. It was as if no one had spoken. I asked Marie. She said, "to help us get out of hospital." I asked if that's what the others thought. They all looked up, and Beverly's voice became louder. I said, "You've all be here a long time and it must be upsetting to think I might expect you to leave if you're not ready." Quiet. I said to Marie that some group members, like herself, might want to leave the hospital. She nodded. I said we could talk about that, either in the group or individually. She smiled. I said then that leaving the hospital was not the purpose of the group, but a place for us to understand and help each other. I asked them what kinds of things they had done together: Rhoda?— "bake cakes"; Arlene?—"go to the store"; Marie?—"make coffee"; Golda?—no answer; Beverly?—no answer. I stated we could continue to do those things together, adding that being in group would be a good chance for them to do things for themselves, too—that they couldn't make their own coffee in the cafeteria. Marie and Rhoda smiled here. I asked if they understood what I was saying.

Slight nods. I asked if there were any questions. Silence. I said, speaking of coffee. I had brought some and wondered if they'd like to make some. Rhoda, Marie, and Arlene nodded. Golda looked at me briefly. Beverly resumed babbling. We prepared and drank the instant coffee, though it was apparent how disorganized and severely functionally impaired most of them were.

The above process excerpt illustrates the worker's difficulty in making a clear, direct contractual statement of service. The worker's own feelings of insecurity and fear of precipitating unknown reactions, particularly Beverly's hostile wrath, contributed to her prematurely moving on to "feed" the group, perhaps joining in with their mode of nonverbal expression, illustrating the group's purpose without words.

An unclear or ambiguous statement of purpose can contribute to a group's feeling anxiety and apprehension, making it more difficult to enter the work phase of the group's life. A clear statement of service for this group may have been, "I am here to try and help you make your life in the hospital a little better. We can talk, have snacks, take walks together, and learn how to understand and help one another."

Beverly soon confronted the worker with the issue of authority, which became an important part of early limit setting and behavioral expectations for her and the others.

I asked who wanted sugar for their coffee. Beverly's mumblings became louder. Her back was to the group. I asked if she wanted sugar. She got even louder. I said I wished I could understand what she was saying, and asked the others if they could. Rhoda said, "one word—mother." They seemed to react to Beverly with little concern and more tolerance than the worker felt. I told Beverly I could understand that she may be upset about being in the group, especially since she said she hates groups and didn't want to come in the first place. I said it would take a while to get used to the change—but that I wanted everyone to come three times before deciding whether or not they wanted to keep coming. I would not force them to stay in the group if they really didn't want to. I heard the word "bitch" from Beverly. I said to her that I would like to have her join us and speak so we could understand what she was saying—she got louder—but if she didn't want to, I'd have to ask her to be quiet so the others could talk and hear. To my surprise, she quieted. Marie told Beverly to drink her coffee before it got cold. Beverly seemed to ignore her but soon had turned enough to snatch her cup and turn away again. Upon leaving, Beverly brushed against me, muttering "bitch," and dropped her crumpled cup on the floor next to the wastebasket.

Beverly's hostility, retrospectively understood as a fear reaction to environmental stress (a change in her routine), made it difficult for the worker to move beyond the behavioral manifestations to understanding her feelings. The desire to understand the feelings underlying disruptive behavior needs to be clearly expressed along with the attempts at limit setting, in order to support a basic beginning purpose of the group, that of encouraging members to communicate with and be aware of each other.

Work Phase

Group members continued for a number of weeks (one meeting per week) to demonstrate behavior similar to that described in the first meeting. The structure increasingly included a clear focus around cooperative task division and provided an opportunity for activities they were familiar with such as knitting, embroidering, and drawing. Since it was imme-

diately gratifying and very special, the group readily accepted participation in coffee preparation. Other activities were less enthusiastically received.

The group began to change around Thanksgiving, when they were able to share with one another and the worker some painful feelings about holidays. Focused observation and listening, tuning in to and reaching for feelings underlying the silence, understanding these feelings by focusing on the nonverbal language, and putting the members' feelings into words are skills illustrated by the following group process excerpt, six weeks after the group began.

The group meets on Thursdays. Since Thanksgiving was on Thursday and I felt it was important for the group to meet consistently, I held it on Wednesday, Thanksgiving Eve.

The group members slowly came into the meeting room. Beverly sat with her back to the rest of the group, muttering an occasional "fuckin' mishugana." (It had by now lost its original hostility.) The women made their instant coffee and drank it, all silently. They were much quieter and still today than usual; they appeared depressed and showed it by their slouched postures and lowered heads. I felt it might have something to do with feelings about Thanksgiving. I said everyone looked quite sad and wondered if they might want to talk about it. Rhoda furrowed her brows and moved her lips. I asked her if she wanted to say something. She shook her head. Another pause. All kept their heads lowered and Arlene, who usually talks to herself, was silent. I said they may all be having thoughts and feelings that the rest of the group might share with them. Silence. I finally said that sometimes it's hard to talk about things that are painful, like being in the hospital on holidays and maybe feeling lonely. Most of the members reacted to this by moving around in their chairs a little. I said I wondered if they did feel sad about tomorrow being a holiday. Rhoda nodded very slightly to herself, but kept her head lowered and didn't speak. Another lengthy pause, with all the ladies looking up at me briefly but not speaking.

When it was time for the group to end, I commented that sometimes it's very hard to talk, like today—and especially when they might be feeling sad. I said I thought next week would be easier. They all looked up at me, and Rhoda smiled, saying, "Have a nice Thanksgiving."

This group meeting illustrates an element in working with the mentally ill that is difficult for workers. For most of us, holidays are happy occasions. We look forward to time with our families and a respite from working. It is difficult, holiday after holiday, to confront the opposite reactions in clients and to be able to tune in to their real feelings. Workers can feel "dragged down" in their own holiday spirit by clients' (en masse) increased feelings of sadness, loss, anger, withdrawal, and depression. During these times, it is essential to focus on the feelings presented and not encourage clients to deny their real feelings for the sake of the worker's wish to experience the holidays "normally"—without undue stress. The hospital unit staff was alerted to the group's sadness and loneliness, and efforts were made to include the women more actively in preparations on the unit. Following holidays, clients frequently express positive feelings about any holiday activities they participated in. Workers should acknowledge feelings (theirs as well as their clients'), while not colluding with the apathy by canceling holiday planning, an act which could reveal the worker's anger toward clients' increased neediness and depression, reflections of their struggles with the life-cycle tasks of intimacy and loss.

The pre-Thanksgiving meeting described above was sad for the worker to experience. Their feelings could not be altered in this meeting, but they could be acknowledged and validated. This group was like sitting with a grieving family—grieving over lost families, friends, youth, and holidays belonging to the past.

The process of development in the group was slow, and interaction remained visibly minimal for several months. It took time for trust to build in order to allow them to risk expressing their feelings.

In response to a death on the unit, the following process illustrates the gradual change in the ability of the group members to verbalize. The worker introduces a difficult topic, observes verbal and nonverbal responses, reaches for their feelings, and promotes direct, physical interaction, thereby reinforcing the feeling that the members can help one another. This is meeting number 18, four and a half months after the group began.

I said something had happened on the unit on Friday that I felt they must have feelings about and wondered if they wanted to talk about it—that was, Mrs. James, a patient, had died on the unit Friday (natural death). Pause. Beverly said, "Mrs. James died?" I nodded and asked if they all knew who she was. Nods. I asked if they knew she'd died. Beverly said, "I heard about it—it's a sad thing to think about." I said it is a sad thing to think about and asked if they had any questions or thoughts about it they wanted to share with the others. Rhoda had tears coming to her eyes, and I gently pointed this out to her, asking if she was feeling sad. She said, "No." Beverly again said, "It *is* sad." I nodded. I said it's kind of a scary feeling, wondering if it will happen to someone else—and maybe to us. Marie and Beverly nodded. Arlene was extremely calm and silent today. Beverly said, "I don't feel scared—just sad." She said, "It 'minds me of my father and mother who died; my father five years ago and my mother three years ago," and held up her fingers to indicate the years. She said, "But I still have my brother, who visits on Sundays." I said that was good. Rhoda was again tearing, and I asked gently if she was thinking about someone who had died. She said, "Yeah—my father died." I asked if it made her feel sad to think about it. This time she said "Yes" and wiped her eyes. When we'd finished the coffee and toast, the group was quiet and there was a sort of gloom in the room. I said we'd talked about some hard things today, like Mrs. James's death, and about how it made us think of people that we've loved who died, and how sad that is to think about. Beverly wiped her eyes. I asked if it made them feel they'd like to have someone to hang onto. Beverly said, "Yeah—I'd like to have someone to hang onto." I said maybe we could hold onto each other for a bit to get some comfort. I asked if they'd like to hold onto each other's hands. Rhoda immediately held out her hands to Beverly and Marie, who took them. Beverly reached toward Golda, who stiffened and looked scared. Beverly said, "Aw, c'm'on, Goldie, let me hang onta yer hand." Golda pulled away, and Beverly looked hurt; she looked down and dropped Rhoda's hand. I reached over to Golda and touched her hand. She looked at me and smiled briefly. As I held her hand, she seemed to relax. I explained that Beverly wanted to hold onto her hand so she'd feel better. Golda raised her brow and smiled a little. I asked her if Beverly could hold onto her hand. She said softly, "Yes." Beverly then took Golda's hand and Rhoda's again, smiling. We all held hands for about twenty seconds, during which I suggested that we all give little squeezes, which they did, and looked at each other. Then hands dropped, and it seemed as if a cloud had been removed from the group; the tension was greatly relieved. I asked if holding onto each other had made them feel better. They all nodded. Marie announced it was time to clean up. Beverly said, "Let's wait a minute." Others nodded. We sat together for a short time.

This group meeting illustrated a change in the group members' ability to respond directly to one another's need for comfort and support and their growing abili-

ty to provide mutual aid. Beverly's participation in this group marked a significant turning point for her in terms of her ability to relate positively to others in the group. The group theme had touched them and their struggle to master their current life-cycle issues of intimacy and loss.

The group now exhibited an ability to express their feelings and an ability and a willingness to participate in a mutual aid contract. However, they continued to have difficulty talking as the primary means of expression. Making coffee and toast or cake together had become routine. They had achieved mastery over these tasks and appeared ready to move on to new areas of work together.

Various activities were introduced to the group, as an indirect means of facilitating the group's work.[23] It became important to use program which would be both age- and skill-appropriate and with potential for enhancing communication and mutual aid.

After some experimentation, modeling clay was introduced, and was positively received by all. It provided an opportunity for individual expression as well as group interaction, as can be seen in the next process excerpt, where the group was preparing for the worker's upcoming spring vacation, five months after the group began.

The group members were busy enjoying working with the multicolored clay, when I reminded them again that I wouldn't be here next week because of spring vacation. Marie looked at me and crumpled the person she'd made from clay into a ball. I pointed out her action to her, and asked what that was about. She shrugged. I asked if she was feeling angry. She shook her head. Disappointed? She nodded, and looked at me. I asked how the others felt. Beverly said, "Will ya be here next week?" I explained it again and showed them on the calendar when I'd be away and when I'd be back. Beverly said, "Will ya be here tomorrow?" Marie said, "No—just Monday, Wednesday, and Thursday." Beverly said, "Not Friday?" I said not Friday. I said it's hard to say good-bye, even for just a week. Beverly said wistfully, "Ya—it's sad to say good-bye." I asked if they would like to meet next week with Ms. L. as they had during my Christmas vacation. Marie broke in with, "We wait 'til you come back." Beverly said, "I'll be all right." Rhoda said, "If we have something to do, it's not so bad." Golda said, "We wait." Arlene nodded at Golda.

This group showed how the use of activity (clay) allowed the worker to observe Marie's reaction to her anticipation of the worker's not being there and to reach for feelings that might not have been observable without this activity. It also illustrated the growing sense of self-sufficiency and strength, in their clear statements about being able to wait.

Based on our previous work around separations, and considering the major developmental issues of this age group (intimacy and loss), it was anticipated that the termination process would be a long and difficult one. In order for them to experience the various stages in the termination process and to preserve the gains they had made, it would be important to have sufficient time to work on this issue.

The Ending Phase

The following excerpt shows the early beginning of the termination process; the worker reaches for their feelings about it, recognizes the difficulty in accepting it, focuses on and supports their efforts, and holds them to working on it. This is meeting number 24, nearly six months after the group began, and seven weeks before termination date.

I said I had something important I wanted to talk with them about. They all looked up from working on the clay. I asked if they remember when we started working together, a long time ago, that I said I'd be here until June. Silence. I said that June will be here in a few weeks—six weeks after today, when I will be leaving the hospital. Beverly said, "Why do ya have ta leave?" I explained about school, and that it ends in June. Beverly said, "When will ya be back after that?" I explained that my leaving in six weeks wouldn't be like the vacations I've had, when I was gone for awhile and came back; that I would be leaving for good in June, not coming back. Beverly said, "Ya mean ya won't come back—ever?" I nodded. Silence. I said they were very quiet, and wondered if they were thinking about what I'd said. Nods. I said I'd wanted to tell them now, since we'd been working together a long time and it's taken them a long time to be able to talk about some very hard things—but they could talk about them now—and it will take time for us to think about and talk about my leaving. Beverly said, "Six more weeks?—that's good." She then said, "What will happen to the group?" I said the group could still meet together, with another worker, and asked if they wanted to talk about that now. Silence. I said it's a hard thing to talk about. Beverly said, "Ya, talk later." When it was time to clean up, they sat longer than usual. I said I felt what we'd talked about today—my leaving soon—made it harder to leave today. Nods.

The worker had to recognize and own up to her own feelings about terminating from the group, which had made such positive gains. The termination work had to be handled well, so that it would represent growth rather than contributing to an accumulation of bitter associations.

The group had achieved a sense of safety, a mutuality of warmth, caring, and concern. It would be crucial, for the preservation of their progress, to help them recognize that their progress had come from them. The worker's role must now be clarified as one of a facilitator, not as the central and only source of strength and support in the group. If the members devalued their contributions, the devastation of the worker's leaving would render them again helpless, isolated, and fearful—full cycle back to the beginning phase of the work. It is critical during the termination phase that the group members feel a sense of collective strength, separate from the worker. If accomplished, this enables them to experience mastery and growth sufficient to preserving gains and continuing progress.

The following process excerpt indicates how, through activity and humor, the worker struggles to help the members identify their feelings about her and about her leaving, attempting to move beyond their initial denial.

Holding her clay in her hand, Beverly said she didn't know what to make. She asked Marie what she was making. Marie pointed to the clay box, depicting a variety of dinosaurs. Beverly said she wanted to make that, too, and asked if I'd help her with it. She said it was a "mean monster." I asked them if they were going to name their monsters. Shrugs. Beverly said, "I don't know what to call it." I said "me?" She laughed and said, "No, I couldn't name it you." I asked why they'd decided to make monsters today. Marie said, "It's on box." I said, "But the box and pictures have been there for weeks." Beverly said, "I wish my monster could yell." I asked about what. She said, "Nuthin'." I said they sure do look mean. They both smiled, and stood them boldly in the center of the table. Beverly picked up her monster to show Rhoda, saying, "See what I made, Rhodie—a monster." Then, laughing, "[worker] said I could call it her." Rhoda smiled. I asked if they maybe thought I was a monster for leaving. Beverly said, "What's a big idea—why do ya have ta leave?" I asked how it made them feel. Beverly said, "Awful." I asked if they could remember other people leaving the group. Beverly said, "Last year." I said, "The worker last year?" Nods.

I asked how they'd felt when she left. Rhoda said, "I don't know where she is." I said, "It's like she just disappeared?" Nods. I asked if it felt like she didn't care and forgot about them when she left. Nods. I said they probably felt the same about me. Slight nods. I said that I did care about them, and that it would be hard for me to leave because I do care about them, and that I won't forget about them. . . . Beverly said, "My brother visits me 'most every Sunday." Then sadly, "But my father and mother are dead." I said, "By dying, they left you." She said, "Ya, they left; but they was too good to die." I asked if others had relatives or someone they loved leave or die. Rhoda said, "My father died." Golda said very softly, "I wasn't there." I said, "You were in the hospital?" She nodded. Beverly picked up on this and said that had happened to her, too, and made it harder. Silence. I said that even though we know things like this must happen, it doesn't make it much easier, and it's still sad to think about. Nods. Beverly said, "When's your last day—six more weeks?—that's good."

The worker's rather abrupt refocusing the group away from their feelings about her leaving onto recollections of feelings about others leaving was, in retrospect, a response to the worker's renewed feelings of insecurity in dealing with the members' expected anger toward her for leaving them. The worker's fear of regression on the part of the members was met with the worker's own regression, to an earlier method of indirect expression, perhaps a safe vehicle for evaluating potential reactions to the current situation.

In the meeting following this, group members demonstrated regression to earlier patterns, such as arriving late or "forgetting" the time of the group, a marked decrease in talking, and a sense of quiet irritability. In this group, four weeks prior to ending, the group gave the worker a clear second chance to work with them and their anger.

Beverly and Arlene had progressed markedly in their ability to share and cooperate with one another. In this group Beverly had "stolen" cigarettes from Arlene, and when asked how she felt about it, Arlene said, "She doesn't care anymore." I commented that we'd been talking about how the group has moved backwards a little since we've been talking about ending and asked if they could remember how things had been when we first started meeting together. Beverly said, "I used ta mop." Why? "So I didn't have ta come ta group." I said she really didn't like the group much then. She said, "That's right—but now I like it." Arlene was talking loud and fast to her reflection in the coffee pot. I asked if she'd like to share something with the rest of us. She looked at me and said, "Shut up." I said (a bit taken aback), "You want me to shut up?" She said, "Sure." I asked why. She went on talking, mentioning a lot of names, "Today her name's Arlene, tomorrow it's Frank, Kevin, then it's Matilda." I said it sounds like Arlene's talking about changes. She looked at me and said, "She is." I said changes are tough and asked others how they felt about changes. Rhoda shook her head hard. Beverly said, "Things should stay like they are." I said, "What things?" She said, "You're too good ta leave." I said it will be hard for me to leave them, because I care about them all. Beverly said, "Ya, I like everyone here." Arlene looked at me and said, "She likes herself but not you." I said I felt Arlene was feeling angry with me today. She gave an abrupt, coarse laugh. I said that it was O.K. to feel angry—it was part of endings too; different people can have different feelings, and that we will try to understand these feelings before I leave. Arlene was talking again, incoherently. I reached over and rested my hand on her arm, which had a calming effect. She quieted. Beverly put her arm around Arlene's shoulder. Arlene smiled at her.

Arlene's reactions reflected her anger and pain over change and loss. Her stated wish ("shut up") that the worker would stop reminding them of their imminent loss while simultaneously bringing the anger into clear, unavoidable focus, indicated a capability and willingness to deal with her feelings. She did not exit from the group during this meeting, a behavior which would have been consistent with her previous pattern of dealing with strong feelings. She chose to remain in group and struggle to find words to express her feelings.

Arlene's use of the third person illustrates her vulnerable sense of self, as well as her use of projection as a defense to help her cope with difficult feelings. Her use of a variety of names may have symbolized the numbers of people moving in and out of her life, as well as a fusion of her self with others she had depended on, thereby causing her to feel the loss of even her primary identity—her name—with the loss of the other person. It was important to recognize and validate Arlene's feelings of anger and also to point out to the group that a diversity of feelings is possible and acceptable, thereby promoting a sense of individualization within the group.

The following process excerpt illustrates the movement toward resolution of the termination issue—following the denial, anger, apathy, and sadness, the group was able to accept the reality of the situation in a more mature, positive manner. This meeting took place one week prior to the final session.

The group was calm today. There was a quiet element, but without anger or sadness. Arlene was covering herself in chalk dust from a "crepe paper design" she was coloring. I asked if she used to make things out of crepe paper. She said, "She sure did—dolls and dresses and coats." Beverly said she couldn't draw anything. With encouragement, she drew what she decided looked like an apple and a pear. I asked if she was hungry, drawing all that good-looking fruit. She laughed. They worked in silence; then Beverly said, "Is next time the last group?" Marie said it was. I asked how that made them feel, to have just one more group together after today. Beverly said, "It's too bad it's over." I agreed, saying it's been such a good group. Beverly again asked where I'd be going and what I'd be doing. She asked if I'd be going to another hospital. I said I wasn't sure yet, but wherever I go, I hope I'll find people as nice as they are. Smiles and nods. As the group was ending, Beverly asked if I'd like to have the picture she'd drawn. I said I'd be pleased to have it and had a good place to hang it at home. She beamed. Arlene, handing me her picture said, "Would you like to have this?" I said I sure would, and thanked her. She smiled. Golda, who had been producing snake-like figures in clay for weeks, had been laboriously working on one small (two-inch) figure for two weeks. During this group she had quietly struggled to make it stand. She even put a face on it for the first time. When it could stand on its own, she gave it to me, saying, "For you to keep." I was very moved here. I told Golda I would treasure it always, and would think of her being able to stand straighter and talk more every time I look at it. She smiled at me and said, "Good."

The spontaneous gift giving here seemed to indicate the growing ability of the women to emerge from their self-involved manner of relating to reach out actively and give of themselves. Golda's effort to make her "person" stand firmly was perhaps her way of thanking the worker for helping her feel she could stand more on her own.

The group members' sharing and giving prompted thoughts regarding the appropriateness of the worker giving them something. After discussion with the staff team, it was decided that small tokens would be appropriate. They could help the members preserve concretely their positive feelings about the group and could serve as transitional objects between this group experience and their next one.

The next excerpt illustrates the final meeting (number 30), seven months after the group began.

Everyone arrived at group early. Several other patients came into the room, asking if they could share the cake. The members were pleased it was all theirs. Beverly said, "Is it bought or did you make it?" I said I'd baked it, like we'd talked about last week. Smiles and nods. They all demonstrated their accomplished skills at dividing the tasks for coffee preparation. After we'd eaten, I said I'd brought them each something today, to show how much I've liked working with them and how much I'll miss them. The small gifts (small bottles of perfume and necklaces with their names engraved on them) were readily accepted and put on. Beverly said, "Ya can't come back to us any more?" I again gently went over that I would be leaving for good today, that I wouldn't be seeing them again, that I would miss them very much, and would think about them a lot. Marie asked about the new worker, and I again told them her name and that she'd be coming in about two weeks. Beverly said, "I won't yell at her too much," and laughed. All smiled at her and nodded. I said, "It sounds like you all want to keep meeting together." All nodded. I said I liked hearing that—that even though I'm leaving, they will have each other, and the group. Beverly said, "Ya, this is a good group." I agreed and added that because they liked this group, it'll be easier for them to be in other groups, too. Smiles and nods. We talked again about the progress each one had made in the group. As I was leaving the unit later in the day, all the group members were watching for me. Beverly shouted from the other end of the hall, "Take good care of yourself." We all waved goodbyes.

CONCLUSION

Hospital settings are rich with material which lends a here-and-now focus to issues which institutionalized individuals struggle with, often in fearful, unnoticed isolation. The group themes which touched the members of this group most significantly centered around life issues which have affected them deeply—deprivation and loss. They expressed their feelings and formed a mutual bond, allowing them to sense that they have each other with whom they can provide and receive comfort and companionship even though many people pass in and out of their lives.

When a milieu setting is conceptualized as a microcosm of the larger world, one can see the importance of helping its members cope with and master their environment. For example, Golda had remained in her "space," sandwiched between two tall supply closets, for many years, always the first to arrive in the morning, and the last to be led to the dorm at night. It was interesting to note that she never needed help in getting to her space, only in leaving it. Her initial reluctance to come to the group and her need to be the first out of the room came to be viewed in light of her fear of being displaced from her space on the unit. If another patient sat in her chair while she was away, she would stand patiently waiting for them to leave. When the worker encouraged Golda to bring her chair with her to the group (and the worker physically did this for her for a few times), her willingness to attend increased markedly. She eventually was able to transfer this increased control over her environment to include moving her chair to other parts of the unit and was frequently observed sitting near other group members. For Golda, this was a monumental achievement, undoubtedly contributing to increased feelings of mastery and autonomy, demonstrated by her ability finally to produce a firmly standing clay figure.

Marie's personal hygiene improved significantly, and she was being considered for a new adult foster home placement when the worker left. Rhoda stated she was looking forward to another group experience. Arlene had ceased being incontinent for nearly two months, the first time in many years. Beverly was considered "pleasant" for the first time in years by staff and other patients and was therefore treated with increased respect and more adult-like expectations.

The ability of these women to make the kind of progress they made in such a short period of time (seven months) may in part be a result of their many years' contact with each other and their previous group experience. Their ability to express themselves, nonverbally and verbally, around difficult life issues, was greater than had been expected, considering their chronicity and level of functioning. Perhaps the difficulty lies in the common predisposition to connote "chronic" synonymously with "hopeless." Potential for growth and change with this population may be underestimated. Many chronic institutionalized individuals may have the potential for growth sufficient to free them from their emotional bondage to a hospital system and enable them to live and work together in supportive environments of a less restrictive nature.

NOTES

1. See, for example, Donald J. Scherl, M.D., and Lee B. Macht, M.D., "Deinstitutionalization in the Absence of Consensus," in *Hospital and Community Psychiatry* 30, no. 9 (September 1979): 599-604; Geoffrey A.W. DiBella, G. Wayne Weitz, Dorothy Poynter-Berg, and Judith L. Yurmark, *Handbook of Partial Hospitalization* (New York: Brunner/Mazel, 1982), pp. 6, 7, 18; and Leona L. Bachrach, ed., "An Overview of Deinstitutionalization," in *Deinstitutionalization: New Directions for Mental Health Services,* ed. H. Richard Lamb (San Francisco: Jossey-Bass, 1983), pp. 5-14.

2. Bachrach, "Overview of Deinstitutionalization," p. 8.

3. President's Commission on Mental Health, *Report to the President,* vol. 1 (Washington, D.C.: Government Printing Office, 1978).

4. See W. Goldman, "Introductory Comments, Session on Deinstitutionalization," paper presented at the annual meeting of the American Orthopsychiatric Association, Atlanta, Georgia, March 5, 1976.

5. See Bachrach, "Overview of Deinstitutionalization," p. 6., citing unpublished data from the National Institute of Mental Health.

6. Miles F. Shore and Robert Shapiro, "The Effect of Deinstitutionalization on the State Hospital," *Hospital and Community Psychiatry* 30, no. 9 (September 1979): 607.

7. See, for example, H. H. Goldman, "Mental Illness and Family Burden: A Public Health Perspective," *Hospital and Community Psychiatry* 33, no. 7 (1982): 557-560.

8. See, for examples, C. P. O'Brien, "Group Therapy for Schizophrenia: A Practical Approach," *Schizophrenia Bulletin* 1, no. 13 (1975): 119-130; C. P. O'Brien, K. B. Hamm, B. A. Ray, J. F. Pierce, L. Luborsky, and J. Mintz, "Group vs. Individual Psychotherapy with Schizophrenics," *Archives of General Psychiatry* 27, no. 4 (1972): 474-478; P. R. May, "Rational Treatment for an Irrational Disorder: What Does the Schizophrenic Patient Need?" *The American Journal of Psychiatry* 133, no. 9 (1976): 1008-1011; William Schwartz

and Serapio R. Zalba, "Introduction," in *The Practice of Group Work* (New York: Columbia University Press, 1971), pp. 3-24; and Alex Gitterman, "Development of Group Services," in *Social Work with Groups in Maternal and Child Health: Conference Proceedings,* (New York: Columbia University School of Social Work and Roosevelt Hospital Department of Social Work, 1979), pp. 15-21.

9. Theodore Lidz, "The Middle Years," in *The Person* (New York: Basic Books, 1968), p. 495.

10. Ibid., p. 498.

11. Ibid., p. 509.

12. Ping-Nie Pao, "On the Formation of Schizophrenic Symptoms" (Rockville, Md.: Chestnut Lodge, n.d.).

13. Ibid., p. 393.

14. Ibid., p. 394.

15. See Margaret Mahler, "On Child Psychosis and Schizophrenia," *Psychoanalytic Study of the Child* 7 (1952), and idem., *On Human Symbiosis and the Vicissitudes of Individuation* (New York: International Universities Press, 1968).

16. Pao, "On the Formation of Schizophrenic Symptoms," p. 394.

17. See Shore and Shapiro, "Effect of Deinstitutionalization," and Bachrach, "Overview of Deinstitutionalization," for examples of which patients remain institutionalized and why.

18. See Michael S. Olmsted, *The Small Group* (New York: Random House, 1959).

19. See, for example, Arthur S. Abramson et al., "A Therapeutic Community in a General Hospital: Adaptation to a Rehabilitation Service," *Journal of Chronic Diseases* 16, no. 179 (February 1963): 179-186; J. Cumming and E. Cumming, *Ego and Milieu* (New York: Atherton Press, 1967); Irving Gootnick, "Transference in Psychotherapy with Schizophrenic Patients," *International Journal of Group Psychotherapy* 25, no. 4 (1975): 379-388; and O'Brien, "Group Therapy for Schizophrenia."

20. May, "Rational Treatment for an Irrational Disorder."

21. Alex Gitterman, "Development of Group Services," p. 15.

22. Olmsted, *The Small Group,* p. 78.

23. For examples of the use of program in social group work, see Lawrence Shulman, "Program in Group Work: Another Look," in *The Practice of Group Work,* ed. William Schwartz and Serapio Zalba (New York: Columbia University Press, 1971), pp. 221-240.

BIBLIOGRAPHY

Abramson, A. S., et al. "A Therapeutic Community in a General Hospital: Adaptation to a Rehabilitation Service." *Journal of Chronic Diseases* 16, no. 179 (February 1963).

Bachrach, L., ed. "An Overview of Deinstitutionalization." In *Deinstitutionalization: New Directions for Mental Health Services.* Edited by H. R. Lamb. San Francisco: Jossey-Bass, 1983.

Cumming, J., and E. Cumming. *Ego and Milieu.* New York: Atherton Press, 1967.

DiBella, A. W., G. Weitz, D. Poynter-Berg, and J. Yurmark. *Handbook of Partial Hospitalization.* New York: Brunner/Mazel, 1982.

Garland, J., H. Jones, and R. L. Kolodny. "A Model for Stages of Development in Social Work Groups." In *Explorations in Group Work.* Edited by S. Berstein. Boston: Boston University School of Social Work, 1968.

Gitterman, A. "Development of Group Services." In *Social Work with Groups in Maternal and Child Health: Conference Proceedings.* New York: Columbia University School of Social Work and Roosevelt Hospital Department of Social Work, 1979.

Goldman, H. H. "Mental Illness and Family Burden: A Public Health Perspective," *Hospital and Community Psychiatry* 3, no. 7 (1982).

Goldman, W. "Introductory Comments, Session on Deinstitutionalization." Paper presented at the annual meeting of the American Orthopsychiatric Association, Atlanta, Ga., March 1976.

Gootnick, I. "Transference in Psychotherapy with Schizophrenic Patients," *International Journal of Group Psychotherapy* 25, no. 4 (1975).

Lidz, T. *The Person.* New York: Basic Books, 1968.

Mahler, Margaret. "On Child Psychosis and Schizophrenia," *Psychoanalytic Study of the Child* 7 (1952).

_____.*On Human Symbiosis and the Vicissitudes of Individuation.* New York: International Universities Press, 1968.

May, P. R. "Rational Treatment for an Irrational Disorder: What Does the Schizophrenic Patient Need?" *The American Journal of Psychiatry* 133, no. 9 (1976).

O'Brien, C. "Group Therapy for Schizophrenia: A Practical Approach," *Schizophrenia Bulletin* 1, no. 13 (1975): 119-130.

O'Brien, C. P., et al. "Group vs. Individual Psychotherapy with Schizophrenics," *Archives of General Psychiatry* 27, no. 4 (1972).

Olmsted, M. *The Small Group.* New York: Random House, 1959.

Pao, Ping-Nie. "On the Formation of Schizophrenic Symptoms." Rockville, Md.: Chestnut Lodge, 1975.

President's Commission on Mental Health. *Report to the President,* vol. 1. Washington, D.C.: Government Printing Office, 1978.

Scherl, D., and D. Macht. "Deinstitutionalization in the Absence of Consensus." *Hospital and Community Psychiatry* 30, no. 9 (1979).

Schwartz, W., and S. Zalba. *The Practice of Group Work.* New York: Columbia University Press, 1971.

Shore, M., and R. Shapiro. "The Effect of Deinstitutionalization on the State Hospital." *Hospital and Community Psychiatry* 30, no. 9 (September 1979).

Shulman, L. "Program in Group Work: Another Look." In *The Practice of Group Work.* Edited by W. Schwartz and S. Zalba. New York: Columbia University Press, 1971.

Derryl Lubell

CHAPTER 15

Living with a Lifeline:
Peritoneal Dialysis Patients

Chronic physical illness affects and permeates all parts of a person's life; it interferes in the normal development patterns and usually means major changes in lifestyle. Chronic renal failure adds the additional stress of choosing between either a life-intrusive treatment program or no life at all—dialysis or death. The particular treatment described in this paper, in-hospital peritoneal dialysis,[1] makes especially severe demands on the patient's time and energy levels, playing havoc with relationships both in and outside the family, affecting work and changing leisure activities. The individual's response to these demands will vary according to age, personality, physical condition, and developmental level. For example, a chronic illness that prevents a man from pursuing his work goals will be perceived differently by an eighteen-year-old who is just beginning to formulate his interests, than by a fifty-year-old who is well established in a job he has no desire to change. Developmental levels affect how people define and approach problems and how they then cope with them. Although the issues associated with chronic illness appear universal, those entering early adulthood, passing through midlife transitions, or approaching retirement are

often working on very different aspects of the same problem.

Any services offered to this diverse population must take into account the wide disparity in needs, goals, life-styles, developmental stages, and treatment situations. This article describes an in-hospital group for peritoneal patients, a group geared to helping them deal more effectively with their life situations within the context of the treatment program, using as the theoretical orientation Schwartz's interactional model of social work practice.

ADULT DEVELOPMENT AND DIALYSIS

People on peritoneal dialysis are making many major adjustments simultaneously. They must figure out how to live with the implications of their disease and the demands of the treatment program, and still preserve their own identity. Where they are developmentally will greatly influence how they manage these tasks; life-cycle issues will affect their perception of and adjustment to dialysis as a way of life. Chronic illness magnifies the importance of the developmental stage as these patients cope with concerns about dependence, loss, cultural and community expectations, employment, and family and marital relationships.[2]

For the young adult, dependency issues mean feeling caught between parents and the patient's own needs. The young person who has been emancipating from family is suddenly relying on them again and being pulled back into the fold. Such a person may well feel that adolescence is being unbearably prolonged but feels helpless to change the situation. Peers, not hampered by these problems, are performing the tasks, separations, and self-care that may now seem impossible to achieve. The younger patients' concerns about death and loss also separate them from their age-mates — peers rarely even think about death; yet, its presence is a major factor in the patients' lives. They tend to feel cut off from their social network because their concerns and issues are so different. Younger patients must grieve the loss of easy camaraderie, of "fitting in." They must also mourn their lost work potential; because they may have worked only a short time, they are less likely to have employer loyalty and a proven track record, giving them less to offset the boss's fears about impaired performance or treatment-related absences and other concerns. Because their career goals may have to be more radically modified than those of older patients, they may feel defeated before they begin.

In contrast, the middle-aged patient is "cut down as he begins to stand up."[3] Such patients are too old to lean on their parents, too young to depend on their children. Just as the middle-age person is establishing and enjoying the separate life that he has created, he must again depend on others. Culturally he is told "to take care of things himself," but realistically he needs help for sheer survival.

The middle-age patient often loses options both at home and at work: it should be a time of life to assess what one has done and what one hopes to accomplish, knowing they have time to make changes. Yet, the midlife dialysis patient, rather than dreaming of new starts, is struggling to maintain the status quo. On the job he must worry about productivity and mourn lost opportunities. In his life, he is different from his peers because the immediacy of his anxiety about death is not yet shared by his cohorts. His awareness of the fragility of his life inhibits his future planning, forcing him more into the unsatisfactory present. The illness and its associated losses have become the major determinant in his life.

For the older chronically ill person, dependency issues revolve around fears of losing control of their lives now and of being unable to care for themselves in the future. For some, the transition from fully functioning member of society to "hospitalized patient" has been very rapid. Although remaining independent is important, many can accept assistance from their families as they grew up with the cultural belief that children help care for aged parents. Yet, this raises concerns about imposing too much on families, of overstressing children and frail spouses. The older person must cope with role changes in family, community, and at work whether ill or not. The infringement of the illness on outside involvements may be just another step on the long road of "retirement." Yet, even here, such patients may need to give up fantasies of travel or moving because they find they cannot sustain the effort; they mourn their dreams. They must prepare for the end of their own life — recognizing the closeness of death as they experience losing their contemporaries and family. Older patients review their own life both to establish its meaning and to help them face their own death.

Some issues, such as marital and family relationships, cut across developmental levels. For example, patients of all ages worry about their role performance, sexual dysfunction, fear of rejection from spouses, and ramifications of body changes, and other matters. They question whether their marital relationship is strong enough to handle the stress or, conversely, feel trapped in a poor relationship because "who else would have them?" The younger patient may not "compete" for a spouse; they may believe it is unfair for them to marry, or depending on the genetic components, unfair to have children, as they don't measure up to the ideal. Middle-age patients are concerned about stress on family, but they may worry about having enough time to spend with children and to share in their care, about burdening their family both financially and emotionally, and some wonder if their death might not really be a relief for their stressed spouse. The older patients fear burdening spouses or family who should be living their own lives. They may be more lonely and more dependent on family now than in the past, at a time when family resources are depleted and scattered.

When examining developmental levels, it is also important to consider not only the age-related issues, but also the time when the illness struck—how many developmental levels have been affected. For example, to be a young adult confronting renal failure for the first time is very different from being a young adult who has been chronically ill since childhood. For the latter, having had to deal with physical impairment, peer rejection, and difficulty in leaving home, dramatically affects adult development. The person may be struggling with a prolonged ado-

lescent dependency, accompanying parental overinvolvement, and poor peer relationships. In contrast, the twenty-five-year-old suddenly hit with a major illness, while grieving loss of health, restrictions, and so on, has more resources. This patient may have a supportive spouse and family to help provide motivation, as well as a work identity. Life-cycle tasks will be more appropriate for the age level than will those of the chronically ill adult who must bring the baggage of past illness to present struggles.

AGENCY CONTEXT AND THE GROUP MODALITY

At the hospital, one of the treatment options for chronic renal failure is peritoneal dialysis. At the time of this group, most new patients first began dialysis on the Peritoneal Dialysis Unit (P.D.U.). This unit consisted of two four-bed wards, not segregated by sex, run by specially trained staff who dialyze each person over a forty-eight-hour period. Patients always "run" the same two days each week. During their first three months in the unit, the patient, with the help of the staff, decides either to stay permanently on peritoneal dialysis or to transfer to hemodialysis.[4] With hemodialysis, because there are fewer days between runs for the wastes to build up in the body and the actual time spent in treatment is less, many people seem to feel better. And those who want transplants must be on this form of treatment first. However, the blood, machinery, isolation, and dependence on the equipment can be quite frightening. For medical, social, or religious reasons, patients may choose to remain in the P.D.U. or to transfer to hemodialysis as they, the staff, and the hospital's resources dictate. Usually the older, more settled patients or those with either physical or emotional difficulties with hemodialysis elect to remain in the P.D.U. The younger, more active patients tend to choose hemodialysis/transplant but must wait up to three months in the P.D.U. for a place in the other program. Thus, those undergoing treatment in the P.D.U. at any one time vary in their service needs and their demands. Beside a veteran of the program whose biggest concern is whether a favorite nurse is on holiday may be someone who is dialyzing for the first time and is very ill. This mix of needs can create conflict. While the long-term patient may have few specific questions, someone new to the program will be trying to sort out the overwhelming medical, social, and emotional experiences. The veteran patient may take certain kinds of service for granted, while the newer one may feel overwhelmed by needs and frightened to ask staff for help.

Although the range of the development and treatment stages does create enormous differences, P.D.U. patients also share many common experiences and emotions. All patients and families are coping with the same incredible stresses—the stress of being dependent on machines and the medical system to stay alive, the stress of adjusting to an ongoing regime of medicines, diets, and restrictions, and the stress of major changes in life-style and family situations.

In conversations with the social worker, all patients reported that they and their families had difficulty accepting the need for treatment; they described feeling extremely dependent and depressed at the commencement of dialysis, questioning "why me?", "why am I singled out for this disease?", fantasizing that a mistake had been made in their case and that they soon would be told they really were O.K. They directed anger at past, inadequate medical care and although grateful, were apprehensive about the quality of the present assistance. They were grieving over the real and perceived losses in the health and functioning. Some people used this experience of illness as an opportunity to examine their priorities and reorganize their lives, trying to live each day more fully. While stating it was difficult to accept help from strangers, the patients felt being with the "family" in the P.D.U. was comforting, since "they are the only people who really understand what it is like." The issues they were struggling with included: (1) accepting their illness and its resulting disruptions of their lives, (2) adjusting to the lifelong involvement with the treatment program, and (3) finding the appropriate level of dependency/independency within both the program and their own family units in light of their new situation.

In addition to listening to the expressed concerns, the social worker observed that the patients in the P.D.U. fit very well into "the sick role." Although the treatment did not necessitate special clothing, all the patients immediately changed into pajamas and lay on their beds, mostly watching TV, for the forty-eight hours. Although regulating their own equipment would give them more mobility and freedom, the patients depended on the staff for total care. Even after the initial adjustment period, the patients continued to see themselves as sick and needing this help, perhaps because they saw the other, more established patients behaving that way. The experienced P.D.U. patients used the very active grapevine to give their opinions, answer questions, and pass on to the newer ones their perceptions of the proper way to act. While this support was vital, not only was their viewpoint not always appropriate for the newer, more active patients but it discouraged them from taking their concerns directly to staff. Here, the patient community proved that it is possible to live with renal failure while also erecting a wall between the new patients and staff. The longer people remained in the P.D.U., the more they became assimilated into the role of a sick, dependent patient.

The patient, while running in the P.D.U., is a "captive audience" available to talk. Yet after the initial integration into the program, most people are reluctant to spend any more time than absolutely necessary in the hospital. Because the social worker covers all the treatment programs, the demands on her time from other patients and staff are quite heavy; she felt she was unable either to meet the P.D.U. patient's needs or to capitalize on the community feeling already existing in the unit. Yet, because she was the only nonmedical staff, patients found certain issues easier to discuss with her, since they worried neither about jeopardizing their care nor about appearing as bad patients to her. Therefore, holding a group for P.D.U. patients during their run time appeared to offer some unique advantages.

First, having the group on the ward recognizes the importance of the community feeling and uses it. Less time is needed to establish common ground, introduce each other, and build basic trust, while rewards from the mutual aid process would soon be obvious. The older patients would benefit from recognition of their role as "elder statesmen," and new patients would benefit from their experience as well as garnering hope about their own futures. Both would enjoy giving to others instead of always receiving the help. Younger patients might stimulate older ones to reexamine their priorities while the more mature could share their stabil-

ity with those still floundering. The information exchanged among patients would be more accurate as staff could correct or add to it during group. This would reinforce the message that staff care and are available to help, while also keeping them up to date about patient issues in the unit. Strengthening bonds among the members might mean benefits from the group experience would carry over into the rest of the shared hospital time. And, for at least the length of the group, patients would have to be active to participate.

However, there are some major drawbacks to a group comprised of people who have no choice about continuing to see each other. While positive spillover from the shared group experience might enhance the sense of family in the P.D.U., this physical and emotional closeness may make it more difficult for group members to share intimate or significant thoughts. For example, if a member shares something during a session that makes him anxious or uncomfortable, because he will continue to see the others for at least twenty-four hours, he may feel as if the group never ends. It can be hard to confront each other, if like family, you must continue to live together; both patients and staff may fear upsetting the atmosphere in the P.D.U. for an extended period of time, not just the period of the group meeting. In addition, it is hard to discuss concerns about one's family when those people will be visiting in an hour and have an ongoing relationship with the other group members. In this situation, the group must respect members' privacy and right to it must be well established.

The P.D.U. staff itself at first reacted negatively to the idea of this group. Changing and increasing the social worker's involvement with P.D.U. patients was perceived as a threat to the staff; they worried that she would usurp their role with the patients, upset well-established modes and customs on the unit, and make their job more difficult. The medical staff does not necessarily see patients' needs in the same way as the nonmedical social worker or give those needs the same priority when they do. However, after much discussion of the possible pros and cons for the staff, the unit, and the particular patients, the staff did support the group and agree with its goals. All hoped the group would enable the members, by establishing an atmosphere of mutual aid and trust, to move toward more functional and pleasurable life-styles both in and outside of the treatment program. The patients, with the help of the leaders, would accomplish this goal by sharing, discussing, and examining: (1) their reactions to both the disease and dialysis, (2) their adjustments to their medical situation, (3) their level of self-care and responsibility both with their treatment and with their family and peer units, and (4) their ability to obtain what they needed from the health professionals.

The group was scheduled during the hospital runs, so that it would not infringe on patients' limited time at home. The worker hoped that group attendance would be more inviting if the group actually took place in front of the patients and required little effort to attend. Therefore, she structured the group as a series of eight meetings, each forty-five minutes long, to take place on the day when the most patients could be present—Tuesdays. The sessions were held in the middle of a ward room, so that even immobile patients could attend. The staff scheduled the meetings for a time when the necessary equipment regulation could easily be handled by the patients. The social worker also invited the head nurse

to join her as a coleader, both because of her technical knowledge and her rapport with the patients, but also because of her previous ambivalence about the group. As she had been quite concerned about what the patients might say about her and her staff, she welcomed the opportunity to be directly involved and to know exactly what was going on!

Although there were changes over time as people moved to hemodialysis, new patients began in the P.D.U., or someone died, the core members were Henry, Victoria, and Maureen, retired workers and homemakers in their fifties and sixties; Charlie, a professional entertainer/disabled pensioner in his forties; Suzanne, in her late twenties, who remained in the P.D.U. because of religious beliefs; and Brad and Patty, who are both in their early twenties and unemployed. Although Maureen, Suzanne, and Patty were new to the dialysis program, only Patty planned to transfer to hemodialysis; the other members expected to remain long-term in the P.D.U.

Interestingly, the group members' ages correspond to key adult developmental milestones. For example, Brad and Patty were both dealing with entering adulthood and making life choices, yet continued to live at home. Suzanne, with deteriorating health, felt acutely alone as she watched her cohorts attain job and family satisfactions she never would. Maureen, forced to retire prematurely at fifty-five, resented experiencing the transition into late adulthood before she felt chronologically and emotionally ready, while Charlie, in the same situation, felt relieved. The senior members, Henry and Victoria, saw dialysis as just one more experience to assimilate in a series of recent major changes in family and social roles. They felt "lucky" their illness began so late in life. Yet all the P.D.U. patients felt the only people who could truly share and understand their experience were the other group members.

GROUP THEMES

As the group met and worked together and the members developed an atmosphere of trust, the group moved through various stages. When they first began meeting together, the members felt safest discussing the medical aspects of their situation; they focused on concrete problems such as how dialysis restricted and changed their life-style and questioned nursing or treatment procedures. As the members became more comfortable with the process and with each other, they risked discussing the more emotional aspects of their situation, focusing on the tremendous sense of loss and isolation they were experiencing, sharing how they coped with their feelings about dependency and death. Because one of the group members died while the group was tentatively exploring this area, the group process became even more relevant to their lives. The members' sense of connection with each other supported them as the group broadened its focus from individual areas to more system-related issues. They combined both by discussing their concerns about their families, how they and their relatives coped with their illness and the changes in family structure. Although the members had always acknowledged the importance of family, they had to feel very safe as a group before this topic could be explored. Because all had ongoing involvement with each other's families during visiting hours, the contact, not necessarily the content, had made family issues too threatening to explore earlier. When the group successfully handled this topic, they felt ready to examine problems in

their "other family," the hospital proper. Over the course of the group, the patients moved from focusing on physical concerns to dealing with individual and family emotionally laden issues to working on more public problems that affected them all. The following examples illustrate these themes of concerns and the group process.

Medical Aspects

The group began by searching for its common ground, the areas in which the illness issues overrode the differences among them in development levels. In this early part they focused on their difficulties adapting to and living with medical restrictions. They devoted much meeting time to discussing their illnesses, treatments, medical histories, and to asking questions about present procedures, hemodialysis, and kidney transplants. They shared distress about problems such as the limited diet and minimal fluid intake, which cut across all developmental levels. The following case example from this beginning phase shows group members helping one another deal with their individual problems.

During a discussion of how hard it was to stick to the diet, Charlie, a professional entertainer, offered to sing a song. The others laughed and encouraged him. I acknowledged how much easier it was to sing and joke than to deal with the sometimes overwhelming problems they were all facing. When Charlie continued to clown, I pointed out that although he was usually the one to distract the group, he also had the most difficulty in following the diet. The others agreed, but Charlie began to give excuses. Brad told him he'd have to change some of his habits and added that he himself no longer went to the pub where he was tempted to drink, but arranged to see his friends at other times instead.

Suzanne added that Charlie did not take the diet seriously enough—that he was the only one to abuse it flagrantly every week. Charlie again claimed that he had to accept drinks from patrons between shows and rejected Maureen's suggestions about how he might explain the situation. When asked how she handled similar situations, Maureen gave an example of how she had responded to dinner invitations adding that if she acted matter of factly, people accepted it easily. I pointed out that it is hard to deal with other people's reactions unless you are feeling comfortable with the situation and have accepted it yourself. There were general nods.

In this vignette, the group members' different responses to their restrictions appear more related to their temperament than their ages. Yet, a contributing factor to Charlie's difficulties is his sense of failure both personally and in terms of typical middle-aged goals. Charlie receives little satisfaction from his family life and has abandoned his breadwinner's role—both important aspects of a successful midlife period. While his singing was the most enjoyable part of his life, Charlie could not or would not explore it as a viable alternative career. Perhaps Charlie's difficulty with his diet reflects not only his inabilty to accept his illness but also his inability to see himself as a middle-age man with family and career responsibilities, roles he had not been filling well.

Emotional Aspects

As the group members became more comfortable with each other, they were able to move into more highly charged areas. Discussions which in the beginning had centered on physical issues soon broadened to include more emotional areas and the range of development levels became more apparent. For example,

while all expressed concern about their increasing dependence on staff for support, the older patients appeared more able to accept it, both because they felt they had earned it and because at their age they found it more culturally acceptable to be cared for by others. As they discussed these dependency issues, the chronicity of their condition and the loss of "quality of life," their sadness began to emerge. All had to mourn the changes in their functioning. And all had to acknowledge and cope with the close and real proximity of death.

Because of his increasing debilitation, John was no longer able to drive or to care for himself at home. The group spent much intensive time with him, trying to involve him in hospital activities, discussing nonthreatening ways he could ask for his family's help, and supporting any efforts he made on his own behalf. Although he told group members how important their efforts had been to him, his depression had not abated significantly when he died a few weeks later. At the next group meeting, the patients included an empty chair in the circle.

When I commented on it, Victoria said it must be for John, who had just died. I said, "It is hard when someone dies with whom you were close." Victoria acknowledged that you get to know everyone in the program very well. Others nodded. They discussed how depressed John had been. I asked, "Does his death make you think more about your own situation?" There was silence. Suzanne said she worried about it a lot. Others shared their fear of being alone and their preoccupation with death. Then they started to recount the details of every death that had occurred among patients in the unit. Victoria said most people who died were depressed at the time or just could not accept dialysis. I asked whether it made it easier for them to accept someone's death if that person were somehow different from the other patients in the P.D.U., if they could attribute the death to something other than kidney failure. The patients agreed. Then they started to say that "we all have to go sometime," and Henry commented that he might be killed crossing the street. I acknowledged that most people never confront death as directly as they had to, which they seconded avidly. I then added that they had been handling a difficult and stressful situation very well and asked what kinds of things made it easier for them to deal with it. Victoria began to talk about getting support and satisfaction from her religion, Maureen about her continued ability to function and give to others, and Henry about the pleasure he received from his children and grandchildren.

The older patients responded more directly to the death on the unit, both because it was their contemporary who died and because even prior to their illness they had been more aware of death as part of their life. Old age meant they had already suffered many losses, including retirement, reduced income, changes in numbers and kinds of life roles, decrease in social interactions, and loss of respect accorded to them by the community. But most importantly, with age came declining health and death in their own friends and family. For the older group members, awareness of death permeated their lives. The younger members were not as aware of it, since in the general community they were usually the one at high risk. Unless they chose to focus on their own situation, death was not as constant a companion.

Family Problems

There appeared to be two main kinds of family problems. The patients worried about what they were doing to their families and conversely what the families were doing for them. For example, some pa-

tients complained that their families were overprotective while others felt that theirs didn't appreciate enough how hard life was for them. With both issues, the group discussed struggling with unexpected dependencies. Staff urged them to function normally in the community at the same time they depended on this same staff for survival. A similar dilemma often existed at home where the patients both wanted and resented needing their family's extra support and help. They asked more from their others and constantly worried what this demand meant to themselves and to their families.

It was hard for the members to discuss the stresses between them and their families. They expressed reluctance to expose these kinds of problems in the group because their relatives had extended contact with the other patients during visiting hours. But it is also likely that their reluctance was due to the worker's difficulty in focusing on this area. When intensively involved with patients, seeing them frequently as individuals, it is easy for a social worker to ignore the family that is continuing to function on the outside. After recognizing this omission, the worker more effectively helped the group discuss this tough area.

Brad was scheduled to transfer to hemodialysis in a few weeks. He was quite nervous about the change and asked many questions about the procedures. When the group began to review what peritoneal dialysis had been like for him, Brad stated that his mother had been his main problem. When the worker asked him to clarify, he explained that his mother babied him, complained to everyone around how sick her boy was, and never acknowledged when he was getting along well. Patty allowed that it must be tough for him, saying, "At least my parents don't talk about it all the time." Maureen felt that Brad's mother had never accepted the disease or the dialysis. Brad then reported that his mother, who had several psychiatric hospitalizations, did not believe the doctors and blamed them for his condition. He added that her behavior on the ward embarrassed him. When Charlie asked if his father could help, Brad replied he was not often home. The worker asked Brad if he were worried about his mother's reaction to his transfer to hemodialysis. Brad nodded and said she would upset the entire staff. The group then spent a few minutes discussing how Brad could tell his mother about hemodialysis, and Maureen asked if his mother had seen the hemodialysis unit. Brad replied that he did not want her to come to the hospital. The worker suggested that if his mother had a special explanation from the staff during her first visit, she might be less nervous about hemodialysis and therefore less disruptive. Brad liked the idea and asked the worker to arrange to show his mother the unit.

In this vignette, Brad is struggling with the dual issues of a difficult and disruptive mother and his own ambivalence about dependency. Once he had assurance of help for his mother, Brad felt freer to discuss some of his own fears about leaving the P.D.U. and by extension, his home. He wanted the further independence of hemodialysis but was afraid to leave the security and safety of the P.D.U. He wanted to live at home where his mother fusses over him and he doesn't have to assume adult responsibilities, but recognized his allowing the situation to continue means he can't meet either his own goals or community expectations. Brad is caught between his need to grow up and his desire to regress, between his chronological age and the pull of chronic illness.

Hospital Issues

The group began by dealing with more individual issues. With success in these areas they moved from fearing that the differences in age and life experiences would make mutual understanding and help impossible, to experiencing the joys and satisfactions of working together. The group became a cohesive unit as the bonds between them grew. They began to examine more effective ways of dealing with the larger systems around them. After the first eight-session contract, the group requested to extend the meetings for another eight weeks to focus on ward problems. Even though the head nurse could not continue to attend, she and the other staff were supportive of the group continuing. Again the difference in development levels meant different perceptions of what is a problem, but all were able to work together toward common goals. During the extended time, the group first tackled the boredom and lack of facilities on the ward. The younger patients organized a film program, showing movies one night a week on the ward walls. All were involved in inviting in a Kidney Foundation representative, trying to improve the television rental service, and conferring with the dieticians about menus. In perhaps the biggest change from previous approaches, the older patients spearheaded a move to be more involved in the planning and organization of their treatment. The following note shows how the group worked together as well as the social worker's role in mediating between systems—here, between the patient group and the hospital staff.

During one group meeting, the patients complained of pain when using a new dialysis machine and of the nurses' refusal to disconnect them. Many patients, especially the middle-aged and older ones, expressed reluctance to confront the nurses directly for fear of antagonizing the staff and appearing ungrateful or jeopardizing their treatment. They were concerned about the implications of these new machines and possible loss of mobility or changes in the P.D.U. structure and routine. After exploring some of the issues, I suggested that the patients invite the head nurse and the physician to a meeting, so that they could discuss these issues directly with them. With hesitation, group members supported this idea and asked me to extend the invitation to the staff. I then described this invitation to the doctor and nurse as an opportunity both to enlist the patients' support for the planned changes and to encourage them to move toward responsible self-care. I also warned staff that they should expect some anger and demands, as I had done with the patients, and discussed briefly with them ways of handling the situation. The staff appeared pleased with the opportunity to present some of their thinking to the patients, and the meeting went well. Together, staff and patients decided that as soon as patients complained of pain, the nurse could disconnect them from their machines without waiting for the physician's permission. In turn, the patients agreed to tolerate the discomfort as long as possible while the staff made various technical adjustments. Although they were not enthusiastic about the possible future changes, the patients did thank the staff for coming and listening. Later, they commented how pleased they were by the staff members' response.

Although the group members worked well together here, their interests in changing the ward appear to correspond to their developmental ages. The younger patients became more involved in the film program because they felt so bored during their runs—they had few visitors during their runs while the older group members had regular outside contacts. The younger patients had had less time to build their own social networks, and their friends were more likely to be fully occupied with their own needs and concerns, more likely to have jobs and young families themselves. The older patients, in contrast, could call on forty or fifty years of friendships as well as extended family. So the younger ones, with fewer outside resources, had to make the P.D.U. "a home away from home," however temporary. In contrast, as most of the younger patients were "only passing through," it was the older ones who worried more about changes in structure or treatment, since they would be dealing with it on a long-term basis. All worried about the quality of treatment life, and their disparate interests, when combined in mutual care, made a powerful force.

CONCLUSION

The most powerful benefit appeared to derive from the experience that a group of people representing several different life stages and styles could combine in such a way to benefit from each other's knowledge and expertise. The sense of accomplishment and enhanced independence seemed to overflow into the rest of the patients' in-hospital time, resulting in some personal and ward changes. For example, some of the patients now wear street clothes while dialyzing, several have trained for home dialysis, and all at least know how to regulate their equipment. The ward atmosphere also seemed to change; the patients' information about their own and alternate treatments was more accurate, they directly approached the staff with questions and concerns about both medical and emotional issues, and the sense of community became stronger. Newer patients appeared to be having fewer difficulties with the restrictions, and there was less general "depression." Victoria even said, "It would have saved me eight months of depression if I had been able to share like this when I first began the program." The best indication of the group's effectiveness was their desire first to extend their contract for eight more sessions and then to meet monthly on an indefinite basis. In addition, the patients running on another day requested similar group meetings and reported feeling positively about their experience as well.

The group experience seems to offer more to the newer patients in the program. After a while, attendance of some of the older, long-term people declined. Quite possibly, once they satisfied their own needs, the pleasure of being an "elder statesman" wanes. For the younger patients, the group remained an important social event, as well as a place to assess their personal and treatment future realistically. Because of the difference in energy and focus, with the younger patients directed outwardly and the older ones inwardly, all received different benefits from the group.

The staff found the group increased their awareness of possible problem areas, thus enabling them to provide preventative care and avert crisis. For the social worker, meeting regularly with so many patients kept her in close touch with their immediate concerns, made her more responsive to their needs and enhanced her ability to mediate effectively between the patients and the hospital system. She was better able to order her service priorities because she had a overall picture of the unit as well as each patient's specific concerns.

For both patients and staff, the group's very existence meant recognition of the emotional and social as well as physical aspects of dialysis treatment. The sharing among all those involved in P.D.U. helped make it a more comfortable and effective place to work and live. As one patient said, "Hearing that I'm not alone—that other people have gotten through—this gives me the strength to continue."

NOTES

1. In this form of dialysis a patient first has a permanent catheter or plastic tube inserted into the abdomen. During treatment, the catheter is connected to a bag of special solution— dialyzate—which hangs from a high wheeled pole. The dialyzate runs or flows into the patient's abdomen where the body's waste products, which can no longer be excreted by the damaged kidneys, pass into it by diffusion. After one hour, the dialyzate is drained out and the whole procedure is repeated forty-eight times a "run" or treatment period. Because of the wheeled poles and simplicity of the equipment, patients can be mobile during most of their run.

2. The following discussion draws on the work of many authors, both those working with dialysis patients and those focused on adult developmental stages. The most significant chronic illness references are: Neil Alex, "The Impact of End-Stage Renal Disease on the Young Adult," Melanie Landsman, "Adjustment to Dialysis: The Middle Years," and Patricia McKevitt and Dean Kappel, "Psychological Needs and Concerns of the Elderly on Dialysis," in *Perspectives, The Journal of Nephrology Social Workers* 2 (November 1977): 29-50; Rudolph Moos, *Coping with Physical Illness* (New York: Plenum Medical Book Co., 1977). For the adult developmental stages, this section draws most heavily on: Douglas Kimmel, *Adulthood and Aging: An Interdisciplinary Development View* (Toronto: John Wiley and Sons, 1980); K. Warner Schaie and James Geuvitz, eds., *Adult Development and Aging* (Toronto: Little, Brown & Co., 1982); Norman Zinberg and Irving Kaufman, eds., *Normal Psychology of the Aging Process* (New York: International Universities Press Inc., 1978).

3. Melanie Landsman, "Adjustment to Dialysis: The Middle Years," in *Perspectives: The Journal of the Council of Nephrology Social Workers* 2 (November 1972): 34.

4. On hemodialysis, the artificial kidney machine filters the waste products directly from blood by bringing the blood to the machine, cleaning it, and returning it to their body. The process takes up to six hours two or three times a week.

BIBLIOGRAPHY

Alex, Neil. "The Impact of End-Stage Renal Disease on the Young Adult." *Perspectives: Journal of the Council of Nephrology Social Workers* 2:1 (November 1977): 29-33.

Carter, Susan; MacLeod, Evangeline; and Lubell, Derryl. "Team Home Visiting. A Pilot Project." *Dialysis and Transplantation* 6 (June 1977): 40-41, 66.

Czaczkes, J. W., and De-Nour, A. Kaplan. *Chronic Hemodialysis as a Way of Life.* New York: Brunner/Mazel, 1978.

Fortner-Frazier, Carrie. *Social Work and Dialysis.* Berkeley: University of California Press, 1981.

Hollon, Thomas. "Modified Group Therapy in the Treatment of Patients on Chronic Hemodialysis." *American Journal of Psychotherapy* 4 (October 1972): 501-510.

Kimmel, Douglas. *Adulthood and Aging: An Interdisciplinary Development View.* Toronto: John Wiley & Sons, 1980.

Landsman, Melanie. "Adjustment to Dialysis: The Middle Years." *Perspectives: Journal of the Council of Nephrology Social Workers* 2:1 (November 1977): 34-38.

Levinson, Daniel. *Seasons of a Man's Life.* New York: Ballantine, 1979.

Lubell, Derryl. "Pre-Dialysis Counselling." *Perspectives: The Journal of the Council of Nephrology Social Workers* 3 (1978): 24-31.

Mass, Henry, and Kuyperc, Joseph. *From Thirty to Seventy.* San Francisco: Jossey-Bass Publishers, 1974.

McKevitt, Patricia, and Kappel, Dean. "Psychological Needs and Concerns of the Elderly on Dialysis." *Perspectives: The Journal of the Council of Nephrology Social Workers* 2 (November 1977): 39-50.

Moos, Rudolph. *Coping with Physical Illness.* New York: Plenum Medical Book Co., 1977.

Schaie, K. Warner, and Geuvitz, James, eds. *Adult Development and Aging.* Toronto: Little, Brown & Co., 1982.

Schwartz, William, and Zalba, Serapio, eds. *The Practice of Group Work.* New York: Columbia University Press, 1971.

Shea, Eileen; Gobdan, Donald; Freeman, Richard; and Schreiner, George. "Hemodialysis for Chronic Renal Failure: IV. Psychological Considerations." *Annals of Internal Medicine* 62 (March 1965): 558-563.

Shulman, Lawrence. *Skills for Helping Individuals and Groups, Second Edition,* Itasca, Ill.: F. E. Peacock Publishers, 1984.

Wijsenbuk, H., and Munitz, H. "Group Treatment in a Hemodialysis Center." *Psychiatria, Neurologia, Neurochirurgia* 73 (1970): 213-220.

Zinberg, Norman, and Kaufman, Irving, eds. *Normal Psychology of the Aging Process.* New York: International Universities Press, 1978.

Diana S. Schaefer
Daniella Pozzaglia

CHAPTER 16

Coping with a Nightmare: Hispanic Parents of Children with Cancer

The parent of a child who has a life-threatening disease such as cancer undergoes a uniquely devastating experience. A large body of literature addresses the multiple stresses in coping with childhood cancer and the need for psychosocial interventions.[1] A Spanish-speaking, nonnative Hispanic parent is separated from extended family, friends, and home. Economic difficulties often prevail. These factors exacerbate the crisis, thus furthering the need for social work services. At our cancer center Hispanic families must make major adjustments not only to the illness and its effects on family life, but to life in an unfamiliar urban area. They have limited opportunity to acculturate, since families view the environment as "temporary."[2] Hispanic families who live locally encounter some of the same difficulties in language, discrimination, and economic hardship, as those experienced by island Puerto Ricans, South and Central Americans, or European Spanish-speaking clients. Spanish-speaking people constitute a heterogeneous group. The term "Hispanic" includes many subdivisions of nationality, class, color, beliefs, customs, and race. However, important cultural commonalities do exist. While all families experience a sense of social isolation due to their child's disease and treatment, Hispanics additionally suffer from linguistic and cultural isolation. Hispanic families respond by grouping together informally for translating and support. Spanish-speaking pediatric social workers decided to enhance the observable, supportive cohesiveness of the Hispanic parents by offering a mutual aid group. The effectiveness of the group modality in providing mutual support for people with common concerns has been reported in the literature.[3] We decided that the group modality would be the most efficient and effective approach to minimize the parents' sense of isolation, to allow for the ventilation of feelings, to gain information, and to share problems and solutions.

THE DEVELOPMENTAL TASKS AND NEEDS

There are clearly differentiated roles in traditional Hispanic families which often cause additional stress on the mother with a sick child. In many Hispanic families, the father is the head of the household. He is the provider and protector and is allowed to make decisions without consulting the rest of the family.[4] The young children tend to be indulged while the older children are expected to assist in caring for the younger ones. The mother's role is to care for both the physical and emotional needs of the family. But often her mother or other extended family members assist her in child rearing.

Hispanics traditionally marry young and have many children.[5] Consequently, the couple is not only adjusting to their relationship but to the difficult task of parenthood. Numerous new demands and responsibilities are placed on the young couple. When a child becomes ill, the family is faced with a devastating crisis which puts a tremendous strain on a new marriage. The family members, both nuclear and extended, must be capable of handling the added duties of caring for the sick child, caring for the other children, maintaining employment, and caring for the household. Often, the parents become so busy with their distinct roles and additional duties that they have no time together, causing acute marital discord.

When a child is diagnosed as having cancer, it is typically the mother's responsibility to bring him or her for treatment and to stay during hospitalizations. Often these mothers are young women who may not have enough experience to acquire the necessary ego skills to cope with being the primary caretaker for the sick child.[6] Additionally, she might have several other children to care for. Divorced or separated mothers experience additional stress. The young Hispanic mothers, like all mothers, need to feel competent in their role as caretaker of their sick child in spite of the strange environment and lack of usual emotional supports. This requires a development of new ego skills such as mastering of medical terminology, development of supportive relationships and open communication with the family.[7]

For all families preexisting problems are exacerbated by the onset of a child's illness and treatment.[8] But, Hispanics rely more heavily on the family for support in stressful circumstances.[9] The Hispanic "family" consists of both the nuclear family and extended family including those related by blood and marriage, godparents, and close friends.[10] Each family member is obligated to help the other. Hispanic parents who bring their child with cancer to the United States to obtain specialized medical treatment leave behind this vital support system. Those Hispanics who already reside in the New York metropolitan area may have also left behind their extended family in their country of origin. Still others discover that some extended family members have difficulty coping with the child's disease and consequently stay away. In these circumstances, Hispanic parents (usually mothers) look to friends acquired in the hospital and hospital staff for support.[11]

At our hospital, we have seen Hispanic families cope in ways that are often variant with the Anglo majority. Our experience suggests that Hispanics tend to be more emotive of their feelings. When the child is hospitalized and is critically ill, family members congregate in the child's room crying and praying together. Under these stressful situations many Hispanics react with somatic complaints and *atagues de nervios* (nervous attacks). The person experiences something similar to an epileptic seizure.[12] This intense expression of feeling is sometimes misinterpreted by non-Hispanics as hysterical. Unlike their uninhibited expression of grief and sadness, Hispanics try to control their anger. This, however, is not necessarily the case with white, middle-class families who are more comfortable in openly expressing their anger at the disease and their frustration with the hospital system. The Hispanic family's strong belief in God and His will is used to explain why the child is ill and minimizes their anger. For these reasons, in addition to the language barrier, the preexisting parent support groups were ineffective in meeting the Hispanic parents' special needs.

Parents must also understand and meet their children's emotional needs. Hispanics, even more than non-Hispanics, want to protect their children from discovering their diagnosis. In Latin countries where treatment is less advanced, cancer is perceived as a "death sentence."[13] Our experience suggests, however, that all children seem to know something about their illness without being told; their fantasies about the illness are usually worse than the reality. The wish to withhold disease-related information more often reflects the parents' rather than the child's difficulty in coping with the diagnosis. Children need to understand what they can about their disease according to the limits of their developmental stage.[14]

Siblings who have a hard time adjusting to parental absence also need to feel included and to understand their brother's or sister's illness. Siblings in this situation often feel neglected, scared, and angry. Most of the attention is being paid to their sick brother or sister. They are expected to be understanding of the circumstances and make fewer demands. Often we find siblings are frightened that this could happen to them and may also feel unloved.

AGENCY CONTEXT AND THE GROUP MODALITY

The hospital as an institution impacts on Hispanic families in important environmental ways.[15] Many Hispanic families who come to our institution from Puerto Rico and other Latin American nations lived in rural areas. Here, they are confronted with adjusting not only to urban life, but to a complex health-care system. The city-dwelling Hispanic families experience much stress, too, in addition to the economic pressure of paying for their child's medical expenses without relief from third-party insurance or government benefits.

In a primarily white, Anglo health-care facility, these families are confronted with culture shock.[16] Misunderstandings caused by inadequate communication are common. Non-Spanish-speaking staff members, unable to meet the Hispanic patient's needs, often become frustrated and angry.[17] Despite communication difficulties, Hispanic families characteristically need to trust hospital staff as individuals. This *"confianza"* or trust must be established over time. Hispanics prefer to relate to staff who are flexible in their approach and who are able to minimize the impact of the impersonal quality of a large institution.[18] This tendency is called *"personalismo"* and comes from their being accustomed to personalized health care delivery in their countries.[19] *Confianza* is difficult to achieve in an American teaching hospital where much of the medical staff rotates. Hispanics use institutions as a last resort to solve their problems, probably due to this discomfort and mistrust.[20]

Hispanic families tend to see submissiveness, passivity, and deferring to others as "proper" behavior toward authority.[21] We find that in a large hospital complex aggressive behavior among the parents is reinforced with attention from staff, but Hispanic families value respect and dignity. However, when *confianza* is established with the hospital staff, the families begin to rely and depend upon individuals for assistance in caring for their sick child, which helps them adapt and cope.

Another important aspect of adjusting to the hospital and the child's disease is understanding the treatment of the illness. While Hispanic families place more emphasis on trust than medical terminology, informational pamphlets and consent forms in Spanish are essential to their understanding.[22] A consistent repetition of information from professionals in the primary language strengthens understanding. Reading is often not sufficient. Some family members may not be able to read, and others may need help in integrating the information they receive.[23] Information about childhood cancer and its treatment can help the Hispanic family modify its pessimistic outlook on the outcome of treatment and thereby maintain realistic hope. In a group setting this educational component can facilitate informational exchange for a greater number of parents.

The hospital's physical environment also affects the family's adaptation to the institution.[24] Hispanic parents describe the "blinding whiteness" of the treatments rooms where their children receive medical procedures (such as bone marrow aspirations and spinal taps). Additionally, professional hospital staff (doctors, nurse practitioners, and social workers) wear white lab coats which immediately differentiate them from the family members who may be already mistrustful of "professionals" due to past experiences in public agencies. Young children begin to associate the white coats with pain and intrusion and cry in anticipation when they see someone wearing one. Of course, these factors also affect non-Hispanic families, but they may be more accustomed to them. The group setting allows parents to share their feelings regarding the physical environment and discuss previous encounters with professionals in order to separate past and present and to form better relationships with staff.

A family's traditional coping mechanisms may prove ineffective in the face of this crisis or even undermine a family's adjustment to the illness. For this reason, parents need assistance to explore how they have coped in past crises and to learn new coping methods. The parents' response to guilt and anger and the ability to intellectualize and maintain hope determines its adaptation to the situation.[25] A safe, nonthreatening atmosphere for family members to learn and attempt new behaviors is facilitated in a group comprised of parents of oncology patients.[26] The literature supports the importance of groups in helping parents cope with their children's life-threatening disease.[27] Social work staff observed that Hispanic parents shared concerns and problems in their own language in the clinic, exchanging solutions as well as some misconceptions. In this situation, their identification with each other limits their feeling of isolation.

The Hispanic parents' group was planned with the following goals: (1) to encourage parents to share experiences, (2) to help parents learn ways of coping with the stresses of having a child with cancer, and (3) to educate parents regarding the care of their child. It enhances communication with staff and increases mutual trust, provides information regarding the children's disease, and helps in fostering adaptive coping patterns in a stressful situation, within the context of their own cultural milieu.

Our Hispanic parents' group is provided weekly for parents as well as extended family members. It is conducted in Spanish. The group size varies from three to eight participants. Sessions last one hour and take place in a treatment room in the Pediatric Day Hospital.

Group members are recruited by the social workers fifteen minutes before the start of the session. Social workers canvass the clinic waiting area and inpatient floor and personally invite parents who are recognized from the caseload of the center's Spanish-speaking social worker. Signs written in Spanish announce meeting time and place. The signs are posted in the waiting area.

Parents are encouraged to discuss their child's illness and share how each child was diagnosed as having cancer. This gives the members an emotional and information basis from which the group develops. As they move on to discussing the coping tasks of dealing with this life crisis, the worker must always integrate the interpersonal processes and group dynamics, as well as the cultural components. Hispanic parents have special needs and circumstances and different customs depending on their backgrounds. However, there are many commonalities. The social worker must encourage the identification of mutual concerns by the group while helping members with their individual developmental tasks.[28] Developing a therapeutic relationship with the group members is vital to providing the ongoing individual assistance to these families. It also provides them with a personal link to the hospital system.

GROUP THEMES

Continuity among participants varies greatly. The content of the group meeting varies accordingly, based on the participant's particular needs at that time. Flexibility is paramount. But even with the fluctuation of members, certain common themes emerge. These can be categorized into four major areas: (1) environmental concerns, (2) family issues, (3) illness and treatment concerns, and (4) death and dying.

Environmental Concerns

Environmental or practical concerns are the issues most frequently brought up by the members in the group discussion. While these are certainly legitimate problems, they are also less threatening issues to discuss. They can, therefore, be raised by the worker early in the session. A discussion on practical concerns (such as transportation, housing, finances, or the language barrier) can elicit strong emotional content on issues more difficult to raise directly. Establishing a temporary home close to the hospital is terribly difficult and stressful. Housing costs are much greater than in Hispanic countries, and suitable housing is not readily available. Many Hispanic families use a temporary residence for children with cancer and their families. Others try to sublet apartments close to the hospital. Some families move in together to share support and costs. The following group excerpt exemplifies these points:

Mrs. Jimenez: Oh, you're from Chile, so where are you living now?
Mr. Pena: In a hotel.
Mrs. Jimenez: (To Mr. P.) You live in a hotel and not an apartment?
Mr. Pena: Yes, because all of the apartments are either very far away from the hospital or if they're close, they're too expensive. So, we are living on 32nd Street, but it is still far and taxis are expensive.
Mrs. Martinez: (To Mr. P.) You can catch a bus right out front.
Mr. Pena: No, because of Gloria's disease, she could get an infection being around so many other people on the bus with her low white blood cell count.
Social Worker: How have others of you managed to find housing with the high cost of rents around here?
Mrs. Martinez: I finally gave up looking for a place near the hospital. I have cousins in Queens who helped us get an apartment there.

Mr. Pena: Yes, but Queens is very far away. I wouldn't know what to do in an emergency if Gloria needed to get to the hospital quickly.

Mrs. Jimenez: You can always get a cab to rush you in.

Mr. Pena: Then the cab fare would even be *more* expensive!

Social Worker: There are agencies to assist in the cost of transportation to the hospital, but there is no assistance for foreign families to pay rent, and given your rent is high now, maybe living farther away but getting help with transportation could solve the problem. What do you think?

Mr. Pena: Can you give me the information about the agency?

Social Worker: For those of you who haven't heard about it . . . will give grants to families for transportation or home care costs.

In this session, the social worker elicited suggestions regarding the common problem of housing for relocating families. As exemplified here, families who arc unfamiliar with the New York metropolitan area are often frightened and reluctant to move out of Manhattan or even the costly surrounding area of the hospital for fear that in an emergency they won't be able to get their child to the hospital in time. The social worker provided information on an agency which assists with the transportation costs to help Mr. Pena and the group.

Financial concerns are important to many Hispanic families. Those who are not American citizens often have limited resources to cover their children's medical treatment. The burden of payment can be staggering for families ineligible for assistance. Their anger over the financial strain often is ventilated in the sessions.

Language is cited as a barrier at most meetings. It emerges as a major concern because Hispanics are constantly frustrated at the difficulty in communicating. For some the primary doctor speaks Spanish, but other staff have limited command of the language. Often, the young patient is in school and has more knowledge of English than the parents. Children are expected to help with translating daily scheduling, procedures, and medical terminology. Caution must be exercised in using the child as an interpreter, given the inappropriateness of some topics and the age of the child.[29]

The language barrier also inhibits socializing with the urban community around the hospital and thereby increases the sense of isolation. Even though there are a large number of Hispanics in the New York area, English is the primary language used. New York can be an overwhelming environment in contrast with small towns in other countries. The pace and speed are different. Parents remark that they rarely venture from their known area of the hospital and apartment. In the following group discussion two mothers, Mrs. Garcia and Mrs. Ramos, and Pat, an older sister of a patient, discuss their frustration regarding language and communication with their doctors.

Mrs. Garcia: My biggest problem is the language. I think if I spoke English, it would be so much easier.

Mrs. Ramos: I tried taking an English course at the high school at night, but now that Maria is sick, I just don't have the time or the energy, and I'm afraid to go out at night.

Pat: I've been trying to get my sister to take a class with me, but she usually feels too sick from chemotherapy, but I still think it would help her spirits and help us talk with Dr. R. It's hard to get a chance to ask questions because he's so busy, and then to have to find a translator—so sometimes we just never ask.

Mrs. Ramos: Yeah, and really, you never know if you're getting the entire answer, and the question just can't be put the way I would.

Mrs. Garcia: The only way I can tell what is being said is by the look on the doctor's face.

Social Worker: It must be awful not to understand exactly what is being said or be able to ask questions directly.

Pat: It is, but after a while you *do* find a way to get your point across.

Social Worker: What suggestions would you give the group on how best to communicate with your doctor?

Pat: Well, we sometimes try to bring a friend who speaks English with us to translate or we look for you or Maria to help.

Mrs. Garcia: I really don't know anyone I could bring with me who could translate, and sometimes I can't find anyone here who could do it.

Social Worker: I can see this is a real problem. What could you say or do to be assured someone could be with you when you see the doctor?

Mrs. Garcia: I don't know.

Social Worker: Mrs. Ramos, you've always seemed to be able to get around this communication problem. Any ideas?

Mrs. Ramos: Actually, the only way I've been able to talk to Joanne's doctor who is always *so* busy in the clinic is to set up an appointment with him in his office. It's easier that way to get someone to come with me to translate.

Social Worker: Mrs. G., what do you think?

Mrs. Garcia: Yeah, but could you help me set up the appointment?

Social Worker: Sure, I'd be glad to.

In this discussion, the worker first reacts to the group members' feelings of helplessness and frustration regarding the language barrier and subsequently turns general ideas to specific examples or suggestions on how they go about minimizing the language restraint.

Family Issues

Group members are encouraged to discuss the impact the illness has on their family, including the siblings and the marital relationship. Feelings of frustration and guilt often arise because parents are faced with very real, stressful situations and each may cope differently. Mothers complain of separation from their other children. They express sadness that others are caring for the patient's siblings or that they cannot divide their attention adequately among all their children.

When most of the parents' energy goes into caring for the patient and less is available to the other children, sibling rivalry is intensified. Brothers and sisters feel neglected because all the attention is paid to the sick one. Parents are emotionally drained because of hospital treatments for the sick child. They have limited time and energy to give the siblings.

Since the group is primarily comprised of mothers, workers attempt to elicit suggestions of family management to mitigate the stresses. They suggest activities that permit family members to communicate feelings and information about the illness and the hospital at age-appropriate levels. Siblings may demonstrate acting-out behavior that is difficult for parents to control. Such issues are raised in the group, and families with more experience offer suggestions to cope with the siblings' behavior. In the following discussion, Mrs. Gutierrez is able to help Mr. and Mrs. Martinez with their other children.

Mrs. Gutierrez: Do you have any other children?

Mrs. Martinez: Yes, two boys, five and nine.

Mrs. Gutierrez: How are they doing?

Mr. Martinez: Well, more or less O.K.

Social Worker: What do you mean?

Mr. Martinez: They really are too young to understand what is going on. The five-year-old doesn't seem bothered, but the nine-year-old is complaining of headaches and not going to school, which has us very worried because that is how we discovered Jaime's brain tumor.

Mrs. Gutierrez: How old is Jaime?

Mr. Martinez: He's eight. They share a room together and go to the same school.

Mrs. Martinez: They are very close.

Mrs. Gutierrez: You know, my younger one complained of being sick when Felix was in the hospital, and what she really wanted was attention because she saw how much attention and presents he got. It's hard when you have to be at the hospital all the time and you're so worried about your sick child.

Social Worker: So what did you decide to do?

Mrs. Gutierrez: I explained to her what was wrong with her brother and told her she wouldn't catch it and if it was her instead of him, she'd get just as many presents. (To Mr. M.) If I were you, I'd tell your children. They need to know, too.

Mr. Martinez: But they're too young to understand about cancer, and I'm afraid it will scare them more to know.

Social Worker: Well, like Mrs. Gutierrez said, the other children are already scared because they know things have changed and they need to understand why. It's our experience too that siblings benefit from the reassurance that everything possible is being done to help the patient, that they will not get sick, and that you still love them.

In this discussion, Mr. and Mrs. Martinez have identified a reactive distress which their two other children were experiencing. However, they, like many other parents, were reluctant to tell their children about their son's tumor. Mrs. Gutierrez is able to explain the reaction her younger child experienced and informed them on how she handled the jealousy and worry her other child had. A helpful suggestion from another parent is more often heard by parents than one from a professional. In this case, though, the worker restated what was said by Mrs. Gutierrez and added her experience from working with other families in this situation to reinforce it.

Marriages are often strained with the stress of dealing with the disease and treatment of the sick child. The father must continue working while the mother is the one caring for the sick child. When the child is hospitalized, they might alternate their night stay with the child and rarely see one another. For some Hispanic families, the father must return to their home country to work and continue to support the family while the mother stays in New York with the child. The treatment can cause them to be separated for a year or longer, which may have a devastating effect on the marriage. Even for Hispanic families living in New York the strain is great. The family equilibrium and normal roles change, and both parents may respond differently to the stress. Traditional Hispanic sex roles remain relatively intact. The father is still usually the provider and protector of his family while the mother's role is to be the nurturing caretaker. With the added dimension of having a child with cancer, mothers often complain that their husbands are not supportive to them or are unwilling to be more involved with the child. However, we have discovered that often the wives just have not communicated the need adequately. Here is an example of a discussion around the issue of marital conflict:

Mrs. Ramirez: We had to move here from Puerto Rico to get treatment for Joanne. My husband gave up his job as a police officer and we've been living with family since we came.

Social Worker: That must be very hard for you.

Mrs. Sanchez: I didn't know your husband was here too. I've never seen him.

Mrs. Ramirez: Oh, I'll introduce you when he comes. He is at home with our other two boys. You know, it is really hard for him staying home with the children when he was used to working, but I'm afraid I don't have much sympathy when I've had to stay two months in the hospital day after day with Joanne and I'm so tired!

Mrs. Torrez: Why don't you take a break? Go home and see your boys and let him come and stay.

Mrs. Ramirez: He won't. He won't come and stay anymore. I even left one afternoon, which I never do, to go home and see the boys and cook. He got mad because I had left Joanne alone! I can't win.

Social Worker: Have you and he discussed how you're feeling and that you need his help?

Mrs. Ramirez: I've tried telling him, but nothing has changed.

Mrs. Garcia: You know how men are. Not working must have hit him hard, and none of them want to care for the kids.

Mrs. Ramirez: Yes, but I have seen some fathers here. Even if he'd just come for the weekend, I'd have a chance to get out.

Social Worker: Let's find a way you can let him know you understand his circumstances and feelings but also get your own needs across. Maybe he is frightened to be here.

Mrs. Ramirez: Yes, I think so. Because the last time he did stay, she had a seizure, and he just didn't know what to do.

Mrs. Torrez: They have so much more trouble handling those situations.

Mrs. Sanchez: You know, the social worker has helped get a volunteer to stay with Tanya so I could leave. Why don't you do that?

Social Worker: Good idea. What do you think, Mrs. Ramirez?

Mrs. Ramirez: Thank you, I would just like to see my husband, Jorge, and talk to him.

Mrs. Garcia: Then, maybe you could ask him to come in every other weekend to give you a rest.

Mrs. Ramirez: I'll try it.

Social Worker: Then the two of you could meet with me to discuss this problem further.

In the beginning phase of this discussion the worker displays an understanding of Mrs. Ramirez's situation, which is then discussed by the other group members. Suggestions are made about what she can do to get a break from the hospi-

tal, but these do not address the underlying problem of marital stress. The social worker then gets the group to work on the problem and come up with ideas. This allows the group to focus and conclude with more helpful suggestions.

Illness and Treatment Concerns

Hispanic parents, like all parents, experience feelings of fear, anger, helplessness, guilt, and sadness when their children are diagnosed as having cancer. They are concerned about caring for the sick child and issues of death and dying. They use their religious beliefs to cope. Hispanics often express feelings of guilt and responsibility in considering the origin of the disease. The following excerpt from a group discussion illustrates this point. The three group members have just finished discussing each of their children's medical situations:

Mrs. Gomez: Children get this leukemia as early as four months old. I knew one. And yet they say it is not hereditary. I knew another child who was born with this disease and my own son got it, and he's only one year old.

Social Worker: (To the group) Do you wonder how your children got sick?

Mrs. Martinez: Yes, they [doctors] told me it isn't the food I gave her or anything that happened during the pregnancy like I thought.

Mrs. Gomez: I also thought that.

Social Worker: I realize it is so hard to know why. In fact, because there is no explanation, many parents feel they may be responsible.

Mr. Perez: That's exactly how I felt. I kept wondering about all the times before when she didn't feel well and I thought it was a cold or something like that. I never expected this, so I waited before we went to a doctor and then it took a month before he took a blood test and diagnosed it. I felt terrible. Why didn't we go sooner?

Mrs. Gomez: I asked if it was the food I gave him or something he ate. I felt so guilty, but the doctor told me I was not to blame—it wasn't the food. I guess it's destiny. If God decides to take Jose, then it's His will.

Social Worker: You hope he will live, but you are afraid he could die.

Mrs. Gomez: Yes, it happened when he was so young. He should have so much more of life to live. But my faith in God helps me believe he will get better.

The other parents supported Mr. Perez and shared their same feelings of responsibility. They finally came to the conclusion that it isn't their fault but something which is "God's will." The leader focused on their explicit feelings of self-blame, addressed them directly, and the group responded by seeking an answer.

In Hispanic families religion plays a major role in life. Hispanics tend to view the world in a fatalistic way, since life is controlled by God, and, therefore, whatever happens in life is destined.[30] This outlook can lessen a parent's feeling of guilt and anger but can also serve to make them more passive regarding treatment. If the outcome is predestined, putting the child through more pain is futile.

Their different belief systems are reflected in their views on life, illness, and death.[31] While Catholicism still dominates as the major religion in Puerto Rico, Protestant and Pentecostal groups are growing in number.[32] But even their Catholicism differs in beliefs and practices from those in North America. As with the health-care system, they tend to distrust the church as an institution and personalize their relationship with God. This is done through developing special relationships with saints who become their connection to God.[33]

Three mothers, one with a two-year-old newly diagnosed son with acute mylogenous leukemia, and two more ex-perienced mothers came to the group meeting. Mrs. Munoz was refusing to allow the surgeons to put in a broviac catheter or central line which would relieve her son from being stuck for IVs for his chemotherapy. The following discussion took place:

Mrs. Munoz: (Said tearfully) . . . and I was against the idea [of the catheter] from the moment Dr. S. explained it. How can I allow my son to go through more pain when I know he's going to die anyway?

Mrs. Lopez: You know something? I felt the same way when Dr. A. wanted to put a broviac in Maria. I thought, "What's the use if she's just going to die? Better to leave her alone." But I finally agreed, and she had her chemo without having to get stuck much, and I've had her well for six months. Now she's not doing as well, but it's given her some time with me.

Mrs. Ramirez: I look at it this way: why would God give man medicine if it wasn't for us to use and improve our lives? Whatever is going to happen to Joanne is in God's hands, but I believe He shows the doctors the way.

Mrs. Lopez: Maria really prefers the catheter and she knows which is best because she's been sick one and a half years. Why don't you come to my room after we're finished and I'll show you Maria's broviac.

Social Worker: (To Mrs. L.) That's a wonderful idea. What do you think, Mrs. Munoz?

Mrs. Munoz: Yes, I'd like to see what it looks like. At least then I'll understand what they're talking about. Thank you.

In this discussion the experienced mothers became an important resource for Mrs. Munoz in coping with a new procedure such as the broviac. They also were able to minimize her fatalistic pessimism and instill hope.

In addition to their belief and worship of saints, many Hispanics also believe in spirits and *"espiritualismo."* Spiritualism is the belief that dead spirits can communicate with the living and make their presence known through a medium or "esperitista."[34] Spirits can prevent or cause both physical and mental illness and influence behavior. This belief also can provide an explanation for misfortune, in this case, the child's illness. Health professionals must support the belief in faith healers along with conventional treatment to demonstrate acceptance of the Hispanic family's faith.

In the same session described above, Mrs. Martinez states her strong religious affiliation and belief in spirits.

Mrs. Martinez: When I heard Jose has leukemia, I prayed to God and called to Jesus over and over again until I felt relieved. I fasted for five days to prove that I really wanted my son to live and meant it.

Mrs. Lopez: But didn't you get sick? I could never do that. I tried once.

Mrs. Martinez: Yes, they had to start an IV on me because I fainted, but that was a sign that my son would be saved.

While this behavior would seem extreme, inappropriate, and even magical to non-Hispanics, in the group it was accepted as Mrs. Martinez's way of being active in a situation where she felt helpless and overwhelmed.

Another common group theme is how to care for the sick child. Hispanic families tend to be indulgent of their young children, especially when the child becomes critically ill.[35] Fewer limits are set, which can hamper the child's adjustment and cause numerous problems for the hospital staff caring for the child as well as for the family. Children need limits on their behavior to feel they are protected and secure. Children who learn they can manipulate and get attention will continue to do so at home as well as in the hospital.[36] However, respect for authority is an extremely important value for Hispanic children. Therefore, when behavior is perceived as disrespectful, children are reprimanded. The following excerpt illustrates a typical discussion about discipline and the need for respect. Mrs. Ramos, Mrs. Vasquez, and Pat, an older sibling, discuss discipline.

Mrs. Ramos: My son is really getting out of hand. He is lashing out at his brothers and sisters and constantly in fights at school. I honestly don't know what to do anymore!

Social Worker: Have others of you had a similar problem with your children and, if so, how did you handle it?

Mrs. Vasquez: Juan was always hitting my younger boy, and I finally had to get my husband to punish him by hitting him. He knows how to be respectful, but just seemed to forget.

Mrs. Ramos: I know it would be different if he had a father around. He would never be like this then.

Social Worker: Why do you think he might be doing this?

Pat: Even though my sister is older, I know she gets angry a lot, and I think she has a right, given all she's gone through. But sometimes I think she gets mad because she can't do the things I can do because she's sick and I'm well. Maybe your son feels the same way.

Mrs. Ramos: Well, that might be part of it, but I think he is also angry at me like he thinks it's my fault he got sick.

Social Worker: Children often expect that their parents can protect them, and when something like this happens, it's the parents that often get blamed.

Mrs. Vasquez: Same with mine, yes. I finally told my son that I know all this was hard for him, but it was to make him well. It wasn't mine or his father's fault. He finally settled down, but it's difficult when his grandmother gives in to his every whim.

The social worker in this session engages the group to share their experiences in handling disciplinary problems with their well children and explore the reasons why they might be acting out. Good suggestions are made on how the siblings are reacting and what a parent can do to mitigate their reaction in an understanding way.

Death and Dying

Even though there are significant medical advances and over half of the children diagnosed with cancer will survive the illness, parents know death is a possibility.[37] Hispanic parents who view life in a fatalistic way seem even less optimistic than other parents in the beginning phases of treatment regarding treatment outcomes. Friedrich and Copeland compared issues raised in both a Spanish-speaking and an English-speaking parents' group.[38] They found that the Spanish-speaking group spent more time discussing death, either related to their own children or another child's death in the hospital, than the English-speaking group, which was more hesitant in discussing death. The social workers leading parents' groups at our hospital have also found this to be true.

The following segment of a group session with Mr. Pena, Mrs. Jimenez, and Mrs. Martinez reveals their preoccupation with death.

Mrs. Jimenez: How long has Gloria been sick?

Mr. Pena: One and a half years, and Jose?

Mrs. Jimenez: (Frantically) Four months. First he was in one hospital; then another. He got all kinds of medicines. Some worked for awhile and others didn't help at all. When his leukemia relapsed, we were sent here because they have more medicines and better ones. But I was sure he would die.

Social Worker: That's a nightmare. And how was it with Gloria?

Mr. Pena: She received treatment, but the disease came back in the bone marrow and

they could do practically nothing. They were good doctors in Chile, but they just didn't have the resources.

Social Worker: (To Mr. Pena) How sad that was for you when you learned it came back and there was nothing they could do. How did you react?

Mr. Pena: I felt helpless because with this disease they cannot do much in my country. My wife wanted to stay, but I insisted we come here. At least there is some hope.

Mrs. Martinez: It is the same in Santo Domingo because over there nearly everyone dies who has this disease. So many come here for a cure like us. I know Jose is getting the best treatment. His doctor is understanding and such a good person. It's in God's hands whether Jose will live or die.

In this discussion, they share many painful and sad feelings and provide mutual support with guidance from the group leader. They need to talk about this common fear and also benefit by discussions around other children's deaths and how other parents have managed. These discussions help to reassure them that they, too, will be able to handle their child's death if it should happen.

CONCLUSION

Hispanic families faced with the devastating life crisis of a child diagnosed with cancer experience great stress. This is compounded by their language and cultural differences, adaptation to a strange new environment, disruption of normal family roles, and often financial difficulties. We as social work professionals recognize the opportunity this crisis provides for significant change and growth for the family and its individual members. Additionally, it provides an opportunity for connection with others in similar circumstances and mutual aid among them to develop solutions to the different problems of estrangement in the hospital system, family difficulties, and coping with illness, treatment, and death.

The Hispanic parents' group is an effective approach to minimize feelings of isolation, and provides a wide range of psychosocial interventions and needed medical information. It is available to all Spanish-speaking parents and extended family members on a weekly basis with the members responsible for the agenda.

The need for such a group and its effectiveness has been demonstrated by the number of parents who have participated in the program and found it to be a helpful addition to the already existing social work support systems. Almost all Hispanic family members have participated in this program. Our goal is to have all Hispanic parents participate since the group effectively enhances communication and coping.

NOTES

1. See, for example, Margaret Adams, "Helping the Parents of Children with Malignancy," *The Journal of Pediatrics* 93 (1978): 734-738; Judith Ross, "Coping with Childhood Cancer: Group Intervention—An Aid to Parents," *Social Work in Health Care* 4 (1979): 347-359; John J. Spinetta, "Adjustment and Adaptation in Children with Cancer: A Three-Year Study," in *Living with Childhood Cancer,* ed. John J. Spinetta and Patricia Deasy Spinetta (St. Louis, Mo.: C. V. Mosby Co., 1981), pp. 5-17; Diana S. Schaefer, "Issues Related to Intervention with Hispanic Families in a Pediatric Cancer Setting," *Journal of Psychosocial Oncology* (1983): 39-46.

2. Judith Landau, "Therapy with Families in Cultural Transition," *Ethnicity and Family Therapy,* ed. Monica McGoldrick et al. (New York: Guilford Press, 1982), pp. 12-27.

3. As discussed in Helen Northern, *Social Work with Groups* (New York: Columbia University Press, 1969); William Schwartz and Serapio R. Zalba, eds., *The Practice of Group Work* (New York: Columbia University, 1971).

4. See, for example, M. D. Abad, J. Ramos, and E. Boyce, "A Model for Delivery of Mental Health Services to Spanish Speaking Minorities," *American Journal of Orthopsychology* 44 (1974): 584-595; Nyudia Garcia-Preto, "Puerto Rican Families," *Ethnicity and Family Therapy,* ed. Monica McGoldrick et al. (New York: Guilford Press, 1982): 164-185.

5. Garcia-Preto, "Puerto Rican Families."
6. F. A. Guerra, "Hispanic Child Health Issues," *Child Today* 9 (1980): 19-22.
7. Alex Gitterman and Carel B. Germain, "Social Work Practice: A Life Model," *Social Service Review* 50 (1976): 601-610.
8. See Grace H. Christ and Margaret Adams, "Therapeutic Interventions at Psychosocial Crisis Points in the Treatment of Childhood Cancer," in *Psychosocial Oncology in Pediatrics,* ed. A. Christ and K. Flomenhaft (New York: Plenum, 1983), pp. 85-96; Ross, "Coping with Childhood Cancer," pp. 347-359.
9. Garcia-Preto, "Puerto Rican Families," pp. 164-185.
10. Ibid.
11. Spinetta, "Adjustment and Adaptation," pp. 5-17.
12. Garcia-Preto, "Puerto Rican Families," pp. 164-185.
13. Schaefer, "Issues Related to Intervention," pp. 39-46.
14. Adams, "Helping the Parents," pp. 734-738.
15. Sylvia Guendelman, "Developing Responsiveness to the Health Needs of Hispanic Children and Families," *Social Work in Health Care* 8 (1983): 1-15.
16. Thomas C. Timmereck and Lorum H. Strattan, "The Health Opinion Survey Translated into Spanish as a Measure of Stress for Hispanic Cultures," *Journal of Psychiatric Nursing* 19:1 (1981): 9-13.

17. See, for example, Elaine J. Cooper, and Margarita Hernandez Centro, "Group and the Hispanic Prenatal Patient," *American Journal of Orthopsychology* 4 (1977): 689-700; Schaefer, "Issues Related to Intervention," pp. 39-46.

18. Abad, Ramos, and Boyce, "A Model for Delivery," pp. 584-595; Cooper and Centro, "Group and the Hispanic Prenatal Patient," pp. 689-700.

19. Guendelman, "Developing Responsiveness," pp. 1-15.

20. Sonia Badillo Ghali, "Cultural Sensitivity and the Puerto Rican Client," *Social Casework* 58 (1977): 459-468.

21. Ibid.

22. Guendelman, "Developing Responsiveness," pp. 1-15.

23. Schaefer, "Issues Related to Intervention," pp. 39-46.

24. Gitterman and Germain, "Social Work Practice," pp. 601-610.

25. Adams, "Helping the Parents," pp. 734-738.

26. Arnold Stolberg and Joseph Cunningham, "Support Groups for Parents of Leukemic Children: Evaluation of Current Programs and Enumeration of Participants' Emotional Needs," in *The Child with Cancer—Clinical Approaches to Psychosocial Care—Research in Psychosocial Aspects,* ed. Jerome Schulman and Mary Jo Kupst (Springfield, Ill.: Charles C Thomas, Publisher, 1980), pp. 58-75.

27. See, for example, ibid.; Adams, "Helping the Parents," pp. 734-738; Ross, "Coping with Childhood Cancer," pp. 347-359.

28. Gitterman and Germain, "Social Work Practice," pp. 601-610; P. M. Levenson, B. J. Pfefferbaum, D. R. Copeland, and Y. Silberberg, "Informational Preferences of Cancer Patients Ages 11-20 Years," *Journal of Adolescent Health Care* 3 (1982): 9-13.

29. Schaefer, "Issues Related to Intervention," pp. 39-47.

30. See Spinetta, "Adjustment and Adaptation," pp. 5-17; E. Cohen, "Principles of Preventive Mental Health and Health Programs for Ethnic Minority Populations: The Acculturation of Puerto Ricans to the U.S.,"
American Journal of Psychiatry 928 (1972): 1529-1533.

31. Abad, Ramos, and Boyce, "A Model for Delivery," pp. 584-595.

32. Garcia-Preto, "Puerto Rican Families," pp. 164-185.

33. Ibid.

34. Melvin Delgado, "Puerto Rican Spiritualism and the Social Work Profession," *Social Casework* 58 (1977): 451-458.

35. Schaefer, "Issues Related to Intervention," pp. 39-46.

36. Adams, "Helping the Parents," pp. 734-738.

37. Ibid.

38. William Friedrich and Donna Copeland, "Children's Health Care: Brief Report—Cultural Differences in Groups of Children with Cancer: English and Spanish-Speaking," *Journal of Association for Care of Children's Health* 11 (1982): 21.

BIBLIOGRAPHY

Abad, M.D.; Ramos, J.; and E. Boyce. "A Model for Delivery of Mental Health Services to Spanish Speaking Minorities." *American Journal of Orthopsychology* 44 (1974): 584-595.

Adams, Margaret. "Helping the Parents of Children with Malignancy." *The Journal of Pediatrics* 93 (1978): 734-738.

Christ, Grace H., and Margaret Adams. "Therapeutic Interventions at Psychosocial Crisis Points in the Treatment of Childhood Cancer." In *Psychosocial Oncology in Pediatrics.* Edited by A. Christ and K. Flomenhaft. New York: Plenum, 1983, pp. 85-96.

Cohen, E. "Principles of Preventive Mental Health and Health Programs for Ethnic Minority Populations: The Acculturation of Puerto Ricans to the U.S." *American Journal of Psychiatry* 928 (1972): 1529-1533.

Cooper, Elaine J., and Margarita Hernandez Centro. "Group and the Hispanic Prenatal Patient." *American Journal of Orthopsychology* 4 (1977): 689-700.

Delgado, Melvin. "Puerto Rican Spiritualism and the Social Work Profession." *Social Casework* 58 (1977): 451-458.

Friedrich, William, and Donna Copeland. "Children's Health Care: Brief Report—Cultural Differences in Groups of Children with Cancer: English and Spanish-Speaking." *Journal of Association for Care of Children's Health* 11 (1982): 21.

Garcia-Preto, Nyudia. "Puerto Rican Families." *Ethnicity and Family Therapy,* edited by Monica McGoldrick et al. New York: Guilford Press, 1982, pp. 164-185.

Ghali, Sonia Badillo. "Cultural Sensitivity and the Puerto Rican Client." *Social Casework* 58 (1977): 459-468.

Gitterman, Alex, and Carel B. Germain. "Social Work Practice: A Life Model." *Social Service Review* 50 (1976): 601-610.

Guendelman, Sylvia. "Developing Responsiveness to the Health Needs of Hispanic Children and Families." *Social Work in Health Care* 8 (1983): 1-15.

Guerra, F. A. "Hispanic Child Health Issues." *Child Today* 9 (1980): 19-22.

Hartford, Margaret. *Groups in Social Work.* New York: Columbia University Press, 1972.

Johnson, Edith M., and Doretta E. Stark. "A Group Program for Cancer Patients and Their Family Members in an Acute Care Teaching Hospital." *Social Work in Health Care* 5 (1980): 335-349.

Landau, Judith. "Therapy with Families in Cultural Transition." In *Ethnicity and Family Therapy.* Edited by Monica McGoldrick et al. New York: Guilford Press, 1982, pp. 12-27.

Northern, Helen. *Social Work with Groups.* New York: Columbia University Press, 1969.

Ross, Judith. "Coping with Childhood Cancer: Group Intervention—An Aid to Parents." *Social Work in Health Care* 4 (1979): 347-359.

Schaefer, Diana S. "Issues Related to Intervention with Hispanic Families in a Pediatric Cancer Setting." *Journal of Psychosocial Oncology* 1 (1983): 39-46.

Schwartz, William, and Serapio R. Zalba, eds. *The Practice of Group Work.* New York: Columbia University Press, 1971.

Spinetta, John J. "Adjustment and Adaptation in Children with Cancer: A Three Year Study." In *Living with Childhood Cancer.* Edited by John J. Spinetta and Patricia Deasy Spinetta. St. Louis, Mo.: The C. V. Mosby Co., 1981, pp. 7-15.

Stolberg, Arnold, and Joseph Cunningham. "Support Groups for Parents of Leukemic Children: Evaluation of Current Programs and Enumeration of Praticipants' Emotional Needs." In *The Child with Cancer—Clinical Approaches to Psychosocial Care —Research in Psychosocial Aspects.* Edited by Jerome Schulman and Mary Jo Kupst. Springfield, Ill.: Charles C Thomas, Publisher, 1980, pp. 58-75.

Part Five
Mutual Aid and the Elderly

Alberta Orr

CHAPTER 17

Dealing with the Death of a Group Member: Visually Impaired Elderly in the Community

For the 95 percent of the population over the age of sixty-five in this country who live independently or semi-independently in the community, a community-based facility such as a local senior center can serve as a primary resource. Attending a senior center is synonymous with group involvement, whether the older person actively participates in various group activities or programs, or merely attends the center for a hot meal in a congregate setting. Both formally and informally, older people are involved in mutual aid in the senior center. Many may not even perceive their involvement as such, nor may the professionals who plan and implement the service think of it as mutual aid, but indeed it is. The informal groups which naturally form around an activity or topic of mutual interest (these can range from a crafts program to a lobbying effort) informally serve as mutual aid for the members of the group.

In New York City, senior centers are plentiful. Those elderly people who attend represent an extremely diverse group, ranging from the newly retired professional to the physically and/or mentally frail older person from early sixties to the late nineties. All in one way or another seek to find a network of peers with whom they can share identified common ground. Those who attend do so for a broad range of reasons: to find companionship, to use time productively and satisfactorily, to make a contribution, to discover new areas of interest or skills, or to rediscover and maximize old ones. In some centers, groups are organized for the purpose of helping members deal with a situation of stress or concern. The frequently offered widows and widowers group is organized as a network to enable these older people who have lost their spouses to share their experiences and common life crises and to develop strategies for coping with loss. The English-as-a-second language (ESL) class not only serves to teach the language, but establishes a mutual aid network for those who speak another primary language and share a common culture. The men's group represents another mutual aid support system frequently organized in centers by men who seek the companionship of other males, since they are routinely outnumbered by older women in the center ten to one.

The mutual aid group which is the focus of this chapter is comprised of visually impaired senior citizens. Originally, the mutual aid group was formed to provide older people with a forum in which to address the problems and concerns imposed by recent vision loss. While the group was formed to help these older people share their frustrations and fears around this particular loss, the group's process of mutual aid expanded to include more generalized concerns encompassing a broad range of losses. Members have used the group as a place to bring and share their feelings related to the loss of a spouse or significant other, or the loss of physical functioning based on a health problem.

The focus of the group meeting presented here deals with the death of a group member and the group's struggle to express their feelings about this loss, to reminisce about previous traumatic losses, and to consider and verbalize their fears related to their own impending death. The function, tasks, and skills of the social worker in enabling the group as a whole, as well as individual group members, to express their feelings openly are presented, followed by a set of practice principles to guide the worker through a mutual aid group's attempt to deal with the death of a group member. While this group deals with a special population of elderly people, those who are visually impaired or blind, much of the content is applicable to any group of older people dealing with the same or similar situation of stress. Hopefully, therefore, the material presented will be helpful to those social workers working with all groups of older people. Special attention is also given to the needs of the hearing impaired older group member—a major service concern to all social workers working with groups of older people, where invariably at least one member if not a substantial percentage of group members experience varying degrees of hearing impairments.

THE DEVELOPMENTAL TASKS AND NEEDS OF THE ELDERLY

Life after sixty-five for many is a period of tremendous satisfaction. Those of us working in geriatric social work settings, particularly community-based services, witness the degree of activity, productivity, and life satisfaction among older clients daily. We see older people assume new contributing roles, senior citizens involved in political and social action activities, the beginnings of new significant relationships—all of which make working with the elderly professionally satisfying, rewarding, and invigorating. While many older people still maintain an amazing vitality and zest for life, the future, and its infinite potential, others feel that the best years of their lives are long past. In the midst of tremendous growth and development and potential for such positive satisfying experiences, we recognize that at this last stage of the life cycle, the primary developmental task for all older people is to deal with the preponderance of losses which dramatically impact on their lives. For all older people, no matter what else is occurring at this stage of the life cycle, no matter how successful or productive or how withdrawn or isolated, losses begin to occur in many areas of their lives at a rate never before so dramatically experienced. These older people may have ten, twenty, or thirty more years of their lives yet to live; yet, they live these years experiencing one loss after another. This accumulation of losses may appear quite obvious in some older people and in others not obvious at all because of the differences in individual ability to cope and resources available to motivate the older person to develop coping strategies. The task at this stage is to adjust to these losses, to incorporate *having had* and *having lost* something or someone so significant into one's sense of self and identity in order to be able to continue to experience life as still worth living, as holding the potential for growth and development, and as having a future. The capacity to cope with so many losses, and the availability of essential supports to enable such coping, are critical factors for the older person to live with satisfaction, dignity, self-confidence, and self-esteem, which are severely shaken by each loss.

The task then, at this stage, is to deal with loss in a psychologically healthy manner in order to be able to invest in other areas of interest, or to be able to develop other areas of interest. The need is to be able to replace, or attempt to replace, the losses with other significant people and activities. This bombardment of losses has been referred to by Cath as an "omniconvergence" of losses.[1] The stresses and strains characteristic of the older person are represented by loss of income and financial security, loss of the work role and sense of productivity, loss of spouse and/or significant others, loss of other meaningful interpersonal relationships such as friends and neighbors, loss of close geographic proximity to children, loss of health through physical illness or impairment, loss of physical functioning, such as that experienced by those with severe arthritis or heart disease, or less commonly thought of, visual impairment, loss of opportunities for self-expression—and the list goes on. Loss of these positive elements characteristic of previous stages of the life cycle are or can be replaced by feelings of physical and psychological dependence, social isolation, and loneliness, dramatically reduced self-confidence and self-esteem, hopelessness, helplessness, and uselessness. The result is a state of dependence or perceived dependence. These dependencies are referred to by Blenkner as the normal dependencies of aging occurring in the areas of economic, physical, mental, and social dependence.[2] As one loss is compounded by each additional loss the life crisis intensifies.

Understanding the nature and scope of the developmental tasks and needs of the elderly and the developmental life crises and situations of stress related to the elderly is essential for all social workers and human service professionals, including those not working exclusively in geriatric settings. This is the segment of the population expanding at the greatest rate and requiring the broadest range of social services.

This "omniconvergence" of losses places the older person in a state of jeopardy or potential jeopardy, which may be further compounded by a serious disability, such as severe visual impairment or blindness. The majority of older visually impaired people today are newly visually impaired as a concomitant of the aging process. They, too, experience this loss at a time when they are experiencing losses in other areas of their lives. One of the most devastating and commonly reported combinations of losses occurs when older people lose their vision and begin to depend on their spouses for help with daily living activities and then lose their spouse soon after the onset of severe visual impairment. When this essential link to involvement and activity is pulled out from under the older newly visually impaired person, the results are devastating. Independence feels like an impossibility. A mutual aid group for this even more specialized segment of the special population may serve as the critical network to enable these older people to cope with this most difficult combination of losses.

The loss of independent mobility is the most devastating loss for the older visually impaired person according to Lessner.[3] This loss of physical freedom leads to feelings of both physical and psychological dependence, dependence on someone else where frequently there is no one else. Dependence on something, like a white cane, is frequently psychologically unthinkable and it seems totally out of the question for the older blind person to consider carrying this stigmatizing symbol of dependence and defectiveness.

Older visually impaired people who lose their vision later on in life have lived sixty, seventy, or eighty years as sighted people and bring with them to this stage of the life cycle all they have learned about disabled people throughout their lifetime. They enter the myths about blindness and act out societal stereotypes— that all blind people are dependent, that they are not productive, that they are a burden to someone, either their family or society, and that they are out of the mainstream of life. A struggle ensues within older blind persons as they attempt to adjust and identify where they are on the independence/dependence continuum.

As they enter this line of thinking, it becomes increasingly difficult to replace the loss of independence with substitutes for renewed independence. If allowed to perpetuate, this state of dependence leads to dramatically lowered self-confidence and self-esteem. Thoughts of premature and unnecessary nursing home placements run rampant as a natural consequence.

As older people lose their vision, very frequently through a gradual deterioration, they perceive themselves as less and less capable of remaining in the main-stream of community life. Many withdraw from the community to their homes or apartments because they are unable to cope with the stresses which accompany remaining actively involved in a neighborhood. This withdrawal from neighborhood involvement leads to both physical and social isolation so detrimental to the emotional, psychological, and social well-being of any older person.

After a period of time, older visually impaired people begin to perceive of themselves as homebound and to describe themselves as homebound to others. This helps to perpetuate the thinking on the part of other people, even service providers to the elderly, that to be blind is to be homebound.

One blind woman's request for help speaks to just this issue. Mrs. Q. called me indicating that she was blind and homebound, asking for help in locating an appropriate nursing home placement. Since she was visually impaired, she was seeking a nursing home knowledgeable about working with blind people and therefore, called an agency for the blind for this help. Mrs. Q. sounded young, bright, articulate, and healthy, and it was initially incomprehensible to me why she would be seeking a nursing home placement. Exploration of Mrs. Q.'s living situation revealed a spry woman, sixty-three years of age, who had gradually lost her vision, but had no physical or mental health problems to speak of, who became her own victim of her own environment. Mrs. Q. described that she used to (two years before) travel independently on public vehicles, walk around her neighborhood to stores and community center, but "gave it all up." Like many visually impaired elderly people, Mrs. Q. had been trained to use a cane, but was embarrassed to be seen among her sighted neighbors as needing "that white thing" in a community where she was once like everyone else. She was frightened to walk the streets with a cane. "It tells everybody that you are less able to take care of yourself; you're an easy target, especially in a neighborhood where old people get mugged." "I used to ride the bus. Sometimes I stood in the wrong place, and the bus would pass me by. If I got the bus, I'd ask the driver to let me know when I got where I was going, but he'd forget and then I was terribly lost in a totally unfamiliar place. So I just don't go anywhere. I'm captive of my apartment. Don't you call that homebound?" And of course, to some extent, she was; but most importantly, she need not be. This represents what can happen to any older person experiencing any dramatic change. Involvement with others in similar circumstances can make a significant difference.

The need for group involvement with others experiencing the same or similar set of circumstances goes without saying. Mummah, Barber, and Galler have each described the needs of visually impaired elderly for the social support of other visually impaired older people in order to adjust to their vision loss.[4] Minkoff, in describing a community-based program to integrate blind elderly people, expressed the need for a separate support group (as a mutual aid network) within that context.[5] Several have called for the need for group therapy to work through the depression and reactions resulting from vision loss.[6] In the program presented here, visually impaired clients' requests for services to this agency for the blind represent a direct call for group services, group support, and mutual aid, as seen below.

AGENCY CONTEXT AND THE GROUP MODALITY

This agency for the blind has an interesting and inspirational history in relation to the development of group services for the blind elderly. The agency began in 1926 as a camp for blind adults offering visually impaired adults of all ages, eighteen to one hundred and more, the opportunity for a vacation in an environment where physical adaptations enabled visually impaired people to move about independently. As the need for year-round services became evident, this agency became a year-round social service agency where visually impaired adults could receive assistance with individual social service needs related to their visual impairment.

Many visually impaired older people who attended the agency's camp discussed with social work staff their need for year-round services, beyond individual social services. The requests for services were represented by a common theme. One client's request is representative of this theme.

I look forward to coming back to camp from the time I board the bus to go home each summer. The two weeks at camp mean so much to older blind people like us, because we have a chance to be reunited with old friends we otherwise rarely get to see. The other fifty weeks of the year we never see each other. There are five of us who literally live within a ten-block area, but it could be ten miles for all we know. We can't get to each other's apartments. We use the telephone—thank God—otherwise we're really very isolated. I used to go to the senior center when I could see, but now I can't go. It's only four blocks from my apartment, but I can't get there. Besides, "they" don't know what to do with blind people if we could get there. Maybe you [the agency] could do something for us, get us out of the house, so we could get together to talk about what it's like being blind. Fifty weeks is a long time. We need something.

The theme of the requests became crystallized: the need to be with other people, no longer to be socially isolated, to get out of the house, to see other blind people who were sharing common concerns and stresses associated with vision loss, and to have access to a once-utilized local resource, the senior center, like other older people in the neighborhood. For the majority of older people experiencing recent vision loss, a state of ambivalence exists. Visually impaired older people want two things simultaneously: (1) to have access to a local senior center they once had when they could see, and (2) to withdraw from the mainstream of community life to the protected environment of a segregated service for the blind. The underlying psychological stresses remain: to be like everyone else, to be accepted within the mainstream of community life, but to recognize one's self as different and in need of special services. The agency's community-based senior center programs are an attempt to minimize the state of ambivalence. The requests were twofold: the need for a special group of visually impaired seniors as a mutual aid system and access to a once-utilized resource. The outgrowth was a combination of services in one setting in an attempt to close the gap. The agency's community-based programs take place in senior centers in over twenty-five local neighborhoods. The community-based design grows out of a particular value base which views older blind people first as senior citizens, and second as older people who happen to be visually impaired. The program is comprised of two components: (1) the mutual aid group for the visually impaired elderly, and (2) opportunities for older blind people to participate in programs and activities in the center with their sighted peers.

The need to provide group services to visually impaired older people, as well as all older people, speaks for itself: the need for a group of peers with whom to identify, who are experiencing common life stresses, and with whom one can easily identify the common themes of concern. The comfort, support, and strength acquired from peers as part of the mutual aid process cannot be replicated by professionals or friends or children. Group participation also allows the development of new relationships which can ease the pain just by knowing this life stress is shared by other older people. The multiplicity of helping relationships which develop in a mutual aid group have greater support potential than the singular relationship between client and worker.

In general, the use of groups in work with the elderly is essential and is considered the primary service modality among many social workers in the field of gerontology. It lessens the social isolation and loneliness which are so devastating at this stage of the life cycle. The mutual aid group is frequently the primary social and support network, a replacement for lost support, a reconstituted family.

This mutual aid group has been meeting for four years, once a week each Friday morning for an hour. The group serves as each group member's primary and in most cases only source of support. It is the place where members bring and deal with the losses in all other areas of their lives. Dealing with the loss of significant others is one of the major crisis events individual members bring to the group. Dealing with the death of a group member, which is the focus of the work presented here, demonstrates how the mutual aid group enables members to support each other and develop coping strategies for dealing with a loss group members are experiencing simultaneously as a group.

The mutual aid group is composed of twelve visually impaired or blind senior citizens, four of whom are also hearing impaired, one severely. They range in age from sixty-one to ninety-two; nine are women, three are men; nine are Jewish, two Italian Catholic, one Protestant; ten are widowed; ten live alone; six are lower middle class, and six are middle class. Members are dependent on door-to-door transportation to participate in the group and in the center in general. The mutual aid group is the lifeline for many who are otherwise physically and emotionally isolated. For ten of the twelve members, the mutual aid group is their only source of support and the center their only source of socialization and recreation. Many experience the devastating emptiness of the weekend, and for several, the weekend has become a time of emotional crisis.

Since the mutual aid group is perceived as a lifeline, the death of a member is experienced as a weakening of the support system. A link is now missing in the mutual aid system. This represents a tremendous threat and is experienced as an individual concern by each member and as a group concern by the group as a whole. Each individual group member's sense of integrity and self-worth is severely threatened. When confronted with the death of a group member, members must deal with past, current, and potential losses, and the ultimate—their own impending death, as all losses come into play simultaneously. The harsh realities of being left behind as others die, of being abandoned by a member of a support system, of dying alone, and not being remembered because everyone else has died before, represent the themes of con-

cern involved in this life-cycle crisis. Members are faced with the fear of their own impending death. Such a crisis event triggers the feeling that little time is left and that time will be spent waiting for death. Life loses its meaning as a member of the support system is lost.

The worker's role is to enable the group members to make use of the mutual aid group. The worker's plan throughout is to intervene as little as possible, only to step in where the helping process will either stop or go astray without intervention. Each of the group members takes on a distinct role in facilitating or inhibiting the mutual aid process.

GROUP THEMES

Members of the group arrive at the center, having been informed by the driver of the van that Maddie, a seventy-five-year-old woman who had been a member of the group for the past year, died the day before of a massive heart attack. This was the first member of the group to die this year (last year four members died). As the members arrive, one member, Goldie, whispers to the worker that Maddie died the day before. As people settle into their seats with coffee and cake, the worker attempts to tune in to what individual group members are feeling and the dynamics of the group as a whole. The following represents the worker's stream of thoughts as she begins to tune in to her clients.

It really hits hard when a member of the group dies; it hits so close to home. I could be next. So Maddie died; I'll hear about two more people soon, you know how they always happen in threes. It's not just Maddie; Maddie's death reminds me of when my two closest friends died, not so long ago. It makes me go back to when I lost my husband. That was so terribly difficult for me. Whenever someone else dies,

I remember how long it took me to get over it. You never get over a death that close to you. Maddie's husband will certainly have a hard time. He was devoted to her. That's how it was with my husband. It makes you feel so empty, like the world's caving in . . . like there is no way of knowing when your time is up.

I remember when my daughter died last spring. Nothing can be worse than losing your only child, your only daughter. Nothing is left. I'd lost everything. It's only been a few weeks that Maddie's been sick. Now she's gone. Everyone liked her so much. She was such a quiet stabilizer. But she's gone now; what can we do? Just stand up in a moment of silence, donate money to the center like we always do, and pretend she was never with us. It hurts too much to talk about it. Talking about it would just make me think too much about all the other people I've lost. I'll try to forget. What else can I do? I hope no one gets upset in the group. Some people show so much emotion. That just makes it harder for me when I'm trying to forget. When you're old, there really is very little to life than watching people die and waiting for your turn, very little else. It makes me want to do nothing, Maddie's death. It takes the meaning out of the day. It makes me feel hollow inside—no it's not really emptiness. It's a painful sadness down deep in the pit of my stomach. No one else can possibly feel this way. No one else has lost what I've lost over the years. I hope we don't talk about it; I hope no one cries—or I may cry, too.

But I want to talk about it; sometimes talking makes it better. You can remember the things that were positive. I want to talk about it, and I don't want to talk about it. It's hard to know which hurts more. There's enough pain in my life day to day. I never forget for a minute how different my life was when my husband was here, when I could see. He won't be here when I die; no one may be here when I die; God forbid, I should outlive them all. Who will be left to say that I meant anything to them . . . that I made life worthwhile . . . that I made a difference? I'll try to forget about what I've heard today. Maddie hasn't been here for a few weeks. That makes it easier. I'm

eighty-eight years old; how much longer can it be? The doctor said Maddie was a fighter, but ultimately there is one fight you lose. Maddie lost. I'll lose. We'll all lose. That's what life's about when you're old. I could just cry. It's just one loss after another. So little time left. I never did everything I wanted to do in my life. Maddie had a hard time being blind these past two years. It was hard for her to adjust. They never got to do the traveling they'd planned because she lost her sight. Life's so cruel. Where's the comfort?

Dealing with the Loss

This group session had no formal beginning as group members arrived and settled in, in the midst of discussion.

Tessie: I just can't believe Maddie died; I've been calling her house every day to speak to her husband and no answer. I knew something was wrong (said softly and with despair).

Brief silence . . .

Rose: Are you crying, Tessie?

Tessie: I don't know whether I'm crying or not (said with frustration).

Goldie: Don't cry, Tessie; you'll only get all upset.

Tessie: How can I not cry? Now it's Maddie; every week it's someone else (begins to cry openly). Rose leans over, reaches out to find Tessie, and puts her arm around her.

Rose: But we are upset, Goldie, why shouldn't she cry? Why shouldn't we? I cried this morning when I found out in the van. We're all upset.

Hannah (who is severely hearing impaired): Who's crying?

Goldie: (whispers to the worker) We shouldn't tell Hannah; she lives in the nursing home; she gets upset when people die there. She doesn't have to know. (then loudly to Hannah) No, nothing, everything is fine. No one's upset.

Worker: (to Goldie) How do you think Hannah will feel when she finds out?

Goldie: (after a long pause) She'll be upset.

Worker: I think Rose is right, that we're all upset. Hannah is part of the group.

Goldie: (loudly to Hannah) Maddie died yesterday.

Hannah: I knew something was wrong. I could feel it. Oh, my . . . that's terrible about Maddie.

The worker's first task is to help the group, primarily Goldie, realize the need to include Hannah in the mutual aid process and to help Goldie tell Hannah about Maddie herself. While the death of a group member is experienced as an individual loss and a group loss, it is a group issue. A basic underlying value in group work in general is "we're all in this together," and in order to share the experience together, we must all have access to the same information, as painful as that information may be, and as much as one member or all the members may want to exclude one member for whatever reason. Because Goldie realizes that Hannah cannot hear what is going on, the temptation is to try to get away without telling her, to protect Hannah and to protect herself—to avoid saying out loud "Maddie died yesterday." Goldie initially assumes the role of "don't make it hurt more than it has to" on behalf of herself and her friend, or at least so she thinks.

This is neither Goldie's nor the group's usual manner of relating to Hannah. Normally group members repeat significant information loudly to Hannah or remind the worker to tell her individually. While not telling Hannah something so difficult seems like the easiest thing to do at the moment, particularly to Goldie, it would ultimately be the worst choice. Emphasis in work with the elderly, and in group work with the elderly in particular, stresses the need to confront real issues directly, to deal with real things representative of

life at this stage of the life cycle. Death is probably the most real of these issues.

The worker is really saying to Goldie, "Hannah's your friend; she trusts you, and even though she'll be upset, listen to what Rose is saying, that everyone's upset. And upset is the most natural, most appropriate response right now. Hannah has no way of knowing what the most appropriate response can be unless we tell her the issue. She can't even participate in the group today, because we're not letting her; we're denying her information, infantilizing her, denying her the right to participate, the right to respond, to feel, to share, and to be equal . . . because we can get away with it—for a little while."

Rather than the skill of facilitative confrontation, the worker uses the skill referred to by this writer as "posing the ultimate question" to enable Goldie to consider the outcome herself. Goldie is able to think beyond the moment and to inform Hannah about Maddie's death. The following principles should guide the worker working under similar circumstances.

1. Even when the content of the group process is emotionally laden, members should not be viewed as so frail that they are overprotected by the worker or other members of the group and kept uninformed.

2. When the communication process of group members is hampered by hearing loss, every effort must be made on the part of the worker and other group members to insure the fullest participation possible for these members, so that they feel they are an equal and integral part of the group process.

3. The worker must initially model this behavior on behalf of all members of the group.

4. The worker needs to encourage members to enhance the participation and in-

volvement of hearing impaired members and not assume all of the responsibility for this.

5. Not only must the worker be critically self-aware of the pitfalls of ageism in herself, but she must also be aware of ageism manifested by young elderly members of a group, where other members may be thirty years their senior. The worker must strive to combat ageism and the biological and cultural determinism which permit a stereotypic view of the old elderly among the young elderly.

An interesting phenomenon occurs in work with the elderly where the group spans thirty years or more, really two generations: *ageism*. Goldie's inclination to protect Hannah is representative of ageism among the young elderly toward the old elderly. Ageism has been identified in the literature by Blank as an obstacle among workers with the elderly.[7] Goldie's view of Hannah is that she is too frail, too much at risk, too vulnerable to burden her with yet another tragedy. Goldie stereotypically believes that Hannah's ninety years, previous losses, limited support, and living situation make her less able to handle this information than those members in their sixties. The reality is more often the reverse. As the elderly live longer and experience more life stresses and losses, they establish coping strategies which make it easier for them to adjust to loss than for younger elderly people who are just beginning to experience this preponderance of losses. Loss becomes a given (though a most difficult reality), a part of life, more readily incorporated into the individual's sense of self at ninety than at sixty. At ninety, most older people recognize that more than likely they do not have thirty more years to live. At sixty, thoughts readily go to "I could die tomorrow, or I could live ten, twenty, or thirty more years, and who knows in what

condition?" As a result, it is easy for Goldie or others in her position to project their own fears of what it must be like at ninety onto Hannah, or someone in Hannah's situation.

Such ageist thinking operates out of a perception of biological and cultural determinism often identified in the worker with the elderly, and in this instance, among the younger elderly.[8] Biological determinism views old age as a time of regression and decline in capacities at all levels. Cultural determinism holds that old age is seen as a decline in personal worth. However, it is only by sharing the information with Hannah that her personal worth and dignity can be permitted, by treating her as equally capable of participating in the group's crisis. The value underlying this knowledge base in work with the elderly is that to deprive one member of the group of human dignity is to deprive the whole group. What may be viewed, then, as protective intervention by an elderly group member may actually be a threat to human dignity. Overprotection is one of the primary roadblocks in work with the elderly and can thwart mutual aid on behalf of every member.[9] As each older person is treated equally, every member has the knowledge that they too would be treated with dignity as they grow older. It is the worker's task to insure that this occurs.

Kastenbaum and Cameron have pointed to the need for cognitive supports in old age, the need for information often denied older people in the disguise of protection.[10] A reduction of cognitive support has been shown to affect dependency greatly in later life, diminishing self-esteem and intensifying feelings of dependency, and so the cycle goes. Cognitive support for Hannah is essential here and equally essential for everyone to experience.

Perceptual losses, that is, vision and hearing loss, have dramatic effects on social functioning and emotional and psychological well-being. Hearing loss results in even greater social isolation than blindness as reported by Butler and Lewis,[11] and because communication is more difficult, a sense of belonging is that much harder to achieve for the hearing impaired member(s) of a group. If self-esteem is enhanced by a feeling of belonging, of giving and receiving within the context of a group, informing Hannah is essential to her self-esteem. As Goldie considers and reconsiders, she is able to share this difficult news with Hannah, to say the hard words out loud.

It is important to note that Hannah is only blind and hearing impaired. Her mental capacity is not at issue, though a lower level of involvement caused by hearing impairment is sometimes attributed to mental dysfunction in group work with the elderly. Had Hannah been mentally frail or shown signs of senility or intermittent inability to process information, it would have been equally important to inform her, to give her the chance to hear the information and the opportunity to filter out whatever she chose at the time, as each of the other members of the group is doing. Such cognitive reinforcement is ego-enhancing to the mentally frail in particular. The group continues.

Ruth: I don't think we should talk about it any more. She's gone now and I'm sorry, but talking about it won't help her any.

Rose: We should all stand up for a moment of silence in memory of Maddie.

Belle: And we can donate ten dollars to the center in Maddie's memory.

Ruth: And then we can stop talking about it. Tessie's upset and Josephine's upset and I'm getting upset too. Talking about it won't help. We can go on to something else. We had something on the agenda.

Worker: What are we going to do with all that we're feeling, though, if we don't talk about it here, in the group? I'm thinking that it's Friday, and we've done a lot of talking over the past few months about how difficult the weekends alone are for so many of you, and especially when something upsetting has happened. Are we going to take all that sadness and pain and emptiness home with us for the weekend?

Rose: That's right, I open my door and no one's there. No one says let's talk about it, or what kind of day did you have? I know I'll think about it this weekend.

Sarah: It makes you think about other people who have died, people very close to you that you lost (said softly, almost in a whisper). Silence . . .

Worker: That's right, Sarah, and that's hard. But you know . . . this is a loss which we're all experiencing together. If we let ourselves talk about Maddie's death together and about Maddie, it may make it easier later on.

A brief silence follows.

Mary: She was someone we all really cared about. She meant a great deal to us and losing her certainly means something to me.

Tessie: It's that so many people have died the past few months. My two best friends, my friend Sam; he did so much for me . . . the woman upstairs. I just can't stand losing so many people. I just can't stand hearing about anyone else dying (continues to cry).

The worker walks over to Tessie, puts her arm around her and around Goldie who is sitting next to her and stands behind them as the discussion continues.

Allan: Remember when Sol died last spring; we were upset then. He'd been here since the beginning of the group; it was three years then; now it's four. That was a big loss.

Ruth: That's what happens when you get old, you just keep losing people, one right after the other.

Hannah: Until it's your turn. I know my turn is coming; it's closer every day.

Josephine: You know it's turn your when

it seems like everyone you ever cared about has died.

Rose: It's closer every day for all of us, but we have to keep going; I go out every day, I make the best of all of it. But this is an especially hard day.

Goldie: Are you O.K., Tessie?

Tessie: No, I'm not O.K. It hits so hard and hurts so much. Hannah's right, it just makes you think that you've got to be next.

Ruth: I try not to think about it.

Rose: But it's always there, even if you pretend it isn't, even if you don't talk about it.

According to Burnside, when the death of a group member occurs, workers are faced with two tasks simultaneously: they must deal with their own personal feelings about losing a client and begin to move to help the group deal with the loss.[12] The worker's personal and professional orientation to dealing with death and professional values regarding work with the elderly around the issue of death converge, intermingling to determine steps toward enabling the group to confront what has happened.

As Ruth takes on the role of mutual aid inhibitor and begins to set the tone for putting the issue to rest and Belle calls for the group's traditional ritual response to acknowledging death, the worker's thoughts race to reaching for a way to challenge the group to consider another method of coping.

While we may not often admit it to anyone, or even to ourselves, we enter the mutual aid process with a preconceived image of how we would like to see it benefit the group. Based on previous experience with the group and knowledge of individual group members' patterned responses to such crises, the worker fears that the group will not be able to work through the pain to completion. Yet the worker believes in the potential of the mutual aid process, in the members' ability to express their most painful thoughts and feelings, and in her own ability to enable this to be a reality. Ruth's call for moving on to whatever is on the agenda indicates that it is time for the worker to intervene, to present an alternative to this movement in the "wrong" direction.

The worker's statement, "what are we going to do with all we are feeling?" is an attempt to lend the group an opportunity to consider another way of dealing with Maddie's death, not instead of their traditional standing in a moment of silence and donating money to the center to perpetuate Maddie's memory, but in addition to this standardized ritual observance. Krupp states that such ritual ceremonies as this group's standing in a moment of silence serve to channel and legitimize the normal flow of emotions, and as such, can be extremely functional in a crisis.[13] The primary issue here is one of timing. Emotions have not even gotten to the surface for most group members. Many members are still trying not to express their pain openly in order to go on in the group as they have been socialized. But to put these emotions in check by standing in a moment of silence would be to bury them prematurely.

When Ruth, in her role as mutual aid inhibitor, calls for moving on to something else, the worker's fear is that the group will enter into a state of mutual denial, rather than mutual aid. According to Weisman denial is a social act.[14] In a group situation, it may originate in one member, be encouraged by a second member, and develop into a mutual strategy to maintain individual and group integrity. When reality becomes too immense, the natural response is to withdraw and avoid contact with it. While the group viewed standing up in a moment of silence as tackling the loss straight on, it was a structured, familiar, and comfortable way of keeping the pain of one more loss in check. The group was not denying Maddie's death, but some members wanted, and needed, to deny the impact. They wanted to withdraw from the meaning and significance of this death for each of them and for the group as a whole. Such denial can serve as an adaptive response, a strategic defense in the face of a crisis.

Of particular importance is the worker's thinking about the moment of silence as it impacts on blind people in particular. Standing in a moment of silence even further isolates the members of the group from experiencing a shared experience, particularly because communication among blind people is so dependent on verbal communication and physical contact, since the visual cues are inoperative. The lack of interpersonal interaction during the moment of silence is a roadblock to the work of the group and therefore cannot be the only attempt at acknowledging Maddie's death.[15]

The worker poses the ultimate question and reaches for clients' feelings by asking "What are we going to do with all we are feeling?" She hopes the members will consider the impending weekend which many will spend alone and begin to think, "What am I going to do with all that I'm feeling?" and begin to share their feelings, pain, and fears with each other, to engage in the process of mutual aid.

Rose gets the point. It hits home for her, and Sarah is able to move on to verbalize what she has been thinking during the morning, about old losses. The worker moves quickly to validate Sarah's risk to say what is really painful and moves to "lend a vision" for their work together and the potential for a positive outcome. By adding that the group consider talking about what Maddie meant to them, not solely what her death means to them,

members are able to consider the impact on their lives. They begin to share the impact of previous losses, fears about their own impending death, and what the time between now and that death holds for them.

Supporting clients in taboo areas is an essential skill in work with groups of elderly people. The underlying value here is that death should not be a taboo area for discussion in a group of elderly people where death and losses are part of living, part of the developmental tasks at this stage of the life cycle. The worker also wants to present the group with a choice about how to respond to Maddie's death. Such choices and alternatives are significant elements in moral behavior in work with the elderly.[16] The worker's role in such work with the elderly is to assist in a process of growth that does not resemble the kind of development which took place during the preceding stages of the life cycle. Growth at this stage occurs by integration rather than expansion, and is concerned with the constant imperative to seek out the meaning of life and affirm its value, even in the face of life's impending termination. Butler and Lewis eloquently state that this is not what it means to be old, but a deep understanding of what it means to be human.[17]

The worker's conscious use of the word "WE" in "what are we going to do?" points to the fact that "we" (the worker and the members of the mutual aid group) are all in this together. While there are conflicting points of view about the role of the group worker, about whether the worker is solely leader, never member, or can ever become a member-level participant in the mutual aid process, the worker's perception is that she does not relinquish her role as "worker" by expression and demonstration of the fact that she too has been touched by a member's death, and that indeed, she is part of the "we." While the worker's role remains intellectually apparent during the work, emotional support flows from worker to members and from group member to member. Members demonstrate a tremendous capacity to survive repeated painful experiences, loss after loss. This flow of feelings enhances the worker's ability to keep working as worker and group members experience together the loss of a member.

The worker also contributes facts, data, ideas, values, and information essential in all group work. Particularly in group work with the elderly where the need for cognitive supports has been identified, an emphasis on supplying information, such as the reminder to the group "you know how difficult the weekends have been for you," demonstrates this information-sharing skill which the worker has learned through her work with this group. Here, by such sharing, the worker serves as a catalyst, "lending a direction" to the work, to challenge the traditional patterns of dealing with difficult subject matter, of coping with a crisis, and of giving hope for the future. In this way, the worker as confidante, leader, and participant builds future into the life of the group.[18]

A motivating element in the worker's intervention here is previous knowledge through individual work with many members of the group about how they have experienced previous losses and the tremendous pain and unresolved grief many have been living with for too long. The knowledge of these histories and struggles and patterned responses greatly contributed to the worker's intervention by her understanding of individual needs, as well as the group's needs. Had this information not been available, such as in the case of a newly formed group or a worker new to the group, it would have been essential for the worker to pose questions which would provide such understanding of individual and group needs.

It is important to stop for a moment and call special attention to Ruth. In the life of every group there is a member who takes on the role assumed by Ruth, who wants to move in the opposite direction, inhibit the work, and create roadblocks. The worker's experience with Ruth led her to believe that while loss was extremely painful for her, so painful that her patterned response was to push the pain aside and pretend it was not there, that it would be better to let Ruth continue in her pattern and be moved by the momentum of the group rather than the worker's intervention. Ruth makes one comment, that "that's what happens when you get old, you just keep losing people," demonstrating that she has begun to enter into the mutual aid process. Considerable time was spent with Ruth by the worker after the group session.

The worker's anticipated outcome to the suggestion for discussion, in addition to the moment of silence, is that people will begin to talk about what they are experiencing in response to Maddie's death, to remember past losses in the group, and the value of sharing. The worker also anticipates that members will be able to go back to past losses in their private lives and to begin to reminisce about some of these painful pieces of their lives which Maddie's death revives. These hoped-for outcomes are derived from the thinking that by sharing such experiences, the group will achieve greater closeness, the closeness which grows out of crisis, and is necessary to close the gap in the mutual aid network.

The worker's skill throughout is an active reaching out, an invitation to begin to talk, to demonstrate to the group their own strengths in dealing with loss, and their capacity to survive, and to lend a vision for the future. The worker is saying to the group, our time shared together is not time waiting for death, but a time to grow, and grow closer. In this way the worker establishes a precedent for future work together around equally difficult issues and thus builds future into the life of the group.

The following practice principles guided these interventions.

1. The worker must establish a safe space and climate for any group of older people to begin to discuss openly issues previously believed to be taboo areas.

2. Death should not be a taboo topic in group work with the elderly, since it is a primary element involved in this stage of the life cycle.

3. While group members may have been socialized to think of death as a taboo area, the worker must strive to challenge this thinking and enable members to begin to express thoughts and feelings in response to death.

4. In group work with blind elderly people, verbal communication must be emphasized because of the missing nonverbal and visual cues which are taken for granted as part of the communication process.

5. The worker must model physical contact with group members as a supportive skill on behalf of the group.

6. The worker should enable the group to experience a level of closeness through mutual aid in the common group task of dealing with an emotionally charged issue, such as death and loss.

7. The worker should never remove the group's standard ritual of coping behavior, but rather can supplement the patterned response with an alternative coping strategy, where appropriate or necessary.

The mutual aid process continues:

Belle: Sadie was the only one with a husband here. It's odd that she should have to die and leave him. It's so hard for a man.

Sarah: I didn't know how I would ever survive when my only daughter died last year. My husband's been dead forty years already. I'm ninety years old and my only daughter has to die, too. I thought there was no one left for me. I even stopped coming to the group last spring (in tears).

People continue to talk about how they have experienced other losses over the years.

Harry: I think we should stand up for a moment of silence now.

(Silence)

Worker: Would you like to stand up for a moment of silence?

The group and I stood up; several people said "may she rest in peace," followed by a series of Amens.

A long, intense silence followed as we sat down.

Worker: I guess what's always most difficult for me is when I feel there was no closure, that I didn't have a chance to say good-bye, and a feeling that I've been deprived of having that person here with me longer.

Tessie: That's what hurts so much about Maddie, that I tried and tried to call and couldn't get through. They didn't know I was calling. That's what I feel deprived of, making sure that she knew that I cared.

Allan: But you've called so many times while she was sick. She knew you cared.

Ruth: A lot of us called. At least we can feel good about that. You should feel good that she knew you cared, Tessie.

Goldie: That's how I felt, deprived, when my brother died this fall. Only sixty-eight years old and so many more years to live, and died just like that of a heart attack . . . still working. I felt he was deprived, and I was deprived, and his wife . . . and children.

Harry: Even though it isn't logical, we feel deprived, even if you know it was better for the one who died so they didn't have to go through so much pain. You're still deprived of having them any more. That's how it was with my wife.

Belle: That's how it happens, Etta, most of the time, just like that.

Josephine: Maddie wasn't well, she had a bad heart, but she was always cheerful, didn't talk about how she felt; she really kept us going, and now she's gone.

Tessie: It's always good to know someone didn't suffer long, it's just hard not to have Maddie here any more.

Worker: We've lost someone very special. Maddie touched each of our lives in a very special way. I think we've all touched each other's lives today. We've shared an awful lot of what we're feeling.

Since it was the worker who tried to delay the moment of silence and it is now called for again after a long and intense session of sharing, it is important that the worker support this last call for the silence when no one is quite sure how to respond to Harry.

All of us know just how difficult silence can be ... as thoughts run to how will it be broken, by whom, and what is less painful—prolonged silence or an attempt to break it. The worker's task is to attempt to reach inside the silence here. It will be difficult to go on. So much has already been said, and there is a need now to begin to pull together in order for the members to be able to go on with their lives.

It is often debated how much and just what the worker should share of herself about personal information or feelings with clients, particularly in a group. The worker's willingness to share her own source of pain during such work with the elderly is essential to the elderly's sense of worth. This worker holds strongly to the theory that when sharing is done to move the group from where it is stuck or past a difficult moment, the expression of the worker's own feelings is facilitating

and serves as a mobilizer. It was extremely difficult for the worker to know what to say at the end of the silence. The silence was probably more difficult for her than for the members, for whom it was probably momentary relief from the steady flow of emotion. Sitting down again was difficult, as though it symbolically said, "Okay, we've said our farewells." The worker felt (or projected) that the group was probably experiencing something similar. The worker could only think that while the group stood in silence, members must have been considering how the day impacted on their lives, about what Maddie meant to each of them and to the group as a whole. Tessie had struggled with not having been able to reach Maddie's husband to express her concern. The worker is thinking how closely her thinking matches Tessie's: "I never had the chance to say you've been such a pleasure to know and I've learned so much from the opportunity to work with you. Thank you for that." At this point, the worker decides to reach inside the silence, to share her own feelings, and simultaneously to display understanding of clients' feelings. By saying what was always most difficult for her, the worker anticipated that members might be able to say what was most difficult for them at the moment or what typically presents a serious problem for them. The group carried its own momentum from there.

Sharing a piece of self in work with the elderly is essential, but for more than just to move or accelerate the work. According to Burnside the worker is expected to share herself.[19] This represents symbolic giving—symbolically to replace meaning to the group where meaning is lost. The worker is constantly assessing how much to intervene, how much to share, but in group work with the elderly, sharing the worker's own feelings helps to equalize the relationship where age difference is frequently quite obvious. It does for the worker what reminiscence does for the aged client: it establishes a working equilibrium where both the worker and members of the group feel the comfort of a safe space in which to share. It is important to achieve the right combination of personal and professional elements in the work. The right balance is experienced as genuine and human caring by the elderly.

The worker's role in the last statement is to convey a sense of accomplishment, of succeeding in what was initially unthinkable for some members and essential to others. The worker attempts to convey that everyone has invested in the mutual aid process and achieved a sense of the closeness established through this mutual aid. When the worker says "we've touched each others' lives," she is saying we all had something to give each other and we have all benefited from each other's humanity. Practice principles guiding these interventions may be useful for work with all age levels, but are essential in work with groups of elderly people.

1. The worker should share her own feelings in group work with the elderly in order to enable members to begin to share.

2. It is not only appropriate but essential that the worker share her own feelings with the group when the group is trying to cope with emotionally charged material in a nonpatterned response to crisis.

3. When the group experiences highly emotionally charged material, it is helpful for the worker to pull together for the group elements of the process and bring the work to a closure (unless a member is able to assume this role).

CONCLUSION

Work with the elderly around issues of loss and death is emotionally and physically intense for both the older person and the social worker. It requires the ability and willingness to tackle the pain straight on—to say what hurts—to relate the current pain to past pain—and to not only survive, but continue to grow through the mutual-aid process. The mutual aid process has tremendous potential to build life, vitality and future into the life of the group.

For the worker, the ability to "tune-in" to each individual group member's situation of stress and that of the group as a whole is key to successfully facilitating the mutual aid process. For the older person, the support of a mutual aid network is a lifeline.

NOTES

1. Stanley Cath, "Some Dynamics of Middle and Later Years," in *Crisis Intervention,* ed. Howard Parad (New York: Family Service Association of America, 1971).

2. Margaret Blenkner, "The Normal Dependencies of Aging," in *The Dependence of Old People,* ed. R. A. Kalish (Detroit, Mich.: Institute of Gerontology, Wayne State University, 1969).

3. Robert Lessner, "A Declaration of Independence for Geriatric Blind Persons,"

The New Outlook for the Blind 67 (April 1973): 181.

4. H. R. Mummah, "Group Work with the Aged Blind Japanese in the Nursing Home and in the Community," *The New Outlook for the Blind* 69, no. 4 (April 1975): 160-167; A. Barber, "Meeting the Needs of Older Blind Adults: A Method of Accountability," *The New Outlook for the Blind* 70, no. 4 (April 1976): 166-167; E. H. Galler, "A Long Term Support Group for Elderly People with Low

Vision," *Journal of Visual Impairment and Blindness* 75 (April 1972): 14-76.

5. J. Minkoff, "An Approach to Providing Services to Aged Blind Persons," *The New Outlook for the Blind* 66, no. 3 (April 1972): 104-109.

6. E. L. Wilson, "Programming Individual and Adjunctive Therapeutic Services for Visually Impaired Clients in a Rehabilitation Center," *The New Outlook for the Blind* 66 (September 1972): 215-220; C. Harshbarger, "Group Work with Elderly Visually Impaired Persons," *Journal of Visual Impairment and Blindness* 74 (June 1980): 221-224; R. L. Evans and B. M. Jaureguy, "Group Therapy by Phone: A Cognitive Behavioral Program for Visually Impaired Elderly," *Social Work in Health Care* 7 (Winter 1981): 79-89.

7. Marie Blank, "Ageism in Gerontologyland," *Journal of Gerontological Social Work* 2, no. 1 (Fall 1979): 5-9.

8. Fred Berl, "Growing Up to Be Old," *Social Work* 8, no. 1 (January 1963): 85-91.

9. Louis Lowy, "Roadblocks in Social Work Practice with Older People," *The Gerontologist* 7, no. 2 (June 1967): 109-114.

10. Robert Kastenbaum and Paul Cameron, "Cognitive and Emotional Dependency in Later Life," in R. A. Kalish, *The Dependence of Old People,* ed. R. A. Kalish (Detroit, Mich.: Institute of Gerontology, Wayne State University, 1969), p. 41.

11. Robert N. Butler and Myrna I. Lewis, *Aging and Mental Health: Positive Psychosocial Approaches* (St. Louis, Mo.: The C. V. Mosby Company, 1977), p. 111.

12. Irene Mortenson Burnside, "Principles from Yalom," in *Working with the Elderly: Group Process and Techniques* (North Scituate, Mass.: Duxbury Press, 1978).

13. George Krupp, "Maladaptive Reactions to the Death of a Family Member," *Social Casework* 53, no. 7 (July 1972): 425.

14. Avery Weisman, "Denial as a Social Act," in *On Dying and Denying* (New York: Behavioral Publications, 1972).

15. Lowy, "Roadblocks."

16. Harold Lewis, "Morality and the Politics of Practice," *Social Casework* 53, no. 7 (July 1972): 404-418.

17. Butler and Lewis, *Aging and Mental Health.*

18. Louis Lowy, "The Group in Social Work with the Aged," *Social Work* 7, no. 4 (October 1962): 43-50.

19. Irene Burnside, "Principles of the Preceptor," in *Working with the Elderly: Group Process and Techniques* (North Scituate, Mass.: Duxbury Press, 1978), chapter 6.

Toby Berman-Rossi

CHAPTER 18

The Fight Against Hopelessness and Despair: Institutionalized Aged

Group association has always been an important part of the lives of institution-alized residents of long-term care facilities. Fueled with the common human need to be part of the social fabric of their collective lives, older residential inhabitants are naturally drawn to each other. For the 4 to 5 percent of the older population who for a complex of reasons can no longer live in their own homes or the homes and setting of those to whom they are known, group association has special meaning.[1] This complicated interrelationship between the elderly and their institutional world sets the context for the mutual aid group. This interplay between people and their environment represents the setting within which the need for group association receives such pre-eminence. The resulting interplay of needs provides the focus toward which social workers necessarily direct their attention.

NORMATIVE ASPECTS OF AGING

Our grasp of the special needs of older, institutionalized people is set against an understanding of the normative aspects of aging. In considering the later years of people's lives, Blenkner writes of the "nor-mal dependencies of aging" and suggests that as the older person ages, increases in dependency occur in four areas: economic, physical, mental, and social.[2] The concept of "older" includes people from sixty-five to one hundred and more years, with dependency intensifying as age advances. Economic changes are pressing for the retired elderly, as they move from producer to consumer. By any standard, the aged are one of the most economically deprived segment of our population with virtually no potential for altering that state.[3] In 1971, almost 25 percent were below the poverty level, with 15 percent at the poverty level.[4] Considering the minimum standards of these established criteria, most older people experience grave hardships once retirement sets in. Overnight one can become poor. Even the previously employed discover that 92 percent of those enrolled in private pension plans, working eleven or more years, did not receive expected pensions at the time of retirement.[5] Adding the plight of women and minorities of younger ages, minority older women are the poorest group in our country.[6]

Both Butler and Brody suggest there is an intricate relationship among socioeconomic status and social services, health

333

factors, and health services.[7] As poverty increases, so does dependence upon institutional supports such as Medicaid, Medicare, welfare, clinics, and hospitals. Both note as poverty increases, so does illness; as preventive nutrition rises, illness declines. Therefore, for older people who struggle to make ends meet, the normal process of physical aging will be compounded. While Medicare and Medicaid have increased medical options, Medicaid's hard line eligibility criteria leave many people too ashamed to apply, while Medicare's crisis orientation leaves certain services uncovered.[8] Mrs. Brenlowsky is an example of such a plight.

In speaking about her problems of managing her frequent doctor visits and medication on her limited Social Security income, I mentioned that I thought she was eligible for Medicaid benefits. "No, no," she cried. "I will not." What was bothering her so much? I wondered. She said she would not go there; she could not. "Why?" I asked, persisting. She lowered her head and began to cry softly. I reached over, placing my hand on hers, and said, "Tell me." She said, "I have been here for thirty years and my English is not good. I would not understand." Her feelings of shame came through clearly. I said, "The papers are hard for many people. I will go with you. I will help you." She smiled reassuringly, and said, "I know you want to help, but I cannot go. It would be too much for my heart. I will manage." She moved on to another area of discussion, and I suggested that if she wanted, we could speak again about medicaid in the future. She said, "Perhaps." I knew she meant no. War years in Germany had convinced her that the least amount of contact with government institutions was best.

For Mrs. Brenlowsky and many Mrs. Brenlowskys there will be no Medicaid, even when possible. Mistrust of institutional programs and exacerbated feelings of inadequacy in the face of complex bureaucratic systems are too hard to transcend. She would manage as she had, living at the poverty level. At least she felt it was a world which was known and therefore one upon which she could count.

A world and a self upon which one could count. The sense of stability which becomes so important to us through our growing years becomes even more precious as we age, precious because uncertainty and unpredictability increase. The existential nature of life begins to predominate.

Many years ago, at the end of my first group meeting with older people (average age eighty-four), I said to the members that I would see them next week. Mrs. Gross rose slowly, turned, looked at me and said, "God willing." She slowly continued walking. I was stunned. Could it mean that she did not know from week to week whether she would be alive? What was it like to live with the reality that life might end at any instant? I was only twenty-nine years old and had just given birth to my first daughter. I could hardly grasp the meaning of what had just occurred between us. It would be a while before I understood how this incident would affect our work together, individually and in the group.

While retirement is a predictable point in life, physical, mental, and social changes associated with aging are less predictable. The physical abilities of a sixty-five year-old are not the abilities of a seventy-five, eighty-five, or ninety-five-year-old. How and when these abilities will change remains unknown. One does know, however, that change will occur. Illness may appear at any time. Death may strike at any moment. Decline in mental powers can occur as can parallel changes in physical status. A stroke with resultant expressive and/or receptive aphasia and decreased reasoning powers or even Alzheimer's disease could suddenly appear. One would never know.

One daughter said, "You should have seen Mother before. She was a pillar of strength to us. We thought she would never change. Then one day she did not visit as expected. We frantically searched for her. The police found her wandering in the street, unable to say where she lived. Perhaps there were little signs before, but nothing like this. I felt devastated. Our lives were never the same."

And

A seventy-three-year-old daughter with a ninety-seven-year-old institutionalized mother with Alzheimer's disease said as she was struggling with the pain of their separation, "My mother is lucky to have me. Whom do I have? My husband is dead. I have no family. What happens if I wake up one morning and I cannot manage? Who will care for me? Who will even know? I have no one."

"Who will care for me?" and "for whom will I care?" represent the essence of changes in social role as aging occurs. When one is no longer a wage earner or a primary caretaker, social relationships increase in importance. They begin to occupy a more central position in the older person's life. Blenkner indicates that the pain of change in this area is triggered by loss, loss of people who offered and received love, people who provided assistance, and people who were part of a social world. With each loss roles change, become redefined, and shrink unless avenues to continued opportunity are maintained. A diminution of status and power are a necessary accompaniment of a depletion of roles.[9] If, as she suggests, sources of help are self, kind, and societal, then loss of kin and friends, coupled with diminishing personal abilities, leave one increasingly dependent upon variable institutional supports. George suggests that while role changes and transitions are not the same for all people, they

do pose challenges for all. The normative aspects of the challenges are influenced by four features of role shifts: (1) their normative meaning, (2) their personal meaning, (3) their impact upon previously instituted norms of conduct, and (4) the degree to which the individual has been prepared for the change in role. Once again, while the impact of role changes and role shifts remain unpredictable, even the most predictable change can be traumatic.[10] The meaning to the individual must be established. In considering the meaning of the role challenges of aging, the relationship between individuals and the world around them must be considered. What the older person brings to the situation, coupled with the response of the external world, determines the ultimate meaning of this change. The interaction between need and opportunity becomes increasingly important.

Feelings of loss are influenced by other opportunities for gratification that exist presently or may exist in the future. Many years ago, as a social worker new to working with older people in groups, I hesitantly approached my group with the announcement that social work services were being reorganized and we would no longer be working together. Very shortly after making the announcement and after hearing their expressions of sadness about my leaving and helping them evaluate our work together, members asked: Will someone else be coming? Who will it be? Will our group continue? My initial reaction was surprise. Did they not really mean it when they said they cared about me and about our working together for the last two years? When thinking about our exchange, several essential elements began to appear: (1) In their long lives they had experienced many losses. Loss and change were a more accustomed part of their lives. (2) If the group was not continuing, then the loss of our relationship would have had different meaning. (3) Loss exists within the context of opportunity. If future opportunities for group association were to continue, then the ending of our working relationship represented change in group services, not an end of them. This experience of residents handling loss in this manner was repeated just recently with a group with which I had been working for seven years. This time, residents' reactions did not come as a surprise.

Similarly, the experience of loss of a spouse will be influenced not only by the nature of that marital relationship but also by the context of that loss. Does the loss occur within a network of relationships? Is there close and available family? Does the possibility for other meaningful friendships exist? If not, can it be created? If paid employment has ended, are there other opportunities for work and satisfying activity which the individual would value?

The import of a particular loss is related to the remaining network of interactional relationships. As social workers focusing on the contribution of group services, we seek to provide maximum opportunities for continued social growth so that loss is not experienced in the context of ever-diminishing opportunities. This interactional focus has additional meaning when we consider role shifts and transitions experienced by the person living within an institutional setting. The relationship between loss and opportunity is critical to understand.

The experience of loss is the phenomenon most pressing for the older person and generates three significant developmental tasks: (1) carrying on in the face of ever diminishing abilities, (2) living with growing uncertainty and unpredictability, and (3) trying to maintain a meaningful life as the death of loved ones and

one's own death move increasingly near. The existential nature of life is never felt as acutely as it is by those contemplating the last period of their lives. Moving forward in the face of ongoing loss is a considerable life task. Aging places life tasks in a context; it does not eliminate them. Creating the sustaining opportunities in the face of loss is the arena in which the energies of the older person and the social worker meet.

While those more privileged economically can mitigate some of the negative aspects of aging, none can escape the challenge of contending with loss and change. The sense of loss, the hardness of life, and the closeness of death are felt even more acutely by institutionalized older people.

AGENCY CONTEXT AND THE GROUP MODALITY

Our setting is a nonprofit, long-term care facility. It has tradition going back more than 110 years of serving older people in New York City by providing a wide range of community and institutional services at two locations. It is toward a group of thirty-eight long-term residents, living on the same skilled nursing floor, that our attention is directed.

Wesson points out four characteristics of a long-term-care facility which are reflective of the population under discussion: (1) chronicity of illness, (2) predomination of sickness and illness, (3) unhappy prognosis, and (4) major role disruption for participants.[11] Gottesman and Hutchinson in their extensive survey of the literature, on attributes of the institutionalized aged, cite characteristics consistent with Wesson's description.[12] They indicate that those no longer living in the community are likely to be older, white, unmarried or widowed, and poor, with a multiplicity of physical disorders and frequent mental disorders. The thirty-eight residents under discussion closely fit this description: their average age is eighty-six, 87 percent are single (18.5 percent unmarried, 68.5 percent widowed), 92 percent (thirty-five) are supported primarily by public funds (medicaid), and all suffer from a multiplicity of chronic physical illnesses. Signs of emotional stress and cognitive limitations are present in most.

For these residents, this nursing home is their last home. What kind of world is a home for the aged? Toward what does it aspire? A long-term-care facility combines elements of two kinds of institutional settings: a hospital and a residential treatment center, both of which are total institutions. The treatment of illness and the sense of total residence have profound effects on the lives of inhabitants. Goffman identifies homes for the aged as one kind of "total institution." As a total institution, a home for the aged cuts off residents from the greater society, formally directs and administers maximal aspects of inhabitants' lives, provides a life of incredible sameness for most participants, and dispenses its authority from above through a formal system of rules and regulations.[13] The net result is "a kind of dead sea in which little islands of vivid encapturing activity appear. Such activity can help the individuals withstand the psychological stress usually engendered upon the self."[14]

Both Zelditch and Kahana share Goffman's concern about the effects of "totality" upon institutional occupants.[15] Kahana suggests that the lower the "totalistic" features the more congruence there is with an individual's needs.[16] Coe also believes that the higher the institutional totality, the higher the withdrawal and depersonalization on the part of the older person.[17] The fit between person

and environment is also noted by Turner, Tobin, and Lieberman, who suggest that while it was previously thought that admission to a nursing home per se increased morbidity and mortality rates, it is rather the person-environment fit which is the crucial variable.[18] If the occupants have personality traits that are congruent with environmental demands, then they will experience less stress. Personality and behavioral characteristics that are not in harmony with environmental demands induce stress in both staff and residents as both work toward harmony between the needs of the older person and the demands of the institution. Consequently, institutional environments are sought which will allow, as much as possible, the influence of residents as a mitigating force against institutional totality. A highly valued milieu seeks to strike a better balance between the concentration of power in staff and the consequent loss of decision making on the part of inhabitants. Institutionalization removes older people from the life situation in which they previously maintained the role of decision maker. It does not change the need of the elderly to remain meaningfully involved in thinking about, working on and planning for their lives. The need to be in charge of one's life is a common human need. Institutionalization does not eliminate this need, though the expression of it and opportunities for satisfaction of it might change.

Into an institutional atmosphere with its elements of totality enter those for whom available community health care services are not sufficient to offset dwindling physical, mental, social, emotional, and economic resources.[19] As with the community aged, experiences of loss predominate. Fried, in speaking about the effects of forced relocation (are there ever any truly voluntary permanent relocations to nursing homes?), poignantly writes that responses to loss

> are manifest in the feelings of painful loss, the continued longing, the general depressive tone, frequency of psychological or social or somatic distress, the active work required in adapting to the altered situation, the sense of helplessness, the occasional expressions of both direct and displaced anger, and tendencies to idealize the lost place. At their most extreme, these reactions of grief are intense, deeply felt, and, at times, overwhelming.[20]

Imagine a projected short stay in a hospital resulting in a permanent stay in a nursing home, never to see one's home, possessions, pets, or neighbors again! In the process of applying to a long-term-care facility, the person may become psychologically institutionalized prior to actual admission. The older person in the anticipatory process looks institutionalized.[21]

This phenomenon can be thought of as part of a preparatory adaptive process in which older people begin to test out what they believe it will feel like to be institutionalized. This process might be likened to those entering religious orders who begin to divest themselves of "worldly" possessions, thereby beginning a process of decathection. In the anticipatory process, the older person "tries on" the issue of separation, "tries on" the experience of loss, "tries on" an increase in dependence. We see the effects of institutionalization indirectly. There is a rise in disequilibrium which continues into admission and begins to characterize the first few months of institutional life. The psychological state is one of lessened hope, more body preoccupation, a view of oneself as powerless and vulnerable, and an identification with the frail elderly. It is as if the older person searches to understand and integrate the forthcoming role and status. Prior roles do not prepare the aged for institutional life because within their community lives they are among the least regimented, least structured, and least observed members of society.[22] Prior to that time, it becomes extremely difficult to factor out the interplay between what the older person brings to institutional life and the actual effects of institutional living.[23] This depressive view poses special challenges to the long-term-care facility during the first two months of the older person's institutional life.

While Tobin and Lieberman caution us with regard to the concept of causation, they also state that "even the best of long-term care institutional environments for the elderly induce harmful institutional effects."[24] Though believing that the effects of admission are less than what was previously considered, they state there is no way for the older person to escape (1) identifying with those who are sicker, (2) perceiving their own increasing need for care, (3) being closer to death, (4) possessing a limited and uncontrollable future, (5) participating with others which sometimes leads to an increase in conflict, and (6) experiencing receding family members. While inescapable, there is a wide range of responses to institutionalization, which again suggests the person-environment fit mentioned earlier. The major task of the institutionalized aged, as with the community aged, is continuance of a meaningful life in the face of pervasive loss and an uncertain future. In the first year of placement, a significant percentage of those admitted die or deteriorate mentally and physically. Passive individuals are particularly vulnerable.[25]

The following story will illustrate. Miss Anspacher, a ninety-one-year-old woman, was transferred to the long-term-care facility after a six-month hospitalization following a hip fracture. She was admitted weighing seventy-six pounds, with a barely audible voice and multiple decubiti, and was severely contracted. Her eighty-nine-year old sister, with whom she had lived all her life, had recently died, unbeknownst to her. Her only living relative, a seventy-three-year-old niece, was stressed from visiting both aunts, giving up their apartment containing a lifetime's possessions, and contending with her own aging. While we provided a high level of medical and nursing care, ministering to Miss Anspacher's emotional wounds became harder as time passed. She rarely spoke verbally. As she withdrew further, so did the home's staff, finding it increasingly more difficult to sustain both sides of the relationship. The technical services offered by medicine and nursing could not counter Miss Anspacher's persistent feeling that "no one special" loved her and therefore life was not worth living. She slipped quietly to her death one evening during sleep, three months after admission. While the institution did not cause her death, it could not prevent it. Unable and not desiring to make demands upon her institutional world, Miss Anspacher became increasingly dependent upon the advances of a team already working hard to attend to the demands of the thirty-seven other more vocal residents. Encouraging her to assert herself on her own behalf became more difficult and less frequent. Assertion *is* required for survival in institutional life. Passivity, depression, and withdrawal are all more likely to be associated with decline and death. Believing that one's life is over can actually help that life to end.

Acknowledging the hardness of institutional life, we may ask several questions of this setting serving older people:

1. To what extent will this "new society" reflect the old? To what extent will it attempt to generate and create new life? Is the institution a place to wait for death, or is it a place to look forward to for the rest of one's life?
2. Can the home for the aged stop this continuous process of loss of significant people by helping to supply meaningful others?
3. To what extent can the long-term-care facility increase productivity and increase the aged person's repertoire of roles?
4. To what extent can it increase feelings of self-worth?
5. And finally can it help to restore a lost sense of dignity with which life once again will be worth living?

The institution therefore can mirror and collude with the older person's dreaded view of institutional life as a "holding place" prior to death, or it can align itself with the older person's hope that institutional life will indeed be meaningful. To align itself with the positive side of the aged resident's ambivalence would result in acknowledging, but working against, the feared belief that nursing home admission is tantamount to death.

Like the immigrants most of them once were, newly admitted residents again become strangers in a strange land. Entering alone, without status and with a predominance of liabilities, new residents find the uncertain future requiring the tasks of establishing friendships, becoming oriented to surroundings, establishing role identities, and responding to the unequal balance of power between care givers and care receivers. While the long-term resident has generally arrived at some resolution in relation to these tasks, life in this new home never really becomes easy. The unknown always looms ahead for the institutionalized, highlighting the existential nature of their lives. A calm can be abruptly altered by staff reassignments, the death of a friend, the admission of a new roommate, changes in the menu, or countless unknown possibilities.

In a pattern similar to the newly arriving immigrants and those deeply affected by the growing industrial economy at the turn of the century, group association becomes a mainstay in the lives of the institutionalized aged.[26] Historically, groups became a way of reaffirming connections among people, fostering the development of group services for both normative aspects of life, that is, Y's, settlements, play and church groups, and camping, as well as helping with special needs of the ill or newly arrived or unorganized within newly developing communities.[27] The group became a countervailing force against the abuses of a developing capitalist state and a means for inducting newcomers into the ways of their new land. Organizing, opposing, educating, and enjoying reached new dimensions as people with common concerns and interest banded together to work toward shared purposes. Schwartz's definition of "group" for social work purposes reflects his reading of history and is consistent with his ideas on symbiosis. It emphasizes interdependence of need, mutual aid, commonness of task and an agency hospitable to the group's endeavor.[28]

Within the long-term facility, group association is fueled by needs which have always stimulated movement toward collectivity. Taken away from their previous society and denied familiar supports, the sense of insecurity in the older person rises dramatically. The impetus to band together against "the powers that be" is a natural outcome of the need to survive and reflects heightened vulnerability. Interestingly, while group association offers a buffer against institutional life, it also simultaneously provides an organized means for making use of agency service. In fact, it becomes the mode of institutional living. Schwartz has described this impetus as follows:

> In the individual's struggle to negotiate the various systems of demand and opportunity that his society offers him, he will, whenever it is made possible, enlist the aid of people with similar systems to manage. The peer group—or the mutual aid system—then becomes a way of helping him negotiate the larger system and getting what it was designed to offer him.[29]

If allowed and even encouraged, the movement of people will be toward each other. Forman would agree, suggesting that:

> The peer group can become the most important and influential environmental factor for a resident, particularly if it is the only social system available to him in which he can experience an ego-building alternative to the deprecatory image presented to him by the institution.[30]

Institutionalized residents face the challenge of establishing and living within their new society. Whether this new world will reflect the old, with its increasing alienation and estrangement from the mainstream of life, or will offer new opportunities for friendship, meaningful activity, and mutuality is critical in determining the quality of life offered those living in homes for the aged.[31]

The quality of life offered inhabitants will be heavily influenced by the long-term-care facility itself. The facility stands as a microcosm of the larger society, reflecting both positives and negatives. With its hierarchically ordered structure, ministering to an increasingly infirm population within a medical setting, it also becomes subject to the abuses of power.

Understanding the life-giving potential of mutual aid groups, the nursing home assigned social workers to floors, not to individual residents. Resident floor groups were established on each unit, based upon the thinking that each floor represented a building, a block, a community of like people among whom the ties were potentially quite strong. A unit of thirty-eight residents needing skilled nursing care would become like family to each other, and like family would reflect all the advantages and liabilities inherent within that close association.

The resident floor group was to be a weekly, open-ended, voluntary group, having the function of helping residents work on troubles, concerns, and issues which arose out of their being older people living on the same floor in a long-term-care facility. The range of issues would be potentially vast, as vast as the real issues in their lives: aging, illness, loss, service-delivery problems, peer relationships, family, and friendships, to name but a few. The meetings might resemble a town meeting or a more intimate family gathering, depending upon the issues with which the group was working. The social worker's role would be to help residents do *their* work, as the elderly struggled to make their way through issues of importance in their lives. The group would be a living testimony to the reality that older people, like people of all ages, could join together to try and think through ways of improving their lives. As such, the group would allow for the development of positive social roles, would give continued expression for the creative talents of its members, and most importantly would serve to provide a source of hope, countering the potential isolation and estrangement so possible within the institution.

The theme of "the group as a source of hope" is illustrated in the following section from a resident floor group meeting.

About fifteen minutes of discussion occurred in which Mr. Posner and Mr. Katz raised for discussion the behavior of a group member, who due to his severe Alzheimer's could no longer distinguish between his property and that of others. Mrs. Brophy, another resident whose husband also was suffering from Alzheimer's, seemed stressed by the discussion. The worker noticed that Mrs. Brophy was getting upset and said that he could see that what was happening had upset her greatly. She said "Yes, yes, it does. He is obviously very limited and not sure of what he is doing. He's not stealing because he wants to steal. He is stealing because he doesn't know any better and perhaps this should have been brought up privately with him some time." Mr. Marlin quickly came to the man's defense in the same way. "He really doesn't know what he is doing." Most of the group was shaking their heads, but Mr. Posner and Mr. Katz were still angry. . . . Mr. Posner said to them, "We trust each other here in the group and this is about the only place we can talk about anything like this. We all understand that Mr. Schwerner is a limited person. We're not going to hurt him or anything like that . . . but we have no other place."[32]

The group provides the opportunity for real work to occur. Unpleasant work, conflictual work, angry work, tender work—all must have avenues for expression. The resident floor group provides that avenue.

While the group offers continued opportunity for communion, social work efforts are very much influenced by the special meaning of group experience for the aged. Five characteristics stand out:

1. Each person is dealing very painfully with the feeling that he is a loser. None will forget that he entered the institution in a position of loss. The resi-

dent's sense of worth is at an all-time low.

2. Each person is dealing with the feeling that it just may be better to be part of a group of "losers" than to be a "loser" alone.

3. Group members are dealing with their awareness that this is their last chance to create a new society. They are closer to death than they have ever been before.

4. Their needs have a greater possibility of being met through alliance with a peer group than in working individually.

5. The group is the only real avenue for the creation of this new society—a society in which feelings of self-worth can rise and alienation decline.

These characteristics of group experience for the institutionalized aged have serious implications for practice, as we labor to help the elderly in their work. They prompt the need for the social work practitioner to:

1. Recognize and deal with feelings which are a result of the psychological, biological, and social changes in the aged.

2. Understand the very real existential nature of our practice, since work can be cut off at any point by death.

3. Recognize and respond to the tremendous potential of the group experience for the aged, as well as the ongoing fear that this enterprise may simply be one more failure.

4. And finally, to view the group and the long-term-care facility as a microcosm of the larger society and through our efforts join with the aged in the creation of their new world.

GROUP THEMES

While themes in the resident floor groups are many, environmental themes predominate.[33] The negotiation of one's world remains an overriding concern for institutional inhabitants. Such discussion offers the possibility of exercising some control in their lives. During fourteen years of working with residents in such groups, food-related concerns have been a central part of the content of group meetings. For this reason efforts to deal with food-related issues will be focused upon.

Meals and Mealtimes

Meals and mealtimes were an important part of institutional life. In the main, they were felt to be a constant, something on which residents could count. Perceived problems in food preparation, meal presentation, and menu selection were experienced harshly by residents. Having had a lifetime of preparing their own meals in their own kitchens, residents approached food with a highly developed sense of how it ought to be. For many, particularly the women, meal preparation was an area of former competence. While they could no longer carry out their own food preparations, they had not lost a sense of how they felt they would, if they had the opportunity. The Dietary Department, in recognition of varied food preferences and the value of choice in activities of daily living, presented a wide assortment of foods from which to choose. Residents who were able made out menus for all meals. Others had their food preferences communicated to the floor dietician. Dieticians appeared at lunch and dinner, trying to be available for ongoing reactions.

Understanding how strongly residents

felt about their food, as well as the complexity of diminishing taste sensations, prevalence of dentures, and various special diets ordered by the medical staff, the Dietary Department agreed to meet regularly with the chief of social service and a committee of Resident Council delegates to work on food-related concerns. This joint committee, which had been in existence for several years, had been successful in bringing about many satisfying changes. It was not unusual for new recipes to be brought to meetings for sampling prior to being served throughout the house. Residents could even have their favorite recipes tested for use. One could conclude that much was being done to make meals satisfying.

Nonetheless, most of the intact, verbal residents on this floor (the most alert SNF floor) who did complain did so bitterly. They continued to feel that "if the home cared" about them, things would be better. Why did problems persist? they asked over and over. Explanations of the complexity of feeding 514 people carried little weight.

9/10
Food problems were again raised. Problem enumerated. I said that previously they had brought up these complaints many times. What did they want to do about them? Without too much deliberation, they indicated they wanted to have the director of Dietary attend the meeting. I discussed their request with the director, who agreed to her staff attending the meeting.

9/24
Two weeks later the floor dietician and the supervising dietician appeared. Problems were identified. ... Discussion was fast and furious. The meeting ended on a hopeful note.

In the next few weeks, food problems were overshadowed by discussion of the death of a favorite member and the difficulties of living with a new admission with Alzheimer's. In addition, the residents prided themselves on their sense of fair play and wanted to give Dietary "a chance."

10/15
A momentary quiet in the group meeting was broken by Mrs. Mann who once again brought up problems with the food. She said that things were always the same, nothing ever changed. There was no point in trying, she insisted; they had been trying for years and nothing ever changed. Her comments brought forth a flood of similarly negative comments. Residents spoke about the futility of further efforts.

It was at that moment that I sensed something different in the group's life. Discouragement had mounted. Residents were sitting dead center on their feelings. I sensed that my vision as to the possibility of change was being called upon in a way that it had not been before.[34] If the residents were to continue working on a matter of concern to them, I would need both to acknowledge and to help them move beyond their discouragement. Reaching inside the silence was important. Within the quiet were nagging feelings of despair and discouragement. The power of these feelings obscured all hope. Within myself I, too, was not sure how change would occur. Much effort was already being put forth on the home's part; yet, residents were still not satisfied. Although the steps were unclear to me, I firmly believed that through the process of engagement between residents and the home, change could occur. Perhaps the three-minute eggs would never be perfect, and the toast might never stay warm and soft by the time it reached the floor, but some positive change could occur. And so the work continued.

What's the Use?

10/15

After a barrage of negatives and the elaboration of discouragement, the following occurred: I listened for a while and when there was a lull I said, "I have been listening to you express these complaints for a long time. . . . Even though you just spoke with Dietary staff a few weeks ago in the group meeting, you still feel things are not better?" Similar negatives came forth. "What do you want to do about feelings that things aren't getting better?" Many people began talking at the same time: "Why bother? What's the use? There's no point." Comments were not new. There was a silence, and I sensed they were waiting for me to speak. I said I know how discouraged they became, how they hated it when meals were not better for them, or not enough better, and while I didn't know if things would get better, I did think that what they were feeling didn't feel very good. I was concerned that those feelings would just fester and grow if they didn't try and make things better. Once again all the discouragement was expressed. I was struck by the reality that no one in the group was saying something positive.

Finally someone challenged me and asked if I thought they *could* make things better. I said I wasn't sure, but I had worked at the home for a long time and I did think the Dietary Department wanted their meals to be satisfying, but there were real, hard problems on which they were working, which were not easy to resolve. I quickly méntioned some. I further said that if they withdrew from working with Dietary, that department would be left to figure things out all by themselves, and then what they felt and wanted might not even be known to the kitchen.

They thought for a moment, seemed challenged, and asked to whom they should speak. We went through the various possibilities: floor dietician, supervisor, assistant director, director, and ultimately administration. They said they had spoken with all those people. What made it so hard for them to try again, I wondered? A combination of: "There's no point," to "we don't want them to turn us down,"

came forth. "Are you afraid they won't care?" "Yes, yes," they replied. "If Dietary cared, the problem wouldn't be there to begin with." I was silent for a moment as the force of what they were saying struck me. I said I wasn't sure I agreed with them, though I could understand that it felt that way. I thought institutions were complex places and it wasn't always easy to figure out things.

They continued listening. Didn't they sometimes think I didn't do what they wanted me to do? Yet, they pretty much thought I cared. They seemed thoughtful. I waited. The room was hushed. All twenty-four people seemed to be in thought, though I certainly wasn't sure what they were thinking. I broke the silence and said, "How about one more chance? One more try! Not doing anything leaves you in a lousy spot. I know you are worried about no one listening, but I do think the home cares, and I would like to help you talk to them one more time." Reluctantly the members agreed. I helped them strategize about whom to contact. They asked me to speak with the director of Dietary for them. I agreed, sensing that to insist they invite her directly would have taxed them beyond their present ability. Further feelings of impotence might have developed. If they could feel they were activating me on their behalf, they might feel more potent. After all, the social service system was not beyond the systems they had to negotiate, but rather was part of them. My role included helping them use me. There was a pause. I told them I thought they were terrific and that I really thought they had a chance by sticking together and joining forces as they were going to do now. The mood in the group had lifted. Some members recalled other things which had gotten better after they had worked on them in the group. People left on a more hopeful note.

I found myself working very hard during this meeting. Discouragement was a formidable force. I sensed strongly that this was the time to confront their hopelessness head on. To allow it to go unchallenged would have had consequences beyond their concerns about food. If they could not challenge food issues in their lives, how could they challenge the harder, more subtle aspects of living within an institution? Those issues such as resident-staff relationships, family relationships, and diminishing abilities all needed strength to engage. Strength could come from successfully working on more "manageable" aspects of their lives. Though it would have been easy to tell residents that I thought things would definitely get better, an illusion about change would have been destructive. All I could really offer was my belief that the agency cared and that working on troubles would feel better than not. I would credit even the smallest efforts, hoping to encourage their viewing themselves as potent. My contribution was to help in the process, not to guarantee outcomes.

And so a year of concerted work in this area began. Of course, many other issues were also worked on throughout the year but none so consistently offered the opportunity for residents to develop their collective strength, determine what was of importance to them, and think through ways of articulating their needs. I was also beginning to see that if work on food concerns was to continue, it would take discipline, belief in group process, a vision of service, and a focus upon the dialogue between residents' needs and agency service. Without worker attentiveness, residents could easily lapse into their discouraged frame of mind.

Engaging the System

During the next few weeks, at the residents' request, I sent an invitation to the director of Dietary, inviting her to a floor group meeting on November 13. Prior to the meeting, she and I reviewed particular problems residents had cited, some prior sources of discouragement, and my pressing hard for them to move beyond their weariness to agree to invite her. It was most important that both residents and Dietary be tuned in to the issues for discussion, as well as possible obstacles in the process of working together. Feelings would be riding high on both sides. Feelings of discouragement, anger, rejection, disappointment, and some tiny rays of hope might be present. My function would be to attend to the dialogue between residents and Dietary. Despite the pulls, I could not side with either party but would focus attention on the talk between them. To do less would be to lose the other. I recalled a previous discussion with residents where:

In the midst of a heated discussion of their relationship with some nursing staff members, Mrs. Mann said she thought I should go and tell them off, for them. Mrs. Rosen said she didn't agree, because if I did, the staff would never listen to me again. They would think I was on the residents' side. There was a hush, and Mrs. Mann looked at me and said, "Aren't you on our sides? Don't you agree with us?" I said that I thought she was asking an important question. I said that actually I thought I was on neither side, but rather on the side of working out the troubles between them and nursing. To do that, I had to have a special relationship with each, where each knew I was listening to them, while not siding with the other. Mrs. Mann thought and said, "That's pretty tricky." I said I agreed. I thought she had put her finger on what was the hardest part of being a social worker— listening hard to both sides in a conflict, siding with neither, while working in the middle to help with the conflict between them. Mrs. Mann winked at me, smiled, and said, "But you really know we are right." We all laughed. I let the comment go as I recalled staff making a similar bid for my allegiance. We moved on to thinking through next steps in their work with nursing staff.

The question of my allegiance was not one which lent itself to "solving." It was one which would find its meaning as it was re-enacted in actual experience in the forthcoming meeting, each time residents and Dietary pulled apart, vying for my support in their struggle to ultimately remain engaged. Both Miss James, the assistant director, and Mrs. Hill, the floor dietician, welcomed the opportunity.

11/13

Miss James and Mrs. Hill were present. Residents were prepared for the meeting by discussions in the previous weeks about the particulars of their complaints. Whether they would speak up or not remained to be seen. After we were all assembled, I turned to Miss James and Mrs. Hill and said, "I think it is important for you to know that many residents are feeling discouraged about food problems getting better, and I had to urge them to allow me to invite you." Miss James said she could understand discouragement, but she really did want to hear. Her department would continue to work on the problems, and to do that, it was important to hear what the residents had to say. I asked for someone to start us off.

After a bit of sluggishness, the problems began to be mentioned. As each of the problems was mentioned, I repeated them over the loudspeaker for all to hear. Discussion went freely between Miss James, Mrs. Hill, and residents. Mrs. Esman was hanging her head and speaking her complaints angrily to herself. I said that I knew Mrs. Esman felt especially bad about the food, and I wondered if she would share some of her feelings. She just kept shaking her head and repeated that it was no good, no good. What in particular? She mentioned, "Why no blintzes? I love them." Then she hung her head and said, "What's the use?" I said, "Your discouragement is very strong." "Yes," she said, "I've given up." "But it's not as if you don't care. You stay mad, and I see you are bothered about the food all the time." "Yes," she answered quietly.

There was a hush in the room. I turned to Miss James and Mrs. Hill and said that I thought they were hearing the kind of feeling from Mrs. Esman that many residents feel. Miss James softly said, "I can understand that. Food is important. It's something to which you look forward. I bet you were a good cook, Mrs. Esman, and preparing the table was important to you." "Yes," she said as her mood began to soften. After her stroke she could no longer do it. Again the room was hushed. One sensed that many recalled pleasures no longer possible. I said, "And now that you can no longer prepare the table, you have to take what the home provides." Mrs. Esman looked up but said nothing. I turned to the group and asked, "Does not being able to do things as you did before make the problem worse?" There was a round of commiseration with how it was different. When they came to a nursing home, they had to be grateful for what they got; they were sick and couldn't do for themselves. Some of the people said they were glad they no longer had to cook. I returned us to the particulars of food problems. The complaints were exhausted, and residents reaffirmed their desire for the traditional Friday-night supper. Miss James said that she had heard them last month and had made plans for some of their favorite foods to be returned. The menus were just in the middle of being typed. Eyes picked up, smiles returned. I said I thought that was terrific. "See, bringing your issues to Miss James and Mrs. Hill did result in Dietary changing the menus as you wanted." She also mentioned the return of the blintzes and cautioned that it was hard to cook blintzes for so many people. I looked at Mrs. Esman and asked her if she wanted them even if they were hard sometimes. She said, "Yes." Miss James said, "O.K." I smiled and said, "How about three cheers for the blintzes and the Friday-night dinner return." The mood had lightened considerably, and we all cheered. I said that it seemed to me that their bringing up complaints and problems together did make a difference and that we ought to offer another round of cheers for them and Miss James, Mrs. Hill, and the Dietary Department. The mood felt hopeful. Tension had lessened.

After the cheers had subsided, I said that I had the feeling that one of the things which made it harder for them was having the feeling that they couldn't talk with Dietary frequently enough. They answered yes. I turned to Mrs. Hill and said, "I see you running around, and I know that you have four floors to get to during meals. I imagine that it must be a frustration to you not to have enough time to spend with residents at meals." Mrs. Hill said it was. At my suggestion, we then strategized about the idea of a monthly meeting with Mrs. Hill, which would lend some stability and regularity to food disussions. All agreed. Mrs. Hill and I agreed to work out the details.

After Miss James and Mrs. Hill left and we reviewed the problems and the next steps in relation to them, I asked the residents how they felt about the meeting. They were pretty discouraged when we started. How did they feel now? There was quiet and then many positives began to come through: maybe Dietary did listen; maybe change is possible; I'm glad we had the meeting; we voiced our ideas together, and they listen more when it's from a group.

Did they think that was true that it was different when they spoke as a group? Lots of reactions this time ... strength in numbers; they think complaints are more real; people don't feel so alone; the group really helps. We had been meeting for over one and a half hours now and people were getting antsy to leave before the change of shift time. Many would need help in going to the bathroom. I said that I knew people wanted to leave, but I wanted them to know I was interested in speaking with them further, at some point, about how they thought the home was able to listen more when they spoke as a group. They said fine. I said I thought they had worked hard today and had done something to help them get what they wanted. The meeting ended on a high note with lots of small talk amongst the residents.

This was an important meeting. A lot was riding on it. It was important that there be an atmosphere in which residents could "level" with Dietary, bringing forth the full extent of their feelings. Dealing with the authority of Dietary would not be easy. Preliminary work with Dietary, in addition to their own sensitivity, helped prepare them somewhat for what was coming. Both sides were tuned in to the problems and the possible obstacles to successful working together. Listening was deeper, responses fuller. Moving from the general to the specific was helpful in this listening process. Vague comments about the food would not help to improve problems. Questioning the particulars of "what" and "when" allowed for detailed, problem-focused attention. Answers would be found in specifics, not generalities.

Eliciting hidden feelings and comments was also important. Mrs. Esman's blood pressure rose sharply whenever she felt victimized. Her heart literally needed her to express what was within. She could not express rage at the fates for her stroke, but she could be helped to express anger at the blintzes. At least that was a beginning. While displacement was apparent, nonetheless the object of displacement was real. Helping residents see the connection between their current feelings about food and their feelings of loss at not being able to prepare as they had allowed them new insights into their reactions. Here was a synthesis of the expressive and instrumental aspects of our work with people in groups. The concrete, situational issues gave rise to feelings which became an important part of our work together. Not only was it important that we hear Mrs. Esman's actual complaint about the blintzes, but that we also hear her feelings about them. The blintzes problem mirrored Mrs. Esman's feelings toward institutionalization, her stroke, and the resultant loss of control over her body and her life.

I thought it probably would have been sufficient, in the beginning, for residents to "see" that they could meaningfully talk with Dietary. I also hoped we could focus upon some of the obstacles which made that talk hard. Viewing the structural arrangement of contact between residents and Dietary allowed for this opportunity. And finally, it was most important to credit residents' efforts. They had worked hard, had pushed beyond their fears, and had accomplished what they set out to do. Summarizing and determining next steps left us a continuing focus. Although the future remained uncertain, I thought we had made a good start together.

I was exhausted after the meeting. In addition to the work described I also had to attend to many environmental and personal variables: using the loudspeaker so people could hear, watching for those who had to go to the bathroom, sitting up those who slumped and needed assistance, comforting those who did not understand, and all the time watching the relationship between the group as a whole and the individuals within it.

12/3

Menu and food problems again arose for discussion in group meetings. This time they just wanted Mrs. Hill to come to a meeting.

12/10

Mrs. Hill was present; problems were once again discussed, information given. Each time residents felt problems were made better, other problems appeared. Some laughed and said at least they weren't falling behind. Residents once again didn't feel too hopeful, but did experience a sense of working on problems. I sensed a difference too.

The work continued into the new year.

1/1 to 2/11

While food remained a concern, other problems came to the fore more strongly during this period: the resignation of a favorite head nurse, the death of a resident, noise in the dining room. It began to appear as if discussion of food was the mainstay content of the group except if another strong issue appeared.

2/18

Most of the meeting concerned itself with Mrs. Lowry's death. They had been concerned about her for a long time.... We spoke of their missing her and their relationship with her.... The residents pointed to her disinterest in food and wondered whether her death was a result of the food. They angrily told me that if the food was tastier, Mrs. Lowry would have eaten and would not have died. I said I heard their sorrow very clearly. I too would miss Mrs. Lowry; I had known her for eight years. We paused together in recognition of our mutual loss. I said I also heard them questioning whether the home had contributed to her death by not providing food which was enticing to her. Mrs. Burke said she really didn't think they meant that. They all knew how Mrs. Hill had prepared special malteds and treats each day. They also knew how nursing had encouraged her to eat at meals. I said what they were saying was true, but was there also some lingering thought that we didn't do all we could have to help Mrs. Lowry? Mrs. Cohen said she thought Mrs. Lowry had died from depression. The group began to share their understanding of the sources of pain in Mrs. Lowry's life and moved away from food as a contributor. I said that I thought they showed great understanding of Mrs. Lowry and had been quite sensitive to her during her life. I wanted to reassure them that she had not died from depression, but rather from a serious physical illness which sometimes showed itself in lack of appetite.

Once again the theme of the institution's power to harm raised its head. It was important to draw that theme out directly, not mincing words, reaching for the strength of the residents' feelings, no matter how "taboo." Lingering thoughts that we had contributed to Mrs. Lowry's death would have been very destructive to residents. In truth, their comments about Mrs. Lowry were another way of speaking about the food, the resolution of which to them seemed entirely within the home's control: The home had the power to give or withold life.

2/25
When food problems appeared in this meeting, I asked residents how they wanted to work on the issues. Mrs. Mann and Mrs. Burke said that things had been promised to them but they had yet to see results. Others echoed the sentiment. I said I thought they had some very important questions to ask. I too had heard certain commitments, and while I knew, as they did, that the new menus weren't ready yet, perhaps they wanted to ask when they would be. Much self-conscious talk ensued: we don't want to be seen as complainers; why don't other floors say as much as we? I said I understood their self-consciousness, but I hoped they could get beyond it. They were involved in serious work with the Dietary Department and I thought it important that they hold that department and all staff, including myself, accountable for the work we were doing together. They asked me to invite Miss James and Mrs. Hill to the next meeting.

Each time we spoke, I had the sense of the group's becoming stronger. The quickness with which the members took to the idea of accountability was suggestive of their growing collective strength and their increasing view that they were not only recipients of what was given to them within the home, but rather a potentially active force in creating the kind of home in which they wanted to live. It was important that I help them hold me accountable for my performance as well as others. Within a relationship of trust it would be easy to neglect negatives. My power within the group was evident. Checks and balances remained essential. Even within

a well-meaning relationship abuses of power could develop.[35] I continued to feel that their regressive potential was ever present and that vigilance was required to keep the possibility of improvement before them. I would need to believe change was possible even when their hope dwindled. There was *always* a next step, even if it was unknown.

3/4
Miss James and Mrs. Hill were present. Residents felt engaged; alienation had lessened.

3/25
There was quiet in the meeting. Mrs. Mann said the sunnyside eggs were good the other day. All eyes were on her. She was the group member *most* critical about food. I broke into a smile and said, "I don't believe it!" Mrs. Mann grinned and smiled and said, "I know—they were terrific!" We were all quiet for a moment, as if soaking in Mrs. Mann's comments. I touched Mrs. Mann's hand, smiled and turned to the group and said, "Boy, there's no telling what can happen now if Mrs. Mann liked the eggs." Lots of laughter. Others began to share positives about the food.

This was an important moment for the group. If an item as delicate as sunnyside eggs was deemed excellent by the group's most critical member, then improvement was really possible. The laughter felt terrific. They took my teasing good-naturedly, joining in with their own. My use of humor de-escalated tension and allowed the members to feel pleasure together. Noting positives had become an important part of our work together.

4/1
During the past two months, Mrs. Burke and Mrs. Mann were critical of Mr. Delato's performance as a Food Committee delegate. For Mr. Delato, a shy, retiring man, unaccustomed to group living, the acceptance of this position reflected increased comfort with group

life. Nonetheless, though he wanted to do well, he felt it hard to represent residents' issues. He did not volunteer to resign and residents would not ask him to.

... Mrs. Burke asked what were they going to do? She was on another committee and therefore couldn't be on both. I looked around the room and said, "Well, what do you think about Mrs. Burke's question?" Various people were suggested to "assist" Mr. Delato. All refused. I looked at Mrs. Mann and said "What about you?" She reviewed her limitations. With annoyance she said she had refused for months; why did I keep bothering her? I said, "Because I'm not convinced you can't do the job." "But I can't see or hear," she insisted. I said that seeing wasn't necessary and she heard fine in our group. She said our group was different. She sat next to me, and I catered to her hearing problems. She was worried that she wouldn't be able to manage in a strange group. The residents likened the floor group to being with family and spoke of fear of "being with strangers." I said I could speak with the chief of social service and perhaps she could sit next to her. Mrs. Mann said "O.K., you win, I'll try it one time." The members congratulated Mrs. Mann, who all along cautioned them not to get too excited. I reviewed the terms of our contract: one try, my talking with the chief of social service. We reviewed problems for the food committee meeting next week....

4/22

More work on food problems. Residents still dependent upon me to urge them to invite Dietary to group meetings.... After the meeting I spoke with Miss James. She felt worn by all the criticism. She and her staff really were trying. Some problems are just so hard to correct. Could she share that with them, I wondered? She had leveled with them all along, and I thought her honesty was helpful. Residents felt a part of her department that way. Miss James mentioned the new items on the menu which they would like. She would give Mrs. Hill the pleasure of sharing the good news.

The work is really difficult for Dietary. Miss

James's department is one with hard-to-solve problems. Often things were beyond her control as when a tough cut of liver was sent or the distributor was out of something. Perhaps as residents felt less "at the mercy" of the institution, they would be more forgiving. Perhaps forgiveness was a feeling possible only between equals. Perhaps as engagement rose and alienation declined, forgiveness would be more possible.

4/29

Mrs. Hill announced all the new items soon to be on the menu. The merriment was broken by Mrs. Esman who said it was too bad that Miss Idel died before these changes were put into effect. She would have been happy. She ate so little. There was an embarrassed silence. I said, "Yes, it was sad that the changes came too late for Miss Idel, but knowing they did come would have made her happy." Silence. I said, "Something just struck me. Is part of your pushing on food so much because you don't know how long you will be here?" Mrs. Burke looked at me incredulously. "Of course," she answered, "we never know when we will die." We then moved on to a discussion of the seeming difference between institutional time and resident time.

I felt we had hit upon a critical underlying dynamic affecting our work together—different temporal clocks. While it was now seven months since our initial group meeting in which residents appeared so discouraged, desired changes were just now being put into the menus. These changes came too late for residents who had died. Institutional time and resident time were clearly disparate. The home's saying "change takes time" must fill residents with feelings of contradiction; while they intellectually understood that change took time, time was the one thing of which they didn't have much.

May

During May residents discussed other concerns: whether life was better in the community or in the home, a depressed resident, table arrangements, and whether life was worth living. Mrs. Mann reported on the two Food Committee meetings she had attended, saying the sessions were really hard on her, despite everyone's efforts to be of help to her. She hoped someone else would take the job. She felt the job was worthwhile. We spoke of how it might be better for her. There were no takers, and as if to avoid too much tension, the issue was tabled until June.

6/17
Mrs. Burke said she felt Mr. Delato should resign as Food Committee delegate. She told him she liked him very much but thought that speaking up went again his grain and that he might feel better if he didn't feel obligated to do a job he really didn't want to do. Discussion ensued and Mr. Delato said he felt he should step down. Residents thanked him for trying. I said, "I think being a Food Committee delegate is hard for Mr. Delato, but he should be pleased at his trying something new. He helped the group when no one else was willing to take on that responsibility." He smiled, feeling good about what he had done. He spoke a little of what was hard for him. He didn't expect it to get easier. Mrs. Burke then said, "O.K., who will be our next delegate?" Dead silence. Mrs. Mann made it clear she would not continue. After much discussion and encouragement, Mrs. Frank agreed. Her trepidation in her new role was apparent, but she was willing to try.

The assertion with which Mrs. Burke confronted Mr. Delato with his lack of performance was impressive. Her act seemed symbolic of the growing strength of the members. They were more hopeful and were taking their work seriously. Food and residents sharing the work were real issues in their lives. Mrs. Frank's agreement, after a year of refusal, appeared to be part of this growing strength. Interestingly, the stronger the group, the stronger the individuals, and the stronger the individuals, the stronger the group. Food, as an environmental problem, had given rise to both inter-and intra-group issues. If the members were to continue their dialogue with Dietary, then the group as a whole would also have to work simultaneously on internal member-to-member relationships. Members had to make demands upon each other and had to provide support once leaders emerged. Otherwise, there would be no one to carry on the group's mission.

July
After my return from vacation, work was devoted to nursing concerns and helping to prepare Mrs. Frank for her first Food Committee meeting. I took notes for her because she could no longer write. It had also become my role to keep track of both the issues and the process of working on the issues. With my trusty notebook, I could be counted upon to preserve our collective memory. Many residents could no longer remember from week to week.

8/5
Mrs. Frank gave her Food Committee report. She was articulate and confident. She inspired residents' confidence in her and the Food Committee. I said she sounded as if she enjoyed going. It was not as hard as she had thought. Preparatory discussion last week had helped. I suggested that in the meeting prior to the Food Committee Mrs. Frank chair a discussion on matters residents wished her to take back. I would continue to take notes for her. They agreed and said that discussion would be helpful. The rest of the meeting was taken up with reactions to my announcement that during September I was to be assigned to another floor. We had worked together for six years. . . .

8/12
More separation work. Mrs. Frank seriously ill with congestive heart failure.

8/12-8/15

Mrs. Frank continued to be quite ill. At one point when she, her family, and I were visiting together, she said, "When I get back," then hung her head as if feeling too arrogant, "*If* I get back to the group meeting, I really want to hear those food problems." I said, "Yes, you really were terrific when you presented your report. The residents have great respect for your abilities. They see you as a fighter." Mrs. Frank smiled and said, "I think it's important that we stick together and fight for what we think is right." We all smiled in recognition of what had become so important to her. She began to rest.

8/16

Mrs. Frank died. She was alert and conscious to the end. She died as she had lived, with continued recommendations for how to make the lives of others better.

8/19

My last group meeting before vacation. In September I would introduce the new worker. Mrs. Schwartz had died in addition to Mrs. Frank. Three residents were transferred to the hospital on an emergency basis. I felt filled with emotion. I imagined residents might be feeling that way also. Life was so uncertain, especially for the residents.

There was silence at the beginning. It had become our tradition that I would make the acknowledgment of a death on the floor. I began the meeting by saying that I imagined this was a hard week for them; they had lost two residents. Both Mrs. Schwartz and Mrs. Frank had died. Reactions came forth easily. They had been close to each in different ways. Mrs. Frank had been a hard-working group member. Mrs. Schwartz had not attended but had been part of the floor life outside the group. I said I would miss them. Mrs. Tisch said Mrs. Frank had worked hard for them. Yes, I said, I admired her courage. I didn't think it was easy for her to complain to all the different people to whom she had to bring criticism. Mrs. Burke said they were all afraid of being seen as complainers. I said perhaps in the future I could help them share those

feelings and thoughts with their new social worker. They agreed.... Toward the end of the meeting I said, "I'd like to take a moment to tell you about a study I read a few years ago." They were interested and I told them about Tobin and Lieberman's findings that assertion, not passivity, was associated with longevity in institutional life. Some said they found that hard to believe. "Imagine, the complainers live longer." After a short discussion about the findings, Mrs. Burke, with tears in her eyes, said, "I want to thank you for what you have just shared with us. You have given me strength to complain. I always was a complainer, but now I know it is the right thing to do." The mood in the group was quite attentive. It was hard for me to speak. I felt as if a year's work culminated in that moment.

Before I could respond, perhaps sensing my emotion, Mrs. Burke said, "Well, life goes on and now we need another Food Committee delegate to take Mrs. Frank's place." There were immediate refusals. Mrs. Burke shouted, "Well, someone *has* to be a delegate." No takers. I said, "Several residents who might might be delegates are not at the meeting. Mrs. Burke, how about speaking to people in the next two weeks while I am away and raise the discussion at our next meeting?" Mrs. Burke and the other residents agreed.

What a powerful meeting! Acknowledgment of death and the continuance of life side by side!

CONCLUSION

During the year the group members worked hard on food concerns. Initial discouragement was understandable. Only seeing the problems inherent in institutional living and not feeling enough a part of the process of making things better had the effect of alienating residents from the very institution designed to serve them. They had spoken about food many times. I was never sure why they became so discouraged when they did. There were obviously many variables influencing how they felt, some related to Dietary and some not. Their feelings of alienation were striking, especially since the Food Committee was working well. Mr. Delato, as a Food Committee delegate, did not strengthen their sense of productivity. However, he offered when no one else would take the job.

Many residents were hesitant to take additional responsibility within the group. Although a resident for two years, Mrs. Frank felt like a newcomer. Though esteemed by others, she doubted her abilities and found it difficult to take on new group tasks and responsibilities. She accepted the role of alternate delegate. Only by taking the Food Committee job was she convinced of how well she could do and how highly esteemed she was by others. She, like many women of her generation, did not see herself in a leadership role.

Mrs. Mann, though of high status and comfortable with the floor group (which she considered family), feared failure within the Resident Council. With decreasing physical abilities, she could not imagine a role of increasing responsibility. Her decision to "assist" Mr. Delato represented a gift to the group and to me.

Mr. Delato, in response to a request from his peers and with considerable group support, took responsibility uncharacteristic of him. His venture deeper into group life reflected growing trust and the pull to belong to the "family" of the group members.

These residents and many others who shared their thinking and feelings in the group grew closer by sharing their lives together. I was constantly impressed with how hard residents worked and how important a part of their lives the group was.

The floor group contained the fuel with which residents rekindled old abilities and developed new ones. What was most noticeable was that new roles and abilities were developed in relation to real work. Tasks were not fabricated "to make people feel better" or "less depressed" or "happier." The pressing reality of work to be done, which reflected the reality of residents' lives, provided the urgent impetus for many to move beyond their fears of inadequacy, discouragement, and self-criticism.

This movement took place within an atmosphere of mutual aid. Their encouragement, their crediting of each other's abilities, and their promise of support in the process of working on troubles were crucial components of group life. Their collective desire for solutions to food problems provided energy week after week.

This mutual aid group helped residents feel more in control over their lives through direct engagement with peers and their environment. Increased feelings of self-worth were apparent as their repertoire of social roles expanded. Residents were once again involved in creating the kind of world in which they wanted to live.

My activity was guided by the five professional tasks identified by Schwartz as the tasks required of social workers as they carry out their function within the group.[36]

Searching Out the Common Ground

Residents' belief that their views were unimportant and unwelcomed ran counter to my belief that there was a symbiotic tie between them and the Dietary Department. In my experience, I observed that Dietary did their work better through dialogue with residents. They wanted to hear complaints and suggestions. In fact, they knew that if residents were to feel more satisfied, their ideas and preferences would have to be included. That the common ground between residents and Dietary sometimes appeared obscured seemed unremarkable to me. This muting was a function of the complexity of institutional life and bureaucratic organization. My simultaneous work with residents and Dietary sought to make the common ground visible to both. I knew if I kept this tie in the foreground, it would become increasingly apparent to the residents. In reality, as residents experienced Dietary's concern and saw some visible signs of change, they too came to believe that their voices were not only accepted, but actually needed for problem resolution.

Detecting and Challenging the Obstacles

Throughout the year, residents' discouragement was a major obstacle blocking the quality and quantity of their work together. When they placed responsibility outside themselves, they failed to see their contribution to the lack of resolution of problems. While responsibility for improving food lay with the Dietary Department, residents did bear responsibility for their contribution to that effort. When they felt like victims, they acted victimized. If Dietary changed their way of making fish and residents refused to try it, how would Dietary ever know if the new way was preferred? If residents were too angry to help, things would be that much harder for Dietary.

A dual emphasis upon the content of the meeting as well as the process of working on troubles was essential. Residents needed me to help them "own" their discouragement and then to see the connection between discouragement and

inactivity. Asking group members to come to grips with the obstacles to their activity and then moving beyond was critical. Initially, residents were better able to acknowledge their discouragement than they were able to do anything about it. Time and time again they needed me to help them move on by saying, "Enough! What are you going to do?" Sometimes they did nothing. They needed my patience in their process of such hard work. Much was at stake. It was easier for residents to find fault than to exercise their hope, one more time, by being active on their own behalf.

Contributing Data

Since residents felt so "stuck," contributing my ideas and thinking about the possible ways to proceed became imperative. What was equally critical was *not* telling them which path to take. I might urge them to act, but when they decided, they had to "own" their decision. This process of owning would help them in the work to come.

Lending a Vision

This task was most crucial in helping the group work together. My belief in the possibility of change was continuously called upon by the members. "Is change possible? Will things get better?" These feelings were present in each meeting. I found it necessary to maintain a high energy level in this area. I needed to have "faith" for all of us. Sometimes I found myself impatient. Why did certain things take so long? I doubted my helping strategy. Perhaps residents should not have complained only to Dietary. Perhaps it was I who was holding them back. These thoughts prompted me to explore alternative strategies with the members. With hindsight I might have "leveled" more with Miss James and Mrs. Hill, pushing past initial explanations for why things weren't happening sooner. I suppose I felt I was always treading a thin line between resident needs and institutional possibilities. It was important to me not to be seen as overidentified with either side.

Establishing the Bounds and Limits of Our Working Relationship

While an overall agreement existed, the particulars of our working agreement — or contract — seemed to be defined during each meeting. Each new problem demanded that the terms of our agreement be determined, in process, in the moment. I would make a recommendation, but I would not tell them what to do. I would do what was too hard for them but only if it really was too hard. I would have faith in the process of working together even when they lost theirs. I would help Dietary and the group work together, but I would not join either side. I would do my work but could not do theirs. If no one would be a Food Committee deletate, then the floor would not be represented. I would do all I could to help that possibility come to pass, but it was their job to produce the delegate.

Group association remains an inherent part of institutional living. The impetus for collectivity has its origin in two main sources: (1) the natural impetus of people who need each other to join together, and (2) the recognition by institutional inhabitants that groups offer a buffer against institutional stress as well as a structural means for engagement with the institution. The institution bears special responsibility for furthering the life-giving potential of group association based upon their recognition of the possible alienating and isolating components of institutional living and the need for a structured means for furthering ongoing dialogue with consumers. Group service offers assistance both to clients and agency. This dual focus upon resident and environment identifies the purview of social workers. Their focus remains upon the dialogue between client need and agency service, seeking to lessen the distance between the two. The social worker's practice in groups with older institutionalized people is influenced by (1) the meaning of institutionalization, (2) the high degree of uncertainty, unpredictability, and loss experienced, (3) the existential nature of life, and (4) the need to continue a meaningful life in the face of loss and ongoing uncertainty. Older people, like people of all ages, possess the ability to work on issues of importance in their lives. The mutual aid group represents a significant means for working on important issues encountered in the lives of older, institutionalized people. The collective whole is indeed much greater than the sum of its parts.

NOTES

1. Elaine M. Brody, "Aging," in *Encyclopedia of Social Work*, 16th ed., ed. R. Morris (New York; National Association of Social Workers, 1971), pp. 51-74.

2. Margaret Blenkner, "The Normal Dependencies of Aging," in *The Later Years: Social Applications of Gerontology*, ed. Richard A. Kalish (Monterey, Calif.: Brooks/Cole Publishing Co., 1977).

3. Many document the poverty of the aged. See for example: Brody, "Aging"; Robert N. Butler, *Why Survive: Being Old in America*

(New York: Harper & Row, 1955); Caroll L. Estes, *The Aging Enterprise* (San Francisco: Jossey-Bass Publishers, 1979).

4. Brody, "Aging," p. 53.

5. Butler, "Why Survive," p. 47.

6. Ibid., pp. 29-32.

7. Ibid.; Brody, "Aging."

8. Brody, "Aging," and Butler, *Why Survive.*

9. Blenkner, "Normative Dependencies of Aging," p. 79.

10. Linda K. George, *Role Transitions in Later Life* (Monterey, Calif.: Brooks/Cole Publishing Co., 1980), p. 7.

11. Albert F. Wesson, "Some Sociological Characteristics of Long-Term Care," in *Older People and Their Social World,* ed. Arnold M. Rose and Warren A. Peterson (Philadelphia: F. A. Davis Company, 1965).

12. Leonard E. Gottesman and Evelyn Hutchinson, "Characteristics of the Institutionalized Elderly," in *A Social Work Guide for Long-Term Care Facilities,* ed. Elaine M. Brody (Rockville, Md.: National Institute of Mental Health, 1974).

13. Erving Goffman, *Asylums* (Garden City, N.Y.: Anchor Books, Doubleday and Company, 1961).

14. Ibid., p. 69.

15. Morris Zelditch, "The Home for the Aged —A Community," *The Gerontologist* 2, no. 1 (1962): 37-41, and Eva Kahana, "Matching Environments to the Needs of the Aged: A Conceptual Scheme," in *Late Life: Communities and Environmental Policy,* ed. Jaber F. Gubrium (Springfield, Ill.: Charles C Thomas, 1974).

16. Kahana, "Matching Environments," p. 206.

17. Rodney M. Coe, "Self-Conceptions and Institutionalization," in *Older People and their Social World,* ed. Rose and Peterson.

18. Barbara F. Turner, Sheldon S. Tobin, and Morton A. Lieberman, "Personality Traits as Predictors of Institutional Adaption Among the Aged," *Journal of Gerontology* 27, no. 1 (1972): 61-68.

19. The issue of who must be institutionalized is becoming a more difficult question to answer as community health care pro-
grams increasingly provide service to those previously thought of as appropriate candidates for institutionalization. The Long-Term Home Health Care Program at Jewish Home and Hospital for Aged, New York, is one such community health care program.

20. Marc Fried, "Grieving for a Lost Home," in *The Urban Condition,* ed. Leonard Jo Duhl (New York: Basic Books, 1963), p. 151.

21. See Sheldon S. Tobin and Morton A. Lieberman, *Last Home for the Aged* (San Francisco: Jossey-Bass, 1976) for a description of their landmark study on the effects of institutionalization.

22. Ruth Bennett, "The Meaning of Institutional Life," *The Gerontologist* 3, no. 3 (1963): 117-125.

23. Tobin and Lieberman, *Last Home for the Aged.*

24. Ibid., p. 215.

25. Ibid.

26. William Schwartz, "Social Group Work: The Interactionist Approach," in *Encyclopedia of Social Work,* 16th ed. Ed. R. Morris (New York: National Association of Social Workers, 1971), pp. 1252-1262.

27. Ibid., p. 1253.

28. Ibid., p. 1258.

29. William Schwartz, "Private Troubles and Public Issues: One Social Work Job or Two?" *The Social Welfare Forum* (New York: Columbia University Press, 1969), p. 38.

30. Mark Forman, "The Alienated Resident and the Alienating Institution: A Case for Peer Group Intervention," *Social Work* 16, no. 2 (1971): 48.

31. See, for example, Stephen Z. Cohen and Jerome Hammerman, "Social Work with Groups," in *Social Work Guide,* ed. Brody.

32. Ken Tarabelli, student process recording, Jewish Home and Hospital for Aged, Spring 1973.

33. The "Record of Service" developed by William Schwartz provides an excellent recording means of conceptualizing and describing a group's work on a particular theme over time. The emphasis is upon what workers do, rather than on what they know or feel. For a discussion of the Record of Service see Goodwin P. Garfied and Carol R. Irizarry, "The

'Record of Service': Describing Social Work Practice," in *The Practice of Group Work*, ed. William Schwartz and Serapio R. Zalba (New York: Columbia University Press, 1971).
34. See William Schwartz, "The Social Worker in the Group," *The Social Welfare Forum* (New York: Columbia University Press, 1961) for a discussion of the function of the social worker as mediator. For a further elaboration of the practice implications of this conceptualization of function see Harold Lipton and Sidney Malter, "The Social Worker as Mediator on a Hospital Ward," in *The Practice of Group Work*, ed. Schwartz and Zalba.
35. Charles S. Levy, *Social Work Ethics* (New York: Human Sciences Press, 1976) devotes considerable attention to elements of power within a fiduciary relationship. See especially chapters 5 and 6.
36. Schwartz, "Social Worker in the Group."

BIBLIOGRAPHY

Bennett, Ruth. "The Meaning of Institutional Life." *The Gerontologist* 3, no. 3 (1963): 117-125.
Blenkner, Margaret. "The Normal Dependencies of Aging." In *The Later Years: Social Applications of Gerontology*. Edited by Richard A. Kalish. Monterey, Calif.: Brooks/Cole Publishing Company, 1977.
Brody, Elaine M. "Aging." In *Encyclopedia of Social Work*, 16th ed. New York: National Association of Social Workers, 1971.
Butler, Robert N. *Why Survive: Being Old In America*. New York: Harper & Row, 1955.
Coe, Rodney M. "Self-Conceptions and Institutionalization." In *Older People and Their Social World*. Edited by Arnold M. Rose and Warren A. Peterson. Philadelphia: F. A. Davis Company, 1965.
Cohen, Stephen Z., and Jerome Hammerman. "Social Work with Groups." In *A Social Work Guide for Long-Term Care Facilities*. Edited by Elaine M. Brody. Rockville, Md.: National Institute for Mental Health, 1974, pp. 27-45.
Estes, Caroll L. *The Aging Enterprise*. San Francisco: Jossey-Bass Publishers, 1979.

Forman, Mark. "The Alienated Resident and the Alienating Institution." *Social Work* 16, no. 2 (1971): 47-54.
Fried, Marc. "Grieving for a Lost Home." In *The Urban Condition*. Edited by Leonard J. Duhl. New York: Basic Books, Inc., 1963.
Garfied, Goodwin P., and Carol R. Irizarry. "The 'Record of Service': Describing Social Work Practice." In *The Practice of Group Work*. Edited by William Schwartz and Serapio R. Zalba. New York: Columbia University Press, 1971.
George, Linda K. *Role Transitions in Later Life*. Monterey, Calif.: Brooks/Cole Publishing Company, 1980.
Goffman, Erving. *Asylums*. Garden City, N.Y.: Anchor Books, Doubleday & Company, 1961.
Gottesman, Leonard E., and Evelyn Hutchinson. "Characteristics of the Institutionalized Elderly." In *A Social Work Guide for Long-Term Care Facilities*. Edited by Elaine M. Brody. Rockville, Md.: National Institute for Mental Health, 1974.
Kahana, Eva. "Matching Environments to the Needs of the Aged: A Conceptual Scheme." In *Late Life: Communities and Environmental Policy*. Edited by Jaber F. Gubrium. Springfield, Ill.: Charles C Thomas, 1974.
Levy, Charles S. *Social Work Ethics*. New York: Human Sciences Press, 1976.
Lipton, Harold, and Sidney Malter. "The Social Worker as Mediator on a Hospital Ward." In *The Practice of Group Work*. Edited by William Schwartz and Serapio R. Zalba. New York: Columbia University Press, 1971.
Schwartz, William. "The Social Worker in the Group." *The Social Welfare Forum*. New York: Columbia University Press, 1961.
———. "Private Troubles and Public Issues: One Social Work Job or Two?" *The Social Welfare Forum*. New York: Columbia University Press, 1969.
———. "Social Group Work: The Interactionist Approach." In *Encyclopedia of Social Work*, 16th ed. New York: National Association of Social Workers, 1971.
Tarabelli, Ken. Student Process Recording.

Spring 1973. Jewish Home and Hospital for Aged.

Tobin, Sheldon S., and Morton A. Lieberman. *Last Home for the Aged.* San Francisco: Jossey-Bass, 1976.

Turner, Barbara F., Sheldon S. Tobin, and Morton A. Lieberman. "Personality Traits as Predictors of Institutional Adaption Among the Aged." *Journal of Gerontology* 27, no. 1 (1972): 61-68.

Wesson, Albert F. "Some Sociological Characteristics of Long Term Care." In *Older People and Their Social World.* Edited by Arnold M. Rose and Warren A. Peterson. Philadelphia.: F. A. Davis Company, 1965.

Zelditch, Morris. "The Home for the Aged— A Community." *The Gerontologist* 2, no. 1 (1962): 37-41.

Part Six
Rediscovering Our Roots

Judith A. B. Lee
Carol R. Swenson

CHAPTER 19

The Concept of Mutual Aid

William Schwartz noted, "Professions have a way of moving periodically through eras of rediscovery in which an old truth comes alive with the vigor and freshness of a new idea."[1] His own discovery and rediscovery of concepts basic to the heart of social group work and to the theoretical development of social work contain just such relevance and excitement. They resonate in us on the level of the "ah ha!" experience which characterizes discovery: "Yes, that is what I have been doing all along!" or "That is exactly what is important!" Schwartz's "generic vision," development of the concept of mediation, and emphasis on the primacy of skill, on process, on the importance of affect (both worker's and client's), on reciprocity, and on the group as "an enterprise in mutual aid" are concepts of that order. In tracing the evolution of concepts with a profession, it is difficult to delineate moments of exciting rediscovery from moments of originality or discovery. If, however, bringing focus and clarity to previously diffuse ideas can vitalize them, it was Schwartz's contribution to bring these concepts to life. His teaching and writings raised some of the basic but half-hidden truths which social workers have always known, or even used without "knowing," to the level of a coherent theoretical approach which can guide practice.

It is difficult to separate the interrelated concepts of the interactionist approach. Like a group, this theoretical approach is more than the sum of its parts and becomes a whole in a unique way. So, in highlighting the concept of mutual aid here, we view it as if we were looking at an individual within a group, ever mindful of each part's uniqueness, and yet its relatedness to the other parts which make up the whole. The concept of mediation, for example, is central to this approach, for it clarifies the social work function itself, forming the base from which all else follows. It moves social work thinking forward dramatically, by overcoming dichotomies such as the individual and society, the one and the many, the individual and the group, change of individuals and social reform, and even the so-called "intrapsychic" and "interpersonal." This concept of the social work function, mediating "the process by which the individual and his society reach out for each other through a mutual need for self fulfillment," places us in a new arena of practice.[2] We are "at the point where the two forces meet"—in the interactional arena. This does not allow us to choose "either-or" but requires "both," thus giving new clarity to the term "psychosocial."

It is Schwartz's concept of the "mutual

need for self-fulfillment" of people and their systems that gives further meaning to his emphasis on mutual aid. People need each other and the social groupings of which they are a part; there is no wholeness or real existence in isolation. According to Shulman, Schwartz's view of the individual-social interaction is a statement of interdependence which is fundamental to our belief in a social responsibility for the welfare of each individual.[3] Gitterman defines the mutual aid system in the group as one in

> which people share relevant concerns and ideas, and begin to experience others in the same "boat," moving through "the rocky waters of life." ... As they confide, share and move into taboo areas, they feel less singled-out, their concerns/problems become less unique, less unusual, and often less pathological. By its very nature the group mutual aid system universalizes people's problems, reducing isolation and stigma.... This unleashes a group's inherent potential for "multiplicity of helping relationships"; with all members invested and participating in the helping process.[4]

The concept of mutual aid does not belong to social work alone, but it is inherent in most of the early group work formulations. It was clearly Schwartz, however, who gave primacy to the concept. In one salient passage he stated:

> *First*, the group is *an enterprise in mutual aid*, an alliance of individuals *who need each other*, in varying degrees, *to work on common problems*. The important fact is that this is a helping system in which the clients need each other as well as the worker. This need to use each other, to create not one but many helping relationships, is a vital ingredient of the group process, and constitutes a common need over and above the specific task for which the group was formed.[5]

The primacy of mutual aid relates to Schwartz's thinking about the nature of the helping process as well. He was clear that change resides in the client, not in the helper.

> the uneasy attempt to take over the language and the sequence-of-treatment concept of the medical profession has confused and retarded our own attempts to find terms and concepts which would truly describe the helping process in social work. For the helping relationship as we know it is one in which the client possesses the only real and lasting means to his own ends. The worker is but one resource in a life situation which encompasses many significant relationships.[6]

The tasks of the worker in helping the client to work follow from this premise. This view of the client as the source of help and this division of labor in the helping relationship differentiate interactionist and later related approaches from "medical model" approaches where the helper studies, diagnoses, treats, and prescribes.[7] The emphasis on the need and potential of people for mutual aid also bespeaks a faith in the ability of the client not only to help himself/herself, but also to help others. It moves us beyond the self-centeredness of our age, so aptly called an "age of narcissism," to a social-centeredness which emphasizes the *relationship between the one and the many*.[8] In offering the concept of mutual aid and in transcending the dichotomy between the individual and his social groupings, Schwartz captures the essence of group work history and, we think, the primary contribution of group work to social work.

A practice example illuminates our understanding of the powerful nature of the mutual aid process. It is drawn from "No Place To Go: Homeless Women," about a small group of women who resided in a temporary public shelter (described in chapter 13). The group members are four women ranging in age from twenty-six to forty-five. Nina, who speaks first, is a black, mildly retarded twenty-eight-year-old who ran away from a physically abusive, alcoholic mother and found herself in the shelter. Carla is a bright, heavy, twenty-six-year-old, middle-class black woman who was cast out of her family after she was raped. Lorna is a forty-five-year-old observant Jewish woman who became depressed and agoraphobic, and eventually homeless, after the death of her parents. Donna is a bright and artistically creative thirty-year-old black woman who had two psychiatric hospitalizations after being beaten by her boyfriend. The common ground these women met on was that they all found themselves alone and homeless, and they shared several months together in the women's shelter. The worker formed the group to promote friendship and a mutual aid system, which would help them leave the shelter and support them once they were on their own. This meeting marked a new step in the intimacy they were developing. The group members had spent a lot of time sharing how difficult life was in the shelter and how they tried to cope.

Nina then said that she was not afraid to express her depressed feelings, because when they hurt, they hurt. The way she was treated here hurt a lot, but the way she was treated at home hurt more. And the workers here kept telling her to go home; they didn't want to know why she couldn't do that. In a lengthy and somewhat vague way she alluded to handcuffs, ropes, and a big dog at home. The others very patiently listened as Nina tried to find words for what happened to her. They kept saying supportive things like "yeah, it sounds hard." I did the same, encouraging her to tell her story, which I knew already, to the others. Donna then said, "It sounds like you had a very hard life, and you did have good

reason to leave home, but could you try to tell us about it a little more clearly?" In response to this support and demand for work, Nina struggled on. "My mother was nice sometimes and then suddenly she was mean. . . . She would tie me up . . . to the hot radiator . . . all alone . . . and make the dog guard me. I had no food, either." Lorna held Nina's hand. They were all outraged for her and let her know that.

Carla said, "I know just how you feel. I was in the same boat. My father beat me bad, too. I ran away first when I was thirteen. My mother would give me candy to smooth it over, but I never forgot the pain, never." Donna said, "I know, too. People put their hands on you and try to control your life, but they can't get your soul. You leave and run away, you can't let them get you, and then your family blames you for it." Carla said, "Exactly. They didn't cause me being here, but they add to my pain by blaming me for it." Lorna added, "Yes, when I was well, I was a sister. I cooked for them, and babysat for them. Now I bring them shame, and I'm not a sister any more." Carla said, "Right, I have parents and six brothers and sisters, but I'm all alone."

Donna said, "Well, maybe not *all* alone," and smiled shyly at the others. It was a close moment. Nina said, "I don't know if I will have you all forever, but I can say I have you to talk to now." Carla said that without us she'd have no one. She said we brought her hope. She said she loved me for helping them. I said that I was very moved by their caring for each other and the help they gave today. I loved them all, too, and I knew they had what it takes to make it. Carla then cracked a joke about the mayor of the city trying to live in a shelter, and "how would he fare?"

This moving excerpt exemplifies exactly what Schwartz, Gitterman, Shulman, and others describe as the mutual aid process. At that moment, the group was theirs. *They* were the helpers: reaching each other, sharing pain, healing old and present wounds, and mobilizing coping abilities and hope as the process unfolded.

Schwartz said that our times have "compelled social workers to look again at the forces of mutual aid and peer group association."[9] This chapter will examine these forces through tracing the concept of mutual aid in the writings and the programs of the helping professions. In so doing, we hope to reaffirm mutual aid as a critical concept for social work practice at the current time.

MUTUAL AID IN SOCIAL WORK

Historical Precursors

Prior to the industrialization of England and America, the family and clan were self-sufficient units of mutual aid which assured survival.[10] As time passed, other formal and informal means of protecting people from pauperism evolved, some taking the form of mutual aid. We know more, however, about the historic provision of economic aid than of social or emotional support. The English Poor Law emerged in early seventeenth-century England to take care of the exceptional cases where the family could not meet its obligations. Under the Poor Law, the "truly indigent and helpless," such as orphaned children, were differentiated from the "idle, able-bodied, and unworthy" poor. The former were provided for, while the latter were considered a threat to the community and were treated harshly.

In colonial America "the early deprivations were so extreme that sheer survival was dependent upon mutual aid." Records from Plymouth and other early colonies indicate individual and institutional responses to need in the form of mutual aid obligations to family and kin, to other members of the community, and even to "all accessible people in trouble, whether they be kin, neighbors, or strangers."[11] Mutual aid, then, flowed side by side with organized efforts to deal with need and its assumed causes and effects.

As early as the seventeenth century, Friendly Societies existed, which "as well as meeting a threefold desire for security in sickness, a lump sum to spend at a future date, and avoidance of a pauper funeral—were social clubs for members."[12] Since people were providing for themselves through mutual aid, such attempts at self-help were viewed as posing no threat to the social order; in fact they were seen as desirable. These societies were important forerunners of more organized group work efforts such as the YMCA's, Sunday schools, and other youth movements in nineteenth-century England and America. In America, in addition, the Jewish Youth Movement was also the forerunner of the Jewish Center Movement. All provided group-oriented solutions to the problems of a rapidly changing social scene dominated by the effects of the Industrial Revolution.[13]

Simultaneously, organized private charities were attempting to deal with the same social changes. This resulted in a proliferation of diverse and uncoordinated efforts which, many felt, pauperized the poor and proved an expense to the rich. The Charity Organization Society sprang out of this chaos to bring "scientific order" to the giving of charity. Both social casework and community organization can trace their roots to this common source, though the former located the problem more in the individual and the latter more in society, emphasizing social processes, social control, and social reform.[14] Group work shared the passion for social reform with community organization and the concern for the individual with casework. It also shared a history of religious motivation, philanthropy, and an emphasis on morality. Many of the early ancestors of group work were dedicated to "character building."

The Three Major Influences on Social Group Work

The origins of social group work are most clearly to be found, however, in nineteenth-century England when the impetus to social work first arose in the awakening of social conscience. Changes in political thought occurred, as people began to recognize laissez-faire as an inadequate basis for social reform. Philanthropy was the first motive behind social group work, while the second was even older, the motive of mutual aid. Mutual self-help developed spontaneously and indigenously within communities to mitigate against the proliferating effects of industrialization. This heritage became part of social group work and may well represent its most important legacy.[15]

Group work in its modern American form emerged during the 1920s with its roots in the settlement, recreation, and progressive education movements. As Gitterman stated, "From settlements, the group work method derived its institutional base. . . . From the recreation movement, social group work gained its interest in the value of play and activities. . . . [And] from the progressive education movement group work acquired a philosophic base."[16] John Dewey, who was a frequent visitor to settlements, influenced them in the direction of democratic group life. The group, whether in the classroom or the settlement house or in informal living, represented the microcosm of a democratic society. To Dewey, the group was an experience in practicing the ideals of democracy. It was the organized recreation movement, however, that promoted leisure-time group activities as a step toward personal development and the acquisition of desired social skills.[17] Nonetheless, the Settlement Movement was the most prominent ancestor of social group work.

The Settlement Movement

Placing emphasis on the economic and social conditions of the day as more problematic than individual weakness, the Settlement Movement added two important and unique dimensions to social work. These were the provision of service to the competent as well as those in need, and an incorporation of mutual aid into formalized social welfare efforts. In using mutual aid, we can say that the settlements formed a bridge between informal and formal social welfare organizations.

The American version of the Settlement Movement also added an emphasis on the small group as "the building block of democracy" and had "a fierce passion for social reform."[18] Such leaders as Jane Addams, Florence Kelley, Lillian D. Wald, and others brought about changes in local conditions and remedial legislation in areas of female and child labor, education, sanitation, recreation, housing, industrial relations, and discrimination against immigrants.[19] The emphasis on reform and mutual aid differed sharply from the philosophy of individual causation of the Charity Organization Society, and the two movements were often antagonistic around the turn of the century. Some interests merged, however, and Jane Addams was elected to the presidency of the National Conference of Charities and Corrections in 1909.[20] In serving individuals in small groups with an emphasis on mutual aid, in all areas from child care to clubs for the aged, and in organizing for social reform, the settlements themselves formed an early context for the practical and conceptual healing of this split.

The settlements also left a profound mark on our understanding of the nature of the helping process in social work through including the client-worker relationship as a mutual aid relationship. Reciprocity occurred not only between clients working together but in the worker-client relationship as well. Woodroofe observed that

> Settlements were designed, not only to bring culture and light into the hard, hopeless lives of the East End, but to deepen the University men's understanding of the poor and their problems.[21]

Canon Samuel Barnett, who founded Toynbee Hall in 1884, emphasized that the residents (workers) should take up civic duties which would "bring them into contact with others and put them in a position both to learn and to teach."[22] While "teaching" was a clear goal of all early social workers, learning from the poor was a rather unique notion involving reciprocity. Indeed, many American settlements provided the locations for leading thinkers such as John Dewey and his cohorts meeting with the neighborhood residents for open sharing and mutual discourse.[23] The purpose was not only for the more well-to-do to give to the poor, but to foster "a solemn sense of relationship," as Octavia Hill has said.[24]

This concept of relationship emphasizes reciprocity. While some of the founders of the first settlements had a sense of noblesse oblige and most had no conception of the massive economic and sociopolitical shifts necessary really to bridge the gaps, they must be given credit for a vision of reciprocity, mutual aid, and social unity which crossed class barriers. Jane Addams even hoped that this reciprocity and collective action would help level "the overaccumulation at one end of society and the destitution at the other." Addams said of her workers that they "must be content to live quietly side by side with their neighbors, until they *grow into* a sense of *relationship* and *mutual interests.*"[25] And Canon Barnett said of Toynbee Hall

> We have too . . . the opportunity of building up a new system of relationships side by side with our old . . . forming around the Hall a new world of student-friends and guest friends, acting and reacting on one another, by whose means refinement and knowledge may pass electrically as from friend to friend, and not professionally as from tutor to pupil.[26]

This vision of a new world, which had mutual aid as its underpinning and reciprocity as its hallmark, was the unique contribution of the settlements to social group work and to social work's philosophy of helping.

Community

Further, settlements and other group work agencies reaffirmed for society and our profession the importance of belonging, of community, of collective action for the collective good. Woodroofe noted that the existence of group work agencies was

> based on the realization that, faced with demoralizing hugeness of the modern industrial state, men and women often laboured under a sense of disability, for they felt that, having lost social control, they stood alone and unprotected. Groups, consciously organized around selected interests, could compensate for this sense of loss . . . they could recreate that sense of intimate purpose which had once belonged to the village of an earlier age.[27]

From the nineteenth century to the present day, group work agencies and group workers have been aware of this compensatory and healing power of the group.

Innovative social caseworkers were convinced of this as well. Bertha Reynolds, for example, pioneered service delivery arrangements based organizationally and theoretically in a context of mutual aid. She recognized the importance of groups, saying

> We have taken our clients aside for individual treatment, not knowing their usual group relationships, or those through which they might find better solutions than are possible for them to work out alone.[28]

She was very concerned about diminishing stigma and offering services in the ordinary life-space of people: in her case, in the labor union. Reynolds touched on many issues, such as the nature of reciprocity, the conditions of altruistic helping, the power of the helper's role and its potential abuse, and the context of social relationships in which helping occurs. She said

> Outside of social work ... people seem to look upon taking and giving help as they do any other activity of life.... Among friends, the repayment may not be immediate nor to the same person, even, but the possibility and the will to do as much must be felt.... It is not hard to take help in a circle in which one feels sure of belonging.... It hurts to be helped when one is thereby relegated to the status of a child....[29]

In 1943 Reynolds called for a generic base for social work and suggested that group work and community work should be the cutting edge of our professional growth.[30]

As group work developed and drew from the emerging science of small-group dynamics, the mutual aid concept continued to be important, though it was often couched in other language, such as morale and cohesion, group problem solving, efficiency and productivity, and group

integration.[31] The recognition of people as beings whose essence was quintessentially social, that is to say, reciprocally interactive, was fundamental. The recognition gradually emerged that the relationships between the members in a group were the primary resource in accomplishing the aims of the group and its members.

In the 1930s Grace Coyle stated that

> Human beings ... cannot live without social contacts and without the expression of common interests. The decline of the neighborhood as a significant unity has meant inevitably the growth of organizations which provide psychological neighborhoods of a specialized sort.[32]

Coyle and others represented what Papell and Rothman later called the "social goals model" of group work,[33] with its objectives described by Germain and Gitterman as:

> the development of personality to its greatest capacity; the fostering of creative self-expression; the building of character and the improvement of interpersonal skills. For them group work functions also included the development of cultural and ethnic contributions; the teaching of democratic values; the support of active and mature participation in community life; the mobilizing of neighborhoods for social reform; and the preservation of ethical values.[34]

Also in the 1930s Samuel R. Slavson used the metaphor of a family, with its implied interdependence and intimacy, to describe the helping qualities of the planned group. He said, "The general plan in the conduct of a therapy group is to simulate as closely as possible family relationships with the members as siblings and the worker as a substitute parent."[35] While he suggested this as a compensatory measure for children and youth with serious emotional difficulties, he also recognized that all groups go through a stage of high levels of mutual aid, intimacy, and interdependence. Studies of the stages of group development also show that achieving a high level of mutual aid and intimacy precedes growing into more separated, but still interdependent, individuals.[36]

RELATED CONCEPTUALIZATIONS

Social Support

When mutual aid is given attention by the mental health professions, it is often conceptualized as informal social support. "Informal" support is distinguished from help offered through formal community institutions or by professional helpers.

Social support has been variously defined. Caplan, one of the prime developers of the concept, defined support as follows:

> (a) the significant others help the individual mobilize his psychological resources and master emotional burdens; (b) they share his tasks; and (c) they provide him with extra supplies of money, materials, tools, skills, and cognitive guidance to improve his handling of his situation.[37]

Tolsdorf has described support as having both instrumental and emotional dimensions. He said, "Instrumental support refers to the provision of tangible resources such as advice, money, the loan of equipment, or the provision of a job. Nurturant support, on the other hand, describes warmth, understanding, empathy, or encouragement."[38]

Cobb took a somewhat unique position in arguing that social support is information only. He excluded goods and services on the grounds that they may foster dependency, whereas information encourages independence. In this view, "social support is information leading the subject to believe that he is cared for and loved, esteemed, and a member of a network of mutual obligations."[39]

Interest in social support has been greatly influenced by research on crisis, stress, and coping. Social support was identified early as one of the variables which facilitates a return to precrisis functioning. Social support was also identified as an intervening variable between stressful life events and adverse health consequences. It appears that support is particularly important in influencing outcomes under conditions of high stress and makes less difference when the stress is lower.[40]

The "Helper Therapy" Principle

Riessman, in 1965, drew the attention of helping professionals to the notion that it could be help*ful* to be a help*er*. He observed that there was a distinct lack of research in this area, but that many self-help groups (Alcoholics Anonymous, Recovery, Inc., Synanon) operated effectively on this principle. He pointed out that deriving positive effects from helping is consistent with the behavioral principle that action in support of something is more reinforcing than passively taking it in.[41]

About ten years later, Skovholt energetically developed the same theme, noting that changes occur in nonprofessional helpers which are like changes associated with successful counseling. He referred to data from foster grandparents, drug-dependent youth, correctional settings, and so on. Skovholt explained that helping enhances the helper's sense of effectance and competence, and maturity is enhanced by being able to give as well as receive. The helper principle also affirms reciprocity and mutual aid as an effective way to live. The helper has a sense of social balance between doing for others and receiving from them. The help*er* also learns about talking personally, as is being modeled by the help*ee*.[42]

Orlando, who was concerned about the dehumanizing aspects of many institutions, particularly mental hospitals, and the "pathological" quality of the relationships among the patients, sought to alter patient-to-patient relationships. She taught basic nondirective counseling skills, such as attending visually, communicating empathy, and reflecting feelings. The connection to the "helper therapy" principle is clearest in Orlando's decision to focus on evaluating the help*er*'s changes. Orlando reported impressionistic findings that the subjects improved in their ability to relate. She felt that subjects showed more self-integration, a greater sense of personal significance, and increased awareness of themselves as compassionate and caring persons.[43]

A second, even more direct application of the helper principle was reported by Ho and Norlin. They used the helper principle in a children's residential center. They observed

> Since meaningful living and encounter require the reciprocal processes of giving and receiving, the helper role provides [residents] ... the opportunity to reverse their customary role ... unless they are afforded the opportunity to give, further efforts to help them tend to become futile and dehumanizing.[44]

This concept is operationalized in a pairing system where older residents are assigned as orientors and guides to new residents, and as cotherapists in family treatment and aftercare. The principle is also extended beyond the residents. Parents are involved as helpers in multifamily therapy. Staff are involved in defining criteria for new staff and in screening new applicants. The authors stated that the helper principle evokes responsiveness because it actively engages clients and coworkers and convinces them that they are worthy of acceptance, trust, and esteem.

The Self-Help Concept

In some literature, self-help and mutual aid seem virtually synonymous—an equation of "people helping themselves" with "people helping each other." Nevertheless, beginning in the 1960s self-help began to acquire the meaning of more or less formalized associations of people sharing common statuses, conditions, or predicaments. Self-help groups explicitly use such concepts as mutual aid and helper therapy in an ideology which emphasizes people's need for each other. Katz and Bender described self-help groups, saying

> Self-help groups are voluntary, small group structures for mutual aid and the accomplishment of a special purpose. They are usually formed by peers who have come together for mutual assistance in satisfying a common need, overcoming a common handicap or life-disrupting problem, and bringing about desired social and/or personal change. The initiators and members of such groups perceive that their needs are not, or cannot be, met by or through existing social institutions. Self-help groups emphasize face-to-face social interactions and the assumption of personal responsibility by members. They often provide material assistance, as well as emotional support; they are frequently "cause" oriented, and promulgate an ideology or values through which members may attain an enhanced sense of personal identity.[45]

Historically, self-help groups probably go back to the earliest stirrings of civilization; Kropotkin certainly thought so.[46] Currently, there appears to be a self-help group for every conceivable type of need or interest. Levy has organized self-help groups into four types: those dealing with some form of conduct reorganization or enhancement of self-control (Alcoholics Anonymous), those offering mutual support to ameliorate the stress of a common stress or predicament (Parents Without Partners), those enhancing the well-being of people whose life-style or subculture is generally discriminated against (black pride groups, gay organizations, women's groups), and groups with a personal growth focus (Integrity Groups). Groups vary widely in their interest in social as well as personal change.[47]

Implicit in the self-help concept is a reevaluation of professional helping. This may be expressed in positive form, emphasizing those positive qualities of self-help which arise from egalitarian relationships, from the common ground of shared predicaments, from experiential knowledge, and from the power of collective action. The reevaluation may also be expressed in negative form. According to Katz and Bender, "the initiators and members of such groups perceive that their needs are not, or cannot be, met through existing institutions."[48] At its sharpest, the critique would maintain that professionals are actively involved in maintaining the misery or devalued status of the self-help group members. The conflicts between some homosexual and some feminist groups and mental health professionals, and between some welfare rights groups and social welfare agencies are examples. The stance of the worker in the interactionist approach, however, may well be compatible with the aims of self-help groups, for the worker's job is not to define or take over the tasks of clients, but to help the group achieve its own ends.

Ideas about why self-help is effective have varied. Of course, all of the ideas about helper therapy would apply. Also, Katz has suggested that self-help makes it easier to communicate feelings, to accept one's problems, to want to change, and to relearn or resume social roles and competencies.[49] We note that these are the very assumptions that social group workers have made about the social group-work process. Professional responses to self-help have varied greatly, ranging from hostility, to disinterest, to co-optation, to excessive enthusiasm. Nonetheless, there are many professionals who are optimistically, if cautiously, supportive of self-help. They are seeking respectful and mutually satisfactory relationships with self-help groups. Let us now turn our attention to programs developed by professionals for a variety of purposes that use mutual aid and related concepts.

PROFESSIONALLY PLANNED PROGRAMS

There are many programs that are explicitly or implicitly based on mutual aid and reciprocal help. Sometimes the literature on such programs is simply descriptive; sometimes the program is linked to a theoretical rationale; and sometimes research or evaluation is also reported. It would be impossible to review these programs exhaustively, but we will note a few such endeavors. In view of the focus of this volume, we have organized this discussion around the life cycle.

Programs Particularly for Children and Adolescents

Numerous programs include mutual aid groups for children and adolescents. Lee reported the use of groups with mentally retarded adolescents and, with Park, with depressed adolescent girls in foster care.[50] Chardarelle reported a group for children whose parents had died.[51] Through sharing their common experiences and feelings, they gave and received help. This concept of forming groups around shared experiences can, of course, be applied in any setting, with any population sharing a common situation.

Another example is Lipton's work with dying children and their families.[52] Moving flexibly between modalities and age groups, he capitalized upon the healing potential of peers for the ill children, their well siblings, and for the parents. The potential for mutual aid within the family unit was also mobilized. Again, it would seem that most practitioners could include elements of such work in their existing positions.

On a more comprehensive scale, the *Unitas* program has been developed, implicitly using mutual aid concepts, for the children of a "burned-out" area of the South Bronx. It has expanded to the point that almost a hundred children are involved at any one time. Teenagers are taught to be helpers for the younger children, and the theoretical base is concepts of helping and sharing, though the language is that of the therapeutic community and open systems. The "catalysts" are social workers, but the children identify the older children as their helpers. *Unitas* includes some children who are growing up relatively smoothly, some who are having difficulty, and some who are seriously troubled or even psychotic.[53]

Programs Particularly for Adults

The Companion Program is one of the most creative programs developed for young adults. It was designed to offer a peer relationship to college students, such as foreign students, handicapped students, and others, who are known to be at high risk of dropping out and other problems. The at-risk student was invited to request a Companion, who then developed whatever relationship the two found mutually satisfying. The only guideline was that the Companion attend regular group discussions and remain willing to discuss the relationship.[54]

Other programs for adults are organized around developmental tasks such as parenting or transitions such as widowhood. Increasingly, health problems, whether chronic or acute, are the focus of support groups. In addition, most self-help groups orient themselves primarily toward adults.[55]

There has been considerable application of mutual aid concepts in programs for psychiatric patients. Early work grew from the concept of the therapeutic community, moving "outside" into halfway houses and so forth. More recently, efforts have been directed to helping ex-patients construct a community support network for themselves and each other. In his research Gordon found that, among patients with less than four months' hospitalization, the "network" group had about half as many rehospitalizations, and only a *quarter* as many days of rehospitalization, as a control group.[56]

Programs Particularly for Elders

Programs for elders may be oriented toward the elders themselves, and, as the number of impaired elders grows, toward their caretakers as well. Becker and Zarit reported training older people successfully as "peer counselors," using measures of unconditional regard, empathy, and genuineness as their indicators of change.[57] The Benton Hill project employed community workers to organize small social groups in neighborhoods. Participants in these groups showed more friendships, visiting, helping, and community involvement than the group which received conventional social services.[58] An example of an extensive mutual aid group program with the elderly, the Elmhurst General Hospital Senior Program, was also described and analyzed by Lee.[59]

The Foster Grandparents Program provides a nice link between children and elders. This program was found to have positive effects upon the well-being of the volunteer "grandparents" and on the development of institutionalized, handicapped children as well.[60]

Increasing attention is being given to the caretakers of frail or impaired elderly, especially the family. One such program is the Natural Supports Program. This emphasizes group programs for the caretakers, built on mutual aid concepts. The professionals go to great lengths not to supplant the natural helpers, but to supplement their efforts.[61]

Programs Organized Within Ecological Units

There are many programs emphasizing mutual aid concepts which are oriented to ecological units, such as a school, the workplace, a hospital ward, or a neighborhood. All these programs use the existing web of relationships and seek to enhance its supportive qualities.

Lela Costin, for example, has conceptualized social work in the school in a systemic fashion, seeking to exploit the potentials in relationships among students, between students and teachers, and among teachers.[62] Elliott Studt has applied similar concepts in a correctional setting. Studt has helped inmates discover that they can make things better for themselves through group action and that they can actually benefit by helping one another.[63]

Joan Shapiro has applied mutual aid concepts in relation to another difficult setting—the socially and physically impoverished environment of the single-room occupancy hotel. Careful study of naturally occurring relationships indicated the existence of natural leaders, processes of caring for the most damaged members, and cooperative efforts at negotiating the "outside world." Shapiro described processes of entry, observation, and intervention based on profound respect for the existing social arrangements and their positive aspects.[64]

Weiner, Akabas, and Somer have reported the application of mutual aid concepts in the world of work. They conceptualized a program based on maximizing job functioning, which is a common ground for employees, union, and employer. They were thus able to engage supportive help from many directions to prevent a worker's problems from intensifying and to enhance the operation of the work unit. Weiner and his associates emphasized the delicate processes of gaining entry and legitimation in such organizations. Intervention strategies included training union stewards in case finding and referral, consultation to key union and management personnel, and mediating with workers and coworkers around interpersonal obstacles right at the job site. Members of the organization were seen as the most effective resources for helping, and the professional's role was to facilitate their efforts.[65]

At the level of the neighborhood, Lee

and Swenson have described a small social service agency which attempted to apply interactionist and ecological concepts in a large housing project. This community was plagued by all of the problems of discrimination, joblessness, and despair of the urban ghetto. Nonetheless, sources of hope and mutual aid were to be found, and residents proved highly responsive to helping based upon promoting reciprocity and competence.[66]

Schwartz and Zalba have reported a number of programs that use mutual aid concepts and show the mediating function of the social worker in a variety of settings. These include further examples from schools, prisons, hotels, single room occupancies (SROs), and neighborhoods, as well as hospital, foster care, residential treatment, and trade union settings. Many of the interventions described can be undertaken by the creative social worker in any setting; they do not require elaborate programmatic supports.[67]

To this point, we have considered several streams of thought which converge on the concept of mutual aid. We have offered a conceptualization of mutual aid and briefly examined altruism and reciprocity as these concepts have been studied in psychology and sociology. We have discussed a series of related concepts such as social support, helper therapy, and self-help. Finally, planned programs using processes of reciprocity and mutual aid have been discussed.

Several researchers have begun to delineate empirically what mutual aid consists of. They have attempted to develop classifications of "natural" helping processes, just as others have worked on developing classifications of professional helping processes.[68] This knowledge is important if helping professionals are to continue to develop practice strategies based upon processes of mutual aid and natural

helping. Swenson's work is among the most recent in this area. In this study, natural helpers were found to help with needs ranging from practical matters, to relationships with organizations and with other people, to developmental tasks, to feelings about the self. Skills used included sustaining emotionally, helping with problem solving, mediating with organizations and individuals, providing tangible services, sharing material resources.[69]

Clearly, people need each other and helping is a moral, social, psychological, and spiritual "good." Moreover, people have helped each other throughout human history, and in every corner of the earth.[70] It appears, however, that helping is not effortless. People seem to need norms or beliefs; modeling, teaching, or encouragement; or the awareness of some benefit to themselves to engage in helping. The mediating role and skills of the social worker in developing the mutual aid group, and in challenging obstacles to its growth, are critical.[71] However, the worker's faith in the helping and healing potential of the group itself, through the process of mutual aid, is the most essential ingredient. It is his faith in the process that is the heart of Schwartz's interactionist approach.

CONCLUSION

Groups as Counterbalances

Schwartz saw the rise of group work agencies and the mutual aid group as a balance to the countervailing forces of industrialization, to the "mobility and rootlessness, the stultifying non-creative work, the rising rates of delinquency and crime, the patterns of neighborhood segregation, and pervading all, the inability of transient and disorganized populations to pool their interests and take action in their own behalf." He felt that one of the outstanding contributions of group work was the "shared belief in the salutory social and personal effects of group association."[72]

It is interesting to note that Alvin Toffler, a prominent current writer, identifies similar social problems as a result of industrialization and comes to similar conclusions about how to cope with these. He says,

> To create an environment in which change enlivens and enriches the individual but does not overwhelm him, we must employ not merely personal tactics but social strategies. If we are to carry people through the accelerative period, we must begin now to build "future shock absorbers" into the very fabric of superindustrial society.[73]

Toffler suggests that "situational groupings" of people going through similar life experiences/transitions "may well become one of the key social services of the future." While he is quite right that this idea "has never been systematically exploited," he fails to note that the use of the group as just such a shock absorber has been around for a very long time, doing what he suggests. Schwartz's method of forming mutual aid groups around commonalities serves exactly that function. Toffler explains that

> Members might hear from others who are more advanced in the transition than they are. In short, they are given the opportunity to pool their personal experiences and ideas before the moment of change is upon them.[74]

He is speaking of the mutual aid group which, as we have shown, is not new in day-to-day experience or recorded social

thought, and particularly had been developed in the profession of social group work. Toffler says that "the suggestion that we systematically honeycomb the society with such 'coping classrooms' " is new. From the group worker's point of view, group work agencies have been doing this for a long time, though it may well be time to revitalize that effort.

It is refreshing to see one of the leading thinkers of our day emphasize the importance of the mutual aid group in helping people cope with the times. It is a needed balance in an "age of narcissism." In 1959, well before this label was applied to the times, Schwartz saw the handwriting on the wall:

> The call for a new individualism is an attempt to find a solution to the loss of human dignity; but in its plea for a new assertion of self, it proposes the one against the many and seeks the sources of freedom in man's liberation from his fellows rather than in the combined efforts of men to control their environment.[75]

He further suggested that group workers have made a special contribution to social work and society:

> Having developed their outlook on life in an age which had clearly identified the common interest of man and men, group workers built their practice on this insight and were certain, even in bad times, that worthwhile ends could be achieved if men trusted the process by which, together, they could find the means.[76]

Schwartz's faith in this process and in mutual aid shaped his approach to social work practice. The interactionist approach is old and it is new. It is firmly based in social work history and in human history, and it is also able to invigorate and focus social work practice in these present difficult times.

NOTES

1. William Schwartz, "The Social Worker in the Group," in *The Practice of Social Work*, 2nd ed., ed. Robert W. Klenk and Robert M. Ryan (Belmont, Calif.: Wadsworth Publishers, 1974), p. 208.

2. Ibid., p. 215.

3. Lawrence Shulman, *The Skills of Helping Individuals and Groups, Second Edition*, (Itasca, Ill.: F. E. Peacock Publishers, Inc., 1984), p. 7.

4. Alex Gitterman, "Social Work with Groups in Maternal and Child Health," Columbia University School of Social Work and Roosevelt Hospital Department of Social Work, Conference Proceedings, June 14-15, 1979, p. 15; see also Shulman, *Skills of Helping Individuals and Groups*, pp. 110-116.

5. Schwartz, "The Social Worker in the Group," p. 218. Emphasis added.

6. Ibid., p. 214.

7. One such recent approach is the "life model of social work practice." See Carel B. Germain and Alex Gitterman, *The Life Model of Social Work Practice* (New York: Columbia University Press, 1980).

8. Christopher Lasch, *The Age of Narcissism* (New York: Norton, 1978).

9. William Schwartz and Serapio Zalba, *The Practice of Group Work* (New York: Columbia University Press, 1971), p. 4.

10. Peter Kuenstler, ed., *Social Group Work in Great Britain* (London: Faber and Faber, 1975), esp. John Spencer, "Historical Development," pp. 29-48.

11. Ralph E. Pumphrey and Muriel W. Pumphrey, *The Heritage of American Social Work* (New York: Columbia University Press, 1961), p. 90.

12. Kathleen Woodroofe, *From Charity to Social Work* (London: Routledge and Kegan Paul, 1962), p. 63. See also Spencer, "Historical Development."

13. Gertrude Wilson and Gladys Ryland, *Social Group Work Practice* (Boston: Houghton Mifflin, 1949).

14. Spencer, "Historical Development," pp. 132, 136, 137.

15. Ibid.

16. Germain and Gitterman, *The Life Model of Social Work Practice*, pp. 353-354.

17. Ibid.

18. Eduard C. Lindeman, "Group Work and Democracy—A Philosophical Note," in *Perspectives on Social Group Work Practice*, ed. Albert S. Alissi (New York: Free Press, 1980), pp. 77-82; Arthur E. Fink, *The Field of Social Work* (New York: Henry Holt, 1942), p. 401.

19. Woodroofe, *From Charity to Social Work*, pp. 69-70.

20. Albert S. Alissi, "Social Group Work: Commitment and Perspectives," in Alissi, *Perspectives on Social Group Work Practice*, pp. 11-15.

21. Woodroofe, *From Charity to Social Work*, p. 68.

22. Ibid., p. 69.

23. Jane Addams, *Twenty Years at Hull House* (New York: Macmillan, Signet Classic, 1961), p. 299.

24. Woodroofe, *From Charity to Social Work*, p. 65.

25. Addams, *Twenty Years at Hull House*, p. 98 (emphasis added). See also Fink, *The Field of Social Work*, p. 401.

26. Woodroofe, *From Charity to Social Work*, p. 73.

27. William Schwartz, "Group Work and the Social Scene," in *Issues in American Social Work*, ed. Alfred J. Kahn (New York: Columbia University Press, 1959), pp. 110-137.

28. Bertha Reynolds, *Social Work and Social Living* (Washington, D.C.: National Association of Social Workers, 1975), pp. 22, 25.

29. Ibid., p. 10.

30. Bertha Reynolds, *Learning and Teaching in the Practice of Social Work* (New York: Russell and Russell, 1970).

31. Charles C. Cooley, *Social Organization* (New York: Charles Scribner's and Sons, 1909); Eduard C. Lindeman, *Social Discovery* (New York: Republic Press, 1924); George C. Homans, *The Human Group* (New York: Harcourt Brace Jovanovich, 1950); Ken Heap, *Group Theory for Social Workers* (Oxford: Pergamon Press, 1977).

32. Grace Longwell Coyle, *Social Processes*

in Organized Groups (Hebron, Conn.: Practitioner's Press, 1979), p. 11.

33. Catherine P. Papell and Beulah Rothman, "Social Group Work Models: Possession and Heritage," in *Perspectives on Social Group Work Practice*, ed. Alissi, pp. 66-77.

34. Germain and Gitterman, *The Life Model of Social Work Practice,* p. 354.

35. Samuel R. Slavson, "Meaningful Personal Relations," in *Creative Group Education* (New York: Association Press, 1937), pp. 368-370.

36. James Garland, Hubert Jones, and Ralph Kolodny, "A Model for Stages of Development in Social Work Groups," in *Explorations in Group Work,* ed. Saul Bernstein (Boston: Boston University School of Social Work, 1965); James K. Whittaker, "Models of Group Development: Implications for Social Group Work Practice," in *Perspectives on Social Group Work*, ed. Alissi, pp. 133-153.

37. Gerald Caplan, *Support Systems and Community Mental Health* (New York: Behavioral Publications, 1974) pp. 5-6.

38. Christopher Tolsdorf, "Social Networks, Support, and Psychopathology," paper presented at a meeting of the American Psychological Association, Chicago, Illinois, September 1, 1975, p. 3.

39. Sidney Cobb, "Social Support as a Moderator of Life Stress," *Psychosomatic Medicine* 38 (September/October 1976): 300.

40. Ibid., pp. 300-314. See also Berton H. Kaplan, John C. Cassell, and Susan Gore, "Social Support and Health," *Medical Care* 15 (May 1977) Supplement: 47-58; Richard L. Leavy, "Social Support and Psychological Disorder: A Review," *Journal of Community Psychology* 11 (January 1983): 3-21.

41. Frank Riessman, "The 'Helper' Therapy Principle," *Social Work* 10 (April 1965): 27-32.

42. Thomas J. Skovholt, "The Client as Helper: A Means to Promote Psychological Growth," *Counselling Psychologist* 4 (1974): 58.

43. Norma Jean Orlando, "The Mental Patient as Therapeutic Change Agent," *Psychotherapy* 11 (Spring 1974): 58-62.

44. Man Keung Ho and Judy Norlin, "The Helper Principle and the Creation of a Therapeutic Milieu," *Child Care Quarterly* 3 (Summer 1974): 109-118.

45. Alfred Katz and Eugene I. Bender, *The Strength in Us: Self-Help in the Modern World* (New York: Franklin Watts Press, 1976), p. 9.

46. Petr Kropotkin is generally viewed as the first person to study mutual aid scientifically. His book, *Mutual Aid: A Factor in Evolution,* written in 1902 (Boston: Extending Horizons Books, n.d.), has become a classic. In it, among other memorable quotations, is the following:

> Sociability and the need of mutual aid are such inherent parts of human nature that at no time of history can we discover men living in small, isolated families, fighting for the means of subsistence.... In its widest extension, even at the present time, we also see the best guarantee of a still loftier evolution of our race. (pp. 153, 300)

47. Leon H. Levy, *Self-Help Groups as Mental Health Resources* (Bloomington, Ind.: Indiana University Press, 1973).

48. Katz and Bender, *The Strength in Us,* p. 9.

49. Alfred J. Katz, "Applications of Self-Help Concepts in Current Social Welfare," *Social Work* 10 (July 1965): 68-74.

50. Judith A. B. Lee, "Group Work with Mentally Retarded Foster Adolescents," *Social Casework* 58 (March 1977): 164-173; and Judith A. B. Lee and Danielle N. Park, "A Group Approach to the Depressed Adolescent Girl in Foster Care," *American Journal of Orthopsychiatry* 48 (July 1978): 516-527.

51. James A. Chardarelle, "A Group for Children with Deceased Parents," *Social Work* 20 (July 1975): 328-330.

52. Hal Lipton, "The Dying Child and the Family," in *The Child and Death*, ed. Q. J. Sahler (St. Louis, Mo: The C. V. Mosby Company, 1978), pp. 52-71.

53. Edward Eismann, "Children's Views of Therapeutic Gains and Therapeutic Change Agents in an Open-System Therapeutic Community" (Bronx, N.Y.: Lincoln Community Mental Health Center, 1975).

54. E. Robert Boylin, "The Companion Program: Students as Helpers," *Psychotherapy* 10 (Fall 1973): 242-244.

55. Just a few examples of the literally hundreds of support groups are: groups for dialysis patients and spouses, cardiac patients, families of stroke and Alzheimer's victims, divorced mothers, battering men, separated adults, recent widows and widowers, parents of retarded children, phobics, and employees with substance-abuse problems.

56. Richard Gordon et al., "Utilizing Peer Management and Support to Reduce Rehospitalization of Mental Patients" (Tampa, Fl.: Human Resources Institute, University of South Florida, 1979).

57. Francoise Becker and Steven H. Zarit, "Training Older Adults as Peer Counsellors," *Educational Gerontology* 3 (July-September 1978): 241-250.

58. Phyllis Ehrlich, "Mutual Help for Community Elderly" (Carbondale, Ill.: Southern Illinois University Rehabilitation Institute, 1979).

59. Judith A. B. Lee, "The Group: A Chance at Human Connection for the Mentally Impaired Older Person," *Social Work with Groups* 5 (Summer 1982): 43-55.

60. Cited in Skovholt, "The Client as Helper."

61. Natural Supports Program, "Strengthening Informal Supports for the Aging" (New York: Community Service Society, 1981).

62. Lela Costin, "School Social Work Practice: A New Model," *Social Work* 20 (March 1975): 135-139.

63. Elliott Studt, "Social Work Theory and Implications for the Practice of Methods," *Social Work Education Reporter* 16 (June 1968): 22-24 and 42-46.

64. Joan Shapiro, *Communities of the Alone* (New York: Association Press, 1971).

65. Hyman G. Weiner, Sheila Akabas, and John Somer, *Mental Health in the World of Work* (New York: Association Press, 1973).

66. Judith A. B. Lee and Carol R. Swenson, "Theory in Action: A Community Social Service Agency," *Social Casework* 59 (June 1978): 359-370.

67. William Schwartz and Serapio Zalba, *The Practice of Group Work* (New York: Columbia University Press, 1971).

68. Edwina Andrews and Doris Norton, "Summary of Preliminary Natural Helper Interviews: Neighborhood Self-Help Project" (Chicago: University of Chicago, School of Social Service Administration, 1979); Ruby Abrahams, "Mutual Helping: Styles of Caregiving in a Mutual Aid Program," in *Support Systems and Mutual Help*, ed. Gerald Caplan and Marie Killilea (New York: Grune and Stratton, 1976), pp. 245-259; Emory L. Cowen et al., "Hairdressers as Caregivers," *American Journal of Community Psychology* 7 (December 1979): 633-648; Shirley L. Patterson et al., "Utilization of Human Resources for Mental Health" (Lawrence, Kans.: University of Kansas, School of Social Welfare, 1972); Mary Ellen Colten and Richard Kulka, "The Nature and Perceived Helpfulness of Formal and Informal Support," paper presented at a meeting of the American Psychological Association, New York, September, 1979; Community Helpers Project, "Community Survey" (University Park, Penna.: Pennsylvania State University, College of Human Development, n.d.); Benjamin H. Gottlieb, "The Development and Application of a Classification Scheme of Informal Helping," *Canadian Journal of Behavioural Science* 10 (1978): 105-115.

69. Carol R. Swenson, "Natural Helping Processes" (Doctoral dissertation, Columbia University School of Social Work, 1983).

70. For examples of mutual aid in this and other cultures, see Swenson, "Natural Helping Processes," Chapter 2.

71. Shulman, *Skills of Helping Individuals and Groups*; Germain and Gitterman, *The Life Model*.

72. Schwartz, "Group Work and the Social Scene," pp. 114-115.

73. Alvin Toffler, *Future Shock* (New York: Bantam Books, 1971), p. 383.

74. Ibid., p. 385.

75. Schwartz, "Group Work and the Social Scene," p. 127.

76. Ibid.

BIBLIOGRAPHY

Abrahams, Ruby. "Mutual Helping: Styles of Caregiving in a Mutual Aid Program." In *Support Systems and Mutual Help.* Edited by Gerald Caplan and Marie Killilea. New York: Grune and Stratton, 1976, pp. 245-259.

Addams, Jane. *Twenty Years At Hull House.* New York: Macmillan, Signet Classic, 1961.

Alissi, Albert S. "Social Group Work: Commitment and Perspectives." In *Perspectives on Social Group Work Practice.* Edited by Alissi. New York: Free Press, 1980, pp. 11-15.

Andrews, Edwina, and Doris Norton. "Summary of Preliminary Natural Helper Interviews: Neighborhood Self-Help Project." Chicago: University of Chicago, School of Social Service Administration, 1979.

Boylin, E. Robert. "The Companion Program: Students as Helpers." *Psychotherapy* 10 (Fall 1973): 242-244.

Becker, Francoise, and Steven H. Zarit. "Training Older Adults as Peer Counsellors." *Educational Gerontology* 3 (July-September 1978): 241-250.

Caplan, Gerald. *Support Systems and Community Mental Health.* New York: Behavioral Publications, 1974.

Chardarelle, James A. "A Group for Children with Deceased Parents." *Social Work* 20 (July 1975): 328-330.

Cobb, Sidney. "Social Support as a Moderator of Life Stress." *Psychosomatic Medicine* 38 (September/October 1976): 300-314.

Colten, Mary Ellen, and Richard Kulka. "The Nature and Perceived Helpfulness of Formal and Informal Support." Paper presented at a meeting of the American Psychological Association, New York, September 1979.

Community Helpers Project. "Community Survey." University Park, Penna.: Pennsylvania State University, College of Human Development, n.d.

Cooley, Charles C. *Social Organization.* New York: Charles Scribner's and Sons, 1909.

Costin, Lela. "School Social Work Practice: A New Model." *Social Work* 20 (March 1975): 135-139.

Cowen, Emory L., et al. "Hairdressers as Caregivers." *American Journal of Community Psychology* 7 (December 1979): 633-648.

Coyle, Grace Longwell. *Social Processes in Organized Groups.* Hebron, Conn.: Practitioner's Press, 1979.

Ehrlich, Phyllis. "Mutual Help for Community Elderly." Carbondale, Ill.: Southern Illinois University Rehabilitation Institute, 1979.

Eismann, Edward. "Children's Views of Therapeutic Gains and Therapeutic Change Agents in an Open-System Therapeutic Community" (mimeo). Bronx, N.Y.: Lincoln Community Mental Health Center, 1975.

Fink, Arthur E. *The Field of Social Work.* New York: Henry Holt, 1942.

Garland, James, Hubert Jones, and Ralph Kolodny. "A Model for Stages of Development in Social Work Groups." In *Explorations in Group Work.* Edited by Saul Bernstein. Boston: Boston University School of Social Work, 1965, pp. 21-30.

Germain, Carel B., and Alex Gitterman. *The Life Model of Social Work Practice.* New York: Columbia University Press, 1980.

Gitterman, Alex. "Social Work with Groups in Maternal and Child Health." Columbia University School of Social Work and Roosevelt Hospital Department of Social Work, Conference Proceedings, June 14-15, 1979.

Gordon, Richard, et al. "Utilizing Peer Management and Support to Reduce Rehospitalization of Mental Patients." Tampa, Fla.: Human Resources Institute, University of South Florida, 1979.

Gottlieb, Benjamin H. "The Development and Application of a Classification Scheme of Informal Helping." *Canadian Journal of Behavioural Science* 10 (1978): 105-115.

Heap, Ken. *Group Theory for Social Workers.* Oxford: Pergamon Press, 1977.

Ho, Man Keung, and Judy Norlin. "The Helper Principle and the Creation of a Therapeutic Milieu." *Child Care Quarterly* 3 (Summer 1974): 109-118.

Homans, George C. *The Human Group.* New York: Harcourt Brace Jovanovich, 1950.

Kaplan, Berton H., John C. Cassell, and Susan Gore. "Social Support and Health." *Medical Care* 15 (May 1977) Supplement: 47-58.

Katz, Alfred J. "Applications of Self-Help Concepts in Current Social Welfare." *Social Work* 10 (July 1965): 68-74.

_____, and Eugene I. Bender. *The Strength in Us: Self-Help in the Modern World.* New York: Franklin Watts Press, 1976.

Kropotkin, Petr. *Mutual Aid: A Factor in Evolution.* Boston: Extending Horizons Books, n.d.

Kuenstler, Peter. *Social Group Work in Great Britain.* London: Faber and Faber, 1975.

Lasch, Christopher. *The Age of Narcissism.* New York: Norton, 1978.

Leavy, Richard L. "Social Support and Psychological Disorder: A Review." *Journal of Community Psychology* 11 (January 1983): 3-21.

Lee, Judith A. B. "Group Work with Mentally Retarded Foster Adolescents." *Social Casework* 58 (March 1977): 164-173.

_____. "The Group: A Chance at Human Connection for the Mentally Impaired Older Person." *Social Work with Groups* 5 (Summer 1982): 43-55.

_____, and Danielle N. Park. "A Group Approach to the Depressed Adolescent Girl in Foster Care." *American Journal of Orthopsychiatry* 48 (July 1978): 516-527.

Lee, Judith A. B., and Carol R. Swenson. "Theory in Action: A Community Social Service Agency." *Social Casework* 59 (June 1978): 359-370.

Levy, Leon H. *Self-Help Groups as Mental Health Resources.* Bloomington, Ind.: Indiana University Press, 1973.

Lindeman, Eduard C. *Social Discovery.* New York: Republic Press, 1924.

_____. "Group Work and Democracy—A Philosophical Note." In *Perspectives on Social Group Work Practice.* Edited by Albert S. Alissi. New York: Free Press, 1980, pp. 77-82.

Lipton, Hal. "The Dying Child and the Family." In *The Child and Death.* Edited by Q. J. Sahler. St. Louis, Mo.: The C.V. Mosby Company, 1978, pp. 52-71.

Natural Supports Program. "Strengthening Informal Supports for the Aging." New York: Community Service Society, 1981.

Orlando, Norma Jean. "The Mental Patient as Therapeutic Change Agent." *Psychotherapy* 11 (Spring, 1974): 58-62.

Papell, Catherine P., and Beulah Rothman. "Social Group Work Models: Possession and Heritage." In *Perspectives on Social Group Work Practice.* Edited by Alfred S. Alissi. New York: Free Press, 1980, pp. 66-77.

Patterson, Shirley L., et al. "Utilization of Human Resources for Mental Health." Lawrence, Kans.: University of Kansas, School of Social Welfare, 1972.

Pumphrey, Ralph E., and Muriel W. Pumphrey. *The Heritage of American Social Work.* New York: Columbia University Press, 1961.

Reynolds, Bertha. *Learning and Teaching in the Practice of Social Work.* New York: Russell and Russell, 1970.

_____. *Social Work and Social Living.* Washington, D. C.: National Association of Social Workers, 1975.

Riessman, Frank. "The 'Helper' Therapy Principle." *Social Work* 10 (April 1965): 27-32.

Shulman, Lawrence. *The Skills of Helping Individuals and Groups, Second Edition,* Itasca, Ill.: F. E. Peacock Publishers, Inc., 1984.

Schwartz, William. "Group Work and the Social Scene." In *Issues in American Social Work.* Edited by Alfred J. Kahn. New York: Columbia University Press, 1959, pp. 110-137.

Schwartz, William. "The Social Worker in the Group." In *The Practice of Social Work,* 2nd ed. Edited by Robert W. Klenk and Robert M. Ryan. Belmont, Calif.: Wadsworth Publishers, 1974, pp. 208-228.

_____, and Serapio Zalba. *The Practice of Group Work.* New York: Columbia University Press, 1971.

Shapiro, Joan. *Communities of the Alone.* New York: Association Press, 1971.

Skovholt, Thomas A. "The Client as Helper: A Means to Psychological Growth." *Counselling Psychologist* 4 (1974): 58-64.

Slavson, Samuel R. *Creative Group Education.* New York: Association Press, 1937.

Spencer, John. "Historical Development." In *Social Group Work in Great Britain.* Edited by Peter Kuenstler. London: Faber and Faber, 1975, pp. 29-48.

Studt, Elliott. "Social Work Theory and Implications for the Practice of Methods." *Social Work Education Reporter* 16 (June 1968): 22-24, 42-46.

Swenson, Carol R. "Natural Helping Processes." Doctoral dissertation, Columbia University School of Social Work, 1983.

Toffler, Alvin. *Future Shock.* New York: Bantam Books, 1971.

Tolsdorf, Christopher. "Social Networks, Support, and Psychopathology." Paper presented at a meeting of the American Psychological Association, Chicago, Illinois, September 1, 1975.

Weiner, Hyman G., Sheila Akabas, and John Somer. *Mental Health in the World of Work.* New York: Association Press, 1973.

Whittaker, James K. "Models of Group Development: Implications for Social Group Work Practice." In *Perspectives on Social Group Work.* Edited by Alfred S. Alissi. New York: Free Press, 1980, pp. 133-153.

Wilson, Gertrude, and Gladys Ryland. *Social Group Work Practice.* New York: Houghton Mifflin, 1949.

Woodroofe, Kathleen. *From Charity to Social Work.* London: Routledge and Kegan Paul, 1962.

Index

THE BOOK MANUFACTURE

Mutual Aid Groups and the Life Cycle, was typeset at Compositors, Cedar Rapids, Iowa. Printing and binding was by Kingsport Press, Kingsport, Tennessee. Cover design was by Jane Brown, Chicago, Illinois. Internal design was by F.E. Peacock Publishers' art department. The typeface is Times Roman.